A water colour of turkeys by C. F. Tunnicliffe. Courtesy of British United Turkeys Ltd.

Recent Advances in Turkey Science
Poultry Science Symposium Number Twenty-one

Poultry Science Symposium Series

Executive Editor (Volumes 1–18): B. M. Freeman

1   Physiology of the Domestic Fowl*
2   Protein Utilization by Poultry*
3   Environmental Control in Poultry Production*
4   Egg Quality — A Study of the Hen's Egg*
5   The Fertility and Hatchability of the Hen's Egg*
6   i. Factors Affecting Egg Grading*
    ii. Aspects of Poultry Behaviour*
7   Poultry Disease and World Economy
8   Egg Formation and Production
9   Energy Requirements of Poultry*
10 Economic Factors Affecting Egg Production
11 Digestion in the Fowl
12 Growth and Poultry Meat Production
13 Avian Coccidiosis
14 Food Intake Regulation in Poultry
15 Meat Quality in Poultry and Game Birds
16 Avian Immunology
17 Reproductive Biology of Poultry
18 Poultry Genetics and Breeding
19 Nutrient Requirements of Poultry and Nutritional Research
20 Egg Quality — Current Problems and Recent Advances
21 Recent Advances in Turkey Science
*Out of print

Volumes 1–18 may be ordered from

Carfax Publishing Company
PO Box 25, Abingdon, Oxfordshire OX14 3UE, England

Volumes 19, 20 and 21 may be ordered from

Butterworth & Co. (Publishers) Ltd
Borough Green, Sevenoaks, Kent TN15 8PH, England

The cover design shows a mosaic of a cockerel from 1st Century BC (Burrell Collection, Glasgow)

Recent Advances in Turkey Science

Poultry Science Symposium Number Twenty-one

C. Nixey
British United Turkeys Ltd, Hockenhull Hall, Tarvin, Cheshire

T. C. Grey
AFRC Institute of Food Research — Bristol Laboratory, Langford, Bristol

Butterworths
London   Boston   Singapore   Sydney   Toronto   Wellington

First published, 1989

© **Butterworth & Co. (Publishers) Ltd, 1989**

British Library Cataloguing in Publication Data

Recent advances in turkey science.
   1. Livestock. Turkeys. Production
   I. Nixey, C.   II. Grey, T. C.   III. Series
   636.5'920883

ISBN 0-408-00971-3

Library of Congress Cataloging in Publication Data

Recent advances in turkey science / [edited by] C. Nixey, T.C. Grey.
      p.   cm. -- (Poultry science symposium : no. 21)
    Papers from the 21st Poultry Science Symposium held at Harper Adams Agricultural College, Newport, Shropshire, 8–11 Sept. 1987 and organized by the United Kingdom Branch of the World's Poultry Science Association in collaboration with Working Group No. 10 of the European Federation of the Association.
    Bibliography: p.
    Includes index.
    ISBN 0-408-00971-3
    1. Turkeys--Congresses.   I. Nixey, C. II. Grey, T. C. III. Poultry Science Symposium (21st : 1987 : Harper Adams Agricultural College)   IV. World's Poultry Science Association United Kingdom Branch.   V. European Federation of the World Poultry Science Association. Working Group No. 10. VI. Series.
SF507.R43 1989
636.5'92--dc19   88-24154

Photoset by Butterworths Litho Preparation Department
Printed and bound in Great Britain by Anchor Press Ltd, Tiptree, Essex

Preface

This volume contains the papers of the 21st Poultry Science Symposium which was held at Harper Adams Agricultural College, Newport, Shropshire on 8–11 September 1987. This series of Symposia is now organized by the United Kingdom Branch of the World's Poultry Science Association. The 21st was run in collaboration with Working Group No. 10 of the European Federation of the Association. Members of the Organizing Committee are listed below.

The 21st Symposium was on 'Recent Advances in Turkey Science' and had four main sections. The first was devoted to aspects of breeding, covering genetics, nutrition, embryology, both male and female reproduction and management. The following section was concerned with growing the commercial turkey, including the physiology and biology of growth. In section three, the major health concerns of the turkey were covered. The final section dealt with turkey meat science, discussing aspects which affect meat yield, texture, flavour and taints, and finishing with a paper on the further processing of turkey meat.

Also included are summaries of the various poster papers presented at the Symposium on a variety of subjects.

The 19 chapters of this volume have been written by acknowledged experts in their field, drawn from Canada, the USA and the UK. There is a dearth of published material on turkey science. This volume remedies this deficiency and should be of great value to anyone involved in any aspect of turkey production.

Organizing Committee
21st Poultry Science Symposium

C. Nixey (Chairman)
T. E. Whittle (Treasurer)
C. G. Belyavin
D. R. Charles
C. Fisher
T. C. Grey
Helen D. Raine
R. G. Wells

Acknowledgements

Financial support for this symposium is gratefully acknowledged from:

AMS Turkeys Ltd
J. Bibby Agriculture Ltd
British Turkey Federation
British United Turkeys Ltd
Dalgety Agriculture Ltd
MSD Agvet
Pauls Agriculture Ltd

Contributors

L. G. Bagley

Hybrid Turkeys Inc., 9 Centennial Drive, Kitchener, Ontario N2B 3E9, Canada

C. Baxter-Jones

British United Turkeys Ltd, Veterinary Laboratory, Platts Lane, Old Moss, Stapleford, Tarvin, Cheshire CH3 8HR, UK

E. G. Buss

The Pennsylvania State University, Room 2 Agricultural Engineering Building, University Park, Pennsylvania, PA 16802, USA

D. R. Charles

Agricultural Development and Advisory Service, Block 7, Chalfont Drive, Nottingham NG8 3SN, UK

V. L. Christensen

School of Agriculture and Life Sciences, North Carolina State University, Department of Poultry Science, Box 7608, Raleigh, NC 27695-7608, USA

G. C. Emmans

Edinburgh School of Agriculture, West Mains Road, Edinburgh EH9 3JG, UK

J. Gascoyne

British United Turkeys of America, PO Box 727, Lewisburg, West Virginia 24901, USA

T. C. Grey

AFRC Institute of Food Research — Bristol Laboratory, Langford, Bristol BS18 7DY, UK

N. E. Horrox

Nigel Horrox Veterinary Group, Driffield, Humberside YO25 8BJ, UK

J. M. Jones

18 Sywell Close, Old Catton, Norwich, Norfolk NR6 7EW, UK

R. C. Jones

Department of Veterinary Pathology, University of Liverpool, Leahurst, Neston, South Wirral L64 7TE, UK

P. E. Lake

AFRC Institute of Animal Physiology and Genetics Research, Edinburgh Research Station, Roslin, Midlothian EH25 9PS, UK

T. R. Morris

Department of Agriculture, University of Reading, Earley Gate, PO Box 236, Reading RG6 2AT, UK

C. Nixey

British United Turkeys Ltd, Hockenhull Hall, Tarvin, Cheshire CH3 8LE

Sally L. Noll

Department of Animal Science, University of Minnesota, 120 Peters Hall, 1404 Gortner Avenue, St Paul, MN 55108, USA

D. L. Reynolds

Veterinary Medical Research Institute, College of Veterinary Medicine, Iowa State University, Ames, IA 50011, USA

R. I. Richardson

AFRC Institute of Food Research — Bristol Laboratory, Langford, Bristol BS18 7DY, UK

L. J. Saif

Food Animal Health Research Program, Ohio Agricultural Research and Development Center, Ohio State University, Wooster, OH 44691, USA

Y. M. Saif

Food Animal Health Research Program, Ohio Agricultural Research and Development Center, Ohio State University, Wooster, OH 44691, USA

P. J. Sharp

AFRC Institute of Animal Physiology and Genetics Research, Edinburgh Research Station, Roslin, Midlothian EH25 9PS, UK

J. C. Stuart

Chapelfield Veterinary Partnership, 21 Chapelfield Road, Norwich, Norfolk NR2 1RR, UK

H. J. Swatland

Department of Animal and Poultry Science, University of Guelph, Guelph, Ontario N1G 2W1, Canada

K. W. Theil

Food Animal Health Research Program, Ohio Agricultural Research and Development Center, Ohio State University, Wooster, OH 44691, USA

C. C. Whitehead

Poultry Division, Institute for Grassland and Animal Production, Roslin, Midlothian EH25 9PS, UK

J. D. Wood

AFRC Institute of Food Research — Bristol Laboratory, Langford, Bristol BS18 7DY, UK

Contents

I Aspects of breeding

1 The world turkey industry, structure and production 3
 J. Gascoyne

2 Genetics of turkeys: origin and development 11
 E. G. Buss

3 Physiology of egg production 31
 P. J. Sharp

4 Recent research in male reproduction 55
 P. E. Lake

5 Embryology of the turkey 69
 V. L. Christensen and L. G. Bagley

6 Nutrition of turkey breeding stock 91
 C. C. Whitehead

7 Management of breeding stock 119
 Sally L. Noll

II Growing the commercial turkey

8 The growth of turkeys 135
 G. C. Emmans

9 Physiology of muscle growth 167
 H. J. Swatland

10 Nutritional responses of growing turkeys 183
 C. Nixey

11 Environmental responses of growing turkeys 201
 D. R. Charles

III   Health of the turkey

12 Rhinotracheitis: Turkey rhinotracheitis (TRT) in Great Britain   217
    J. C. Stuart

    Laboratory investigations   224
    C. Baxter-Jones and R. C. Jones

13 Enteric viruses of turkeys   235
    Y. M. Saif, K. W. Theil, D. L. Reynolds and L. J. Saif

14 The general health status of turkeys   263
    N. E. Horrox

IV   Turkey meat science

15 Meat yield and carcass composition in turkeys   271
    J. D. Wood

16 Turkey meat texture   289
    T. C. Grey

17 Flavour and taint in turkey meat   313
    J. M. Jones

18 Further processing of turkey meat   331
    R. I. Richardson

19 The place of the turkey in the animal industry of the future   351
    T. R. Morris

20 Poster papers   357

    Index   365

Part I

Aspects of breeding

Chapter 1

The world turkey industry, structure and production

J. Gascoyne

Introduction

Of the many wonders of the New World, turkeys were one of those items taken back to Europe by the early explorers. As a result of this, domestic turkey production is recorded in Europe from the sixteenth century and this 'technology' was applied to the native stock by the founding fathers of the USA. Christmas consumption of turkey is a tradition which was spread to other countries by British and Spanish settlers.

The turkey, with its unusual appearance and relatively large size, lent itself to consumption on special occasions when extra funds were available.

To meet increasing demand, individual farms ran small turkey breeder flocks and the surplus production from local demand was sent to the local town at holiday time. The traditional form of sale was for the turkey to be dead, with all feathers removed except for the neck and for it to be displayed hanging from its feet in the retail outlet.

Early photographs reveal that the turkey probably looked much better with its feathers on, as these featherless turkeys showed very prominent keel bones and every indication of having a rather low meat yield. The turkey's original and continued asset however, was its eating quality which was widely acceptable to consumers.

As is the nature of supply and demand, backyard farmers began to grow turkeys on a larger scale and some larger companies began to be developed. However, turkey production was very much dictated by nature. Better stock for breeding would be retained in the summer of one year, grown through the winter stimulated into egg production by the naturally increasing daylength in the following spring, with the progeny being placed from spring into summer giving a range of killing weights for the year-end holiday season. The two significant consumption areas were North America for Thanksgiving and Christmas celebrations, and in Britain, France and Spain for Christmas consumption. Turkey consumption also began to grow in the South American and Australian continents.

It was in the second quarter of the twentieth century that the industry began to change. The development of artificial incubation meant that turkey eggs could be handled more efficiently and larger groups of birds could be placed. After the Second World War, turkey breeding began to move from being an activity centred around individual farmers to one that became centred around processing plants. The widespread distribution of freezers in retail outlets and, in due course, freezers

3

in homes meant that turkeys did not have to be produced to be timed to consumption; they could, in fact, be produced year-round and stored for consumption at a later date. This enabled the turkey season to be extended. Development of more sophisticated incubators and of artificial insemination meant that breeders could produce a more reliable supply of poults and companies existed purely to provide the hatchery function and supply poults to growers. Often these hatcheries had their own breed of turkey.

With increasing demand for turkey meat which, in real terms, reduced in cost in response to improvements resulting from selective breeding, opportunities presented themselves to market turkeys in the growing cities of North America and Europe. Small family companies became much larger turkey processors and large corporations began to invest in the turkey business.

In the mid 1960s, the industry was marketing its product to meet a primarily year-end demand. The story of the last 20 years is how turkey began to become a year-round rather than a year-end meat and the opportunities this presents for future expansion.

Structure

The turkey industry is concentrated geographically. Not only is 90% of the world's turkey industry in North America and Europe, but the production locations are limited within these areas. Published statistics do not all have the same parameters and definitions. It has therefore been necessary to try to standardize the information when constructing tables or figures. The statistics quoted in this chapter are my interpretation of statistics published by governmental departments and trade magazines and refer to the situation in 1986. (I am also grateful for additional material supplied by British United Turkeys Ltd.)

The three states with the largest production in the USA are responsible for 46% of production (*Table 1.1*), the first three countries with the largest production in

Table 1.1 The distribution of turkey production within the USA

State	Million turkeys per annum	% of total production
North Carolina	39	19
Minnesota	34	16
California	22	11
Arkansas	16.5	8
Virginia	14	7
Missouri	13.5	6.5
Indiana	9.4	4.5
Pennsylvania	7.8	4
Iowa	7	3.5
Wisconsin	6	3
South Carolina	4	2
Texas	4	2
Colorado	4	2
Utah	3	1.5
TOTAL	184.2	90.0

Table 1.2 The distribution of turkey production within the EEC

Country	Million turkeys per annum	% of total production
France	65	46
UK	32	23
Italy	23	16
West Germany	8.5	6
Spain	3.0	2
Holland	2.7	2
Ireland	2.5	2
Portugal	2.5	2
TOTAL	139.2	99

Europe supply 85% of production (*Table 1.2*), and the first three provinces in Canada supply 76% of national production.

Within these concentrated producing areas, there are only a limited number of companies engaged in producing the turkeys.

The top three companies in the USA produce over 20% of the turkey meat; the top three in Europe similarly are responsible for 20% of the turkey meat production.

This concentration is not always obvious from the total numbers of units involved in production. Of the 7000 producing farms in the USA, 11% are responsible for 70% of the production.

One of the main forces in concentrating the industry has been the economics of turkey processing and compound feed manufacturing. Both activities benefit from increasing volume at one location, and the economics of transporting limit the area in which turkeys can be grown around the feed mill and processing plant.

The actual location of turkey production in North America and Europe is linked to local favourable factors. The large midwest production of turkeys in the USA is linked to the availability of cheap feed raw materials; California has the largest US population and a good producing climate for turkeys which offsets some of the feed cost disadvantage. The southeast USA has a climate which is favourable for feed conversion and year-round production. In Europe, the Brittany area of France offered a large number of small farmers, looking for extra activity, with a supply of capital to construct poultry housing while the Veneto region of Italy had feed raw materials available and feed mill capacity to supply a growing turkey industry.

Only limited quantities of turkey meat are exported from producing countries.

Principal characteristics of the turkey producing areas

First, the producers bring in primary breeding stock from the outside. Secondly, they ship out end product to supply the major production centres of the country of production. The principal sectors of the industry are as follows:

(1) primary breeding,
(2) multiplication/hatchery,
(3) turkey growing,
(4) turkey processing, further processing, and marketing.

Primary breeding

Primary breeding reflects the same trends as the rest of the industry. Primary turkey breeding has gone from a situation where everybody bred their own turkeys to one where 90% of all turkeys in the world come from three primary breeding companies.

Tracing the developments since 1965, as the industry became organized into larger groups, choices developed about the source of breeding stock used. There was significant elimination of primary breeders in the 1960s. One of the major determinants for survival was whether they were successful in eliminating respiratory disease. Those companies who did not eradicate *Mycoplasma gallisepticum* could not find customers for their stock and left the business. Those who successfully eradicated it had a chance to participate in supplying stock in the 1970s.

It is estimated that ten primary breeders entered the 1970s (the definition used here for a primary breeder would be a company that sold more breeding stock than it used itself). Today there are three primary breeders left. These companies are divisions of multinational firms which now specialize in the activity of developing and marketing more efficient turkeys. The other characteristic they share is that they all have lines of turkeys under development which are not currently sold and they therefore represent the industry's future in terms of meeting future, and as yet unspecified, needs.

The acquisition of the breeding companies by multinationals during the 1970s reflected an increasing need for research and development funds and biological expertise to enable these companies to provide the required stock for the 1980s and 1990s.

The largest single breeding stock demand on a worldwide basis is for a 23–25 lb breeder hen which can produce at least 90 eggs in a 24-week production cycle which in turn would yield at least 68 poults.

Male line toms, which provide the growth element to the breeding package, would average at 65 lb or more at the end of the breeding cycle if not feed restricted.

Breeding stock is free of *Mycoplasma gallisepticum, synoviae* and *meleagridis*, three primary sources of economic loss.

At present the European-headquartered turkey breeder supplies three-quarters of the parent needs of that market, while the two North American-based turkey breeders supply 90% of the North American market. This largely seems to be for historical reasons and it is expected that there will be changes in this balance of market penetration in the very near future.

Multipliers and hatcheries

In the 1960s, there were a number of independent hatcheries which either held breeders or purchased eggs on contract, and existed to provide larger groups of turkeys to larger growers who were emerging. This was not always the structure in Europe; in the UK there was early emphasis on total integration whereby companies that processed turkeys had their own breeders and hatcheries.

This has become the case in other markets such as France and Italy, and there has been significant movement in this direction in the USA. Two major independent hatchery companies in the USA have become major processors between 1982 and 1987. The trend is for processing companies to control the breeders by either ownership or contract and to own the hatcheries, therefore being responsible for the poult supply to growers. It is anticipated that there will always be independent growers for filling specialized needs, but that 90% of the industry will be totally integrated, as margins on turkey production become lower in real terms.

The average size of flock held by multipliers would normally range from 5000–12000 hens in production, and it is limited by the intensive labour requirement of egg collection and artificial insemination. In recent years there have been attempts to automate collection of eggs from turkeys, and this is a potentially economic proposition.

While there have been management changes which have led to males being kept on specialized farms where the males themselves and the semen production can be individually evaluated, the job of artificially inseminating hens depends on them being handled individually and given the correct dose of semen in the correct manner. There seems no immediate possibility of significantly automating this operation.

At the hatchery level, while hatchery machines have got bigger, there has been very little change in the basic methodology. In Europe there is rather more emphasis on single stage machines containing eggs all at the same stage of incubation. Hatchability everywhere has been increasing so that a good producing flock can average over 80% hatch of eggs incubated in a laying cycle.

Growing farms

There were many thousands of small growers involved in turkey production in North America in the 1960s. While total numbers remain large, 1600 farms, which produce 30000 or more turkeys per annum, are responsible for 90% of the production. While data are incomplete, there would appear to be a similar situation in Europe. This increasing size of grower reduces the programming aspect of the hatchery function, in turn helping to lead to the integration of the hatchery.

The main financial arrangement for growing turkeys in the world is one of contract growing. At current prices, one and a half times the live value of each turkey produced needs to be invested for each growing turkey space; the capital requirement to grow the whole turkey flock is therefore significant. Processors have an interest to contract the farm and the labour of the grower rather than investing in housing themselves. The contracts between processors and growers are cost-based. They are linked to the price of the poult supplied by the processor, the price of feed supplied by the processor, the cost of utilities and sundry items, the capital cost of the building, the growers' labour, an adjustment which is based on the success of the grower in livability of the turkeys and the feed conversion. Most contracts are regulated by an average production cost for all growers, and then individual growers are paid according to how much better or worse their performance is in relation to the average. This type of contract would be usual in the USA, Italy and France. In the UK the integrator would tend to own the growing farm; in Germany the grower would tend to fund his own production. The contract grower system has proved very effective at times of industry expansion in creating significant additional housing area for production.

Processors

The nature of turkey killing and processing is such that turkeys can be killed and processed in one place and be distributed over a wide area.

Beginning with the branding of whole bird products, processors began to distribute nationally in their markets. As whole bird production has grown into further processing, the need to increase the marketing area has become more significant. Processors now control the industry in deciding production levels by controlling the feed and poult supply. In the USA an average size processing plant may be killing 8–10 million turkeys per year at one location. On present trends, the growth of the industry will be met by expansion of existing plants.

Table 1.3 Turkey meat consumption per capita per annum and the percentage represented by whole turkey sales in 1986

Country	Turkey meat consumed per capita per annum (kg)	% whole turkeys of total production
USA	6.1	42
France	4.5	15
Canada	4.3	46
Italy	4.0	10
UK	2.9	45
West Germany	1.5	5

The whole bird turkey market (*Table 1.3*) is not seen as increasing. There are a limited number of holidays in a year and with the large unit size of turkeys, it is hard to increase whole bird consumption outside this period. By cutting up turkeys and developing further processed products, turkey meat is brought into the weekly budget. While turkey breast is a distinct product, it leaves part of the turkey unsold — the thighs, the legs, and carcass meat. The challenge of further processing has been to develop products for this part of the carcass. Turkey has lost some of its identity in the process by becoming involved in ham, salami, and sausage products but has gained access to the much larger red meat market and is showing signs of having significantly greater consumption in the future.

Turkey production has shifted from being production-led to being marketing-led. Marketing needs are transmitted back to the production level through the totally or partially integrated processing plant.

Turkey meat — the future

As a percentage of all meat consumed, turkey remains at a low level in the major producing countries, normally at 5–6% (*Figure 1.1*). While the growth in turkey meat consumption has been significant, the proportion of the red meat market that it now occupies suggests that there is at least the same potential for future growth. In Israel, where pork is not consumed and beef production is difficult, turkey meat consumption is at 10 kg per capita, indicating that there is consumer willingness to increase consumption. With the present strong growth in turkey meat consumption, a similar level of uptake by 1995 is possible.

While the whole bird market helps the total consumption, it is not necessary for significant consumption of turkey meat. With turkey meat's natural ability to be flavoured to compete with red meat, the future growth opportunities are for further

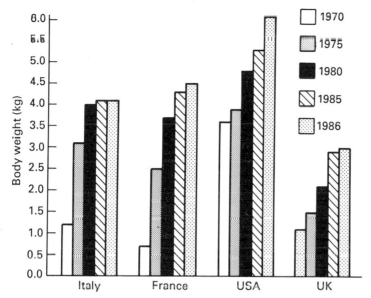

Figure 1.1 Per capita consumption of turkey

processed products directly competing with red meat as opposed to whole birds which have a finite market.

Turkey is lower in fat and cholesterol compared with red meat and is therefore a good raw material for products to be made for an increasingly sedentary and informed consumer. Turkey meat products are already being marketed as being 95–99% fat-free which has consumer appeal.

The future will be of food marketeers having an increasing role in shaping the industry with a highly integrated production system buying in parent breeding stock which will have been subjected to specific selection programmes with meat processing qualities increasingly an objective.

Chapter 2

Genetics of turkeys: origin and development

E. G. Buss

Origin

Historical

A remarkable attempt to provide a comprehensive history of the wild turkey was
made by Schorger (1966). Approximately 2500 references were cited in his book
that starts with the earliest of recorded history nearly five centuries ago. North
America's most important avian contribution to the economy of the world began
when the Spanish explorers took the turkey from Central America to Spain early in
the sixteenth century. When the English colonists came to America, they brought
the turkey back to its native land.

The life histories of gallinaceous birds in North America were studied extensively
by Bent (1932). The family Meleagrididae was divided into four races of *Meleagris
gallopavo*; namely, *merriami* of south-western USA; *silvestris* of north-eastern
United States and Ontario; *osceola* of the southern half of Florida; and *intermedia*
of the Rio Grande Valley. *Gallopavo* of Vera Cruz in Mexico was added by Moore
(1938); Schorger (1966) added *mexicana* in Bolanos, *jalisco* of mexico and *onusta* in
Guayachi, *chihushua* of Mexico. The designations of races were determined largely
by the places in which the turkeys were found; however, some slight variations in
pigmentation of feathers were noted. *Silvestris* had extremely dark feathers
whereas *gallopavo* has pure white tips in the rectrices and tail coverts.

Leopold (1948) claimed there were two species of turkey native to Mexico. The
wild turkey (*Meleagris gallopavo*) occupied areas in the USA and south to central
Mexico, and the ocellated turkey (*Agriocharis ocellata*) occupied the Yucatan
Peninsula of Mexico.

Nature of turkeys at the beginning of commercial development

The number of turkeys and farms with turkeys, plus the known varieties of turkeys
in the 1920s and 1930s in the USA was presented by Marsden and Knox (1937). The
years in which seven varieties of turkeys were recognized were during the
nineteenth century, and the varieties include the Cambridgeshire Bronze and
Norfolk Black from England, Narragansett, White Holland, Slate, Buff and
Bourbon Red. Body weights for Bronze were shown to be greater than for the
other varities.

The varieties and breeding system employed in 1933 to develop the Beltsville
Small White (BSW) turkey during the following ten years were described by

11

Marsden (1967). Bronze, Narragansetts, Blacks and White Hollands were used, and nine objectives were pursued. Commercial adoption of the BSW turkey peaked in 1954.

Development

Gene mutations

Some mutant genes may have a useful characteristic, e.g. white feather pigmentation. Others may be deleterious. In breeding programmes they will be selected against but as such genes are invariably recessive they may remain in a population, albeit at a low level.

The following gene mutants have been described by workers. The mode of inheritance is indicated by: A, autosomal; S, sex linked; A*, S*, co-dominance.

Trait: Feather pigmentation

Description	Symbol	Mode of inheritance	Reference
Non-barring	1	A*	Asmundson, 1939a
Black-winged Bronze	(b' in lieu of 1 above)		Asmundson, 1945b
Slate[a]	s1	A*	Asmundson, 1940
Black	B	A*	Robertson, Bohren and Warren, 1943
Red	r	A*	Robertson, Bohren and Warren, 1943
Slate[a]	D	A*	Robertson, Bohren and Warren, 1943
White	c	A	Robertson, Bohren and Warren, 1943
Narragansett	m	S*	Robertson, Bohren and Warren, 1943
Brown	e	S	Asmundson, 1945b
Faded	–	A	Keeler, Hoffman and Shearer, 1949
Spotting	up	A*	Asmundson, 1955
Pale	–	?	Williams, 1964
Grey	c^g	A	Nestor and Renner, 1979

The genotypes for wild-type female, Bronze, is: b/b, C/C, R/R, S1/S1, Sp/Sp, E/-, N/-

Three alleles at the B locus are:
B
b
b'   Asmundson, 1945b

Three alleles at the N locus are:
N
n
n[a]   Asmundson, 1950

[a] The author of this paper has worked with the locus for slate for 25 years and concludes that the mutation should be referred to as an autosomal recessive, sl, proposed by Asmundson (1940). The colour of the heterozygote is a distinct slate, and it is darker with a few spots of black pigment. Thus, the gene expression is that of visible co-dominance.

Trait: Feather structure

Hairy	Hairy	A	Smyth, 1954

Trait: Feathering

Late feathering	K	S	Asmundson and Abbott, 1961
Naked	na	A	Poole and Marsden, 1961

Trait: Skin

Melanization	m	A	Harper, Bernier and Babcock, 1964

Description	Symbol	Mode of inheritance	Reference
Trait: Muscle			
Muscular dystrophy	dy	A	Harper and Parker, 1967
Degenerative myopathy	–	polygenic	Harper et al., 1975
Trait: Pendulous crop			
Enlarged crop	–	A*	Asmundson and Hinshaw, 1938
Trait: Nerves			
Congenital loco	lo	A*	Cole, 1957
Vibrator	vi	S	Coleman et al., 1960
Trait: Calcified tissues			
Shortening of bones	s	A*	Asmundson, 1944b
Crooked-neck dwarf	–	A	Asmundson and Pun, 1956
Supernumerary spurs	–	?	Williams, 1967
Trait: Eyes			
Albinism	al	S	Hutt and Mueller, 1942
Trait: Blood			
Binucleated red cells	bn	A	Bloom, Buss and Strother, 1970
Trait: Embryonic lethals			
Knobby	kn	A	Smith and Smyth, 1970
Chondrodystrophy	ch	A	Gaffney, 1975
Chondrodystrophy	cn^m	A	Nestor, 1978
16–17 day	–	A	Stout and Buss, 1979a
Ring	rl	A	Savage and Harper, 1985
Swollen plumules	sdp	A	Savage, Wallner-Pendleton and Harper, 1986

b. Pleiotrophy

Description	Reference
Clubbed down – occurs with black pigment, B*	Hawes and Buss, 1963
Red (r/r) reduced body weight and egg weight	
Spotted (sp/sp) – reduced body weight	
White (c/c) – reduced semen volume and sperm concentration	Nestor and Renner, 1979

c. Developmental features noted for some of the mutants

Description	Reference
Albinism	Hutt and Mueller, 1942
Shortening of bones	Asmundson, 1944b
Spotted	Asmundson, 1955
Knobby	Smith and Smyth, 1970

Trait: Increased or total mortality after hatching

Faded Bronze	Keeler, Hoffman and Shearer, 1949
Hairy	Smyth, 1954
Congenital loco	Cole, 1957
Vibrator	Kulenkamp, Coleman and Peterson, 1968

Description	*Reference*
Trait: Reduced rate of growth	
Spotted	Asmundson, 1955
Crooked neck dwarf	Asmundson and Pun, 1956
Muscular dystrophy	Harper and Parker, 1967
Trait: Extra hind toes and joint abnormalities	
Naked	Poole and Marsden, 1961
Trait: Sex influence, higher incidence in females	
Binucleated red blood cells	Bloom, Buss and Strother, 1970
Trait: Parabionts do not alter expression	
Binucleated red blood cells	Searle and Bloom, 1974
Trait: Age in embryonic development at which defect can be identified	
Chondrodystrophy	Stout and Buss, 1979b
Trait: Measure of degree of retardation of embryonic weight and bone growth	
Chondrodystrophy	Lange and Buss, 1984
Trait: Myelin sheath and Purkinji cells	
Vibrator	Peterson, Ringer and Coleman, 1963
Trait: Appearance in commercial flocks	
Crooked neck dwarf	Moorehead and Mohamed, 1968
Trait: Variable penetrance and expressivity	
Degenerative myopathy	Harper *et al.*, 1975
Trait: Variable penetrance	
Pendulous crop	Asmundson and Hinshaw, 1938

The mutant genes observed have prevented expression of the wild-type phenotype; furthermore, limitations to more than one trait have been observed for some mutants. Embryonic or post-hatching mortality is often increased by action of the mutant alleles; also, growth rate is frequently reduced. Some mutations, especially for feather pigmentation, are clearly evident in the heterozygotes. Further observations of all mutants may reveal some degree of phenotypic modification in the respective heterozygotes. Co-dominance may be more ubiquitous than has been observed and reported, therefore, all mutations should be considered as recessive.

Cytogenetics

The various cytological studies (Werner, 1931; Sokolow, Tiniakow and Trofimov, 1936; Stenius, Christian and Ohno, 1963) have elucidated various features regarding numbers, morphology, species differences, appearance in hybrids, constitution in parthenogenetically produced embryos and turkeys and the effect of a mutation on mitotic cell divisions. The morphological studies suggest that the turkey and pheasant resemble each other closely whereas the chromosomes of the chicken are distinctly different. However, the differences in morphology and number do not preclude the production of viable hybrids (Asmundson and Lorenz, 1955; Barraud, 1958; Harada and Buss, 1981a). The 2N chromosome number for turkeys is generally considered to be 80, but various investigators have reported differing 2N numbers (Stenius, Christian and Ohno, 1963; Krishan, 1964; Abroyan and Chilingaryan, 1974). All have found variation among cells. This illustrates the long period of time that is necessary to learn the many intricacies in employing appropriate techniques. The ploidy of cells in parthenogenetically produced embryos has been studied (Yao and Olsen, 1955; Poole, 1959; Sato and Kosin, 1960; Harada and Buss, 1981b) with the result that their origin is more reasonably described.

Autosomes and sex chromosomes have been studied for the position of the centromere as well as sizes. Therefore, the idiogram can be used as a cytotaxonomic feature and as a diagnostic tool.

Genetic control of biochemical parameters has received only limited attention. The majority of the studies have been on comparisons of species, strains and varieties. Generally, when differences were found, the more precise nature of the genetic influence has not been pursued. Two exceptions, one with albumen phenotypes (Quinteros et al., 1964) and the other with adenosine deaminase (Grunder and Hollands, 1978), revealed that a single pair of alleles existed for each of these traits. Several loci and alleles have been discovered for blood groups.

Association of biochemical traits and economic traits have been investigated, but the results have not indicated striking relationships. One blood group allele and body weight allele appeared to merit further study (Stevens and Asmundson, 1968). Only one significant study of amino acid sequences has been found for turkeys (Grant, Sanders and Hood, 1971). With the vast amount of research for other species in this area, it seems reasonable to suggest that more should be done in the turkey, especially as related to disease susceptibility, resistance and diagnosis.

Physiological assessments

Krista et al. (1969) and (1970) demonstrated that differences existed between strains for systolic blood pressure and that this could be influenced by selection. Aortic rupture was five times higher in the hypertensive than in the hypotensive line. Heritability estimates of blood pressure averaged about 0.30. Simialr work was carried out by Shoffner et al. (1971).

Two lines of turkeys differing greatly in body weight and egg production were studied by Nestor, Bacon and Renner (1970). Ovarian weight was larger in the meat line. Within lines, there were significant differences in ovarian weight and period of rapid development. However it was concluded that yolk production is not the limiting factor in the lower egg production characteristic of heavier meat lines. Further studies by Bacon, Nestor and Renner (1972) confirmed this; also there were more atretic follicles in more females in the meat line.

Parthenogenesis

Parthenogenesis in turkeys occurs naturally (Olsen and Marsden, 1954a; 1954b; 1956). The incidence can be increased by selection, and an increase in incidence is accompanied by a higher proportion of embryos and embryos that hatch (Olsen,

1960a; 1960b). Hundreds of parthenogens have been reared and high levels of fertility have been recorded for parthenogenically-produced males. All parthenogens are males, and the advanced embryos and hatched poults are diploid (Olsen, 1965). As studies have advanced, the evidence indicates that most parthenogens are isozygous; however, some questions remain unanswered. Parthenogenesis appears to begin with a haploid gamete (Harada and Buss, 1981b), but diploidy results from some mechanism not described thus far. Embryonic development has been advanced by the use of live fowl pox vaccinations (Olsen and Buss, 1967), but the onset of development in parthenogenetic development is retarded. Polyembryony is a striking event that suggests mitotic divisions among cells of a large population on the surface of the yolk. Isozygous males are, by genotype, free of lethals and potentially valuable as breeders. Females producing eggs with a high incidence of parthenogens can be recognized as to embryonic lethals they carry. Chromosomes segregate in a 1:1 fashion; hence, one-half of the embryos may exhibit the one, two, three or more lethals carried. Parthenogenesis affords a remarkable way of purging embryonic lethals from turkeys (Olsen, 1969).

Economic traits

Body weight

Selection has been demonstrated to be effective for increasing body weight. Performance goals for growth rate are now more than double those reported in a survey by Marsden and Knox in 1937.

The most desirable age for selection appears to be at or near the age the turkeys are marketed (Johnson and Gowe, 1962; Abplanalp, Ogasawara and Asmundson, 1963). As a percentage of male body weights, females may be as low as 50% and as high as 85% (Shaklee, Knox and Marsen, 1952). Body weights of neither the males nor the females were indications of the magnitude of the differences between the sexes.

Heritabilities for females in 17 studies were reported by Arthur and Abplanalp (1975). The average was 0.41. Nestor (1984) reported a lower heritability of 0.24 for females in the sixteenth generation of turkeys selected for increased body weight at 16 weeks of age. Differences in sexes indicate that estimates may be slightly higher for males (MacLaury et al., 1954; Goodman, Brunson and Godfrey, 1954; Nestor, 1984). Results of variety and strain crosses have been mixed, but, generally, F_1s do not exceed the better parent and more normally will be intermediate between the parents (Hassan, Kosba and Zaiden, 1984).

Body conformation

Asmundson (1944a) studied three strains of Bronze and concluded that width of breast at a definite distance from the anterior end could be used to differentiate strains, and it is the only body feature other than weight that needs to be used. At 24 weeks, one-half of the variation in width of breast is determined by variation in weight. Asmundson (1945a) reported on the inheritance of breast width. Two strains were crossed, and the F_1s were intermediate. Furthermore, reciprocal backcrosses were intermediate between the F_1 and the respective parents. El-Ibiary (1948) found that the turkeys having wider breasts are likely to have slightly shorter shanks than narrower breasted birds of the same weight. El-Ibiary and Jull (1948) concluded that it is possible to establish strains differing significantly in plumpness of breast by selecting breeders on a progeny-test basis. The influence of sires in transmitting breast width to progeny was more pronounced than that of the females. An exceptional study with many correlations among traits was published by Lasley (1949). Determination of the width of breast was superior to other skeletal measurements. The degree of fleshing becomes increasingly important in determining body weight. Nestor (1971) did not find any heterosis for breast width at 24 weeks in the progeny from two large commercial strains. Andrews (1972) reported that greater body weight was associated with well-rounded breasts. Correlations for males and females differed. Bird (1948) described equipment for measurement of the roundness of breast. The critical point for measurement of breast width is one-fifth of body from the crest of the keel to the spinal column. Arthur and Abplanalp (1975) reported an estimate of heritability for conformation as 0.28, and a genetic correlation of conformation with body weight of 0.58.

Body characteristics

Jaap (1938) studied conformation in 27- and 28-week-old turkeys. Many correlations of body characteristics were reported. In both sexes, those with shorter shanks and thighs in proportion to body weight were considered to have better fleshing. Jaap, Thompson and Milby (1939) found shorter shanks and less depth of body, at all ages, in progeny selected for greater body weight. The growth of shank length stopped at 20–22 weeks in females while the length continued to 24–26 weeks in the male. Asmundson and Lerner (1942) found a high correlation between logarithmic body weight and logarithmic shank length up to the time growth ceased for shank length. All bones are expected to be shorter per unit of body weight in larger birds. Asmundson (1944a) concluded that length of shank, length of keel and depth of body and keel length is not correlated with depth of body. Knox and Marsden (1944) studied four varieties, F_1s and F_2s. Shank length, breast type and body weight were found to exhibit blending inheritance. Asmundson (1948) determined that, per unit of body weight, males have shorter shanks than females, and, in general, heavier birds have longer shanks. El-Ibiary and Jull (1948) concluded that it is possible to establish strains, with widely differing skeletal proportions. However, correlations between keel length and body depth or shank length were high — 0.87. Correlations of body characteristics with breast width were low. An extensive study of some body measurements was conducted by Kondra and Shoffner (1955a). It was concluded that breeders would gain very little by taking into account body measurements in addition to selection for body weight. Using hybrids of turkeys, chickens and pheasants, Asmundson and Lorenz (1957) showed evidence of additive gene expression for bone length. Johnson and Asmundson (1957a) reported many correlations among traits. They found that selection for longer bones has little effect on breast width. Also, no consistent changes in heritability estimates of body characteristics with age were found. In another paper, Johnson and Asmundson (1957b) studied muscles, and they found that the growth of muscle continues after the skeleton has diminished or stopped. In males and females, the total breast muscle as a percentage of body weight was 16% at 8 weeks and 19% at 24 weeks. Keel length and breast width were found to be significantly correlated with the weight of breast muscle when the variation due to body weight was removed. McCartney (1961) reported many correlations among body characteristics and between these traits and body weight. Nearly all correlations between body measurements and between these traits and body weight were positive and quite high, >0.50. Another aspect of measurements of body characteristics is repeatability. This has been examined by Nestor and Chamberlain (1966) who found that, for the caliper, repeatability was over 0.60 for shank length and body depth but only 0.31 for keel length and breast width. McCartney, Nestor and Harvey (1968) increased all body measurements at 24 weeks in two lines by selection. Mukherjee and Friars (1970) selected for 7 years in two commercial strains. No time trends for heritability were observed for body weight and body measurements. Nestor, McCartney and Harvey (1967) reported many heritabilities for body characteristics and body weight. These values were all near 0.50, except for body weight which was only 0.28. Kreuger et al. (1972) selected primarily for reproductive performance in a strain of Broad Breasted Bronze for 5 years. Body measurements did not change materially. Body weight did show a consistent upward trend. Heritabilities for all traits were reported. Nestor (1971) did not find any significant indications for heterosis of shank length, keel length and body depth at 24 weeks of age. Nestor et al. (1985) mass selected to increase shank length. A significant increase was achieved only for the males. Shank width was determined to be significantly different between two lines; it increased consistently with increase in length due to selection. Average heritabilities reported for females by Arthur and Abplanalp (1975) are 0.51 for shank length ($n=7$), 0.36 keel length ($n=10$), 0.41 for body weight ($n=10$) and 0.23 for breast width ($n=11$); also, average estimates for genetic correlation of these traits with body weight are given. The correlations are 0.57 for shank length ($n=5$), 0.50 for keel length ($n=5$), 0.64 for body depth ($n=5$), 0.64 for body depth and 0.57 for breast width ($n=6$). Nestor et al. (1985) found the heritability for shank width to be 0.29, and Popescu-Vifor and Puscatu (1977) reported 0.55 as an estimate of heritability for chest width.

Shank length, keel length, body depth and breast width appear to be expressed by additive gene action. Although the proportions may be changed by selection, the evidence for the worth of these traits to improve body weight does not merit their being included as traits for selection in a breeding programme.

Sexual maturity

Females

Early work on this subject (Asmundson, 1939b; Whitson, Marsden and Titus, 1944) did not eliminate the influence of seasonal daylength pattern on sexual maturity.

Harper (1949) ranked hens into seven groups for days to first egg following the beginning of artificial lights for lengthening the light period of the day. Hens starting to lay after only 19 days of extra light produced 64 eggs while those taking more than 30 days produced only 31 eggs. An increase in days to first egg was clearly associated with fewer eggs. Mukherjee and Friars (1970) selected two lines for increased weight at 12 weeks for four generations. The heritability for age at first egg was reported as 0.32 for the larger and 0.15 for the smaller line. Nestor (1972) used four strains in a 9-year study. Days to first egg and eggs produced were negatively correlated, -0.42.

Heritability for days to first egg was determined to be 0.81. However, in another paper in 1972, Nestor, Brown and Weaver reported an estimate for heritability to be 0.31 for days to first egg. Koneva (1976) reported heritability estimates of 0.43

and 0.40 for days to first egg in two varieties. Bacon and Nestor (1977) found the number of days to first egg to be 22 and 23 as averages for four medium-sized and for seven large-bodied strains respectively.

Males

Inheritance of sexual maturity in male turkeys was investigated by Lorenz and Lerner (1946). The onset of semen production ranged from 137 to 293 days. Analyses of data left little doubt about the conclusion that the age at which semen is produced is inherited.

Carson, Lorenz and Asmundson (1955) found significant differences in age at maturity for males and from two strains and among sire families. Differences between strains were increased from 12 to 44 days by selection in only 1 year. Date of hatch had less effect on mean age at maturity of the early than of the late strain. Heritability was found to be 0.50 for age at which a first collection contained 500 million sperm.

Semen production

Selection has been demonstrated to be effective in altering the volume of semen produced (Nestor 1976; Shanskova, 1976). Strains vary in average volume of semen (Cherms, 1968). There is some indication that concentration may be increased when volume is increased by selection (Nestor, Brown and Renner, 1979). However it has been shown that larger males have larger testes and diameters of seminiferous tubules (Kresan, 1983). The volume of semen at the peak may be at least 0.3 million per collection, and it may decline as the season advances (Pingel *et al.*, 1984). An average of heritability estimates for semen volume is 0.36 and 0.40 for sperm concentration.

Broodiness and pauses

Broodiness has been reduced when selection for increased egg production was effective (Knox and Marsden, 1954; McCartney, Nestor and Harvey, 1968). Hens that respond more quickly, less than 3 weeks, to artificial lights given 14 h of daylight, have few days lost to broodiness (Nestor, 1972). As days to first egg increase, the days lost to broodiness increase. Strains differ in the incidence of broodiness (Bacon and Nestor, 1977). Body weight does not appear to be associated with broodiness (Nestor, 1977). High levels of prolactin may be found in highly productive hens (Bacon, Nestor and Renner, 1986), so it is not a reliable indicator. Broodiness within a population can be reduced by identifying broody birds and removing to pens without nests (Nestor, Bacon and Renner, 1986); however, such treatment appears to be unaffected by genetic differences among strains. Nestor (1972) estimated the heritability for broody pauses was 0.33 and that for days lost from broodiness was 0.46.

Number of eggs

The early work on eggs numbers was greatly influenced by the season of the year over which the hens were laying. Strains and varieties differ for egg production (Kondra and Shoffner, 1955a and b; McCartney, Chamberlain and Wyne, 1956).

Heritability of egg numbers has been estimated by many researchers. Arthur and Abplanalp (1975) summarized 18 reported heritabilities for egg number and arrived at an average of 0.22. The more recent work (Nestor, 1972; Nestor, Brown and Weaver, 1972; Kunev, Bachev and Todorova, 1975; Koneva, 1976; Desmarais, 1984) would indicate a higher value, sometimes in excess of 0.30. This may be the result of the improved health and management of the modern strains of turkey.

Days to first egg is an indicator of production, the fewer the days the more eggs produced. Persistency is an important factor in the total number of eggs. Strong and Nestor (1978) found significant differences in egg production between five lines but no significant differences in plasma phosphorus, plasma calcium and lipophosphoprotein concentrations among the five lines were found.

Single trait selections have generally found that as egg production was increased, body weight declined (Nestor, 1977; Nestor, 1980). Likewise, selection for increased body weight generally results in a lower number of eggs (Nestor, 1984; Nestor and Bacon, 1986). However, Robel (1981), comparing a large with a small strain for egg production over a 23-week period, found a positive association of egg production with body weight. Nearly all of the selection experiments have been based on mass or individual selections. A limited use of an index for egg number and body weight has been reported and the results suggest that progress in both traits can be accomplished simultaneously (Clayton, 1971; Desmarais, 1984).

Clayton (1970) reported an exceptionally fine analysis on the genetics of egg production. The flock used was fully pedigreed. In the analysis, the sire components of variance were consistently and highly significant, suggesting that the principal source of genetic variation for egg production resides in the sex chromosome. It was suggested that males be selected from superior dam families on the basis of 12-week records. Females should be selected on the basis of their own record combined with that of their dam and sire family averages. Part season records that are meaningful will most likely require a schedule that exceeds 52 weeks.

Results from two- and three-way crosses have generally yielded results that were intermediate to the parental lines. The best use of crossing appears to be a two-way to produce a female that is then crossed with a male of a third line.

Fertility

It is now universal commercial practice to use artificial insemination to fertilize eggs. A wealth of data on the genetics of fertility results from the use of artificial matings.

Maw and McCartney (1956) found variation between individuals in the length of duration of fertility following a single insemination. The average number of days for duration in all birds was 36; 5% of the hens had a duration exceeding 50 days. The correlation of fertility and duration of fertility was 0.40, which was significant.

Nestor, Brown and Weaver (1972) determined an estimate of heritability for fertility to be 0.34; also, the genetic correlation for fertility and egg production was 0.59. Koneva (1976) compared two varieties of turkeys and estimated heritabilities for fertility to be 0.28 for one and 0.39 for the other.

Nestor (1976) selected for increased semen yield for five generations. There was no consistent change in percentage fertility. Shanskova (1976) selected for 4 years to maintain body weight while increasing semen quality. Percentage fertility increased slightly, 89% to 92%. Nestor (1977) mass selected two lines for 9 years to increase body weight. No significant correlation of body weight with percentage fertility was found. Nestor (1980) selected to establish a line for increased clutch length and one for few days lost due to broodiness. In the seventh generation, the clutch line had lost 7% fertility and the reduced broodiness line lost 1%. Nestor (1984) selected for 16 generations to improve 16-week body weight. The effect on fertility was inconsistent. Selection based on families has been suggested by some of those who have studied this rather independent trait.

Hatchability

From a review of the literature, it is evident that varieties and strains differ for hatchability with some exceeding 80% with others more than 20% less. Abplanalp and Kosin (1953) used three lines of Broad Breasted Bronze; hatchability was 82, 78 and 74%. Storage effects of 1 week versus 2 weeks were compared. The greatest loss was for the line having the highest hatchability. Kosin (1964) also found genetic variation in the rate of loss in hatchability due to storage before incubation.

Crossing of strains and varieties yields inconsistent results but generally the better parent is not exceeded (Kondra and Shoffner, 1955b; Rooney, 1957). Frequently, maternal influence is observed (McCartney and Chamberlain, 1961) and hatchability of the cross is similar to the female's parent. F_1 females mated to males of a third strain offer the best use of crosses to bring hatchability near that of the better parental line used in producing the F_1 female. Hatchability appears to be a female characteristic that is not greatly affected by the male.

Work on the influence of body weight and other body characteristics on hatchability presents a contradictory picture. Some workers could find no influence on hatchability (Ogasawara, Abplanalp and Asmundson, 1963; Nestor, 1977; Nestor, 1984). Other work (McCartney, Nestor and Harvey, 1968; Mymrin and Krivich, 1972; Cramer, 1975) suggests an adverse effect on hatchability resulting from increased body weights. Heritability estimates vary greatly. Mukherjee and Friars (1970) using two commercial strains estimated it to be 0.24 for the larger strain and 0.30 for the smaller. Koneva (1976) estimated heritability for hatchability in two varieties; in the white, it was 0.10 and in the Bronze it was 0.40. Nestor, Brown and Weaver (1972) estimated heritability for hatchability to be 0.17. The genetic correlation of hatchability with egg number was determined to be 0.52 and 0.94 with fertility.

Nestor (1980) found hatchability to be negatively correlated with days lost to broodiness, -0.62. Selection of a line for longer clutch length resulted in a decrease of 2% in hatchability. Selection for fewer days lost to broodiness resulted in an increase of 1% in hatchability. Strong and Nestor (1980) used four medium-sized and seven large lines in a study of egg traits and any associated effects with hatchability. The relationship of various egg characteristics and components differed between medium and large lines. No conclusion could be drawn. Christensen and McCorkle (1982) used three lines, one control, one for increased egg weight and one for decreased egg weight. It was concluded that each strain may require a unique environmental condition for embryonic viability.

Viability

From the very limited information published, it does not appear that viability is enhanced by crossing varieties and strains (Kondra and Shoffner, 1955b; Clark, 1961). Cahaner, Abplanalp and Shultz (1980) found that viability was reduced by 1.4% when inbreeding was increased by 10%.

Egg weight

Selection on an individual basis for increased egg number generally results in a decrease in egg weight (Arthur and Abplanalp, 1975; Nestor, 1980). A similar selection procedure for increased body weight results in an increase in egg weight (Kunev, Bachev and Todorova, 1975; Strong and Nestor, 1980; Nestor and Bacon, 1986). An average for estimates of heritability for egg weight is 0.50.

Feed efficiency

No recent work on this topic is available. In early work (Headley, 1948; Lasley, 1949; Lucas, Seeger and Tomhave, 1949; McCartney, 1952) comparisons of varieties and strains reaching various body weights are consistent in showing that the largest turkeys attain the weight with less feed per unit of gain. Clark (1961) made reciprocal crosses among varieties of turkey. Feed efficiency varied only slightly between purebreds and crossbreds. Wolford et al. (1963) found that total feed consumption was positively correlated with total egg production and with body weight, 0.32 and 0.46 respectively. The effect of body size on feed consumption was lessened as the rate of production increased.

Yield of edible meat

The yield of breast meat on a percentage basis tends to increase as the body weight increases. Work on this subject has included measurements of physical characteristics and it seems likely that breast width has also increased as body weight has increased. Considerable variation in meat yield exists between strains (McCartney, 1952; Orr, Hunt and Snyder, 1956; Taylor and Fry, 1967; Hayse and Moreng, 1973; Orr et al., 1974).

Using 12 strains from a Random Sample Test, Taylor and Fry (1967) found significant differences in yield of both breast and thighs. Skinless breasts varied from 23.4 to 29.7% for males and 22.8 to 27.7% for females. Skinless thighs varied from 12.9 to 14.1% for males and 13.3 to 14.8% for females.

The percentage skin varies between varieties and increases with age. As the percentage goes up, the percentage breast meat goes down while thigh meat remains unaffected by the reciprocal relationship of skin and meat (MacNeil and Buss, 1968; Hartung and Froning, 1968).

The fat content as expressed by abdominal fat and indirectly by percentage skin with its accompanying subcutaneous fat shows considerable variation between strains (Nestor, 1982; Marquez et al., 1983; Bacon, Nestor and Renner, 1986) and appears worthy of selection for a reduced amount. Bacon, Nestor and Renner (1986) found the genetic correlation between body weight and weight of abdominal fat pad and total carcass fat is positive, 0.39.

Both Clark (1961) and MacNeil and Buss (1968) found that breast meat and total meat yield of the F_1s were intermediate to that of the parents. However Scerbina (1969) found that the meat yield of F_1s from White parents and Bronze males was 46% better than the intermediate of that of the parents, but the yield of F_1s from the reciprocal mating were less than that of the parent lines. The details of the parent lines were not given.

In view of the growth of further processing of turkeys into meat products, there is a need for more information on the genetics of factors affecting meat yields.

Phenotypic deformation

Of most economic importance are leg deformities and foot pad lesions. Experimental evidence is lacking to show that growth rate is associated with leg defects. Riddell (1981) reviewed many papers concerned with skeletal deformities in poultry. It was concluded that there is no experimental evidence that rapid growth is the primary cause of skeletal deformities.

Nestor et al. (1985) observed the influence of genetic increases in body weight with walking ability. A line selected for shank width and another selected for increased weight were compared with a heavy control line. The walking ability of the weight line was judged to be poorer than the control, whereas the line selected for increased shank width was considered to walk better than the control. LeBlanc et al. (1986) studied the histology and histocompatibility of tibia growth in two strains, one small without leg problems and the other large with an incidence of 10–30% of leg problems. The results supported the hypothesis than an inadequate metaphysical vascular supply may be the primary defect in the development of tibial dyschondroplasis.

While the incidence of foot pad lesions varies among strains, there is no evidence to indicate that it is a primary genetic deformity.

Selection

Suggested breeding programmes have been outlined by various workers (Marsden, 1948; Clayton, 1962; Shannon and Armour, 1962; Nestor, McCartney and Bachev, 1969). Body weight and body characteristics are amenable to noticeable change whereas it is difficult to improve reproductive characteristics. Multitrait and index selection has been suggested. The number of individuals needed has received sparse comment. The use of fully pedigreed dam and sire families is mentioned but the mode of selection lacks data. Clayton (1974) discussed the effect of size on efficiency and progress in turkey breeding — with emphasis being given to the importance of developing one or possibly two male lines and a stable of female lines.

Feed efficiency and edible meat yield are traits emerging with greater importance. Employment of biochemical, physiological and cytological techniques do not appear among recommendations for commercial breeding programmes. Studies of molecular methods for their worth in breeding programmes have not been employed, except for the possibility in vaccine production.

Many estimates of heritability have been determined for economic traits, and a few have been reported for a vast array of other traits. Continuing this practice does not appear to be justified.

Additional experiments using single traits appear to be highly questionable. The use of mass selection for traits leaves doubt about the efficiency with which these traits may be modified by pedigreed and family selection. The numbers of individuals and families needed for a breeding programme remains a question. Many papers have recorded associated effects on traits other than the ones selected for. How many of these associations are chance events is not known. From F_1s, F_2 populations need to be produced so that sibs may be compared to determine if associations of traits do in fact segregate together.

The research papers do not suggest that studies of the characteristics of populations and associations of traits were carried out before selections were initiated. Furthermore, there is no indication that large populations were used whereby maximum genotypic differences could be available for more divergent selections in the initial generation. Hence, selection for differences may have been limited, because the initial generation did not differ greatly.

Recommendation

Much closer relationships should be established between the researchers of government and universities with the professionally trained geneticists directing commercial pedigreed breeding programmes to determine problems for which there are no answers and merit investment of research funds.

References

Abplanalp, H. and Kosin, I. L. (1953). Genetic variation of fertility and hatchability in the Broad Breasted Bronze turkey. *Poultry Science, 32*, 321–331

Abplanalp, H., Ogasawara, F. X. and Asmundson, V. S. (1963). Influence of selection for body weight at different ages on growth of turkeys. *British Poultry Science, 4*, 71–82

Abroyan, L. O. and Chilingaryan, A. A. (1974). Chromosome complement of domestic fowls, turkeys and their hybrids. *Biologicheskii Zhurnal Armenii, 27*, 47–51. In *Animal Breeding Abstracts* (1975), 9, 484, no. 4269

Andrews, L. D. (1972). Phenotypic correlations for certain turkey parameters. *Poultry Science, 51*, 1270–1275

Arthur, J. A. and Abplanalp, H. (1975). Linear estimates of heritability and genetic correlation for egg production, body weight, conformation and egg weights of turkeys. *Poultry Science, 54*, 11–23

Asmundson, V. S. (1939a). Inherited non-barring in the flight feathers in turkeys. *Journal of Heredity, 30*, 342–348

Asmundson, V. S. (1939b). On the measurements and inheritance of sexual maturity in turkeys (*Meleagris gallopavo*). *American Naturalist, 73*, 365–374

Asmundson, V. S. (1940). A recessive slate plumage color of turkeys. *Journal of Heredity, 31*, 215–217

Asmundson, V. S. (1944a). Measuring strain differences in the conformation of turkeys. *Poultry Science, 23*, 21–29

Asmundson, V. S. (1944b). Inherited shortening of the bones in the turkey. *Journal of Heredity, 35*, 295–299

Asmundson, V. S. (1945a). Inheritance of breast width in turkeys. *Poultry Science, 24*, 150–154

Asmundson, V. S. (1945b). A triple-allele series and plumage color in turkeys. *Genetics, 30*, 305–322

Asmundson, V. S. (1948). Inherited differences in weight and conformation of Bronze turkeys. *Poultry Science, 27*, 695–708

Asmundson, V. S. (1950). Sex-linkage in the turkey. *Journal of Heredity, 41*, 205–207

Asmundson, V. S. (1955). Inheritance of spotting in the plumage of turkeys. *Journal of Heredity*, **46**, 285–288

Asmundson, V. S. and Abbott, U. K. (1961). Dominant sex-linked late feathering in the turkey. *Journal of Heredity*, **52**, 99–104

Asmundson, V. S. and Hinshaw, W. R. (1938). On the inheritance of pendulous crop in turkeys (*Meleagris gallopavo*). *Poultry Science*, **17**, 276–285

Asmundson, V. S. and Lerner, I. M. (1942). Growth of turkeys. II. Relative growth of the tarsometatarsus. *Poultry Science*, **21**, 505–510

Asmundson, V. S. and Lorenz, F. W. (1955). Pheasant-turkey hybrids. *Science*, **121**, 307–308

Asmundson, V. S. and Lorenz, F. W. (1957). Hybrids of ring-necked pheasants, turkeys and domestic fowl. *Poultry Science*, **36**, 1323–1334

Asmundson, V. S. and Pun, C. F. (1956). Crooked neck dwarf in the turkey. *Journal of Experimental Zoology*, **131**, 225–237

Bacon, W. L. and Nestor, K. E. (1977). The effect of various lighting treatments or the presence of toms on reproductive performance of hen turkeys. *Poultry Science*, **56**, 415–420

Bacon, W. L., Nestor, K. E. and Renner, P. A. (1972). Further studies on ovarian follicular development in egg and meat type turkeys. *Poultry Science*, **51**, 398–401

Bacon, W. L., Nestor, K. E.. and Renner, P. A. (1986). The influence of genetic increases in body weight and shank width on the abdominal fat pad and carcass composition of turkeys. *Poultry Science*, **65**, 391–397

Barraud, C. (1958). On a case of hybridization between the turkey and the guinea fowl. Doctoral thesis, Veterinary Faculty Medicine, University of Paris, pp. 1–59. In *Animal Breeding Abstracts*, **27**, 101, No. 470

Bent, A. C. (1932). Life histories of North American gallinaceous birds; orders galliformes and columbiformes. *United States National Museum Bulletin*, **162**, 1–490

Bird, S. (1948). Quantitative determination and segregation of breast conformation in poultry. *Poultry Science*, **27**, 506–508

Bloom, S. E., Buss, E. G. and Strother, G. K. (1970). Cytological and cytophotometric analysis of binucleated red blood cell mutants (bn) in turkeys (*Meleagris gallopavo*). *Genetics*, **65**, 51–63

Cahaner, A., Abplanalp, H. and Shultz, F. T. (1980). Effects of inbreeding on production traits in turkeys. *Poultry Science*, **59**, 1353–1362

Carson, J. D., Lorenz, F. W. and Asmundson, V. S. (1955). Semen production in the turkey male. 2. Age at sexual maturity. *Poultry Science*, **34**, 344–347

Cherms, F. L. (1968). Variations in semen quality and the relationships of semen quality of fertility of turkeys. *Poultry Science*, **47**, 746–754

Christensen, V. L. and McCorkle, F. M. (1982). Characterization of incubational egg weight losses in three types of turkeys. *Poultry Science*, **61**, 848–854

Clark, T. B. (1961). Crossbreeding in turkeys. II. Summary of studies on hatchability, growth and body characteristics. *West Virginia Unive;rsity Agricultural Experiment Station Bulletin*, **455T**, 1–30

Clayton, G. A. (1962). A system of turkey breeding. *London Bulletin*, **185**, 1–29. London, MAFF

Clayton, G. A. (1970). Genetics of egg production in turkeys. *Proceedings XIV World Poultry Congress*, **2**, 27–35

Clayton, G. A. (1971). Egg production in turkeys. *British Poultry Science*, **12**, 463–474

Clayton, G. A. (1974). Turkey breeding. *World's Poultry Science Journal*, **30**, 290–300

Cole, R. K. (1957). Congenital loco in turkeys. *Journal of Heredity*, **48**, 173–175

Coleman, T. H., Ringer, R. K., Mathey, W. J., Rood, K. G. and Pope, C. W. (1960). Vibrator, a recessive sex-linked mutation in turkeys. *Journal of Heredity*, **51**, 158–160

Cramer, J. L. (1975). Genetics and physiological parameters related to body size in five strains and crosses of the domestic turkey, *Meleagris gallopavo*. *Dissertation Abstracts International*, **B35**, 5938

Desmarais, M. (1984). Selection of a broiler turkey strain for egg production. *Proceedings XVII World's Poultry Congress*, 97–99

El-Ibiary, H. M. (1948). Body confirmation in turkeys. *Poultry Science*, **27**, 825–826

El-Ibiary, H. M. and Jull, M. A. (1948). Criteria and genetic variation of live body conformation in turnkeys. *Poultry Science*, **27**, 40–52

Gaffney, L. J. (1975). Chondrodystrophy: an inherited lethal condition in turkey embryos. *Journal of Heredity*, **66**, 339–343

Goodman, B. L., Brunson, C. C. and Godfrey, G. F. (1954). Heritability of 25-week body weight in turkeys. *Poultry Science*, **33**,305–307

Grant, J. A., Sanders, B. and Hood, L. (1971). Partial amino acid sequences of chicken and turkey immunoglobulin light chains. Homology with mammalian k chains. *Biochemistry*, **10**, 3123–3132

Grunder, A. A. and Hollands, K. G. (1978). Inheritance of adenosine deaminase variants in chickens and turkeys. *Animal Blood Groups and Biochemical Genetics*, **9**, 215–222

Harada, K. and Buss, E. G. (1981a). Turkey-chicken hybrids: A cytological study of early development. *Journal of Heredity*, **72**, 264–266

Harada, K. and Buss, E. G. (1981b). The chromosomes of turkey embryos during early stages of parthenogenetic development. *Genetics*, **98**, 335–345

Harper, J. A. (1949). The rate of response of turkey hens to artificial light as related to reproduction. *Poultry Science*, **28**, 312–314

Harper, J. A. and Parker, J. E. (1967). Hereditary muscular dystrophy in the domestic turkey. *Journal of Heredity*, **58**, 189–193

Harper, J. A., Bernier, P. E. and Babcock, W. E. (1964). Skin melanization in the domestic turkey, *Meleagris gallopavo*. *Poultry Science*, **43**, 577–583

Harper, J. A., Bernier, P. E., Helfer, D. H. and Schmitz, J. A. (1975). Degenerative myopathy of the deep pectoral muscle in the turkey. *Journal of Heredity*, **66**, 362–366

Hartung, T. E. and Froning, G. W . (1968). Variation of physical components of turkey carcasses as influenced by sex, age and strain. *Poultry Science*, **47**, 1348–1355

Hassan, M. F., Kosba, M. A. and Zaidan, S. A. (1984). Heterosis and heritability estimates of body weight in turkeys. *Beitrage zur Tropischen Landwirtschaft und Veterinarmedizin*, **22**, 427. In *Animal Breeding Abstracts*, **53**, 987, No. 7957

Hawes, R. O. and Buss, E. G. (1963). The association of a clubbed down condition with black down-color in the turkey. *Poultry Science*, **42**, 50–58

Hayse, P. L. and Moreng, R. E. (1973). The influence of genetic strain on growth performance and meat yield of large White turkeys. *Poultry Science*, **52**, 1552–1556

Headley, F. B. (1948). Relation of size of turkeys to economy of production, edible meat in carcass and weights of parts of carcass. *Nevada Agricultural Experiment Station Bulletin*, **180**, 1–14

Hutt, F. B. and Mueller, C. D. (1942). Sex-linked albinism in the turkey, *Meleagris gallopavo*. *Journal of Heredity*, **33**, 69–77

Jaap, R. G. (1938). Body conformation of the live market turkey. *Poultry Science*, **17**, 120–125

Jaap, R. G., Thompson, R. B. and Milby, T. T. (1939). Heritable body shape of the domestic turkey. *Proceedings VI World's Poultry Congress*, 68–70

Johnson, A. S. and Asmundson, V. S. (1957a). Genetic and environmental factors affecting size of body and body parts of turkeys. 1. The heritability and interrelationships of body size and live body measurements. *Poultry Science*, **36**, 296–301

Johnson, A. S. and Asmundson, V. S. (1957b). Genetic and environmental factors affecting size of body and body parts of turkeys. 2. The relation of body weight and certain body measurements to pectoral and tibial muscle weights. *Poultry Science*, **36**, 959–966

Johnson, A. S. and Gowe, R. S. (1962). Modification of the growth pattern of the domestic turkey by selection at two ages. *Proceedings XII World's Poultry Congress*, Section Papers 57, 62, No. 1542

Keeler, C. E., Hoffman, E. and Shearer, R. K. (1949). Faded Bronze plumage: an autosomal mutant in the turkey. *Poultry Science*, **28**, 633–635

Knox, C. W. and Marsden, S. J. (1944). The inheritance of some quantitative characteristics in turkeys. *Journal of Heredity*, **35**, 89–96

Knox, C. W. and Marsden, S. J. (1954). Breeding for increased egg production in Beltsville Small White turkeys. *Poultry Science*, **33**, 443–447

Kondra, P. A. and Shoffner, R. N. (1955a). Heritability of some body measurements and reproductive characters in turkeys. *Poultry Science*, **34**, 1262–1267

Kondra, P. A. and Shoffner, R. N. (1955b). Crossing strains and breeds of turkeys. *Poultry Science*, **34**, 1268–1274

Koneva, A. F. (1976). Heritability of basic production traits and physicomorphological egg traits of North Caucasus turkeys. *Trudy*, **8**, 135–138. In *Animal Breeding Abstracts*, **45**, 253, No. 2084

Kosin, I. L. (1964). Recent research trends in hatchability-related problems of the domestic fowl. *World's Poultry Science Journal*, **20**, 254–268

Kresan, J. (1983). The morphogenesis and growth of testes in turkeys after hatching. *Acta Zootechnica Nitra*, **39**, 233–244. In *Animal Breeding Abstracts*, **52**, 635, No. 5011

Krishan, A. (1964). Microchromosomes in the spermatogenesis of the domestic turkey. *Experimental Cell Research*, **33**, 1–17

Krista, L. M., Waible, P. E., Sautter, J. H. and Shoffner, R. N. (1969). Aortic rupture, body weight and blood pressure in the turkey as influenced by strain, dietary fat, Beta-aminopropionitrile fumarate and diethylstilbestrol. *Poultry Science*, **48**, 1954–1960

Krista, L. M., Waible, P. E., Shoffner, R. N. and Sautter, J. H. (1970). A study of aortic rupture and performance as influenced by selection for hypertension and hypotension in the turkey. *Poultry Science*, **49**, 405–411

Krueger, W. F., Atkinson, R. L., Quisenberry, J. H. and Bradley, J. W. (1972). Heritability of body weight and conformation traits and their genetic association in turkeys. *Poultry Science*, **51**, 1276–1282

Kulenkamp, A. W., Coleman, T. H. and Peterson, R. A. (1968). Some comparisons of 'vibrator' and 'normal' turkeys. *Poultry Science*, **47**, 1459–1463

Kunev, K., Bachev, N. and Todorova, V. (1975). Heritability and relationship between some production characters of Beltsville White turkeys. *Zhivotnov dni Nauki*, **12**, 101–196. In *Animal Breeding Abstracts*, **45**, 587, No. 6281

Lange, A. and Buss, E. G. (1984). A comparison of bone length and bone weight with embryo weight in chondrodystrophic and normal Beltsville small white turkey embryos. *Poultry Science*, **63**, 578–579

Lasley, E. L. (1949). A comparison of skeletal and fleshing development in three types of domestic turkeys. *North Dakota Agricultural Experiment Station Bulletin*, **335**, 1–50

LeBlanc, B., Wyers, M., Cohn-Bendit, F., Legall, J. M. and Thibault, E. (1986). Histology and histomorphometry of the tibia growth in two turkey strains. *Poultry Science*, **65**, 1787–1795

Leopold, A. S. (1948). The wild turkeys of Mexico. *Transactions of the 13th North American Wildlife Conference*, (Quee, E. M., ed.), pp. 393–400. Washington, DC, Wildlife Management Institute

Lorenz, F. W. and Lerner, I. M. (1946). Inheritance of sexual maturity in male chickens and turkeys *Poultry Science*, **25**, 188–189

Lucas, W. C., Seeger, K. C. and Tomhave, A. E. (1949). Production factors of six varieties of turkeys. *Delaware Agricultural Experiment Station Bulletin*, **279**, 1–19

McCartney, M. G. (1952). Rate of growth, efficiency of feed utilization and market quality in three varieties of turkeys to eighteen weeks. *Poultry Science*, **31**, 838–843

McCartney, M. G. (1961). Heritabilities and correlations for body weight and conformation in a randombred population of turkeys. *Poultry Science*, **40**, 1694–1700

McCartney, M. G. and Chamberlain, V. D. (1961). Crossbreeding turkeys. 1. Effect of mating system on reproductive performance. *Poultry Science*, **40**, 163–171

McCartney, M. G., Chamberlain, V. D. and Wyne, J. W. (1956). Turkey strains are compared for reproductive performance. *Ohio Agricultural Experiment Station Farm and Home Research*, **41**, 93–95

McCartney, M. G., Nestor, K. E. and Harvey, W. R. (1968). Genetics of growth and reproduction in the turkey. Selection for increased body weight and egg production. *Poultry Science*, **47**, 981–990

MacLaury, D. W., Insko, W. M., Jr., Steele, D. G. and Wightman, E. T. (1954). Turkey breeding investigations. *Kentucky Agricultural Experiment Station Bulletin*, **616**, 1–14

MacNeil, J. H. and Buss, E. G. (1968). Skin and meat yields of turkeys as influenced by strain. *Poultry Science*, **47**, 1566–1570

Marquez, O. V., Ochoa, G. P., Barranco, C. J. and Romano, P. J. J. (1983). Carcass characteristics in two types of turkey reared in two environments. *Veterinaria, Mexico*, **14**, 63–68. In *Animal Breeding Abstracts*, **52**, 790, No. 6156

Marsden, S. J. (1948). Selecting breeding turkeys. *World's Poultry Science Journal*, **4**, 262–265

Marsden, S. J. (1967). The Beltsville Small White turkey. *World's Poultry Science Journal*, **23**, 32–42

Marsden, S. J. and Knox, C. W. (1937). The breeding of turkeys. *USDA Yearbook*, pp. 1350–1366

Maw, A. J. G. and McCartney, M. G. (1956). Variation in fertility on inbred chickens and of fertility and hatchability in White Holland turkeys. *Poultry Science*, **35**, 1185–1190

Moore, R. T. (1938). A new race of wild turkey. *Auk*, **55**, 112–115

Moorhead, P. D. and Mohamed, Y. S. (1968). Case report: pathologic and microbiologic studies of crooked-neck in a turkey flock. *Avian Diseases*, **12**, 476–482

Mukherjee, T. K. and Friars, G. W. (1970). Heritability estimates and selection responses of some growth and reproductive traits in control and early growth selected strains of turkeys. *Poultry Science*, **49**, 1215–1222

Mymrin, I. A. and Krivich, G. (1972). Production characters of Broad Breasted White turkeys selected for different traits. *Ptakhivnitstvo*, **13**, 19–25. In *Animal Breeding Abstracts*, **41**, 263, No. 2385

Nestor, K. E. (1971). Genetics of growth and reproduction in the turkey. 4. Strain crosses for improvement of growth and reproduction. *Poultry Science*, **50**, 1683–1689

Nestor, K. E. (1972). Broodiness, intensity of lay and total egg production of turkeys. *Poultry Science*, **51**, 86–92

Nestor, K. E. (1976). Selection for increased semen yield in the turkey. *Poultry Science*, **55**, 2263–2369

Nestor, K. E. (1977). Genetics of growth and reproduction in the turkey. 5. Selection for increased body weight alone and in combination with increased egg production. *Poultry Science*, **56**, 337–347

Nestor, K. E. (1978). Hereditary chondrodystrophy in the turkey. *Poultry Science*, **55**, 577–580

Nestor, K. E. (1980). Genetics of growth and reproduction in the turkey. 7. Relationship of total egg production intensity of lay, broodiness and body weight. *Poultry Science*, **59**, 1385–1294

Nestor, K. E. (1982). The influence of genetic increases in body weight on the abdominal fat pad of turkeys. *Poultry Science*, **61**, 2301–2304

Nestor, K. E. (1984). Genetics of growth and reproduction in the turkey. 9. Long-term selection for increased 16-week body weight. *Poultry Science*, **63**, 2114–2122

Nestor, K. E. and Bacon, W. L. (1986). The influence of genetic increases in egg production and body weight on egg mass production and biological efficiency of turkey hens. *Poultry Science*, **65**, 1410–1412

Nestor, K. E. and Chamberlain, V. D. (1966). Repeatability of body measurements in the turkey. *Poultry Science*, **45**, 1059–1060

Nestor, K. E. and Renner, P. A. (1979). Genetics of growth and reproduction in the turkey. 6. Influence of plumage color pattern genes on mortality, body weight and egg and semen production. *Poultry Science*, **58**, 1137–1142

Nestor, K. E., Bacon, W. L. and Renner, P. A. (1970). Ovarian follicular development in egg and meat type turkeys. *Poultry Science*, **49**, 775–780

Nestor, K. E., Bacon, W. L. and Renner, P. A. (1986). The influence of time of application of broody hen treatments on egg production of turkeys. *Poultry Science*, **65**, 1405–1409

Nestor, K. E., Brown, K. I. and Renner, P. A. (1979). The influence of molting during the reproduction period on semen production of turkey males. *Poultry Science*, **58**, 1592–1598

Nestor, K. E., Brown, K. I. and Weaver, C. R. (1972). Egg quality and poult production in turkeys. 2. Inheritance and relationship among traits. *Poultry Science*, **51**, 147–158

Nestor, K. E., McCartney, M. G. and Bachev, N. (1969). Relative contributions of genetic and environment to turkey improvement. *Poultry Science*, **48**, 1944–1949

Nestor, K. E., McCartney, M. G. and Harvey, W. R. (1967). Genetics of growth and reproduction in the turkey. 1. Genetic and non-genetic variation in body weight and body measurements. *Poultry Science*, **46**, 1374–1384

Nestor, K. E., Bacon, W. L., Saif, Y. M. and Renner, P. A. (1985). The influence of genetic increase in shank on body weight, walking ability and reproduction of turkeys. *Poultry Science*, **64**, 2248–2255

Ogasawara, F. X., Abplanalp, H. and Asmundson, V. S. (1963). Effect of selection for body weight on reproduction in turkey hens. *Poultry Science*, **42**, 838–842

Olsen, M. W. (1960a). Performance record of a parthenogenetic turkey male. *Science*, **132**, 1661

Olsen, M. W. (1960b). Nine year summary of parthenogenesis in turkeys. *Proceedings of the Society for Experimental Biology*, **105**, 279–287

Olsen, M. W. (1965). Twelve year summary of selection for parthenogenesis in Beltsville Small White turkeys. *British Poultry Science*, **6**, 1–6

Olsen, M. W. (1969). Potential uses of parthenogenetic development in turkeys. *Journal of Heredity,* **60**, 346–348

Olsen, M. W. and Buss, E. G. (1967). Role of genetic factors and fowl pox virus in parthenogenesis in turkey eggs. *Genetics,* **56**, 727–732

Olsen, M. W. and Marsden, S. J. (1954a). Natural parthenogenesis in turkey eggs. *Science,* **120**, 545–546

Olsen, M. W. and Marsden, S. J. (1954b). Development in unfertilized turkey eggs. *Journal of Experimental Zoology,* **126**, 337–347

Olsen, M. W. and Marsden, S. J. (1956). Parthenogenesis in eggs of Beltsville Small White turkeys. *Poultry Science,* **35**, 674–682

Orr, H. L., Gillis, W. A., Usborne, W. R. and Stevens, R. W. C. (1974). Influence of strain and age on the grade and yield of component parts of turkey broilers. *Poultry Science,* **53**, 1382–1386

Orr, H. L., Hunt, E. C. and Snyder, E. S. (1956). A comparison of dressing percentage and yield of edible cooked meat in five strains of turkeys as broilers and as mature stock. *Poultry Science,* **35**, 333–338

Peterson, R. A., Ringer, R. K. and Coleman, T. H. (1963). A study of the central nervous system of 'vibrator' turkeys. *Michigan Agricultural Experiment Station Quarterly Bulletin,* **46**, 119–123

Pingel, H., Schubert, C., Stubs, M. and Henker, W. (1984). Genetic effects of fertilization, persistency and quantitative sperm characteristics. *Proceedings XVII World's Poultry Congress,* 280–281

Poole, H. K. (1959). The mitotic chromosomes of parthenogenetic and normal turkeys. *Journal of Heredity,* **50**, 150–154

Poole, H. K. and Marsden, S. J. (1961). An autosomal naked mutation and associated polydactylism in Beltsville Small White turkeys. *Journal of Heredity,* **52**, 183–185

Popescu-Vifor, S. and Puscatu, I. (1977). Genetic parameters of some external characters in turkey broilers. *Lucrari Stunfice, Institute Agronomic 'N. Balcescu, D(Zootehnie),* **20/21**, 75–80. In *Animal Breeding Abstracts,* **48**, 239, No. 2235

Quinteros, I. R., Stevens, R. W. C., Stormont, C. and Asmundson, V. S. (1964). Albumin phenotypes in turkeys. *Genetics,* **50**, 579–582

Riddell, C. (1981). Skeletal deformities in poultry. *Advances in Veterinary Science and Comparative Medicine,* **25**, 227–310. New York, Academic Press

Robel, E. J. (1981). Relationships of age and body weight to reproductive traits in turkey hens. *Poultry Science,* **60**, 2709–2712

Robertson, W. R. B., Bohren, B. B. and Warren, D. C. (1943). The inheritance of plumage color in the turkey. *Journal of Heredity,* **34**, 246–256

Rooney, W. F. (1957). Body weight and reproduction in turkeys. *Poultry Science,* **36**, 229–231

Sato, I. and Kosin, I. L. (1960). A cytological study of the parthenogenetically developing turkey germ discs and embryos. *Cytologia (Tokyo),* **25**, 256–266

Savage, T. F. and Harper, J. A. (1985). Ring lethal: An early embryonic failure in Medium White turkeys. *Journal of Heredity,* **76**, 474–476

Savage, T. E., Wallner-Pendelton, E. and Harper, J. A. (1986). Swollen down plumules, an autosomal recessive lethal in turkeys. *Poultry Science,* **65**, 823–828

Scerbina, P. F. (1969). Heterosis in reciprocal crossing of turkeys. *Problemy Zootekhnicheskoi Genetik N'auka,* **304**, 251–261. In *Animal Breeding Abstracts,* **38**, 685, No. 4324

Schorger, A. W. (1966). *The Wild Turkey: Its History and Domestication,* pp. 1–625. Norman, Oklahoma, University of Oklahoma Press

Searle, B. M. and Bloom, S. E. (1974). Expression of the bn turkey mutant gene in a chicken parabiant. *Proceedings XV World's Poultry Congress,* 499–500

Shaklee, W. F., Knox, C. W. and Marsden, S. J. (1952). Inheritance of the sex differences of body weight in turkeys. *Poultry Science,* **31**, 822–825

Shannon, W. G. and Armour, D. M. (1962). The breeding and selection of turkeys and ordinary fowl for improvement in meat qualities. *Proceedings XII World's Poultry Congress,* 54–56

Shanskova, A. M. (1976). The effectiveness of selecting turkeys for body weight and semen quality. *Trudy,* **123**, 50–53. In *Animal Breeding Abstracts,* **46**, 65, No. 499

Shoffner, R. N., Krista, L. M., Waibel, P. E. and Quarfoth, G. J. (1971). Strain crosses within and between lines of turkeys selected for high and low blood pressure. *Poultry Science,* **50**, 342–345

Smith, J. C. and Smyth, J. R., Jr. (1970). Knobby, a semi lethal mutation resulting in defective down in the turkey. *Journal of Heredity*, **61**, 119–122

Smyth, J. R., Jr. (1954). Hairy, a gene causing abnormal plumage in the turkey. *Journal of Heredity*, **45**, 196–200

Sokolow, N. N., Tiniakow, G. G. and Trofimov, J. E. (1936). On the morphology of the chromosomes in Gallinaceae. *Cytologia*, **7**, 466–489

Stenius, C., Christian, L. C. and Ohno, S. (1963). Comparative cytological study of *Phasianus colchicus, Meleagris gallopavo* and *Gallus domesticus. Chromosoma*, **13**, 515–520

Stevens, R. W. C. and Asmundson, V. S. (1968). Test for association between blood groups and performance traits in turkeys. *Poultry Science*, **47**, 800–806

Stout, J. T. and Buss, E. G. (1979a). Identification of a 16–17 day lethal factor in a chondrodystrophic stock of turkeys. *Journal of Heredity*, **70**, 62–64

Stout, J. T. and Buss, E. G. (1979b). Initial identification of chondrodystrophy turkey embryos. *Journal of Heredity*, **70**, 139–141

Strong, C. F., Jr. and Nestor, K. E. (1978). Changes in the plasma content of calcium, phosphorus and yolk lipophosphoprotein precursor during the production season in turkeys. *Poultry Science*, **57**, 1710–1719

Strong, C. F., Jr. and Nestor, K. E. (1980). Egg quality and reproduction in turkeys. 5. Relationship among traits in medium- and large-bodied lines. *Poultry Science*, **59**, 417–423

Taylor, M. H. and Fry, J. L. (1967). Yield of turkey parts in relation to turkey roll compositions. *Poultry Science*, **46**, 374–378

Werner, O. S. (1931). The chromosomes of the domestic turkey. *Biological Bulletin*, **61**, 157–164

Whitson, D., Marsden, S. J. and Titus, H. W. (1944). A comparison of the performance of four varieties of turkeys during the breeding season. *Poultry Science*, **23**, 314–320

Williams, L. E. (1964). A recurrent color aberrancy in the wild turkey. *Journal Wildlife Management*, **28**, 148–152

Williams, L. E. (1967). Wild turkeys (*Meleagris gallopavo*) with supernumerary leg spurs. *Auk*, **84**, 113–114

Wolford, J. H., Ringer, R. K., Coleman, T. H. and Zindel, H. C. (1963). Individual feed consumption of turkey breeder hens and correlation of feed intake, body weight and egg production. *Poultry Science*, **42**, 599–604

Yao, T. S. and Olsen, M. W. (1955). Microscopic observation of parthenogenetic embryonic tissues from virgin turkey eggs. *Journal of Heredity*, **46**, 133–134

Chapter 3

Physiology of egg production

P. J. Sharp

Introduction

The ancestors of the domestic turkey, being native to North America and Mexico, were adapted to breed at lower temperate zone latitudes. The climate at these latitudes permits a long breeding season, making it possible to produce two broods each year. A wild turkey lays a clutch of 10–25 eggs before becoming broody, with early clutches being larger than those laid later in the breeding season (Schorger, 1966). The wild turkey may thus have the capacity to produce well in excess of 50 eggs in a breeding season, particularly if it is not allowed to become broody and the food supply is of sufficient quantity and quality. The number of eggs produced by a hen reflects the number of yellow-yolky follicles which develop in the ovary in an orderly hierarchy, and ovulate. The growth of these follicles depends on increased concentrations of plasma gonadotrophins which are regulated by changes in daylength. The physiological mechanisms involved in this photoperiodic response make it possible for seasonal breeding to be initiated and terminated at precise times of the year and persist in a modified form in domesticated turkeys. They must be taken into account when devising lighting patterns for maximum egg production. In addition to being influenced by changes in daylength, egg production is also affected by the development of broodiness. Egg production must stop at the onset of broodiness to allow the synchronous development and hatch of each brood of chicks. Since the survival of the turkey as a species depends, in part, on the quality of parental behaviour, it is not surprising that the broody trait persists in domesticated birds.

In this review, emphasis is placed on the endocrine and neuroendocrine control of ovarian follicular growth and ovulation. Particular attention is given to recent advances in understanding of two major physiological mechanisms, photorefractoriness and broodiness, which are responsible for poor persistency of lay after photostimulation.

Endocrine control of ovarian function

Most of what is known about the structure, function and growth of the ovary, and of the mechanism of ovulation in birds is based on studies on the domestic fowl (Gilbert and Wells, 1984; Wilson and Cunningham, 1984; Johnson, 1986) and probably applies in general, to the turkey. However, there is a substantial although fragmented, literature dealing with ovarian function in turkeys.

Ovarian follicular growth

The ovary is on the left side of the abdominal cavity and contains hundreds of thousands of microscopic oocytes, which are present at hatch. They represent a capacity for egg production far in excess of what can be achieved. Prior to the onset of egg production, a small proportion of these oocytes begins to enlarge to about 1–5 mm in diameter as the result of the deposition of white proteinaceous primordial yolk. When the follicles reach 5–8 mm diameter, they enter the final rapid growth phase which is characterized by the rapid deposition of yellow yolk. The yellow-yolky follicles form an orderly hierarchy of different sizes so that at the peak of egg production, the ovary produces a single ovulable follicle of about 40–45 mm diameter, nearly every day. The major precursor of yellow yolk is very low density lipoprotein (VLDL) which is produced by the liver in response to oestrogen stimulation (Neilson and Simpson, 1973) and is transported to the ovary in the blood. The yolk in a turkey egg weighs about 20 g and of this, 8.7 g is VLDL (Bacon, 1986). This lipoprotein is metabolized differently in laying hens than in immature hens or males, resulting in lipid deposition being directed to the ovary rather than to the adipose tissue (Bacon, 1981). In a study on the turnover of VLDL in the turkey, Bacon (1986) found that 30% of the VLDL in circulation is deposited in the developing follicles: the fate of the remaining 70% is unknown. The uptake of VLDL is independent of plasma concentrations, fractional clearance rate, distribution volume or body weight (Bacon, 1986).

Studies in the domestic fowl (Gilbert and Wells, 1984) indicate that selection of follicles which will eventually ovulate occurs at the white-yolky stage of follicular development by a process of differential atresia. Thus, the ovarian follicular hierarchy forms before the formation of the smaller (~8 mm) rapidly growing yellow-yolky follicles. This view is supported by a study in the turkey where it was shown that the numbers of atretic 1–2 mm sized white-yolky follicles are negatively related to the number of yellow-yolky follicles (Hocking et al., 1988a).

The growth of yellow-yolky follicles can be readily investigated by feeding a fat soluble dye which is deposited in a ring in the yolk marking the day of feeding. Using this technique, follicles have been shown to require 11–13 days to grow from 8 mm diameter to an ovulable size (Bacon and Cherms, 1968; Nestor, Bacon and Renner, 1970; Hocking et al., 1988b). A fully developed ovary from a hen at peak of lay contains 9–10 yellow-yolky follicles. During the laying year the weight of the ovum at ovulation progressively increases reflecting an increase in the time taken for a yellow-yolky follicle to reach an ovulable size (Table 3.1). This increase in ovum weight is directly related to an increase in egg size (Bacon, Nestor and Renner, 1972).

Table 3.1 Effect of period in production on ovum weight at ovulation and the time taken for a yellow-yolky follicle to grow to ovulable size

	Weeks after transfer to stimulatory daylength[a]				
	1–4	5–8	9–12	13–16	17–20
Ovum weight at ovulation (g)	23.1	25.2	25.7	27.6	28.3
Duration of rapid follicular growth (days)	11.8	13.0	13.2	13.0	13.7

After Bacon and Cherms (1968)

[a] Based on seven hens photostimulated at 34 weeks; an analysis of variance showed a significant ($P<0.01$) interaction between time and ovum weight, and between time and duration of rapid follicular growth.

Selection for increased egg production (egg lines) or growth rate (meat-lines) affects ovarian follicular development (Nestor, Bacon and Renner, 1970, 1980; Bacon, Nestor and Renner, 1972). Selection for increased egg production has been achieved by increasing sequence length or by reducing broodiness (*Table 3.2*). A genetic increase in sequence length results in an increase in the number of rapidly growing yellow-yolky follicles (*Table 3.2*) but not in total follicular weight. As a consequence, the increase in egg numbers is off-set by a decrease in average ovum weight. A genetic decrease in broodiness has no effect on numbers or total weight of developing follicles, but reduces the numbers of follicles developing in pairs (*Table 3.2*).

Table 3.2 Effect of selection for egg production or increased 16-week body weight on ovarian follicular growth after an 80-day production period

Selection line[a]	Control[b] (RBC2)	Increased sequence length (C)	Reduced broodiness (B)	Increased body weight (F)
Body weight (kg)	9.39	9.16	8.26[c]	12.25[c]
Number of follicles in pairs/hens	0.2	0.1	0.1[c]	0.4[d]
Number of yellow-yolky follicles/hen	8.3	8.9[c]	8.4	10.0[c]
Egg production/hen	103	112[c]	111[c]	84[c]
Number of atretic follicles/hen	0.5	0.5	0.2	0.2

After Nestor, Bacon and Renner, 1980

[a] The birds were selected for these traits for between five and eight generations
[b] In the original paper, different control groups were used for each selection line. The values shown here are for the control group for the 'C' line and are representative of the other control groups in the experiment
[c] $P<0.05$ compared with the control group
[d] Selection for a further four generations resulted in this value becoming significantly ($P<0.05$) greater than in the control line

Selection for increased body weight results in an increase in the numbers and total weight of yellow-yolky ovarian follicles (*Table 3.2*) which is most pronounced during the initial period of egg production (Nestor, Bacon and Renner, 1970; Bacon, Nestor and Renner, 1972). This trait is further enhanced if the hens are photostimulated at 24 rather than at 30 weeks of age (Hocking *et al.*, 1988a). Despite this increase in follicle numbers, egg production is depressed. The most significant feature associated with this reduced egg production is an increase in the number of pairs of membraneous eggs being laid in a 24-h period (Nestor and Bacon, 1972). The production of two membraneous eggs is typically associated in the domestic fowl, with the ovulation of two ovarian follicles of the same size within a few hours of each other, in response to a single pre-ovulatory release of luteinizing hormone (Sharp, Beuving and van Middelkoop, 1976). A similar situation probably occurs in meat-lines of turkeys in which the number of ovarian follicles developing in pairs is greater than in egg-lines (Nestor, Bacon and Renner, 1970; Bacon, Nestor and Renner, 1972; *Table 3.2*). A further factor contributing to reduced egg production in meat-lines in the middle of the laying period is an increase in the incidence of atresia of yellow-yolky follicles (Bacon, Nestor and Renner, 1972). The increase in ovarian follicular numbers in meat-line birds is not related to differences between egg- and meat-line turkeys in circulating levels of VLDL (Bacon, Nestor and Musser, 1973). It thus seems that increased yolk deposition in meat-lines is not due to increased concentrations of the precursors of yolk in the blood.

The growth of ovarian follicles depends on the secretion of gonadotrophins by the anterior pituitary gland. Surgical removal of the pituitary gland from laying turkeys thus results in the regression of the ovary (Opel, 1974). Conversely, daily administration of a mixture of mammalian follicle stimulating hormone (FSH) and luteinizing hormone (LH) to out-of-lay turkeys stimulates ovarian growth and oviduct development (Burke and Cogger, 1977). Two distinct gonadotrophins, designated FSH and LH on the basis of their activities in several bioassay systems, have been purified from turkey pituitary glands (Wentworth, 1971; Farmer, Papkoff and Licht, 1975; Burke et al., 1979). Studies on turkey gonadotrophins indicate that there is an overlap in the biological properties of turkey LH and FSH with turkey LH showing significant FSH-like activity (Burke et al., 1979).

Injection of mammalian LH and FSH in laying turkeys results in an increase in the concentrations of plasma oestrogen and progesterone (Camper and Burke, 1977). It is likely that both steroids originate from the ovary and in particular, the rapidly growing follicles. Studies on the domestic fowl show that during the rapid growth phase, oestrogen and progesterone are produced, respectively, in the theca and granulosa layers of the ovarian follicular wall (Bahr et al., 1983). As the follicle approaches ovulable size, progesterone production increases while oestrogen production decreases (Bahr et al., 1983). Similar endocrine changes probably also occur during ovarian follicular maturation in the turkey. In support of this view, turkey LH stimulates more progesterone release from cultured turkey granulosa cells taken from mature than from less mature ovarian follicles (Asem et al., 1983).

The secretion of gonadotrophins is controlled by the release of the neuropeptide, gonadotrophin releasing hormone (GnRH) produced in neurons in the hypothalamus (Sharp, 1983). This neuropeptide provides the link between the reproductive system and the central nervous system and hence between the bird's internal and external environments. The observations that electrolytic lesions or knife cuts in the hypothalamus of the laying turkey induces ovarian regression (Opel, 1979a, b) and that administration of synthetic mammalian GnRH stimulates the release of LH in turkey hens (Burke and Cogger, 1977; El Halawani, Fehrer and Silsby, 1987) are consistent with the production of a similar neuropeptide in this bird.

The commercial availability of synthetic GnRH suggests a possible treatment to bring non-laying turkeys back into production. Attempts to use GnRH in this way have been unsuccessful (Burke and Cogger, 1977) possibly because prolonged administration of the neuropeptide or its long-acting analogues, results in a loss of pituitary gland responsiveness (Sharp et al., 1986a).

The ovulatory cycle

A series of eggs laid on successive days is known as a 'sequence' while days on which no eggs are laid are 'pause days'. In turkeys held on a 14-h daylength, between 80 and 90% of eggs are laid between 4 and 14 h after the beginning of the light period with a peak occurring between 7 and 9 h (Woodard, Wilson and Mather, 1963; Wolford, Ringer and Coleman, 1964). Successive eggs in a sequence are laid later on successive days. As a consequence, the first eggs of long sequences are laid earlier in the day than the first egg of short sequences (Woodard, Wilson and Mather, 1963). The daily distribution of egg laying is entrained by the light–dark cycle and can be readily advanced or delayed by advancing or delaying the beginning of the photoperiod (Bixler and Ringer, 1968).

The restriction of egg laying to a 10–11-h period each day is a reflection of an underlying neuroendocrine control mechanism which limits the initiation of pre-ovulatory releases of LH to a daily 10–11-h 'open period' of the ovulatory cycle. The limits of this 'open period' have been determined in laying turkeys exposed to 14 h of light per day by measuring changes in plasma LH over 24 h (Sharp *et al.*, 1981). Pre-ovulatory releases of LH are only initiated between the onset of darkness and about 1 h after the onset of the light period. As has been shown in the domestic fowl (Sharp, 1980; Wilson and Cunningham, 1984) the exact position of the 'open period' of the ovulatory cycle is determined by the way in which the underlying circadian rhythm is entrained by the lighting cycle.

Ovulation of a mature ovarian follicle is preceded by an increase in the concentrations of plasma LH and progesterone (Mashaly *et al.*, 1976; Hammond *et al.*, 1981; Sharp *et al.*, 1981). There are no such increases on days when ovulation does not occur. The pre-ovulatory release of LH is thought to be responsible for ovulation. It can be deduced from studies on the domestic fowl (Sharp, 1980; Wilson and Cunningham, 1984; Johnson, 1986) that the pre-ovulatory releases of LH and progesterone are caused by a positive feedback interaction. Progesterone stimulates the release of GnRH and hence LH which, in turn, stimulates the secretion of more progesterone from the highly responsive granulosa layer (see above) in the mature pre-ovulatory follicle. In this way a pre-ovulatory cascade of plasma progesterone and LH builds up and is finally terminated by ovulation. The pre-ovulatory releases of LH and progesterone are initiated 12–10 h before ovulation with a peak of LH occurring 8–6 h, and of progesterone, 4–2 h, before ovulation (Sharp *et al.*, 1981). The interval between the pre-ovulatory LH peak and the resulting oviposition of a hard-shelled egg is about 36 h (Sharp *et al.*, 1981) resulting, in birds held on a 14-h daylength, in most ovipositions occurring in the middle or towards the end of the photoperiod.

The neural mechanism responsible for the 'open period' of the ovulatory cycle is not understood but is of practical interest because it places a constraint on egg production. At peak of lay a turkey ovary is capable of producing a mature follicle every 25–28 h. This means that there is a lack of synchronization between the 'open period' which occurs every 24 h and the development of an ovulable follicle in the ovary. As a consequence, at regular intervals, a follicle achieves an ovulable condition outside the 'open period' and must wait until the next 'open period' before ovulation can occur. This results in 'pause days' which separate orderly sequences of eggs. 'Pause days' can also becaused in other ways, for example, by internal ovulation, production of membraneous or soft shelled eggs and gaps, caused by atresia, in the yellow-yolky follicular hierarchy. Such 'pause days' result in unpredictable irregularities in otherwise orderly sequences of eggs.

The expulsion of a hard-shelled egg from the shell gland is mediated by an increase in the concentration of plasma prostaglandins (Hammond *et al.*, 1981). Studies on domestic fowl suggest that this increase in prostaglandins is part of a mechanism whereby pre- or post-ovulatory follicles play a role in the timing of oviposition (Shimada, Neldon and Koike, 1986).

Photoperiodic responses

Changes in daylength play a crucial role in determining the rate and persistency of lay (Sharp, 1984). Albright and Thompson (1933) were among the first to demonstrate that turkeys can be brought into lay in the winter by providing artificial light to extend the daily photoperiod. Subsequently, the basic principles involved in commercial lighting patterns for turkeys were established in studies carried out between the 1940s and 1960s. Recent studies relevant to a better understanding of photorefractoriness in turkeys have been carried out in wild birds.

Photoinduced gonadotrophin release

Early studies on winter lighting of turkeys established that daylength should be increased to a minimum of 13 h to stimulate maximum egg production (*Table 3.3*). A photoperiod of 12 h is also stimulatory but the reproductive response is slow and peak egg production is depressed (Ogasawara, Wilson and Asmundson, 1962; *Table 3.3*). Transfer to daylengths in excess of 13 or 14 h does not improve egg

Table 3.3 Effect of daylength on egg production in 31–33 week old turkeys reared on natural daylength (at latitude 39°N) and photostimulated on 30 November ($n = 7$–10)

Fixed lighting pattern	Average number of eggs per hen per month					
	Dec	*Jan*	*Feb*	*March*	*April*	*May*
9L:15D[a]	0	0	1.1	_[b]	_[b]	_[b]
11L:13D	0	1.6	6.0	_[b]	_[b]	_[b]
12L:12D	1.3	10.0	10.4	12.5	11.5	9.3
13L:11D	1.4	18.0	14.6	14.2	13.0	11.5
14L:10D	1.5	20.3	17.1	17.8	14.0	8.7
15L: 9D	2.0	19.5	14.7	13.9	10.5	10.2
24L: 0D	4.8	18.2	13.7	14.8	11.4	7.3

After Asmundson and Moses, 1950

[a] 9 h light: 15 h darkness
[b] No data

production (Asmundson and Moses, 1950). Comparisons of step-wise and abrupt increases in daylength suggest that the latter procedure is preferable (e.g. Marsden, Cowen and Lucas, 1962). A study involving the daily administration of dyes to follow the pattern of yellow-yolk deposition showed that in 34-week-old turkeys transferred from 6 h to 14 h light per day, rapid growth of ovarian follicles begins after 8.6 days (range 4–12 days) and the first eggs are laid after 25.2 days (range 19–31 days) (Bacon and Cherms, 1968). Ovarian growth and function are associated with increases in the concentrations of plasma LH and FSH within 2–3 days of photostimulation (Godden and Scanes, 1977; Burke and Dennison, 1980; Lea and Sharp, 1982; El Halawani *et al.*, 1984). This increase in plasma gonadotrophins presumably stimulates the growth of the yellow-yolky ovarian follicles which in turn, secrete increased amounts of oestrogens and progesterone. The development of yellow-yolky ovarian follicles is thus marked by increases in plasma oestrogens (Bajpayee and Brown, 1972; Wineland and Wentworth, 1975) and progesterone (Mashaly and Wentworth, 1974; Godden and Scanes, 1977). The principal plasma eostrogen appears to be oestrone although concentrations of 17β oestradiol are also elevated. In addition, there are significant concentrations of 15α OH-oestriol and 15α-OH oestradiol which have not been observed in the blood of other species (Brown *et al.*, 1979). This increase in ovarian steroids is associated with increases in plasma calcium and total free fatty acids in preparation for egg formation (Bajpayee and Brown, 1972).

The minimum daylength required to stimulate gonadotrophin release in turkey hens held on short daylengths has been re-investigated by measuring photoinduced LH release (*Figure 3.1*). In agreement with earlier studies, the minimum daylength required is between 10 and 12 h. However, in contrast with earlier studies, transfer to 12 h was as stimulatory as transfer to 14 h light per day (*Figure 3.1*). It is possible that 12-h daylengths may not necessarily be sub-optimal in some lines of turkeys given an appropriate lighting history.

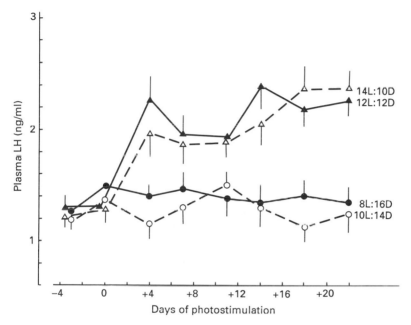

Figure 3.1 Changes in concentrations of plasma luteinizing hormone (LH) in groups of out-of-lay turkey hens (*n* − 5) transferred from 8 h of light per day to fixed daylengths of 10, 12 and 14 h. The hens had been previously exposed to 8 h light per day for 12 weeks in order to dissipate photorefractoriness after one photoinduced laying cycle. Vertical lines represent the standard error of the mean (P. J. Sharp, unpublished observation)

The response to an increase in daylength is influenced by several factors, including age and the quality of light. If turkey hens held on short days are photostimulated before being fully grown, the onset of egg production is slow and the first eggs are small (e.g. Leighton and Shoffner, 1961b; Sexton and McCartney, 1973). Thus, Leighton and Shoffner (1961b) found that turkeys exposed to 6 h light per day for 4 weeks and transferred to 15 h light per day at 28, 26, 24 and 22 weeks came into lay after 32, 34, 37 and 44 days, respectively.

It is likely that egg production is inhibited in juvenile hens by a central nervous inhibitory input to the GnRH neurons in the hypothalamus. Such an inhibitory input has been demonstrated in juvenile male turkeys in which precocious puberty is stimulated by cutting the lateral neural inputs to the hypothalamus (Kuenzel and Lake, 1984). This inhibitory system may become progressively less important in opposing the stimulatory effects of increasing daylength as the hen approaches full body weight.

Changes in daylength influence the activity of the GnRH neurons and hence egg production by a neural pathway which does not involve the eyes. Thus, blinded turkeys held on short days respond to an increase in daylength and lay as many eggs as intact hens (Siopes and Underwood, 1987). The pineal gland can also be discounted as the photoreceptor for photoinduced egg production. Pinealecto-mized turkey hens also respond to photostimulation although they come into lay more slowly, and total egg production is lower than in intact hens (Siopes and Underwood, 1987). Changes in daylength are thus detected by an extraretinal photoreceptor. Since brain tissues are penetrated about 30 times more readily by red (~650 nm wavelength) than by green (~500 nm) light (Foster and Follett, 1985) it is not surprising that turkeys can be more readily stimulated into egg production with the longer wavelengths of the visible spectrum (Jones, Hughes and Thurston, 1982). The amount of light a turkey requires for maximum photostimulation can not be defined without reference to the spectrum of the light source. However, Thomason, Leighton and Mason (1972) found that 5.4 and 86.1 lx of incandescent light in a 16-h photoperiod were equally effective in stimulating and maintaining egg production. Siopes (1984a) compared the proportion of light energy in the red spectrum in incandescent and full-spectrum fluorescent lamps and found it to be 43 and 27% respectively. As a consequence, birds exposed to 76 lx of incandescent or full spectrum fluorescent light received respectively, 20.8 and 8.3 lx of red light (600–700 nm wavelength). Despite this difference, both methods of lighting resulted in similar reproductive responses (Siopes, 1984a). It might be supposed that the extraretinal photoreceptor would be more sensitive to red, than to green or blue light since red light penetrates the brain more readily than light with shorter wavelengths. However, this may not be the case. In quail, the extraretinal photoreceptor is most sensitive to green (500 nm wavelength) light (Foster and Follett, 1985).

Juvenile photorefractoriness

Many birds breeding at temperate latitudes do not come into full reproductive condition in the year in which they are hatched despite the fact that by late summer, they may be fully grown and exposed to long daylengths. It thus seems that, like their parents, juvenile birds are insensitive to the stimulatory effects of long days in late summer and are therefore photorefractory. In the turkey, this juvenile insensitivity to long days may have decreased as a consequence of domestication. Juvenile photorefractoriness was first noted in turkeys in the 1930s (e.g. Asmundson and Lloyd, 1935) when it was observed that hens hatched in December and January came into lay slowly in summer and thereafter, did not lay well. Egg production drops when daylength decreases in autumn but can be maintained although not very satisfactorily, by increasing the daylength (Clayton and Robertson, 1960; Leighton and Shoffner, 1961a).

Knowing that photorefractoriness can be dissipated in wild birds by exposure to short daylengths, Marr et al. (1956) were among the first to use a short-day treatment to dissipate juvenile photorefractoriness in turkeys. They found that egg production improved in hens hatched in January if they were subjected to 8 h light per day between 14–16 weeks and 28–30 weeks and then exposed to 14 h light per day. Subsequent studies confirmed and elaborated upon this finding (Harper and Parker, 1957, 1960, 1965; Clayton and Robertson, 1960; Leighton and Shoffner, 1961a, b; McCartney et al., 1961; Marsden, Cowen and Lucas, 1962; Ogasawara, Wilson and Asmundson, 1962; Shoffner et al., 1962; Wilson, Ogasawara and

Asmundson, 1962; Marsden and Lucas, 1964). Most authors conclude that 3–6 weeks exposure to 6–8 h light per day before photostimulation substantially dissipates juvenile photorefractoriness. However, Shoffner *et al.* (1962) showed that the effects of long days during the growing period on subsequent egg production are remarkably persistent and suggested that longer periods of short-day treatments are necessary to ensure complete dissipation of juvenile photorefractoriness. Since it is not always practical to subject turkeys to short daylengths before the onset of lay, several attempts have been made to find an alternative to short-day treatment. These include starvation, and treatment with progesterone, corticosterone, diethylstilboestrol, methyltestosterone and the catecholamine antagonist, reserpine (Harper and Parker, 1965; 1973). None of the treatments provided a satisfactory alternative to exposure to short daylengths.

Adult photorefractoriness

The decline in egg production with age in turkeys maintained on a stimulatory daylength is not due only to age but to the development of photorefractoriness. The development of this condition is important in terminating reproductive activity at temperate latitudes since it allows juveniles to grow sufficiently to face the rigours of winter or to migrate. Experimental studies in the 1940s showed, in wild birds,

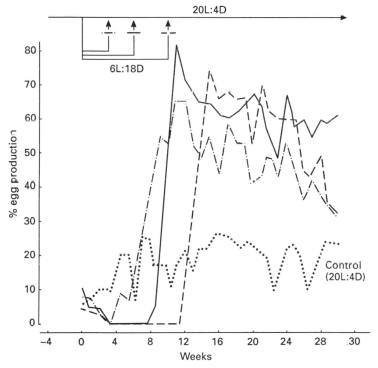

Figure 3.2 A comparison of the relative ability of 3, 6 or 10 weeks' exposure to 8 h of light per day to dissipate photorefractoriness in turkeys (*n* = 8–10) at the end of a first photoinduced lay cycle. The photoperiodic responsiveness of the hens is indicated by numbers of eggs laid. The hens were photostimulated into production with a 20-h day length (P. J. Sharp, unpublished observation)

that photorefractoriness can be dissipated by exposure to short daylengths (e.g. Burger, 1947; Damsté, 1947; Wolfson, 1952). These observations encouraged the development of short-day treatments to dissipate photorefractoriness in commercial turkeys. As discussed previously, short-day treatments are routinely used to dissipate juvenile photorefractoriness but are not so widely used to dissipate adult photorefractoriness. The dissipation of this condition using short daylengths to bring hens back into a second cycle of egg production is usually discussed in relation to the induction of moult at the end of a laying year (e.g. Harper and Parker, 1957; Leighton and Shoffner, 1964; Leighton et al., 1971; Ferguson et al., 1975; Cleaver, Christensen and Ort, 1986). Attempts to dissipate photorefractoriness using 6–9 h light per day for 3–5 weeks have generally been unsatisfactory (Harper and Parker, 1957; Leighton and Shoffner, 1964). However, longer periods of light restriction of 8 weeks or more have resulted in a second photoinduced cycle of egg production almost identical to the first (Leighton et al., 1971; Cleaver, Christensen and Ort, 1986). A small study comparing the relative effectiveness of 3, 6 or 10 weeks of short-day treatments in dissipating photorefractoriness confirms the finding of Cleaver, Christensen and Ort (1986) that about 8 weeks' exposure to short daylengths should be adequate (*Figure 3.2*).

Photorefractoriness can also be dissipated by reducing light intensity to about 0.5 lx of incandescent light rather than decreasing the photoperiod (Siopes, 1984b). Presumably at this lighting intensity, light is unable to penetrate the brain sufficiently to stimulate the extraretinal photoreceptors and hence the birds are deprived of photoperiodic stimulation.

Photorefractoriness is not primarily due to a loss of pituitary gland or gonadal function but to a central nervous inhibition of GnRH synthesis and release (Sharp, 1983). This view has been confirmed in the starling where the concentration of hypothalamic GnRH decreases dramatically in photorefractory birds in association with decreases in the concentrations of pituitary gland and plasma FSH (Dawson et al., 1985). The development of photorefractoriness is progressive rather than sudden, reflecting a progressive long-day dependent development of a central nervous inhibitory input to the GnRH neurons in the hypothalamus. This view is supported by the finding in the Willow ptarmigan, that the LH response to castration is greater at the beginning than at the end of the breeding season (*Figure 3.3*). The difference in response to castration is interpreted to reflect an increase in the central nervous inhibitory input to the GnRH neurons. This build-up in inhibitory input is not reflected in a decrease in plasma LH levels until the breeding season is almost complete (*Figure 3.3*).

The progressive development of photorefractoriness in turkeys, as indicated by a progressive fall in egg production, is marked by a reduction in rapidly growing yellow-yolky follicles in the ovary (Hocking et al., 1988a) and a progressive fall in concentrations of plasma progesterone during the laying period (Mashaly and Wentworth, 1974; Mashaly et al., 1976). Although this decrease in ovarian follicular activity would be expected to be caused by a decrease in circulating gonadotrophins, such a decrease has not been observed (Lea and Sharp, 1982; El Halawani et al., 1984).

Recent studies directed towards a better understanding of the neuroendocrine control of photorefractoriness have used wild birds as experimental models. A change in hypothalamic sensitivity to the inhibitory feedback action of gonadal steroids on gonadotrophin release has been shown not to be the primary cause of photorefractoriness in several wild birds including the Willow ptarmigan (Stokkan

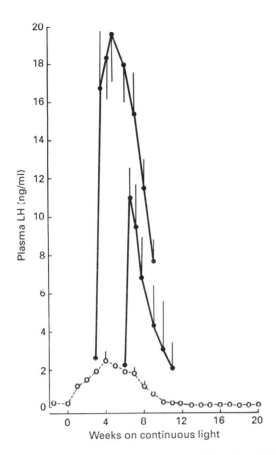

Figure 3.3 Changes in concentrations of plasma luteinizing hormone (LH) in photosensitive Willow ptarmigan castrated at 3 (*n* = 6) or 6 (*n* = 6) weeks after transfer from 6 h light per day to continuous light (●). The changes in plasma LH levels in intact birds exposed to the same lighting pattern are also shown (○). The reduction in LH response to castration after 6 as opposed to 3 weeks' exposure to continuous light marks the progressive development of photorefractoriness which is not so evident from measurements of plasma LH in intact birds. Vertical lines represent the standard error of the mean (Adapted from Stokkan and Sharp, 1984)

and Sharp, 1984) which is a Galliform species related to the turkey. In the starling, the development of photorefractoriness is dependent on the presence of the thyroid glands and can be dissipated by thyroidectomy (Dawson, Goldsmith and Nicholls, 1985). On the other hand, thyroidectomy in another passerine species, the red-headed bunting, does not prevent the development of photorefractoriness (Thapliyal and Lal, 1984).

A progressive increase in plasma prolactin is associated with the development of photorefractoriness in all wild birds studied so far, including three Galliform species, the Grey partridge, the Willow ptarmigan and Spitzbergen ptarmigan (Sharp *et al.*, 1986b; Stokkan *et al.*, 1988). A role for prolactin in the development of photorefractoriness is an attractive possibility since this hormone has anti-gonadotrophic activity (e.g. Opel and Proudman, 1980). However, in contrast to the studies on wild birds, a large increase in plasma prolactin does not mark the

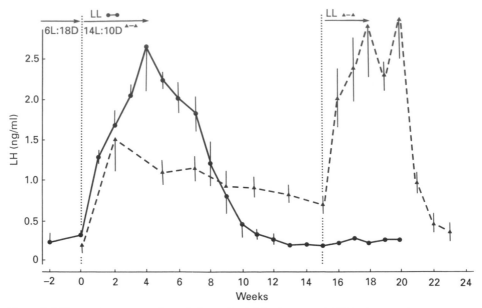

Figure 3.4 Changes in concentrations of plasma luteinizing hormone (LH) in photosensitive Willow ptarmigan (*n* = 5) transferred at week 0 from 6 h light per day to a sub-optimal stimulatory 14 h of light per day (▲–▲). At 15 weeks the birds were transferred to continuous light (LL). A control group (*n* = 6) was transferred at week 0 to continuous light (●–●). Note the development of photorefractoriness, as marked by the steep fall in plasma LH, after 8–10 weeks of exposure to continuous light. Birds exposed to 14-h light per day did not become photorefractory at this time. Vertical lines represent the standard error of the mean (Adapted from Stokkan, Sharp and Moss, 1982)

development of photorefractoriness in the turkey (Lea and Sharp, 1982; Bacon *et al.*, 1983; Zadworny, Walton and Etches, 1986).

It has long been known that the time taken for photorefractoriness to develop is inversely related to the duration of the daily photoperiod (Sharp, 1983). In some birds, exposure to sub-optimal photoperiods may prevent the development of photorefractoriness (Stokkan, Sharp and Moss, 1982; Dawson and Goldsmith, 1983). This point is illustrated by a study on Willow ptarmigan photostimulated into breeding condition with a sub-optimal 14-h daylength (*Figure 3.4*). Although concentrations of plasma LH never increased as much as in the fully photostimulated control birds, they were sufficient to maintain full breeding condition until after the control birds had become photorefractory. Birds exposed to 14-h daylengths remained responsive to a further increase in photoperiod although this increase resulted in the development of photorefractoriness. In this study, control birds were in breeding condition for about 8 weeks whereas the experimental birds were in breeding condition for about 16 weeks. It thus seems possible that novel lighting patterns might be devised to extend the laying period of commercial turkeys.

Broodiness

Potential egg production is lost in many lines of turkeys when kept on the floor, because of the development of broodiness. This problem particularly affects heavier meat-lines but can be overcome by careful management. The search for more economical ways of controlling broodiness in turkeys has recently encouraged strategic research into the endocrine and neuroendocrine control of this behaviour.

Endocrine interactions

Broodiness is characterized by increased nesting behaviour which is usually associated with regression of the ovary and oviduct. The chief endocrine features of the development of broodiness are an increase in the concentration of plasma prolactin (Burke and Dennison, 1980; Proudman and Opel, 1981; Etches and Cheng, 1982; *Figure 3.5*) and, when egg production stops, a fall in the plasma LH and ovarian steroids (Cogger, Burke and Ogren, 1979; Burke and Dennison, 1980; El Halawani, Burke and Dennison, 1980b; Harvey, Bedrak and Chadwick, 1981; *Figure 3.5*).

In laying hens, nesting behaviour usually only occurs around the time of oviposition. Studies on the induction of nesting behaviour in ovariectomized turkeys show that it depends on an interaction between oestrogen and progesterone (El Halawani *et al.*, 1986). These studies suggest that oestrogen coming from the

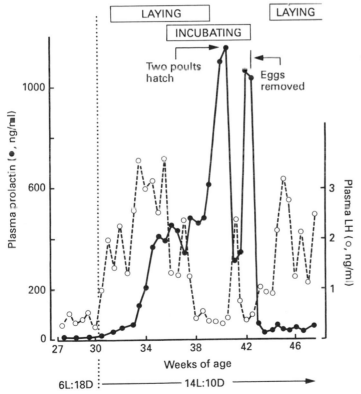

Figure 3.5 Changes in the concentrations of plasma luteinizing hormone (LH) and prolactin during a cycle of broodiness in a turkey. The hen was kept in a floor pen with a nest box and allowed to accumulate a clutch of eggs. She was artificially inseminated at 4 weeks after transfer from 6 h of light per day (6L:18D) to 14-h light per day (14L:10D) (Adapted from Lea, Sharp and Chadwick, 1982)

rapidly growing yellow-yolky follicles 'primes' a neural mechanism controlling nesting behaviour, making it responsive to a pre-ovulatory release of progesterone. Nesting behaviour in response to an increase in plasma progesterone is not immediate, but occurs after a delay of about 24 h. A pre-ovulatory release of progesterone thus triggers the nesting behaviour associated with the oviposition of the resulting ovulated ovum. El Halawani *et al.* (1986) showed that nesting behaviour induced in ovariectomized turkeys after treatment with oestrogen and progesterone can be maintained by injections of ovine prolactin. Thus, prolactin treatment of oestrogen–progesterone-primed turkeys increases the persistency of nesting behaviour transforming it into broody or, more precisely, incubation behaviour. Once incubation behaviour is initiated, it further enhances prolactin release which in turn serves to reinforce the behaviour.

Evidence that incubation behaviour maintains prolactin release is based on the observation that plasma prolactin levels drop rapidly after nest deprivation and increase after the nests are returned (El Halawani, Burke and Dennison, 1980a). Readiness to incubate persists for between 2 and 3 days after nest deprivation (El Halawani, Burke and Dennison, 1980a). It thus appears that prolactin must be withdrawn for this period before it loses its ability to maintain readiness to incubate. The view that prolactin maintains incubation behaviour, is reinforced by the findings in the Ring Dove (Janik and Buntin, 1985) and Bantam (P. J. Sharp *et al.*, 1988) that injections of ovine prolactin maintain readiness to incubate in broody birds deprived of their nests.

Nesting frequency increases in turkey hens 9–7 days before the onset of broodiness (Haller and Cherms, 1961) and this increase is associated with rising concentrations of plasma prolactin (Burke and Dennison, 1980; Proudman and Opel, 1981). Attempts to determine which comes first, an increase in plasma prolactin or an increase in nesting frequency, have been inconclusive. The most detailed study has been done on Bantam hens (Lea *et al.*, 1981; Lea, Sharp and Chadwick, 1982). A few days before the onset of incubation, nocturnal surges of plasma prolactin develop in association with a switch from roosting on a perch to nesting at night. On successive days before the onset of incubation these nocturnal surges of prolactin extend progressively into the light period as nesting becomes more persistent.

In view of these observations it may be misleading to think of the initiation of increased nesting prior to onset of incubation as being an immediate response to an increase in plasma prolactin. An alternative hypothesis is that the initiation of prolonged nesting might be the result of a progressive lowering of a prolactin-dependent neural threshold to a variety of environmental factors which encourage broodiness (*Figure 3.6*). According to this view, an increase in base-line concentrations of plasma prolactin predisposes a hen to broodiness rather than directly initiates it. An examination of base-line plasma prolactin levels during a photoinduced laying cycle in turkeys is consistent with this view. Base-line concentrations of plasma prolactin are at their highest between about 4–8 weeks of egg production (Etches and Cheng, 1982; Bacon *et al.*, 1983) which corresponds with the period when broodiness is most likely to occur (Nestor, Bacon and Renner, 1986).

Several factors cause base-line concentrations of plasma prolactin to increase at the beginning of the laying period. One is a direct effect of stimulatory daylengths which is independent of the ovarian steroid environment since an increase in plasma prolactin is seen immediately after photostimulation in intact and ovariectomized turkeys (El Halawani *et al.*, 1984; Saeed and El Halawani, 1986).

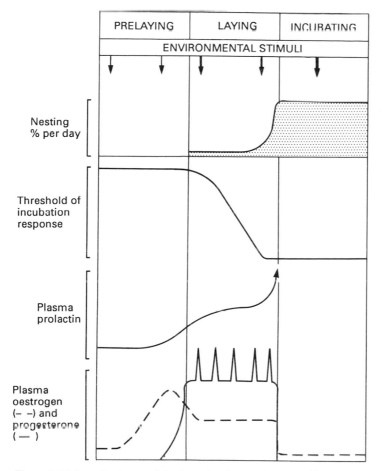

Figure 3.6 A hypothesis to explain the endocrine–environmental interactions which induce broodiness. Oestrogen and progesterone from rapidly growing ovarian follicles induce the development of nesting behaviour associated with each oviposition. Oestrogen also facilitates the release of prolactin from the anterior pituitary gland causing base-line concentrations of plasma prolactin to increase. It is proposed that this increase in base-line concentrations of prolactin progressively lowers a neural threshold to a variety of environmental factors (e.g. a nest site, clutch of eggs) which encourage increased nesting. An increase in nesting behaviour stimulates further prolactin release which maintains the behaviour and transforms it into incubation behaviour

Another factor is an oestrogen-dependent increase in the release of prolactin from the pituitary gland (El Halawani *et al.*, 1986; Saeed and El Halawani, 1986). It appears that as turkeys come into lay, increasing concentrations of oestrogens produced by rapidly growing ovarian follicles enhance the release of prolactin from the pituitary gland either directly, or indirectly by increasing responsiveness to hypothalamic prolactin releasing factor (PRF).

It is not known why base-line concentrations of prolactin fall towards the end of the laying period (Etches and Cheng, 1982; Bacon *et al.*, 1983). Since the number of rapidly growing ovarian follicles decreases during this period, ovarian oestrogen production might be decreasing thereby reducing the facilitatory action of oestrogens on the release of prolactin.

High ambient temperature is often associated with an accelerated incidence of broodiness (Thomason, Leighton and Mason, 1972) and it is likely that this temperature effect is mediated by a rapid increase in base-line plasma prolactin. Thus, El Halawani *et al.* (1984) found in turkeys kept on the floor, that plasma prolactin increased more rapidly after photostimulation in groups exposed to 30°C than in groups exposed to 24 or 19°C. This observation is consistent with the view that raised base-line plasma prolactin may increase responsiveness to environmental factors which encourage broodiness.

In addition to maintaining incubation behaviour, high concentrations of plasma prolactin in broody turkeys may depress food intake (Denbow, 1986) and depress the release of LH (Lea *et al.*, 1981; Sharp *et al.*, 1988). The inhibitory effect of prolactin on LH release is mediated at the hypothalamic rather than the pituitary gland level of control since the pituitary gland of incubating hens is fully responsive to GnRH (Sharp and Lea, 1981; El Halawani *et al.*, 1987). Prolactin does not appear to be involved in the changes in intermediary or water metabolism which occur in broody turkeys (Zadworny, Walton and Etches, 1985).

The concentration of plasma prolactin required to maintain incubation behaviour is not necessarily the same as that required to inhibit egg production (*Figure 3.5*, Proudman and Opel, 1981; Zadworny, Walton and Etches, 1986). As shown in *Figure 3.5*, incubation behaviour can be maintained by moderately elevated levels of plasma prolactin without inhibiting egg production. Egg production is only inhibited after a further increase in concentrations of plasma prolactin. It is possible that selection against broodiness or increased egg production may differentially alter the thresholds of response to the behavioural and anti-gonadotrophic effects of prolactin (Bacon *et al.*, 1983). Thus, selection for egg production may make the hens less responsive to the anti-gonadotrophic effects of prolactin but have less of an effect on the minimum concentration of prolactin required to maintain incubation behaviour. A comparison of base-line concentrations of prolactin within a meat-line failed to establish any correlation between groups that become broody and those which did not become broody (Bacon *et al.*, 1983). This observation suggests that the base-line levels of prolactin can not be used as a marker for a broody genotype.

Neuroendocrine control mechanisms

Prolactin secretion is controlled predominantly by hypothalamic prolactin releasing factors (Fehrer, Silsby and El Halawani, 1985; Fehrer *et al.*, 1985a, b; El Halawani *et al.*, 1987), the identity of which are not fully established. Research interest has focused on two neuropeptides, thyrotrophin-releasing hormone (TRH), vasoactive intestinal polypeptide (VIP), and two neurotransmitters, dopamine and serotonin.

Thyrotrophin releasing hormone stimulates the release of prolactin in young turkeys when administered *in vivo* but does not release prolactin from cultured turkey pituitary gland cells *in vitro* (Fehrer *et al.*, 1985b). It can therefore be deduced that the stimulatory effects of TRH on prolactin release are mediated by a second releasing factor. One such factor could be VIP since this neuropeptide releases prolactin directly from turkey pituitary gland cells *in vitro* (Proudman and Opel, 1983). Further support for VIP as a prolactin releasing factor acting directly on the pituitary gland comes from a study on broody bantams. In the bantam, VIP releases prolactin from cultured pituitary gland cells and a VIP-like peptide is localized in neurons and nerve terminals in hypothalamic structures known to be involved in the regulation of anterior pituitary gland function (Macnamee *et al.*, 1986).

The stimulatory action of TRH on prolactin release *in vivo* is enhanced in ovariectomized turkeys after treatment with oestrogen (Saeed and El Halawani, 1986). This observation suggests that the oestrogen-dependent increase in base-line levels of plasma prolactin at the beginning of the laying period may be due, in part, to an increased response of the pituitary gland to hypothalamic prolactin releasing factor(s).

A stimulatory role for dopamine in the regulation of prolactin release in turkeys is suggested by the finding that the turnover of this neurotransmitter increases in the hypothalamus during the transition from laying to incubation (El Halawani and Burke, 1976). Further, injection of dopamine into the third cerebroventricle of non-broody post-laying turkeys stimulates an increase in plasma prolactin (Hargis and Burke, 1986). The stimulatory effect of dopamine on prolactin release is not mediated by a direct stimulatory action on the pituitary gland. The neurotransmitter suppresses prolactin release from turkey pituitary glands *in vitro* (Fehrer, 1984).

Of the neurotransmitters studied to date, there is no doubt about the stimulatory role of serotonin in the regulation of prolactin release. In turkeys, the turnover of serotonin in the hypothalamus increases in broody hens (El Halawani and Burke, 1976) while systemic or cerebroventricular injection of serotonin, serotonin precursor, or serotonin agonists, stimulate prolactin release (Fehrer, Silsby and El Halawani, 1983; Hargis and Burke, 1984). Administration of the serotonin synthesis inhibitor, *p*-chlorophenylalanine (PCPA) inhibits prolactin release in re-nesting and incubating turkeys (El Halawani, Burke and Dennison, 1980b; El Halawani *et al.*, 1983) which is consistent with a stimulatory role of serotonin in prolactin release. Like dopamine and TRH, serotonin does not exert its stimulatory effect on prolactin release by acting directly on the pituitary gland (Fehrer, Silsby and El Halawani, 1985).

Pharmacological treatments

The traditional approach to the treatment of broodiness involves careful monitoring of each hen's nesting behaviour. Those showing signs of increased nesting are subjected to a novel environment to disrupt or inhibit development of broody behaviour (Nestor, Bacon and Renner, 1986). This approach can be made more efficient by applying broody hen treatment only from 4 to 8 weeks of production when the birds are most likely to become broody (Nestor, Bacon and Renner, 1986).

Early successful pharmacological treatments of broodiness were based on the administration of gonadal steroids or gonadotrophins (Haller and Cherms, 1961). While gonadal steroids disrupt broody behaviour, they delay the return to lay. This observation has recently been confirmed in bantam hens (Sharp and Sterling, 1986). Treatment with gonadotrophins brings broody turkeys quickly back into lay but is too expensive for practical use. An alternative might be to treat broody turkeys with synthetic GnRH. However, treatment of broody bantams with various doses and concentrations of GnRH analogues failed to stimulate ovarian growth (Sharp and Sterling, 1986). It is therefore doubtful if GnRH treatment offers a practical way of bringing broody turkeys back into lay.

Another approach to the treatment of broodiness is based on the use of the anti-oestrogen, clomiphene citrate. The anti-oestrogen might be expected to antagonize the inhibitory feedback action of oestrogen on gonadotrophin release (Sharp, 1983) and to prevent oestrogen acting on the pituitary to potentiate the release of prolactin. Robinzon *et al.* (1984) found that clomiphene treatment brought nest-deprived broody turkeys back into lay more quickly, and with a higher rate of egg production than control birds. However, these observations were not confirmed in a subsequent study by Renner *et al.* (1987).

An attempt has been made to disrupt broodiness in bantams by treating broody hens with anti-prolactin serum to neutralize the biological effects of plasma prolactin (Lea *et al.*, 1981). This treatment resulted in a rapid increase in concentration of plasma luteinizing hormone, (LH) but, over the 2-day period of the study, it did not disrupt broodiness (*Figure 3.7*). This may not be surprising since in bantams (P. J. Sharp *et al.*, 1988) as in turkeys (El Halawani, Burke and Dennison, 1980a) readiness to incubate persists, despite lowered levels of plasma prolactin, for 2–3 days after nest deprivation. Due to the shortage of anti-prolactin serum it was not possible to establish whether passive immunization against prolactin for a longer period would disrupt broodiness and stimulate egg production.

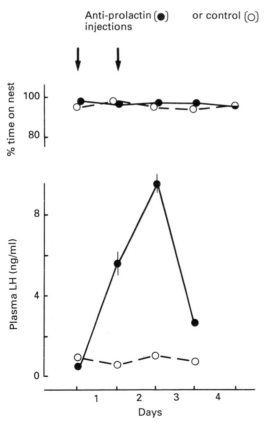

Figure 3.7 The effect of two daily intravenous injections of anti-chicken prolactin serum (●) on the concentration of plasma luteinizing hormone (LH) and incubation behaviour in broody bantam hens (*n* = 5). Control broody bantams were injected with non-immune serum (0, *n* = 5). Vertical lines represent the standard error the mean. (Based on data from Lea *et al.* (1981) and R. W. Lea and P. J. Sharp, unpublished observations)

Studies on the role of dopamine and serotonin in the regulation of prolactin secretion (see above) suggest other pharmacological treatment of broodiness. Attempts have been made to inhibit the stimulatory effect of dopamine on the release of prolactin immediately prior to the onset of broodiness by treatment with pimozide, a dopamine receptor blocking agent (Millam, Burke and Ogren, 1980). Treatment of turkeys showing increased nesting frequency with pimozide decreased the incidence of broodiness and increased egg production. However, weekly treatment of a flock of turkeys with pimozide, without regard to nesting frequency, had no effect on the incidence of broodiness (Millam, Burke and Ogren, 1980).

Daily treatment of incubating turkeys with oral doses of the serotonin synthesis inhibitor, p-chlorophenylalanine, for 3 days abolished nesting behaviour within 12 days and stimulated the resumption of egg production in 24.7 ± 1.7 days in seven out of eight hens (El Halawani *et al.*, 1983). The success of this treatment suggests that a practical pharmacological approach to broodiness might yet be found, given the appropriate research effort.

References

Albright, W. P. and Thompson, R. B. (1933). Securing early turkeys by stimulated egg production. *Poultry Science*, **12**, 124–128

Asem, E. K., Lintner, F., Biellier, H. V., Burke, W. H. and Hertelendey, F. (1983). Comparison of turkey leutinizing hormone (LH) and ovine LH-induced progesterone production in granulosa cells of the turkey (*Meleagris gallopavo*) and of the domestic fowl (*Gallus domesticus*). *General and Comparative Endocrinology*, **52**, 445–451

Asmundson, V. S. and Lloyd, W. E. (1935). The effect of age on reproduction of the turkey hen. *Poultry Science*, **14**, 259–265

Asmundson, V. S. and Moses, B. D. (1950). Influence of length of day on reproduction in turkey hens. *Poultry Science*, **29**, 34–41

Bacon, W. L. (1981). Metabolism of lipid labeled very low density lipoprotein from laying turkey hens in laying turkey hens and immature turkeys. *Poultry Science*, **60**, 1525–1536

Bacon, W. L. (1986). Metabolism and ovarian follicular uptake of the major yolk precursor in laying turkey hens. *Poultry Science*, **65**, 1184–1192

Bacon, W. L. and Cherms, F. L. (1968). Ovarian follicular growth and maturation in the domestic turkey. *Poultry Science*, **47**, 1303–1314

Bacon, W. L., Nestor, K. E. and Musser, M. A. (1973). Relative concentration and plasma content of yolk lipoprotein precursor in three lines of turkeys. *Poultry Science*, **52**, 1175–1187

Bacon, W. L., Nestor, K. E. and Renner, P. H. (1972). Further studies on ovarian follicular development in egg and meat type turkeys. *Poultry Science*, **51**, 398–401

Bacon, W. L., Burke, W. H., Nestor, K. E. and Brown, K. I. (1983). Influence of genetic increases in egg production on traits associated with broodiness in turkeys. *Poultry Science*, **62**, 2460–2473

Bahr, J. M., Wang, S. C., Huang, M. Y. and Calvo, F. O. (1983). Steroid concentrations in isolated theca and granulosa layers of pre-ovulatory follicles during the ovulatory cycle of the domestic hen. *Biology of Reproduction*, **29**, 326–334

Bajpayee, D. P. and Brown, K. I. (1972). Effect of photoperiodicity on the circulating levels of oestrogens, corticosterone, calcium and free fatty acids in female domestic turkeys (*Meleagris gallopavo*). *Poultry Science*, **51**, 1157–1165

Bixler, E. J. and Ringer, R. K. (1968). Effects of light regime upon time of oviposition in turkey hens. *Poultry Science*, **17**, 1027–1028

Brown, K. I., Long, D. W., Bacon, W. L. and Braselton, W. E. (1979). Evidence for the presence of 15-hydroxylated estrogens in the peripheral plasma of the laying turkey. *General and Comparative Endocrinology*, **39**, 552–560

Burger, J. W. (1947). On the relation of day-length to the phases of testicular involution and inactivity of the spermatogenetic cycle of the starling. *Journal of Experimental Zoology*, **105**, 259–267

Burke, W. H. and Cogger, E. A. (1977). The effect of luteinizing hormone releasing hormone on serum LH and ovarian growth in turkeys. *Poultry Science*, **56**, 234–242

Burke, W. H. and Denrison, P. T. (1980). Prolactin and luteinizing hormone levels in female turkeys (*Meleagris gallopavo*) during a photoinduced reproductive cycle and broodiness. *General and Comparative Endocrinology*, **41**, 92–100

Burke, W. H., Licht, P., Papkoff, H. and Bona Gallo, A. (1979). Isolation and characterization of luteinizing hormone and follicle stimulating hormone from the pituitary glands of the turkey (*Meleagris gallopavo*). *General and Comparative Endocrinology*, **37**, 508–520

Camper, P. M. and Burke, W. H. (1977). Serum estradiol and progesterone levels of the laying turkey hen following acute treatment with mammalian luteinizing hormone or follicle-stimulating hormone. *General and Comparative Endocrinology*, **31**, 224–232

Clayton, G. A. and Robertson, A. (1960). Light induction of out of season reproduction in the turkey. *British Poultry Science*, **1**, 17–23

Cleaver, W. T., Christensen, V. L. and Ort, J. F. (1986). Physiological characteristics of a molt and second cycle of egg laying in turkey breeder hens. *Poultry Science*, **65**, 2335–2342

Cogger, E. A., Burke, W. H. and Ogren, L. A. (1979). Serum luteinizing hormone, progesterone and estradiol levels in relation to broodiness in the turkey (*Meleagris gallopavo*). *Poultry Science*, **58**, 1355–1360

Damsté, P. H. (1947). Experimental modification of the sexual cycle of the greenfinch. *Journal of Experimental Biology*, **24**, 20–35

Dawson, A. and Goldsmith, A. R. (1983). Plasma prolactin and gonadotrophins during gonadal development and the onset of photorefractoriness in male and female starlings (*Sturnus vulgaris*) on artificial photoperiods. *Journal of Endocrinology*, **97**, 253–260

Dawson, A., Goldsmith, A. R. and Nicholls, T. J. (1985). Thyroidectomy results in termination of photorefractoriness in starlings kept on long daylengths. *Journal of Reproduction and Fertility*, **74**, 527–533

Dawson, A., Follett, B. K., Goldsmith, A. R. and Nicholls, T. J. (1985). Hypothalamic gonadotrophin-releasing hormone and pituitary and plasma FSH and prolactin during photostimulation and photorefractoriness in intact and thyroidectomized starlings (*Sturnus vulgaris*). *Journal of Endocrinology*, **105**, 71–77

Denbow, D. M. (1986). The influence of prolactin on food intake of turkey hens. *Poultry Science*, **65**, 1197–1200

El Halawani, M. E. and Burke, W. H. (1976). Brain monoamine metabolism of turkey hens in various stages of their reproductive cycle. *Biology of Reproduction*, **23**, 118–123

El Halawani, M. E., Burke, W. H. and Dennison, P. T. (1980a). Effect of nest deprivation on serum prolactin levels in nesting female turkeys. *Biology of Reproduction*, **23**, 118–123

El Halawani, M. E., Burke, W. H. and Dennison, P. T. (1980b). Effects of *p*-chlorophenylalanine on the rise in serum prolactin associated with nesting in broody turkeys. *Biology of Reproduction*, **23**, 815–819

El Halawani, M. E., Fehrer, S. C. and Silsby, J. L. (1987). Enhanced luteinizing hormone release by luteinizing hormone releasing hormone in incubating female turkeys. (*Meleagris gallopavo*). *Biology of Reproduction*, **36**, 884–889

El Halawani, M. E., Silsby, J. L., Fehrer, S . C. and Behnke, E. J. (1983). Reinitiation of ovulatory cycles in incubating female turkeys by an inhibitor of serotonin synthesis, *p*-chlorophenylalanine. *Biology of Reproduction*, **28**, 221–228

El Halawani, M. E., Silsby, J. L., Behnke, E. J. and Fehrer, S. C. (1984). Effect of ambient temperatures on serum prolactin and luteinizing hormone levels during the reproductive life cycle of the female turkey (*Meleagris gallopavo*). *Biology of Reproduction*, **30**, 809–815

El Halawani, M. E., Silsby, J. L., Behnke, E. J. and Fehrer, S. C. (1986). Hormonal induction of incubation behaviour in ovariectomized female turkeys (*Meleagris gallopavo*). *Biology of Reproduction*, **35**, 59–67

El Halawani, M. E., Youngren, O. M., Silsby, J. L. and Phillips, R. E. (1987). Prolactin release following electrical stimulation of the brain in female turkeys (*Meleagris gallopavo*). *General and Comparative Endocrinology*, **65**, 1–8

Etches, R. J. and Cheng, K. W. (1982). A homologous radioimmunoassay for turkey prolactin: changes during the reproductive and ovulatory cycle. *Poultry Science*, **61**, 1354–1362

Farmer, S. W., Papkoff, H. and Licht, P. (1975). Purification of turkey gonadotrophins. *Biology of Reproduction*, **12**, 415–422

Fehrer, S. C. (1984). Quoted in Hargis and Burke (1986)

Fehrer, S. C., Silsby, J. L. and El Halawani, M. E. (1983). Serotonergic stimulation of prolactin release in the young turkey (*Meleagris gallopavo*). *General and Comparative Endocrinology*, **52**, 400–408

Fehrer, S. C., Silsby, J. L. and El Halawani, M. E. (1985). Serotonergic influences on pituitary gland and hypothalamic induction of prolactin and luteinizing hormone release in the young turkey (*Meleagris gallopavo*). *Biology of Reproduction*, **33**, 1064–1072

Fehrer, S. C., Silsby, J. L., Behnke, E. J. and El Halawani, M. E. (1985a). Hypothalamic and serum factors influence on prolactin and luteinizing hormone release by the pituitary gland of the young turkey (*Meleagris gallopavo*). *General and Comparative Endocrinology*, **59**, 73–81

Fehrer, S. C., Silsby, J. L., Behnke, E. J. and El Halawani, M. E. (1985b). The influence of thyrotropin releasing hormone on *in vivo* prolactin release and *in vitro* prolactin, luteinizing hormone and growth hormone release from dispersed pituitary cells of the young turkey (*Meleagris gallopavo*). *General and Comparative Endocrinology*, **59**, 64–72

Ferguson, T. M., Atkinson, R. L., Bradley, J. W. and Miller, D. H. (1975). Reproductive performance of caged Beltsville Small White turkeys as affected by choline, bird density and forced molting. *Poultry Science*, **54**, 1679–1684

Foster, R. G. and Follett, B. K. (1985). The involvement of a rhodopsin-like photopigment in the photoperiodic response of the Japanese quail. *Journal of Comparative Physiology*, Part A, **157**, 519–528

Gilbert, A. B. and Wells, J. W. (1984). Structure and function of the ovary. In *Reproductive Biology of Poultry*. (Cunningham, F. J., Lake, P. E. and Hewitt, D., eds), pp. 15–27. Edinburgh, British Poultry Science Ltd, Longmans

Godden, P. M. M. and Scanes, C. G. (1977). Effect of photoperiod on gonadotrophin concentrations in domestic turkeys. *British Poultry Science*, **18**, 687–694

Haller, R. W. and Cherms, F. L. (1961). A comparison of several treatments on terminating broodiness in Broad Breasted Bronze turkeys. *Poultry Science*, **40**, 155–163

Hammond, R. W., Koelkebeck, K. W., Scanes, C. G., Biellier, H. V. and Hertelendy, F. (1981). Plasma prostaglandin, LH and progesterone levels during the ovulation cycle of the turkey *Meleagris gallopavo*. *General and Comparative Endocrinology*, **44**, 400–403

Hargis, B. M. and Burke, W. H. (1984). Prolactin and luteinizing hormone levels of pre-laying, laying and post-laying turkey hens following central administration of serotonin and peripheral administration of quipazine maleate. *General and Comparative Endocrinology*, **55**, 12–19

Hargis, B. M. and Burke, W. H. (1986). Influence of cerebroventricular injection of dopamine on plasma prolactin and LH levels of post-laying and broody turkey hens. *General and Comparative Endocrinology*, **61**, 142–147

Harper, J. A. and Parker, J. E. (1957). Changes in seasonal egg production of turkeys induced through controlled light exposure and force moulting. *Poultry Science*, **36**, 967–973

Harper, J. A. and Parker, J. E. (1960). Effect of restricted light and hormones on subsequent egg production of winter hatched turkeys. *Poultry Science*, **37**, 900–903

Harper, J. A. and Parker, J. E. (1965). Effect of light and drugs in controlling egg production in turkeys. *Poultry Science*, **44**, 778–784

Harper, J. A. and Parker, J. E. (1973). Pre-laying use of reserpine for control of light refractoriness in young turkey females. *Poultry Science*, **52**, 1745–1748

Harvey, S., Bedrak, E. and Chadwick, A. (1981). Serum concentrations of prolactin, luteinizing hormone, growth hormone, corticosterone, progesterone, testosterone and oestradiol in relation to broodiness in domestic turkeys (*Meleagris gallopavo*). *Journal of Endocrinology*, **89**, 187–195

Hocking, P. M., Gilbert, A. B., Whitehead, C. C. and Walker, M. A. (1988a). Effects of age and of early lighting on ovarian function in breeding turkeys. *British Poultry Science*, **29**, 223–229

Hocking, P. M., Walker, M. A., Waddington, D. and Gilbert, A. B. (1988b). Observations on the size of the follicular hierarchy in the turkey hen and a case of arrested follicular growth. *British Poultry Science*, **28**, 755–757

Janik, D. S. and Buntin, J. D. (1985). Behavioural and physiological effectsd of prolactin in incubating ring doves. *Journal of Endocrinology,* **105**, 201–209

Jones, J. E., Hughes, R. J. and Thurston, R. A. (1982). The effects of red and white light during the prebreeder and breeder periods on egg production and feed consumption in Large White turkeys. *Poultry Science,* **61**, 1930–1932

Johnson, A. L. (1986). Reproduction in the female. In *Avian Physiology* (Sturkie, P. D., ed.), pp. 403–431. New York, Berlin, Springer-Verlag

Kuenzel, W. J. and Lake, P. E. (1984). Advanced gonadal development in male turkeys following knife cuts directed to the hypothalamus. *Poultry Science,* **63**, 568–572

Lea, R. W. and Sharp, P. J. (1982). Plasma prolactin concentrations in broody turkeys: lack of agreement between homologous chicken and turkey prolactin radioimmunoassays. *British Poultry Science,* **23**, 451–459

Lea, R. W., Dods, A. S. M., Sharp, P. J. and Chadwick, A. (1981). The possible role of prolactin in the regulation of nesting behaviour and the secretion of luteinizing hormone in broody bantams. *Journal of Endocrinology,* **91**, 89–97

Lea, R. W., Sharp, P. J. and Chadwick, A. (1982). Daily variations in the concentrations of plasma prolactin in broody bantams. *General and Comparative Endocrinology,* **48**, 275–284

Leighton, A. T. and Shoffner, R. N. (1961a). Effect of light regime and age on reproduction of turkeys. 1. Effect of 15, 24 hour and restricted light treatment. *Poultry Science,* **40**, 861–870

Leighton, A. T. and Shoffner, R. N. (1961b). Effect of light regime and age on reproduction of turkeys. 2. Restricted vs unrestricted light. *Poultry Science,* **40**, 871–884

Leighton, A. T. and Shoffner, R. N. (1964). Effect of light and age on reproduction of turkeys. 3. Restricted light on yearling hens. *Poultry Science,* **43**, 49–53

Leighton, A. T., Van Krey, H. P., Moyer, D. D. and Potter, M. (1971). Reproductive performance of force molted turkey breeder hens. *Poultry Science,* **50**, 119–126

McCartney, M. C., Sanger, V. L., Brown, K. I. and Chamberlin, V. D. (1961). Photoperiodism as a factor in the reproduction of the turkey. *Poultry Science,* **40**, 368–376

Macnamee, M. C., Sharp, P. J., Lea, R. W., Sterling, R. J. and Harvey, S. (1986). Evidence that vasoactive intestinal polypeptide is a physiological prolactin releasing factor in the bantam hen. *General and Comparative Endocrinology,* **62**, 470–478

Marr, J. E., Garland, F. W. Jr., Milligan, J. L. and Wilcke, H. L. (1956). Effect of controlled light during the growing period upon subsequent performance of breeder turkeys. *Poultry Science,* **35**, 1156

Marsden, S. J. and Lucas, L. M. (1964). Effects of short-day and low-intensity light treatments on reproduction of fall-hatched turkeys in two environments. *Poultry Science,* **43**, 435–441

Marsden, S. J., Cowen, N. S. and Lucas, L. M. (1962). Effect of gradual and abrupt lengthening of photoperiod on reproductive response of turkeys. *Poultry Science,* **41**, 1864–1868

Mashaly, M. M. and Wentworth, B. C. (1974). A profile of progesterone in turkey sera. *Poultry Science,* **53**, 2034–2035

Mashaly, M. M., Birrenkott, G. P., El-Begearmi, M. M. and Wentworth, B. L. (1976). Plasma LH and progesterone concentrations in the turkey hen during the ovulatory cycle. *Poultry Science,* **55**, 1226–1234

Millam, J. R., Burke, W. H. and Ogren, L. A. (1980). Preventing broodiness in turkey hens with a dopamine receptor blocking agent. *Poultry Science,* **59**, 1126–1131

Neilson, J. T. McL. and Simpson, C. F. (1973). Plasma lipoproteins of turkeys injected with a single dose of diethylstilbesterol. *Atherosclearosis,* **18**, 445–450

Nestor, K. E. and Bacon, W. L. (1972). Production of defective eggs by egg and meat type hens. *Poultry Science,* **51**, 1361–1365

Nestor, K. E., Bacon, W. L. and Renner, P. A. (1970). Ovarian follicular development in egg and meat type turkeys. *Poultry Science,* **49**, 775–780

Nestor, K. E., Bacon, W. L. and Renner, P. A. (1980). The influence of genetic changes in total egg production, clutch length, broodiness and body weight on ovarian follicular development in turkeys. *Poultry Science,* **59**, 1694–1699

Nestor, K. E., Bacon, W. L. and Renner, P. A. (1986). The influence of time of application of broody hen treatments on egg production of turkeys. *Poultry Science,* **65**, 1405–1409

Ogasawara, F. X., Wilson, W. O. and Asmundson, V. S. (1962). The effect of restricting light during the adolescent period on reproductive performance in turkeys subsequently exposed to a 12-, 14- and 20-hour day. *Poultry Science*, **41**, 1858–1863

Opel, H. (1974). Rate of follicular atresia following hypophysectomy of the turkeys. *Poultry Science*, **53**, 825–827

Opel, H. (1979a). On hypothalamic control of ovulation in the turkey. *Poultry Science*, **58**, 717–724

Opel, H. (1979b). Effects of hypothalamic deafferentation on light-stimulated ovarian function in turkeys. *Poultry Science*, **58**, 1382–1391

Opel, H. and Proudman, J. A. (1980). Failure of mammalian prolactin to induce incubation behaviour in chickens and turkeys. *Poultry Science*, **59**, 2550–2558

Proudman, J. A. and Opel, H. (1981). Turkey prolactin: validation of a radioimmunoassay and measurement of changes associated with broodiness. *Biology of Reproduction*, **35**, 573–580

Proudman, J. and Opel, H. (1983). Stimulation of prolactin and growth hormone secretion from turkey pituitary cells. *Poultry Science*, **62**, 1484–1485

Renner, P. II., Nestor, K. E., Bacon, W. L. and Havenstein, G. B. (1987). Clomiphene-citrate does not reduce broodiness in turkey hens. *Poultry Science*, **66**, 558–560

Robinson, B., Shafir, Z., Perek, M. and Snapir, N. (1984). The effects of clomiphene-citrate on broody turkey hens. *Poultry Science*, **63**, 2268–2270

Saeed, W. and El Halawani, M. E. (1986). Modulation of the prolactin response to thyrotrophin releasing hormone by ovarian steroids. *General and Comparative Endocrinology*, **62**, 129–136

Schorger, N. (1966). *The Wild Turkey. Its History and Domestication*. Oklahoma, University of Oklahoma Press

Sexton, W. E. and Mccartney, M. G. (1973). The effect of age and lighting on reproduction in the turkey hen. *Poultry Science*, **52**, 516–520

Sharp, P. J. (1980). Female reproduction. In *Avian Endocrinology*, (Epple, A. and Stetson, M. H., eds), pp. 435–454. New York and London, Academic Press

Sharp, P. J. (1983). Hypothalamic control of gonadotrophin secretion in birds. In *Recent Progress in Non mammalian Brain Research*, (Nistico, G. and Bolis, L., eds), pp. 124–164. Boca Raton, Florida, USA, CRC Press

Sharp, P. J. (1984). Seasonal breeding and sexual maturation. In *Reproductive Biology of Poultry*, (Cunningham, F. J. and Hewitt, D., eds), pp. 203–218. Edinburgh, British Poultry Science Ltd, Longmans

Sharp, P. J. and Lea, R. W. (1981). The response of the pituitary gland to luteinizing hormone-releasing hormone in broody bantams. *General and Comparative Endocrinology*, **45**, 131–133

Sharp, P. J. and Sterling, R. J. (1986). Approaches to the pharmacological control of broodiness. *Proceedings 7th European Poultry Conference*, Paris, World Poultry Science Association, French Branch, 1029–1033

Sharp, P. J., Beuving, G. and van Middelkoop, J. H. (1976). Plasma luteinising hormone and ovarian structure in multiple ovulating hens. *Proceedings 5th European Poultry Conference*, Malta, 1259–1267

Sharp, P. J., MacNamee, M. C., Sterling, P. J., Lea, R. W. and Pedersen, H. C. (1988) Relationships between prolactin, LH and broody behaviour in bantam hens. *Journal of Endocrinology*, **118**, 279–286

Sharp, P. J., Lea, R. W., Chadwick, A. and Lake, P. E. (1981). Concentrations of plasma luteinising hormone, prolactin, progesterone and androgens during the ovulatory cycle of the turkey. *British Poultry Science*, **22**, 375–383

Sharp, P. J., Sterling, R. J., Milton, R. C. deL. and Miller, R. P. (1986a). Effect of luteinising hormone releasing hormone and its analogues on plasma luteinising hormone concentrations in incubating bantam hens. *British Poultry Science*, **27**, 129–135

Sharp, P. J., Massa, R., Bottoni, L., Lucini, V., Lea, R. W., Dunn, I. C. and Trocchi, V. (1986b). Photoperiodic and endocrine control of seasonal breeding in Grey partridge (*Perdix perdix*). *Journal of Zoology, London (A)*, **209**, 187–200

Shimada, K., Nelson, H. J. and Koike, T. J. (1986). Arginine vasotocin (AVT) release in relation to uterine contractility in the hen. *General and Comparative Endocrinology*, **64**, 362–367

Shoffner, R. N., Polley, C. R., Burger, R. E. and Johnson, E. L. (1962). Light regulation in turkey management. 2. Female reproductive performance. *Poultry Science*, **41**, 1563–1573

Siopes, T. D. (1984a). The effect of full-spectrum fluorescent lighting on reproductive traits of caged turkey hens. *Poultry Science, 63*, 1122–1128

Siopes, T. D. (1984b). Recycling turkey hens with low light intensity. *Poultry Science, 63*, 1449–1452

Siopes, T. D. and Underwood, H. A. (1987). Pineal gland and ocular influences on turkey breeder hens. 1. Reproductive performance. *Poultry Science, 66*, 521–527

Stokkan, K-A. and Sharp, P. J. (1984). The development of photorefractoriness in castrated Willow Ptarmigan (*Lagopus lagopus lagopus*). *General and Comparative Endocrinology, 54*, 402–408

Stokkan, K-A., Sharp, P. J. and Moss, R. (1982). Development of photorefractoriness in Willow Ptarmigan (*Lagopus lagopus lagopus*) exposed to different photoperiods. *General and Comparative Endocrinology, 46*, 281–287

Stokkan, K-A., Sharp, P. J., Dunn, I. C. and Lea, R. W. (1988). Endocrine changes in photostimulated Willow Ptarmigan (*Lagopus lagopus lagopus*) and Svalbard Ptarmigan (*Lagopus mutus hyperboreus*). *General and Comparative Endocrinology* (in press)

Thapliyal, J. P. and Lal, P. (1984). Light, thyroid, gonad and photorefractory state in the migratory Redheaded Bunting *Emberiza bruniceps*. *General and Comparative Endocrinology, 56*, 41–52

Thomason, D. M., Leighton, A. T. and Mason, J. P. (1972). A study of certain environmental factors on the reproductive performance of Large White turkeys. *Poultry Science, 51*, 1438–1449

Wentworth, B. C. (1971). Isolation and purification of follicle stimulating hormone and luteinizing hormone from turkey pituitary glands. *Biology of Reproduction, 5*, 107–108

Wilson, S. C. and Cunningham, F. J. (1984). Endocrine control of the ovulation cycle. In *Reproductive Biology of Poultry*, (Cunningham, F. J., Lake, P. E. and Hewitt, D., eds), pp. 29–49. Edinburgh, British Poultry Science Ltd, Longman Group

Wilson, W. O., Ogasawara, F. X. and Asmundson, V. S. (1962). Artificial control of egg production in turkeys by photoperiods. *Poultry Science, 41*, 1168–1175

Wineland, M. J. and Wentworth, B. C. (1975). Peripheral serum levels of 17β estradiol in growing turkey hens. *Poultry Science, 53*, 381–387

Wolford, J. H., Ringer, R. K. and Coleman, T. H. (1964). Lag time, interval between successive eggs and oviposition time in the turkey. *Poultry Science, 43*, 612–615

Wolfson, A. (1952). The occurrence and regulation of the refractory period in the gonadal and fat cycles of the junco. *Journal of Experimental Zoology, 121*, 311–326

Woodard, A. E., Wilson, W. O. and Mather, F. B. (1963). The egg laying rhythm of turkeys in cages. *Poultry Science, 42*, 1131–1133

Zadworny, D., Walton, J. S. and Etches, R. J. (1985). Effect of feed and water deprivation or force-feeding on plasma prolactin concentration in turkey hens. *Biology of Reproduction, 32*, 241–247

Zadworny, D., Walton, J. S. and Etches, R. J. (1986). Effect of environment on the intake of food and water, body weight, egg production and plasma concentrations of corticosterone and prolactin in turkey hens. *British Poultry Science, 27*, 639–650

Chapter 4

Recent research in male reproduction

P. E. Lake

The future turkey industry is predicted to assume ever-increasing importance in providing quality meat very competitively with that of large farm animals. In this endeavour the male can be expected to play a large part in maintaining and improving performance traits, such as food conversion efficiency and growth. This will apply particularly in those sectors where there is an emphasis on trade in meat portions, when there will be a quest for still further increases in the size of the bird. The male of some modern strains of turkey is already very heavy (about 30 kg), and breeding with these extreme types presents the farmer with an arduous task since artificial insemination involves lifting and man-handling the male for semen collection. Also, biologically, amongst many types of domestic animals there is a trend for increased body weight to be inversely correlated with reproductive organ size. In this respect, the heavier types of domestic birds, such as the broiler fowl, medium-weight layer fowl, turkey and Muscovy duck are inferior in testis size to the lightweight Leghorn type of fowl selected for eating-egg production.

Artificial insemination (AI) is obligatory for breeding. Thus, it is an advantage to obtain from the male a high yield of good quality semen in terms of quantity of spermatozoa of high fertilizing ability and to minimize the loss of spermatozoa held *in vitro* under all circumstances. Thus, it is important to recognize the factors about the biology of the male and his management that are likely to limit the reproductive activity in these respects. Recent research has been motivated by these considerations.

Basic anatomical features of the turkey male relating to reproduction

At the outset it is interesting to recognize that the ratio of mean testis weight to mean body weight in the turkey is much less than that of the broiler fowl, which in turn is less than that of the type of fowl selected intensively for eating-egg production. For example, in our laboratories recent observations showed that the ratio of mean testes weight (g) to mean body weight (kg), at comparable age of full sexual maturity, of a heavy turkey, broiler fowl and Leghorn-type fowl was 1.7, 8.1 and 12.7, respectively. While about the same mean volume of semen is obtained from these types of domestic birds, the total output of spermatozoa tends to be greater in the turkey, as in our experience the average density of spermatozoa in the semen of the turkey is about 11 million compared with 4 million/mm^3 in the different types of fowl. Nevertheless, it would be a great advantage to the breeder if

55

turkey reproductive organs were larger and the total output of spermatozoa could be increased greatly. Amongst other things, this would reduce the number of males to be man-handled to obtain sufficient semen for an AI session. It would also extend greatly the genetic influence of individual males. Perhaps future physiological studies into the interaction of cell growth factors, output of pituitary hormones and tissue receptors should be encouraged hoping that such work may lead to the development of methods for the manipulation of reproductive organ growth and semen output.

There has been little recent work on the male reproductive organs of the turkey, and no detailed information exists on the mechanism of the maturation of the spermatozoa therein. Long ago, Saeki and Brown (1962) suggested that spermatozoa were more likely to be able to fertilize eggs when they reached the distal regions of the ductus deferens. However, this warrants further consideration because Bakst and Cecil (1981) indicated that spermatozoa from the proximal and distal *ductus deferens* were able to fertilize eggs.

Like the fowl, the reproductive system of the male turkey consists of paired testes, located at the cranial end of the kidneys in the anterior abdominal cavity, and their excurrent duct systems. The latter originate with the epididymal region on the dorso-medial region of each testis and continue posteriorly with the *ductus deferens* which opens in the urodaeum of the cloaca through a projecting papilla (*papilla ductus deferentis*) (Hess, Thurston and Biellier, 1976; Hess and Thurston, 1977; Bakst, 1980). There are no accessory sex organs, e.g. seminal vesicles and prostate gland, which contribute large volumes of fluid to semen at ejaculation in some mammals and the human.

King (1981a,b) discusses the anatomy of the cloaca and phallus and the significance of their presence in different types of vertebrates including the birds. This anatomical feature in the turkey has attracted attention since fluids from the cloaca may contribute to the semen at ejaculation, especially during massage for artificial semen collection. Aspects of recent work to define the anatomy of the turkey cloaca are referred to by Bakst and Cecil (1986) in a study of the embryonic development of the turkey male genitalia in this region. This work confirmed the absence in the turkey of the central, ventral *corpus phallicum medianum* and more prominent *corpora phallica laterale* in the *phallus nonprotudens*, which contrasts with the situation in the fowl. Knight, Bakst and Cecil (1984) discuss the mechanism of tumescence and detumescence of the *phallus nonprotudens* involving an inflow of blood and lymph-like fluid into the tissue structures associated with the cloaca. Fujihara and Nishiyama (1984) and Fujihara, Nishiyama and Koga (1985a,b) suggested that some of this fluid exudes into the cloaca and contributes to the semen at ejaculation, together with a minute amount of frothy fluid emanating from a triangular fold in the mucosa of the mid-dorsal proctodeum. Bakst and Cecil (1985) made a detailed microscopical study of this latter tissue, properly known as the proctodeal gland (*glandula proctodealis dorsalis*). It occurs in all galliform birds. In the sexually active male quail it is extensively developed and produces the well-known foamy secretion. Further investigation is needed on the significance of this gland to the reproductive process. Bakst and Cecil (1985) considered that there was no real evidence of an association between ejaculation and the release of the proctodeal gland muco-substance in the turkey. If ejected it was likely to be a miniscule amount. However, of interest to the reproductive process, they suggested that further consideration should be given to the possibility of anti-sperm antibodies being formed in this tissue, particularly if damaged by pressure applied during manual semen collection. If so, it may account for the occasional agglutination of spermatozoa seen in semen samples collected by massage.

Of importance to the breeding of turkeys, dependent on AI, and the collection of semen by massage, is that damage may be caused to the tumescent phallic structures in the cloaca by pressure during massage for semen collection (Bakst and Cecil, 1983a,b). This could lead to down-grading of semen quality or, at worst, impotence of the male. With regard to obtaining the average quantity of semen by massage without affecting quality, judged by fertilizing ability, not more than two massage strokes per ejaculate is recommended (Cecil and Bakst, 1985).

Physiology of turkey semen

Three years ago, Lake and Wishart (1984) reviewed aspects of the comparative physiology of turkey and fowl semen in which they emphasized basic features of the morphology, biochemistry and metabolism of turkey spermatozoa. They indicated the implications of this knowledge for the development of *in vitro* semen storage techniques. Since 1984 a few further facts have been described concerning the inherent control mechanisms of the function of the spermatozoa of the turkey and factors influencing their activity *in vitro*. The need to use AI more effectively for perpetuating the modern strains of turkeys continues to prompt the exploration of biological and environmental factors affecting the function of spermatozoa.

Environmental factors influencing the activity of spermatozoa

A bizarre study on turkey spermatozoa was prompted by concern for the expansion of microwave radiation applications in many facets of modern life, and also by a preliminary uncertain observation that treatment of spermatozoa with microwave radiation (50 mW/g) enhanced fertility. Turkey spermatozoa were considered suitable material to test effects of such radiation on the functional capacity of a cell since the semen provided an easily accessible dense suspension of cells, each identical in its haploid set of chromosomes, whose malfunction could be tested after radiation by insemination into hens and observing egg fertilization rate. Microwave radiation (30 min exposure; 25°C; 2.45 GHz at 10 or 5 mW/g) was shown not to alter the ability of spermatozoa to function normally (Hall *et al.*, 1983).

The neural mechanisms governing the output of gonadotrophic hormones and reproductive activity appear to involve monoaminergic systems. Serotonin (5-HT) appears to be anti-gonadotrophic under certain circumstances and increases prolactin release which causes gonadal regression in the female. Berg *et al.* (1984) tested the effect of atmospheric negative air ions on semen quality and serum levels of luteinizing hormone and prolactin in male turkeys because of reports that a high negative ion concentration caused a reduction in circulating levels of 5-HT. Abundant negative air ionization produced no effect on either semen quality or serum hormone levels when compared with controls. However, it was suggested that if birds were under unfavourable environmental conditions and had lowered hormone levels then, perhaps, treatment with negative air ions may have had a remedial effect.

Since semen is likely to be kept *in vitro* for a few hours for dilution and storage during the application of AI, there has been a renewed interest in whether light *per se* affects the viability of spermatozoa. Conflicting reports exist on the detrimental or beneficial effects of light on the spermatozoa of different species of animals (see Williams and Siopes, 1985). These authors emphasized that many interacting factors, e.g. duration, intensity and quality of light exposure, diluent composition, temperature and source-animal influence the reaction of suspended spermatozoa and could account for conflicting reports on observations of spermatozoal function in the presence of light. The criterion for reporting a beneficial effect of a light treatment is the maintenance of fertilizing ability of spermatozoa kept *in vitro*, suspended in a diluent at a particular temperature. Williams and Siopes (1985) showed that spermatozoa in neat and diluted semen and stored for up to 6 h appeared to benefit from being exposed to light (20 W, cool-white fluorescence; 38 cm distance; 2500 lx). The stimulatory effect of light was dependent upon wavelength, i.e. greater at 450 nm than at 650 nm. However, there was an indication of an interaction of light and temperature in some cases. For example, light was more effective at low temperature with neat semen. This may suggest that light enhanced metabolism which was otherwise reduced by the low temperature. It was shown that neat semen stored for 6 h at 15°C under light gave very low fertility on insemination but was, nevertheless, better than the same semen kept in the dark. It may be worth considering whether light causes agitation and, therefore, greater aeration of the semen sample, because there is evidence that turkey spermatozoa survive better *in vitro* when oxygenated by agitation (see Wishart and Lake, 1984). Whether there is a specific light effect has yet to be determined in view of possible interactive factors of the environment confounding the observations made on spermatozoal activity.

An interesting report of an environmental factor possibly interacting with a physical condition of the bird to affect turkey semen characters was given by Krista *et al.* (1985). They studied two groups of males selected for high and low blood pressure, a proportion of each being caused to walk about one mile per day for 6 weeks. They examined the effect of this stressful exercise on semen characteristics during weeks 40 to 46 of semen collection. The work was motivated by the knowledge that the mobility of mature turkey males under commercial conditions is severely restricted by confinement and any activity can be considered stressful. Also, exercise is an integral part of sire management in stallions and bulls. The results with turkeys did not show a clear beneficial effect of exercise, although the hypertensive males showed generally a higher output of spermatozoa. No fertility testing was carried out to verify the functional integrity of the spermatozoa from the various groups of males.

Physiological and biochemical factors controlling the function of spermatozoa

It has been emphasized by Thurston (1984) and K. Krueger and O. Dobrescu (personal communications) that in the past, with the obligatory use of AI, turkey breeders were forced to develop farms with males and females in the same premises. The use of pooled semen and expressing genetic contributions mainly in terms of 'male-line' performance rather than the abilities of individual males has not been a spur to seeking knowledge of individual male performance in terms of semen quality.

This situation may partly account for the paucity of research on spermatozoal function and quality, other than that related to work on the development of techniques for semen preservation. The little new work reported since the review of

Lake and Wishart (1984) has been prompted, particularly in the USA, by recent interests in establishing stud farms to use AI more directly for improving genetic gain. Therefore, there is a need to be able to monitor individual male semen quality, and to transport and/or hold semen for several hours.

Knowledge from the few recent studies on the physiology of turkey semen, showing effects of temperature, pH and oxygenation on spermatozoal activity, has led to the development of methods for holding semen *in vitro* for varying periods up to 48 h. The pH of a diluent influences the retention of fertilizing ability of turkey spermatozoa stored *in vitro* with around 6.8 to 7.3 being optimum depending upon the desired period of storage and basic diluent composition. A degree of oxygenation during storage is also essential (Lake and Ravie, 1982; Sexton and Giesen, 1982; Giesen and Sexton, 1983; Lake, Cherms and Wishart, 1984; Pinto *et al.*, 1984; Wishart and Lake, 1984; Huyghebaert, Van Wambeke and De Groote, 1984, 1985).

Studies of the activities of several enzymes in turkey spermatozoa and the utilization of glucose confirmed that the spermatozoa require oxygen to maintain optimal ATP concentrations, essential to sustaining their integrity *in vitro* for long periods (Wishart, 1982; Wishart and Carver, 1984) Lactic dehydrogenase activity was confirmed to be low in the spermatozoa.

The futile conversion of glucose to fructose, during incubation *in vitro*, by turkey spermatozoa occurs only under aerobic conditions (Amir *et al.*, 1985). The reason for the conversion remains obscure. The latter authors observed the utilization of the formed fructose when turkey spermatozoa metabolized glucose and noted certain consequent effects on the motility of the spermatozoa *in vitro*. Fructose and glucose, and their presence or absence, have different effects on the respiration rate of spermatozoa and motility. However, Pinto *et al.* (1985) found that fertility for 15 days post-insemination was not affected by the presence or absence of glucose or fructose in the medium, or storage, after 4 h at 15°C.

For many years, extremely yellow-coloured semen has been recognized to be of poor quality. Recently, Hess and Thurston (1984) identified degenerative changes in the epithelia of the *ductuli efferentes* and blebbing of cytoplasmic material into the ductal lumen in males producing yellow semen. They observed associated repercussions on some biochemical features of the seminal plasma. The protein, cholesterol (free and esterified), aspartate aminotransaminase and acid phosphatase levels were all raised above those of normal semen. Dobrescu (1986) observed that a group of turkeys maintained on a lighting regime of 8-h light, 16-h dark from 16 to 52 weeks of age had an endemic yellow semen syndrome by 40 weeks of age, characterized by a combination of an elevated seminal plasma protein concentration (5.9–19.8 g/100 ml), abnormal spermatozoa and numerous macrophages. It appeared to be reversible in some males when they were given 14-h light/24 h. It would be of interest to observe whether the males on a short photoperiod had reduced humoral androgens since Froman and Thurston (1982) suggested that such a status might be associated with semen protein changes in males producing yellow semen. It is essential to use only good quality semen in breeding practices where holding semen *in vitro* is adopted and, therefore, yellow semen should be avoided in such circumstances as it may be detrimental to the survival of spermatozoa.

A limited amount of work has been done to examine the plasma membrane of the turkey spermatozoa, prompted by the relative difficulty of cryopreserving turkey semen compared with the fowl (see Lake, 1986). Fujihara, Buckland and

Koga (1983) using observations on the uptake of α-aminoisobutyric acid indicated a possible dissimilarity in the properties of the membrane between the turkey and fowl spermatozoon which may be one factor contributing to the greater problem of cryopreserving the turkey spermatozoon. However, there is no specific work on how this factor may be linked to the problem. Ravie and Lake (1985) explored the ratio of the polyunsaturated:saturated fatty acids bound to phospholipids in the turkey spermatozoa since previous work with spermatozoa of many animal species had shown that there was a low ratio in types of spermatozoa which were less susceptible to cold shock. However, the results were inconclusive since, compared with the fowl (easier to cryopreserve), the ratio was only slightly different although low. Interestingly, the low ratio was comparable to that found for mammalian epididymal spermatozoa which are more resistant to cold shock than ejaculated spermatozoa. This may be significant in view of the fact that semen collected by massage from the fowl and turkey is obtained directly from the papillae of the *ducti deferentes* which project into the cloaca and is not mixed with accessory reproductive fluids on ejaculation.

Recently, Wishart and Palmer (1986), following on from their previously quoted studies, showed that rigorous tests have to be performed on spermatozoa to determine precisely the quality of cell function under different circumstances, e.g. only after incubation of frozen-thawed spermatozoa at 40°C for 3 h, and then an examination of the state of their mechanisms to maintain ATP content, motility (Wishart and Ross, 1985), lactic dehydrogenase and morphology could one discover damage consistent with the true lowered fertilizing ability of the frozen-thawed spermatozoa. These tests are likely to be valuable in future work to improve semen storage techniques or even to evaluate objectively fresh semen of different sires.

Bakst and Richards (1985) and Bakst (1987a) emphasized that little is known of the mechanisms governing the acceptance, survival and release of spermatozoa from the uterovaginal sperm-storage tubules in the hen vital to sustaining high fertility after insemination. This prompted them to seek information on possible specific regulators of the function of spermatozoa which might influence their ability to survive in the oviduct and fertilize eggs. Previously, Howarth (1984) discussed aspects of the phenomena relating to the domestic fowl. The presence of selected chemical ions were examined in the serum and oviductal mucosa of the turkey hen by Bakst and Richards (1985) since they were known to be involved in events which might control the survival of spermatozoa, e.g. suppression of metabolism, stabilization of acrosomal and other membranes and suppression of immune responses to spermatozoa. They found variations in serum ions, including zinc, magnesium and copper with time around oviposition and with age. Whether, they could be related to the mobilization of spermatozoa was not considered. They speculated that the influence of zinc on spermatozoal survival may be worth further investigation because persistently high levels were found in the sperm-storage area of the oviduct. Furthermore, zinc, as well as calcium, is known in other animals to affect the above-mentioned biological phenomena suspected of being involved in the survival of spermatozoa in the oviduct. Bakst (1985) found also that oxygen uptake by turkey spermatozoa *in vitro* was reduced by zinc. Further work is required to verify the role of chemical ions influencing the sojourn of spermatozoa in the oviduct. Van Krey *et al.* (1987) suggested that it was necessary to explore the possibility of host lymphocytes in the sperm-storage sites acting as regulatory suppressor T-cells, thus rendering the female tolerant immunologically of continual exposure to antigenic spermatozoa during repetitive inseminations. Bakst (1987a) confirmed the presence of lymphocytes in the sperm-storage sites, but considers that further work is required to determine whether they have any significance in an immunological role related to infertility (Bakst, 1987b).

An intact acrosome is vital for the process of fusion of the spermatozoon with the ovum to bring about a successful fertilization. It is known that an influx of calcium ions is required for the acrosome reaction (preparation for fertilization) in a variety of animals. Froman and Thurston (1985) were interested to explore whether circumstances of storing semen *in vitro*, which lead to poor fertility after insemination, prematurely altered the permeability of turkey spermatozoa to calcium and whether, simultaneously, acrosin activity of spermatozoa was altered. They found a greatly increased influx of calcium ions into spermatozoa and an increase in acrosin enzyme activity when diluted semen was stored at 4°C for 24 h without agitation which was associated with a marked loss of fertilizing ability of the spermatozoa. It was suggested that a premature influx of calcium in their experimental circumstances may cause antecedent acrosin formation detrimental to the fecundity of the spermatozoon. They also considered whether the importance of oxygenation for successful *in vitro* storage of turkey spermatozoa (see Lake and Wishart, 1984) might be explained by the need for oxygen to maintain ATP levels for efficient functioning of the calcium–adenosine triphosphatase pump, which prevents intracellular calcium accumulation. Lowering the temperature of the turkey spermatozoon induces a decrease in ATP under anaerobic condition (Wishart, 1984).

Sexton (1986a) confirmed recently in fertility tests, using semen stored for 6 h at 5°C whilst agitating, that ageing of the male is another physiologial factor influencing the activity of spermatozoa. He found that the minimal number of spermatozoa needed to produce optimal fertility over a 14-week period increased with time with weekly inseminations. It was associated with a decline in the number of viable spermatozoa after a time in successive weekly semen samples as judged by a sperm-membrane integrity test. Moreover, it appeared that males used for breeding in the spring–summer yielded higher fertility than those in the autumn–winter. Future research is needed to determine the influence of pre-breeder management on the subsequent reproductive ability of breeder males. For example, it was suggested by Sexton (1986a,b) that high ambient temperatures during the pre-breeder period may affect development of the male sex organs, reflected in the production of viable spermatozoa late in the season.

Effect of some management practices on semen production

A series of investigations has been made on the reserves of spermatozoa in the turkey male reproductive tract with respect to body weight, age, testis weight, and the content of spermatozoa in the testes and *ducti deferentes* under the influence of particular management conditions. The aim of the work was to determine the physiological limits to harvesting semen for use in AI and whether these parameters could be manipulated with advantage to maximize breeding efficiency using AI.

Body reserves of spermatozoa and limits to the extraction of semen for breeding purposes

Cecil and Bakst (1984) examined the amount of semen collected routinely by massage compared to that available in the male reproductive organs. They studied high (0.3 ml semen collected by massage) and low semen producers (0.22 ml) in a group of Large White breeder males. The size of the testes were similar in both types. It appeared that differences in the male's ejaculation response to manual stimulation determined the yield of semen rather than the available amount of semen in the distal region of the *ducti deferentes*, which was much greater than that collected in the ejaculate of both types of male. They suggested that an understanding of the factors controlling the production of spermatozoa in the male organs and ejaculation may lead to novel developments of male management and semen collection techniques to obtain a greater yield of available semen from the distal regions of the *ducti deferentes*. The fertilizing capacity of the ejaculated semen and that obtained surgically from the distal regions of the *ducti* was the same. With respect to seeking physiological factors affecting semen production, Cecil and Bakst (1986) found no relationship between the serum testosterone levels of males producing high and low volumes of semen when extracted by massage.

Above, Cecil and Bakst (1984) indicated that not all available semen is extracted by massage from the distal region of the *ductus deferens*. With regard to maximizing the use of the male, there has been some renewed interest in examining the effect of different rates of semen collection on the output of good quality spermatozoa. Bakst and Cecil (1981) observed the time required to refill the *ductus deferens*, and some physiological characteristics of ejaculated and *ductus deferens* semen, after successive and/or exhaustive ejaculations. With multiple ejaculations (three and five times at 30 and 60 min intervals, respectively), the pH of successive ejaculations increased (a change from about pH 7.4 to 8.3) parallel with a reduced volume of ejaculate and density of spermatozoa, and an increased amount of transparent fluid from the cloaca. The volume of semen in the *ductus deferens* was not replenished until 4 or 5 days after five successive ejaculations at 30 min intervals. Using 200×10^6 spermatozoa, the fertilizing ability of spermatozoa from the proximal and distal *ductus deferens* in the first and third ejaculations, and in 24 and 72 h post-exhaustive ejaculations, were not significantly different. From a practical breeding point of view, collecting at these frequencies is clearly not useful. Thrice weekly collections appear to be optimal and possible with respect to quality of ejaculate and total weekly outputs, although the volume per ejaculate was slightly less than with once weekly collections. Ansah *et al.* (1984) were broadly in agreement when they found thrice weekly collections of semen optimum with respect to output of spermatozoa and their fertilizing ability.

Effects of feed and protein restriction on semen production

The possibility of reducing the weight of breeding males as a means of obtaining more semen and stimulating heavy males to persist in producing semen for a longer period has been explored. Restrictive feeding and/or reducing protein levels in the diet are two practices that have been examined for these purposes.

Cherms *et al.* (1981), Brown (1982), Cecil (1984, 1986), Dobrescu (1986), Hulet and Brody (1986) and Sexton (1986b) have reviewed and investigated recently the effects of restricted feeding and/or different protein levels in the diet on age of onset and seasonal pattern of semen production. It is difficult to identify a single dietary or feeding regime which maximizes semen output for all types of turkeys in all circumstances with respect to quantity of spermatozoa produced from an early age and persisting for a prolonged period. The interpretation of results reported in some of the studies are confounded by the simultaneous imposition of lighting treatments.

Charms *et al.* (1981), using a Nicholas Large White male line, compared semen production and body weight in birds full-fed or 20% restricted from 2 weeks to 32 weeks of age, full-fed (2–20 weeks) then 20% restricted (21–32 weeks) and restricted then full-fed. Birds were exposed to natural daylength to 22 weeks (hatched June) and then to 12-h light/24 h with an intensity of 0.5 foot candle (5.4 lx). A comparison of the effect of the management treatments showed that, overall, the average semen output per male to 365 days was the same in all cases. It appeared that 20% restriction during 21–32 weeks had a depressing effect on semen production from 30 weeks onwards even when full-fed earlier. Full-fed continuously gave highest semen output to 39–40 weeks but then it fell off rapidly. The restricted and then full-fed group persisted longest in semen production but was not as high as the full-fed (continuous) group.

A low protein diet dropping to 17% by 10 weeks and reaching 9% by 18 weeks of age and then holding at about 12.8% to 58 weeks also depressed semen production. In general, reducing body weight, by whatever method, appears to cause a delay in the attainment of maximum semen production (Cecil, 1981, 1984, 1986), which is a handicap to breeders who like to have early high poult production. Overall there is no difference in average semen production per male unless there is a drastic feed restriction (Cecil, 1984). Fertility *per se* is not affected by low protein or restrictive feeding practices (Sexton, 1986b). These problems were highlighted by Cecil (1986). Earlier, Cecil (1984) reported that feeding the large male with 17% protein from 8 to 28 weeks, and then 8% protein, resulted in satisfactory semen production at the end of the breeding season (47–52 weeks of age). Dobrescu (1986) also showed that a low protein level (10%) in the diet was satisfactory once the males were in good reproductive condition. Hulet and Brody (1986) confirmed that after a delay in onset of semen production, there was no difference in semen output between restricted and control males.

It is clear from the literature that with all the modern types of turkeys, varying greatly in shape and size, work is still required on feeding practices to achieve correct body weight gain during the pre-breeder period in order to obtain improved testis growth and quality semen output for a desired start to a breeding period and for sustained semen production for a longer period.

Effect on light on semen production

Light is a well-known physical factor controlling the reproductive activity of birds. Brown (1982), Siopes (1983), Leighton and Meyer (1984), Lee *et al.* (1984, 1985), Cecil (1986), Dobrescu (1986) and Lu *et al.* (1986, 1987) have recently reviewed and investigated the effects of light on aspects of the semen production of the turkey male. The age of onset of semen production and subsequent production (level of output and persistency over the breeding period) is affected by the lighting applied during the pre-pubertal phase of life, the age at which stimulatory lighting is given and the lighting after sexual maturity.

El Halawani *et al.* (1980) studied the age of onset of the post-castration rise in serum luteinizing hormone in pre-pubertal turkeys kept on long days (16 h light/24 h). They concluded that photosensitivity in the male occurred by 8 weeks of age.

In general, for the satisfactory response of males for breeding, the photoperiod must not be restricted to 8 h/24 h for longer than 16–18 weeks of age in order to obtain a good response to later stimulatory lighting.

The growth of males is a factor determining the response to light with respect to producing semen. After rearing males to 30 weeks on 12 to 14 h light/24 h, Cecil (1986) applied light (15 h/24 h) of different intensities (6.5 and 100 lx) to groups of males which achieved different body sizes (12.6 and 19.4 kg) at 32 weeks of age. Semen production was examined at 33 and 49 weeks of age. On average, it was found that thet low-weight males were delayed in the onset of semen production and gave a lower output of spermatozoa. Unlike the normal-weight birds, high light intensity increased their semen production. It was confirmed that the production of normal-sized males was not influenced by light intensities between 5.3 and 100 lx in the breeding period. Cherms et al. (1981) indicated previously that 160 lx, compared with 10.8 lx, at 22 weeks of age depressed semen production over the breeding season.

In general, semen production during the breeding period (28 to 39 weeks of age onwards) of normal-weight males seems to be satisfactory after experiencing photoperiods varying between 8 to 12 h/24 h during adolescence and then given 14 h/24 h with a power range of 6–40 lx. The extent of the response may depend upon genetic type (Leighton and Meyer, 1984; Hulet and Brody, 1986; Sexton, 1986b).

A constant 12 h light/24 h (5.4 lx) from an early age (6 weeks) has been found to be compatible with satisfactory semen production, or light restriction of 8 h/24 h during adolescence (6–18 weeks) followed by 16 h/24 h (Lee et al., 1985; Brown, 1982). Too much light (above 12 h/24 h) during adolescence (to 18 weeks), and continued beyond, may be a disadvantage to the level of semen production eventually achieved and the persistency of output (Lee et al., 1985; Lu et al., 1987). Leighton and Meyer (1984) found that if males were on a naturally increasing daylength (details not given) during adolescence, they gave satisfactory semen output on subsequent exposure to a low intensity (32 lx), 14 h/24 h daylight regime from 28 to 31 weeks of age.

Any drastic reduction in light must be applied to a male at an early age (around 6 weeks) to avoid a subsequent deleterious response in gonad development. On a 12 h light/24 h regime there could be an advantage for semen production in increasing intensity from 5.4 (6–17 weeks), through 10.8 (18–25 weeks) to 54 lx (26 weeks onwards) (Lu et al., 1987).

Siopes (1983) found that after growing turkey males on restricted light (6 h/24 h) from 24 to 34 weeks of age and then subjecting them to intermittent lighting, giving total periods of 4, 6 and 8 h/24 h and 40 lx illumination power, semen production was similar to controls given constant 15 h light/24 h. He suggested that the beneficial effect was due to light falling in the photosensitive phases of the bird's daily rhythm. The possibility of using intermittent lighting has implications for energy saving in the breeding industry.

It can be concluded from the literature that further carefully designed studies of the application of light to males are necessary to explore the possibility of greatly improving semen production. As yet, it is difficult to identify a satisfactory single lighting programme that can be applied to all types of turkeys for commercial gains. Also, a lighting pattern has not yet been devised that will cause a combined early onset of sexual maturation, a greatly raised yield of spermatozoa and prolonged production of semen. Often it is difficult to glean from the literature a specific effect of light because some studies of this physical factor have been confounded by simultaneous alterations in feeding at different ages.

References

Amir, D., Pinto, O., Schindler, A. and Hurwitz, S. (1985). Metabolism and motility of turkey (*Meleagris gallopavo*) spermatozoa in the presence or absence of oxygen, glucose and fructose. *Comparative Biochemistry and Physiology*, **80A**, 325–327

Ansah, G. A., Buckland, R. B., Chan, C. W. and Touchburn, S. P. (1984). Effects of frequency of semen collection and insemination, and number of spermatozoa inseminated on reproductive performance of turkeys. *Canadian Journal of Animal Science*, **64**, 351–356

Bakst, M. R. (1980). Luminal topography of the male chicken and turkey excurrent duct system. *Scanning Electron Microscopy*, **3**, 419–425

Bakst, M. R. (1985). Zinc reduces turkey sperm oxygen uptake *in vitro*. *Poultry Science*, **64**, 564–566

Bakst, M. R. (1987a). Anatomical basis of sperm-storage in the avian oviduct. *Scanning Microscopy*, **1**, 1257–1266

Bakst, M. R. (1987b). Quantification of intraepithelial lymphocytes in the turkey uterovaginal junction. *Poultry Science*, **66**, 2036–2038

Bakst, M. R. and Cecil, H. C. (1981). Changes in the characteristics of turkey ejaculated semen and ductus deferens semen with repeated ejaculations. *Reproduction, Nutrition, Développement*, **21**, 1095–1103

Bakst, M. R. and Cecil, H. C. (1983a). Histology of turkey papillae after manual semen collection. *Poultry Science*, **62**, 690–696

Bakst, M. R. and Cecil, H. C. (1983b). Gross appearance of turkey cloacae before and after single or multiple manual semen collection. *Poultry Science*, **62**, 683–689

Bakst, M. R. and Cecil, H. C. (1985). A microscopic examination of the male turkey proctodeal gland. *Journal of Morphology*, **186**, 361–368

Bakst, M. R. and Cecil, H. C. (1986). Embryonic development of the turkey male genitalia. *Poultry Science*, **65**, 1623–1630

Bakst, M. R. and Richards, M. P. (1985). Concentrations of selected cations in turkey serum and oviductal mucosae. *Poultry Science*, **64**, 555–563

Berg, R. W., El Halawani, M. E., Crabo, B. G., Loseth, K. J. and Silsby, J. L. (1984). Sperm output, serum prolactin and luteinizing hormone in male turkeys under conventional management and air ionization. *10th International Congress of Animal Reproduction and Artificial Insemination*, Urbana, pp 130–132

Brown, K. I. (1982). Lighting male turkeys and other management factors affecting semen production. *Turkeys*, **30**(4), 21–26

Cecil, H. C. (1981). Effects of dietary protein on body weight and reproductive performance of male turkeys. *Poultry Science*, **60**, 1049–1055

Cecil, H. C. (1984). Effect of dietary protein and light restriction on body weight and semen production of breeder male turkeys. *Poultry Science*, **63**, 1173–1183

Cecil, H. C. (1986). Effect of light intensity during the breeder period on semen production of low weight and normal weight breeder turkeys. *Poultry Science*, **65**, 1900–1904

Cecil, H. C. and Bakst, M. R. (1984). Testicular weights, ductus deferens semen volumes, and sperm concentration of turkeys with high and low ejaculate volumes. *Poultry Science*, **63**, 1432–1437

Cecil, H. C. and Bakst, M. R. (1985). Volume, sperm concentration, and fertilizing capacity of turkey ejaculates obtained from successive cloacal strokes during semen collection. *Poultry Science*, **64**, 1219–1222

Cecil, H. C. and Bakst, M. R. (1986). Serum testosterone concentration during two breeding cycles of turkeys with low and high ejaculate volumes. *Domestic Animal Endocrinology*, **3**, 27–32

Cherms, F. L., Stoller, M. G., MacIlwraith, J. J., Africa, K. C. and Halloran, H. R. (1981). Reduction of body weight during growing and holding periods and subsequent semen production and fertility in turkeys. *Reproduction, Nutrition, Développement*, **21**, 1049–1058

Dobrescu, O. (1986). Photoperiod, diet and method of feeding in reproduction. *Poultry Science*, **65**, 559–564

El Halawani, M. E., Burke, W. H., Ogren, L. A. and Millam, J. R. (1980). Developmental changes in the photosensitivity of male turkeys. *General and Comparative Endocrinology*, **40**, 226–231

Froman, D. P. and Thurston, R. J. (1982). The influence of testosterone propionate on semen quality and testes morphology in the domestic turkey, *Meleagris gallopavo*. *Poultry Science*, **62**, 169–174

Froman, D. P. and Thurston, R. J. (1985). Effects of incubation at 4°C on calcium uptake and acrosin activity in turkey spermatozoa. *Poultry Science*, **64**, 396–400

Fujihara, N., Buckland, R. B. and Koga, O. (1983). Transport of α-amino-isobutyric acid into chicken and turkey spermatozoa. *5th World Conference on Animal Production*, Tokyo, **2**, 185–186

Fujihara, N. and Nishiyama, H. (1984). Addition to semen of a fluid derived from the cloacal region by male turkeys. *Poultry Science*, **63**, 554–557

Fujihara, N., Nishiyama, H. and Koga, O. (1985a). Studies on the accessory reproductive organs in the male turkey. *3rd Asian–Australasian Association of Animal Production Animal Science Congress*, Seoul, **1**, 393–395

Fujihara, N., Nishiyama, H. and Koga, O. (1985b). The mechanism of the ejection of a frothy liquid from the cloaca in the male turkey. *Poultry Science*, **64**, 1377–1381

Giesen, A. F. and Sexton, T. J. (1983). Beltsville Poultry Semen Extender. 9. Effect of storage temperature on turkey semen held eighteen hours. *Poultry Science*, **62**, 1305–1311

Hall, C. A., McRee, D. I., Galvin, M. J., White, N. B., Thaxton, J. P. and Christensen, V. L. (1983). Influence of *in vitro* microwave radiation on the fertilizing capacity of turkey sperm. *Bioelectromagnetics*, **4**, 43–54

Hess, R. A. and Thurston, R. J. (1977). Ultrastructure of the epithelial cells in the epididymal region of the turkey (*Meleagris gallopavo*). *Journal of Anatomy*, **124**, 765–778

Hess, R. A. and Thurston, R. J. (1984). Protein, cholesterol, acid phosphatase and aspartate amino transaminase in the seminal plasma of turkeys (*Meleagris gallopavo*) producing normal white and abnormal yellow semen. *Biology of Reproduction*, **31**, 239–243

Hess, R. A., Thurston, R. J. and Biellier, H. V. (1976). Morphology of the epididymal region and ductus deferens of the turkey (*Meleagris gallopavo*). *Journal of Anatomy*, **122**, 241–252

Howarth, B. (1984). Maturation of spermatozoa and mechanism of fertilisation. In *Reproductive Biology of Poultry*, (Cunningham, F. J., Lake, P. E. and Hewitt, D., eds), pp. 161–174. Harlow, Essex, Longman Group

Hulet, R. M. and Brody, T. B. (1986). Semen quality and fat accumulation in prepuberal and postpuberal male turkeys as affected by restricted feeding. *Poultry Science*, **65**, 1972–1976

Huyghebaert, G., Van Wambeke, F. and De Groote, G. (1984). The effect of pH of diluent, number of spermatozoa and storage method on fertility and hatchability obtained with turkey semen stored for 6 and 24 hours. *Archives fur Geflugelkunde*, **48**, 142–150

Huyghebaert, G., Van Wambeke, F. and De Groote, G. (1985). The effect of different storage methods of turkey semen on fertility and hatchability. *Archives fur Geflugelkunde*, **49**, 205–211

King, A. S. (1981a). Cloaca. In *Form and Function in Birds*, (King, A. S. and McLelland, J., eds), **2**, 63–105. London, Academic Press

King, A. S. (1981b). Phallus. In *Form and Function in Birds*, (King, A. S. and McLelland, J., eds), **2**, 107–147. London, Academic Press

Knight, C. E., Bakst, M. R. and Cecil, H. C. (1984). Anatomy of the *Corpus vasculare paracloacale* of the male turkey. *Poultry Science*, **63**, 1883–1891

Krista, L. M., Pierson, E. E. M., McDaniel, G. R., Mora, E. C., McGuire, J. A., Bolden, S. L. and Miller, L. E. (1985). Effects of exercise conditioning on semen characteristics from hyper- and hypotensive lines of turkeys. *British Poultry Science*, **26**, 349–356

Lake, P. E. (1986). The history and future of the cryopreservation of avian germ plasm. *Poultry Science*, **65**, 1–15

Lake, P. E. and Ravie, O. (1982). Effect on fertility of storing turkey semen for 24 hours at 10°C in fluids of different pH. *British Poultry Science*, **23**, 41–47

Lake, P. E. and Wishart, G. J. (1984). Comparative physiology of turkey and fowl semen. In *Reproductive Biology of Poultry*, (Cunningham, F. J., Lake, P. E. and Hewitt, D. eds), pp. 151–160. Harlow, Essex, Longman Group

Lake, P. E., Cherms, F. L. and Wishart, G. J. (1984). Effect of aeration on the fertilising ability of turkey semen stored for 48 hours at 5 and 15°C: A study from the 33rd to the 47th week of age. *Reproduction, Nutrition, Developpement*, **24**, 147–153

Lee, C. W., Ansah, G. A., Buckland, R. B., Chan, C. W. and Touchburn, S. P. (1984). Effects of lighting programs on reproductive performance of turkey males. *Research Reports, Department of Animal Science, McGill University*, Montreal, Canada, pp. 58–60

Lee, C. W., Ansah, G. A., Chan, C. W., Touchburn, S. P. and Buckland, R. B. (1985). The effects of lighting programs on reproductive performance of turkey males, II. *Research Reports, Department of Animal Science, McGill University*, Montreal, Canada, pp. 62–63

Leighton, A. T. and Meyer, G. B. (1984). Effect of light environment during the adolescent period on subsequent semen volume and concentration of male turkeys. *Poultry Science*, **63**, 806–812

Lu, L. C., Chan, C. W., McNiven, M. A. and Buckland, R. B. (1986). The effects of lighting programs on reproductive performance of turkey males, III. *Research Reports, Department of Animal Science, McGill University*, Montreal, Canada, pp. 40–42

Lu, L. C., Chan, C. W., McNiven, M. A. and Buckland, R. B. (1987). The effects of lighting programs on reproductive performance of turkey males. IV. *Research Reports, Department of Animal Science, McGill University*, Montreal, Canada, pp. 41–44

Pinto, O., Amir, D., Schindler, H. and Hurwitz, S. (1984). Effect of pH on the metabolism and fertility of turkey spermatozoa. *Journal of Reproduction and Fertility*, **70**, 437–442

Pinto, O., Amir, D., Schindler, H. and Hurwitz, S. (1985). Fertility of fresh and stored turkey spermatozoa in the presence or absence of glucose or fructose in the suspension medium. *Poultry Science*, **64**, 1388–1390

Ravie, O. and Lake, P. E. (1985). The phospholipid-bound fatty acids of fowl and turkey spermatozoa. *Animal Reproduction Science*, **9**, 189–192

Saeki, Y. and Brown, K. I. (1962). Fertilizing ability and laboratory evaluation of ejaculated and vasa deferentia semen in turkeys. *Poultry Science*, **41**, 905–909

Sexton, T. J. (1986a). Relationship of the number of spermatozoa inseminated to fertility of turkey semen stored 6 h at 5°C. *British Poultry Science*, **27**, 237–246

Sexton, T. J. (1986b). Effect of dietary protein and season on fertility of turkey semen stored 18 hours at 5°C. *Poultry Science*, **65**, 604–606

Sexton, T. J. and Giesen, A. F. (1982). Beltsville Poultry Semen Extender. 6. Holding turkey semen for six hours at 15°C. *Poultry Science*, **61**, 1202–1208

Siopes, T. D. (1983). Effects of intermittent lighting on energy savings and semen characteristics of breeder tom turkeys. *Poultry Science*, **62**, 2265–2270

Thurston, R. J. (1984). Semen — its biochemical and cellular properties and storage methods as determinants of its fertilizing capacity. *Turkeys*, **32**(4), 26–27

Van Krey, H. P., Schuppin, G. T., Denbow, D. M. and Hulet, R. M. (1987). Turkey breeder hen infertility associated with plasma cells in the uterovaginal sperm storage glands. *Theriogenology*, **27**, 913–921

Williams, C. J. and Siopes, T. D. (1985). Effects of artificial illumination on turkey sperm viability. *Poultry Science*, **64**, 2351–2357

Wishart, G. J. (1982). Maintenance of ATP concentrations in and of fertilising ability of fowl and turkey spermatozoa *in vitro*. *Journal of Reproduction and Fertility*, **66**, 457–462

Wishart, G. J. (1984). Metabolism of fowl and turkey spermatozoa at low temperatures. *Journal of Reproduction and Fertility*, **70**, 145–149

Wishart, G. J. and Carver, L. (1984). Glycolytic enzymes of fowl and turkey spermatozoa. *Comparative Biochemistry and Physiology*, **79B**, 453–455

Wishart, G. J. and Lake, P. E. (1984). Oxidative metabolism of spermatozoa and success in turkey semen storage. *17th World's Poultry Congress*, Helsinki, pp. 216–218

Wishart, G. J. and Palmer, F. H. (1986). The effect of cryopreservation at −196°C on the viability of fowl and turkey spermatozoa assessed *in vitro*. *Animal Reproduction Science*, **10**, 317–324

Wishart, G. J. and Ross, F. H. (1985). Characterization of a spectrophotometric technique for the estimation of fowl and turkey sperm motility. *Gamete Research*, **11**, 169–178

Chapter 5

Embryology of the turkey

V. L. Christensen and L. G. Bagley

Introduction

The hatchability of turkey eggs is notoriously poor and this report is intended to focus on the development of the turkey embryo with emphasis on factors which affect hatchability. Data have been collected for years on the embryology of avian species and a complete description of the development of turkey embryos is beyond the scope of this chapter. For further information the reader is referred to the book by Freeman and Vince, *Development of the Avian Embryo* (1974).

George (1978) defined hatching as the event that marks the termination of embryogenesis and involves a complex sequence of events including initiation of pulmonary ventilation, pipping of the eggshell and emergence of the hatchling. However, hatchability defines a broader sequence of events than simply hatching. When a turkey egg is fertilized, all of the chemicals and mechanisms are present to form a new poult with the notable exception of oxygen. Heat must also be applied to the eggs to synchronize the development. Hatchability, or the rate of success of these mechanisms, could be defined as the ability of each egg and embryo to synchronize heat, oxygen and biochemicals to emerge from the shell in a given time frame.

Three conditions must be satisfied for a turkey egg to hatch (Rahn, 1981); these occur independent of egg size and incubation time and must be met at the time of incubation when oxygen consumption plateaus (at 24, 25, and 26 days of incubation for turkeys). The first hatching requirement is that the incubating egg must have consumed 100 ml of oxygen for every g of initial egg mass. The second requirement is that the gas conductance properties of the eggshell be exceeded such that the partial pressure of oxygen inside the air space of the egg declines to 14% while the partial pressure of carbon dioxide increases to 6%, and finally, the egg must have lost approximately 15% of its mass as water.

Time of embryonic mortality in the domestic turkey

Embryonic development of the turkey poult is marked by critical periods in which mortality peaks. Few researchers have examined the temporal pattern of embryonic turkey deaths. Insko and Martin (1935) reported on one-time samples of eggs. Christensen (1978) and Cherms (1981) have reported on larger samples of non-hatching turkey eggs. Christensen (1978) reported data collected over a 3-year period of genetic selection for hatchability.

Because embryonic mortality is a non-random event, the chance of an embryonic death occurring is not equal on all days of incubation. Two peaks of critical periods in mortality have been observed for embryonic turkeys (Christensen, 1978). In the early incubation period, from days 1 to 6 of incubation, approximately 38.5% of all deaths occur, whereas, late in incubation from days 24 to 28 of incubation, 39.6% of all embryonic deaths occur. More embryonic deaths occurred on the 28th day of incubation than on any other day. With the exception of the 28th day of incubation, significantly ($P<0.01$) more deaths occurred at days 3 and 4 of incubation than all others followed by day 6 and day 25 whose frequencies were significantly ($P<0.01$) greater than all other days. Previous observations indicated a decline in the number of deaths between days 5 and 6 of incubation (Insko and Martin, 1935).

The age of the hens producing the eggs has been examined as a factor in embryonic mortality (Christensen, 1978). At days 4 and 28 embryonic mortality increased with hen age, but day 3 deaths declined. In general, early deaths were more prevalent earlier in lay, and late deaths more prevalent among older hens. When the totals for the two peaks were compared the pattern of embryonic mortality was clear by the eighth week of lay when proportionally more deaths began to occur in the late mortality peak than in the early. The reason for this reversal in times of embryonic mortality is unknown. More research is needed in the area of declining hatchability with the age of turkey breeder hens. Older hens produce eggs with thinner shells, greater conductance, higher water vapour loss, and altered oxygen/carbon dioxide exchange.

Horn and Pereyni (1974) reported early mortality increased as the season progressed, but not attempt was made to discriminate between true infertiles and embryonic deaths. Cherms (1981) reported on the incidence of malpositions through a 20-week laying cycle for Large White turkey hens. The incidence of malpositions in each 4-week period from the start of lay to the end of lay was 1.6%, 1.7%, 2.8%, 2.7% and 3.7%. The increase in malpositions over time occurred mainly from the increase in the two malpositions of head over right wing and head between the legs. Terata (abnormal embryonic development) occurred in the following frequencies: 0.6%, 0.6%, 0.9%, 0.9% and 1.9% from the start to the end of lay. Abnormalities of the beak accounted for most of the increase in terata.

Genetic selection for reduced embryonic mortality results in slow improvement (McCartney, 1962) but selection to increase embryonic deaths in turkeys is effective (Shook, Stephenson and Biellier, 1971). Arora and Kosin (1966) found that selection for high and low hatchability was influenced mostly by improved fertility, and decreased pre-oviposital and early post-oviposital embryonic mortality. Christensen (1978) noted that mortality at days 3, 4 and 6 decreased with increased selection pressure for hatchability over a 3-year period. No consistent improvement in the late embryonic mortality was noted.

Pre-incubation storage of turkey eggs for longer than 8 days depresses the hatchability of turkey eggs (Asmundson, 1947). Christensen (1978) studied the effect of egg storage on developmental deaths among turkey embryos. Embryonic mortality during incubation was increased daily for every day past 8 days of storage but an interesting observation reported was that turkey eggs stored for shorter periods than 2 days did not hatch well. Apparently, a short pre-incubation storage period enhances the hatchability of turkey eggs. Eggs stored longer than 8 days, had increased numbers of incubation deaths in both early and late incubation. The storage of hatching eggs increased death rates on the more critical days of incubation (3, 4 and 28) to a greater degree than it did the less critical days. The greatest increase occurred in late incubation death on day 28 of incubation.

Kosin and Mun (1960, 1965) observed that turkey eggs laid in multiple egg clutches hatched better and also had the greatest embryonic development at the time of oviposition. Christensen (1978) examined the position of an egg in a laying sequence and its subsequent effect on the time of embryonic mortality. In the combined sequence positions, 4 to 33, a significant decrease in mortality occurred between days 24 and 28 of incubation. A lesser decline in the number of embryos dying between days 1 and 6 of incubation was seen as the length of the clutch or sequence increased.

The time of day that an egg is oviposited is related to its sequence position. Kosin and Munn (1960) noted that eggs laid during the later parts of all sequences were held in the oviduct for progressively longer periods of time. The progressively longer time spent in the oviduct would increase developmental age at the time of oviposition. Eggs laid later in the day would presumably be eggs incubated for longer periods of time prior to oviposition. More embryonic deaths occurred in eggs oviposited between 17.00 h on the previous day and 08.00 h on the day of collection (Christensen, 1978). The increased mortality occurred principally on days 24–28 of incubation. Increased mortality occurring in eggs laid after 17.00 h may be due to several factors. The care of hatching eggs may be inadequate at that time because the eggs may have remained in the laying house overnight without proper temperature or humidity controls. Alternatively, many of the eggs laid late in the day may be primarily abnormal eggs.

Today, peaks in embryonic mortality of turkeys are chronologically as well as quantitatively similar to those reported nearly 50 years ago (Insko and Martin, 1935), suggesting that genetic improvement in reducing embryonic mortality has been limited. Mortality occurring between days 24 and 28 of incubation still accounts for the greatest proportion of all deaths. The late embryonic mortality may represent a lack of synchronization of physiological events which normally occur at the time of hatching (George, 1978).

Comparison of wild and domestic turkey eggs

Eggs produced by wild turkeys hatch well and, if eggs that are lost to predators are not counted, essentially all eggs laid by wild turkeys, and incubated naturally, hatch (Schorger, 1966). Conversely, eggs produced by domesticated turkeys and incubated artificially hatch poorly. The reasons why hatchability declined with domestication are not clear.

Artificial incubation

When turkeys were domesticated it involved changing from natural to artificial incubation of eggs. Insko (1949) described four environmental factors during artificial incubation that would have an effect on turkey egg hatchability. These factors are temperature, humidity, turning of the eggs and ventilation. Each one of these factors and its effect on hatchability will be considered.

Temperature

The current normal practice in multistage incubators is to incubate turkey eggs at 37.5°C for 25 days then to decrease the temperature to 36.9°C during the actual hatching process for days 26, 27 and 28 of incubation. In single stage incubators a variety of temperatures are used to incubate turkey eggs.

Temperature plays an important role in embryonic development. Any ambient thermal deviation from an optimum incubation temperature constitutes a stress on embryos, disturbing body temperature, metabolic rate, blood acid-base status and cardiac output (Tazawa, 1973; Tazawa and Mochizuki, 1978). These observed physiological aberrations support the hatchability data of Barott (1937) who reported that hatchability declined rapidly with departures from optimum incubation temperature.

Temperature is the most critical physical factor of artificial incubation affecting hatchability. There is a paucity of data concerning the proper incubation temperature for turkey eggs. Optimum hatchability has been observed in turkey eggs incubated in a natural-draft incubator at temperatures of 38.1°C the first week, 38.6°C the second week, 39.2°C the third week and 39.4°C the fourth week (Insko, 1949). Romanoff, Smith and Sullivan (1938) suggested that optimum hatchability in a forced-draft incubator would be achieved at 37.5°C. The ratio of the weight of the chick at hatching to the original weight of the egg was highest at those temperatures which yielded the best hatch. Romanoff (1936) suggested that at the optimum incubation temperature the developing chick can utilize the nutrient supplies available in the egg to its greatest advantage.

Landauer (1967) reviewed the literature on the effects of cooling eggs during incubation on hatchability. He reported that a chick embryo's resistance to cooling is greatest during the first week compared to the last 2 weeks of incubation. Moreng and Shaffner (1951) showed the sensitivity of developing embryos to cold was related to the stage of development, as well as the genetics of the embryo. Deuchar (1952) demonstrated that there was a lack of thermoregulation in the embryo prior to 7 days of incubation. The lack of thermoregulation may explain the decreased sensitivity to cooling during the first week of incubation. Buckland (1969) allowed chicken eggs to cool to approximately 21.2°C for periods of 4–24 h during the 17th day of incubation without any detrimental effects. However, when the egg temperature was lowered to 11.3 or 5.2°C for more than 4 h, the hatchability was rapidly reduced. Hatchability has been improved when eggs from meat type chickens were allowed to cool to 22.0°C for a 24-h period (Sarpong and Reinhart, 1985). The improvement in hatchability came from a reduction in late embryonic mortality. Conversely, lowering the incubation temperature for a limited span of time is likely to reduce the percentage of hatching only slightly (Buckland, 1970). However, Kaufman (1948) reported that temporary cooling that does not produce an entire cessation of development may be more harmful than complete stoppage. He suggested that it may lead to disharmonious growth of various organs, ending in death of the embryo. Similar observations have been reported by Harrison and Klein (1954) and Rott (1957). Tazawa and Nakagawa (1985) suggested that the extra-embryonic fluids may act as a thermal buffer in embryonal eggs. This may help explain why late in incubation the embryo is able to withstand mild cold stress for only short periods.

Higher incubation temperatures also depress hatchability. Landauer (1967) reported that chick embryos may have relatively high resistance to temporary cooling, but they are very sensitive to even slight increases in temperature. Thus, a slight change in temperature above optimum may disturb normal development more than a slight change below optimum temperature. Hatchability has been decreased in a force-draft incubator when eggs were incubated at 43.3°C for 6 h

(Wilson et al., 1975). If the exposure period at the same temperature was extended to 24 h, all embryos were killed but they observed that a temperature of 40.6°C in a force-draft incubator had no effect on hatchability. This agreed with the work of Martin and Insko (1935) who noted increased embryonic mortality in turkey eggs when the temperature of the incubator was above 39.4°C during the fourth week of incubation. Increased embryonic mortality occurred mainly at day 25 of incubation.

Increasing the temperature only 3 or 4°C may cause microvascular changes in developing embryos. Nilsen (1984) showed the physiological effect of slight (3 or 4°C) hyperthermia on developing 2 and 3 day chick embryos. He observed significant microvascular changes and prevascular oedema and suggested that these microvascular changes with pathological leakage may play an important role in abnormal vascular and embryonic development.

Humidity

Humidity during artificial incubation is the second physical factor to be considered. Optimum hatchability of turkey eggs results when they are incubated at 54% relative humidity ((Insko and Martin, 1935). This is true if eggs are incubated in single or multiple stage incubators. Landauer (1967) and Lundy (1969) published excellent reviews of the early research on the role of humidity in incubation. Hatchability is reduced in low humidity because of excessive dehydration, but the reason high humidity reduces hatchability is not clear. Landauer (1967) and Lundy (1969) concluded from their reviews that optimum hatchability results when relative humidity (RH) in the incubation cabinet is 50% and satisfactory hatchability results within a range between 40 and 70% RH. Lundy (1969) in his review concluded that maximum hatchability for chicken eggs was associated with humidity which gave a weight loss of 300 mg/egg/day. Differences in hatchability of turkey eggs were noted when eggs were transferred at 25 days of incubation from 66 or 65% RH into increased or decreased relative humidities ranging from 68 to 47% (Krueger, Corral and Quisenberry, 1956). Conversely, Kirk et al. (1980) showed that 82% RH was significantly superior to either 66 or 95% RH during the hatching period (19–21 days) for chicken eggs.

Flock age may determine the optimum RH during incubation. Kirk et al. (1980) suggested that as the flock aged a decrease in RH during incubation improved hatchability because of the concomitant egg weight increase. They recommended 55% RH in young flocks and 45% in older flocks.

Research has concentrated on the effect of humidity on egg weight loss. Weight loss from the egg depends on a vapour pressure gradient across the shell (Thompson, 1952, Ar and Rahn, 1980). The relative water content of the egg must increase since lipids are metabolized during development, and metabolic water is created thereby increasing the relative water content (Rahn, 1981). Ar and Rahn (1980) presented evidence that showed the relative water fraction of hatchlings of 32 avian species was essentially the same as found in the freshly laid egg in spite of an incubation water loss which typically averaged 15% of the initial egg mass. Therefore, eggs from almost any species of bird need to lose approximately 12–15% of their weight as water (Rahn, Ar and Paganelli, 1979). Christensen and Bagley (1987) showed optimum water loss of turkey eggs during incubation was approximately 12%. Christensen and McCorkle (1982b) reported a 9.6% loss of turkey egg initial mass as water reduced hatch with peak mortality at 25 days of incubation, but a 10.4% loss of initial mass as water hatched more successfully.

Hays and Spear (1951) found that egg weight loss could vary between 6.5 and 12% without significantly affecting hatchability, but weight losses greater than 12% induced a marked decline in hatchability. Likewise, Kirk *et al.* (1980) showed that eggs can hatch reasonably well over a wide range of weight losses during incubation. Simkiss (1980) suggested that most physiological processes have a considerable safety factor and that most organisms possess regulatory mechanisms that limit their dependence on environmental variables. He observed that many embryos can survive abnormally high water losses.

The relative humidity may interact with developmental age to affect hatchability. Gildersleeve (1984) observed that minor, short-term relative humidity changes during early incubation influenced egg weight losses, but similar changes had no significant effect on weight losses during late incubation. The minor RH changes did not affect hatchability.

The age of hens producing eggs influences egg size and may affect incubational egg weight loss. Kirk *et al.* (1980) showed that at a constant relative humidity in the incubator the proportional egg weight lost in the first 2 weeks of incubation was inversely related to dam age and egg weight. Similarly, Reinhart and Hurnik (1984) showed a flock age by humidity interaction on egg weight loss during the first 8 days of incubation which was inversely related to egg size. They recommended that for most efficient utilization of modern technology, eggs with similar weights and flock history should be incubated in the same incubator.

Research to determine proper humidity for artificially incubating turkey eggs has not received as much attention as the chicken egg. Recent work indicated optimum hatchability for turkeys occurred when an egg lost approximately 12% of its initial egg weight as water (Meir, Nir and Ar, 1984; Hulet, Christensen and Bagley, 1987). Hulet, Christensen and Bagley (1987) programmed RH and weekly egg weight losses so the weight loss of the eggs at the end of incubation would be approximately 12%. The eggs incubated to regulate their weight loss hatched 3–4% higher than control eggs incubated at recommended relative humidity.

Turning the eggs

The third physical factor of artificial incubation is turning. Turkey eggs are turned approximately eight times per day under normal commercial practice. Landauer (1967) and Lundy (1969) reviewed the effects of egg turning during incubation, describe different aspects of turning during incubation. These aspects include the frequency of turning, the angle of turning, the axis of setting and rotation and the developmental age at which the eggs are turned.

Landauer (1967) expressed the view that in otherwise satisfactory incubation conditions, it is unlikely that turning more than eight times/day would effect an appreciable improvement in hatchability. Lundy (1969) reported that hatchability increased rapidly with turning frequency up to 8–12 times/day. Thereafter, further increases in frequency yielded progressively smaller gains in hatchability.

The best hatchability can be observed when eggs are set with large ends up (Lundy, 1969). Cain and Abbott (1971) reported turkey egg hatchability was reduced by 40% when the small end is set up compared to control eggs which were incubated with their large ends up.

Hatchability has been reported in two experiments to be greatest when eggs are turned at an angle of ±45 degrees (Funk and Forward, 1953 and 1960). Funk and Forward (1952) subjected eggs to rotation in one, two or three different planes.

The principal result of multiplane turning was a reduction in malpositions and an improvement in hatchling quality. The literature suggests that turning is not necessary throughout incubation, but it seems to be most important during the second week of incubation. It can be said that the pattern of turning before the 18th day is particularly important in determining events after 18 days of incubation (Lundy, 1969). Robertson (1961) observed that mortality was reduced throughout incubation, but the greatest reduction occurred between days 18 and 23 of incubation.

The physiological benefits derived from turning are still unclear. However, Tyrrell et al. (1954) reported that failure to turn eggs caused a reduction of the chorioallantoic area attached to the eggshell. This is in agreement with more recent work by Tazawa (1980) who observed in unturned eggs that the chorioallantoic area attached to the eggshell was reduced by the albumen interposing between the chorioallantois and inner shell membrane. This would cause a decreased arterialized oxygen pressure and an increased haematocrit. Freeman and Vince (1974) reported that avian eggs must be turned periodically during incubation to prevent premature adhesions between the extra-embryonic membranes and embryos which caused distortions in subsequent development.

Ventilation

The fourth and final physical factor of artificial incubation is ventilation. Turkey eggs require a minimum of $2\,ft^3$ of fresh air/min/1000 eggs in the incubator. Most commercial incubators provide more than the minimum amount. Care must be taken not to overventilate carbon dioxide which plays an important physiological role in embryonic development. Landauer (1967) and Lundy (1969) have also published reviews of the effect of ventilation during artificial incubation. Rahn, Paganelli and Ar (1974) showed that oxygen crosses the eggshell via diffusion. The diffusion of gases is dependent on gas concentration gradients inside and outside the eggshell. Therefore, in modern incubators a strong flow of air must be maintained during incubation to optimize hatch. This movement of air serves to provide the ventilation needed inside the incubation cabinet and outside the eggshell for the developing embryo and to maintain a homogeneous environment.

The aforementioned reviews suggest that good hatchability can be obtained between 18 and 50% oxygen and not greater than 0.5% carbon dioxide. The maximum hatchability has been reported when the oxygen concentration was maintained at 21% (Landauer, 1967).

The atmospheric concentration of carbon dioxide that will affect hatchability is still unknown. Romanoff (1930) and Barott (1937) found that an atmospheric carbon dioxide concentration above 1% resulted in slow growth, formation of abnormalities and early death. Wilgus and Sadler (1954) observed the greatest hatchability of chicken eggs at a 0.5% carbon dioxide level. They suggested that carbon dioxide may have a stimulating effect on embryonic development within certain limits. Ramm and La Blanc (1964) suggested that the presence of traces of carbon dioxide has a stimulating effect during incubation and especially the initial stages of development. Gildersleeve and Boeschen (1983) reported that more turkey embryos were viable during incubation when the carbon dioxide inside the incubator was maintained at 0.3%. They further suggested that carbon dioxide concentration is an important environmental variable during the early part of incubation.

A developmental age by atmospheric carbon dioxide concentration interaction has been suggested. In a series of experiments the 21-day incubation time of the chicken egg was examined in each of five periods (Taylor, Sjodin and Gunns, 1956; Taylor and Kreutziger, 1965, 1966, 1969; Taylor, Kreutziger and Abercrombie, 1971). The periods were: (1) days 1–4, (2) days 5–8, (3) days 9–12, (4) days 13–16, and (5) days 17–21. In each of these periods the atmospheric concentrations of oxygen and carbon dioxide were determined in which hatchability was optimum. During the first 4 days of incubation normal hatchability resulted from carbon dioxide levels from 0 to 1%, whereas hatchability was reduced at concentrations greater than 1.1%. The embryos during this time appeared to be very resistant to high oxygen concentrations but very susceptible to low oxygen concentrations. They reported normal hatchability occurred between oxygen concentrations of 18 to 50% for period 1 (Taylor and Kreutziger, 1965).

Taylor and Kreutziger (1966) showed during the third experimental period, days 9–12 of incubation, that the embryos became even more tolerant to carbon dioxide. The embryos also showed an increased tolerance to oxygen. Hatchability was unaffected by levels of carbon dioxide up to 6%. The range of oxygen concentrations in which hatchability was not affected was 15–60%. They suggested that the apparent growth of the respiratory system was responsible for the increased tolerance.

During days 13–16 (experimental period 4) there was an increased tolerance to greater concentrations of carbon dioxide and oxygen. Atmospheric carbon dioxide could rise to 8% before hatchability was affected and the atmospheric oxygen concentration varied from 15 to 85% with little reduction in hatchability (Taylor and Kreutziger, 1969). Similar results were obtained during the last experimental period (days 17–21 of incubation). Concentrations in excess of 7% carbon dioxide reduced hatchability. The atmospheric concentrations of oxygen which did not reduce hatchability varied from 16.5 to 45% (Taylor, Kreutziger and Abercrombie, 1971). Synergistic interactions between carbon dioxide and oxygen concentrations were found in these experiments. When levels of carbon dioxide were high, oxygen concentrations maintained at normal atmospheric conditions (21%) significantly improved hatchability. Conversely, hatchability was reduced when carbon dioxide levels were high and oxygen levels were low. A reduction in hatchability was also observed when oxygen, carbon dioxide concentrations were simultaneously high (Taylor, Sjodin and Gunns, 1956; Taylor and Kreutziger, 1965, 1966, 1969; Taylor, Kreutziger and Abercrombie, 1971).

Kaltofen (1969) detected no unfavourable influence of fan speeds on hatchability. However, he observed the best hatching resulted in incubators with stirrer speeds of 180 rev/min. Spotilla, Weinheimer and Paganelli (1981) observed no effect of wind speed on the rate of evaporative water loss from chicken eggs suggesting the wind velocity of ventilation has little effect on vital gas exchange.

Eggs incubating at high altitudes have different needs for ventilation than eggs incubating at sea level. The partial pressure of oxygen is reduced at high altitude and early work showed that hatchability could be improved through oxygen supplementation to the incubators (Ells and Morris, 1947; Meshew, 1949; Stephenson, 1950; Wilgus and Sadler, 1954). It was concluded by Ells and Morris (1947) that poor hatchability at high elevations was due to oxygen starvation indicating that ventilation in itself was not adequate to supply the proper concentration of oxygen.

Embryonic respiration

Turkey eggs are cleidoic, i.e. they contain everything needed to develop and hatch. The only major component missing is oxygen for fuel to drive metabolism. The embryo itself does not participate in respiration as it does later in life. The shell functions as the embryonic lung and gases are exchanged by diffusion without the aid of convection.

There are three distinguishable periods of respiration during incubation: the prenatal period, the perinatal period and the postnatal period (Ar et al., 1980). The prenatal period is characterized by diffusional gas transport across the shell membranes overlying the chorioallantois. The perinatal period is characterized by a gradual transition between gas transport by diffusion and by convection from the lung. The postnatal period gas transport is limited to convection of the lung.

Near the middle of the 25th day of incubation in the turkey egg, internal pipping takes place when the break of the embryo pierces the inner shell membrane into the air cell. This marks the end of the prenatal and the beginning of the perinatal period (Ar et al., 1980). Prior to this time all oxygen and carbon dioxide exchange has taken place by diffusion between ambient air and the chorioallantois. Now an additional transport mechanism is initiated, namely, convection, where gas is actively pumped in and out of the pulmonary system (Rahn, 1981). The perinatal period is usually between the 25th or 26th day of incubation in the turkey. Romijn and Roos (1938) described the perinatal period as lasting 24 h or more and as a period in which respiratory rhythm and general muscular activity are further developed. During the first half of incubation the oxygen uptake is minimal. Later it becomes exponential and reaches a plateau which is 3 days prior to the perinatal period. The plateau phase is maintained until internal pipping occurs (Christensen, 1978; Rahn, 1981). The plateau phase in oxygen consumption is thought to aid in initiating lung ventilation and pipping (Rahn, Paganelli and Ar, 1974).

Beattie (1964) measured the oxygen uptake and carbon dioxide output during the last 36 h of incubation. He observed that the exchange of these two gases increased progressively from the start of pulmonary respiration until hatching. He suggested that prior to the penetration of the shell by the beak of the embryo there was marked hypoxia (lack of oxygen) and hypercapnia (excess of carbon dioxide) which were relieved when the embryo gained access to atmospheric air. Visschedijk (1968a) observed that during the perinatal period, respiratory exchange through the air cell became progressively more important than through the chorioallantois. There was a sudden and obvious increase in total carbon dioxide production and oxygen consumption which continued during the whole perinatal period. He concluded that the chorioallantoic function is not reduced during the perinatal period, but after pipping of the eggshell has taken place the chorioallantois begins to dry and its circulation rapidly ceases. Rahn, Paganelli and Ar (1974) observed similar results. They reported that as the beak penetrated into the air cell and the lung system filled, the blood supply of the chorioallantoic membrane over the air cell was disrupted by the ever greater penetration of the beak into the air cell. However, the chorioallantois over the remaining surface is still intact and provides for the major gas exchange.

Some research has been conducted to determine response when the environment during the perinatal period was altered. Windle, Scharpenberg and Steele (1938) reported that as long as the chorioallantois served adequately as a respiratory mechanism, the embryo made little or no attempt to execute respiratory movements during the perinatal period. They suggested that whenever the normal embryo's requirements surpassed the capacity of the chorioallantois to furnish oxygen and dispose of carbon dioxide, respiratory movements began. Windle and Barcroft (1938) observed that the addition of 0.8 to 1.6% of carbon dioxide initiated rhythmic respiratory movements 4–6 days prematurely. Visschedijk (1968b) observed that the time at which pipping took place in eggs was accelerated by an average of 7.6 h by preventing gaseous exchange through the shell over the air cell after 17.5 to 19.5 days of incubation. In contrast the time of pipping was delayed an average of 6.0 h when gaseous exchange was increased by drilling a hole at the top of the air cell. However, the time of hatching was not changed.

Diffusion

Oxygen and carbon dioxide cross the shell by diffusion through pores and follow Fick's First Law of Diffusion (Wangensteen and Rahn, 1970/71). Wangensteen and Rahn (1970/71) summarized Fick's law as it relates to transport of gases across the eggshell. It was stated in general as follows:

Gas flux across the shell = Shell permeability × Shell surface area ×
Gas tension difference across the shell

Oxygen, therefore, must diffuse from a greater concentration in the air outside the shell through pores spread across the shell itself and through two underlying shell membranes to reach the blood in the dense capillary network of the chorioallantoic membrane.

Eggshell permeability

Wangensteen and Rahn (1970/71) defined permeability as a measure of the shell's resistance to the diffusion of a particular gas. They also reported that the permeability depended on the number and size of the pores in the shell. Wangensteen (1972) observed that shell permeability is one of the factors that is responsible for the final gas tension in the air cell. As mentioned previously, the final tension of oxygen must decline to 14% and the final carbon dioxide tension must increase to 6% for hatching to occur (Rahn, 1981).

Recently, Tranter, Sparks and Board (1983) suggested that three barriers resist the inward diffusion of oxygen once the gas has passed through the pores of the shell. The three resistances are the inner, outer and limiting membranes. Bellairs and Boyde (1969) found in studies of fine structures with the electron microscope that the inner surface of the inner shell membrane is covered with electron dense material, which they called the limiting membrane.

There are currently two theories describing permeability of the eggshell and membranes. One theory suggests that permeability is minimal at the time of oviposition and is insufficient to permit the increase in oxygen consumption which occurs in the later development of the embryo. During incubation, permeability increases to insure that the rate of oxygen consumption and carbon dioxide loss can also increase (Romijn, 1950; Romanoff, 1960; Fromm, 1963; Kutchai and Steen, 1971; Tullett and Board, 1976; Bissonnette and Metcalfe, 1978; Tranter, Sparks and Board, 1983). Kutchai and Steen (1971) observed that the oxygen permeability of the eggshell of fertile eggs increased dramatically between the 2nd and 5th days of incubation. Permeability increased to a level sufficient to allow oxygen uptake at the rate required by the developing embryo late in incubation. Tullett and Board (1976) concluded that the increased oxygen flux seen during early incubation was the result of drying of the inner shell membrane. It is generally agreed among researchers that the permeability of the shell and outer membrane is fixed at the time of laying (Romijn and Roos, 1938; Romijn, 1950; Romanoff, 1960; Fromm, 1963; Wangensteen and Rahn, 1970/71; Kutchai and Steen, 1971; Tullett and Board, 1976; Paganelli, Ackerman and Rahn, 1977; Bissonnette and Metcalfe, 1978; Rahn, Ar and Paganelli, 1979; Tranter, Sparks and Board, 1983).

Tullett and Board (1976) measured the oxygen flux across the integument of eggs from several species of birds during the first week of incubation. They observed a tenfold increase during the first week of incubation in all species. In the turkey this increased permeability to oxygen occurred at days 6–8 of incubation. Kayar et al. (1981) reported similar results in chicken eggs. They partitioned out the resistances of the outer and inner membrane to oxygen throughout the developmental period. The outer membrane added 6% to the resistance of the shell and the inner membrane initially accounted for 88%, but fell to 12% of the resistance by the end of incubation. The work of Tullett and Board (1976) and Kayar et al. (1981) suggests that the action of ventilation on the physiology of hatching may be concentrated in the shell and its membranes rather than the embryo itself.

The alternative theory of eggshell and membrane permeability is that permeability is fixed at the time of laying and that the optimal porosity was engineered by the hen producing the egg and has been fixed by evolution (Romijn and Roos, 1938; Wangensteen and Rahn, 1970/71; Paganelli, Ackerman and Rahn, 1977; Rahn, Ar and Paganelli, 1979). Rahn, Ar and Paganelli (1979) offered as evidence for the latter theory the fact that eggshell permeability does not change because under constant humidity and temperature the loss of water from fertilized eggs remains remarkably constant throughout incubation.

Tranter, Sparks and Board (1983) concluded that the decrease in the resistance of the integument of the fertile egg to oxygen diffusion is caused either wholly or in part by changes in the limiting membrane. They observed cracks in the limiting membrane only in fertile eggs which had been incubated for more than 4 days and in which normal embryo development occurred. Moreover, there was an absolute correlation between a decrease in membrane resistance in oxygen diffusion and the occurrence of cracks. They suggested that the cracks occurring in the limiting membrane are caused by mechanical stress due to egg turning.

Eggshell surface area

Surface area is the second factor in Fick's law. Gases traverse the shell through pores which penetrate the shell. Domestication and genetic selection of turkeys for body size has resulted in a larger egg without an increase in the number of pores on an egg (Paganelli, Olszowka and Ar, 1974; Christensen, Beillier and Forward, 1982). Non-functional egg characteristics of turkey eggs have increased in proportion to the egg mass. However, functional characteristics of domesticated turkey eggs have not changed in proportion to each other. Total pore numbers have not increased, therefore, increased pore radius and shortened pore length must be responsible for maintaining the constant functional pore area in wild and domestic turkey eggs. Because a larger embryonic tissue mass (53% larger) must exchange vital gases over the constant functional pore area, it is suggested that domestic turkey embryos may have a more difficult time respiring than wild turkey embryos.

The average total shell area of turkey eggs is over $90 \, cm^2$ and contains an average of 9600 pores. In spite of the large number of pores their total functional area is only $2.2 \, mm^2$. Thus the total communication channel is only 0.024 of 1% of the total shell area (Rahn, 1981).

Christensen and McCorkle (1982a) and Tullett (1981) observed that surface area of turkey eggs increased as the laying cycle of the hen progressed. Consequently, the pores on an egg from a domestic turkey are more dispersed and each pore must serve a greater area as turkey hens age. Pore spreading may cause insufficient gas volumes to be exchanged by the embryos in large eggs (Christensen and Biellier, 1982; Christensen and McCorkle, 1982b). Christensen (1983) further proposed that the distribution of pores on a turkey egg contributes to embryonic livability. Fewer pores per cm^2 were found on eggshells containing embryos which died late in incubation further suggesting inadequate eggshell permeability or egg surface area in domesticated turkeys. The would be expected if the turkey embryo is truly suffering from hypoxia late in the incubation period.

Gas tension difference across the shell

Oxygen transport across the shell is driven by an oxygen gradient. This is also true for carbon dioxide and water vapour. Eggs have been incubated at various oxygen concentrations to determine which concentration yields the best hatchability (Landauer, 1967). Optimum hatchability was obtained with a concentration of 21% oxygen maintained continuously during incubation. It appears that the embryo is more sensitive to reduced oxygen concentrations than increased oxygen concentrations (Taylor, Sjodin and Gunns, 1956 and Taylor, Kreutziger and Abercrombie, 1971; Taylor and Kreutziger, 1965, 1966 and 1969).

As incubation progresses and the embryo's need for oxygen increases, it uses more of the oxygen inside the pores. This decreases the partial pressure of oxygen in the air space of the pores. Thus, the oxygen gradient between the outside and inside of the shell is greater and more oxygen enters the egg. The reverse is essentially true for carbon dioxide (Wangensteen and Rahn, 1970/71). The metabolic products of the embryo are carbon dioxide and water. Therefore, a gradient exists for carbon dioxide and water vapour from the inside of the shell to the outside. Thus, there is an important relationship between metabolic rate and shell permeability in determining the oxygen and carbon dioxide tensions in the air space (Wangensteen and Rahn, 1970/71; Wangensteen, 1972; Rahn, 1981). The inside of the egg is saturated with water, and water is also a metabolic by-product. Therefore, metabolic water must be lost during incubation from the egg to maintain proper water balance (Paganelli, Ackerman and Rahn, 1977; Rahn, 1981) and hatchability (Meir, Nir and Ar, 1984; Hulet, Christensen and Bagley, 1987).

Chapman–Enskog relation

It has been shown that gases follow the Chapman–Enskog relation (Reid and Sherwood, 1966). The Chapman–Enskog equation describes the inverse relationship between barometric pressure and gas flow. As the barometric pressure decreases at high altitude, the velocity or rate of flow of gases increases. This represents a partial compensation for the decreased partial pressure of vital gases at high altitude. The enhanced diffusion of oxygen into the egg may compensate in part for the detrimental effects of hypoxia on metabolism (Visschedijk et al., 1980;

Carey *et al*, 1982) However, increased rates of diffusion of carbon dioxide and water vapour from the egg during incubation may be harmful to normal embryonic growth (Rahn *et al.*, 1977; Carey, 1980; Carey *et al.*, 1982).

The environmental and eggshell interaction

It is clear that the successful development of a turkey egg into a new animal, in an appropriate time frame, is dependent upon the interaction of the environmental factors of heat, humidity, turning and ventilation with the factors determined by the structure of the eggshell. The equation or function which describes the interaction is called Fick's First Law of Diffusion although some have suggested that Stefan's Law might be more appropriate (Simkiss, 1986).

In order to satisfy the three requirements for hatching, a series of events which are interrelated and complex must occur (Rahn, 1981). For example, an embryo with a greater metabolic rate will produce water more rapidly. Thus increased metabolic water increases the requirement for water vapour loss. Therefore, the entire process must be coordinated with shell permeability, egg surface area, and the gas tension differential across the shell. Christensen, Beillier and Forward (1982) and Christensen and Bagley (1987) have suggested that a possible asynchrony due to domestication may exist in the balance between water vapour, carbon dioxide and oxygen uptake in turkey eggs.

Further support for this hypothesis comes from the work of Rahn and Ar (1974) who suggested that eggshell conductance and egg weight could be used in a relationship to determine length of the incubation period. They suggested that for any given egg weight, the incubation time was inversely proportional to (1) the water vapour conductance of the egg, which in turn is set by pore area and thickness of the shell, and (2) to the rate of water loss. The equation given is $I = 5.2(W/G_{H_2O})$. If we assume that I = length of the incubation period and the G_{H_2O}, or water vapour conductance of turkey eggshells, to be $14.5 \, mgH_2O/day/torr$ (Rahn, Christensen and Edens, 1981) and the average weight of a turkey egg (W) to be $93.5 \, g$ (Rahn, Christensen and Edens, 1981) then the incubation period should be = 33.5 days. Turkey eggs are incubated commercially for 28 days but many hatchery managers utilize 27 days and 20h to optimize labour use and improve poult quality. These incubation periods are much shorter than predicted biologically. The nature of the asynchrony will be discussed for the remainder of this chapter.

Embryo physiology

The asynchrony resulting from the interaction of environmental and eggshell factors results in asynchrony of several physiological systems during the latter stages of incubation. Most of the aberrations occur during the pre- and perinatal periods when synchronization of several physiological events (George, 1978) is imperative for survival. Some of these events will be summarized briefly.

Heart and haematology

Grabowski and Schroeder (1968) observed that hypoxia affected the embryonic heart distension and the rate of contraction which may be related to increased levels of blood potassium caused as a consequence of hypoxia. Gross distensions of the heart occurred during a period of rapid morphogenesis and, thus, it may have permanent effects on the heart. Smith, Burton and Besch (1969) reported that embryonic heart development is biphasic. An early rapid growth occurring for the first 2 weeks is followed by a slower growth during the third week. They reported that the latter growth phase was greater at high altitude compared to sea level. This would indicate that factors leading to cardiac hypertrophy at high altitude become effective only after 2 weeks of incubation. McCutcheon *et al.* (1982) observed that heart growth was stimulated most compared to other organs by increased oxygen, but was retarded least by hypoxic conditions.

Beattie (1964) showed that the chick heart contained appreciable amounts of glycogen by the 19th day of incubation. These cardiac glycogen stores are particularly important in enabling the embryo to overcome periods of anoxic stress (Beattie, 1964; Freeman, 1965). Therefore, hypoxia causes a precipitous decline in the cardiac stores of glycogen (Beattie, 1964) resulting in death. Glycogen stores in the pipping muscle (*Musculus complexus*) of turkey embryos can be maintained if glucose is injected into the egg (John, George and Moran, 1987). Perhaps additional glucose could increase glycogen stores in the heart and improve hatchability.

The number of red blood cells (RBC) in the chick embryo increases directly with the age of the embryo (Zorn and Dalton, 1937; Macpherson and Deamer, 1964; Romanoff, 1967). Macpherson and Deamer (1964) showed that the concentration of red blood cells started from 1 million cells/mm^3 on the 8th day of incubation and climbed steadily to a level of 2.7 million cells/mm^3 immediately after hatching. The rate of increase slows at about the 15th day. The count reaches its highest level at about the 18th day, quite often above 3 million cells/mm^3 (Macpherson and Deamer, 1964; Romanoff, 1967).

Christensen, Biellier and Forward (1982) observed that the RBC concentration in blood of poult embryos increased from days 24 to 27 of incubation then decreased from the 27th to 28th day of incubation. The average values for the poult embryo between days 24 and 28 as reported by Christensen, Biellier and Forward (1982) were 1.95, 2.14, 2.28, 2.35, and 2.27 million cells/mm^3 on days 24, 25, 26, 27 and 28, respectively. RBC values in the poult embryo at all days of incubation examined were greater than those in the chick embryo (Zorn and Dalton, 1937; Barnes and Jensen, 1959; Macpherson and Deamer, 1964; Romanoff, 1967). Romanoff (1967) reported that the amount of haemoglobin (Hb) in the developing embryo continually increased reaching a maximum on the 18th day. This Hb peak corresponded with the peak RBC concentration. However, Macpherson and Deamer (1964) reported that the curve derived by plotting Hb concentration by day of incubation is rather flat to day 13 then shows a peak, on day 16, of nearly 9 g/dl of blood, which is approximately the Hb concentration seen at the time of hatching.

The Hb concentrations increased from 9.4 to 11.1 g/dl in the poult embryo as hatching approached (Christensen, Biellier and Forward, 1982). Hb concentrations were observed to be greater in poult embryos than chicks during the hatching process (Zorn and Dalton, 1937; Macpherson and Deamer, 1964).

Christensen, Biellier and Forward (1982) measured mean cellular haemoglobin (MCH) and mean cellular haemoglobin concentration (MCHC) in the poult embryo. MCH was significantly greater on day 24 and day 28 of incubation than all other days. MCHC declined significantly from days 24 to 25, then increased in a significant daily sequence. These results are similar to the results obtained by Grima and Girard (1981).

The haematocrit (HCT) in the poult embryo increases significantly between days 24 and 25 of incubation from 33.7 to 37.4% (Christensen, Biellier and Forward, 1982). No other significant changes were observed until days 27 and 28 when the HCT decreased significantly from 36.2 to 33.6% (Christensen, Biellier and Forward, 1982). These values were higher than those observed in chick embryos (Zorn and Dalton, 1937; Johnston, 1955; Barnes and Jensen, 1959; Macpherson and Deamer, 1964).

Christensen, Biellier and Forward (1982) measured mean corpuscular volume (MCV) in poult embryos. The MCV value is an estimate of the size of the red blood cell or erythrocyte measured in μm^3. They observed a significant decline in MCV as development proceeded. The MCV values for days 24, 25, 26, 27, and 28 of incubation were 173.0, 174.7, 158.2, and 148.2, respectively.

Hypoxic environments have been shown to increase RBC, Hb, HCT, MCH, and MCHC in developing poult embryos (Bagley, 1987). A failure in any of these physiological mechanisms may result in embryonic death.

Lung

The development of the embryonic lung has been reviewed by Duncker (1977) and Timmwood, Hyde and Plopper (1987a,b). Smith, Burton and Besch (1969) observed that lung weights were somewhat depressed by incubation at high altitude. Hylka and Doncen (1983) reported some evidence that suggests important roles for the pituitary and adrenal hormones in the ontogeny of the avian lung. They demonstrated that pituitary hormones and corticosterone can influence growth, hydration and lipid content of the lung of the chick embryo. They concluded that corticosterone had the most prominent effect both on pulmonary growth and on surfactant synthesis. Administration of corticosterone caused a reduction in lung size and weight in the chick embryo. Bagley (1987) showed that lung size and weight in the turkey embryos were affected by hypoxia.

El-Ibiary, Shaffner and Godfrey (1966) reported that lung inflation occurred quickly and can be safely considered an all-or-none or a threshold occurrence. However, Vince and Tolhurst (1975) noted that lung ventilation began slowly. The lungs do not become completely functional following the first breaths. Their results suggested that complete aeration was not found in all individuals for several hours after the first appearance of respiratory movements. It was also concluded that both lungs do not necessarily become functional at the same time or at the same rate.

Liver

The liver is the metabolic centre of the body and thus the probable target of a host of contradictory signals from the rest of the embryo. It seems to respond to both an excess and a deficit of oxygen by slowing its growth relative to that of the embryo. Smith, Burton and Besch (1969) noted that liver development appeared to be unaffected by altitude. Conversely, McCutcheon et al. (1982) reported that the liver was sensitive to hypoxia, and thus, there was a weight reduction in the liver when exposed to hypoxic conditions. Bagley (1987) saw similar results with poult embryos.

Like the heart, the liver has appreciable amounts of glycogen stored by the 19th day of incubation. Even during times when the stores are being depleted there is indirect evidence that glycogen synthesis continues and the carbohydrates mobilized from the stores are being utilized anaerobically (Beattie, 1964; Freeman, 1965).

Intestinal digestive function

The final growth of the small intestine and the appearance of the microvilli which line the intestine to increase absorptive area occurs late in incubation (Moog, 1950; Hinni and Watterson, 1963; Overton and Shoup, 1964). Thyroid and adrenal hormones, whose availability is dependent upon oxygenation, play significant roles in the development of duodenal morphology and induce the production of the digestive enzymes, maltase and alkaline phosphatase (Black and Moog, 1977; Black, 1978; Black and Moog, 1978; Black, Yoneyana and Moog, 1980). Hydrocortisone and thyroxine treatments also increase sugar absorption in the duodenum of chick embryos (Mallon and Betz, 1982). Retarded intestinal development in turkey embryos may be carried into the postnatal period (Phelps, Edens and Christensen, 1987). This may be a cause of 'starve-out' mortality in poults.

Adrenal and thyroid function

During the perinatal period there are increased blood concentrations of both thyroxine (T_4) and triiodothyronine (T_3) as well as increases in the T_3/T_4 ratio (Davison, 1976; Thommes and Hylka, 1978; Christensen and Biellier, 1982). Adrenal hormones (corticosterone) in blood peak in concentration late in incubation (Wentworth and Hussein, 1985). Christensen and Biellier (1982) showed that a lack of thyroid output in turkey embryos was characteristic of turkey embryos with poor hatchability. There are a multitude of physiological functions attributed to these hormones during development but, in general, it can be stated that they assist the turkey embryo in surviving the hypoxia of pipping and hatching (McCartney and Shaffner, 1949). Injection of thyroid hormones into turkey eggs immediately prior to pipping improves the hatchability of turkey eggs (Christensen, 1986).

Conclusions

This review has attempted to describe the development of the turkey embryo. Rather than take the traditional approach as in the academic discipline of embryology, I have opted to describe the entire development period of the turkey embryo. Reports have focused on studies relating incubation environment to genetics of the modern type of turkey and its egg and how the embryo responds physiologically to its environment. It is hoped that this review will serve as a basis for discussions and research that may improve the hatchability of turkey eggs in the future.

References

Ar, A., Visschedijk, A. H. J., Rahn, H. and Pipper, J. (1980). Carbon dioxide in the chick embryo towards end of development: Effects of He and SP_6 in breathing mixture. *Respiratory Physiology,* **40**, 293–307

Ar, A. and Rahn, H. (1980). Water in the avian egg: overall budget of incubation. *American Zoology,* **20**, 373–384

Arora, K. L. and Kosin, I. J. (1966). Developmental responses of early turkey and chicken embryos to preincubation holding on eggs: Inter- and intra-species differences. *Poultry Science,* **45**, 958–970

Asmundson, V. S. (1947). Time held prior to incubation and hatchability of turkey eggs. *Poultry Science,* **26**, 305–307

Bagley, L. G. (1987). Embryonic respiration and hatchability of turkey eggs. PhD Thesis. North Carolina State University Raleigh, NC

Barnes, A. E. and Jensen, W. N. (1959). Blood volume and red cell concentration in the normal chick embryo. *American Journal of Physiology,* **197**, 403–405

Barott, H. G. (1937). Effect of temperature, humidity and other factors on hatch of hen's eggs and on energy metabolism of chick embryos. *Technical Bulletin,* USDA, 553

Beattie, J. (1964). The glycogen content of skeletal muscle, liver and heart in late chick embryos. *British Poultry Science,* **5**, 285–293

Bellaires, R. and Boyde, A. (1969). Scanning electron microscopy of the shell membranes of the hen's egg. *Z. Zellforsch,* **96**, 237–249

Bissonnette, J. M. and Metcalfe, J. (1978). Gas exchange of the fertile hen's egg: Components of resistance. *Respiratory Physiology,* **34**, 209–218

Black, B. L. (1978). Morphological development of the epithelium of the embryonic chick intestine in culture: Influence of thyroxine and hydrocortisone. *American Journal of Anatomy,* **153**, 573–600

Black, B. L. and Moog, F. (1977). Goblet cells in embryonic intestine: accelerated differentiation in culture. *Science,* **197**, 368–370

Black, B. L. and Moog, F. (1978). Alkaline phosphatase and maltase activity in the embryonic chick intestine in culture. *Developmental Biology,* **66**, 232–249

Black, B. L., Yoneyana, Y. and Moog, F. (1980). Microvillous membrane vesicle accumulation in media during culture of intestine of chick embryo. *Biochimica et Biophysica Acta,* **601**, 343–348

Buckland, R. B. (1969). Effect of cold stressing chicken embryos on hatchability and post-hatching body weight. *Canadian Journal of Animal Science,* **49**, 132–134

Buckland, R. B. (1970). Effect of cold stressing chicken embryos and preincubation storage on hatchability, post-hatching body weight, mortality and sex ratio. *Canadian Journal of Animal Science,* **50**, 243–352

Cain, J. R. and Abbott, U. K. (1971). Incubation of avian eggs in an inverted position. *Poultry Science,* **50**, 1223–1226

Carey, C. (1980). Adaptation of the avian egg to high altitude. *American Zoology,* **20**, 449–459

Carey, C., Thompson, E. L., Vleck, C. M. and James, F. C. (1982). Avian reproduction over an altitudinal gradient: Incubation period, hatchling mass, and embryonic oxygen consumption. *The Auk,* **99**, 710–718

Cherms, F. L., Jr. (1981). Incidence of embryonic malpositions and terata in turkeys. *Poultry Science,* **60**, 1638 (abstract)

Christensen, V. L. (1978). Physiological parameters limiting hatchability in domestic fowl (*Gallus domesticus*) and domestic turkey (*Meleagris gallopavo*). PhD Thesis. University of Missouri, Columbia, MO

Christensen, V. L. (1983). Distribution of pores on hatching and non-hatching turkey eggs. *Poultry Science,* **62**, 1312–1316

Christensen, V. L. (1986). Supplemental thyroid hormones and hatchability of turkey eggs. *Poultry Science,* **64**, 2202–2210

Christensen, V. L. and Bagley, L. G. (1987). Water balance in incubating turkey eggs. *Poultry Science* (In press)

Christensen, V. L. and Biellier, H. V. (1982). Physiology of turkey embryos during pipping and hatching. IV. Thyroid function in embryos from selected hens. *Poultry Science,* **61**, 2482–2488

Christensen, V. L. and McCorkle, F. M. (1982a). Characterization of incubational egg weight losses in three types of turkeys. *Poultry Science*, **61**, 848–854

Christensen, V. L. and McCorkle, F. M. (1982b). Turkey egg weight losses and embryonic mortality during incubation. *Poultry Science*, **61**, 1209–1213

Christensen, V. L., Biellier, H. V. and Forward, J. F. (1982). Physiology of turkey embryos during pipping and hatching. I. Hematology. *Poultry Science*, **61**, 135–142

Christensen, V. L., Biellier, H. V. and Forward, J. F. (1982). Physiology of turkey embryos during pipping and hatching. III. Thyroid function. *Poultry Science*, **61**, 367–374

Christensen, V. L., Parkhurst, C. R. and Edens, F. W. (1982). Conductance and qualities of wild and domestic turkey eggs. *Poultry Science*, **61**, 1753–1758

Davison, F. F. (1976). Circulating thyroid hormones in the chicken before and after hatching. *Gen. Comp. Endo.*, **29**, 21–28

Deucher, C. (1952). The effect of high temperature shock on early morphogenesis in chick embryo. *Journal of Anatomy*, **86**, 443–458

Duncker, H. R. (1977). Development of the avian respiratory and circulatory systems. In *Respiratory Function in Birds, Adult and Embryonic*, (Pipper, J., ed.), pp. 261–273. New York

El-Ibiary, H. M., Shaffner, C. M. and Godfrey, E. F. (1966). Pulmonary ventilation in a population of hatching chick embryos. *British Poultry Science*, **7**, 165–176

Ells, J. B. and Morris, L. (1947). Factors involved in hatching chicken and turkey eggs at high elevations. *Poultry Science*, **26**, 635–638

Freeman, B. M. (1965). The importance of glycogen at the termination of the embryonic existence of *Gallus domesticus*. *Comparative Biochemistry and Physiology*, **14**, 217–222

Freeman, B. M. and Vince, V. A. (1974). *Development of the Avian Embryo*. London, Chapman and Hall

Fromm, D. (1963). Permeability of the hen's egg shell. *Poultry Science*, **42**, 1271 (abstract)

Funk, E. M. and Forward, J. F. (1952). Effect of multiple plane turning of eggs during incubation on hatchability. *Res. Bul. Mo. Agr. Exp. Sta.*, 599

Funk, E. M. and Forward, J. F. (1953). The effect of angle of turning eggs during incubation on hatchability. *Bul. Mo. Agr. Exp. Sta.*, 599

Funk, E. M. and Forward, J. F. (1960). The relation of angle of turning and position of the egg to hatchability of chicken eggs. *Poultry Science*, **39**, 784–785

George, J. C. (1978). The mechanism and physiology of hatching in birds. *Pavo*, **16**, 179–192

Gildersleeve, R. P. (1984). The effect of humidity and broiler strain on egg weight losses during incubation. *Poultry Science*, **63**, 2140–2144

Gildersleeve, R. P. and Boeschen, D. P. (1983). The effects of incubator carbon dioxide level on turkey hatchability. *Poultry Science*, **63**, 779–784

Grabowski, C. T. and Schroeder, R. E. (1968) A time-lapse photographic study of chick embryos exposed to teratogenic doses of hypoxic. *Journal of Embryology and Experimental Morphology*, **19**, 347–362

Grima, M. and Girard, H. (1981). Oxygen consumption by chick blood cells during embryonic and post-hatch growth. *Comparative Biochemistry and Physiology*, **69**, 437–442

Harrison, J. R. and Klein, I. (1954). Effect of lowered incubation temperature on growth and differentiation of the chick embryo. *Biology Bulletin*, **106**, 48–59

Hays, F. A. and Spear, E. W. (1951). Losses in egg weight during incubation associated with hatchability. *Poultry Science*, **30**, 106–107

Hinni, J. B. and Watterson, R. L. (1963). Modified development of the duodenum of the chick embryo hypophysectomized by partial decapitation. *Journal of Morphology*, **113**, 381–426

Horn, P. and Pereyni, M. (1974). The effects of time in production and season of lay on hatchability parameters of artificially inseminated turkeys. *Proceedings of the XV World's Poultry Congress*, pp. 14–15

Hulet, R. M., Christensen, V. L. and Bagley, L. G. (1987). Controlled egg weight loss during incubation of turkey eggs. *Poultry Science*, **66**, 428–432

Hylka, V. M. and Doneen, B. A. (1983). Ontogeny of embryonic chicken lung: Effects of pituitary gland, corticosterone, and other hormones upon pulmonary growth and synthesis of surfactant phospholipids. *Gen. and Comp. Endo.*, **52**, 108–120

Insko, W. M., Jr. (1949). Physical conditions in incubation. In *Fertility and Hatchability of Chicken and Turkey Eggs*, (Taylor, L. W., ed.). New York, John Wiley and Sons, Inc.

Insko, W. M., Jr. and Martin, J. H. (1935). Mortality of the turkey embryo. *Poultry Science*, **14**, 361–364

John, T. M., George, J. C. and Moran, E. T., Jr. (1987). Pre- and post-hatch ultrastructural and metabolic changes in the hatching muscle of turkey embryos from antibiotic and glucose treated eggs. *Cytobioscience*, **49**, 197–210

Johnston, P. M. (1955). Hematocrit values for the chick embryo at various ages. *American Journal of Physiology*, **180**, 361–362

Kaltofen, R. S. (1969). The effect of air movement on the hatchability of chicken eggs during artificial incubation. *British Poultry Science*, **10**, 1–11

Kaufman, L. (1948). The effect of certain thermic factors on the morphogenesis of fowl embryos. *Official Reports. Eighth World's Poultry Congress, Copenhagen*, **1**, 351–356

Kayar, S. R., Snyder, G. K., Birchard, G. F. and Black, C. P. (1981). Oxygen permeability of the shell and membranes of chicken eggs during development. *Respiratory Physiology*, **46**, 209–221

Kirk, S., Emmans, G. C., McDonald, R. and Arnot, D. (1980). Factors affecting the hatchability of eggs from broiler breeders. *British Poultry Science*, **21**, 37–53

Kosin, I. J. and Mun, A. M. (1960). Clutch size, oviposition time and 'floor' eggs as factors in turkey hatchability. *Poultry Science*, **39**, 82–92

Kosin, I. J. and Mun, A. M. (1965). Some factors affecting the biological quality of turkey hatching eggs. *Poultry Science*, **44**, 31–39

Krueger, W. F., Corral, G. and Quisenberry, J. H. (1956). The effect of increased air exchange during late embryonic development on hatchability of chicken eggs. *Poultry Science*, **39**, 1267 (abstract)

Kutchai, H. and Steen, J. B. (1971). Permeability of the shell and shell membranes of hen's eggs during development. *Respiratory Physiology*, **11**, 265–278

Landauer, W. (1967). *The Hatchability of Chicken Eggs as Influenced by Environment and Heredity*. Storrs Agr. Exp. Sta., Univ. of Conn., Monograph 1

Lundy, H. (1969). A review of the effects of temperature, humidity, turning and gaseous environment in the incubator on the hatchability of the hen's egg. In *The Fertility and Hatchability of the Hen's Egg*, (Carter, T. C. and Freeman, B. M., eds), Edinburgh, Oliver and Boyd

McCartney, M. G. (1962). Heritabilities and correlations for reproductive traits in a randombred population of turkeys. *Poultry Science*, **41**, 168–174

McCartney, M. G. and Shaffner, C. S. (1949). Chick thyroid size and incubation period as influenced by thyroxine, thiouracil and thyroprotein. *Poultry Science*, **28**, 223–228

McCutcheon, I. E., Metcalfe, J., Metzenberg, A. B. and Ettinger, T. (1982). Organ growth in hyperoxic and hypoxic chick embryos. *Respiratory Physiology*, **50**, 153–163

Macpherson, C. R. and Deamer, J. (1964). Some observations on normal erythrocyte development in the chick embryo. *Poultry Science*, **43**, 1587–1594

Mallon, D. L. and Betz, T. W. (1982). The effects of hydrocortisone and thyroxine treatments on development of duodenal morphology, alkaline phosphatase, and sugar transport in chicken (*Gallus gallus*) embryos. *Canadian Journal of Zoology*, **60**, 3447–3455

Martin, J. H. and Insko, W. M., Jr. (1935). Incubation experiments with turkey eggs. *Bul. Ky. Agr. Exp. Station*, 359

Meir, M., Nir, A. and Ar, A . (1984). Increasing hatchability of turkey eggs by matching incubator humidity to shell conductance of individual eggs. *Poultry Science*, **63**, 1489–1496

Meshew, M. H. (1949). The use of oxygen in the hatching of chicken and turkey eggs at high altitudes. *Poultry Science*, **28**, 84–97

Moog, F. (1950). The functional differentiation of the small intestine. 1. The accumulation of alkaline phosphatase in the duodenum of the chick. *Journal of Experimental Zoology*, **15**, 109–130

Moreng, R. E. (1983). Incubation and growth of fowls and turkeys in high altitude environments. *World Poultry Science Journal*, **39**, 47–51

Moreng, R. E. and Shaffner, C. S. (1951). Lethal internal temperatures for the chicken, from fertile egg to mature bird. *Poultry Science*, **30**, 255–266

Nilsen, N. O. (1984). Endothelial changes and microvascular leakage due to hyperthermia in chick embryos. *Cellular Pathology*, **46**, 165–174

Overton, J. and Shoup, J. (1964). Fine structure of the cell surface specializations in the maturing duodenal mucosa of the chick. *Journal of Cell Biology*, **21**, 75–85

Paganelli, C. V., Ackerman, R. A. and Rahn, H. (1977). The avian egg: *In vivo* conductances to oxygen, carbon dioxide, and water vapor in late development. In *Respiratory Function Birds Adult and Embryonic*, (Piper, J., ed.), pp. 212–218. New York, Springer-Verlag

Paganelli, C. V., Olszowka, A. and Ar, A. (1974). The avian egg: Surface area, volume, and density. *The Condor*, **76**, 319–325

Phelps, P. V., Edens, F. W. and Christensen, V. L. (1987a). The posthatch physiology of the turkey poult. 1. Growth and development. *Comparative Biochemistry and Physiology*, **86A**, 739–743

Phelps, P. V., Edens, F. W. and Christensen, V. L. (1987b). The posthatch physiology of the turkey poult. II. Hematology. *Comparative Biochemistry and Physiology*, **86A**, 745–750

Rahn, H. (1981). Gas exchange of avian eggs with special reference to turkey eggs. *Poultry Science*, **60**, 1971–1980

Rahn, H. and Ar, A. (1974). The avian egg: Incubation time and water loss. *The Condor*, **76**, 147–152

Rahn, H., Ar, A. and Paganelli, C. V. (1979). How bird eggs breathe. *Scientific American*, **240**, 46–55

Rahn, H., Carey, C., Balmas, K., Bhatia, B. and Paganelli, C. V. (1977). Reduction in pore area of the avian eggshell as an adaptation to altitude. *Proceedings of the National Academy of Science, USA*, **74**, 3095–3098

Rahn, H., Christensen, V. L. and Edens, F. W. (1981). Changes in shell conductance, pores, and physical dimensions of egg and shell during the first breeding cycle of turkey hens. *Poultry Science*, **60**, 2536–2541

Rahn, H., Paganelli, C. V. and Ar, A. (1974). The avian egg: Air-cell gas tension, metabolism and incubation time. *Respiratory Physiology*, **22**, 297–309

Ramm, G. M. and La Blanc, J. (1964). Development of chick embryos in lowered oxygen atmosphere. *American Zoology*, **4**, 322 (abstract)

Reid, R. C. and Sherwood, T. K. (1966). Ch. 11 In *Properties of Gases and Liquids*, 2nd edn. New York, McGraw-Hill

Reinhart, B. S. and Hurnik, G. I. (1984). Traits affecting hatching performance of commercial chickens broiler eggs. *Poultry Science*, **63**, 240–245

Robertson, I. S. (1961). The influence of turning on hatchability of hen's egg. II. The effect of turning on the pattern of mortality, the incidence of malpositions, malformations and dead embryos with no somatic abnormality. *Journal of Agricultural Science*, **57**, 57–67

Romanoff, A. L. (1930). Biochemistry and biophysics of the developing hen's egg. I. Influence of humidity. *Cornell Univ. Agr. Exp. Sta. Men.*, **132**, 1–27

Romanoff, A. L. (1936). Effects of different temperatures in the incubator on the prenatal and postnatal development of the chick. *Poultry Science*, **15**, 311–315

Romanoff, A. L. (1960). *The Avian Embryo*. New York, Macmillan

Romanoff, A. L. (1967). *Biochemistry of the Avian Embryo*. New York, John Wiley and Sons

Romanoff, A. L., Smith, L. L. and Sullivan, R. A. (1938). Biochemistry and biophysics of the developing hen's egg. III. Influence of temperature. *Cornell Agr. Exp. Sta. Mem.*, 216

Romijn, C. (1950). Fetal respiration in the hen. Gas diffusion through the egg shell. *Poultry Science*, **29**, 43–51

Romijn, C. and Roos, J. (1938). The air space of the hen's egg and its changes during the period of incubation. *Journal of Physiology*, **94**, 365–379

Rott, N. N. (1957). A quantitative study of growth in the chick embryo at different incubation temperatures. Translation of *Doklady Biological Sciences Sections (Doklady Akademy Nauk SSSR)*, **113**, 241–243

Sarpong, S. and Reinhart, B. S. (1985). Broiler hatching stress and subsequent growout performance. *Poultry Science*, **64**, 232–234

Schorger, A. W. (1966). *The Wild Turkey. Its History and Domestication*. Norman, OK, University of Oklahoma Press

Shook, J. G., Stephenson, A. B. and Biellier, H. V. (1971). Heritability estimates of differences in arbitrary and embryonic mortality traits in turkeys. *Poultry Science*, **50**, 1255–1260

Simkiss, K. (1980). Eggshell porosity and the water metabolism of the chick embryo. *Journal of Zoology*, **192**, 1–8

Simkiss, K. (1986). Eggshell conductance — Fick's or Stefan's law. *Respiratory Physiology*, **65**, 213–222

Smith, A. H., Burton, R. R. and Besch, E. L. (1969). Development of the chick embryo at high altitude. *Federation Proceedings*, **2**(8), 1092–1098

Spotilla, J. R., Byers, R. L. and Kayar, S. R. (1984). Effects of hypoxia on tissue capillarity in geese. *Respiratory Physiology of Zoology*, **54**, 195–202

Spotilla, J. R., Weinheimer, C. J. and Paganelli, C. V. (1981). Shell resistance and evaporative water loss from bird eggs: Effects of wind speed and egg size. *Physiology and Zoology*, **54**, 195–202

Stephenson, A. B. (1950). Supplemental oxygen for high altitude incubation. *Poultry Science*, **29**, 781 (abstract)

Taylor, L. W. and Kreutziger, G. O. (1965). The gaseous environment of the chicck embryo in relation to its development and hatchability. 2. Effect of carbon dioxide and oxygen levels during the period of the fifth through the eighth days of incubation. *Poultry Science*, **44**, 98–106

Taylor, L. W. and Kreutziger, G. O. (1966). The gaseous environment of the chick embryo in relation to its development and hatchability. 3. Effect of carbon dioxide and oxygen levels during the period of the ninth through twelfth days of incubation. *Poultry Science*, **45**, 867–884

Taylor, L. W. and Kreutziger, G. O. (1969). The gaseous enviornment of the chick embryo in relation to its development and hatchability. 4. Effect of carbon dioxide and oxygen levels during the period of the thirteenth through the sixteenth days of incubation. *Poultry Science*, **48**, 871–877

Taylor, L. W., Kreutziger, G. O. and Abercrombie, G. L. (1971). The gaseous environment of the chick embryo in relation to its development and hatchability. 5. Effect of carbon dioxide and oxygen levels during the terminal days of incubation. *Poultry Science*, **50**, 66–78

Taylor, L. W., Sjodin, R. A. and Gunns, C. A. (1956). The gaseous environment of the chick embryo in relation to its development and hatchability. 1. Effect of carbon dioxide and oxygen levels during the first four days of incubation upon hatchability. *Poultry Science*, **35**, 1206–1215

Tazawa, H. (1973). Hypothermal effect on the gas exchange in chicken embryo. *Respiratory Physiology*, **17**, 21–31

Tazawa, H. (1980). Adverse effect of failure to turn the avian egg on the embryo oxygen exchange. *Respiratory Physiology*, **41**, 137–142

Tazawa, H. and Mochizuki, M. (1978). Oxygen transport in chicken embryo under hypothermal exposure. *Respiratory Physiology*, **32**, 325–334

Tazawa, H. and Nakagawa, S. (1985). Response of egg temperature, heart rate and blood pressure in the chick embryo to hypothermal stress. *Journal of Comparative Physiology*, **155**, 195–200

Thommes, R. G. and Hylka, V. W. (1978). Hypothalamo-adenohypophyseal-thyroid interrelationships in the chick embryo. 1. TRH and TSH sensitivity. *Gen. Comp. Endo.*, **34**, 193–200

Thompson, R. L. (1952). Incubation at high altitude. The effects of wind, barometric pressure and humidity on fetal mortality in the hen's egg. *Poultry Science*, **31**, 497–502

Timmwood, K. I., Hyde, D. M. and Plopper, C. G. (1987a). Lung growth of the turkey *Meleagris gallopavo*: 1. Morphologic and morphometric description. *American Journal of Anatomy*, **178**, 144–157

Timmwood, K. I., Hyde, D. M. and Plopper, C. G. (1987b). Lung growth of the turkey *Meleagris gallopavo*: II. Comparison of two genetic lines. *American Journal of Anatomy*, **178**, 158–169

Tranter, H. S., Sparks, N. H. C. and Board, R. G. (1983). Changes in structure of the limiting membrane and in oxygen permeability of the chicken egg integument during incubation. *British Poultry Science*, **24**, 537–547

Tullett, S. G. (1981). Theoretical and practical aspects of eggshell porosity. *Turkeys*, **29**, 24–28

Tullett, S . G. and Board, R. G. (1976). Oxygen flux across the integument of the avian egg during incubation. *British Poultry Science*, **17**, 41–450

Tyrell, D. A., Tamm, J. I., Fornman, O. C. and Horsfall, F. L., Jr. (1954). A new count of allantoic cells of the 10-day chick embryo. *Proceedings of the Society for Experimental Biological Medicine*, **86**, 594–598

Vince, M. A. and Tolhurst, B. E. (1975). The establishment of lung ventilation in the avian embryo. The rate at which lungs become aerated. *Comparative Biochemistry Physiology*, **52**, 331–337

Visschedijk, A. H. J. (1968a). The air space and embryonic respiration. 1. The pattern of gaseous exchange in the fertile eggs during the closing stages of incubation. *British Poultry Science*, **9**, 173–184

Visschedijk, A. H. J. (1968b). The air space and embryonic respiration. 2. The times of pipping and hatching as influenced by an artificially changed permeability of the shell over the air space. *British Poultry Science*, **9**, 185–196

Visschedijk, A. H. J., Ar, A., Rahn, H. and Piiper, J. (1980). The independent effects of atmospheric pressure and oxygen partial pressure on gas exchange of the chicken embryo. *Respiratory Physiology*, **39**, 33–44

Wangensteen, O. D. (1972). Gas exchange by a bird's embryo. *Respiratory Physiology*, **14**, 64–74

Wangensteen, O. D. and Rahn, H. (1970/71). Respiratory gas exchange by avian embryo. *Respiratory Physiology*, **11**, 31–45

Wentworth, B. G. and Hussein, M. O. (1985). Serum corticosterone levels in embryos, newly hatched and young turkey poults. *Poultry Science*, **64**, 2195–2201

Wilgus, H. S. and Sadler, W. W. (1954). Incubation factors affecting hatchability of poultry eggs. 1. Levels of oxygen and carbon dioxide at high altitudes. *Poultry Science*, **33**, 460–471

Windle, W. F. and Barcoff, J. (1938). Some factors governing the initiation of respiration in the chick. *American Journal of Physiology*, **121**, 684–691

Windle, W. F., Scharpenberg, L. G. and Steele, A. G. (1938). Influence of carbon dioxide and anoxemia upon respiration in the chick at hatching. *American Journal of Physiology*, **121**, 692–699

Wilson, H. R., Wilcox, C. J., Voitle, R. A., Baird, C. D. and Dorminey, R. W. (1975). Characteristics of white leghorn chickens selected for heat tolerance. *Poultry Science*, **54**, 126–130

Zorn, C. M. and Dalton, A. J. (1937). A chemical study of the blood of the developing chick. *American Journal of Physiology*, **119**, 627–634

Chapter 6

Nutrition of turkey breeding stock

C. C. Whitehead

Introduction

Although there has been considerable research on the nutrition and feeding of turkey breeding stock, mainly in the USA, the high cost of such research and the specialist facilities required mean that there is much less information available on turkey than on chicken breeders. The information on turkeys is also qualitatively inferior. There are few data sets available that allow the same degree of dose-response assessment that has been carried out on chicken data. Indeed, in some areas of nutrition there is little experimental information at all and we are left to make assumptions on turkey requirements on the basis of chicken data.

This review will attempt to present and interpret the data available on the nutrition of breeding stock at different stages. In particular, data from recent European studies will be highlighted. Finally, metabolic and mathematical comparisons will be made with chickens to determine to what extent the same nutritional principles apply to both species.

Nutrition during rearing

The object in feeding young turkey breeding stock is to produce a bird with maximum reproductive potential as economically as possible. The well-established procedure with the broiler breeder involves severe feed restriction during the rearing stage to limit body weight and/or fatness in order to maximize reproductive performance. Research has not been carried out on pre-breeder nutrition of turkeys on such an extensive scale as for broiler breeders, but nevertheless there are several reports to indicate that the principles involved in turkey pre-breeder nutrition differ considerably from those in the broiler.

Feed allowances for females

Several studies have been carried out to determine whether limitation of growth during the rearing stage confers any productive or other advantages on female turkeys. Different nutritional methods have been used to limit growth, quantitatively using feed restriction either on a daily or skip-a-day basis, or qualitatively using diets of low energy content. These methods have been applied under a wide variety of conditions, such as length of time, severity, etc. and to

91

different types of turkeys. The results have not always been consistent with each other, but nevertheless it is possible to establish some general principles.

The results from 13 studies on the restriction of growth during the rearing period are summarized in *Table 6.1*. As can be seen, restriction has not enhanced reproductive capability; it has usually resulted in no or some impairment in reproduction. In the last case, delays in the attainment of sexual maturity and decreases in egg number and, more rarely, egg weight have been reported. Fertility and hatchability have not been impaired by restriction.

Table 6.1 Summary of reports on effects of restriction of feeding or growth during the rearing period on reproductive performance

Reference	Ages of restriction (weeks)	Body weights at end of restriction		Reproductive effect
		Control (kg)	Restricted (kg)	
Mitchell *et al*. (1962)	19–34	8.4	7.0	Smaller eggs
Touchburn *et al*. (1968)	12–28	Feed intake	80% of controls	Fewer eggs
		Feed intake	70% of controls	Even fewer eggs
Potter and Leighton (1973)	20–32	5.4	5.1	None
Balloun (1974)	20–31	7.5	6.7	More eggs
	18–30	8.2	6.8	None
Borron *et al*. (1974)	8–32			Delayed maturity
Jones *et al*. (1976)	12–32	8.3	7.6	Fewer eggs
McCartney *et al*. (1977)	10–28, 32	8.7	6.9	More eggs
	18–42	10.8	10.3	None
Voitle and Harms (1978)	10–30	8.2	7.2	None
			5.0	Fewer eggs
Krueger *et al*. (1978)	19–30	9.3	7.7	Delayed maturity Fewer eggs
Andrews and Morrow (1978)	8–32	8.7	7.6	Fewer eggs
Potter *et al*. (1978a)	22–38	10.0	8.3	None
Owongs and Sell (1980)	6–20	7.0	4.8	None
			4.0	None
Nestor *et al*. (1981)	16–40	11.8	10.5	None

Generalizations can be made on these different responses when a consideration is made of the other experimental variables, such as body weight of the birds, degree of restriction of body weight, the ages over which the restriction was applied and the age of photostimulation. It is difficult to separate the influences of body weight and age of photostimulation, since experiments with very heavy bodyweight strains have invariably involved photostimulation at or after 40 weeks of age whereas light or medium bodyweight strains have usually been photostimulated at about 30 weeks. However, when body weight and age of photostimulation are combined as factors, an interaction is seen with bodyweight restriction. Thus, bodyweight restrictions of up to 20% in heavy birds (9.5–11 kg) photostimulated at 40 weeks have not been found to impair reproduction (McCartney, Borron and Brown, 1977; Potter, Shelton and Meyer, 1978a; Nestor *et al.*, 1981). In contrast, an equivalent degree of restriction of lighter bodyweight hens up to photostimulation at about 30 weeks has impaired reproduction (Krueger *et al.*, 1978; Voitle and Harms, 1978). For instance, Krueger *et al.* (1978) limited food intake from 22 to 30 weeks of age to restrict body weight from 9.3 to 7.7 kg (17%). Egg number per bird over 20 weeks of production was depressed significantly from 88.4 to 77.9 as a result.

Severity of bodyweight restriction is obviously a factor that might be expected to influence performance. Indeed it has been observed that decreases in performance have been greater with more severe bodyweight restrictions in birds restricted up to photostimulation at about 30 weeks. Voitle and Harms (1978) found that feed restriction over the period 10–30 weeks to limit body weight from 8.2 to 7.2 kg did not significantly affect egg production but that restriction to 5.0 kg resulted in a significant depression in egg number. Similarly, Touchburn, Naber and Chamberlin (1968) reported that a 20% feed restriction up to 28 weeks depressed egg production slightly and a 30% restriction depressed it significantly.

With birds photostimulated at about 30 weeks, the effects of a more severe bodyweight restriction on subsequent performance are less severe if the restriction is lifted some time prior to photostimulation. Thus Owongs and Sell (1980) feed-restricted birds between 6 and 20 weeks to achieve a body weight of 4.0 kg compared to 7.0 kg for birds fed *ad libitum*. Transferring the restricted birds to full feeding resulted in some catch up in weight but this group was still 16% lighter (6.9 versus 8.5 kg) at 32 weeks when they were photostimulated. However, adverse effects on reproduction were not observed.

From these observations it is apparent that bodyweight restriction during rearing does not improve the reproductive performance of turkey hens. On the contrary, if restriction is too severe and is continued too near to photostimulation at 'normal' ages (about 30 weeks), depressions in performance will occur. However turkey hens can tolerate, without an adverse effect, weight restriction during rearing if (a) restriction is mild, (b) a more severe restriction is not maintained up to the normal age of photostimulation, or (c) photostimulation is delayed to later ages.

These conclusions are useful in two ways. Firstly, they suggest that transient nutritional irregularities or mishaps during rearing will probably not impair reproductive capability. Secondly, they raise the possibility that savings in feed costs could be made during the rearing period by judicious restriction. To determine whether this conveys any overall benefit, it is necessary to consider subsequent responses in body weight and feed intake.

When birds are released from feed restriction, some compensatory growth usually occurs. This is true in turkeys as in chickens and thus some of the feed 'saved' during the period of restriction will be 'lost' thereafter. This occurs even if restriction is maintained up to the time of photostimulation. During the early part of the laying period the unrestricted bird loses weight — 'lives off its fat' — whereas the bird restricted during rearing will lose less weight or even gain weight as well as lay eggs. Thus, feed intake during the breeding period is invariably higher in birds that have been restricted during rearing. The net result of this compensation is that by the end of the laying period there may be little difference in body weight or lifetime feed intake between birds restricted or fed *ad libitum* during rearing.

These relationships and their financial consequences are illustrated in data sets of Potter, Shelton and Meyer (1978a) and Owongs and Sell (1980) presented in *Table 6.2*. The different feed restriction regimes did not affect reproduction adversely in either study. The total feed saving in the case of the heavy bodyweight strain restricted between 23 and 38 weeks (Potter, Shelton and Meyer, 1978a) was small. Indeed if the likely higher cost of breeder feed was taken into account, it is probable there was either no financial benefit or a loss, depending upon the degree of restriction. However, the data of Owongs and Sell (1980) suggest there might be

Table 6.2 Effect of feed restriction during rearing on overall feed intake and body weight

Period of restriction (weeks)	Body weights (kg)			Feed intakes (kg)			Total feed
	38 weeks	62 weeks		–38 weeks	38–62 weeks		
22–38	8.35	9.26		18.01	43.01		61.02
22–38	8.70	9.18		20.8	42.25		63.05
Control	10.05	9.54		23.2	39.85		63.02
(Potter et al., 1978a)							
	20 weeks	32 weeks	52 weeks	–20 weeks	20–32 weeks	32–52 weeks	Total feed
6–20	4.0	6.9	7.2	11.7	16.8	32.6	61.1
6–20	4.8	7.2	7.5	13.9	17.1	32.6	63.6
Control	7.0	8.5	7.8	19.3	17.6	31.0	67.9
(Owongs and Sell, 1980)							

a more substantial financial benefit if restriction starts during the time when more expensive early growing diets are being fed.

Nutrition specifications for rearing diets

Metabolizable energy (ME)

The bodyweight restrictions discussed in the previous section were achieved by restriction of ME intake, usually by limiting the feed allowance. Since such restriction was shown to be not necessarily harmful, it would seem logical to suppose that the ME content of diets for feeding to pre-breeding birds *ad libitum* need not be formulated to achieve best possible growth. This is substantiated by experimental evidence.

There are several reports on the feeding of low ME diets during rearing. The feeding of a low ME diet does not necessarily depress ME intake, for turkeys can adjust their feed intake. Thus, Potter and Leighton (1973) observed a 49% increase in feed consumption when a rearing diet was diluted with 440 g oat hulls/kg. However this adjustment of feed intake is not adequate to maintain the same rate of growth, for birds fed on lower ME diets have invariably been lighter at the end of the rearing period, though the difference has not always been significant. The birds of Potter and Leighton (1973) fed the oat hull diet were marginally smaller at the end of rearing. Bougon et al. (1982a) observed that birds fed a diet containing 9.46–10.04 MJ/kg consumed more than those given 11.47 MJ/kg over the period 7–28 weeks but were still lighter at the end (7.52 versus 7.67 kg, $P<0.05$). McCartney, Borron and Brown (1977) also reported that birds fed 9.62 MJ/kg were lighter than those given 12.55 MJ/kg (10.3 versus 10.8 kg, $P<0.05$). These marginally lower point-of-lay body weights have not generally been associated with poorer reproductive performance. An exception is the study by Bougon et al. (1982a), but these authors speculated that the depressed egg production of the lighter birds might have been due to the rapeseed meal in the laying diet.

The feeding of high ME diets during rearing has also been investigated but has not been found to be advantageous. McCartney, Boron and Brown (1977) did not find a reproductive benefit from feeding 15.5 MJ rather than 12.5 MJ/kg during the second half of the rearing period. Likewise, Potter and Leighton (1973) did not find a reproductive response to a rearing dietary level of 15.5 MJ/kg.

There being no productive advantage to any particular dietary ME level, it follows that rearing diets should be formulated to the most economic ME content. The only exception to this general conclusion might be if birds were going to be photostimulated at relatively early ages. Herron and Whitehead (1985) have provided evidence that breeding performance in birds photostimulated at 24 weeks, rather than the usual 30, was better if they had been reared on diets containing higher levels of ME (12.1–12.4 MJ versus 11.5–10.9 MJ/kg). Presumably the higher dietary nutrient density permitted birds to get into better reproductive condition at the earlier age.

Protein

The feeding of low protein diets (100–120 of crude protein/kg) during rearing has been investigated as a means of limiting growth during rearing. In this objective it has succeeded, but has been uniformly found to depress subsequent breeding performance (Voitle et al., 1973; Cherms, Stoller and MacIlraith, 1978a; Voitle and Harms, 1978; Meyer et al., 1980).

Table 6.3 Dietary specification (g/kg) for turkey breeder hens during the rearing state

Age (weeks)	0–4	4–8	8–12	12–lighting
Metabolizable energy (MJ)	11.5	11.5	11.5	11.5
Crude protein	270	240	200	130
Lysine	16	14	11	5
Methionine + cystine	8.7	7.4	5.8	3.8
Linoleic acid	9	9	9	9
Calcium	12	10	7.5	5
Phosphorus (available)	6	5	3.8	2.5
Sodium	1.7	1.5	1.2	1.2

Evidence is not so readily available on the reproductive consequences of feeding rearing diets whose protein-to-energy ratios are less severely imbalanced, but it seems advisable that dietary protein and amino acids should be provided in relation to ME to allow normal growth at the different ages. This means a relatively high dietary protein level during the first few weeks followed by successive decreases in protein/energy as the birds grow: 140 g crude protein/kg, in conjunction with 12.55 MJ/g, fed from 12 weeks of age to the end of the rearing period has been found to be adequate for subsequent reproduction (Cherms, Stoller and MacIlraith, 1976).

Data on requirements for individual amino acids and other nutrients are not available specifically for pre-breeding turkey hens. Thus recommendations have to be based on information relating to the growth of meat turkeys. Suggestions for dietary specifications for some nutrients for rearing breeders are given in Table 6.3.

Nutrition of the breeding hen

One general principle governs the nutritionist's attitude to feeding the turkey breeder: the value of the output (good quality poults) is high in relation to the cost of turkey breeder feed. This means that the calculation of the incremental change in the value of the output in relation to the cost of additional nutrient input is not so important as in the case of, say, chicken table egg layers. Thus the nutritional philosophy is to provide a sufficient nutrient input so that poult production will lie on the plateau of the dose-response curve. However, the temptation with this approach is to allow diets to contain amounts of nutrients greater than the minima needed reliably to give maximum output.

There is considerably less information available on nutrient requirements and responses in turkey breeders than for other types of poultry, and requirements for many nutrients are still ill-defined. This represents a further temptation for the formulation of diets that contain higher levels of nutrients than might be necessary. However, it is not good business practice to feed diets that are excessive both nutritionally and economically. Nor is it good nutritional practice, for nutrient excesses can lead to imbalances which can have adverse effects on performance.

The following chapters review the extent of knowledge of turkey hen requirements for all nutrients and give recommendations as to optimum dietary nutrient levels. Some uncertainties still exist, partly from inadequate information and partly from the wide range of conditions encountered in turkey breeding. Environmental and husbandry factors can vary; turkey strain characteristics such as body weight and daily egg output can vary widely. The effects of these variations on breeder nutrient requirements have not all been quantified, but some guidelines are given in the text.

Body weight and feed intake

The turkey hen shows some very characteristic changes in body weight and feeding over the laying period and it is interesting to compare these in relation to reproductive performance. Typical patterns of body weight, feed intake and egg production in a medium bodyweight strain photostimulated at 30 weeks are given in *Figure 6.1*. When the birds start to lay their first eggs there is a sharp drop in feed intake. Once egg laying is established, feed intake starts to increase. This increase is maintained over the whole of the reproductive period (up to 55 weeks of age). As might be expected, body weight changes in response to these changes in feeding. It declines, by a mean of about 600 g/bird over the period 30–41 weeks, then remains constant for about 5 weeks before gradually increasing. However, at 55 weeks birds may still be lighter than they were at 30 weeks. These changes are more pronounced than in any other species of poultry and their implications for reproductive efficiency have been investigated.

Turkey hens not maturing sexually until after 30 weeks of age can contain high proportions of body fat and the data given in *Table 6.4* indicate that the bodyweight loss between 30 and 43 weeks is due almost entirely to a decrease in body fatness. Thus the bird may be able to 'live off its fat' in energy terms over this period, but that leaves open the possibility that the supply of other nutrients may be suboptimal for egg production while feed intake is depressed. It has therefore been of interest to determine whether the decrease in body weight is harmful to reproduction or whether the depression in feed intake can be minimized, with resultant benefit to reproduction.

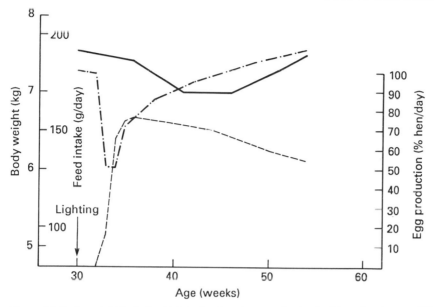

Figure 6.1 Body weight (—), feed intake (–·–) and egg production (––) in turkey hens at different ages

Table 6.4 Body compositional changes during the breeding period in hens photostimulated at 30 weeks

Age (weeks)	Body weight (kg)	Lipid (g/kg)	Protein (g/kg)	Lipid-free body weight (kg)
32	7.48	234	170	5.73
43	7.03	166	182	5.86
55	7.84	186	183	6.38

(C. C. Whitehead, unpublished)

Table 6.5 Correlations between bodyweight characteristics and egg production

Traits	Correlation coefficient
33-week body weight versus egg number	−0.03
43-week body weight versus egg number	−0.16
33–43-week body weight loss versus egg number	0.19
33-week body weight versus egg number	0.07

(Herron and Whitehead, 1985)

Consideration of data from individually-caged hens suggests that these changes in body weight do not influence reproduction. Correlation coefficients between egg number over a 25-week production period and body weight at 33 or 43 weeks or the weight loss between 33 and 43 weeks were all low and insignificant, as shown in *Table 6.5*. It would seem that these bodyweight changes are a normal physiological characteristic of the turkey hen and are not associated with impaired reproduction, provided the hen is being fed adequately.

It is perhaps as well that these bodyweight and feed intake changes are not reproductively disadvantageous because it has proved to be very difficult to influence them by nutritional means. Rearing birds on lower ME diets, thereby conditioning them to higher feed intakes, does not cause them to have higher ME intakes if they are then transferred to higher ME diets at the start of the laying period (Bougon et al., 1982a). Likewise, increasing the dietary density of protein, amino acids or minerals for hens with lower than average feed intakes during the early part of lay has not resulted in reproductive responses (Mather and Harms, 1982). These observations are thus reassuring to the nutritionist that special considerations do not need to be taken into account during the early part of the laying period in relation to the changes in feed intake and body weight that are normal for the turkey.

Metabolizable energy

The theoretical and quantitative basis for energy metabolism is well defined in the chicken. Energy intake can be balanced against energy losses in the forms of egg production, body maintenance, changes in body composition and heat loss. Factors influencing these relationships include dietary ME (which influences feeding) temperature (which affects heat loss) and strain (maintenance requirements are higher in relation to body weight in lighter strains). In general, chickens are able to adjust their ME intakes to meet these different components of their requirement, though this adjustment is not total: for hens fed conventional diets, ME intake can increase by 2–5% for each 10% increase in dietary ME concentration.

The quantitative aspects of energy metabolism are not so well defined in turkey hens. This is partly because turkeys are more complex physiologically; for instance body weights and compositions and feed intakes all change quite markedly with time, as has been discussed earlier. However, qualitative principles appear to be similar to those in the chicken, especially in relation to the adjustment of feed intake by the turkey to meet its perceived energy needs.

Responses of feed intake and reproduction to changes in dietary ME concentration have been investigated in several studies, summarized in *Table 6.6*. The widest range in ME levels (3.8–11.2 MJ/kg) was achieved by Dymsza, Boucher

Table 6.6 Summary of reports on responses in metabolizable energy (ME) intake and reproduction to changes in dietary ME concentration

Reference	Ranges of dietary ME (MJ/kg)	Change in ME intake per 10% increase in diet ME	Reproductive responses to higher dietary ME
Dymsza et al. (1954)	3.8–11.2	+3%	Higher hatchability
Robblee and Clandinin (1959)	9.5–11.3		None
Anderson (1964)	12.1–12.8	0	Small decrease in hatchability
Jones et al. (1976)	11.2–13.0	−2%	Heavier eggs
Potter et al. (1978b)	11.7–13.0	0	None
Menge et al. (1979)	9.6–13.8	+1.5%	None
Harms et al. (1984)	12.2–13.8	−3%	More eggs
Bougon et al. (1985)	11.6–12.4	+1.5%	More eggs

and McCartney (1954) by dietary dilution with fibre. Over this range, ME intake increased by an average of 3% per 10% increase in dietary ME concentration. Loss of body weight was slightly higher over the whole laying period with the lower ME diets but egg production was unaffected. The only adverse productive response observed was a marked decrease in hatchability with the lowest ME diet, though this may have been an indirect effect of the high fibre content of the diet interfering with micronutrient absorption.

Other studies over smaller ranges of dietary ME have shown little or no increase in ME intake with increasing dietary concentration. Thus Menge et al. (1979) observed only a 1.5% increase per 10% increase in dietary ME concentration over the range 9.6–13.8 MJ/kg. Again the higher ME diet resulted in a smaller decline in body weight during lay but there were no effects on egg number, weight or hatchability. Anderson (1964) and Potter, Shelton and Meyer (1978b) did not find any change in ME intake with increases in dietary ME, whilst Jones, Hughes and Barnett (1976) and Harms, Buresh and Wilson (1984) reported decreases in ME intake. Consistent production responses were not observed.

The only European report is by Bougon, Le Ménec and L'Hospitalier (1985) who compared dietary ME levels of 11.6 and 12.4 MJ/kg. There were two treatments at the higher ME level: one gave a significant increase in egg number whereas the other, at a slightly higher dietary protein level, did not. Egg weight was not affected. Protein levels within the ranges studied are unlikely to have affected egg production, so if the data from the two higher ME treatments are combined it becomes probable that the apparent effect of higher ME on egg number was not meaningful.

On the basis of these observations, it seems that the turkey hen can control its intake of ME within very close limits, perhaps even more successfully than the chicken. However, these conclusions are drawn on the basis of studies using relatively well balanced diets. There is little information available on the extent to which a hen will overconsume ME to maintain the intake of some limiting nutrient, either when fed diets of inadequate nutrient: ME ratio or when metabolic energy requirements are decreased by elevated environmental temperature (these two situations can be related). However, observations with growing turkeys fed diets of different ME:CP ratio suggest that the control of ME intake overrules control of both nutrient and feed bulk intake (MacLeod, Fisher and Jewitt, 1984).

The laying turkey can also regulate its ME intake in response to changes in environmental temperature. Bougon, Le Ménec and L'Hospitalier (1985) established the following relationship between ME intake and mean daily temperature (T).

$$\text{ME (MJ/day)} = 3.38 - 0.035\,T(°C) \tag{1}$$

Depressed feed intake at high temperatures can be a problem in turkey production, so a means of predicting ME intake could be helpful in allowing adjustments to be made to the diet to maintain the intake of other essential nutrients. However the above equation is only of limited predictive value, applying to the birds (7.6 kg body weight, egg output 48.5 g/day) in that particular experiment. A more general equation might include terms for metabolic body weight and egg output. However other factors might also have to be considered: there is a school of thought that diurnal temperature variation is also important in influencing the feed intake of turkey hens.

On the basis of these various studies, several conclusions can be drawn about laying turkey hens.

(1) They can regulate their intake of balanced diets of different ME content to maintain total ME intake within very close limits.
(2) Bodyweight loss over the whole laying period is only slightly less with higher ME diets.
(3) Dietary ME *per se* does not affect egg production or weight or hatchability. Changes in some of these traits in individual experiments may have reflected changes in other dietary components (e.g. fibre, fat). Diets can therefore be formulated for ME to least cost.

Fat

Essential fatty acids

Fatty acids of the n3 and n6 series are needed by poultry for normal metabolic processes. However they cannot be synthesized in the body and hence must be provided in the diet. The main roles of n3 fatty acids seem to be as precursors for prostaglandin synthesis and so requirements for them are very small. Essential fatty acid requirements are thus usually expressed as requirements for linoleic acid, the simplest member of the n6 series.

Linoleic acid requirements for normal physiological function seem to be similar in young chickens and turkeys, in the order of 10 g/kg diet, as assessed by growth and normality of tissue ratios of triene to tetraene fatty acids (Hill, Silbernick and McMeans, 1967; Hopkins and Nesheim, 1962; Ketola, Young and Nesheim, 1973).

Requirements are more difficult to determine in adults because of reserves accumulated during rearing, but turnover studies have suggested that 9 g/kg diet is adequate for normal physiological function in laying chickens (Balnave, 1971). However, productive requirements are less certain. Responses in egg weight in laying chickens to dietary supplementation with vegetable oils were attributed originally to an effect of high dietary levels of linoleic acid *per se* (Shutze, Jensen and McGinnis, 1962; Shutze and Jensen, 1963). However, later studies suggested that oleic acid was as effective as linoleic acid in enhancing egg weight (Shannon and Whitehead, 1974) and responses to dietary levels of unsaturated fatty acids have been established (Whitehead, 1981).

There is less information available on linoleic acid requirements or responses in laying turkeys. Cooper and Barnet (1968) reported that 12 g linoleic acid/kg diet

Table 6.7 Reproductive responses to dietary lipid and linoleic acid

Diet (g/kg)					
Total lipid	36	41	51	64	62
Linoleic acid	8.5	11	18	24	11
Responses (33–35 weeks)					
Egg number/hen	98.4	107.7	106.8	105.6	107.4
Hatchability of fertile eggs (%)	80.8	85.6	83.0	85.0	85.7
Poults/hen	64.5	80.4	74.1	76.4	76.4
Mean of egg weight (g)	75.6	75.3	75.2	75.8	76.2

(Whitehead and Herron, 1988)

was adequate for normal egg production and hatchability but that egg weight was increased by dietary supplementation with 50 g maize oil/kg. However conflicting data have come from a recent UK study (Whitehead and Herron, 1988) the results from which are given in *Table 6.7*. A basal diet containing 8.5 g linoleic acid and 36 g total fat/kg was inadequate for reproduction. Optimum egg production and hatchability were achieved with a diet containing 11 g linoleic acid/kg. However, adding 25 g maize or olive oils/kg to the basal diet did not result in any change in egg weight. The conclusion from this study is that egg weight is not so responsive to dietary fat in the turkey as in the chicken.

This conclusion conflicts with the findings of Cooper and Barnet (1968) and it is interesting to speculate why. These authors observed a greater egg number (+12.3%, $P<0.05$) as well as egg weight (+3.7%, $P<0.05$) in the group fed supplemental maize oil. It is shown in the next section that small increases in egg number have been observed frequently in response to dietary fat supplementation. However these increases have usually been much less than 12.3%. It is therefore possible that the greater egg weight was related more to the greater inherent productivity of this group than to the dietary fat addition.

A conclusion common to the studies of Cooper and Barnet (1968) and Whitehead and Herron (1988) is that the linoleic acid requirement for hatchability is met by a dietary level of 11 to 12 g/kg. This requirement is unlikely to be influenced upwards by other nutritional factors — the birds of Whitehead and Herron (1988) were reared on a diet of relatively low linoleic acid content and hence point-of-lay body reserves of this fatty acid would have been minimal for turkeys reared on practical diets.

Dietary fat

Once requirements for essential fatty acids have been met, it is important to consider whether dietary fat itself conveys any reproductive advantages to turkeys. As indicated in *Table 6.6*, many of the experiments on dietary ME level involved feeding diets of different fat content. More information on fat levels in basal and supplemented diets is given in *Table 6.8*.

Table 6.8 Summary of reports on responses in egg number and weight to dietary fat supplementation

Reference	Dietary fat content (g/kg)		% change	
	Basal	Supplement	Egg number	Egg weight
Anderson (1964)	36	40 'fat'	−0.2 (NS)[a]	–
Cooper and Barnet (1968)	30	50 maize oil	+12.3 (NS)	+3.7[b]
Jones *et al.* (1976)	35	60 blended fat	+2.3 (NS)	+1.5[b]
Potter *et al.* (1978b)	40	60 animal/vegetable fat	=1.7 (NS)	0
Menge *et al.* (1979)	100	70 animal/vegetable fat	+0.9 (NS)	−1.0 (NS)
		140 animal/vegetable fat	−2.4 (NS)	−1.3 (NS)
Grizzle *et al.* (1982)	28	20 'fat'	+1.5 (NS)	–
		40 'fat'	+7.4 (NS)	–
Harms *et al.* (1984)	28	80 'fat'	+30.4[b]	−0.2 (NS)
Bougon *et al.* (1985)	37	25 soybean oil	+2.4 (NS)	+0.5 (NS)

[a] NS: not significant
[b] $P<0.05$

Basal diets in all the experiments were thought to be adequate in essential fatty acids and usually contained 30–40 g fat/kg. They were then supplemented with different amounts and types (often unspecified) of fat. Apart from differences in feed intake (where the ME content of diets varied) the only other characteristic to show any frequent response was egg number. These responses listed in *Table 6.8* show considerable variability and were seldom statistically significant. Some experiments showed small declines in egg number in response to added fat (Anderson, 1964; Potter, Shelton and Meyer, 1978b) or no response (Whitehead and Herron, 1988). Other experiments showed such large increases, +12.3% (Cooper and Barnet, 1968), +30.4% (Harms, Buresh and Wilson, 1984) as to suggest that some factor other than dietary fat was involved. Another study, by Menge *et al.* (1979), involved supplementation of a basal diet already containing such a high level of fat, 100 g/kg, that any responses to additional fat were not likely to be meaningful. However, the studies of Jones, Hughes and Barnett (1976), Grizzle, Voitle and Harms (1982) and Bougon, Le Ménec and L'Hospitalier (1985) showed consistent increases (usually 2–3%) in egg number in response to higher dietary fat levels. The general conclusion from these sets of data is that more often than not increasing the dietary fat above minimum levels has resulted in a benefit in egg number. To cater for this response, it is recommended that turkey laying diets should contain a minimum of 50 g total fat/kg.

As can be seen from *Table 6.8*, there is little evidence that supplemental dietary fat has beneficial effects on egg weight.

Amino acids and protein

Experimental evidence for the amino acid requirements of turkey breeders is largely lacking. There are some reports, mainly in abstract form or describing effects of additions of single levels of amino acids to diets (Luther and Waldroup, 1970; Jensen, 1973; Atkinson *et al.*, 1974; Cherms, Stoller and McIlraith, 1978b; Parsons, Leighton and Meyer, 1979). Thus requirement values quoted in tables, such as NRC (1984), are usually extrapolations based on chicken responses, reinforced by observations at critical levels of protein in turkeys fed practical diets. Possible ways of calculating turkey breeder amino acid requirements based on theoretical modifications of chicken responses have been described by Wilgus (1976).

In order to investigate directly the responses of turkeys to dietary amino acids, and to compare these to chicken responses, an experiment was recently carried out on caged turkeys at Roslin. Making some assumptions on the basis of chicken responses, data on egg output, feed intake and body weight from an earlier Roslin turkey breeder flock were used with the Reading Model (Fisher, Morris and Jennings, 1973) to calculate theoretical requirements for lysine and sulphur amino acids. A series of diets were then formulated to be equally limiting or over supplied to varying degrees with these amino acids at the same ME level (11.4 MJ/kg). The observed responses were then analysed with the Reading Model.

Amino acid requirements of an individual bird can be written in the form

$$R = aE + bW$$

where R is the requirement for a particular amino acid (mg/day) at a given level of egg output, E (g/day), by a bird of body weight W (kg). The coefficients of output and maintenance are constants a and b (in mg). The coefficients calculated from experimental data over the period of peak egg output (37–43 weeks) for lysine, methionine and methionine plus cystine were:

	a (mg/g egg)	b (mg/kg body weight)
Lysine	10.6	32.5
Methionine	5.75	10.0
Methionine + cystine	11.2	10.4

Calculation of the efficiencies of utilization of these amino acids for egg output gave values of about 0.61 for lysine and methionine but only 0.52 for methionine plus cystine. This suggests that dietary levels of lysine and methionine were equally limiting but that methionine plus cystine was less limiting. This conclusion is supported by the similarities of the b constants for methionine and methionine plus cystine. The experiment was therefore a better test of lysine and methionine requirements.

Comparison of the a and b constants with chicken values showed some differences. Equivalent values of a for chickens are in the order 10.0 mg/g for lysine and 4.8 mg/g for methionine (McDonald and Morris, 1985). Thus the turkey seems to be slightly less efficient than the chicken in converting these dietary amino acids into egg.

Much larger differences between the species are apparent in maintenance requirements. Values for b were much lower than in laying chickens, where equivalent values are 73 mg/kg for lysine and 31 mg/kg for methionine (McDonald and Morris, 1985). Scaling the values of feather-free body protein raised to the power 0.73 narrows but does not eliminate the difference (laying chicken values become 42 mg/kg for lysine and 13 mg/kg or methionine).

This difference in amino acid maintenance requirement may represent a species difference. Alternatively the explanation may be biochemical, related to the turnover of tissue proteins. The recycling and retention of amino acids may be slower or more efficient in the amino acid pools of large muscles. If this explanation is correct, b is not a constant but is a function of body weight (or perhaps more correctly of body protein) and should decline as body weight increases. Values quoted by Nixey and Boorman (1985) for growing turkeys do indeed show a decrease with increasing age.

Data from the Roslin amino acid response study are summarized in Table 6.9. Estimated daily intakes required for maximum egg output are: lysine 1.1 g,

Table 6.9 Reproductive responses to different dietary levels of lysine, methionine and cystine

Diet (g/kg)						
Lysine	4.1	4.6	5.6	6.2	6.9	7.9
Methionine	1.9	2.2	2.6	3.0	3.6	4.0
Methionine + cystine	3.3	3.9	4.6	5.1	5.9	6.4
Crude protein	93	110	130	140	150	163
Responses (37–43 weeks)						
Egg production (% hen/day)	60.6	65.2	71.9	69.6	70.4	68.7
Mean egg weight (g)	70.3	73.9	75.1	75.5	77.0	76.7
Total egg output (g/day)	42.5	48.3	53.9	52.4	53.4	52.9
Feed intake (g/day)	175	180	194	190	194	194
Body weight at 40 weeks (kg)	7.0	7.5	7.4	7.4	7.7	7.6

methionine 0.57 g, methionine plus cystine 0.97 g. However a consideration of the individual components of egg output indicates that these responded differently, egg weight responding to higher dietary intakes of amino acids than did egg number. Economic models are not available to calculate the most efficient level of turkey breeder output in relation to nutrient input, but on the assumption that maximum poult production is the main objective, the above requirement values should be satisfactory. They should permit maximum egg number and egg weights within 0.2% of the maximum for turkeys weighing about 7.5 kg. At the feed intakes of these hens, these daily intakes corresponded to dietary levels of: lysine 5.7 g/kg, methionine 2.94 g/kg methionine plus cystine 5.1 g/kg. Using the a and b coefficients established with 7.5 kg hens, the calculated requirements for 10 kg hens are: lysine 5.2 g/kg, methionine 2.6 g/kg, methionine plus cystine 4.4 g. However if the b coefficient is smaller in 10 kg hens, for the reasons discussed earlier, these requirement values may be slight overestimates. A summary of amino acid requirements is given in Table 6.10.

Table 6.10 Recommended daily intakes and dietary levels of major nutrients for turkey breeders

	Intake (g/day)		Dietary level (g/kg)	
	A	B	A	B
Metabolizable energy (MJ)			12	
Crude protein	29	34	150	140
Lysine	1.10	1.30	5.7	5.2
Methionine	0.57	0.66	2.9	2.6
Methionine + cystine	0.97	1.10	5.1	4.4
Tryptophan	0.25	0.30	1.3	1.2
Calcium	4.9	5.7	25	23
Phosphorus (available)	0.8	0.95	4.2	3.8
Sodium			1.6	
Potassium			6	
Magnesium			0.6	
Chloride			1	
Total fat			50	
Linoleic acid			12	

A: Recommended values for 7.5 kg hens eating 194 g feed/day and laying 54 g eggs/day
B: Recommended values for 10 g hens eating 250 g feed/day and laying 60 g egg/day

Once amino acid requirements have been established it becomes possible to consider protein requirements. Provided birds receive adequate daily intakes of all essential amino acids, it is unlikely that their protein requirements are higher than the amounts needed to provide these intakes, within the normal range of dietary amino acid supplementation. In the Roslin amino acid experiment already described, a dietary protein intake of 25.2 g CP/day was sufficient for maximum egg number; 29.1 g CP/day was adequate to give egg weight within 0.2% of the maximum. At the feed intakes of the birds, these values corresponded to dietary levels of 130 and 150 g CP/kg respectively.

Results from several other studies on protein requirements are summarized in Table 6.11; further studies have been published in abstract form (e.g. Bradley et al., 1971; Atkinson et al., 1972; Cherms et al., 1978b; Parsons et al., 1979). Most of these studies have compared only two dietary protein levels, hence a dose-response

Table 6.11 Summary of reports on crude protein requirements

Reference	Dietary levels tested (g/kg)	Level found adequate		Body weight (kg)
		Daily intake (g)	Diet levels (g/kg)	
Balloun (1974)	120, 140, 160	31	120	8.0
Cherms et al. (1976)	156, 185	35	156	8.8
Kruegcr et al. (1978)	140, 180	44	140	10.1
Menge et al. (1979)	140, 180	32	180	(heavy)
Bougon et al. (1982b)	140, 160, 180	35	160	8.1

analysis of data is not possible. However the data are generally consistent with the view that optimum performance is possible with conventional breeder diets containing 140–160 g CP/kg. From a review of some of these and other data, Wilgus (1976) concluded that daily protein intakes of 25–27 g were adequate.

Minerals

There is a reasonable amount of information available on calcium and phosphorus requirements of turkey hens but very little evidence on requirements for other major or trace elements. It is therefore only possible to consider requirements and allowances in individual terms; the question of optimum balances such as between electrolytcs is not open to informed discussion.

Calcium

In general terms, a turkey can lay about the same daily weight of eggs as a chicken, but on a much larger feed intake. Calcium requirements as a proportion of the diet are thus likely to be quite different in the two species. However a set of assumptions common to the two species has been used to calculate theoretical requirements. On the basis of an egg content of 34.8 mg Ca/g egg, a maintenance requirement of 55 mg Ca/kg body weight/day and a dietary Ca utilization of 0.50, a WPSA (1984) working party calculated requirements of 3.4 to 5.3 g Ca/day, depending upon the weight of the turkey and the weight of daily egg output. When this method of calculation was applied using data from the Roslin turkey flock described in the previous chapter (egg output 54 g/day, daily feed intake 194 g of diet containing 11.4 MJ ME/kg, body weight 7.6 kg), the theoretical requirement was 4.6 g Ca/day (23.7 g Ca/kg diet). The allowance was 25.0 g/kg. For the heavier turkeys described by Robel (1981), weighing 10 kg and laying a daily egg weight of 60 g on an intake of 250 g, the calculated requirement was 5.1 g Ca/day (20.4 g/kg diet). By comparison, 2 kg chickens eating 110 g/day and laying 54 g/day would require 36 g Ca/kg by this method of estimation.

There are two main limitations to this method of assessing requirements. Firstly, the method is better at calculating the requirement of an individual bird rather than a flock, where different birds may have different input and output characteristics. Output is also irregular, though the large skeletal mass of the turkey might be expected to provide a considerable buffer to short-term fluctuations in calcium supply and demand. The second limitation lies in the assumption of a single value for calcium utilization. No account is taken of the possibilities that (a) individual utilizations may vary, and (b) utilization may be influenced by dietary level. It is therefore advisable also to consider experimental evidence on calcium requirements.

The results of several experimental studies on calcium requirements are summarized in *Table 6.12*. Requirements were assessed using egg number and hatchability as criteria. Daily intakes of 4–6 g Ca have usually been found to be adequate and in dietary terms these intakes have usually been provided by levels of 23–25 g Ca/kg diet. These values might be considered to represent safe minimum levels. There do not appear to be any direct performance penalties associated with a moderate oversupply of calcium; Jensen *et al.* (1964) did not observe any adverse effects of feeding 62.5 g Ca/kg diet. However high levels of dietary calcium are thought to depress the absorption of other nutrients and should be avoided if possible.

Table 6.12 Summary of reports on calcium requirements

Reference	Dietary levels tested (g/kg)	Level found adequate	
		Daily intake (g)	Diet level (g/kg)
Jensen *et al.* (1963)	9.5, 17.6, 25.8, 31.6	5.07	17.6
Balloun and Miller (1964b)	15, 20, 25, 30	5.7	20
Atkinson *et al.* (1967a)	12.4, 19.0, 26.6, 34.3	5.82	26.6
Arends *et al.* (1967)	15, 22.5, 30		22.5
Nestor *et al.* (1972)	2.3, 30	6.0	22.3
Potter *et al.* (1974)	9.9, 17.7, 25.5, 33.3	2.7	17.7
Manley *et al.* (1980)	25, 35		35
Mather and Harms (1982)	26, 40	5.1	26

Phosphorus

Requirements for this element have been assessed in several studies (Ferguson, Sewell and Atkinson, 1974; Potter, Leighton and Chu, 1974; Waldroup, Maxey and Luther, 1974; Atkinson *et al.*, 1967a; Miller, Bradley and Ferguson, 1976; Mather and Harms, 1982). In general, dietary levels of 4.0–4.3 g available phosphorus/kg in diets containing about 12 MJ ME/kg have given optimal performance. Manley, Voitle and Harms (1980) did not observe an interaction between calcium and phosphorus at reasonable dietary levels of either nutrient. WPSA (1984) has suggested levels of 3.5–4.0 g available phosphorus/kg for a diet of similar ME content, depending upon body weight and egg output (the lower end of the range for the heavier birds).

Chloride

The chloride requirement of turkey hens has been studied by Harms, Junqueira and Wilson (1983). They found that a natural dietary content of 0.3 g/kg was adequate for egg production and hatchability but egg weight responded to dietary levels up to 0.9 g/kg.

Sodium

Harms, Buresh and Wilson (1985) have suggested that the sodium requirement of the turkey hen is 0.62 g/kg diet; egg production was the most sensitive criterion of requirement. This experiment involved heavy birds (9 kg) with relatively low rates of lay, so higher dietary levels may be needed by smaller birds or those with more normal rates of egg production. It might be better to assume a minimum requirement of 1 g/kg, and to set an allowance of 1.5 g/kg for breeding diets containing about 12 MJ ME/kg.

Potassium

Experimental evidence on the potassium requirements of turkey breeders is lacking. However when comparisons are made in young birds, it seems that the poult has a higher requirement than the chick (6 versus 2.6 g/kg). On the basis that the laying chicken has a lower requirement than the young chick (1.5 versus 2.6 g/kg), it is assumed that the requirement of the breeding turkey should be met by a dietary level of 6 g/kg (NRC, 1984). This value is probably considerably in excess of the minimum requirement but should be provided by the natural content of most practical diets. Evidence is not available to suggest that such diets benefit from supplementation with potassium.

Magnesium

Requirements of turkey breeders for this element have not been determined. Requirements for the laying chicken are in the order of 0.4 g/kg and turkey breeder requirements have been tentatively set at 0.45 (ARC, 1974) or 0.6 g/kg (NRC, 1984). These requirements are largely academic, since practical cereal-based diets should contain natural magnesium contents of at least twice the higher of these requirement values.

Trace elements

Trace element nutrition of turkey breeders is based on much speculation and little information. There appear to be published reports on experiments involving only two trace elements, manganese and selenium. In the study on the former, Atkinson et al. (1967b) for levels of 27, 54, 108 and 162 mg added per kg to a practical diet probably containing about 15 mg natural Mn/kg. Egg production and hatchability were improved significantly with the supplement of 54 mg/kg and were slightly higher still with 108 mg/kg. Fitting a curvilinear response to the doses suggests the requirement was about 90 mg total Mn/kg diet.

The study on selenium is less satisfactory for quantitative interpretation. Cantor, Moorhead and Brown (1978) reported the results of two experiments where a basal diet, probably containing about 0.02 mg Se/kg and 10 mg vitamin E/kg, was supplemented with 0.20 mg Se/kg. Responses in hatchability were observed in both experiments and were significant in one. However, this study indicates only that 0.02 mg Se/kg (in conjunction with 10 mg vitamin E/kg) was inadequate, and not whether or to what extent a supplement of 0.2 mg Se/kg was adequate.

The requirements of the turkey breeder for copper, iron, zinc and iodine as well as for selenium listed by NRC (1984) are estimated values. In general they are similar to values listed for breeding chickens (some of which are also estimates!). If one considers the likely lower natural levels of trace minerals in typical UK practical diets it can be estimated that such diets are likely to be seriously deficient in manganese and iodine, possibly deficient in selenium, marginal in iron and zinc and probably adequate in copper. However, in view of uncertainties over maternal requirements, and mindful of the need to produce poults with a good nutrient carryover to optimize viability, it is recommended that practical diets should contain supplements of all of these elements: manganese, iodine and selenium to overcome likely deficiencies, zinc and iron to give a margin of safety, and a small amount of copper in view of its role in the aetiology of aortic rupture in poults.

Other trace elements, namely cobalt, molybdenum, nickel, silicon and vanadium may have a nutritional role in poultry but it does not seem necessary to add them as supplements to practical turkey breeding diets.

A summary of mineral requirements, likely minimum dietary levels and allowances are given in *Table 6.13*.

Table 6.13 Dietary levels of trace elements for turkey breeders (mg/kg diet)

Element	Estimated requirement (NRC, 1984)	Suggested allowance	Likely natural dietary content	Suggested dietary supplement
Copper	8	10	12	0–20
Iron	60	90	60	30
Manganese	60	115	15	100
Zinc	65	90	40	50
Iodine	0.4	1	0.1	1
Selenium	0.2	0.2	0.1	0.2

Vitamins

The depth of knowledge on turkey breeder vitamin requirements is little better than that for minerals. Satisfactory reports seem to exist for about only seven vitamins, and most of these originated from the USA over 20 years ago. Most of the values currently quoted in tables of requirements are therefore based most probably on outdated information or extrapolated from chicken data. There is however some evidence that requirements in the two species may differ widely (e.g. vitamin D, as is discussed later). For greater insight into the extent to which the principles of vitamin metabolism or nutrition may be differed in the turkey, it is of interest to consider recent findings on the incorporation of biotin into turkey and chicken eggs.

Incorporation of vitamins into eggs

MECHANISMS OF BIOTIN TRANSFER

All the vitamin needed by the developing embryo and hatching chick must be incorporated into the egg before it is laid. Simple diffusion of vitamins into yolk or albumen from plasma is not an efficient enough process to incorporate the relatively large amounts of vitamins needed. Instead there is an active transport system based on specific vitamin-binding proteins. The relationships between these binding proteins and their vitamins have been shown to differ considerably in the chicken from one vitamin to another (e.g. riboflavin and biotin, White, Armstrong and Whitehead, 1986; White and Whitehead, 1987). However, biotin is the only vitamin for which comparisons have been made in chickens and turkeys. Considerable differences in biotin transport have been found in these species.

Two plasma biotin binding proteins (BBPs) have been found in the laying chicken. Both are synthesized or released in response to biotin, hence unbound BBPs are not found in plasma, nor is unbound biotin over a wide range of dietary intakes. BBP I is produced preferentially at low biotin intakes, but BBP II becomes the major protein at higher biotin intakes. BBP II is better suited for uptake at the membrane of the developing yolk follicle and so transports the majority of the biotin found in chicken egg yolk. The synthesis of BBP II and the incorporation of biotin in the yolk respond to increasing intakes of dietary biotin up to the limit of production of BBP II. Yolk biotin level then plateaus. At higher biotin intakes, free biotin in the plasma becomes bound to another BBP, avidin, in the oviduct and there is then a rapid rise in the biotin incorporated into albumen. Avidin synthesis is not dependent on biotin and biotin deposition in the albumen continues until the limit at which avidin becomes fully saturated (White and Whitehead, 1987).

In contrast the turkey hen has only one plasma BBP, similar in properties to chicken BBP I. The low efficiency with which this protein is incorporated into yolk accounts for the much lower yolk biotin concentrations found in turkeys than in chickens equivalent dietary and plasma biotin levels (typical turkey values may be 0.3–0.5 those of chickens). However, turkeys have a much higher production of avidin in the oviduct. Hence the upper limit of incorporation of biotin into turkey albumen is much greater than in chickens, although within the normal nutritional ranges of biotin the concentrations of biotin in chicken and turkey eggs are similar. The net result is that avidin-bound biotin in albumen makes up a greater proportion of the total biotin in turkey than in chicken eggs; at dietary levels above 160 µg/kg more biotin is present in turkey albumen than in yolk (White, Whitehead and Armstrong, 1987). It is presumed that this avidin-bound biotin is nutritionally available to the embryo and, indeed, Robel (1985) has been able to improve hatchability by injecting biotin into turkey eggs. This may not be the case in the chicken, where attempts to rescue biotin-deficient eggs by injection have not been successful (White and Whitehead, 1987). It is thus apparent that there may be considerable differences in vitamin metabolism between turkeys and chickens. It is therefore not safe to assume vitamin requirements are the same in both species.

EFFECTS OF AGE

Studies on broiler breeders have shown that biotin concentrations in eggs have increased as the hens have aged (Whitehead, 1983). Robel (1983) has reported a similar phenomenon for biotin in turkey eggs. He has also found opposite age effects on other vitamins. For instance egg folate and especially pyridoxine levels declined with age. The nutritional implications of these observations have not yet been established, but it could be possible that the vitamin requirements of turkey hens change with age.

Vitamin requirements

VITAMIN A

The requirement of the turkey hen for maximum egg production and hatchability has been reported to be met by 790 µg retinol/kg (Stoewsand and Scott, 1961). Subsequent data of Jensen (1965) indicated that maximum performance was obtained with a diet containing 1056 µg/kg and this value may be taken as a preferred estimate of the requirement).

VITAMIN D_3

The most recent studies of vitamin D_3 requirements have been by Stevens *et al.* (1984) and Stevens, Blair and Salmon (1984) who compared supplemental levels of 7.5, 22.5 and 67.5 µg cholecalciferol/kg in Large White females. In the first study, egg production, egg weight and hatchability were all depressed at the lowest level but there were no significant differences in these characteristics between the higher levels. However, studies in the second report suggested that 22.5 µg/kg might have been inadequate for poult development. Poults hatching from hens fed this level were lighter and had lower tibia ash values than poults from hens given 67.5 µg/kg. The former poults also had elevated activities of kidney 25-hydroxyvitamin D_3-1-hydroxylase, a characteristic of vitamin D_3, calcium or phosphorus deficiency. There is still much work required to establish the optimum levels and balances involving vitamin D_3, its metabolizing enzymes and metabolites in relation to calcium and phosphorus metabolism and performance in poultry. Nevertheless, the present data may indicate that 22.5 µg/kg is inadequate for breeding turkeys and that 67.5 µg/kg (2700 IU/kg) may be a safer level. The dietary vitamin A level in these experiments was 3 mg retinol/kg (10 000 IU/kg).

VITAMIN E

This vitamin is important for reproduction, especially in relation to hatchability. Atkinson *et al.* (1955) observed an increase in hatchability from 52 to 88% but no change in egg number when 45 mg α-tocopherol acetate/kg was added to a turkey breeder diet containing no animal proteins. However there are no response data available to judge a requirement for vitamin E either alone or in conjunction with selenium.

RIBOFLAVIN

The only report on requirements of breeding turkeys for this vitamin seems to be by Boucher, Patrick and Knandel (1942) who reported that 3.5 mg/kg was needed.

PANTOTHENIC ACID

Kratzer *et al.* (1955) reported that the requirement of the breeding turkey was 16 mg/kg.

BIOTIN

The requirement for biotin seems to be mainly for hatchability. Jensen (1967) found that 110 µg/kg was inadequate for maximum hatchability. However, Waibel *et al.* (1969) and Arends *et al.* (1971) found that supplementing diets containing 145 and 155 µg/kg respectively did not improve the performance of breeders, or of progeny fed adequate diets. On the basis of these studies the requirement has been set at 150 µg/kg (NRC, 1984).

FOLIC ACID

Miller and Balloun (1967) found that the requirement for egg production was met by 0.35 mg/kg but that the requirement for hatchability was higher and influenced by dietary choline content. At a choline level of 1000 mg/kg, the suggested folic acid requirement on the basis of these data is 1.2 mg/kg.

CHOLINE

It has been reported that 1000 mg/kg was adequate for egg production, hatchability and growth and viability of poults (Balloun and Miller, 1964a). Later studies found that supplementing a diet containing 1230 mg/kg did not improve egg production, fertility or hatchability (Ferguson *et al.*, 1975). The preferred estimate of requirement is thus 1000 mg/kg.

VITAMIN ALLOWANCES

Conclusions from the limited vitamin requirement studies are summarized in *Table 6.14*. Also included are values quoted by ARC (1974) and NRC (1984). There are many gaps in the turkey data and these have been filled by estimated values. An experiment has recently been completed at Roslin to test the adequacy of published requirement levels for biotin in particular, and the other vitamins in general.

Table 6.14 Summary of reports on vitamin requirements

Vitamin	Experimental requirement /kg diet (year of report)		Suggested requirements	
			ARC (1974)	NRC (1984)
Vitamin A (µg)	1056	(1965)	810	1200
Vitamin D$_3$ (µg)	67.5	(1984)	50	22.5
Vitamin E (mg)			60	25
Vitamin K (mg)				(1)
Thiamin (mg)				(2)
Riboflavin (mg)	3.5	(1942)	3.5	(4)
Pantothenic acid (mg)	16	(1955)	16	16
Nicotinic acid (mg)				(30)
Pyridoxine (mg)				(4)
Biotin (µg)	150	(1971)	200	150
Folic acid (mg)	1.2	(1967)	0.7	1.0
Vitamin B$_{12}$ (µg)				(3)
Choline (mg)	1000	(1975)	1350	(1000)

NRC (1984) values in parentheses are estimated requirements

The experimental plan is outlined in *Table 6.15*. Female turkeys were reared normally until photostimulated at either 24 or 30 weeks. At these times they were distributed between five dietary treatments. The basal diet contained all vitamins at levels corresponding approximately to ARC (1974)/NRC (1984) values, with appropriate increments to allow for diet storage or processing losses. The other diets contained either increased levels of all vitamins or additional supplements of 350 or 1850 µg biotin/kg. Reproductive performance of the hens was recorded up to 55 weeks of age and responses to treatments are shown in *Table 6.15*.

Table 6.15 Egg number and hatchability in hens photostimulated at 14 or 30 weeks and fed diets containing different levels of biotin or a mixture of all other vitamins

Dietary vitamins		Egg number (24–54 weeks)		Hatchability (%)	
Biotin (µg/kg)	Others	Lit 24 week	Lit 30 week	Lit 24 week	Lit 30 week
150	+	117.8	107.6	74.3	80.3
	++	117.2	95.2	70.1	78.4
500	+	109.7	116.6	70.4	82.1
	++	101.5	112.3	76.6	85.1
2000	+	102.1	88.5	67.2	78.5

Significance of effects

Lighting		NS		$P, 0.001$	
Biotin 150–500		NS		$P, 0.05$	
Biotin 150–2000		$P, 0.05$		$P, 0.05$	
Other vitamins		NS		NS	
Biotin × others		NS		$P, 0.05$	

(C. C. Whitehead, unpublished)

Egg production was affected only by the highest dietary biotin level (2000 µg/kg) which caused a marked decrease. However, hatchability showed several nutritional responses. Increasing the dietary biotin content from 150 to 500 µg/kg increased hatchability by about 3%, but feeding 2000 µg/kg resulted in a considerable depression in hatchability. Increasing the dietary level of all vitamins did not affect hatchability significantly but there was an interaction between the levels of biotin and all other vitamins. Thus best hatchability was achieved with 500 µg biotin/kg and the higher levels of all other vitamins.

The results of this experiment can be interpreted as indicating that the dietary level of 150 µg biotin/kg and the levels of some vitamins in the minimal mixture were marginally inadequate for hatchability. The results also demonstrate the adverse effects of vitamin imbalances, for when either the levels of biotin or the mixture of other vitamins were increased, performance suffered. This was especially noticeable when biotin was increased to the very high level of 2000 µg/kg.

Comparison of the results on the two lighting treatments confirmed previous observations (Herron and Whitehead, 1985) that photostimulation at 24 weeks rather than 30 weeks resulted in greater egg number but lower overall hatchability. However there was no indication that this lower hatchability was related to vitamin status or supply.

From the results of this investigation it can be concluded that some of the vitamin requirement values proposed by NRC (1984)/ARC (1974) are not adequate for maximum reproductive performance. They are likely to be even less adequate for optimum poult quality and viability. Unfortunately, the Roslin experiment did not identify which vitamin levels apart from biotin at 150 µg/kg were inadequate. It has sometimes been argued that it is not necessary to know turkey breeder vitamin requirements accurately; under commercial conditions vitamins are usually supplied considerably in excess of requirement levels and hence deficiencies are unlikely to occur. There are several weaknesses in this argument. Firstly, if the requirement is not known even approximately, it is difficult to know to what extent a fed level is adequate or excessive. Secondly, routine oversupply of vitamins can be wasteful. Finally differing degrees of oversupply can lead to imbalances which, as has been shown, can have deleterious effects on performance. A better knowledge of vitamin requirements might therefore be expected to benefit the practice of turkey nutrition. Until such time, however, it is necessary to base breeder vitamin allowances on existing information. Suggested allowances are given in *Table 6.16*. It is recognized that many local factors may influence the optimum dietary allowances — the values given assume no abnormal losses of vitamins during processing or storage of diets or vitamin premixes.

Table 6.16 Recommendations for dietary vitamin levels for turkey breeders (/kg diet) fed wheat-based diets

	Allowance	Suggested dietary supplement
Vitamin A (µg retinol)	3600	3600
Vitamin D₃ (µg)	75	75
Vitamin E (mg α-tocopherol)	40	35
Vitamin K (mg)	4	4
Thiamin (mg)	5	2
Riboflavin (mg)	15	15
Pantothenic acid (mg)	30	20
Nicotinic acid (mg)	60	50
Pyridoxine (mg)	8	6
Biotin (µg)	300	250
Folic acid (mg)	4	3
Vitamin B₁₂ (µg)	20	20
Choline (mg)	1300	300

Conclusions

The nutritional and metabolic responses in turkey hens differ in many respects from those seen in chickens. There has been a limited amount of research undertaken on the nutrition of turkey breeders, though little under European conditions. Nevertheless some nutritional principles seem well established. For instance, bodyweight restriction during rearing may make some modest feed saving but conveys no reproductive benefit. Likewise there seems good evidence for lack of reproductive response to dietary ME levels. Information on protein requirements is reasonably good, though further data on responses to amino acids, especially in heavyweight hens, would be helpful for the confirmation and refinement of predictive models. However, there are glaring gaps in knowledge of requirements for many trace minerals and vitamins. Summaries of nutrient requirements are presented in the appendices, but some of the values must be regarded as tentative and open to improvement from future research work.

References

Anderson, D. L. (1964). Effect of body size and dietary energy on the protein requirement of turkey breeders. *Poultry Science*, **43**, 59–64

Andrews, L. D. and Morrow, H. D. (1978). Restricted feeding regimes and subsequent reproductive performance in cage and floor housed turkey hens. *Poultry Science*, **57**, 17–21

ARC (1974). *The Nutrient Requirements of Farm Livestock. 1. Poultry.* London, Agricultural Research Council

Arends, L. G., Kienholz, E. W., Shutze, J. M. and Taylor, D. D. (1971). Effect of supplemental biotin on reproductive performance of turkey breeder hens and its effect on the subsequent progeny's performance. *Poultry Science,* **50,** 208–214

Arends, L. G., Miller, D. L. and Balloun, S. P. (1967). Calcium requirements of the turkey breeder hen. *Poultry Science,* **46,** 727–730

Atkinson, R. L., Bradley, J. W. and Quisenberry, J. H. (1972). Effect of protein level and amino acid supplementation on turkey reproduction. *Poultry Science,* **51,** 1780

Atkinson, R. L., Bradley, J. W., Couch, J. R. and Krueger, W. F. (1974). Effect of added lysine and methionine to turkey breeder rations. *Poultry Science,* **53,** 1632

Atkinson, R. L., Bradley, J. W., Couch, J. R. and Quisenberry, J. H. (1967a). The calcium requirements of breeder turkeys. *Poultry Science,* **46,** 207–214

Atkinson, R. L., Bradley, J. W., Couch, J. R. and Quisenberry, J. H. (1967b). Effect of various levels of manganese on the reproductive performance ot turkeys. *Poultry Science,* **46,** 472–475

Atkinson, R. L., Ferguson, T. M., Quisenberry, J. H. and Couch, J. R. (1955). Vitamin E and reproduction in turkeys. *Journal of Nutrition,* **55,** 387–397

Balloun, S. L. (1974). Effect on reproductive performance of turkey breeders of nutrient restriction during the development period. *Poultry Science,* **53,** 625–632

Balloun, S. L. and Miller, D. L. (1964a). Choline requirements of turkey breeder hens. *Poultry Science,* **43,** 64–67

Balloun, S. L. and Miller, D. L. (1964b). Calcium requirements of turkey breeder hens. *Poultry Science,* **43,** 378–381

Balnave, D. (1971). The contribution of absorbed linoleic acid to the metabolism of the mature laying hen. *Comparative Biochemistry and Physiology,* **40A,** 1097–1105

Borron, D. C., McCartney, M. G. and Fuller, H. L. (1974). The effects of restricted energy feeding during the growing period on the reproductive performance of turkey breeder females. *Poultry Science,* **53,** 1485–1493

Boucher, R. V., Patrick, H. and Knandel, H. C. (1942). The riboflavin requirement of turkeys for hatchability and growth. *Poultry Science,* **21,** 466

Bougon, M., Le Ménec, M. and L'Hospitalier, R. (1985). Variations des performances zootechniques des dindes reproductrices en fonction des teneurs des aliments en energie et en protéines. *Bulletin d'Information, Station Experimentale d'Aviculture de Ploufragan,* **25,** 3–17

Bougon, M., L'Hospitalier, R., Le Ménec, M. and Launay, M. (1982a). Influence sur les performances zootechniques de la tenur énergétique des aliments distribués à des dindes reproductrices pendant les periodes d'élevage et de production. *Bulletin d'Information, Station Experimentale d'Aviculture de Ploufragan,* **22,** 47–53

Bougon, M., Le Ménec, M., L'Hospitalier, R. and Quémeneur, P. (1982b). Influence de la teneur en proteines de l'aliment sur les performances zootechniques des dindes reproductrices. *Bulletin d'Information, Station Experimentale d'Aviculture de Ploufragan,* **22,** 142–154

Bradley, J. W., Atkinson, R. L., Couch, J. R. and Quisenberry, J. H. (1971). Relation of protein level and grain type to egg production of turkeys. *Poultry Science,* **50,** 1555

Cantor, A. H., Moorhead, P. D. and Brown, K. I. (1978). Influence of dietary selenium upon reproductive performance of male and female breeder turkeys. *Poultry Science,* **57,** 1337–1345

Cherms, F. L., Stoller, M. G. and MacIlraith, J. J. (1976). Reproduction in turkey hens as influenced by prebreeder and breeder protein intake and the environment. *Poultry Science,* **55,** 1678–1690

Cherms, F. L., Stoller, M. G. and MacIlraith, J. J. (1978a). The influence of low protein during the early growth period and reproduction in turkey hens. *Poultry Science,* **57,** 1127

Cherms, F. L., Stoller, M. G. and MacIlraith, J. J. (1978b). Supplementation of a suboptimal protein diet with lysine and methionine and the effect on reproduction of turkey hens. *Poultry Science,* **57,** 1127

Cooper, J. B. and Barnet, B. D. (1968). Response of turkey hens to dietary linoleic acid fed as corn oil. *Poultry Science,* **47,** 671–677

Dymsza, H., Boucher, R. V. and McCartney, M. G. (1954). Influence of dietary fibre and energy levels on reproductive performance of turkey pullets. *Poultry Science,* **33,** 1159–1163

Ferguson, T. M., Atkinson, R. L., Bradley, J. W. and Miller, D. H. (1975). Reproductive performance of caged Beltsville small white turkeys as affected by choline, bird density and forced moulting. *Poultry Science,* **54**, 1679–1684

Ferguson, T. M., Sewell, C. E. and Atkinson, R. L. (1974). Phosphorus levels in the turkey breeder diet. *Poultry Science,* **53**, 1627–1629

Fisher, C., Morris, T. R. and Jennings, R. C. (1973). A model for the description and prediction of the response of laying hens to amino acid intake. *British Poultry Science,* **14**, 469–484

Grizzle, J. M., Voitle, R. A. and Harms, R. H. (1982). Evaluation of distillers dried grains with solubles in diets of turkey hens. *Poultry Science,* **61**, 1363–1366

Harms, R. H., Buresh, R. E. and Wilson, H. R. (1984). The influence of the grower diet and fat in the layer diet on performance of turkey hens. *Poultry Science,* **63**, 1634–1637

Harms, R. H., Buresh, R. E. and Wilson, H. R. (1985). Sodium requirement of the turkey hen. *British Poultry Science,* **26**, 217–220

Harms, R. H., Junqueira, O. M. and Wilson, H. R. (1983). The chloride requirement of the turkey breeder hen. *Poultry Science,* **62**, 2442–2444

Herron, K. M. and Whitehead, C. C. (1985). Recent studies on turkey breeder nutrition. *Turkeys,* **33**(1), 24–26

Hill, E. G., Silbernick, C. L. and McMeans, E. (1967). Dietary linolete and methionine in chicks. *Poultry Science,* **46**, 523–526

Hopkins, D. T. and Nesheim, M. C. (1962). The effect of linoleic acid depletion on performance of hens and their progeny. *Poultry Science,* **41**, 1651

Jensen, L. S. (1965). Vitamin A requirement of breeding turkeys. *Poultry Science,* **44**, 1609–1610

Jensen, L. S. (1967). Biotin in practical turkey rations. *Proceedings of Pacific Northwest Animal Nutrition Conference,* **3**, 7–11

Jensen, L. S. (1973). Failure to improve the reproductive performance of turkey breeder hens by supplementing a low protein diet with methionine. *Poultry Science,* **52**, 1988–1990

Jensen, L. S., Saxena, H. C. and McGinnis, J. (1963). Nutritional investigation with turkey hens. 4. Quantitative requirement for calcium. *Poultry Science,* **42**, 604–607

Jensen, L. S., Wagstaff, R. K., McGinnis, J. and Parks, F. (1964). Further studies on high calcium diets for turkey hens. *Poultry Science,* **43**, 1577–1581

Jones, J. F., Hughes, B. L. and Barnett, B. D. (1976). Effect of feed regimes on body weight of turkey hens at 32 weeks of age and subsequent reproductive performance. *Poultry Science,* **55**, 1356–1360

Ketola, H. G., Young, R. J. and Nesheim, M. C. (1973). Linoleic acid requirement of turkey poults. *Poultry Science,* **52**, 597–603

Kratzer, F. H., Davis, P. N., Marshall, B. J. and Williams, D. E. (1955). The pantothenic acid requirement of turkey hens. *Poultry Science,* **34**, 68–72

Krueger, K. K., Owen, J. A., Krueger, C. E. and Ferguson, T. M. (1978). Effect of feed and light regimes during the growing period on subsequent reproductive performance of broad breasted white turkeys fed two protein levels. *Poultry Science,* **57**, 27–37

Luther, L. W. and Waldroup, P. W. (1970). Protein, methionine and energy requirements for turkey breeder hens. *Poultry Science,* **49**, 1408

McCartney, M. G., Borron, D. C. and Brown, H. B. (1977). Reproductive performance of turkey females as affected by grower and pre-breeder diets. *Poultry Science,* **56**, 985–991

McDonald, M. W. and Morris, T. R. (1985). Quantitative review of optimum amino acid intakes for young laying pullets. *British Poultry Science,* **26**, 253–264

MacLeod, M. G., Fisher, C. and Jewitt, T. R. (1984). Protein: energy ratio for the growing turkey; effects on energy and nitrogen metabolism. *Proceedings of the XVII World's Poultry Congress,* Helsinki

Manley, J. M., Voitle, R. A. and Harms, R. H. (1980). The influence of dietary calcium and phosphorus on egg production and hatchability of turkey breeder hens. *Poultry Science,* **59**, 2077–2079

Mather, F. B. and Harms, R. H. (1982). Performance of laying turkeys grouped according to daily food intake. *Poultry Science,* **61**, 1818–1822

Menge, H., Frobish, L. T., Weinland, B. T. and Geis, E. G. (1979). Effect of dietary protein and energy on reproductive performance of turkey hens. *Poultry Science,* **58**, 419–426

Meyer, G. B., Props, C. F., Leighton, A. T., Van Krey, H. P. and Potter, L. M. (1980). Influence of dietary protein during the pre-breeder period on subsequent reproductive performance of large white turkeys. 1. Growth, feed consumption and female sex-limited reproductive traits. *Poultry Science*, **59**, 352–357

Miller, D. L. and Balloun, S. L. (1967). Folacin requirements of turkey breeder hens. *Poultry Science*, **46**, 1502–1508

Miller, D. H., Bradley, J. W. and Ferguson, T. M. (1976). Reproductive performance of broad breasted white turkeys in relation to dietary phosphorus. *Poultry Science*, **55**, 2481–2483

Mitchell, R. H., Creger, C. R., Davis, R. E., Atkinson, R. L., Ferguson, T. M. and Couch, J. R. (1962). The effect of restricted feeding of broad breasted, bronze turkeys during the holding period on subsequent reproductive performance. *Poultry Science*, **41**, 91–98

Nestor, K. E., Cantor, A. H., Bacon, W. L. and Brown, K. I. (1981). The influence of body weight restriction during the growing and holding periods on reproduction of turkey females from strains differing in body weight. *Poultry Science*, **60**, 1458–1467

Nestor, K. E., Touchburn, S . P., Musser, M. A. and Naber, E. C. (1972). Egg quality and reproduction in turkeys. 3. Variation in dietary calcium level. *Poultry Science*, **51**, 669–677

Nixey, C. and Boorman, K. N. (1985). The lysine requirements of market turkeys. *Proceedings of 5th European Symposium on Poultry Nutrition, Israel*, 137–144

NRC (1984). *Nutrient Requirements of Poultry*, 8th edn. Washington DC, National Academy Press

Owongs, W. J. and Sell, J. L. (1980). Effect of restricted feeding from 6 to 20 weeks of age on reproductive performance of turkeys. *Poultry Science*, **59**, 77–81

Parsons, M. C., Leighton, A. T. and Meyer, G. B. (1979). Protein and sulphur amino acid requirements of turkey breeder hens. *Poultry Science*, **58**, 1091–1092

Potter, L. M. and Leighton, A. T. (1973). Effects of diet and light during the pre-breeder period and of diet during the breeder period on turkey breeder performance. *Poultry Science*, **52**, 1805–1813

Potter, L. M., Leighton, A. T. and Chu, A. B. (1974). Calcium, phosphorus and Nopgro as variables in diets of breeder turkeys. *Poultry Science*, **53**, 15–22

Potter, L. M., Shelton, J. R. and Meyer, G. B. (1978a). Effects of controlled feeding of turkeys during the pre-breeder period on subsequent performance. *Poultry Science*, **57**, 478–484

Potter, L. M., Shelton, J. R. and Meyer, G. B. (1978b). Added fat, Ipopran and Rofenaid in diets of turkey breeders. *Poultry Science*, **57**, 485–488

Robblee, A. R. and Clandinin, D. R. (1959). The relationship of energy and protein to reproductive performance in turkey breeders. *Poultry Science*, **38**, 141–145

Robel, E. J. (1981). Relationships of age and body weight to reproductive traits in turkey hens. *Poultry Science*, **60**, 2709–2712

Robel, E. J. (1983). The effect of age of breeder hen on the levels of vitamins and minerals in turkey eggs. *Poultry Science*, **62**, 1751–1756

Robel, E. J. (1985). Effect of injecting turkey eggs with biotin on hatchability. *Poultry Science*, **64**, (Suppl. 1), 171

Shannon, D. W. F. and Whitehead, C. C. (1974). Lack of response in egg weight or output to increasing levels of linoleic acid in practical layer's diets. *Journal of the Science of Food and Agriculture*, **25**, 553–561

Shutze, J. V. and Jensen, L. S. (1963). Influence of linoleic acid on egg weight. *Poultry Science*, **42**, 921–924

Shutze, J. V., Jensen, L. S. and McGinnis, J. (1962). Accelerated increase in egg weight of young pullets fed practical diets supplemented with corn oil. *Poultry Science*, **41**, 1846–1851

Stevens, V. I., Blair, R., Salmon, R. E. and Stevens, J. P. (1984a). Effect of varying levels of dietary vitamin D_3 on turkey hen egg production, fertility and hatchability, embryo mortality and incidence of embryo beak malformations. *Poultry Science*, **63**, 760–764

Stevens, V. I., Blair, R. and Salmon, R. E. (1984b). Influence of maternal vitamin D_3 carry-over on kidney 25-hydroxyvitamin. D_3-1-hydroxylase activity of poults. *Poultry Science*, **63**, 765–774

Stoewsand, G. S. and Scott, M. L. (1961). The vitamin A requirements of breeding turkeys and their progeny. *Poultry Science*, **40**, 1255–1262

Touchburn, S. P., Naber, E. C. and Chamberlin, V. D. (1968). Effect of growth restriction on reproductive performance of turkeys. *Poultry Science*, **47**, 547–556

Voitle, R. A. and Harms, R. H. (1978). Performance of broad breasted large white turkey hens grown on restrictive feeding programs. *Poultry Science*, **57**, 752–756

Voitle, R. A., Walter, J. H., Wilson, H. R. and Harms, R. H. (1973). The effect of low protein and skip-a-day grower diets on the subsequent performance of turkey breeder hens. *Poultry Science*, **52**, 543–548

Waibel, P. E., Krista, L. M., Arnold, R. L., Blaylock, L. G. and Neagle, L. M. (1969). Effect of supplementary biotin on performance of turkeys fed corn-soybean meal diets. *Poultry Science*, **48**, 1979–1985

Waldroup, P. W., Maxey, J. F. and Luther, L. W. (1974). Studies on the calcium and phosphorus requirement of caged turkey breeder hens. *Poultry Science*, **53**, 886–888

White, H. B., Armstrong, J. and Whitehead, C. C. (1986). Riboflavin-binding protein: concentration and fractional saturation in chicken eggs as a function of dietary riboflavin. *Biochemical Journal*, **238**, 671–675

White, H. B. and Whitehead, C. C. (1987). Role of avidin and other biotin-binding proteins in the deposition and distribution of biotin in chickens eggs. *Biochemical Journal*, **241**, 677–684

White, H. B., Whitehead, C. C. and Armstrong, J. (1987). Relationship of biotin deposition in turkey eggs to dietary biotin and biotin-binding proteins. *Poultry Science*, **66**, 1236–1241

Whitehead, C. C. (1981). The response of egg weight to the inclusion of different amounts of vegetable oil and linoleic acid in the diet of laying hens. *British Poultry Science*, **22**, 525–532

Whitehead, C. C. (1983). Biotin intake and transfer to the egg and chick in broiler breeder hens housed on litter or in cages. *British Poultry Science*, **25**, 287–292

Whitehead, C. C. and Herron, K. M. (1988). Fatty acid requirements of breeding turkeys. *British Poultry Science*, **29**, 761–768

Wilgus, H. S. (1976). Estimation of the amino acid requirements of turkey breeder hens, with comparisons to those of laying chickens. 1. Estimation of requirements. *Feedstuffs, Minneapolis*, **48**(47), 38–41

WPSA (1984). Mineral requirements and recommendations for adult birds. *World's Poultry Science Journal*, **40**, 183–187

Chapter 7

Management of breeding stock

Sally L. Noll

The management of the turkey breeder flock should have as its objective to maximize the production of poults per hen by maintaining high levels of egg production, fertility and hatchability. Management areas of major impact on poult production would be lighting of breeders and broody control.

As established earlier (Chapter 3) lighting for hens and males is of great importance in initiation and maintenance of egg and semen production. Research on the lighting requirements of the turkey breeder hen and male has indicated the need to consider not only the photoperiod but also the characteristics of the light source (intensity and wavelength) in maximizing reproductive performance. Another management area having major impact on the number of eggs per hen is that of minimizing broodiness in breeder hens.

Lighting for prebreeder hens

Efforts to improve egg production throughout the year have led to better definition of the lighting requirements of the turkey hen during the growing and holding periods prior to light stimulation. Egg production of flocks hatched in the autumn or winter was low. These hens had been reared under natural or increasing daylengths and were determined to be photorefractory when exposed to photoperiods considered to be light stimulatory (Harper and Parker, 1957; Leighton and Shoffner, 1961a).

Photoperiod

Photosensitivity was found to be restored in photorefractory hens by exposing them to short daylengths (Clayton and Robertson, 1960; Leighton and Shoffner, 1961a,b; McCartney et al., 1961; Marsden and Lucas, 1964; Ogasawara, Wilson and Asmundson, 1962; Shoffner et al., 1962; Wilson, Ogasawara and Asmundson, 1962). Darkening or light restriction is accomplished by shortening the daylength for a time period prior to light stimulation.

The lighting schedule during the darkening period needs to not only consider the daily hours of light or photoperiod, but also the duration of the darkening period and the quality of light administered.

Shortening the daylength or hours of light to less than 10 h of light per day appears sufficient to terminate the photorefractory state. Ogasawara, Wilson and

Asmundson (1962) and Wilson, Asmundson and Asmundson (1962) observed better egg production when daylength during the light restriction period was less than 10 h/day. Ogasawara, Wilson and Admundson (1962) found 3 weeks of 6 h was more effective compared with 10 h for 3 weeks. Wilson, Ogasawara and Asmundson (1962) indicated better egg production with 6 h of daily light compared with 4, 8, and 10 h of light per day. Siopes (1987) found no difference in egg production of hens when daily hours of light were restricted to 4, 8 or 10 h/day prior to photostimulation.

Several studies have indicated a trend for improved egg production as the length or duration of the light restriction period was increased. One week of light restriction was insufficient to overcome the refractory condition in studies by Harper and Parker (1957) and Wilson, Ogasawara and Asmundson (1962). Light restriction of 3 weeks' duration appears minimal. Other reports show an additional egg production response as the length of the light restriction period increased over 3 weeks (Harper and Parker, 1957; Leighton and Potter, 1969; McCartney et al., 1961; Shoffner et al., 1962; Wilson, Ogasawara and Asmundson, 1962; Wilson, Ogasawara and Woodard, 1967). A recent report by Siopes (1987) supports increasing the length of the light restriction period to 8 weeks as decreased egg production was found when hens were reared with 6 weeks of light restriction compared with hens light restricted for 8 or 12 weeks.

Light intensity

Light intensity during the periods of rearing and light restriction has been demonstrated to affect later egg production rates. Egg production of hens reared on 0.11 lx from 0 to 30 weeks of age was lower compared with those reared at 32 lx. Egg production tended to increase further as the light intensity was increased to 194 lx during rearing and light restriction (El Halawani et al., 1974, 1975, 1978).

Commercially, interest exists to rear prebreeder hens at low light intensity to save energy costs. Subsequent studies indicated that light intensities in excess of 32 lx were needed starting at 8 weeks of age prior to light restriction at 18 weeks to maximize egg production response (Noll, El Halawani and Waibel, 1981).

Light intensity during the dark or blackout part of the daily light cycle during light restriction has not been shown conclusively to affect subsequent production. Egg production under blackout conditions was numerically greater than under brownout conditions (Leighton and Potter, 1969; Potter and Leighton, 1973). Light intensity during brownout averaged 0.86 lx (Leighton and Potter, 1969). However, Siopes (1987) found a light intensity of 0.5 lx during the dark portion of the photoperiod was detrimental to egg production.

Light sources

The use of light sources other than incandescent lamps for prebreeders has only been explored briefly. Fluorescent lamps were acceptable when light intensity was increased to account for its different spectral distribution in the red wavelength with a warm white type lamp at 731 lx (El Halawani, Waibel and Kramer, 1978) or not adjusted-cool white lamp at 55 lx (Siopes, 1984a) and compared to incandescent lamps. Jones et al. (1982) observed equivalent egg production of hens conditioned on red or white lights at low light intensities of 5 lx. Fluorescent lamps such as the warm white bulb which emits more light in the red wavelength are recommended.

In summary, for prebreeders reared for off-season production or prebreeders reared in confinement, light restriction should be initiated 8–12 weeks prior to light stimulation with daily light hours restricted to 6–8 h/day. Light intensity in excess of 32 lx should be used after 8 weeks of age. Blackout conditions are needed during the light restriction period.

Lighting for breeder hens

Photoperiod

After light restriction, the hours of light or daylength are increased to stimulate the hen into production. Increasing the photoperiod to 11–12 h of light will stimulate egg production but more hours are needed to obtain maximum egg production (Leighton, 1980; Marsden, Cowan and Lucas, 1962; Ogasawara, Wilson and Asmundson, 1962; Wilson, Ogasawara and Asmundson, 1962). Asmundson and Moses (1950) established that 14–16 h of light were required to bring the hen into maximum egg production and this was later confirmed by others (Marsden, Cowan and Lucas, 1962; Ogasawara, Wilson and Asmundson, 1962).

Light stimulation of hens with more than 16 h of light does not appear to result in better production. Egg production of hens given 24 h or 22 h of continuous light was not different from hens lit with 15 h (Leighton and Shoffner, 1961a; McCartney et al., 1961). Ogasawara, Wilson and Asmundson (1962) found that 20 h of light decreased egg production when compared with 14 h.

A few studies have examined if this increase in light hours at the time of light stimulation should be done gradually or abruptly. McCartney et al. (1961) found no production difference with Large White hens when the light hours were increased from 9 to 15 h either abruptly or by increasing the light hours 2 h/week. Marsden, Cowan and Lucas (1962) with Beltsville Small Whites previously restricted with 9 h of light found the abrupt change to 11, 13 or 15 h of light resulted in a shortened time interval to the first egg compared with a gradual increase in light of 30 min/day. Greater egg production was observed at the more minimal hours of stimulatory light of 11 and 13 h with the abrupt changes.

Some attempts have been made to maintain high levels of egg production by increasing the photoperiod gradually throughout the season. Bacon and Nestor (1977) found when the light hours were increased by 15 min every 2 weeks starting at 21 days of production through 180 days of production, egg production was not different compared with the control (14L:10D). Cherms (1982a) increased light hours from 14 to 15 h after 10 weeks of production with no effect on egg production. McCartney et al. (1961) increased light hours by 0.5 h/week starting at 15 h and ending when the daily hours of light reached 22 h/day with no beneficial effects on egg production.

That lighting need not be given continuously was demonstrated by Bacon and Nestor (1977, 1981 and 1982) who utilized an intermittent lighting programme (IL) where the 5 h of light were spaced equally in what would normally be the 14-h light portion of the day followed by a 10-h continuous period of darkness (4(1L:2.25D):1L:10D). Intermittent lighting of hens in floor pens resulted in similar rates of egg production, but hens on the IL programme produced more floor eggs when compared with the control (14L:10D). IL hens were more difficult to nest train and the servicing of the flock during the 1-h light periods presented problems but savings in feed and electricity were noted (Bacon and Nestor, 1977).

When tested in caged hens, IL resulted in more eggs and decreased shell-less egg production (Bacon and Nestor, 1982). Further testing in floor pens indicated that the IL programme could be initiated after lighting with continuous light and that the light periods need not be spaced equally (Bacon and Nestor, 1981).

Other IL programmes have been tested. Cherms (1982b) examined an IL programme in which the light (8.5 h) was given during a 14-h period with no effect on the total egg production of off-season Large White hens. Production for the IL hens was less through 8 weeks of lay and greater during the following 6 weeks of lay compared with the control (14L:10D) with more floor egg production. Krueger, Burnard and McIntyre (1982) compared an IL regime of 2L/6D/8L/8D with a 16L/10D regime. The IL regime resulted in similar egg production levels for Small White hens compared with the controls but significantly lowered egg production in Large White hens.

Light intensity and light source

Light intensity and source also affect egg production levels in breeders as well as the prebreeder hen. Research with intensity is interrelated with light source as light sources contain different spectral distribution or different amounts of light of the red wavelength.

At low levels of light intensity (16 lx versus 32 lx) with incandescent lamps, McCartney (1971) observed similar rates of production. However, within limits, increasing light intensity appears to increase egg production. Leighton (1980) found egg production increased as light intensity increased from 5.4 to 86 lx especially when given for 11 compared with 16 h of light per day. Cherms (1982a) indicated 161 lx (quartz lighting) resulted in 6–9 eggs per hen more than at 54 lx. In studies by Siopes (1984a) and Thomason, Leighton and Mason (1972) egg production of hens at higher light intensities tended to be greater, i.e. 22 versus 108 lx and 5.4 versus 86.1 lx, respectively although no statistically significant differences were detected.

Selection of a light source must not only consider potential costs in terms of installment, fixtures, electrical and replacement lamp costs but must also consider the effects on the reproductive performance which is dependent on the light in the red wavelength of the colour spectrum.

In a comparison of fluorescent (warm white), incandescent and high intensity discharge sodium vapour lighting at equal intensities of 108 lx, similar rates of egg production were observed in an off-season flock (El Halawani et al., 1980b). Use of cool white fluorescent lamps were found to delay sex maturity by 1.4 days and decrease egg production in cage hens lit at 32 weeks (Siopes, 1984a) at two light intensities of 20 and 108 lx. An earlier study by Payne and McDaniel (1958) also found lower egg production which occurred during 10–22 weeks of production for hens with fluorescent lighting compared with incandescent lighting. When full spectrum fluorescent lamps at 76 lx were compared with incandescent lamps, no difference in production was noted for first and second cycle hens (Siopes, 1984b).

Flock production can be adversely affected by light stimulating hens at too young an age. Lower egg production, lower egg weight, a time delay in onset of lay after lighting, greater proportion of non-layers, and more broodiness has been noted in flocks lighted at an early age (Leighton and Shoffner, 1964; McCartney, 1971; Wilson, Ogasawara and Asmundson, 1962; Woodard et al., 1974). For the small and medium type hen, lighting earlier than 26 weeks of age was found to be detrimental (Leighton and Shoffner, 1964; Wilson, Ogasawara and Asmundson,

1962). With large type hens lighting earlier than 28 weeks of age (McCartney, 1971; Wilson, Ogasawara and Asmundson, 1962; Woodard *et al.*, 1974) resulted in poor egg production.

In summary, for breeder hens the hours of light to maximize production were found to be 14–16 h where continuous lighting is used. An intermittent programme can be used with fewer hours of light appropriately spaced. Minimum light intensity is 54 lx with some production responses noted at greater intensities. More energy efficient lamp sources such as fluorescent or sodium vapour lamps can be used as long as the spectral output of the lamp is considered.

Lighting for males

Lighting programmes for breeder males are different from those for breeder hens as they do not require short days to become reproductively active (Ogasawara, Wilson and Asmundson, 1962; Polley *et al.*, 1962). Light programmes still need to consider alteration of photoperiod and light intensity to insure availability of high quality semen at the onset of egg production and at the end of the hatching egg season.

Male breeder candidates can be raised under either 12 h of light (12L:12D) or with restricted lighting (6L:18D). Research results concerning the advantages of using a restricted programme prior to light stimulation have been inconclusive. Restricted lighting can be used as a tool to synchronize semen production in the males or to hold them out of production until needed. Males can begin semen production as early as 22–24 weeks of age when held on 12–15 h of light (Cecil, 1984; Polley *et al.*, 1962). Males on restricted light (6L:18D) during 18–28 weeks of age and light stimulated with 14L:10D at 29 weeks of age had a shorter time interval in reaching peak semen production compared with males reared on 12L:12D (Cecil, 1984).

Some research has indicated greater amounts of semen volume and/or sperm concentration when males are held on short days. Leighton and Meyer (1984) found sperm cell concentration was increased significantly for Large White males light restricted from 12 to 28 weeks of age with 6 h of light (10.8 lx). In another study with Large White males, both semen volume and concentration were increased when the males were light restricted (6L:18D) when compared with those receiving 12 h during rearing from 12 to 30 weeks of age (Leighton and Jones, 1984).

No advantage has been noted with light restriction in studies by McCartney *et al.* (1961), Ogasawara, Wilson and Asmundson (1962) and Polley *et al.* (1962). Some studies have observed poorer performance with restricted lighting of males during rearing. Fertility was found to decrease with the use of restricted lighting (Polley *et al.*, 1962) and Cecil (1984) observed lower numbers of sperm per ejaculate from previously restricted males (6L:18D, 18–28 weeks of age) compared with a programme of 12L:12D from 18 to 28 weeks of age.

Age at lighting

Several studies have noted that light restricted males will have a delay in attaining sexual maturity (McCartney *et al.*, 1961; Nestor and Brown, 1971; Ogasawara, Wilson and Asmundson, 1962; Wall and Jones, 1976). Research (Nestor and Brown, 1971; Wall and Jones, 1976) has indicated that males should be lit 7 weeks in advance of when semen will be needed for insemination to assure adequate semen production.

Optimum body weights

Light restriction used in combination with nutritional programmes designed to limit body weight need further investigation. Restriction of body weight through nutritional means has been noted to delay the start of semen production and lower initial semen production in comparison to full fed males. Reduced testes weight has been observed in restricted fed males (Hulet and Brody, 1986; Krueger *et al.*, 1977), indicating a relationship of onset of sexual maturity with body size. A programme restricting both body weight and light may severely delay the onset of semen production. Reduced semen production of breeder males severely limited in body weight was not corrected for by use of a full lighting regime of 14L:10D (Cecil, 1984) compared with a restricted light programme. There are insufficient data to indicate the interaction between lighting (intensity and programme) and bodyweight restriction although the relationship between the initiation of semen production and light programme suggests the use of a lighting programme without light restriction and using higher light intensity where semen production appears to be suboptimal.

Photostimulation

In situations where the light has been restricted either artificially or through exposure to decreasing natural daylengths, the males will need to be photostimulated 3–4 weeks in advance of the lighting of the hens. The hours of light to stimulate and maintain production covers a range of 8–16 h/day with 8 h appearing minimal. Winter hatched males reared on 8 h of light starting at 18 weeks of age performed as well as males reared on 12 h/day although a slight delay in sexual maturity was observed in winter hatched males at 30 weeks of age (Krueger *et al.*, 1977). Eight hours of light (25 lx) starting at 16 weeks of age was found to be insufficient for Large White males (Dobrescu, 1986). Lowered semen volume and concentration were observed when compared with males receiving 14 h of light. Yellow semen syndrome was also prevalent in the males receiving 8 h of daily light.

Leighton and Jones (1984) found no effect of 12 versus 16 h of light applied during the breeding season with males exposed to 6 or 12 h of light between 12 and 30 weeks of age. Brown (1982) found no difference in semen volume and concentration in males reared at 12 h (20–26 weeks) and maintained at 12 or 14 h light (5.4 lx) from 20 to 60 weeks of age. In studies by Ogasawara, Wilson and Asmundson (1962), 12–14 h of light was found to be sufficient. Increasing daylength to longer hours appears to encourage photorefractoriness. Weekly hourly increases in light from 14 to 20 h/day decreased semen production (Ogasawara, Wilson and Asmundson, 1962).

Males should be maintained on the same light schedule (10–16 h) throughout their life or alternatively be given restricted light followed by increased light. However, they should not be exposed to decreasing light as they approach sexual maturity.

As observed with hens, photostimulatory light need not be given on a continuous basis but can be given intermittently with appropriate spacing of the light periods. Siopes (1983) demonstrated that as little as 4 h of light given intermittently

(2L:11D:2L:9D) resulted in volumes and sperm concentrations similar to those of the controls. In addition, there were reduced electrical and feed costs savings. El Halawani and Graham (1985) also found no difference in semen production between a continuous programme (16L:8D) and an intermittent programme (2(4L:8D)).

Light intensity during production

Light intensity effects on semen production have been noted. Higher light intensity appears to stimulate males into earlier semen production. Males reared under natural light and daylength came into production more quickly than males raised under similar hours of artificial light at 43 lx (Wall and Jones, 1976). Leighton and Meyer (1984) also found males reared under natural and increasing daylength produced more semen (volume and concentration) than males reared at 12 h of light (10.8 lx). Higher light intensity (100 lx) at the time of lighting (30 weeks) improved the semen production of low bodyweight males (12.6 kg) compared with performance at 6.5 lx (Cecil, 1986).

The seasonal decline in semen production of males reared and maintained under natural lighting has been attributed to higher light intensity (Krueger et al., 1977; Wall and Jones, 1976). In the study by Wall and Jones (1976), males reared under naturally increasing light went out of production sooner and semen production decreased when compared with males reared on similar hours of artificial light but at a lower light intensity of 43 lx. When males exposed to natural light starting at 28 weeks of age (from June to November) and supplemented with artificial light (intensities of 5.3 or 43 lx) when needed to provide 14 h of daily light were compared to males kept under artificial light (5.3 and 43 lx), semen volume decreased over the 6-month experimental period (Jones, Hughes and Wall, 1977).

In light controlled buildings, Brown (1982) observed lowered semen volume and concentration in males lit (14L:10D) with a light intensity of 10.8 lx compared with 5.4 lx. In Large White males lighted with 13, 30 or 56 lx, semen volume over a 24-week period was reduced at intensities of 30 or 56 lx (Nestor and Brown, 1971). However for medium size males, higher light intensity (55 lx versus 19 lx) resulted in greater semen volume and initial sperm concentration. Cherms et al. (1981) noted lower semen production at 15 lx compared to 1 lx in different housing environments.

Higher light intensity may not always be detrimental. Light intensity ranging from 10.8 to 86.1 lx during 12–30 weeks at either 6 or 12 h of light had no effect on semen volume or concentration (Leighton and Jones, 1984). In the same study when breeders, increased semen volumes were obtained from males lit with 43 and 86.1 lx compared with 10.8 lx. No differences were found by Jones, Hughes and Wall (1977) in lighting of breeder males with 5.3 and 43 lx. Leighton (1980) also found no differences in the performance of males lit (16L:8D) with either 21.6 or 86.1 lx. Nestor and Brown (1971) noted that with frequent collections (every 2 days) a light intensity of 13 lx was insufficient to maintain semen production at levels observed with 30 lx.

In summary, a lighting programme for breeder males could utilize a restricted lighting programme prior to lighting. Alternatively, males can be reared on light cycles of 12L:12D at minimal intensity of 5.4 lx. Light stimulation should occur 3–4 weeks prior to lighting of the hens with an increase in light hours to 14L:10D. With an intermittent light programme as little as 4 h/day can be used. Light intensities greater than 5.4 lx can bring males into production much more quickly but further information is needed on the effect of high light intensity on late season semen production.

Broodiness

Following light stimulation the hen responds to the increase in daylength by starting to lay approximately 16–21 days later. Broodiness (incubation behaviour) may become a problem after the hens have been in lay for 3–4 weeks with the first major peak occurring at this time. Nestor, Bacon and Renner (1986) noted that 63% of the hens became broody after 4–8 weeks of production. Several periods of broodiness may occur during the egg production season. In one report (Nestor and Renner, 1966), the incidence of broodiness was monitored in two commercial flocks and 1.3 broody periods (that is, pauses of 5 or more consecutive days) were observed per hen in 84 days of production and 2.9 broody periods per hen in 180 days of production.

Broodiness, unless prevented, results in a lapse of egg production for at least 12 to 13 days (Haller and Cherms, 1961) due to ovarian regression. If left untreated, broody hens will stop egg production and exhibit the behaviours of incubation and nest protection. Feed and water consumption will be greatly decreased due to the amount of time spent on the nest. Regression of both the ovarian and reproductive tracts will continue and the hen will exhibit tight, hard pubic bones, and a small, dry cloaca. Eventually, the hen will become photorefractory (El Halawani *et al.*, 1984).

The degree to which broodiness decreases egg production is dependent on the number of days spent broody. Broodiness decreased egg production by 7.5, 12.1, 29.2, and 45.4% compared with non-broody hens as the number of days broody increased to 1–14, 15–28, 29–42 and over 43 days, respectively (Haller and Cherms, 1961). Likewise, treatment for broodiness has resulted in more eggs per hen than with non-treated broody hens (Nestor, Bacon and Renner, 1986). In genetic lines demonstrating high and low incidences of broodiness (RBC1 and RBC2 respectively) treatment for broodiness resulted in an average of 13 eggs per hen more in 180 days of production (5-year average).

Hens which go broody may not necessarily be poor producers prior to the onset of broodiness (Cogger, Burke and Ogren, 1979). For 15 days prior to the onset of broodiness, the egg production of the broody hens averaged 0.63 eggs per hen per day compared with their laying counterparts of 0.51 eggs.

Identification of broodiness is based upon the detection of increased nesting activity of the transitional broody hen. The increase in nesting frequency occurs 7–9 days before the last oviposition. Haller and Cherms (1961) found that nest visits increased from 2.2 per day on the 9th day before the last egg and increased to 3.5 visits per day during the last 3 days. After the last egg was laid, daily nest visits averaged 4.4. Similar results have been reported by Cherms and Stoller (1974) and Cogger, Burke and Ogren (1979).

Successful broody treatment requires removal of the opportunity for the hen to nest since nesting activity encourages high circulating levels of prolactin (El Halawani *et al.*, 1980a), a hormone which is associated with the onset and maintenance of broodiness. Broodiness is discouraged by the removal of the hen from the flock and placing her in an altered environment. Several methods exist such as use of floor pens without nests and different type floors (wire or wood slats), cages, bright continuous lights and noise. Experimental treatment with chemicals has also been tested.

In a comparison of broody treatment it appears several methods are effective but the effectiveness is dependent on early detection of the broody hen. The importance of early detection was observed by Cherms and Stoller (1974). As the number of non-productive days following the onset of broodiness increased from 1 to 3 days, a trend was observed for a lowered success rate of the broody treatment in returning hens to production.

Nestor and Renner (1966) also found that the length of the broody period and total days broody could also be decreased by the early detection of broodiness. In the first study broody hens were identified as those which had not laid an egg for 3 to 4 days or those which were difficult to open at insemination time. In the second study, hens were considered broody if they were on the nest at the end of the photocycle, had not laid an egg that day and were without a hard-shelled egg *in utero* after palpation. All broody hens were placed in a broody pen (wire or wood slatted floor with continuous light for 36 h). Three more eggs per hen were obtained in an 84-day period for the second study than for the first.

Using the above system of broody detection, Nestor, Bacon and Renner (1971) found no difference in effectiveness of the following broody treatments applied for 39 or 63 h: cages (14 h light at 186 lx), wire floor (24 h light at 189 lx), slatted floor (24 h of either low intensity light (40.9 lx) or high intensity light (215 lx) and cages within laying pen (14 h light at 37.7 lx).

In hens that had not laid for 3 days, treatment with continuous lights for 24 h and placing hens in a pen with a wire floor for 7 days brought the treated hens back into production in 13.5 and 14.5 days repectively after treatment had ended. Placement of hens in a litter floor pen was less successful (Haller and Cherms, 1961). Jeannoutot and Adams (1961) found that exposure of hens to sounds of flying jet planes and placement of hens in a broody coup (4 days) decreased the number of days spent on the nest and increased egg production following treatment compared with non-treated controls.

Treatment with bright lights (216 lx) for 72–96 h was found to be more effective than 24–48 h treatment in reducing nesting activity (Cherms and Stoller, 1974). Twenty-four hour light treatment of hens found in the nest at the end of the photocycle and then locked into the nest at that time worsened the incidence of broodiness and increased the number of hens going out of production (Nestor, Bacon and Renner, 1976).

El Halawani *et al.* (1980c) compared three broody treatments: slatted floor broody pen (15 h of light, 55 lx), individual wire cages (24 h light, 200 W bulbs), and moving broody hens outdoors during the cold winter months in Minnesota. All three treatments were equally effective in breaking up broodiness.

Treatment length was demonstrated to be critical by El Halawani *et al.* (1980a) in that broody hens in advanced stages of broodiness (nesting, no eggs for 2 weeks) and placed in cages showed decreases in prolactin levels within 12 h of the change. However, hens quickly resumed nesting when removed from cages after 24 and 48 h of treatment and prolactin levels increased to pre-confinement levels. Hens in cages for 96 h had the lowest of levels of prolactin. Unfortunately the time taken to return to production of these groups was not monitored in this study.

Since the development and maintenance of broodiness is under hormonal control, some treatments have tested the use of chemicals to correct the broody condition. Pimozide (dopamine receptor blocking agent) was administered once by either subcutaneous injection (4 mg/hen) or oral administration (6 mg/hen) to broody hens identified as having nested for four or more times in 1 day. Egg production increased and nesting frequency was decreased when compared with non-treated broody controls (Millam *et al.*, 1980). Treatment of broody hens (incubating) with an oral administration of parachlorophenylalanine (inhibitor of serotonin synthesis) in gelatin capsules (50 mg/kg) for 3 successive days decreased prolactin levels following administration with the lowest levels reached at 7 days. In seven of the eight treated hens oviposition was restored between 18 and 31 days later (El Halawani *et al.*, 1983).

Administration of clomiphene citrate (6 mg/kg body weight) abolished broody behaviour 48 to 72 h after treatment for 5 consecutive days with egg production increased significantly above that of placebo treated controls (Robinzon *et al.*, 1984; Renner *et al.* (1987), with a similar treatment regimen of broody hens (genetic RBC1 and RBC2 lines), detected as being broody at an earlier stage found no effect when compared with broody hens treated for broodiness by the removal to cages under high intensity light for 24 h.

Treatment of broody hens (those hens found on nest in early morning rounds and which could not be everted) with commercial aspirin tablets (one, two or three tablets of 325 mg per tablet) administered orally was unsuccessful in breaking up broodiness (Cattley, Jones and Barnett, 1976).

Due to the high labour requirement of identifying individual broody hens, methods to control broodiness on a flock basis would be preferred. Pimozide given to recycled hens starting 17 days after the first egg on a regular basis (twice weekly for 8 weeks) without regard to nesting status had no effect on egg production, nesting frequency or broodiness (Millam *et al.*, 1980). Application of 2 days continuous light to the regular lighting regime (14L:8D) every 2 weeks, lowered egg production and had no effect on nesting frequency or broodiness (Bacon and Nestor, 1976).

One method which has had some success in the field is rotation of flocks from building to building every 10 to 14 days starting just before the first broody peak. Preliminary results (El Halawani, Noll and Silsby, 1987), where blood levels of prolactin were monitored in commercial flocks prior to rotation and following rotation (5 days later), have indicated a drop in prolactin levels. Individual broody treatment was also effective in this trial.

Other management factors that may encourage broodiness are environmental temperature, age at lighting, nest design and infrequent egg collection. Hens reared at 30°C versus 10°C started production 3 to 4 days earlier and exhibited greater levels of broodiness (El Halawani *et al.*, 1984). Other reports have indicated seasonal differences in egg production and broodiness with broodiness more prevalent in the late spring and summer months. Early lighting of hens (large type) at 28 weeks versus 30 weeks of age was observed to lead to more broody periods (Thomason, Leighton and Mason, 1972).

Nest designs which provide the hen with a darkened warm environment will encourage broodiness. Cherms (1962, 1982a) suggests a nest design to allow good air circulation, and with lights overhead on a separate circuit to allow the nest area to be lit once the hens have become accustomed to using the nest.

In general several broody treatments are effective but successful treatment is dependent on accurate and early detection of broody hens which can be very laborious. Methods are needed that inhibit or slow the development of broodiness on a flock basis.

References

Asmundson, V. S. and Moses, B. D. (1950). Influence of length of day on reproduction in turkey hens. *Poultry Science*, **29**, 34–41

Bacon, W. L. and Nestor, K. E. (1976). Two days of continuous light every two weeks has no beneficial effect on turkey egg production. *Poultry Science*, **55**, 1986–1988

Bacon, W. L. and Nestor, K. E. (1977). The effect of various lighting treatments or the presence of toms on reproductive performance of hen turkeys. *Poultry Science*, **56**, 415–420

Bacon, W. L. and Nestor, K. E. (1981). Modification of an intermittent lighting program for laying turkey hens. *Poultry Science*, **60**, 482–484

Bacon, W. L. and Nestor, K. E. (1982). Intermittent lighting and in-cage broodiness treatment for turkey hens in cages. *Poultry Science*, **61**, 785–789

Brown, K. I. (1982). Lighting male turkeys and other management factors affecting semen production. *Ohio Agricultural Research and Development Center. Dept. Series*, No. **80**, pp. 76–87

Cattley, R. C., Jones, J. E. and Barnett, B. D. (1976). Inefficacy of aspirin in reducing broodiness in turkeys. *Poultry Science*, **55**, 1997–1998

Cecil, H. C. (1984). Effect of dietary protein and light restriction on body weight and semen production of breeder male turkeys. *Poultry Science*, **63**, 1175–1183

Cecil, H. C. (1986). Effect of light intensity during the breeder period on semen production of low weight and normal weight breeder turkeys. *Poultry Science*, **65**, 1900–1904

Cherms, F. L. (1962). Care of hatching eggs and broody hens. *Poultry Fact Sheet* No. 29, University of Wisconsin

Cherms, F. L. (1982a). New look at lighting. *Turkey World*, 14–16

Cherms, F. L. (1982b). Effect of intermittent lighting program on turkey breeder hens. *Poultry Science*, **61**, 1437

Cherms, F. L. and Stoller, M. G. (1974). Effect of intense light on broody turkeys, pp. 427–428 in *Proceedings of XV World Poultry Congress*, New Orleans

Cherms, F. L., Stoller, M. E., MacIlraith, J. J., Africa, K. C. and Halloran, H. R. (1981). Reduction of body weight during growing and holding periods and subsequent semen production and fertility in turkeys. *Reproduction and Nutrition Developments*, **21**(6B), 1049–1058

Clayton, G. A. and Robertson, A. (1960). Light induction of out of season reproduction in the turkey. *British Poultry Science*, **1**, 17–23

Cogger, E. A., Burke, W. H. and Ogren, L. A. (1979). Serum luteinizing hormone, progesterone, and estradiol levels in relation to broodiness in the turkey (*Meleagris gallopavo*). *Poultry Science*, **58**, 1355–1360

Dobrescu, O. (1986). Photoperiod, diet, and method of feeding on reproduction. *Poultry Science*, **65**, 559–564

El Halawani, M. E., Walbel, P. E., Burke, W. H. and Shoffner, R. N. (1974). Influence of ambient environment and nutrition on development of growing turkeys, and their subsequent reproductive performance. *Ohio Agricultural Research and Development Center Summary*, **80**, 134

El Halawani, M. E., Wiabel, P. E., Burke, W. H. and Shoffner, R. N. (1975). Effect of pre-breeder light treatment on egg production in turkey breeders. *Minnesota Agricultural Experiment Station Miscellaneous Report*, **134**, 20–24

El Halawani, M. E., Waibel, P. E. and Kramer, S. L. (1978). Influence of light intensity, range rearing, and nutrition on reproductive performance of turkey breeder hens during the pre-breeding period. *Minnesota Agricultural Experiment Station Miscellaneous Report*, **165**, 19–25

El Halawani, M. E., Burke, W. H. and Dennison, P. T. (1980a). Effect of nest-deprivation on serum prolactin level in nesting female turkeys. *Biology of Reproduction*, **23**, 118–123

El Halawani, M. E., Waibel, P. E. and Noll, S. L. (1980b). Effects of source of light, air cooling and nutrition on breeder hen turkeys' reproductive performance. *Proceedings of Virgina Turkey Days 1980*, 4–8

El Halawani, M. E., Burke, W. H., Dennison, P. T., Silsby, J. L. and Millam, J. R. (1980c). Physiological control of broodiness. *Proceedings of Virginia Turkey Days 1980*, 61–66

El Halawani, M. E., Silsby, J. L., Fehrer, S. C. and Behnke, E. J. (1983). Reinitiation of ovulatory cycles in incubating female turkeys by an inhibitor of serotonin synthesis, *p*-chlorophenylalanine. *Biology of Reproduction*, **28**, 221–228

El Halawani, M. E., Silsby, J. L., Behnke, E. J. and Fehrer, S. C. (1984). Effect of ambient temperature on serum prolactin and luteinizing hormone levels during the reproductive life cycle of the female turkey (*Meleagris gallopavo*). *Biology of Reproduction*, **30**, 809–815

El Halawani, M. E. and Graham, E. (1985). MTGA research progress reports. *Gobbles* (June) 1985, 4

El Halawani, M. E., Noll, S. L. and Silsby, J. L. (1987). Circulating prolactin: An index of broody management program effectiveness. *Proceedings of Minnesota Conference on Turkey Research*, Minnesota Agricultural Experimental Station Miscellaneous Publications 43–1987, pp. 90–92

Haller, R. W. and Cherms, F. L. Jr. (1961). A comparison of several treatments on terminating broodiness in Broad-Breasted Bronze turkeys. *Poultry Science*, **40**, 115–163

Harper, J. A. and Parker, J. E. (1957). Changes in seasonal egg production of turkeys induced through controlled light exposure and forced molting. *Poultry Science*, **36**, 967–973

Hulet, R. M. and Brody, T. B. (1986). Semen quality and fat accumulation in prepuberal and postpuberal male turkeys as affected by restricted feeding. *Poultry Science*, **65**, 1972–1976

Jeannoutot, D. W. and Adams, J. L. (1961). Progesterone *versus* treatment by high intensity sound as methods of controlling broodiness in Broad-Breasted Bronze turkeys. *Poultry Science*, **40**, 517–521

Jones, J. E., Hughes, B. L. and Wall, K. A. (1977). Effect of light intensity and source on tom reproduction. *Poultry Science*, **56**, 1417–1420

Jones, J. E., Hughes, B. L., Thurston, R. J., Hess, R. A. and Froman, D. P. (1982). The effects of red and white light during the prebreeder and breeder periods on egg production and feed consumption in Large White turkeys. *Poultry Science*, **61**, 1930–1932

Krueger, K. K., Owen, J. A., Krueger, C. E. and Ferguson, T. M. (1977). Effect of feed or light restriction during the growing and breeding cycles on the reproductive performance of Broad Breasted White turkey males. *Poultry Science*, **56**, 1566–1574

Krueger, K. K., Burnard, T. P. and McIntyre, D. R. (1982). Effects of continuous versus intermittent light on egg production in turkey hens. *Poultry Science*, **61**, 1495

Leighton, A. T. Jr. (1980). Light environment, semen volume and frequency of insemination on reproduction of turkeys. *Proceedings of 1980 Virginia Turkey Days*, pp. 54–58

Leighton, A. T. and Jones, M. C. (1984). Effect of light environment on semen volume, semen concentration and molting of turkey breeder males. *Poultry Science*, **63** (Suppl. 1), 137

Leighton, A. T. Jr. and Meyer, G. B. (1984). Effect of light environment during the adolescent period on subsequent semen volume and concentration of male turkeys. *Poultry Science*, **63**, 806–812

Leighton, A. T. Jr. and Potter, L. M. (1969). Reproductive performance of turkeys subjected to blackout *versus* brownout restricted light conditions. *Poultry Science*, **48**, 505–514

Leighton, A. T. Jr. and Shoffner, R. N. (1961a). Effect of light regime and age on reproduction of turkeys. 1. Effect of 15, 24 hour and restricted light treatment. *Poultry Science*, **40**, 861–870

Leighton, A. T. Jr. and Shoffner, R. N. (1961b). Effect of light regime and age on reproduction of turkeys. 2. Restricted *vs.* unrestricted light. *Poultry Science*, **40**, 871–884

Leighton, A. T. Jr. and Shoffner, R. N. (1964). Effect of light regime and age on reproduction of turkeys. 3. Restricted light on yearling hens. *Poultry Science*, **43**, 49–53

Marsden, S. J., Cowen, N. S. and Lucas, L. M. (1962). Effect of gradual and abrupt lengthening of photoperiod on reproductive responses of turkeys. *Poultry Science*, **41**, 1864–1868

Marsden, S. J. and Lucas, L. M. (1964). Effect of short-day or low-intensity light treatments on reproduction of fall-hatched turkeys in two environments. *Poultry Science*, **43**, 434–441

McCartney, M. G. (1971). Reproduction of turkeys as affected by age at lighting and light intensity. *Poultry Science*, **50**, 661–662

McCartney, M. G., Sanger, V. L., Brown, K. I. and Chamberlin, V. D. (1961). Photoperiodism as a factor in the reproduction of the turkey. *Poultry Science*, **40**, 368–376

Millam, J. R., Burke, W. H., El Halawani, M. E. and Ogren, L. A. (1980). Preventing broodiness in turkey hens with a dopamine receptor blocking agent. *Poultry Science*, **59**, 1126–1131

Nestor, K. E. and Brown, K. I. (1971). Semen production in turkeys. *Poultry Science*, **50**, 1705–1712

Nestor, K. E. and Renner, P. A. (1966). New management system for broody turkey hens. *Ohio Reports*, **51**, 83–84

Nestor, K. E., Bacon, W. and Renner, P. A. (1971). Influence of light intensity and length of light day in the broody pen on broodiness and egg production of turkeys. *Poultry Science*, **50**, 1689–1693

Nestor, K. E., Bacon, W. L. and Renner, P. A. (1976). Night lighting of nesting turkey hens does not reduce broodiness. *Poultry Science*, **55**, 1989–1990

Nestor, K. E., Bacon, W. L. and Renner, P. A. (1986). The influence of time of application of broody hen treatments on egg production of turkeys. *Poultry Science*, **65**, 1405–1409

Noll, S. L., El Halawani, M. E. and Waibel, P. E. (1981). Influence of prebreeder lighting (source and intensity) and nutritional supplementation on the reproductive performance of turkey hens. *Minnesota Agricultural Experiment Station Miscellaneous Report*, **179**, 42–45

Ogasawara, F. X., Wilson, W. O. and Asmundson, V. S. (1962). The effect of restricting light during the adolescent period on reproductive performance in turkeys subsequently exposed to 12, 14 and 20 hour day. *Poultry Science*, **41**, 1858–1863

Payne, L. F. and McDaniel, G. R. (1958). Fluorescent lights for turkey breeders. *Poultry Science*, **37**, 722–726

Polley, C. R., Shoffner, R. N., Burger, R. E. and Johnson, E. L. (1962). Light restriction in turkey management. 3. Male performance. *Poultry Science*, **41**, 1570–1573

Potter, L. M. and Leighton, A. T. Jr. (1973). Effects of diet and light during the prebreeder period, and of diet during the breeder period on turkey breeder performance. *Poultry Science*, **52**, 1805–1813

Renner, P. A., Nestor, K. E., Bacon, W. L. and Havenstein, G. B. (1987). Research note: clomiphene-citrate does not reduce broodiness of turkey hens. *Poultry Science*, **66**, 558–560

Robinzon, B., Shafir, Z., Perek, M. and Snapir, N. (1984). The effect of clomiphene-citrate on broody turkey hens. *Poultry Science*, **63**, 2268–2270

Shoffner, R. N., Polley, C. R., Burger, R. E. and Johnson, E. L. (1962). Light regulation in turkey management. 2. Female reproductive performance. *Poultry Science*, **41**, 1563–1577

Siopes, T. D. (1983). Effect of intermittent lighting on energy savings and semen characteristics of breeder tom turkeys. *Poultry Science*, **62**, 2265–2270

Siopes, T. D. (1984a). The effect of high and low intensity cool-white fluorescent lighting on the reproductive performance of turkey breeder hens. *Poultry Science*, **63**, 920–926

Siopes, T. D. (1984b). The effect of full-spectrum fluorescent lighting on reproductive traits of caged turkey hens. *Poultry Science*, **63**, 1122–1128

Siopes, T. D. (1987). Personal communication. North Carolina State University, Dept. of Poultry Sci., Raleigh, N.C.

Thomason, D. M., Leighton, A. T. Jr. and Mason, J. P. Jr. (1972). A study of certain environmental factors on the reproductive performance of large white turkeys. *Poultry Science*, **51**, 1438–1449

Wall, K. A. and Jones, J. E. (1976). Effect of restricted daylengths during the growing period on semen quality and fertility of turkey toms. *Poultry Science*, **55**, 425–430

Wilson, W. O., Ogasawara, F. X. and Asmundson, V. S. (1962). Artificial control of egg production by photoperiod. *Poultry Science*, **41**, 1168–1175

Wilson, W. O., Ogasawara, F. X. and Woodard, A. E. (1967). Increasing egg production in winter hatched turkeys by a restricted light treatment. *Poultry Science*, **46**, 46–52

Woodard, A. E., Abplanalp, H., Stinnett, V. and Snyder, R. L. (1974). The effect of age at lighting on egg production and pausing in turkey hens. *Poultry Science*, **53**, 1681–1686

Part II
Growing the commercial turkey

Chapter 8

The growth of turkeys

G. C. Emmans

> One, two
> Miss a few,
> Ninety-nine
> A hundred

  (Children's counting rhyme)

Introduction

An immature turkey can usefully be seen as seeking to progress to a final equilibrium state called maturity; when mature it seeks a zero rate of state change. The first section of this chapter describes the mature state of turkeys in both chemical and physical terms.

A turkey at hatching has a potential path to maturity which it will take providing that it is kept in conditions such that it can. (The description of pre-hatching growth is fascinating but is not dealt with here.) As the immature turkey moves along its potential growth path its composition will change. The second section considers the rates at which an immature turkey will change in size and composition as it progresses along its potential growth path.

To attain its potential growth path a turkey needs resources from its feed (energy and nutrients) and environment (heat dissipation). The next section is concerned with the scaling of these resources and the rates at which they are needed by a given kind of turkey at a given degree of maturity. The problems of variation due to time for a given turkey, and between individuals at a time, are discussed.

A set of actual conditions under which a turkey is kept may not be such that it can attain its potential. Those aspects of feed composition and environment which may prevent the turkey attaining its potential are discussed in the last section.

Some of the arguments put forward are those of Emmans and Fisher (1986).

The mature state

Turkeys vary substantially in mature size. Within a stock males are about twice as big as females and, within a sex, appreciable effects of stock exist. Such large differences in mature size could be accompanied by systematic variations in composition. Hocking *et al.* (1985) reported the compositions of a wide range of chicken stocks but, until recently, no such data existed for turkeys.

Any apparently systematic effects of mature size on composition may be spurious. For example, a stock selected for growth rate, and a high proportion of breast meat, will be both larger at maturity and have a higher yield of breast meat than an unselected stock. But its higher yield of breast meat will not be because it is larger, rather because it has been selected to have a higher yield.

The recently collected data of Oritsegbubemi (1987) are used here to describe the mature composition of turkeys.

Material

Turkeys of both sexes, aged 49 or 50 weeks, were taken from breeder flocks. Of the seven lines, four came from one breeding company and three from another. For each of the 14 kinds of turkey (seven lines × two sexes) four individual birds were physically dissected and a further four chemically analysed after bleeding and plucking. As the losses due to bleeding and plucking were only crudely estimated only the composition of the bled and plucked body (PBW) was considered.

No control over the feeding and management was exercised from hatch to slaughter. It is, therefore, possible that the data reflect, in part, differences which are not genetic. The correlations between the sexes across stocks were calculated as indications of the extent to which the observed differences may well have been truly genetic.

Chemical composition

The empty body — in this case after bleeding and plucking — of an animal can usefully be seen as being composed, in chemical terms, of the lipid-free dry matter (protein, ash and a little carbohydrate), water and lipid. The protein contents of the lipid-free dry matter, and the water contents of the lipid-free bodies of mature turkeys are given in *Table 8.1* (Oritsegbubemi, 1987). There were no appreciable

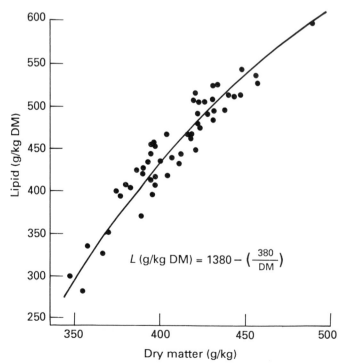

$$L \text{ (g/kg DM)} = 1380 - \left(\frac{380}{DM}\right)$$

Figure 8.1 Lipid in dry matter versus dry matter in mature turkeys (from Oritsegbubemi, 1987)

Table 8.1 The chemical composition of the plucked and bled bodies of both sexes of seven lines of turkey

Line	Plucked, bled weight[a] (kg)		Protein in LFDM[d] (g/kg)		Water in LF body[d] (g/kg)		Lipid (g/kg)		Body protein[b] (kg)	
	Male	Female	Male	Female	Male	Female	Male	Female	Male	Female
3	29.03	15.84	831	825	731	723	185	199	5.29	2.90
7	25.08	12.61	807	823	730	732	148	199	4.66	2.23
4[c]	23.84	12.90	838	798	724	723	195	200	4.30	2.28
2	20.32	9.84	806	819	721	718	185	181	3.72	1.86
6	20.28	9.53	827	827	729	728	244	167	3.44	1.78
5	17.02	8.53	832	834	717	730	209	182	3.16	1.57
1	13.79	6.31	821	814	724	716	184	131	2.55	1.27
Mean			821.5 (3.9)[f]		724.8 (1.0)[f]		186.0 (5.2)[f]			
r_{mf}[e]	0.99		−0.18 NS		0.19 NS		−0.27 NS		0.98	
Male/female	2.01 (0.05)[f]		1.00 (0.01)[f]		1.00 (0.004)[f]		1.10 (0.10)[f]		1.97 (0.03)[f]	

(Oritsegbubemi, 1987)

[a] Means of eight birds of which four were chemically analysed
[b] From mean weights and protein contents
[c] Five males in all, of which two were analysed
[d] LFDM = lipid-free dry matter; LF = lipid free
[e] Correlation between male and female means across lines
[f] SE

differences due to sex or line. The lipid contents of the PBW are also given in *Table 8.1*. There were some significant differences, but these were not systematic as is shown by the low correlation between the male and female values across lines.

The variation in composition between birds was due to the extent that a lipid-free body of constant composition was diluted with lipid. This is indicated by the data for the individual birds in *Figure 8.1* where the lipid content of the dry matter is plotted against the dry matter content of the whole. The data are closely distributed around the line described by the equation:

$$\text{lipid in dry matter} = 1380 - (380/DM) \hspace{3cm} \text{g/kg} \quad (1)$$

which follows from (i) that lipid-free dry matter has 821.5 protein/kg, and (ii) that the water:protein ratio is 3.20:1.

The females had been laying and their lipid contents may reflect, in part, a lipid loss during egg production. The summary of the data in *Table 8.2* has assumed a lipid:protein ratio of 1.4:1 for females at first egg. As shown in *Table 8.1* the males were twice as large as the females in PBW and in bodyprotein weight; line effects on mature size were substantial.

Table 8.2 Summary of the chemical composition of male and female turkeys at maturity[a]

Measure[b]	Males	Females
LFDM/protein	1.22	1.22
Water/protein	3.21	3.21
Lipid/protein	1.0	1.4[c]
Contents (g/kg)		
Protein	184	172
Water	591	551
Lipid	184	240
Rest	41	37

[a] The plucked, bled body
[b] *LFDM* = lipid-free dry matter
[c] Increased from 1.0 at 50 weeks of age to estimate value at first egg

Physical composition

To avoid the inevitable correlations where compositions are expressed as proportions, the weights of the body components were related to that of carcass bone (CB). The component:CB ratios for mature turkeys (Oritsegbubemi, 1987) are shown in *Tables 8.3* and *8.4*.

There are large, and highly significant, differences between the lines in physical composition. These are related mainly to whether they are 'male' lines (lines 3, 4 and 7) or 'female' lines (lines 1, 2, 5 and 6) rather than to mature size *per se*. A summary of body composition is shown in *Table 8.5*.

The relationship between body protein and carcass bone

Body protein weight was taken as the chemical measure of size (*Table 8.1*) and carcass bone weight as the physical measure of size (*Table 8.3*). The relationship

139

Table 8.3 The physical composition of the eviscerated carcasses of male and female turkeys at maturity as component: carcass bone (CB) ratios

Line	Carcass bone (kg)		White meat[a] (g/kg CB)		Dark meat[b] (g/kg CB)		Skin (g/kg CB)		Eviscerated carcass (g/kg CB)	
	Male	Female	Male	Female	Male	Female	Male	Female	Male	Female
3	4.53	2.59	2432	2256	1618	1413	524	493	5574	5162
7	3.78	2.09	2324	2215	1832	1457	575	420	5731	5092
4	3.75	2.12	2265	2290	1456	1361	538	355	5269	5005
2	3.27	1.77	2034	1773	1555	1294	539	478	5128	4545
6	3.39	1.84	1765	1552	1406	1214	539	443	4710	4209
5	3.08	1.62	1580	1478	1358	1214	524	377	4462	4069
1	2.08	1.11	2136	1904	1482	1326	548	449	5166	4679
r_{mf}[c]	1.00		0.96		0.87		−0.05 NS		0.73	
Male/female (SE)	1.83 (0.02)		1.08 (0.02)		1.15 (0.02)		1.27 (0.06)		1.10 (0.01)	

(Oritsejbubemi, 1987)

[a] Breast meat was 0.8586 (SE 0.003) of total white meat
[b] Leg meat was 0.808 (SE 0.006) and 0.771 (SE 0.005) of total dark meat in males and females respectively
[c] Correlation between male and female means across lines

Table 8.4 The non-carcass components of male and female turkeys at maturity as component: carcass bone (CB) ratios

Line [a]	Giblets (g/kg CB)		Abdominal fat (g/kg CB)		Evisceration loss (g/kg CB)	
	Male	Female	Male	Female	Male	Female
3	314	290	47	86	779	581
7	371	287	84	69	737	468
4	324	257	49	98	679	672
2	359	310	50	121	919	580
6	341	326	104	100	773	617
5	352	322	113	119	763	714
1	361	314	31	90	983	624
r_{mf} [b]	0.42 NS		0.20 NS		0.11 NS	
Male/female (SE)	1.15 (0.03)		0.72 (0.13)		1.34 (0.09)	

(Oritsegbubemi, 1987)

[a] Correlation between male and female values across lines
[b] Giblets are neck, liver, heart and gizzard

Table 8.5 Summary of the physical composition of mature turkeys

	Male	Female	$CV\%$ [a]
White meat/carcass bone (g/kg)	2077	1924	16.1
Dark meat/carcass bone (g/kg)	1531	1326	8.7
Skin/carcass bone (g/kg)	541	431	–
Giblets/carcass bone (g/kg)	346	301	–
Abdominal cat/carcass bone (g/kg)	68	98	–
Evisceration loss/carcass bone (g/kg)	805	608	–
Plucked, bled weight/carcass bone (kg/kg)	6.368	5.688	–
Carcass bone/PBW (kg/kg)	0.157	0.176	–

[a] Between line means within a sex

Table 8.6 The relationships between two measures of mature size: protein (BP_m) and carcass bone CB_m) weights

Line	Males			Females		
	BP_m (kg)	CB_m (kg)	CB_m/BP_m	BP_m (kg)	CB_m (kg)	CB_m/BP_m
3	5.29	4.33	0.819	2.90	2.59	0.893
7	4.66	3.62	0.777	2.23	2.13	0.955
4	4.30	3.77	0.877	2.28	2.17	0.952
2	3.72	3.15	0.847	1.86	1.78	0.957
6	3.44	3.42	0.994	1.78	1.80	1.011
5	3.16	3.00	0.949	1.57	1.63	1.038
1	2.55	2.11	0.827	1.27	1.11	0.874

between the two measures of size across the 14 turkey genotypes is shown in *Table 8.6.* The carcass bone:body protein ratio was lower in males than in females. The correlation between the male and female values was 0.75 which supported the idea of true genetic differences. The overall mean value, as a male equivalent, was 0.870 (SE=0.017) with a coefficient of variation among line means of 7.3%.

The path to maturity

When kept in non-limiting conditions an immature turkey will change in size and form with time in a way that defines its potential growth path. The time course of its size change is considered first in terms of live weight. In later sections its changes in composition with size are considered.

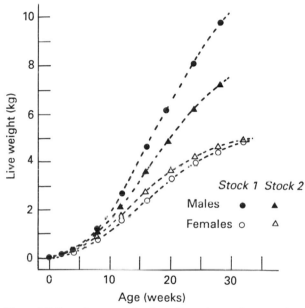

Figure 8.2 Growth curves of turkeys (from Asmundson, 1942)

The potential growth curve

The weight by time curves of both sexes of the smallest (Bourbon Red) and largest (Black × Black-winged Bronze) of the nine turkey stocks of Asmundson (1942) are shown in *Figure 8.2*. The fitted functions, which describe the data quite well, are Gompertz equations of the form:

$$W = A \exp\left(-\exp(-B(t - t^*))\right) \qquad\qquad \text{kg} \quad (2)$$

where 'exp' means 'e to the power of'. The parameter A is the final, mature, weight and t^* is the time (days after hatching) when $W = A/e$, where e, the base of natural logarithms, is 2.718. . . . The rate parameter, B per day, can be seen in several ways. When $t = t^*$ then $W = A/e$ and the growth rate, dW/dt, is then at a maximum given by:

$$(dW/dt)_{max} = B.A/e \qquad\qquad \text{kg/day} \quad (3)$$

The value of B can then be seen as being given by $(dW/dt)_{max} (e/A)/day$.

The estimates of the values of the three parameters for the stocks in *Figure 8.2* are given in *Table 8.7*. The A values for the males are about twice those of the females. The B values are greater for the females. Taylor's (1980) time scaling rule would suggest that a scaled rate parameter, $B^* = B.A^{0.27}$ would be uncorrelated with A and, as shown in *Table 8.7*, B^* is similar for both sexes within a stock. The mean value of B^* for the 1942 turkeys is 0.027.

Table 8.7 Estimated values of the growth parameters A (mature weight), B (rate parameter), and t^* (time constant) in different kinds of turkey

Stock	Ref.	Sex	A (kg)	B (per day)	t^* (days)	$B^* = B.A^{0.27}$	Age range used (weeks)
1	1	M	9.3	0.0153	108.5	0.0279	0–28
		F	5.3	0.0178	87.5	0.0279	0–32
2	1	M	13.3	0.0145	117.8	0.0292	0–28
		F	5.7	0.0153	103.1	0.0240	0–32
3	2	F	10.8	0.0215	72.7	0.0409	0–24
4	3	M	18.0	0.0216	80.3	0.0471	0–8
		F	8.4	0.0248	64.5	0.0440	0–14
5	3	M	25.0	0.0229	77.4	0.0546	0–4
		F	12.0	0.0242	69.5	0.0473	0–16
6	4	M	21.8	0.0218	81.0	0.0501	0–8
		F	10.3	0.0258	64.2	0.0487	0–18 (5 day delay, 8–10 weeks)
7	5	M	22.0	0.0182	–	0.0419	4–28 (4 day delay, 12–16 weeks)
8	6	M	17.7	0.0233	76.1	0.0507	1–6 (A from 34 to 37 weeks)
9	6	M	16.3	0.0229	74.2	0.0486	1–6 (A from 44 to 50 weeks)

1 Asmundson (1942)
2 Leeson and Summers (1980)
3 Bray (unpublished)

3 Jones *et al.* (unpublished)
5 Fisher (unpublished)
6 Okunuga (1980)

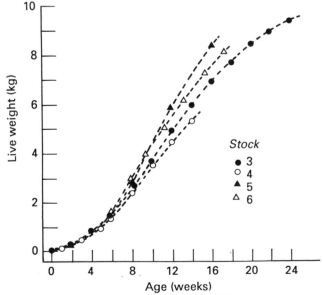

Figure 8.3 The growth curves of four stocks of female turkeys

Figure 8.3 shows the weight by time curves of four modern stocks of turkey females with their fitted Gompertz functions, which describe the data well. The estimated values of the three parameters are in *Table 8.7*.

Comparing the females of modern stocks with those from 1942 (*Table 8.7*), it can be seen that A has increased and that the scaled rate of maturing, B^*, is substantially higher than it was in 1942. Selection for a high weight at an age will tend to increase both A and B^* as birds with higher values of these parameters will be heavier at an age. The large increases in both A and B^* are thus likely to reflect past selection for weight at an age. The age at selection may well have been decreased with time.

Modern female turkeys (*Figure 8.3*) grow in the same way as older female turkeys (*Figure 8.2*) in that their (presumed potential) growth curves can be well described by Gompertz functions. Their absolute growth curves are, however, quite different — and differ from each other — because their values of the inherited growth parameters are different (*Table 8.7*).

Figure 8.4 shows the early part of the growth curves of modern male turkeys of three stocks (T. R. Bray, unpublished; Jones *et al.*, unpublished) kept under conditions presumed to be non-limiting. The data are well described by Gompertz functions with the values of the parameters given in *Table 8.7* for stocks 4, 5 and 6. As for the turkeys of Asmundson (1942) the A values for the males are about twice those of the females and the B^* values a little higher in the males.

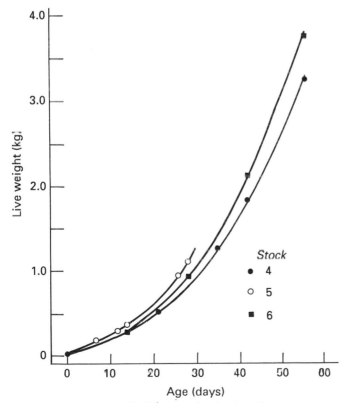

Figure 8.4 The early growth of three stocks of male turkeys

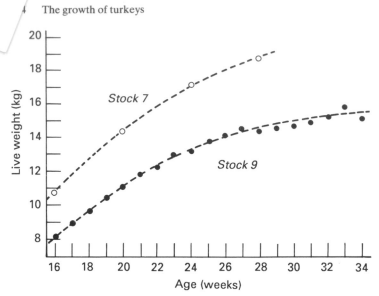

Figure 8.5 Late growth in male turkeys of two stocks

Figure 8.5 shows the later stages of growth for two sets of modern male turkeys (Okunuga, 1980; Fisher, unpublished). The fitted Gompertz functions describe the data well. The parameter values are in *Table 8.7*.

The Gompertz function has been seen to describe the post-hatching growth of modern female turkeys (*Figure 8.3*), that of male and female turkeys from 1942 (*Figure 8.2*) and the early (*Figure 8.4*), and late (*Figure 8.5*), stages of growth of modern male turkeys. It is reasonable to expect it also to describe the entire post-hatching growth of modern male turkeys but, for reasons discussed later, it is hard to demonstrate this from published data.

The Gompertz growth function

The Gompertz growth function can be written:

$$W = A.\exp(-\exp(B(t - t^*)))\qquad\qquad\text{kg}\quad(4)$$

as described earlier. The growth rate, dW/dt kg/day, can be found by differentiation to be:

$$dW/dt = B.W.\log_e(A/W)\qquad\qquad\text{kg/day}\quad(5)$$

It is convenient to define a degree of maturity in weight, u_w, as $u_w = W/A$ so that equation (5) becomes:

$$dW/dt = B.A.u_w\log_e(1/u_w)\qquad\qquad\text{kg/day}\quad(6)$$

The form of this equation is shown in *Figure 8.6*. Such a plot of actual data, where growth rate is measured over short periods of time, is useful in detecting growth checks. Equation (6) shows that, across genotypes, growth rate at a given degree of maturity is proportional to the product $(B.A)$.

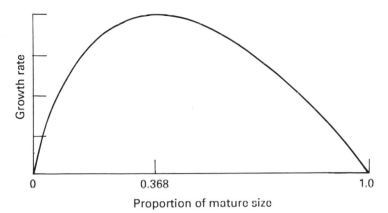

Figure 8.6 Growth rate in relation to size for a Gompertz growth function

The growth of the feather-free chemical body

Table 8.1 supported the idea that the composition of the lipid-free dry matter at maturity was constant across genotypes. The data of Okunuga (1980) and Fisher (unpublished) support the further idea that it does not vary with degree of maturity, as indicated by the data in *Table 8.8*. The small difference between the means in *Tables 8.1* and *8.8* is probably because the latter includes blood while the latter excludes it. The weight of the lipid-free dry matter can thus be estimated from the protein weight, P, as $k.P$ where $k = 1/0.8056 = 1.24$.

Table 8.8 The protein content of the lipid-free dry matter of male turkeys at different ages

Age (weeks)	n	Ref.	Protein in lipid-free dry matter (g/kg) Mean	SE
3, 4, 5	6	1	812	8.7
8	16	1	811	6.8
15	13	1	804	9.4
9	8	2	805	3.5
12	8	2	787	3.4
16	8	2	793	7.7
21	8	2	809	4.7
25	8	2	813	1.4
Overall mean			805.6	
Multiplier			1.24	

1 Okunuga (1980)
2 Fisher (unpublished)

An attractive possibility is that (i) the major components of the feather-free body, taken as protein (P), water (WA) and lipid (L) have potential growth curves which are Gompertz functions of time and, (ii) that each component has the same value for the rate parameter, B, for a given kind of turkey. It then follows that:

$$P = P_m \exp(-\exp(-B(t - t^*)))$$ kg   (7)

$$WA = WA_m \exp(-\exp(-B(t - t^*_{WA}))) \qquad\qquad \text{kg} \quad (8)$$

$$L = L_m \exp(-\exp(-B(t - t^*_l))) \qquad\qquad \text{kg} \quad (9)$$

and that the weight of the feather-free body, FFB, is then:

$$FFB = k.P + WA + L \qquad\qquad \text{kg} \quad (10)$$

The parameters in equations (7), (8) and (9) are the weights of the chemical components at maturity, P_m, WA_m and L_m, the rate parameter, B, and the three respective time constants, t^*_p, t^*_{wa} and t^*_l. If equations (7), (8) and (9) do correctly describe the potential growth curves of the chemical components then three important things follow. The first (the proof is not given here) is that the weights of water and lipid are simple power functions of the weight of protein potential growth:

$$WA = y_1 P^{c+1} \qquad\qquad \text{kg} \quad (11)$$

$$L = y_2 P^{b+1} \qquad\qquad \text{kg} \quad (12)$$

The second is that the values of y_1 and y_2 can be found at maturity, when $P = P_m$, $WA = WA_m$ and $L = L_m$, and equations (11) and (12) written as:

$$WAPR = WAPR_m u^c \qquad\qquad (13)$$

$$LPR = LPR_m u^b \qquad\qquad (14)$$

In these equations $WAPR$ and $WAPR_m$ are the water:protein ratios in growth and at maturity respectively, LPR and LPR_m are the lipid:protein ratios in growth and at maturity respectively and $u = P/P_m$, is a degree of maturity in body protein. Equations (13) and (14) thus relate the values of the two ratios at a given degree of maturity in potential growth, to their values at maturity through the two exponents, b and c.

That equations (7), (8) and (9) may apply can be seen from the data of Doornenbal (1971, 1972, 1975) for castrated male Lacombe pigs. The weights of the three components of the empty body — protein, lipid and the remainder — were given by Doornenbal at different ages. Where C is the weight of any one component we have, by analogy with equation (7):

$$C = C_m \exp(-\exp(-B(t - t^*_c))) \qquad\qquad \text{kg} \quad (15)$$

The degree of maturity in the component is $u_c = C/C_m$ so that:

$$u_c = \exp(-\exp(-B(t - t^*_c))) \qquad\qquad (16)$$

By taking natural logarithms, changing the signs and taking natural logarithms and changing the signs again, equation (16) becomes:

$$G_c = -\ln(-\ln u_c) = (-Bt^*_c) + Bt \qquad\qquad (17)$$

For the castrated pigs the estimates of C_m were $P_m = 29$, $L_m = 147.9$ and $R_m = 94.83$ kg, where R_m is the weight of the remainder of the empty body at maturity.

The graphs of the transformed degrees of maturity, G_c against t for the three components are shown in *Figure 8.7*. The data are all distributed around straight lines of slope 0.0093/day, but the intercepts are different for the three components. When $t_c = t^*_c$, then $G_c = 0$; the estimates of the t^*_c values were $t^*_p = 162.5$, $t^*_1 = 217.2$ and $t^*_r = 150.2$ days, all with a standard error of 1.0 days. The order of maturing is the remainder, followed by protein, followed by lipid as would be

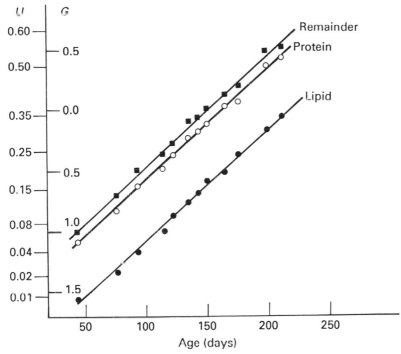

Figure 8.7 The degree of maturity, u, and its transformation, G, for protein, lipid and the remainder of the empty body of castrated pigs against age (from Doornenbal, 1971)

expected. The assumption that equations (7), (8) and (9) hold for animals is not rejected by the data of Doornenbal (1971, 1972, 1975) for his particular castrated male Lacombe pigs.

The third thing that follows from the assumptions (again the proof will not be given here) is that the exponents and the time constants are related by:

$$t^*_{wa} = t^*_p + (\log_e (c + 1))/B \qquad\qquad \text{days} \quad (18)$$

$$t^*_l = t^*_p + (\log_e (b + 1))/B \qquad\qquad \text{days} \quad (19)$$

From a suitably designed serial slaughter experiment, under non-limiting conditions, such as that of Doornenbal for pigs, values of P, WA and L in the plucked body can be collected at different ages for a given kind of turkey in potential growth. Such data allow the estimation of the values of the set of parameters of the equations: P_m, $WAPR_m$, LPR_m, B, t^*_p, b and c, and allow the assumptions underlying the equations to be tested.

The value of P_m was seen to vary appreciably between turkeys (see *Table 8.1*). The values of $WAPR_m$ and LPR_m (see *Tables 8.2* and *8.3*) varied little, except that LPR_m was assumed to be greater in females than in males. The value of B for the chemical component growth curves will be similar to that for weight (*Table 8.7*) so that its variation will be largely, but not entirely, accounted for by differences in mature size across commercial stocks at a given time. The values of the remaining parameters t^*_p, b and c are investigated below.

Testing and parameter estimation

The protein growth curve of Large White female turkeys is given in *Figure 8.8* from the data of Leeson and Summers (1980). The males of Fisher (unpublished), after allowing for an obvious growth check between 12 and 16 weeks of age, also gave data consistent with a Gompertz function for protein growth.

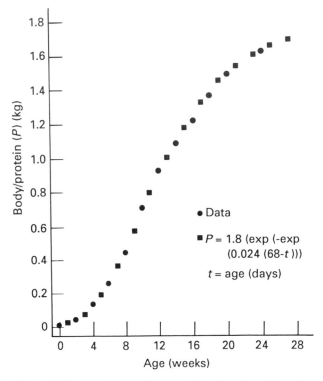

Figure 8.8 The protein growth curve of female turkeys (from Leeson and Summers, 1980)

The weights of water are plotted against the weights of protein for the females of Leeson and Summers (1980) in *Figure 8.9* on log-log scales. The relationship is well described by a straight line of slope 0.90 so that: (i) the assumption that water weight is a simple power function of protein weight is not rejected, and (ii) the value of $(c + 1)$ is estimated as 0.90 so that c is estimated as -0.10. The value of $c = -0.10$ holds for cattle, sheep and pigs as well (Emmans, unpublished). At a protein weight of 1.8 kg, the estimate at maturity from *Figure 8.8*, the water:protein ratio is predicted to be 3.22 which is in agreement with the estimate in *Table 8.2*.

There are more problems involved in estimating the value of the exponent b which relates fatness, as a lipid:protein ratio, to the degree of maturity in protein. The actual fatness of a turkey, as of any animal, is sensitive to its treatment. Departures from non-limiting conditions may cause fatness to be either above or below that of potential growth.

At maturity the values of LPR_m were estimated to be 1.0 for males and 1.4 for females (*Table 8.2*). If the inherent lipid:protein ratio is assumed to be 0.15 at $u_p = 0.0087$ for males and $u_p = 0.0115$ for females, which seem reasonable values, then

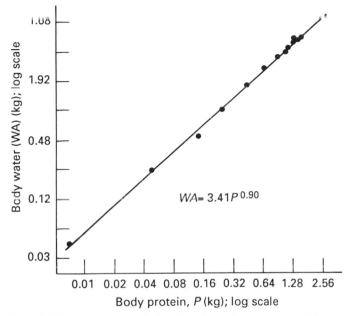

Figure 8.9 Water and protein in female turkeys (from Leeson and Summers, 1980)

the values for b are 0.4 for males and 0.5 for females. These values predict higher body lipid contents at ages between 6 and 20 weeks than those seen in the experiments of Leeson and Summers (1980), Hurwitz *et al.* (1983) and Fisher (unpublished). It is, however, uncertain that the conditions in these experiments were such that the inherent fatness was attained.

The presumed relationship between fatness and degree of maturity in non-limiting conditions needs further testing for turkeys.

The growth of the physical body

The description of the physical body is that already used to describe the mature turkey. The first loss is the blood and feathers (Loss 1). The body, other than the oven-ready carcass (eviscerated carcass + giblets + abdominal fat) and Loss 1 is Loss 2. The eviscerated carcass can be considered as portions — breast, legs, wing and remainder — and each portion as yielding meat, skin and bone. For present purposes the yields of white meat, dark meat, skin, giblets, abdominal fat, evisceration loss and blood and feather loss will be considered in relation to total carcass bone (*CB*).

Estimates of the allometric exponents for component:carcass bone ratios on carcass bone weights were obtained from some of the data from three experiments kindly made available by Trevor Bray of ADAS. Experiments 1 and 3 were of a four protein level × four environmental temperatures design where feed protein contents were changed every 4 weeks. Experiment 1 used a medium weight stock and Experiments 2 and 3 a heavy weight stock; data for the females came only from Experiment 3. Experiment 2 had three treatments. The data on carcass bone and component weights from both younger (12 or 14 weeks of age) and older (24 weeks for males and 16 weeks for females) turkeys were used. The exponents were estimated for each treatment separately in each experiment. As no systematic effects of either feeding programme or temperature on the exponents were present the 16 values from each experiment were averaged with the results shown in *Table 8.9.*

Table 8.9 The maturing exponents for component:carcass bone ratios on carcass bone weight

Component	Males		Stock 2[b]	Females	Value taken
	Stock 1			Stock 1[c]	
	Exp. 1[a]	Exp. 2[a]			
White meat	0.55	0.66 (0.05)[d]	0.74 (0.07)	0.52 (0.08)	0.62
Dark meat	0.38	0.46 (0.05)	0.53 (0.04)	0.30 (0.06)	0.42
Skin	1.26	1.21 (0.07)	1.70 (0.19)	1.05 (0.15)	1.3
Abdominal fat	1.50	1.65 (0.25)	2.40 (0.33)	1.96 (0.31)	1.8
Giblets	−0.03	−0.02 (0.02)	0.05 (0.04)	–	0
Evisceration loss	−0.20	0.05 (0.09)	−0.29 (0.14)	–	−0.15
Blood and feathers	−0.21	−0.02 (0.04)	0.08 (0.04)	–	−0.05

(Bray, unpublished)

[a] Between 12 and 14 weeks of age
[b] Between 14 and 24 weeks of age
[c] Between 12 and 16 weeks of age
[d] ( ) = SE

The results in *Table 8.9* show good agreement between the two stocks for white and dark meats and for giblets and the loss from live weight to the oven-ready carcass. For the two components influenced by fattening — abdominal fat and skin — the values were more variable. This difference may reflect experiments rather than stocks, but it means that these values should not be seen as being as reliable as the others.

The use of the exponents is illustrated in *Table 8.10* where they are used in conjunction with the mean values for mature males in *Tables 8.3* and *8.4* to 'construct' birds at carcass bone weight of different proportions of the mature value of 3.5 kg.

The relationship between carcass bone and body protein

No suitable data were available for turkeys to test the assumption that, in potential growth, there is some simple relationship between the weights of body protein and carcass bone. The data of Hakansson, Eriksson and Svensson (1978) for male broiler chickens were therefore used. Carcass bone weights are plotted against body protein weights in *Figure 8.10* on log-log scales. The assumption of a straight line is not rejected. The equation of the line is:

$$CB = 0.70 \, P^{0.87} \qquad\qquad\qquad \text{kg} \quad (20)$$

As mentioned earlier it can be shown that if (i) one component has a Gompertz growth curve and (ii) the weights of another component are a simple power function of its weights, then the growth curve of the second component is also a

Table 8.10 The predicted mean physical composition of male turkeys at a range of degrees of maturity in carcass bone weight

Component	$(C/CB)_m$ [a]	C_m (kg) [b]	Exponent [c]	$u_{CB} = 0.48$ [d] Weight (kg)	g/kg LW [e]	$u_{CB} = 0.64$ [d] Weight (kg)	g/kg LW [e]	$u_{CB} = 0.80$ [d] Weight (kg)	g/kg LW [e]
Carcass bone	1.00	3.500	0	1.680	187	2.240	172	2.800	160
White meat	2.08	7.280	0.62	2.217	247	3.533	271	5.072	289
Dark meat	1.53	3.355	0.42	1.889	210	2.841	218	3.901	222
Skin	0.54	1.890	1.3	0.349	39	0.677	52	1.131	65
Abdominal fat	0.068	0.238	1.8	0.030	3	0.068	5	0.127	7
Giblets	0.346	1.211	0	0.581	65	0.775	60	0.969	55
Evisceration loss	0.804	2.814	0.15	1.508	169	1.926	148	2.328	133
Blood and feathers	0.430	1.505	0	0.722	80	0.963	74	1.204	69
Live weight (kg)		23.8		8.976		13.023		17.532	
Oven-ready carcass (g/kg)					751		778		798

[a] Component : carcass bone ratio at maturity
[b] Component weight at maturity
[c] Exponent for component : carcass bone ratio on carcass bone weight
[d] U_{CB} = degree of maturity in carcass bone
[e] Proportion of the live weight (g/kg)

Gompertz function. The data in *Figure 8.10* are thus consistent with carcass bone following a Gompertz function, on the reasonable assumption that the body protein weights of these chickens also followed a Gompertz function.

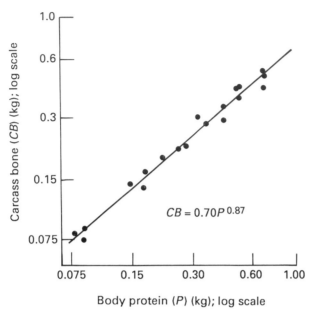

Figure 8.10 Body protein and carcass bone weights in male broiler chickens

The growth of feathers

There are difficulties in describing the growth of feathers: (i) feather weight is not a simple power function of body protein weight, (ii) feathers which have been grown and shed are obviously not present at slaughter, so that feather weights at slaughter under-estimate total feather growth and, (iii) genotypes may differ appreciably in feather growth due to the presence, or absence, of a few single genes.

Hurwitz *et al.* (1983) plotted the proportion of the live weight as feathers in turkeys against age and fitted a quadratic equation. Such an equation while, perhaps, giving a reasonable description of the data from a given experiment, cannot be expected to have any general validity. For example, the quadratic function predicts that at some age there will be no feathers. it is more rational to relate feather weight to some other measure of size, such as body protein weight.

The data of Hurwitz *et al.* (1983) and of Fisher (unpublished) were used to relate feather weight to body protein weight in male turkeys of two stocks. The data are in *Figure 8.11*, plotted on log–log scales. The data suggest a possible model that might be used. Up to a body protein weight of 1.0 kg (a degree of protein maturity of about 0.25) feather protein weight, FP_1, is a simple power function of body protein weight, BP:

$$FP_1 = 0.250 \, BP^{1.21} \qquad\qquad\qquad \text{kg} \quad (21)$$

The two data points from Fisher's turkeys are in quite good agreement with those of Hurwitz *et al.* (*Figure 8.11*). Thereafter the data appear to be distributed around

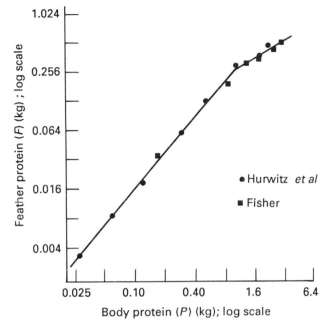

Figure 8.11 Feather and body protein in male turkeys

a second power function with an exponent of lower value, which is close to two-thirds:

$$FB_2 = 0.250\ BP^{2/3} \qquad\qquad\qquad \text{kg} \quad (22)$$

Extrapolation to a mature body protein weight of 4.0 kg gives a prediction of a mature feather protein weight of 0.630 kg. In individually caged laying fowls at 37 weeks of age, Farjo (1981) found a mean feather weight of 0.135 kg with a mean body protein weight of 0.363 kg. Taking the protein content of mature feathers as 0.90 gives an estimate of 0.238 kg feather protein/(body protein weight)$^{2/3}$ which is similar to the value estimated for the male turkeys; the slightly smaller value may reflect some feather loss due to caging.

A possible model for feather protein growth is thus:

$$\text{For } u < u^*: \quad FP_1 = a.BP^{b_1} \qquad\qquad \text{kg} \quad (23)$$

$$\text{For } u < u^*: \quad FP_2 = 0.250\ BP^{2/3} \qquad\qquad \text{kg} \quad (24)$$

where $u = BP/BP_m$.

At $u = u^*$, $FP_1 = FP_2$ so that if both u^* and b_1 are known then the value of 'a' can be calculated. In the absence of other information it is assumed that $u^* = 0.25$ and $b_1 = 1.21$ for turkeys.

While the model appears to be a good representation of feather weight in relation to body protein weight for the male turkeys of Hurwitz *et al.* (1983) and Fisher (*Figure 8.11*), it has the consequence that the derivatives of equations (23) and (24) have different values at $u = u^*$. The derivatives are:

$$dFP_1/dBP = a.b_1\ BP^{1-b_1} \qquad\qquad\qquad (25)$$

$$dFP_2/dBP = (2/3)k.BP^{-1/3} \qquad\qquad\qquad (26)$$

The abrupt change in dFP/dBP at $u = u^*$ predicted by the model may, or may not, be realistic. If judged to be unrealistic the change can be made smooth by a device. The value of dFP/dBP at, say, $u = 0.35$ can be calculated from equation (26) and that at $u = 0.25$ calculated from equation (25). The derivative is then made, say, a linear function of u for $0.25 < u < 0.35$.

As an appreciable proportion of the protein requirements — and a greater proportion of the requirement for the sulphur-containing amino acids — is for feather growth, the problem of predicting feather growth in a satisfactory way deserves attention. The solution proposed here must be seen as a provisional one.

The problem of predicting feather loss and hence total feather growth, remains. It is dealt with here by assuming a rate of loss which is proportional to feather weight at 0.01/day.

The requirements for potential growth

The requirements for potential growth to be attained are, briefly, free access to a balanced feed, which does not constrain intake, and a thermally neutral environment. When treated in this way an immature turkey is expected to eat the offered feed at a rate such that it just meets its requirments for energy and, as the feed is balanced, its requirements for all other feed resources, and to attain its potential growth path. The problems are: (i) to define a general energy scale, (ii) to have a general method of predicting the energy requirement, (ii) to have a general method for calculating the nutrient:energy ratios of a balanced feed, and (iv) to have a general method for calculating the temperature of a thermally neutral environment. The methods need to be general across feeds and degrees of maturity for any given kind of turkey or, preferably, any domestic animal. The problems are considered in turn.

The effective energy scale and energy requirement

The metabolizable energy, ME, apparently yielded by a diet to a monogastric animal, comes from the apparently digested organic components — protein, lipid and carbohydrate. It is conventional to correct the actual ME from digested protein by subtracting 'a' MJ/kg of protein retained. This convention is a useful one if energy retention is also corrected by 'a' MJ/kg of protein retained.

It has been found to be useful (Emmans, 1984 and unpublished) to further adjust the ME, corrected to zero protein retention, for three (in monogastrics) effects in order to remove differences in the effectiveness of the ME between diet compositions. These are:

(1) The ME from digested protein is reduced by the amount of heat that would have been excreted, Z_1, MJ/kg digested protein. The heat that is produced by the retention of protein is also reduced by Z_1 MJ/kg.
(2) The ME is reduced by Z_2 MJ/kg faecal organic matter as an allowance for the heat produced as a result of eating organic matter which yields no ME.
(3) The ME from digested lipid is used more efficiently for lipid retention than that from carbohydrate or (adjusted) protein. This is allowed for by adding $x.Z_3$ MJ/kg digested lipid to the ME of the diet, where x is the proportion of digested lipid directly retained.

The relationship between the effective energy content, FEC MJ/kg, of a feed and its metabolizable energy content (corrected to zero N-retention), MEC_n MJ/kg, is thus:

$$EEC = MEC_n - Z_1 DPC - Z_2 FOMC + x.Z_3 DLC \qquad \text{MJ/kg} \quad (27)$$

where DPC and DLC are the digested protein and lipid contents of the diet (kg/kg), and $FOMC$ is the faecal organic matter content of the diet (kg/kg). The values of $a = 5.63$, $Z_1 = 4.67$, $Z_2 = 3.8$ and $Z_3 = 12$ MJ/kg have been estimated from suitable sets of data from animals other than turkeys. The value of x is a variable, the proportion of digested lipid which is directly retained, and may lie between 0 and 1; for practical cases $x = 0.5$ has been asumed.

The requirement for effective energy

The immature turkey, in a thermally neutral environment, needs effective energy for (i) maintenance, (ii) protein growth, and (iii) lipid retention. A maintenance scaling rule, which appears to apply across domestic animals (Emmans, unpublished), is

$$MH = M_E P_m^{0.73} u \qquad \text{MJ/day} \quad (28)$$

where MH = maintenance heat MJ/day, P_m = mature body protein weight, kg, $u = P/P_m$ and P = body protein weight, kg. The constant, M_E, has been estimated as 1.63 MJ/unit day.

The effective energy requirements for protein and lipid retention have been estimated as 50 and 56 MJ/kg respectively. Protein retention includes protein retained as those feathers which are subsequently lost from the body. The rate of feather loss is taken here to be 0.01 feather weight/day.

Where the rates of protein and lipid retention dP/dt and dL/dt, kg/day respectively, are known the effective energy requirement, $EERQ$, is calculated as:

$$EERQ = MH + 50dP/dt + 56dL/dt \qquad \text{MJ/day} \quad (29)$$

The values of dP/dt and dL/dt can be derived from the equations given earlier for the potential growth of a given kind of turkey, including the feathering equations.

The data of Fisher (unpublished) for male turkeys were used to test the ability of equation (29) to predict the rate at which turkeys would eat a feed given their actual values of P, dP/dt and dL/dt as determined by weighing and chemical analysis of slaughtered birds at a series of weights (roughly eight birds at each 4 weeks to 24 weeks of age). The effective energy yields of the feeds given were calculated from their estimated ME yields and their chemical compositions. The feed intake in a period, PFI, was predicted as $PFI = EERQ/FEEC$ kg/day where $EERQ$ was calculated from equation (29) and $FEEC$ is the estimated effective energy content of the feed. The value of P_m was assumed to be 3.64 kg.

Table 8.11 shows the predicted and measured intake for the age periods. The agreement is good and is consistent with equation (29) applying to turkeys as it does to other animals.

Amino acid requirements

The turkey's requirement for minerals and vitamins will not be considered here. It is, however, important to note that if a mineral or vitamin is the first limiting

Table 8.11 The predicted and actual feed intakes of male turkeys (data of Fisher, unpublished)

Age (weeks)	Body protein[a] (BP, kg)	Actual gains (g/day)		EE required[c] (kJ/day)	Feed EEC[d] (kJ/day)	Feed intake (g/day)	
		Protein (PR)	Lipid (LR)			Predicted[e]	Actual
0–4	0.071	7.85	0.81	564	10.97	51.4	50.7
4–8	0.402	23.1	4.9	1894	11.20	169	167
8–12	1.02	33.3	12.1	3515	11.35	310	295
12–16	1.70	26.9	20.3	4437	11.44	388	388
16–20	2.29	26.7	33.6	5847	11.57	505	505
20–24	2.78	23.8	18.1	5403	11.69	462	471

[a] Mean value for the period
[b] Includes 0.01 of mean feather weight
[c] Effective energy required $1150BP + 50PR + 56LR$ kJ/day
[d] EEC = effective energy yield of feed calculated from feed ME, protein and lipid values
[e] Predicted feed intake = EE required/feed EEC

Table 8.12 The essential amino acid contents of body and feather proteins (g/kg)

Amino acid	Body protein			Feather protein		Values used	
	(1)[a]	(2)[b]	(3)[c]	(1)[a]	(3)[c]	Body	Feather
Arginine	69	64	68	72	61	68	65
Cystine	3	11	11	84	67	11	70
Histidine	30	29	26	7	8	26	8
Leucine	90	73	71	81	66	71	70
Isoleucine	44	42	35	50	37	40	40
Lysine	80	80	66	19	18	75	18
Methionine	27	26	18	7	5	25	6
Phenylalanine	46	36	40	51	40	40	45
Threonine	46	42	42	46	42	42	44
Tryptophan	–	10	–	7	–	10	7
Tyrosine	30	31	31	27	52	31	50
Valine	54	46	42	77	57	44	60

[a] Hurwitz et al. (1983), Table 7; turkeys
[b] Hakansson et al. (1978), edible portion of chickens
[c] Fisher (1986), for poultry

nutrient, rather than an amino acid in a given diet, then data from such a diet cannot be used to estimated amino acid responses nor to test predictions of what these may be.

The essential amino acid compositions of body and feather proteins are given in *Table 8.12*. For both feather, and body protein growth, the net efficiency of using an apparently digested amino acid which is first limiting is assumed to be 0.80 (Fisher, personal communication). The protein needed for body maintenance is assumed to have the same composition as that of the body (*Table 8.12*). Maintenance is scaled in the same way as energy so that the maintenance protein requirement, MP g/day, is given by:

$$MP = M_p P_m^{0.73} u \qquad\qquad \text{g/day} \quad (30)$$

The value of M_p has been estimated at 8 g/unit day.

Amino acids are needed for the growth of feathers which are subsequently lost; this can be seen as a protein requirement for feather maintenance. The amino acid composition of protein for feather maintenance is taken to be that of feathers (*Table 8.12*) and the rate as 0.01 g/g feathers per day.

An example of the calculation of requirements

To calculate the requirements, over time, for a turkey to attain its potential growth it is necessary to describe that turkey. An 'average' male turkey has been assumed to have the following values of the parameters. At maturity $P_m = 4.0$ kg, $LPR_m = 1.0$, $WAPR_m = 3.25$ and, $k = 1.24$, so that the mature plucked body weighs 21.96 kg and has 182 g/kg of both protein and lipid, 43.7 g/kg of lipid-free dry matter other than protein, and 592.0 g/kg of water. Its feather protein weight is 0.630 kg so that it has 0.630/0.90 = 0.700 kg of feathers and, hence, an empty weight of 22.66 kg. The values $B = 0.020$/day, $b = 0.4$, $c = -0.10$ and $t_p{}^* = 91$ days are assumed.

The equations were first solved to predict the effective energy requirement at intervals of 2 weeks. The feed intake was then predicted assuming that all feeds yielded 11.5 MJ/kg of effective energy. The predicted feed intake by time curve is shown in *Figure 8.12*. The lysine requirement was then calculated and converted to a protein requirement assuming a digestibility of 0.88 and that all feeds had 0.05 of their protein as lysine. The computed protein requirement, g/kg feed, is compared with the NRC recommended values in *Figure 8.12*.

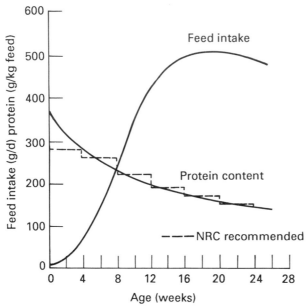

Figure 8.12 Predicted feed intake, and the protein content of a balanced feed, for a male turkey at different ages

The predicted requirements, g/kg feed, for lysine and the sulphur-containing amino acids, were calculated and are plotted against age in *Figure 8.13* where they are compared with the values of Hurwitz *et al.* (1983). From 0 to 8 weeks for lysine, and from 10 to 17 weeks for the sulphur-containing amino acids, the two predictions agree. Otherwise they differ appreciably.

It must be emphasized that *Figures 8.12* and *8.13* apply to a particular turkey with the stated characteristics always growing at its potential and are examples of the use of the method. The requirements of other kinds of turkey will be different functions of age.

Variation in requirement

Figures 8.12 and *8.13* show how the requirements of a particular kind of turkey — described by assigning values to the inherited parameters — vary with time when the bird is attaining its potential growth. An additional source of variation in practice is that between individuals within a flock, which is assumed to be of a single sex.

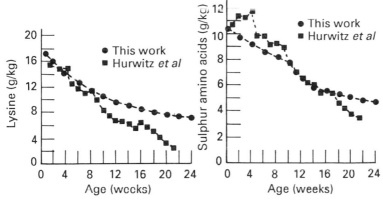

Figure 8.13 The calculated amino acid requirements of a male turkey by two methods

Each individual turkey will have its own characteristic values of the inherited parameters. Those which certainly show some important variation are P_m (or A) and B. It is possible that LPR_m, and hence b, also vary between individuals but this is harder to determine. For the mature turkeys described earlier the mean coefficient of variation in PBW within a line/sex combination was 6.9%. This is essentially the expected value of 7% (Emmans and Fisher, 1986).

To get some indication of the variation in B for turkeys the individual male birds of each of two stocks of Okunuga (1980) were used; there were six of one and eight of the other. The mature weight of each bird was estimated from its late weights and, using this estimate of A, its value of B estimated from its weekly weights from 1 to 6 weeks of age. The results are shown in *Table 8.13*. The coefficient of variation in B^* was 3.2%. The coefficient of variation in A was close to the expected value of 7%.

Table 8.13 Estimates of the variation in the growth parameters between individual male turkeys

Stock	n	Mature weight (A, kg)[a]		Rate parameter (B/day)[b]		Scaled rate parameter (B^*)	
		Mean	*CV%*	*Mean*	*CV%*	*Mean*	*CV%*
8	6	17.7	7.5	0.0233	2.66	0.0507	3.27
9	8	16.3	9.4	0.0229	4.07	0.0486	3.18
Mean			8.5				3.2

(Okunuga, 1980)

[a] Estimated from weights at 34–37 weeks and 44–50 weeks for stocks 8 and 9 respectively
[b] From weekly weights, 1 to 6 weeks, using individual estimates of A

Such variation in A (and hence P_m) and B^*, combined with variation in the degree of maturity at hatching (and hence t_n^*) and, possibly, in LPR_m (and hence b) will lead to a population of lines when the required amino acid content of the feed is plotted against time for each individual. This is shown diagrammatically in *Figure 8.14*.

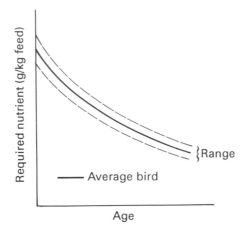

Figure 8.14 Variation in requirement with age and between individuals

Figure 8.14 is a representation of the problem facing someone attempting to devise a feeding programme for a flock of turkeys. Such a feeding programme comprises: (i) a certain number of single feeds given in succession, (ii) rules, usually ages, for changing from one feed to the next, and (iii) the specifications of each of the feeds to be used. It is clear that no such feeding programme can exactly meet the requirements of all birds at all times. The problem is made more difficult if (i) the environmental temperature is varying with time in some unknown way, and (ii) the past treatment of the flock has caused growth checks so that the birds are lighter at a given time than would be predicted by their potential growth curve. The problem of attempting to devise an optimum feeding programme, i.e. that which is most profitable, is thus one of terrifying complexity. A possible alternative approach is described in the next section.

Choice feeding

The requirement of a given kind of turkey, expressed as a nutrient:energy ratio in a feed, changes continually as it grows, as is shown in *Figures 8.12* and *8.13*. The problem of trying to meet such a changing ratio by a feeding programme, where each of a succession of single feeds is given for some periods of time, has been described above. Where there is also (i) variation between birds and (ii) uncertainty about both the line for the average bird in a given case and about the variation between birds, the problem becomes extremely complex.

A different approach has been used at Aberdeen at the North of Scotland College of Agriculture by Michie and his colleagues. The steps are (i) decide to choice feed from some age (such as 6 weeks), (ii) formulate a balanced feed for the birds at, say, 10–12 weeks of age at least cost, subject to it containing at least 500 g/kg of barley or wheat, whichever gives the cheaper feed per unit of energy, (iii) if wheat is used, formulate a balancer by removing 500 g/kg of wheat from the complete feed and give this as a free choice with wheat from 6 weeks of age, (iv) if barley is used formulate a balancer by removing the 500 g/kg of barley from the complete feed and give this as a free choice with oiled barley from 6 weeks. The barley is oiled by adding vegetable oil.

When choice fed is these ways turkeys appear to achieve their potential growth rates, choose balanced diets over time and give high financial margins.

It may be that the rules for formulating the balancers could be improved but, otherwise, the system appears to be highly effective. It could well be that a change to such a feeding system would solve the problems of designing conventional feeding programmes by making such programmes unnecessary.

The climatic environment

A turkey, in order to grow along its potential path, needs an environment to which it can lose the heat produced as an inevitable consequence of attaining that path. If it were to be placed in an environment where hotness varied spatially it would be expected to move to an area where it was comfortable, provided that such an area existed. When the turkey is placed in a quasi-homogeneous environment it is the environment that largely determines the rate at which the turkey can lose, and hence produce, heat.

For a given turkey in a given state the relationship between heat loss and environmental temperature may be as shown in *Figure 8.15*. Its total heat loss, HL, is the sum of its sensible heat loss, SHL, which is dependent on the environment, and its evaporative heat loss, EHL, which is independent of the environment. The turkey is seen as having some measure of control over both SHL and EHL.

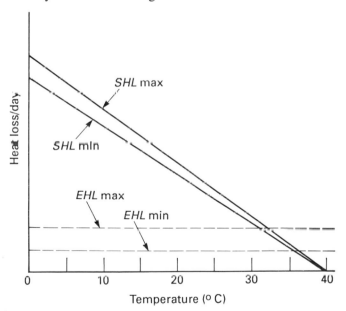

Figure 8.15 Sensible (SHL) and evaporative (EHL) heat loss at different temperatures

The representation in *Figure 8.15*, which is a conventional one, raises several questions:

(1) at what temperature is SHL zero?
(2) what is the value of the slope relating SHL_{min} to T and in what ways does this vary between turkeys?
(3) what is the value of EHL_{min} and in what ways does this vary between turkeys?
(4) what is the ratio of SHL_{max} to SHL_{min}?
(5) what is the ratio of EHL_{max} to EHL_{min}?

Some provisional answers to these questions can be given and applied to the example of the male turkey illustrated in *Figure 8.12*. This bird was assumed to be given feeds which were balanced and which yielded 12.5 MJ/kg of *ME* corrected to zero N retention. Its heat loss was calculated as its *ME* intake less its energy retention as protein and lipid. It was assumed that 0.2 of its heat loss was as *EHL* and that its sensible heat loss would be zero at an environmental temperature of 40°C. The slope of the line relating *SHL*, expressed per (kg plucked weight)$^{2/3}$ to *T*, called *s*, was assumed to be linearly related to feather weight, also expressed per (kg plucked weight)$^{2/3}$, by the expression:

$$S = 64 - 0.5(\text{g feathers/kg}^{2/3}) \qquad\qquad \text{kJ/kg}^{2/3}\,°\text{C day} \quad (31)$$

On these assumptions, and the calculated heat production of potential growth, it was possible to calculate the temperature at which the turkey would be comfortable as a function of age. The results of the calculation are in *Figure 8.16*. From 10 to 18 weeks of age the turkey is calculated to need an environmental temperature of 10–12°C in order to lose the heat produced by its potential growth, and hence to attain its potential growth.

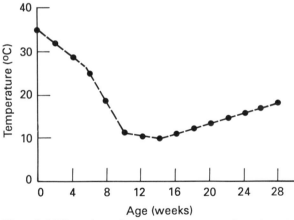

Figure 8.16 The estimated comfort temperature of a male turkey at different ages

Other turkeys, with different potential rates of growth, will have different relationships between their comfortable temperature and age. In general, the required temperature will fall as the potential growth rate, at a weight, is increased by selection. It may be quite simple to find the temperature requirements of a given kind of turkey by placing it in a thermocline, with a range of 0 to 40°C, and recording the temperature that it chooses over time.

Negative aspects of feed composition and environment

The earlier parts of this chapter dealt with a description of the potential growth paths of a turkey to maturity and its requirements for attaining this path. Failure to get what it needs will cause the actual growth path of the turkey to deviate from the potential path. The problem briefly addressed in this final part is: what, in its treatment, may prevent a turkey from getting what it needs to attain its potential growth path, and what will the consequences of this failure be?

Temperature and feed balance

The data for the 8–12 week period for male and female turkeys in *Table 8.14* come from Bray (unpublished). At the lowest temperature used, 12.6°C, and on the feed with the highest protein content 234 g CP/kg feed, the females attained a growth rate calculated to be their potential. Increasing the temperature to 22.7°C, or decreasing the feed protein content to 155 g/kg, or, particularly, doing both of these things together, caused substantial reductions in weight gain. Similar effects of treatment were seen in the males (*Table 8.14*) but, in this case, the estimated potential growth was not achieved, even at the lowest temperature and with the feed with the highest protein content used.

Table 8.14 The weight gains (kg) of turkeys from 8 to 12 weeks of age on two temperatures × two feed protein contents

Sex	Females		Males	
Potential	2.934		5.056	
Feed protein (g/kg)	12.6°C	22.7°C	12.6°C	22.7°C
234	2.988 (100)[a]	2.716 (91)	4.067 (100)	3.557 (87)
155	2.156 (84)	2.090 (70)	3.185 (78)	2.517 (62)

(Data of Bray, unpublished)

[a] Percentage of gain on feed with 234 g protein/kg at 12.6°C

It is likely that, in commercial practice, a common cause of growth failing to be at the potential rate are temperatures that are too high, or feeds of too low a nutrient:energy ratio, or both in combination.

There are many experimental reports (Leeson and Summers, 1980; Behrends, 1980; Siopes *et al.*, 1983; Hurwitz *et al.*, 1983; Bray, unpublished; Jones, unpublished; Moran *et al.*, 1984) where male Large White turkeys on the best treatments used have had growth rates, at live weights of about 10 kg, of 95–130 g/day. Their growth rates at lower, and in some cases higher, weights suggest that their potential growth rate was close to 180 g/day. The most likely cause of the poor growth rates is that the environments used were effectively too hot; it may also be that there is an upper limit to the rate at which the birds can ingest and digest cereal-based feeds.

A possible argument is that the final cause of growth rate being depressed either at higher temperatures, or on feeds with low nutrient:energy ratio, is the same, namely: an upper limit to the bird's capacity to lose heat in a given environment.

If the feed given is imbalanced, or the environment is too hot, or both, a turkey's growth rate will be reduced. In addition, depending on the details of the combination, it may became fatter, or thinner, at a weight than is predicted from its potential.

Other factors

The feed content of a non-protein nutrient — a mineral or a vitamin — in relation to energy, may also limit growth.

If a feed is of such a bulkiness — on whatever scale that bulk should be measured — that the turkey cannot eat it at the rate necessary to meet its requirements, then the potential performance will not be attained. Work is needed to define a suitable scale of feed bulk and the capacities of turkeys for bulk measured on this scale.

A feed may contain some chemical — which may be a nutrient — which would have toxic effects if the feed were to be eaten at the rate necessary for the turkey to meet its requirements. In such a case intake will be depressed and, as a consequence, growth rate.

Finally, high stocking rates may act to reduce growth by a combination of effects: (i) access to feed and water is made more difficult and feeding, for some of the birds at least, may not be truly *ad libitum*; (ii) the proximity of other turkeys will reduce radiant heat loss and the environment will become effectively hotter; (iii) litter condition may deteriorate with effects on foot and skin health, and (iv) the possibility of excess levels of ammonia is increased.

Discussion

An attempt has been made in this chapter to resolve the paradox which can be stated as: all turkeys are the same, but each turkey is different from all others. The resolution was in two parts: (i) those respects in which all turkeys are the same were identified; (ii) given this common framework, differences between turkeys were described and quantified.

The respects in which all turkeys are the same have been described here. In brief they are: (i) the variables describing the mature, and immature, chemical and physical compositions are the same for all turkeys, (ii) the form of the growth function is the same for all turkeys, and (iii) the requirements for units of scaled maintenance, growth and fattening are the same for all turkeys. Differences between turkey genotypes may then arise in the following ways: (i) there may be differences in mature size, however expressed, and in mature chemical composition; the evidence is that, across a wide range of mature sizes, chemical composition differs trivially between stocks. (ii) Within a sex there may be differences between stocks in the physical composition at maturity; the evidence is of substantial differences which, presumably, reflect past selection for conformation, (iii) there may be differences in the value of the scaled rate of maturing parameter, B^*; over time, the value of B^* has increased substantially and differences between current commercial stocks may be small but real.

Providing that a common framework is available the known differences between turkey genotypes can be allowed for in designing feeding programmes, at least in principle. The practical problems of dealing, in some systematic way, with the variation between individuals at a time, and for any one individual over time, are complex. It may well be that these problems can be solved by a change to choice feeding as was briefly discussed.

Although the main parts of the framework are clear there are problems which remain:

(1) The growth curve of body lipid in non-limiting conditions and its relationship to body protein both need to be better defined.
(2) The ability of turkeys, particularly when young, to react to imbalanced feeds by forming extra lipid needs to be explored.

(3) The capacities of turkeys to lose heat in environments of different hotnesses at different degrees of maturity need to be quantified. The emphasis needs to be on the problems that a turkey has in dealing with effectively hot, rather than effectively cold, environments.

(4) Better descriptions of feather growth and loss are needed.

The analysis has identified an apparently serious problem in the failure of modern male turkeys, under 'normal' conditions to achieve their potential growth rates, in the period 8–16 weeks of age. Such failure appears to be due to 'normal' environments being too hot for such animals and leads to an increase in the feed and time needed to get a turkey to a weight. The definition of non-limiting environments for modern male turkeys in the 8–16 week period is worthy of further investigation.

Acknowledgements

I am grateful to Asifo Oritsegbubemi, and his co-supervisor Kingsley Smith, for permission to use material in his MSc thesis on mature turkeys. Trevor Bray kindly let me have access to data from several ADAS turkey experiments and I am grateful to him. Finally, Colin Fisher of IGAP, allowed me access to some of his data and provided encouragement and helpful criticism.

References

Asmundson, V. S. (1942). Crossbreeding and heterosis in turkeys. *Poultry Science*, **21**, 311–316

Behrends, B. R. and Waibel, P. E. (1980). Methionine and cystine requirements of growing turkeys. *Poultry Science*, **59**, 849–859

Doornenbal, H. (1971). Growth, development and chemical composition of the pig. I. Lean tissue and protein. *Growth*, **35**, 281–295

Doornenbal, H. (1972). Growth, development and chemical composition of the pig. II. Fatty tissue and chemical fat. *Growth*, **36**, 185–194

Doornenbal, H. (1975). Growth, development and chemical composition of the pig. III. Bone, ash and moisture. *Growth*, **39**, 427–434

Emmans, G. C. (1984). An additive and linear energy scale. *Animal Production*, **38**, 538

Emmans, G. C. and Fisher, C. (1986). Problems of nutritional theory. In *Nutritional Requirements and Nutritional Theory*. (Fisher, C. and Boorman, K. N., eds), London, Butterworths

Farjo, G. Y. (1981). Studies on the factors affecting food and energy intake of brown egg layers. MSc Thesis. University of Glasgow

Hakansson, J., Eriksson, S. and Svensson, S. A. (1978). The influence of feed energy level on feed consumption, growth and development of different organs of chicks. Reports Nos 57, 59. Swedish University of Agricultural Sciences, Department of Animal Husbandry, Uppsala

Hocking, P. M., Gavora, J. S., Chambers, J. R. and Fortin, A. (1985). Genetic variation in body size, composition, temperature and feed intake in mature chickens. *Poultry Science*, **64**, 6–28

Hurwitz, S., Plavnik, I., Bengal, I., Talpaz, H. and Bartov, I. (1983). The amino acid requirements of growing turkeys. 2. Experimental validation of model-calculated requirements for sulfur amino acids and lysine. *Poultry Science*, **62**, 2387–2393

Leeson, S. and Summers, J. D. (1980). Production and carcass characteristics of the large white turkey. *Poultry Science*, **59**, 1237–1245

Moran, E. T., Poste, L. M., Fernet, P. R. and Agar, V. (1984). Response of large tom turkeys differing in growth characteristics to divergent feeding systems: performance, carcass quality and sensory evaluation. *Poultry Science*, **63**, 1778–1792

Okunuga, K. O. (1980). The effects of early undernutrition and feed protein content on the growth of turkeys. MSc Thesis. University of Glasgow

Oritsegbubemi, A. J. (1987). The relationship between mature body size and body composition of different turkey strains. MSc Thesis. University of Glasgow

Siopes, T. D., Timmons, M. B., Baughman, G. R. and Parkhurst, C. R. (1983). The effect of light intensity on the growth performance of male turkeys. *Poultry Science,* **62**, 2336–2342

Taylor, St. C. S. (1980). Genetic scaling rules in animal growth. *Animal Production,* **30**, 161–165

Chapter 9

Physiology of muscle growth

H. J. Swatland

Introduction

In this brief review of the physiology of muscle growth, the emphasis will be on muscle growth in turkeys. Muscle growth in meat-producing animals is too often regarded solely as a 'faster is better' system and insufficient attention is given to the interactions between the physiology of muscle growth, animal health and meat quality. Poultry meat is not the least expensive way for consumers to acquire their daily protein, even though it may be less expensive than many types of red meat. To safeguard traditional markets it is essential to strive for optimum meat quality at an economically viable cost. Thus, while the emphasis of this review is on turkeys, the theme will be 'quantity versus quality'.

The minimum vocabulary that is required to discuss muscle growth is as follows (*Figure 9.1*).

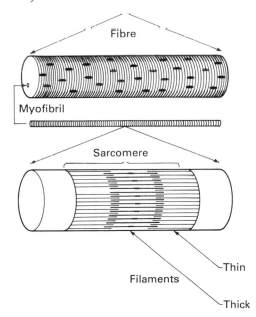

Figure 9.1 Major histological features of skeletal muscle. A cylindrical segment of striated muscle fibre is enlarged to show one of the many striated myofibrils that it contains. A one-sarcomere segment of the myofibril is enlarged to show its composition from sliding thick and thin filaments

167

(1) Muscle fibre — the giant, multinucleate cellular unit of striated skeletal muscle or meat. Bundles of muscle fibres (fasciculi) form the visible grain of the meat.
(2) Myofibrils — the contractile organelles that run longitudinally within muscle fibres.
(3) Thick and thin filaments — the sliding filaments within the myofibril that produce contraction in living muscle and give meat its texture.
(4) Myosin — a protein with a rod-like backbone and two mobile heads. The backbones form the thick filament and the heads protrude to form mobile cross-bridges that cause thick and thin filaments to slide past one another during contraction.
(5) Actin — a globular protein whose molecules are arranged in a double helix to form a thin filament.
(6) Sarcomere — the shortest functional unit long the length of the myofibril. A sarcomere contains a set of thick filaments linked transversely at their midlength by an M line, and two sets of thin filaments terminally embedded in the Z lines that mark the ends of the sarcomere.
(7) Sarcoplasmic reticulum — membranous vesicles that surround the myofibrils. They sequester calcium ions in resting muscle but release them to trigger muscle contraction.
(8) Transverse tubular system — tubular invaginations of the fibre plasma membrane that transmit action potentials from the fibre surface to the sarcoplasmic reticulum, thereby linking the contractile myofibrils to the nervous system.

To save on space, literature citations are kept to a minimum. Any of the general principles that are presented here are fully referenced in the bibliography provided by Swatland (1984). The quantitative data reported here were derived by re-working the data base combined from a series of published experiments on turkey muscle growth (Swatland, 1979a,b,c,d, 1980, 1985; Mullen and Swatland, 1979).

Gross anatomy

Valuable information on the physiology of muscle growth may be obtained by carcass dissection. The data have an obvious commercial interest since they describe the yield of edible meat, but they are also interesting scientifically since the mass of a muscle represents the summation of all the individual cellular and molecular growth processes within the muscle. *Figure 9.2* shows the growth curves of breast muscles from one side (*m. pectoralis* + *supracoracoideus* + *coracobrachialis ventralis*) of both sexes of two commercial strains of turkeys which, for obvious reasons, are identified no further. Sexual dimorphism is strongly developed, to the extent that the male of the lightly muscled strain has more muscle than the female of the heavily muscled strain.

Liveweight gains are important commercially, as in the calculation of feed-conversion efficiency, but how much do they tell us about muscle growth and actual meat production? In the example shown, the answer is — not much (*Figure 9.3*)! The more heavily muscled strain had lower live weights and, hence, a greatly enhanced meat yield when expressed as a percentage of muscle weight over live weight. The data shown are for males, but the trend also held true for females.

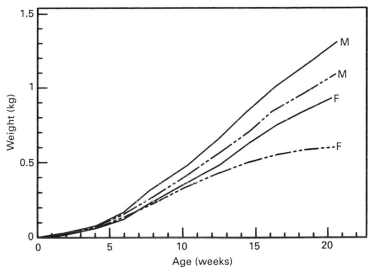

Figure 9.2 Growth curves for breast muscles (*m. pectoralis + supracoracoideus + coracobrachialis ventralis; unilateral*) in heavily muscled (solid lines) and lightly muscled (broken lines) commercial strains of white turkeys showing differences between males (M) and females (F)

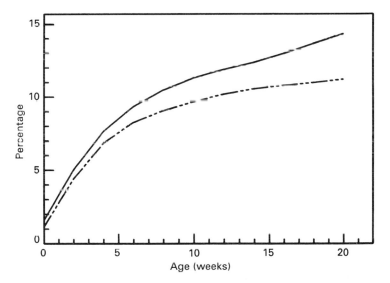

Figure 9.3 Unilateral breast muscle yield (data from *Figure 9.2*) as percentages of live weight in heavily muscled (solid line) and lightly muscled (broken line) male turkeys

Muscle weights are obviously important, but consumers do not know the weights of individual muscles when they select a turkey in a shop. What the consumer sees and probably reacts to is the appearance of muscularity — the way in which the breast muscles bulge outwards over the pectoral girdle. *Figure 9.4* shows the growth curves for a set of linear measurements that describes the shape of the turkey breast (using the more heavily muscled male birds from *Figure 9.2*). These linear measurements are the summation of some complex growth processes. The length of

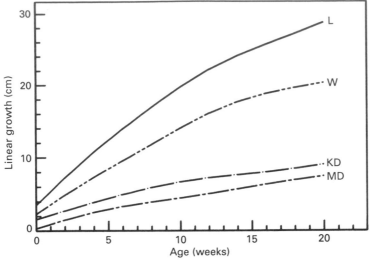

Figure 9.4 Linear growth of breast shape in males of the heavily muscled strain. Maximum length, L; maximum width, W; maximum keel depth, KD; and maximum muscle depth, MD

the breast involves longitudinal growth of the sternum plus matching longitudinal muscle growth and anterior bulging of the muscles. The width of the breast involves sternal growth plus radial growth in the girth of breast muscles. The muscle depth over the sternum is a fair measure of breast muscle mass ($r = 0.97$ in the correlation of the cube root of muscle weight with muscle depth) but, subjectively, its magnitude appears to be altered by the depth of the adjacent keel. For example, in two birds with the same absolute muscle depth, a bird with a shallow keel will appear to have breast muscles that bulge to a greater extent than will a bird with a deep keel.

The gross anatomical structure of muscles may limit the way in which they grow. In turkey carcasses, the two major types of muscles are those with parallel or slightly divergent fasciculi and those with a more complex internal arrangement of fasciculi. The *supracoracoideus*, for example, has a pennate structure in which its fasciculi attach to an internal tendon in a 'V' arrangement. Muscles with a relatively simple structure are less limited in their growth, particularly if they are located superficially in the body.

Different muscles of the body may grow at different rates relative to each other. In turkeys, the allometric growth ratios (which measure differential growth in body proportions) of leg, thigh and wing regions are 0.85, 0.91 and 0.98, respectively, relative to breast muscle weight. Thus, leg muscles, for example, grow at a slower rate than breast muscles so that the proportion of breast muscle in the carcass may increase with age.

Red and white muscle fibres

An interesting paradox in the physiology of muscle growth in turkeys concerns the conflict between muscle inactivity and muscle enlargement. For example, if we, as a species of animal, wished to enlarge our own muscle we might expend considerable amounts of energy in strenuous muscle exercise. Conversely, if we were of a different frame of mind and wished to eat *ad libitum* without exercise beyond that required for basal metabolism, we would not be too surprised if our bodies became obese and our muscles wasted away. With our own species for comparison it is, therefore, rather interesting to observe that well-fed domestic turkeys can develop enormously large, lean breast muscles without using them to any extent.

A speculative explanation of this paradox takes us back to the behaviour of wild turkeys for whom flight is a frantic means of escape from predators. Exceptionally strong breast muscles are required to lift a heavy body to the safety of the skies or to a nearby perch. Wild turkeys escape into the air by a series of strong wing beats and then they glide at a constant altitude with occasional wing beats (Schorger, 1966). Heavy birds are sometimes unable to repeat the lift-off without a period of rest despite the fact that they may have massive fat deposits of stored energy. The energy for lift-off is stored intracellularly as glycogen granules between the myofibrils (*Figure 9.5*) since there is insufficient time to mobilize blood-borne fatty acids and an inadequate supply of oxygen for their complete oxidation. Thus, breast muscles of turkeys have an extreme adaptation for rapid and powerful, yet easily fatigued contraction.

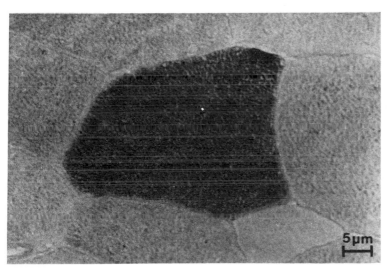

Figure 9.5 Transverse section of a turkey pectoralis muscle fibre loaded with glycogen between its myofibrils. The surrounding fibres depleted their glycogen as the bird was captured. The glycogen is demonstrated by the periodic-acid Schiff reaction

Nearly all the individual muscle fibres of white muscles such as the *m. pectoralis* follow this metabolic pattern in miniature. Thus myosin from white fibres has relatively fast adenosine triphosphatase (ATPase) activity for fast contraction and is histochemically identifiable by its relative resistance to formaldehyde but susceptibility to acetic acid. Fibres are loaded with glycogen (unless depleted just before the bird is killed) and with enzymes such as glycogen phosphorylase that are involved in anaerobic glycolysis. Aerobic features such as: (1) myoglobin content, (2) blood capillary supply to the muscle fibre surface, (3) the presence of intracellular droplets of triglyceride, and (4) the numbers of mitochondria, are very

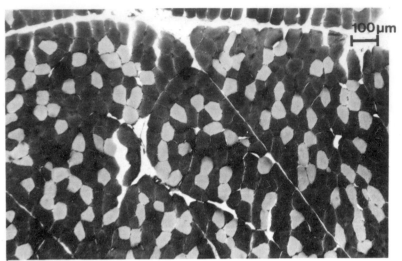

Figure 9.6 Transverse section of turkey sartorius muscle at 22 weeks reacted for myofibrillar ATPase to demonstrate fast-contracting (dark) and slow-contracting (light) fibres

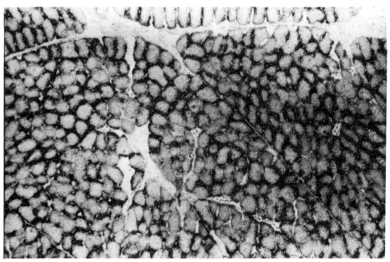

Figure 9.7 Serial section to *Figure 9.6* reacted for succinate dehydrogenase to show the distribution of mitochondria

low relative to the fibres of fatigue-resistant muscles. Leg muscles have a mixture of fast- and slow-contracting muscle fibres, most of which have fairly strong aerobic metabolism (*Figures 9.6* and *9.7*).

The histological and physiological features of red and white muscle have been investigated for over a century. Perhaps the most important accomplishment of recent years has been the combination of these two disciplines. The physiological characteristics of contraction in individual muscle fibres have now been directly correlated with their histochemical characteristics in frozen transverse sections. Thus, we can now be far more certain how histochemical, biochemical and physiological parameters are interrelated.

The subject on which we have made the least progress in this area is understanding the mechanism that controls the physiological differentiation of fibres into the three main types of fibres: (1) fast-contracting anaerobic, (2) fast-contracting aerobic, and (3) slow-contracting aerobic fibres. Control is somehow mediated through the nervous system since experimentally cross-re-innervated fast and slow muscles (the nerve that originally supplied the fast muscle is re-directed to the slow muscle and vice versa) undergo a reversal of their physiological and histochemical characteristics. Whether this happens by the release of trophic substances from the axons at neuromuscular junctions or whether it is mediated by activity patterns imposed by motor neurons remains a subject for debate. Indeed, arguments still continue as to whether the three main histochemical fibre types are distinctly different species of fibres or simply three peaks in an otherwise continuous distribution of histochemical and physiological features.

In cattle, pigs and sheep, all the muscle fibres of the commercial meat carcass are innervated by a sharply localized type of neuromuscular junction usually termed a motor end plate. The situation in poultry is more complicated. Fast-contracting fibres have sharply localized junctions (*en plaque* type neuromuscular junction) whereas slow-contracting fibres may have a more diffuse ending that extends a considerable way along each fibre (*en grappe* type). These histological differences are associated with physiological differences in the ways that membranes respond to acetylcholine released at the neuromuscular junction, but it is reasonable to suppose that the nervous system is still involved in regulating the physiological differentiation of muscle fibres.

From studies on beef and lamb there is evidence that many of the desirable aspects of meat quality that are detected by consumers are related to the percentages of aerobic fibres loaded with myoglobin, mitochondria and triglyceride droplets. In cooked turkeys, the succulence of leg muscles compared to the sometimes problematical dryness of breast muscles suggests that the same relationship may hold true.

In cattle, pigs and sheep, there are often marked changes in the ratios of different physiological fibre types during development. For example, muscles with a postural function that act primarily against gravity may increase their relative proportion of fibres with fatigue-resistant slow contraction. This may happen very rapidly after birth when the neonate is first exposed to gravity, or more slowly later in development when body weight (cubic function) tends to out-grow muscle strength (squared function — muscle cross-sectional area). Developmental changes such as these may involve recruitment of one physiological fibre type from another or allometric radial growth. Allometric longitudinal growth is an unproven possibility, but one that might confound attempts to measure fibre-type ratios in muscle cross-sections. Positive allometric growth of slow-contracting muscle fibres has been detected in turkey leg muscle, but there is no readily available information on changes in fibre type ratios.

Radial growth of muscle fibres

For almost as long as microscopists have been looking at muscle cross sections, it has been appreciated that the diameters of muscle fibres increase as muscles grow larger. The radial growth of muscle fibres is accompanied by an increase in the amount of sarcoplasm (cytoplasm of the muscle fibre) and in the number of myofibrils seen in transverse sections.

Differences in the radial growth of muscle fibres are important in turkeys. Males develop larger diameter fibres than females (*Figure 9.8*) and genetic strains with a high meat yield may also have larger diameter fibres than less muscular strains. Perhaps the most interesting feature about radial growth is that it occurs at a fairly regular rate in turkeys with little or no evidence of reaching an asymptote during the commercial growing period. This differs from the growth pattern in cattle, pigs and sheep where radial growth is often completed before animals reach slaughter weight.

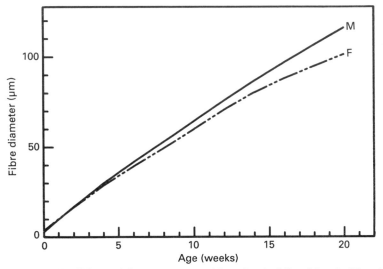

Figure 9.8 Radial growth in *m. supracoracoideus* of male (M) and female (F) turkeys of a well-muscled genetic strain

The method by which myofibrils increase in number is still only poorly understood. The ideas of early histologists such as Heidenhain form the basis of what many of us now believe. As shown in *Figure 9.9*, new filaments appear to be added to the periphery of existing myofibrils so that the diameters of the myofibrils are increased. This probably creates operational problems for the myofibril since it is surrounded by the sarcoplasmic reticulum. The diffusion pathway of calcium ions is thereby increased (calcium ions are released inwards to activate contraction and are re-sequestered outwards by the sarcoplasmic reticulum to allow muscle

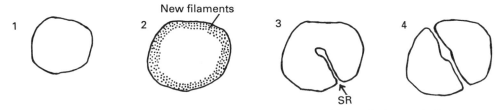

Figure 9.9 Possible stages in the splitting of a myofibril during the radial growth of a muscle fibre. Transverse sections show: (1) starting size, (2) addition or new filaments peripherally, (3) splitting of enlarged myofibril and ingrowth of the sarcoplasmic reticulum (SR), and (4) separated myofibrils

relaxation). This might cause shearing between the peripheral sliding filaments (which are turned on and off rapidly) and the inner filaments (which may respond more slowly). Located within the myofibril is a calcium-activated protease that attacks alpha-actinin, the protein that anchors the thin filaments in the Z line. Whether or not these factors all come together neatly (radial shear forces acting on centrally weakened Z lines caused by persistent calcium ions) or whether this speculation is simplistic is difficult to decide, but what appears to happen is that a fissure (often running through a central hollow in the fibril) may split the fibril into two smaller units that can be properly serviced by an inpushing of the sarcoplasmic reticulum.

When muscle fibres reach a large radius as a result of myofibrillar splitting, the diffusion pathway of oxygen from capillaries on the muscle fibre surface to the central axis of the fibre may become too long for optimal rates of gas exchange. Thus, in some physiological types of muscle fibres, the mitochondria tend to be more densely packed in the periphery of the fibre than in the axis (*Figure 9.10*). The classic physiological model of oxygen movement in skeletal muscle is based on the centrifugal diffusion of oxygen from capillaries surrounded by a matrix of muscle fibres. There is now a movement in favour of an alternative model in which diffusion is based centripetally on the axis of the muscle fibre. The computer mapping of aerobic enzymes, such as that shown for turkey sartorius fibres in *Figure 9.10*, supports the latter model.

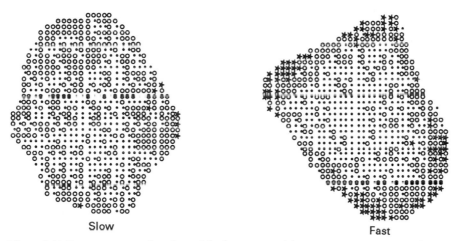

Slow   Fast

Figure 9.10 Computer maps of succinate dehydrogenase activity in slow- and fast-contracting muscle fibres from turkey sartorius muscles. The symbols show the strength of enzyme activity: (*) strong, (O) intermediate and (·) weak

The agricultural important of work in this area relates to the problem of meat quality versus quantity. Both selective breeding and optimum nutrition may encourage the extensive radial growth of muscle fibres so that they reach a very large size. Common sense tells us that there may be an upper limit to the diameter of a muscle fibre (more exactly, for each physiological type of muscle fibre). This leads us to two predictions: (1) that fibres with a very large diameter may have altered patterns of metabolism, and (2) that there may be an upper limit to the extent to which muscularity or meat yield can be improved by increasing muscle fibre diameters.

In the first prediction, the concern relates to meat quality. In the late 1960s and early 1970s, several investigators argued, quite plausibly, that the excessive radial growth of muscle fibres in pigs had contributed to the porcine stress syndrome (PSS). As a generalization, PSS pigs tend to store large amounts of glycogen in their muscles. The pigs over-react to normal stresses such as being transported or crowded together and they metabolize their glycogen to produce lactic acid and heat. This may kill the pig or, if the metabolic reaction occurs during slaughtering when the circulation can no longer flush out the lactate from the musculature, then the rapid accumulation of lactate in the still hot carcasses causes the meat to become pale, soft and exudative (PSE). The only two points which support this hypothesis are that breeds such as the Pietrain that suffer seriously from PSS probably have larger diameter fibres than any other breed, and that the central axes of muscle fibres in heavy pigs of many breeds frequently develop cores of solid glycogen which, if they were present in human muscle, would certainly be regarded as a pathological feature. There are, however, other more profound hypotheses to account for PSS, and the possibility of a relationship between excessive muscle fibre diameters and poor meat quality is more of a worry than a proven fact. The PSE condition has been reported in turkey breast muscles (van Hoof, 1979).

Longitudinal growth

The longitudinal growth of muscle fibres has received very little attention from agricultural scientists since it is a difficult parameter to investigate. Myofibrils are built up from a sequence of structurally independent sarcomeres along their length so that longitudinal growth can only occur by the formation of new sarcomeres at the ends of fibres. To maintain the mechanical continuity of the myofibril (a problem rather like adding links to a chain while it is in use), the myofibrils are attached obliquely to the inner surface of the plasma membrane of the muscle fibre (*Figure 9.11*). While the force of contraction can be transmitted through connections of the Z line to the membrane, new filaments can be added to build up new sarcomeres farther along the myofibril. When completed, the new sarcomere can be added to the functional length of the myofibril and a new attachment at the end of the sarcomere can be put into service. The ends of many muscle fibres are conical to allow a large internal area for the attachment of the myofibrils at an oblique angle. Sometimes the fibre membrane may protrude internally to form finger-like projections into the interior of the fibre. These increase the area for the attachment of myofibrils.

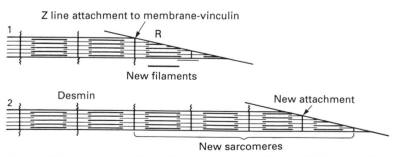

Figure 9.11 Longitudinal sections at the end of a muscle fibre to show how new filaments might be added to form new sarcomeres without disrupting the series continuity of the myofibril

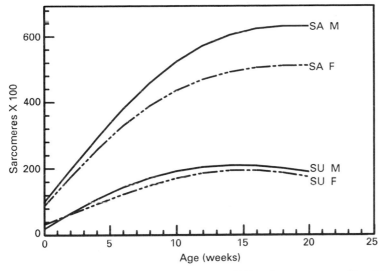

Figure 9.12 Longitudinal growth of *m. sartorius* (SA) and *m. supracoracoideus* (SU) in male (M) and female (F) turkeys measured by the number of sarcomeres along the length of the muscle (fascicular length/mean sarcomere length)

Figure 9.12 shows some curves for the longitudinal growth of turkey muscles. Since it is extremely difficult to dissect out individual muscle fibres to measure their length, the length of the muscle has been measured by the number of sarcomeres along its length (fascicular length/mean sarcomere length). This avoids the problem of trying to decide what constitutes the resting length of the muscle of its sarcomeres. Rates of sarcomere formation vary considerably, as the data show. As an order of magnitude approximation, however, one sarcomere is added to the muscle length about every hour. In contrast to radial growth, longitudinal muscle growth in turkeys reaches an asymptote during the commercial growing period. There might even be a loss of sarcomeres (*Figure 9.12*), as in the supracoracoideus muscle which outgrows its osteofascial compartment and is liable to self-destruct if heavily exercised (Siller, 1985).

It is often assumed that muscle fibres run the complete length of their muscle, from one end to another. While this may be true of the muscles of relatively small animals, it is certainly not the case in the large muscles of meat animals. In large muscles, many fibres terminate intrafascicularly, that is, one or both ends of the fibre may taper over a length of several millimetres to form a very small diameter muscle fibre that is then anchored in the connective tissues that invest an adjacent muscle fibre. The connective tissues around individual muscle fibres are formed by highly branched reticular fibres composed of biochemical Type III collagen.

Numbers of muscle fibres

Intrafascicularly terminating muscle fibres present a formidable problem in studying muscle growth in meat animals. If a muscle is transected at its mid-length and the number of fibres that appears in the transverse section is estimated, there is virtually no way to determine the number of intrafascicularly terminating muscle fibres that have been missed. In the large muscles of meat animals, therefore, the fraction of the real number of muscle fibres that appear in a transverse section at the muscle mid-length may be rather variable. In pigs, for example, the apparent number may increase during growth to slaughter weight while, in cattle, some of the hindlimb muscles show a decrease in apparent numbers of muscle fibres.

Since there is virtually no histological evidence of the formation or destruction of muscle fibres after birth in health muscles, the only tenable explanation of these sometimes dramatic increases in apparent numbers of muscle fibres is that they are a manifestation of the longitudinal growth of intrafascicularly terminating muscle fibres. Thus, when apparent numbers of fibres increase, intrafascicularly terminating muscle fibres may be growing at a faster rate than the overall length of the muscle and, conversely, when apparent numbers decrease, intrafascicularly terminating fibres may be failing to keep pace with the longitudinal growth of the whole muscle. If these ideas are correct, then the formation of new sarcomeres at the ends of intrafascicularly terminating fibres must occur in a way that maintains the structural connection between an intrafascicularly terminating fibre and the normal diameter fibres on which it is anchored. This is not inconceivable since the same problem (that of maintaining series continuity while changing in length) also occurs intracellularly with the formation of new sarcomeres relative to the muscle fibre membrane.

The situation regarding muscle fibre numbers in turkeys is poorly known. In the sartorius muscle there appears to be an increase in the apparent number of muscle fibres at the muscle mid-length just after hatching. There is also evidence that males have a greater apparent number of muscle fibres than females. Whether or not the more heavily muscled genetic strains have a greater number of muscle fibres than lightly muscled strains is unknown at present. Since all the skeletal muscle fibres of the commercial turkey carcass are formed during early development prior to hatching, fibre numbers are likely to be highly heritable and worthy of investigation as a trait for genetic selection.

Formation of muscle fibres

The multinucleate condition of the skeletal muscle fibre originates from the fusion of mononucleate cells — a discovery that dates back to Theodore Schwann in 1839. A population of cells called premyoblasts expands by mitosis. After a particular cell division, which is probably genetically regulated and is called the quantal or critical mitosis, the premyoblast changes from DNA synthesis to large-scale RNA synthesis. It is now called a myoblast and reveals itself by fusing with other myoblasts and by starting to synthesize muscle-specific actin and myosin and to assemble filaments and myofibrils (*Figure 9.13*). The newly formed myofibrils start to surround the nuclei of a string of fused myoblasts so that the resulting multinuclear cell has a tubular appearance (caused by the outer shell of myofibrils) and, thus, is called a myotube.

Myotubes are formed early in embryonic development and soon become arranged in a pattern which is the foundation for later muscle development. At this time, premyoblasts are still actively dividing, becoming myoblasts and contributing to the formation of new multinucleate muscle cells. These later generations of cells utilize the structural framework provided by the myotubes to accelerate the process of becoming correctly aligned and of becoming fused. Younger myoblasts adhere to

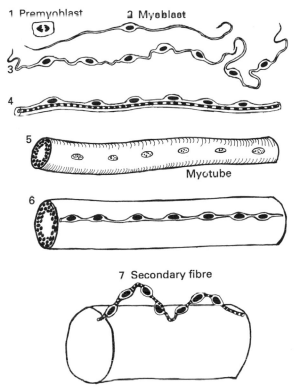

1 Premyoblast   2 Myoblast

3

4

5

Myotube

6

7 Secondary fibre

Figure 9.13 Stages in the formation of muscle fibres before hatching. (1) Premyoblasts capable of mitosis; (2) myoblast switched over to cell fusion and protein synthesis; (3) fusion of myoblasts at the ends of their cytoplasmic extensions; (4) formation of myofibrils; (5) myofibrils surround axial nuclei to form a myotube; (6) a new generation of myoblasts becomes aligned using the primary myotube as a template; and (7) secondary fibres become detached from the surface of the myotube

the surfaces of myotubes which are now innervated and undergoing slow, often rhythmic contractions associated with the formation of skeletal joints. New multinucleate muscle cells form on the surfaces of myotubes and are sheared off as they become independent. These new multinucleate muscle cells seldom develop a neat tubular structure and they are often called secondary fibres rather than myotubes.

By the time of birth or hatching, the nuclei of myotubes move to a peripheral position so that muscle fibres derived from both myotubes and secondary fibres have the same basic structure, although those derived from myotubes are generally larger in diameter. As a generalization, muscle fibres derived from myotubes mostly develop into slow-contracting aerobic fibres while muscle fibres derived from secondary fibres tend to develop into fast-contracting anaerobic fibres. There are, however, plenty of exceptions. In the turkey pectoralis muscle, for example, all the fibres derived from myotubes in the outer regions of the muscle develop into fast-contracting anaerobic fibres.

Much of the recent literature relating to the molecular biology of early muscle development is summarized by Emerson *et al.* (1986). Premyoblasts are now known to go through an exact series of four symmetrical mitoses to generate cohorts of 16 myoblasts, a point which relates to the heritability of muscle fibre numbers. If double-muscling (muscle fibre hyperplasia) in cattle is any guide, then the number of myoblasts that develops embryologically might well determine the number of muscle fibres that can be formed. Other premyoblasts remain quiescent as small satellite cells trapped on the muscle fibre surface. Later in development, they become mitotic again and their daughter cells fuse into the muscle fibre to provide the increasing amounts of DNA found in growing turkey muscles (Kang, Sunde and Swick, 1985).

Another active field of research concerns the environment around the developing myoblasts. The chemical and tactile properties of substrates are particularly important for myoblasts and there are now known to be systematic changes in the relative proportions of different types of proteoglycans in the matrix around the myoblasts. The proteoglycan matrix is involved in the stimulation of muscle growth by as yet unidentified muscle growth factors. The known growth factors now include proteins such as transferrin — an iron-binding protein. Last, but not least impressive, is the growing library of genetic codes for muscle proteins.

The histology of skeletal muscle reached a high degree of sophistication as it developed from the 1830s to about 1900. However, from 1900 until the advent of biological electron microscopy there was an unforgivable decline in the quality of knowledge so that many of the early discoveries were ignored and neither confirmed nor rejected. Before the development of accurate microtomes, most histological studies on muscle were undertaken by microdissection and isolated myofibrils and fibres were examined with a skill that is difficult to match, even today. By dissecting fresh muscle fibres it became known that there was an invisible skeleton within the fibre which held myofibrils together laterally, which bound myofibrils to the inner surface of the muscle fibre membrane, and which bound sarcomeres together longitudinally in series.

The cytoskeleton is one of the most ancient features of animal cells. It consists of monomeric units that can be rapidly polymerized and depolymerized to create a woven framework of fine filaments (typically 10 nm in diameter; Nelson and Traub, 1982). This skeletal framework within the cell provides both movement and structural support. The highly specialized sliding filament system of the myofibril is a highly evolved derivative of the cytoskeleton, but other elements of the cytoskeleton are still present within the muscle fibre. Each Z line is sandwiched between two rings of cytoskeletal filaments and there are connections both laterally, to link adjacent Z lines, and longitudinally (Wang and Ramirez-Mitchell, 1983). Transverse cytoskeletal fibres are woven to form cables that are visible by transmission electron microscopy at the level of the M line as well as the Z line (Pierobon-Bormioli, 1981).

Two of the major proteins of the transverse cytoskeleton are desmin, which forms transverse cables (Granger and Lazarides, 1978), and vimentin, which links the cables to the inner surface of the muscle fibre membrane (Pardo, Siliciano and Craig, 1983; Shear and Bloch, 1985). Major longitudinal linkages are made of connectin (Maruyama *et al.*, 1985). The list of identified proteins in the muscle cytoskeleton continues to grow (vimentin, synemin, spectrin, ankyrin, zeugmatin, amorphin, etc.) and the general belief is that each one of them has a special role to play in providing the structural elements of the cytoskeleton and the 'glues' that hold them together. Thus, in attempting to explain how new filaments are added to growing myofibrils we can now name some of the major proteins that provide the cytoskeletal framework within which myofibrillar growth occurs (*Figure 9.11*).

Progress has also been made in understanding how intrafascicularly terminating muscle fibres might be anchored since the internal cytoskeleton of the muscle fibre appears to be matched by a comparable degree of organization in the connective tissue matrix between the muscle fibres (Orcutt *et al.*, 1986; Loewy *et al.*, 1983; Shear and Bloch, 1985).

Summary

Muscle growth patterns in well-nourished turkeys depend upon the anatomical structure of the muscle, the sex of the bird and its genetic strain. The radial growth of muscle fibres is associated with the longitudinal splitting of myofibrils and tends to occur at a steady rate from hatching to at least 20 weeks. The longitudinal growth of muscle fibres is associated with the formation of new sarcomeres at the ends of muscle fibres and becomes asymptotic before 20 weeks. Recent discoveries in molecular biology, especially studies on the proteins desmin and vinculin, help to explain the physiology of radial and longitudinal muscle growth.

References

Emerson, C., Fischman, D., Nadal-Ginard, B. and Siddiqui, M. A. Q. (1986). *Molecular Biology of Muscle Development.* New York, Alan R. Liss

Granger, B. L. and Lazarides, E. (1978). The existence of an insoluble Z disc scaffold in chicken skeletal muscle. *Cell*, **15**, 1253–1268

Kang, C. W., Sunde, M. L. and Swick, R. W. (1985). Characteristics of growth and protein turnover in skeletal muscle of turkey poults. *Poultry Science*, **64**, 380–387

Loewy, A. G., Wilson, F. J., Taggart, N. M. *et al.* (1983). A covalently cross-linked matrix in skeletal muscle fibers. *Cell Motility*, **3**, 463–483

Maruyama, K., Yoshioka, T., Higuchi, H., Ohashi, K., Kimura, S. and Natori, R. (1985). Connectin filaments link thick filaments and Z lines in frog skeletal muscle as revealed by immunoelectron microscopy. *Journal of Cell Biology*, **101**, 2167–2172

Mullen, K. and Swatland, H. J. (1979). Linear skeletal growth in male and female turkeys. *Growth*, **43**, 151–159

Nelson, W. J. and Traub, P. (1982). Intermediate (10 nm) filament proteins and the Ca^{2+}-activated proteinase specific for vimentin and desmin in the cells from fish to man: an example of evolutionary conservation. *Journal of Cell Science*, **57**, 25–49

Orcutt, M. W., Dutson, T. R., Wu, F. Y. and Smith, S. B. (1986). The fine structure of the endomysium, perimysium and intermyofibrillar connections in muscle. *Food Microstructure*, **5**, 41–51

Pardo, J. V., Siliciano, J. D. and Craig, S. W. (1983). A vinculin-containing cortical lattice in skeletal muscle: transverse lattice elements ('costameres') mark sites of attachment between myofibrils and sarcolemma. *Proceedings of the National Academy of Sciences, USA*, **80**, 1008–1012

Pierobon-Bormioli, S. (1981). Transverse sarcomere filamentous systems: 'Z- and M-cables'. *Journal of Muscle Research and Cell Motility*, **2**, 401–413

Schorger, A. W. (1966). *The Wild Turkey*, pp. 183–187. Norman, Oklahoma, University of Oklahoma Press

Shear, C. R. and Bloch, R. J. (1985). Vinculin in subsarcolemmal densities in chicken skeletal muscle: Localization and relationship to intracellular and extracellular structures. *Journal of Cell Biology*, **101**, 240–256

Siller, W. G. (1985). Deep pectoral myopathy: A penalty of successful selection for muscle growth. *Poultry Science*, **64**, 1591–1595

Swatland, H. J. (1979a). Development of shape in turkey carcasses. *Journal of Agricultural Science, Cambridge*, **93**, 1–6

Swatland, H. J. (1979b). Allometric radial growth in muscle, comparing fibres with strong and with weak adenosine triphosphatase activity. *Journal of Anatomy*, **129**, 591–596

Swatland, H. J. (1979c). Differential growth in the supracoradoideus muscles of male and female turkeys. *Zentralblatt fur Veterinarmedizin, Series C*, **8**, 227–232

Swatland, H. J. (1979d). Differential growth in the sartorius muscles of male and female turkeys. *Zentralblatt fur Veterinarmedizin, Series A*, **26**, 159–164

Swatland, H. J. (1980). A histological basis for differences in breast meat yield between two strains of white turkeys. *Journal of Agricultural Science, Cambridge*, **94**, 383–388

Swatland, H. J. (1984). *Structure and Development of Meat Animals*. New Jersey, Prentice-Hall

Swatland, H. J. (1985). Growth-related changes in the intracellular distribution of succinate dehydrogenase activity in turkey muscle. *Growth*, **49**, 409–416

van Hoof, J. (1979). Influence of ante- and peri-mortem factors on biochemical and physical characteristics of turkey breast muscle. *Veterinary Quarterly*, **1**, 29–36

Wang, K. and Ramirez-Mitchell, R. (1983). A network of transverse and longitudinal intermediate filaments is associated with sarcomeres of adult vertebrate skeletal muscle. *Journal of Cell Biology*, **96**, 562–570

Chapter 10

Nutritional responses of growing turkeys

C. Nixey

Types of nutritional response

Nutritional responses of growing turkeys can take several forms. At its most extreme turkeys can either live or die. This type of response has previously been observed and was found to be due to the presence or absence of individual vitamins in diets. It is also seen most dramatically if a toxic substance is eaten in excess. In practice, the toxin is often a drug present either by mistake or in excess because of an error in the feed mill. The ionophore group of coccidiostats can be particularly toxic to turkeys if there is an excessive quantity in the diet.

The turkey is a very fast growing animal. It will have multiplied its hatching weight by more than 20 times by 28 days of age. By 20 weeks of age, the males will have multiplied their original poult weight by almost 300 times. To achieve this development in a normal manner requires considerable demands on their nutrient intake. If the nutritional response is abnormal, it can have several manifestations. The rapid skeletal growth puts considerable demands on the intake of minerals. Abnormal responses would include rickets in the early weeks of life and twisted leg bones and hock deformities at older ages. A particularly sensitive area of development would appear to be feather growth. Abnormal feathering such as broken feathers, uneven feathering or late development of the feathers can all be symptoms of poor nutrition. The other visual aspect of nutritional responses is in the faeces of the turkey, which are very sensitive to changes in nutrient intake. They may vary in liquid content, colour, stickiness and smell, all aspects the good stockman will regularly assess when inspecting his stock. Sometimes the influence of nutrition via the faeces is an indirect one. If it causes the litter to be wet, this may subsequently result in an increase in leg problems in the flock. This was demonstrated by Martland (1984) who produced wet litter by spraying with water. This resulted in increased leg problems compared with those birds kept on dry litter. The most consistent nutritional response is on the liveweight gain of the turkey and it is intended to concentrate on this aspect for most of this chapter.

Vitamins

If a vitamin is deficient in a diet, the first signs to appear are loss of appetite, retarded growth and diarrhoea. Individual vitamins do result in other symptoms which are quoted as characteristic of a particular vitamin deficiency (NRC, 1984).

183

In addition to the vitamins occurring naturally in ingredients, it is normal to add vitamins via premix. There has been little work of real substance on most of the vitamin requirements of turkeys. It is normal commercial practice to include vitamins in excess of the theoretical requirements (NRC, 1984); the surplus being necessary to allow for the partial destruction during the pelleting process and degradation during storage. It is rare for classic vitamin deficiency symptoms to be seen. The most likely cause will be for the feed mill to omit by mistake the vitamin premix, particularly in the diet fed to very young turkeys.

Minerals

With regard to the mineral requirements of the turkey, the report of the sub-committee of Working Group 2 (Nutrition) of the European Federation of the branches of the World Poultry Science Association on mineral requirements for poultry covers the subject as well as the inadequate information will allow (WPSA, 1985). The sub-committee recommendations for phosphorus are stated as non-phytin phosphorus for the period 0–6 weeks, being 0.5 g/MJ ME. After the starting period, it is presumed that the turkey can partially utilize phytate phosphorus in ingredients (Sauveur, 1983).

In the chicken Mongin and Sauveur (1979) suggest that there is an optimum balance between Na + K − Cl. They suggest this equation should give an approximate value of 250 mEq/kg for optimum growth rate. There is debate about the sensitivity of this balance and even if such a balance is of importance. However, it does seem possible that the relationship between these elements could influence water uptake and subsequently the moisture content of the faeces. This may subsequently influence the litter management and so indirectly, the incidence of leg problems (Martland, 1984). It is an area worthy of further investigation with turkeys.

Amino acids

The turkey is a low fat, high protein containing animal and I make no apology for concentrating most of this chapter on the amino acid responses of the turkey. In my experience, this is an area of nutrition that is responsible for most of the variations in growth rate seen with the same genetic material which I see around the world.

Expression of amino acid requirement

It is only a short time ago that growth responses were ascribed to protein intake. '% protein' is still used as the shorthand description of diets when amino acid levels would be a more accurate but longer description. In some papers the amino acid requirement is expressed as a proportion of the protein. This method of expressing the amino acid requirement has a serious weakness in that the quality of the protein as judged by its lysine content will influence the requirement. For example 1.38% lysine is 4.75% of the protein if contained in a 29% protein diet and 5.5% if in a 25% protein diet. In other papers, the amino acid requirement is expressed as a proportion of the diet. While this is a more independent expression of the requirement, it will be influenced by factors which affect food intake. Three major factors which affect food intake are (1) the metabolizable energy (ME) content of the diet (Booth, 1979), (2) the form of the feed be it mash or pellets (Britzman, 1976) and, (3) the ambient temperature (Albuquerque et al., 1978; Noll and Waibel, 1982). The temperature and the form of the feed can be specified when the requirements are stated. To overcome the influence of the ME content of the diet, the amino acid requirement can be expressed as g of amino acid/MJ ME.

Empirical experimentation

It has been traditional to assess the amino acid requirements directly by empirical experimentation. Most experiments have involved the addition of free amino acid incrementally to a basal diet deficient in the test amino acid to achieve a range of test amino acid concentrations. This technique has two weaknesses. The first is that variation occurs in the amino acid balance of successive diets within a supplementary series. The second criticism is that another amino acid may become limiting before the maximum response to the test amino acid is achieved. The interpretation of some of the data can also be criticized.

Lack of plateau

To ensure that the full potential response to the limiting amino acid has been achieved, the data should give a clear indication of a plateau or 'upper limit'. This criterion has not been met in several experiments where it has been concluded that the requirement for maximum bodyweight gain is the highest level of input in the series (Tuttle and Balloun, 1974; Jensen et al., 1976).

Previous plane of nutrition

It has been shown that the previous plane of nutrition can influence the utilization of protein by the turkey in the subsequent growth periods (Auckland, Morris and Jennings, 1969; Scholtyssek, 1981). In a number of experiments, the amino acid requirements were determined for two or more consecutive periods without randomized re-mixing of the birds. In such a situation, the bodyweight gains and efficiencies of utilization of amino acids during subsequent periods under test are going to be influenced by the treatments previously received (Jensen et al., 1965; Geraedts and Kan, 1981).

Method of interpretation

Even in experiments where the data would appear to be sound, it is important that they are interpreted correctly. A common method of determining the requirement is the 'broken line' least squares method (Robbins, Norton and Baker, 1979). The broken line method determines the requirement point (breakpoint) as the intersection of the sloping line fitted to the growth response section of the curve with the line fitted to the plateau section. The 'broken line' method will tend to underestimate the requirement because it ignores the 'diminishing returns' zone normally seen to the plateau and, assuming the true response is curvilinear, the intersection will not lie on this curve.

It is not therefore surprising that the recommendations derived from research work on the amino acid requirements of the turkey show a wide variation. The research work reported is not very substantial. Most papers cover the lysine requirements with a lesser number on the sulphur amino acids and very few on other amino acids. There are more papers on the protein requirements but, as the first limiting amino acid may vary between the levels of protein compared, the work at the moment is of no value in describing amino acid responses. When more is known about individual amino acid responses, it may be possible in the future to go back to the work on protein levels and use it for verification of descriptions of amino acid responses. In reviewing studies on the lysine response of turkeys, very few papers were found on the requirements of both sexes. By far the most work has been done on the males. The authors' conclusions have been converted where possible to be expressed as g of lysine/MJ ME. This information is shown in *Table 10.1*.

Table 10.1 Lysine requirements of male turkeys

Approximate age range (days)	*No. of data sets*	*Mean indicated lysine requirement[a] (g/MJ ME)[b]*	*Range of indicated requirement*	
			Low	*High*
0–28	6	1.236	1.135	1.328
28–56	3	1.254	1.219	1.278
56–84	10	0.896	0.729	1.110
84–112	3	0.836	0.646	0.978
112–140	9	0.557	0.478	0.717
140–168	2	0.512	0.470	0.569

(Nixey and Boorman, 1985)

[a] The indicated requirement concluded by original authors
[b] The ME is the calculated value as stated in the original paper

A decreasing requirement with age is seen but at each age, there is considerable range in the indicated lysine requirements. If the highest indicated requirements are plotted against age, the correlation is very good ($r = 0.985$) with a regression coefficient of 5.7 mg of lysine/MJ ME for each change in day of age. However the range in the indicated requirement is of concern, and probably originates from the weaknesses in empirical experimentation already discussed.

In reviewing the papers on the sulphur amino acid response of turkeys, even fewer papers were found. There was the added complication that there is a requirement for methionine alone in addition to its contribution to the sulphur amino acids. Turkey diets will contain both methionine and cystine. Cystine has a 'sparing' effect on methionine, i.e. the methionine requirement is dependent on the amount of cystine in the diet. For this chapter it has been found feasible to only analyse the total sulphur amino acid (TSAA) response data in the published papers. Behrends and Waibel (1980) estimated that cystine could replace up to 55, 58 and 57% of the TSAA for starting, growing and finishing turkeys respectively. A summary of the review of the literature is shown in *Table 10.2*.

Very little work has been carried out on the other amino acids. This is included in the section dealing with the interdependence of amino acids below. The case for empirical experimentation has not therefore been helped by its implementation in practice.

Table 10.2 The total sulphur amino acid requirements of male turkeys

Approximate age range (days)	No. of data sets	Mean indicated TSAA requirement[a] (g/MJ ME)[b]	Range of indicated requirement	
			Low	High
0–56	2	0.865	0.814	0.915
0–28	5	0.783	0.664	0.876
28–56	2	0.740	0.696	0.784
56–84	4	0.568	0.492	0.647
84–112	0	–	–	–
112–140	2	0.312	0.282	0.341
140–168	0	–	–	–

(Nixey and Boorman, 1985)

[a] The indicated requirement concluded by original authors
[b] The ME is the calculated value as stated in the original paper

Calculated responses

Fisher and Emmans (1983), argued the case for determining the amino acid requirements indirectly by factorial calculation rather than by empirical experimentation so as to accommodate widely differing situations and also to fill quickly the large gaps in the present state of knowledge. Two groups of workers have attempted to calculate the amino acid requirements of the turkey. Fisher and Emmans (1983) have produced calculations based on the Edinburgh Growth model and Hurwitz et al. (1983) have produced a model based on body composition. The former will be referred to as the Edinburgh model and the latter as the Israeli model.

Growth rate

The two groups have tackled the problem in different ways, using different combinations of empirical and analytical data to produce their model of the turkey. The Israeli model is based on actual measurements made on BUT large white male turkeys so that their calculations relate specifically to that bird. The Edinburgh model uses the Gompertz function, a well established growth equation which gives an estimate of body weight at time t. It requires the definition of two parameters; A, the body weight at maturity and B, the rate of decline in relative growth rate which is a measure of the rate of maturity.

Maintenance

The Israeli model uses maintenance requirements calculated from first principles by measuring tissue loss. The Edinburgh model uses values calculated from data collected on adult cockerels. In the Israeli model, the amino acid requirements are expressed as mg/g body weight$^{2/3}$/day whereas in the Edinburgh model they are expressed as mg/kg body weight/day. The relative comparisons of the predictions of the two models therefore change as the body weight changes. For example the two models give a similar prediction for lysine requirement in the bodyweight range 1.3–1.5 kg. As the body weight increases thereafter the Israeli model predicts progressively less lysine required per kg body weight/day. By 10 kg body weight, the Israeli model uses a lysine prediction which is almost half the figure used in the Edinburgh model.

Bodyweight gain

The method of calculating the net amino acid requirements for weight gain contains major differences between the two models. The Edinburgh model bases its efficiency of conversion of dietary to body amino acid of 64%. The Israeli model does not use a term for biological utilization but contains a term for the efficiency of intestinal absorption, which is a function of the digestibility of the protein. The efficiency of absorption is taken as 85% (Hurwitz *et al.*, 1979). If all other calculations were similar therefore the Israeli model would arrive at a dietary amino acid requirement considerably lower than the Edinburgh model. The Israeli model uses for its protein content of weight gain, data from body composition analysis. This would seem to be more accurate than in the Edinburgh model, where the protein content of the body is calculated by a theoretical formula related to the degree of maturity of the turkey which presumes an increasing protein content up to maturity.

Amino acid profiles

The two models therefore have arrived at amino acid requirements based on different methods of calculation. Some amino acids are likely to be relatively more important for maintenance, e.g. the sulphur amino acids, whereas others, e.g. lysine, are likely to be relatively more important for bodyweight gain. The differing methods of calculation have therefore also resulted in different predicted amino

Table 10.3 A comparison of the amino acid profiles predicted by the Edinburgh and Israeli models for large male turkeys

Age (weeks)	Lysine		Methionine		TSAA		Tryptophan		Threonine	
	Israeli	Edin	Israeli	Edin	Israeli	Edin	Israeli	Edin	Israeli	Edin
4	100	100	36.5	36.0	70.8	64.0	14.7	17.3	78.9	70.3
5	100	100	36.0	36.1	71.6	64.1	14.7	17.3	79.2	70.2
6	100	100	36.1	36.2	75.6	64.2	14.9	17.3	80.8	70.2
7	100	100	36.2	36.4	79.1	64.4	15.2	17.2	82.3	70.1
8	100	100	36.5	36.5	79.3	64.5	15.1	17.2	82.5	70.0
9	100	100	36.6	36.7	83.6	64.7	15.4	17.2	84.1	69.9
10	100	100	36.7	36.9	83.4	64.9	15.5	17.2	84.2	69.8
11	100	100	36.7	37.1	83.6	65.1	15.5	17.1	84.2	69.6
12	100	100	37.2	37.4	90.3	65.4	16.0	17.1	87.0	69.5
13	100	100	37.8	37.6	91.4	65.7	16.2	17.1	87.4	69.4
14	100	100	38.6	37.9	95.5	65.9	16.3	17.0	89.4	69.2
15	100	100	38.7	38.1	97.8	66.3	16.4	17.0	90.2	69.0
16	100	100	39.1	38.6	101.0	66.7	16.9	17.0	91.3	68.8
17	100	100	38.9	39.0	99.5	67.1	16.7	16.9	90.6	68.6
18	100	100	39.1	39.5	96.8	67.5	16.4	16.9	89.9	68.4
19	100	100	38.7	39.9	86.8	68.0	16.0	16.8	85.8	68.2
20	100	100	39.3	40.4	94.2	68.6	16.2	16.7	89.0	67.9
21	100	100	39.4	41.0	90.6	69.2	16.5	16.7	87.0	67.6

acid profiles which changed with age. Basing the amino acid profile on lysine having a value of 100, the predicted profiles are shown in *Table 10.3*. There is close agreement on the methionine value but a large divergence on the total sulphur amino acid value. In view of the work by Behrends and Waibel (1980) which suggested that cystine could only represent up to 55, 58 and 57% of the TSAA for starting, growing and finishing turkeys respectively, the relative values of methionine and TSAA look suspect at the older ages in the Israeli model. There is also a wide divergence between the models in the predicted threonine values.

Table 10.4 The amino acid profiles of ingredients commonly used in turkey diets

Ingredient	Lysine	Methionine	TSAA	Tryprophan	Threonine
Maize	100	83.3	145.8	37.5	162.5
Wheat (soft)	100	48.3	119.4	38.7	103.2
Soya	100	22.2	45.7	22.2	61.7
Fish (white)	100	37.1	53.6	14.8	56.7
Meatmeal	100	25.0	47.0	12.0	58.0
Sunflower	100	50.0	100.0	45.0	105.0
Barley	100	42.5	90.0	35.0	105.0
Oats	100	36.0	80.0	32.0	86.0

(NRC, 1984)

An indication of the significance of these values can be obtained by reference to the amino acid profiles in common ingredients (*Table 10.4*). It will be seen that in high protein diets used early in life which contain large quantities of soya, fish-meal and meat-meal, there is a very real possibility of the threonine level being well below even the Edinburgh model predictions. Tryptophan is unlikely ever to be the first limiting amino acid. With the availability of synthetic methionine, it need never be a problem to obtain the required level, although if the Israeli model is correct, TSAA may well be the first limiting amino acids in diets commonly in use.

Metabolizable energy

The preferred method of expressing the requirement of an amino acid is as g/MJ ME. This requires an estimate of ME daily requirements. In the Israeli model, Hurwitz, Sklan and Bartov (1978) assessed the requirement using temperature controlled chambers and carrying out balance trials. Their conclusion was that at 12°C the maintenance requirement was $2.70 \, \text{kcal/g}^{2/3}$ and the requirement for growth was 0.7 kcal/g weight gain. This was later modified (Hurwitz *et al.*, 1980) to take into account differences in the proportion of the weight gain which was lipid. This equation is $D = 0.6 + (9.3 \times F)$ where D is the requirement for weight gain, in kcal/g and F is the lipid fraction in the bodyweight gain. This is used in the Israeli model.

The Edinburgh model uses the following formula:

$$dM/dt = M.W_t + g.u^{0.08}. dW/dt$$

where dM/dt = ME intake, kJ/day
    M = maintenance requirement = $600A^{0.73}/A$ kJ/kg day

$$
\begin{aligned}
\text{where } A &= \text{mature body weight} \\
g &= \text{growth requirement, kJ/g} \\
u &= \text{degree of maturity} = W_t/A \\
\text{where } W_t &= \text{body weight } W \text{ at time } t \\
dW/dt &= B \cdot W_t \cdot \ln (A/W_t) \\
\text{where } B &= \text{rate of decline of relative growth rate} \\
\ln &= \text{natural logarithm}
\end{aligned}
$$

The two equations indicate broadly similar ME requirements until the birds commence laying down significant quantities of body fat (14 weeks onwards for the males). At that stage the Israeli model commences to indicate a noticeably higher ME requirement than the Edinburgh model.

Predicted requirements

The Edinburgh model cannot be used prior to 4 weeks of age (Fisher and Emmans, 1983). *Table 10.5* compares each model's predictions for g amino acid/MJ ME with the mean indicated requirement from published research. There is more agreement between the empirical research and the Edinburgh model on the lysine requirements while the Israeli model is closer to the empirical research in the TSAA requirement predictions. The situation however is very unsatisfactory, with considerable variations so that nutritionists can have little confidence in the information, when deciding on their turkey formulations.

Table 10.5 A comparison of indicated amino acid requirements (g/MJ ME)

Age period	Lysine			Methionine			TSAA		
	Israeli	Edin	Literature[a]	Israeli	Edin	Literature	Israeli	Edin	Literature[b]
0–4	1.209	–	1.236	0.437	–	–	0.898	–	0.783
4–8	0.926	0.987	1.254	0.339	0.359	–	0.763	0.634	0.740
8–12	0.646	0.880	0.896	0.245	0.326	–	0.603	0.572	0.568
12–16	0.485	0.764	0.836	0.189	0.291	–	0.465	0.505	–
16–20	0.364	0.647	0.557	0.148	0.257	–	0.358	0.439	0.312

[a] See *Table 10.1*
[b] See *Table 10.2*

Reading model analysis

An alternative method of determining nutritional responses between empirical experimentation and calculated models is to use suitable empirical data to produce response equations which can then be used in a calculated model. Fisher, Morris and Jennings (1973) produced a model, now known as the Reading model, to analyse and describe the response curve of egg output by a flock of laying hens to essential amino acids. It has since been proposed for use with growing birds by Clark *et al.* (1982) and Fisher and Emmans (1983). If the broken line method is used to interpret data, the indicated requirement for maximum bodyweight gain occurs at a lower level than that indicated by the Reading model.

In the Reading model, the amino acid requirement for maximum bodyweight gain (AA, mg/day) is calculated as $AA = a.\Delta W + b.W$ where ΔW is the potential bodyweight gain/day and W is the mean body weight. The constant a is defined as the amino acid intake (mg/day) per unit (g/day) bodyweight gain. The constant b is defined as the amino acid intake (mg/day) unit (g) of body weight maintained. These constants are derived from fitting a curve as described by Fisher, Morris and Jennings (1973).

Very few of the papers reviewed gave sufficient data for use in the Reading model for lysine response and even fewer for TSAA. Of those authors who had published usable data, the a and b values have been calculated and these are shown in *Table 10.6*. These confirm that more lysine than TSAA is required to produce 1 g of bodyweight gain. On the other hand more TSAA than lysine is required to maintain 1 g of body weight per day. The relatively greater importance of the maintenance requirement as the birds get older is reflected in the increased TSAA requirements.

Table 10.6 Reading model a and b values derived from suitable data in published papers

Age (days)	a		b	
	Lysine	TSAA	Lysine	TSAA
0–28	22.32	13.745	22.8	64.1
28–56	19.91	No data	17.2	No data
56–84	21.16	11.281	19.3	98.0
84–112	No data	No data	No data	No data
112 140	22.96	10.941	10.5	118.6

The advantage of the Reading model is that the constants a and b can be used to predict the requirements of birds with different genetic potentials for bodyweight gain. An example of the input and output predictions that can be obtained is shown in *Table 10.7*. There are two very significant conclusions which can be drawn from the relationship of the TSAA and lysine inputs as illustrated by the TSAA input expressed as a percentage of the lysine input. As already mentioned lysine is of relatively greater importance for weight gain and TSAA for maintenance. The change in the percentage comparisons illustrates this. As the bird gets bigger, the maintenance requirement grows in significance, hence the indication of an increased TSAA need relative to lysine as the birds get older. However the change in the relationship would appear to be greater than normally used in current commercial formulations. The NRC (1984) recommendations indicate a relationship of 65.6, 57.7 and 68.8% TSAA of the lysine % for 0–4, 8–12 and 16–29-week periods respectively. At near optimal weight gains, the Reading model analysis of available data indicates a relationship of 65, 70 and 96% for those same periods. At the older ages we may be seriously under-formulating for the total sulphur amino acid content of the diet.

This may be more likely to occur when the second conclusion to be drawn from *Table 10.7* is considered. As the actual weight gains achieved, decreases, compared with the potential weight gain for that age period, so relatively more TSAA is required compared to lysine. This drift in the relationship is particularly significant at the older ages when daily bodyweight gain is a smaller percentage of initial body weight at the start of the day. In commercial practice, considerable variations are seen in actual bodyweight gain achieved. This is usually because of a reduction in total protein consumed possibly due to bad pellet quality, high house temperatures, lack of feeder space or wide ME to protein ratios. A reduction of 25% below potential bodyweight gain for the 16–20-week period is not uncommon in certain parts of the world. In such a situation, it would appear likely that the first limiting amino acid will be TSAA as the indications are that at that performance level, the TSAA level should be 110% of the lysine level from 16 to 20 weeks — a much higher TSAA level than is normally used in such a situation. The new situation indicated by the comparison of the Reading model input and output data shown in *Table 10.7* is that the nutritionist is aiming at a moving target. As the level of the first limiting amino acid is increased, resulting in improved bodyweight gain so the optimum relationship between lysine and TSAA also changes. In the ideal world the nutritionist would know the normal food consumption in a particular situation and then adjust both the lysine and TSAA simultaneously to achieve the required intake of each. In the less than ideal world in which we work, there are a variety of situations to be met. As there would appear to be more to be lost from under-formulating TSAA than lysine in the variety of situations, the prudent course would appear to be to presume a growth depression of 10%. *Table 10.7* would indicate that the TSAA should be 65, 71.5 and 100.5% of the lysine content at 0–4, 8–12 and 16–20 weeks of age respectively for large type males at that level of growth depression. This would be a particularly large increase in the level of TSAA used from 16 to 20 weeks. The Israeli model indicated a figure of 94.3% for this age period which would tend to support the Reading model analysis. However the analysis was carried out on insufficient data so more work on the subject is urgently required as this is an age period when the birds are consuming large quantities of food and also laying down potentially large quantities of valuable breast meat. Insufficient data were available to estimate threonine requirements by the Reading model. In view of the indications shown in *Tables 10.3* and *10.4* that threonine is likely to be at least the next limiting amino acid after lysine and TSAA, and in some circumstances may be first limiting, studies with turkeys on their threonine requirements also are needed.

Amino acid balance

The intake of one amino acid cannot be assessed in isolation. Inter-relationships exist between amino acids. The amino acid pattern or profile of a diet may therefore influence the response to individual amino acids.

In early work when the adverse effects on growth of an unbalanced protein, i.e. one amino acid deficient and the others in excess were seen, it was assumed that the condition caused impairment of the utilization of the limiting amino acid. It would now appear that the main effect is a decrease in food intake (Harper, Benevenga and Wohlhuetcr, 1970; Boorman, 1980). If the effect of food intake is taken into account, there would appear to be no large adverse effect of imbalance on the utilization of the limiting amino acid. The adverse effect of excess amino acids on food intake is of commercial importance. Regrettably, our knowledge of the correct amino acid profile at each age and environmental conditions is meagre in the extreme. The amino acid profile may be deleterious in one of three categories — amino acid imbalances, amino acid antagonisms and amino acid toxicities.

Table 10.7 Reading model amino acid input and bodyweight gain output predictions (based on a and b values shown in Table 10.6)

Bodyweight gain (g/bird/day)	Start body weight 55 g 0–4 weeks			4.1 kg 8–12 weeks				12 kg 16–20 weeks			
	Requirement (g/bird/day)	(g/bird/day)	TSAA as % of lysine	Bodyweight gain (g/bird/day)	Requirement (g/bird/day)	(g/bird/day)	TSAA as % of lysine	Bodyweight gain (g/bird/day)	Requirement (g/bird/day)	(g/bird/day)	TSAA as % of lysine
16	0.372	0.263	70.7	80	1.812	1.506	83.1	76	1.892	2.486	131.4
20	0.462	0.318	68.8	88	1.980	1.596	80.6	84	2.075	2.576	124.1
24	0.550	0.373	67.8	96	2.150	1.688	78.5	92	2.260	2.667	118.1
28	0.640	0.428	66.9	104	2.322	1.784	76.8	100	2.445	2.760	112.9
32	0.730	0.483	66.2	112	2.498	1.886	75.5	108	2.640	2.858	108.3
36	0.820	0.540	65.9	120	2.690	1.992	74.1	116	2.850	2.966	104.1
40	0.920	0.602	65.4	128	2.890	2.105	72.8	124	3.065	3.094	100.9
44	1.023	0.665	65.0	136	3.083	2.206	71.6	132	3.284	3.270	99.6
46	1.080	0.703	65.1	140	3.200	2.290	71.5	136	3.590	3.536	98.5
48	1.320	0.860	65.1	146	3.950	2.770	70.1	139	4.130	3.980	96.4

Amino acid imbalances

Harper (1964) proposed that the term amino acid imbalance should be applied to those changes in the amino acid pattern of a diet that caused a decrease in growth rate and food intake which could be completely prevented by a small supplement of the limiting amino acid or acids. The concentrations of the other amino acids within the imbalanced mixtures are such that they could not be considered toxic if they were added individually to the diet.

Amino acid antagonisms

Harper (1964) defined amino acid antagonisms as an amino acid interaction created by the addition of an excess of an individual amino acid to a protein deficient diet. The adverse effects on growth rate and food intake cannot be alleviated merely by the addition of the amino acid which appears limiting. The effects of such an interaction can only be rectified by the addition of a structurally or metabolically related amino acid. D'Mello and Lewis (1970a) clearly demonstrated that the amino acid required to be added to the diet is not necessarily the one most limiting in the diet.

Amino acid toxicities

Under this heading Harper (1964) placed those excessive intakes of individual amino acids which fitted neither the category of amino acid imbalance nor of amino acid antagonism. Amino acid toxicities result in a decrease in food intake and growth rate similar to those observed in the other two categories. Unlike the other two categories there is some suggestion that the decrease in food intake is not wholly responsible for the decreased growth rate (D'Mello, 1967; Daniel and Waisman, 1968).

Commercial diets

In commercial turkey diets, the most common problem will be an amino acid imbalance, with the diet being deficient in an amino acid. As has been discussed earlier, this is likely to be lysine, TSAA or perhaps in some circumstances threonine. There are however two specific amino acid antagonisms which may be encountered.

The lysine–arginine antagonism

This has been shown to exist in the rat (Jones, Wolters and Burnett, 1966), the guinea pig (O'Dell and Regan, 1963), the chick (Jones, 1964; Smith and Lewis, 1966; D'Mello and Lewis, 1970a) and also the turkey (D'Mello and Emmans, 1975). An excess of lysine causes a decrease in food intake and growth rate, an elevation in plasma lysine concentration and a decrease in plasma arginine concentration. It does not seem that the reverse antagonism, i.e. excess arginine, exists. The work by D'Mello and Emmans (1975) clearly demonstrates the antagonism as is shown in Table 10.8. It will be seen that in a diet containing 1.05% lysine, 1% arginine will support maximum weight gain. If the diet contains 1.30% lysine, a level of 1.50% arginine is required for maximum growth rate. If an even higher level of lysine, 1.55% is present, the arginine requirement is increased still further to 1.75%.

Table 10.8 Weight gain[a] of turkey poults fed on diets of different lysine and arginine contents from 7 to 21 days

Dietary arginine content (%)	Dietary lysine content (%)		
	1.05	1.30	1.55
1.00	15.0	18.3	20.8
1.25	14.1	23.3	24.2
1.50	15.1	24.1	26.6
1.75	13.7	21.5	29.4

(D,Mello and Emmans, 1975)

[a] g/bird day

The leucine, isoleucine and valine inter-relationship

The existence of this inter-relationship has been well established in rats and has been shown to exist in chicks (D'Mello and Lewis, 1970b) and in turkeys (D'Mello, 1975). The adverse effects of an excess of leucine can be corrected primarily by the addition of valine but isoleucine is also required for complete restoration of food intake and growth rate. The work by D'Mello (1975) suggested a percentage relationship of leucine 100, isoleucine 59 and valine 85. The relationship between these amino acids in ingredients commonly used in turkey diets (NRC, 1984) would indicate a low valine content or conversely high leucine content of most ingredients but particularly maize judged on the relationship indicated by D'Mello (1975). It is a subject worthy of further investigation particularly with older turkeys where the genetic potential for growth rate is such that it is very sensitive to adverse food intake factors. An excess of an amino acid may also cause food intake depression but no experimental evidence for this is available for the turkey.

It seems likely that in future, turkey nutritionists will become more conscious of the amino acid balance, wishing to avoid one amino acid concentration limiting the performance of diets and avoiding excesses of amino acids which may interact with other amino acids depressing growth rates or excesses of amino acids which themselves depress performance. Considerably more data on the subject is required before diets can be designed with confidence.

Food intake

While the formulation may influence the food intake, it is more sensitive to external factors such as pellet quality, accessibility of the food and temperature. The food intake is also influenced by the energy requirements of the bird (Moran, Summers and Orr, 1960; Owen et al., 1981). A significant influence on energy requirements will be the turkey's maintenance requirements for energy which will be related to the size of the bird. This in turn will be related to the previous growth rate achieved

A recent experiment (Nixey, unpublished data) illustrates the effect some factors, other than diet, can have on the foot intake and growth rate of turkeys. Comparison was made of food fed in mash or crumb form, day-old versus 7-day debeaking, and 'user friendly' food presentation compared with the opposite 'antagonistic' food presentation in a 2 × 2 × 2 factorial experiment, from day-old to 4 weeks of age. All birds were fed the same formulation. The 'user friendly' food presentation treatment involved supplementing the normal plastic tube feeders with food intrays on the floor for 7 days which the poults could walk on. The same plastic tube feeders were kept throughout the 4 weeks, whereas in the 'user antagonistic' food presentation treatment, larger feeders, hung in different positions, were introduced at 2 weeks of age.

Large differences were seen between the body weights of the poults fed food as mash or crumbs. At 28 days the mash-fed birds were 23.3% lighter than those fed crumbs. Even at 7 days a difference of 16% was apparent. While the day-old debeaked poults did not appear to suffer reduced growth rate when fed crumbs, some reduction, around 6%, was seen if the poults were fed mash. This reduction was already apparent by 7 days of age. Giving the poults easier access to the food by placing supplementary food in trays on the floor promoted approximately 8% faster growth rate to 14 days of age. Unfortunately the effect was then confounded by the introduction of different feeders, which rather than having a negative effect, seemed to have had the reverse effect. The feeders were larger with a deeper wider area of food available which may have promoted greater food intake. The difference in 28-day body weight follows closely the differences found in food intake. The experiment illustrated that even when the same formulation is fed to poults, large differences in 28-day body weights can be obtained between treatments, related to factors which affect food intake.

The logical question to then ask is 'what effect does 28-day body weights have on subsequent performance'? To attempt to answer this question, the trial birds were split into two feeding programmes subsequent to 28 days, one was a high protein programme and the other a low protein programme. The results, summarized in *Table 10.9* showed that the 28-day body weight was still exerting a major influence on subsequent body weights at least up to 168 days.

The results contradict the work by Auckland, Morris and Jennings (1969) who found that bodyweight differences obtained at 6 weeks of age had disappeared by 20 weeks. The major difference between the trials was in the type of bird used. The

Table 10.9 The influence of 28-day body weight on subsequent bodyweight gain of BUT Big 6 male turkeys

Age (days)	28	57	86	113	140	169
Protein %	30	27	23	18	18	18
			Body weights (kg)			
0–28 days' treatment						
Crumbs	1.02	4.16	8.76	12.73	16.54	20.00
Mash	0.78	3.67	8.21	11.85	15.63	18.79
Difference	0.24	0.49	0.55	0.88	0.91	1.21
Protein %	30	23	18	18	14	14
0–28 days' treatment						
Crumbs	1.02	3.96	8.12	10.95	14.34	16.74
Mash	0.78	3.42	7.34	10.06	12.91	14.79
Difference	0.24	0.54	0.78	0.89	1.43	1.77

1969 study used male turkeys which only achieved 7.6 kg in 20 weeks compared with 16.54 kg in 1987. The modern turkey not only grows much faster, it is also later maturing, and is still gaining considerable body weight at 24 weeks of age.

Recommended nutrient ratios

In the past nutrient requirements were normally stated as percentages of the diet. The modern trend to state nutrient requirements as g/MJ ME is more meaningful as it attempts to allow for one of the major factors influencing food intake. Despite the gaps in knowledge, the commercial nutritionist has to make decisions on his formulations. The author's suggested nutrient ratios are shown in *Table 10.10*.

Table 10.10 Suggested nutrient ratios for Big 6 males where the conditions and pellet quality are good

Age fed (weeks)	0–4	4–8	8–12	12–16	16–20	20–24
Nutrient ratios (g/MJ ME)						
Lysine	1.57	1.34	1.10	0.89	0.75	0.65
Methionine	0.57	0.53	0.47	0.44	0.43	0.42
TSAA	1.02	0.94	0.82	0.76	0.75	0.71
Tryptophan	0.27	0.23	0.19	0.15	0.13	0.11
Threonine	1.00	0.86	0.75	0.58	0.48	0.42
Arginine	1.69	1.46	1.21	1.02	0.88	0.80
Calcium	1.10	1.05	0.95	0.85	0.80	0.70
Avail. phos.	0.62	0.60	0.55	0.50	0.45	0.40
Sodium	0.13	0.13	0.13	0.13	0.13	0.13
NaCl	0.30	0.30	0.30	0.30	0.30	0.30
EFA	1.27	1.09		No minimum stated		
ME (MJ/kg)	12.0	12.1	12.2	12.4	12.6	12.8

These should be considered only as a starting point and be adjusted according to the situation, particularly when factors occur which adversely affect food intake. The body weight achieved compared to the breed's performance goals are the ultimate judge of the formulation's effectiveness.

References

Albuquerque, K. de, Leighton, A. T. Jr., Mason, J. P. Jr. and Potter, L. M. (1978). The effects of environmental temperature, sex and dietary energy levels on growth performance of Large White Turkeys. *Poultry Science*, **57**, 353–362

Auckland, J. N., Morris, T. R. and Jennings, R. C. (1969). Compensatory growth after under-nutrition in market turkeys. *British Poultry Science*, **10**, 293–302

Behrends, B. R. and Waibel, P. E. (1980). Methionine and cystine requirements of growing turkeys. *Poultry Science*, **59**, 849–859

Boorman, K. N. (1980). Dietary constraints on nitrogen retention in protein deposition in animals. In *Protein Deposition in Animals* (Buttery, P. J. and Lindsay, D. B., eds), pp. 147–166. London, Butterworths

Booth, D. A. (1979). Food intake regulations in poultry. In *Proceedings of Poultry Science Symposium No.14* (Boorman, K. N. and Freeman, B. M., eds), pp. 13–62. Edinburgh, British Poultry Science Ltd

Britzman, D. G. (1976). Comparative performance with pelleted and meal diets for growing turkeys and egg producing chicken. *Proceedings of 37th Minnesota Nutrition Conference*, pp. 139–162

Clark, Felicity, A., Gous, R. M. and Morris, T. R. (1982). Response of broiler chicken to well balanced protein mixtures. *British Poultry Science*, **23**, 433–446

Daniel, R. G. and Waisman, H. A. (1968). The effects of excess of amino acids on the growth of the young rat. *Growth*, **32**, 225–265

D'Mello, J. P. F. (1967). Amino Acid Interactions in Chick Nutrition. PhD Thesis, University of Nottingham

D'Mello, J. P. F. (1975). Amino acid requirements of the young turkey: Leucine, Isoleucine and Valine. *British Poultry Science*, **16**, 607–615

D'Mello, J. P. F. and Emmans, G. C. (1975). Amino acid requirements of the young turkeys: lysine and arginine. *British Poultry Science*, **16**, 297–306

D'Mello, J. P. F. and Lewis, D. (1970a). Amino acid interactions in chick nutrition. 1. Inter-relationships between lysine and arginine. *British Poultry Science*, **11**, 299–311

D'Mello, J. P. F. and Lewis, D. (1970b). Amino acid interactions in chick nutrition. 2. Inter-relationships between leucine, isoleucine and valine. *British Poultry Science*, **11**, 313–323

D'Mello, J. P. F. and Lewis, D. (1970c). Amino acid interactions in chick nutrition. 3. Interdependence in amino acid requirements. *British Poultry Science*, **11**, 367–385

Fisher, C. and Emmans, G. C. (1983). Calculated amino acid requirements for growing turkeys. *Turkeys*, **31**, No.1, 39–43

Fisher, C., Morris, T. R. and Jennings, R. C. (1973). A model for the description and prediction of the response of laying hens to amino acid intake. *British Poultry Science*, **14**, 469–484

Geraedts, L. H. J. and Kan, C. A. (1981). The performance including compensatory growth of male broiler turkeys on different energy and lysine levels in the diet. In *Proceedings of 3rd European Symposium on Poultry Nutrition*, pp. 121–123. Edinburgh

Harper, A. E. (1964). Amino acid toxicities and imbalances. In *Mammalian Protein Metabolism. Vol II* (Monro, H. N. and Allisom, J. B., eds), pp. 87–134. New York, Academy Press

Harper, A. E., Benevenga, N. J. and Wohlhueter, R. M. (1970). Effects of ingestion of disproportionate amounts of amino acids. *Physiological Reviews*, **50**, 428–558

Hurwitz, S., Sklan, D. and Bartov, I. (1978). New formal approaches to the determination of energy and amino acid requirement of chicks. *Poultry Science*, **57**, 197–205

Hurwitz, S., Eisner, U., Dubrov, D., Sklan, D., Riesenfeld, G. and Bar, A. (1979). Protein, fatty acids, calcium and phosphate absorption along the gastro-intestinal tract of the young turkey. *Comparative Biochemistry and Physiology*, **62A**, 847–850

Hurwitz, S., Weiselberg, M., Eisner, U. *et al.* (1980). The energy requirements and performance of growing chickens and turkeys as affected by environmental temperature. *Poultry Science*, **59**, 2290–2299

Hurwitz, S., Frisch, Y., Bar, A., Eisner, U., Bengal, I. and Pines, M. (1983). The amino acid requirements of growing turkeys. 1. Model construction and parameter estimation. *Poultry Science*, **62**, 2208–2217

Jensen, L. S., Manning, B., Falen, L. and McGinnis, J. (1976). Lysine needs of rapidly growing turkeys from 12–22 weeks of age. *Poultry Science*, **55**, 1394–1400

Jensen, L. S., Ranit, G. O., Wagstaff, R. K. and McGinnis, J. (1965). Protein and lysine requirements of developing turkeys as influenced by pelleting. *Poultry Science*, **44**, 1435–1441

Jones, J. D. (1964). Lysine–arginine antagonism in the chick. *Journal of Nutrition*, **84**, 313–321

Jones, J. D., Wolters, R. and Burnett, P. C. (1966). Lysine–arginine–electrolyte relationship in the rat. *Journal of Nutrition*, **89**, 171–188

Martland, M. F. (1984). Wet litter as a cause of Plantar Pododermatitis leading to foot ulceration and lameness in fattening turkeys. *Avian Pathology*, **13**, 241–252

Mongin, P. and Sauveur, B. (1979). Dietary balance and imbalance between Na, K and Cl. Effects on growth, laying rate and tibial dischondroplasia. In *Proceedings of the 2nd European Symposium on Poultry Nutrition* (Kan, C. A. and Simons, P. C. M., eds), pp. 60–63

Moran, E. T., Summers, J. D. and Orr, H. I. (1960). The effect of absolute alteration in energy concentration of developing and finishing diets for the Large White turkey on performance and carcass quality with a note on the correlation of back skin fat and grade of finish. *British Poultry Science*, **10**, 127–138

Nixey, C. and Boorman, K. N. (1985). The lysine requirements of market turkeys. In *Proceedings of the 5th Symposium on Poultry Nutrition* (Bornstein, S., ed.), pp. 137–144. Ma'ale Hachamisha, Israel

NRC (1984). National Research Council. Nutrient requirements of domestic animals. *No.1 Nutrient requirements of poultry* (8th revised edition, 1984), p. 17). Washington DC, USA, National Academy Press

Noll, S. L. and Waibel, P. E. (1982). Influence of environmental temperature on the lysine requirements of growing turkeys. In *Proceedings of 43rd Minnesota Nutrition Conference*, pp. 123–134

O'Dell, B. L. and Regan, W . O. (1963). Effect of lysine and glycine upon arginine requirement of guinea pigs. *Proceedings of Experimental Biology and Medicine*, **112**, 336–337

Owen, J. A., Waldroup, P. W., Mabray, C. J. and Slagter, P. J. (1981). Response of growing turkeys to dietary energy levels. *Poultry Science*, **60**, 418–424

Robbins, K. R., Norton, H. W. and Baker, D. H. (1979). Estimation of nutrient requirements from growth data. *Journal of Nutrition*, **109**, 1710–1714

Sauveur, B. (1983). Bioavailability to poultry of plant origin phosphorus. Methodological criticisms and results. *Proceedings of 4th European Symposium on Poultry Nutrition*, pp. 103–111. Tours, France

Scholtyssek, S. (1981). Mast-und ausschlachturyserque-bnisse schnerer puten nach futterung mit uhterschredlichen nurbrstuffkonzentrationers. *Kraftfuttes*, **64**, 2–4

Smith, G. H. and Lewis, D. (1966). Arginine in poultry nutrition. III Agent and target in amino acid interactions. *British Journal of Nutrition*, **20**, 621–631

Tuttle, W. L. and Balloun, S. L. (1974). Lysine requirements of starting and growing turkeys. *Poultry Science*, **53**, 1698–1704

WPSA (1985). Mineral requirements for poultry — mineral requirements and recommendations for growing birds. *World's Poultry Science Journal*, **41**, No.3, 252–258

Chapter 11

Environmental responses of growing turkeys

D. R. Charles

Introduction

There are two approaches to the recommendation of climatic environmental conditions for poultry. The most popular has been the unsystematic testing of one whole system of housing or ventilation versus another without any real understanding of the effects on the birds, and usually without adequate replication either.

A much better approach, which has been applied to laying hens and broiler chickens (Sutcliffe, King and Charles, 1985), is to recognize that poultry respond to the component physical factors such as temperature, lighting and ventilation. There are four stages to the application of this approach to turkeys. The first is to review the literature on the responses of turkeys to these factors, and to summarize it algebraically. Secondly, the response curves can be evaluated financially by attaching cash values to body weight and feed consumed, and thus estimating the economic optimum conditions and the cost penalties associated with error. Thirdly, practical systems can be designed, appropriate to the magnitude of these penalties. Fourthly, it is useful to monitor the systems to make sure that they are working properly.

Responses of growing turkeys to environmental components

Temperature

Some of the early experimental work on the response of growing turkeys to temperature used replicated pens in paired but unreplicated buildings, and thus could not properly distinguish between temperature and building effects. Blakely and MacGregor (1965) used this technique in tests of 28 days' duration on 21-week-old turkeys. They reported a weight gain of 2.32 kg/bird per 28 days in a cold building (varying between −26°C and 7°C), and 2.10 kg/bird in a warm building (heated to 21–24°C). Food intakes over the test period were 12.23 and 10.43 kg/bird respectively. Due to the experimental method the differences were not analysable, and are quoted merely for comparison with later results.

Hellickson et al. (1967) used eight climate rooms, replicated treatments over time, and fitted quadratic curves to the responses which they obtained, thus

201

permitting the kind of economic analysis mentioned above. Some of the functions obtained for results from 21 to 25 weeks of age were:

$$W_\sigma = 2.2211 + 0.2368T - 0.0069T^2$$
$$W_\varphi = 2.6437 + 0.0279T - 0.0015T^2$$
$$FCR = 12.365 - 0.157T + 0.00106T^2$$

where W_σ = weight gain of males (kg)
$\quad\quad W_\varphi$ = weight gain of females (kg)
$\quad\quad FCR$ = food conversion ratio, both sexes, food eaten/liveweight gain
$\quad\quad T$ = temperature (°C)

Parker, Boone and Knechtes (1972) used four environmental chambers containing male turkeys of 42 weeks of age and 47 weeks (Broad-Breasted Bronze and Broad-Breasted White strains respectively). The tests ran for 28 days. *Table 11.1* shows the body weights obtained.

Table 11.1 Effects of temperature

Temperature (°C)	Body weight (kg/bird)	
	Bronze strain	White strain
10	14.81	13.07
21	13.23	13.57
32	12.47	14.55
38	11.91	14.04

(Parker, Boone and Knechtes, 1972)

Albuquerque *et al.* (1978) used four rooms each containing four pens, ran each room at a different temperature, and repeated the experiments twice. They grew their birds in rooms over longer periods than those used in the experiments reviewed above, so that results for a wide range of ages are available. Linear, quadratic and cubic fits to the data were tested and the results shown graphically.

Table 11.2 Effects of temperature, 8 to 24 weeks of age

Temperature (°C)	Liveweight gain (kg/bird)	Feed efficiency (kg weight gain/ kg feed intake)
10	7.1	0.223
18	7.0	0.246
27	6.7	0.267
35	6.2	0.268

(Albuquerque *et al.*, 1978)

In our own experiments at the Agricultural Development and Advisory Service (ADAS) Gleadthorpe Experimental Husbandry Farm (EHF) in 1980 (Bray and Binstead, 1980), two climate rooms were used for each of four set temperatures (12, 15, 18 and 21°C). Within each room replicated pens were used to test two nutrient densities (calculated analyses 12.2 and 12.4 [low nutrient density]; and 13.0 and 13.3 MJ/kg [high nutrient density] in the grower and finisher stages respectively). The corresponding crude protein levels were 17.6 and 18.8 and 21.4 and 22.2%. Feed intake and liveweight gain of a medium strain of turkeys were recorded weekly, and carcass analysis carried out twice, all data being recorded separately from males and females.

Table 11.3a Coefficients for male turkeys – low nutrient density

	12°C	15°C	18°C	21°C
		Cumulative feed intake		
a	2.351	2.399	2.349	2.444
b	0.0207571	0.02022	0.0197142	0.0197428
		Live weight		
c	0.1046108	0.1039005	0.0986187	0.0947584
d	−2.506804	−2.512793	−2.19301	−2.040105
		Eviscerated carcass		
f	0.1029524	0.083	0.0778095	0.0624761
g	−4.991667	−2.693993	−2.110667	−0.401335
		Total meat		
h	0.0675237	0.057	0.0445237	0.0409524
i	−3.533662	−2.367999	−0.80666	−0.45067
		Dark meat		
j	0.0288571	0.0231904	0.0159047	0.0150475
k	−1.719	−1.099332	−0.112331	0.006667
		White meat		
l	0.0386667	0.0338571	0.028619	0.0245237
m	−1.814668	−1.274999	−0.694332	−0.303663

General forms of the equations

Cumulative feed intake: $Y = a e^{bx}$
Live weight   : $Y = xc + d$
Eviscerated carcass : $Y = fx + g$
Total meat   : $Y = hx + i$
Dark meat   : $Y = jx + k$
White meat   : $Y = lx + m$

In order to facilitate storage of and access to such a large amount of data, curves were fitted by a least squares technique and the coefficients stored as a database. With the age range used (42–133 days) it was decided to regard live weight against age as linear and food intake against age as exponential, after comparative inspection of many functions, and comparison of the goodness of fit. Linearity had to be assumed for the carcass analysis data against age because it was only available

Table 11.3b Coefficients for male turkeys – high nutrient density

	12°C	15°C	18°C	21°C
		Cumulative feed intake		
a	2.312	2.355	2.299	2.222
b	0.0206571	0.0204142	0.0202571	0.0199285
		Live weight		
c	0.1065167	0.1080698	0.102781	0.0988897
d	−2.642325	−2.698548	−2.385641	−2.273681
		Eviscerated carcass		
f	0.0901428	0.0931428	0.099619	0.0762858
g	−3.353002	−3.563993	−4.647335	−1.830014
		Total meat		
h	0.0491904	0.0543332	0.0647618	0.0520475
i	−1.299331	−1.742334	−3.188329	−0.627332
		Dark meat		
j	0.0158095	0.0213334	0.0313332	0.0190475
k	−0.144667	−0.669337	−1.866331	−0.356335
		White meat		
l	0.0333332	0.033	0.0331428	0.0329047
m	−1.149334	−1.073997	−1.289999	−1.250333

General forms of the equations

Cumulative feed intake: $Y = a e^{bx}$
Live weight   : $Y = xc + d$
Eviscerated carcass : $Y = fx + g$
Total meat   : $Y = hx + i$
Dark meat   : $Y = jx + k$
White meat   : $Y = lx + m$

for two ages at the time the model was built. Using the fitted curves a table of coefficients, such as given in *Table 11.3*, can be offered as a concise summary of a large amount of data.

An interactive computer model was constructed in 1981 using these coefficients to provide easy access to the results, and to permit money values to be attached to the inputs and outputs, thus providing an economic appraisal of the results for any set of prices of meat and food.

The experiments cited show that as temperature is increased both rate of bodyweight gain and feed intake are progressively depressed. If databases such as given in *Table 11.3* are used in computer models with money values attached, the economic optimum temperature for growing turkeys is found to vary greatly with market circumstances. It depends upon the ratio between the value of liveweight/kg and the cost of turkey feed/kg. This ratio varies considerably even within any one

Table 11.3c Coefficients for female turkeys – low nutrient density

	12°C	*15°C*	*18°C*	*21°C*
		Cumulative feed intake		
p	1.039	1.043	1.059	0.987
q	0.0273	0.0269142	0.0262857	0.0267714
		Live weight		
r	0.0695	0.0700714	0.0684285	0.0662142
s	−1.421001	−1.449	−1.354	−1.269

High nutrient density

	12°C	*15°C*	*18°C*	*21°C*
		Cumulative feed intake		
p	1.018	1.065	1.029	0.9754
q	0.0270428	0.0264571	0.0265142	0.0265571
		Live weight		
r	0.0732857	0.0710714	0.0723571	0.0699285
s	−1.602	−1.489001	−1.571	−1.421

General forms of the equations

Cumulative feed intake: $Y = p e^{qx}$
Live weight   : $Y = rx + s$
Where x = age in days and e = base of natural logarithms

country at a given time. For example, in the UK at the time of writing the economic optimum temperature for turkeys grown for the frozen trade at relatively low liveweight values is about 19–20°C at typical feed prices. However, for high value fresh turkeys the optimum is often as low as 12–15°C, since the ratio between liveweight value and feed cost is wider, and therefore it is advisable to allow feed intake to increase so as to obtain a higher body weight at a given age. Thus, in the UK it is probably adequate to provide simple housing for turkeys for the fresh trade, though the birds should be protected from the worst excesses of the winter. Tests at Gleadthorpe EHF showed that simple housing, but with carefully constructed and adjusted ventilation baffling (using straw and polythene) was capable of providing near the optimum temperature most of the time in a British winter. For the frozen turkey trade more elaborate controlled environment housing may be justified, because for these lower value birds it is more important to use feed economically, and also because stocking densities may be higher.

It has been hypothesized that the depression in growth rate as temperature is increased may merely follow nutrient intake as feed intake is reduced. For example, in laying hens an important interaction between temperature and dietary formulation was shown by Payne (1967) and confirmed by Emmans and Charles (1977). It was found that egg production could be maintained up to 28–30°C provided that the diet was re-formulated to provide nutrient concentrations that permitted the birds to maintain adequate levels of intake of the essential nutrients other than energy. Whether or not such an interaction exists for growing turkeys was the subject of an experiment carried out by T. S. Bray at Gleadthorpe EHF in 1982.

Four temperatures were used, and at each temperature four isocaloric diets were fed containing four amino acid concentrations. The diets quoted in *Table 11.4* are those fed from 20 to 24 weeks of age. *Table 11.5* shows the complete set of diets used.

Table 11.4 Performance of growing turkey stags as affected by diet and temperature. Results at 24 weeks of age (all diets at 12.5 MJ/kg metabolizable energy)

Diet fed from 20 to 24 weeks of age	% lysine % methionine	0.5 0.2	0.55 0.21	0.64 0.23	0.74 0.25	
		Live weight (kg/bird)				*Mean*
Temperature (°C)	12.7	13.34	15.40	15.18	14.97	14.72
	15.7	12.20	15.07	14.64	14.52	14.11
	19.3	11.00	14.12	13.93	14.47	13.38
	23.0	9.61	13.59	12.85	13.38	12.36
	Mean	11.54	14.54	14.10	14.33	13.64
		Food intake (kg/bird, cumulative)				
Temperature (°C)	12.7	46.56	48.31	50.14	49.09	48.53
	15.7	42.80	46.67	47.70	46.91	46.02
	19.3	36.51	40.84	43.76	43.53	41.16
	23.0	32.48	39.68	39.62	40.55	38.08
	Mean	39.59	43.87	45.31	45.02	43.45

These performance results are as recorded at 24 weeks of age, and the dietary treatments forming columns in the table are those fed at that time. Throughout life the birds received four graded levels of amino acids (as given in detail in *Table 11.5*), but all four levels were gradually reduced with advancing age, reaching the levels in *Table 11.4* at 20 weeks of age

Table 11.5 Diet specifications throughout the experiment

0–4 weeks of age				
Metabolizable energy (MJ/kg)	11.7			
% lysine	1.77			
% methionine	0.58			
4–8 weeks				
ME (MJ/kg)	12.0			
% lysine	1.62			
% methionine	0.53			
8–12 weeks				
ME (MJ/kg)	12.5			
% lysine	0.77	0.92	1.06	1.20
% methionine	0.30	0.34	0.37	0.40
12–16 weeks				
ME (MJ/kg)	12.5			
% lysine	0.64	0.74	0.83	0.96
% methionine	0.28	0.30	0.32	0.35
16–20 weeks				
ME (MJ/kg)	12.5			
% lysine	0.55	0.64	0.74	0.83
% methionine	0.26	0.28	0.30	0.32
20–24 weeks				
ME (MJ/kg)	12.5			
% lysine	0.50	0.55	0.64	0.74
% methionine	0.20	0.21	0.23	0.24

The results, shown in *Table 11.4*, suggest that the depression in growth rate at high temperature can only be partially obviated through dietary formulation.

A difficulty encountered in interpreting and using a review of the effects of temperature on the growth of turkeys is that over the period covered by the review the genetic material has changed. Even if all experimenters had chosen the same nominal breed, which they did not, that breed's genetic characteristics would have gradually changed. Thus, while the signs of the effects of temperature on growth rate and food intake are consistent between experiments, and their magnitudes reasonably consistent as a proportion of body weight, their absolute magnitudes are different. The best that can be done when using such data to make recommendations and to estimate the economics of house temperature, is to choose results relevant to birds of the weight of interest, rather than the age, though even that may be unreliable. Thus this approach unfortunately necessitates periodic updating by repeating the experiments. Emmans (1980) suggested that fundamental biological modelling might avoid this problem and its associated experimental cost, and in due course this may be so. To date fundamental models have not been widely accepted by users, but the gradual improvement in predictive value of such models, and the spread of microcomputers and of computer literacy may change this.

Light

Gill and Leighton (1974) compared dim and bright light (5.4 and 86 lx) and three light colours (white, red and blue). Two stocking densities were used (5.6 and 11.1 birds/m^2 to 14 weeks of age and 2.8 and 5.6 birds/m^2 from 14 to 24 weeks). The lower light intensity was consistently associated with faster growth, without an interaction with stocking density. In early life blue light gave faster growth, but after 16 weeks turkeys grew faster in both white and red lights, and their gonadal development was faster. This is consistent with many observations on other avian species that gonad development is faster when birds are illuminated with light from the red end of the visible spectrum, for example, Foss, Carew and Arnold (1972) with chickens and Benoit and Ott (1944) with ducks.

Siopes *et al.* (1983) found no significant differences in the growth rate to 22 weeks of male turkeys between 11, 110 or 220 lx. For female turkeys both growth rate and food intake to 2 weeks of age were depressed at 1 lx, compared with 11, 110 or 220 lx (Siopes *et al.*, 1984). Birds at 1 lx had significantly enlarged eyes and greater adrenal weights than those on the other treatments. It is difficult to reconcile these results with those of Gill and Leighton (1974) but it might be relevant that in the later experiments the birds received substantial dark periods (the light patterns used being 12L:12D and 2L:2D, whereas Siopes *et al.* (1984) used 23L:1D. Hester, Sutton and Elkin (1987) found superior growth at 20 lx compared with 2.5 lx using 15D:9L.

Klingensmith *et al.* (1986) found less lameness at 20 lx than at 2.5 lx, using three stocking densities. They attributed this result to the promotion of earlier closure of the growth plates of the long bones. Hester, Sutton and Elkin (1987) found no difference in the incidence of leg abnormalities between 20 and 2.5 lx.

At a light intensity of 2.5 lx, a daylength regime of 24L:OD at 12 days, followed by 10L:14D until 133 days was compared with 9L:15D from 4 days to 55 days increased to 15L:9D at 126 days, with the intention of affecting leg weakness through exercise (Hester *et al.*, 1985). The stepped down programme was associated with faster growth and lower food conversion of male turkeys, but although activity was measurably increased there was no consistent effect on leg abnormalities.

Practical recommendations based on such evidence are difficult to make, but presumably it is safe to say that very dim light should be avoided because of the risk of eye damage and lameness, but where electric lights are used there may be little performance advantage to offset the cost of providing very bright light. Perhaps about 10–100 lx might be a suitable target level for houses completely dependent upon artificial lights. White light is probably suitable.

Air

The ventilation of housed livestock is essentially a matter of using air as a diluent for metabolic heat, in an attempt to hold the temperature inside the house at the desired level, subject to the constraints imposed by gaseous composition. Probably the first thorough quantification of the subject, based on physiological measurements, was that by Mitchell and Kelley (1933).

It is inherent in this principle that the design of practical ventilation systems demands knowledge of two air quantity requirements. The maximum quantity of air needed depends upon the metabolic sensible heat output (i.e. total heat generated less that lost by evaporation), and is defined as the quantity which is sufficient to prevent the indoor equilibrium temperature rising more than some arbitrary specified amount (usually 3°C) above outside temperature. Note that at equilibrium, the building cannot be cooler than outside, though due to heat storage equilibrium may take a long time to be achieved.

Thus the maximum ventilation requirement can readily be calculated from the heat capacity of air and the sensible heat output of the birds. Values are given below in the section on physical principles of achieving environments, and the necessary sensible heat outputs are reviewed in that section.

The concept of a minimum air requirement is much more contentious and its calculation is more difficult. Sufficient air must be provided for the provision of oxygen and the removal of moisture (from respiration, excretion, litter metabolism, and sometimes brooder fuel combustion), carbon dioxide, ammonia, dust, odours and air-borne organisms. Mitchell and Kelley (1933) suggested calculations based on keeping carbon dioxide concentration below about 0.5%, but preferably 0.1%. Most practical recommendations on air change rate since this, but in particular those of Davies (1951), have been based on this suggestion. It has usually been assumed that such allowances will not permit oxygen levels to fall low enough to be conceivably harmful, and it is commonly found in practice, as was pointed out by Scorgie and Willis (1952), that when operating on such a basis the first limiting factor is ammonia in most buildings, and ammonia and condensation in poorly insulated buildings. Certainly, high levels of ammonia must be avoided for several reasons. In several species, including turkeys, excess ammonia has been shown to damage the respiratory tract and to predispose chickens to Newcastle disease (Anderson, Beard and Hanson, 1964; Valentine, 1964) and to directly depress growth rate (Charles and Payne, 1966). Furthermore, high levels are unpleasant for staff working in the building, and in the UK there are regulations against permitting staff to work full shifts at concentrations above 25 ppm. There is no evidence on the effects of ammonia on turkey growth rate, but the occurrence of the problem in turkey buildings has been quantitatively studied (Anderson et al., 1964).

Emmans and Charles (1977) kept laying hens in climate rooms at two minimum ventilation settings, in order to check that rates calculated according to the above criteria were also adequate as measured by performance responses. Charles, Scragg and Binstead (1981) repeated the procedure using broilers. They concluded that minimum rates calculated according to the principles of Mitchell and Kelly (1933) and Davies (1951) were probably appropriate for normal commercial levels of

Table 11.6 Ventilation rates for growing turkeys

Live weight		Maximum ventilation		Minimum ventilation	
(kg)	(kg$^{3/4}$)	(m^3/s per 10^4 birds)	(Fans per 10^4 birds)[a]	(m^3/s per 10^4 birds)	(Fans per 10^4 birds)
0.5	0.59	9	3.6	0.9	0.4
2	1.68	27	10.8	2.7	1.1
5	3.34	53	21	5.3	2.1
10	5.62	90	36	9	3.6
20	9.46	150	60	15	6

[a] Fans/10^4 birds refers to 610 mm 900 rev/min agricultural propeller fans, at a working pressure of 50 Pa

performance, that ammonia was likely to be the first limiting factor, and that measured concentrations of carbon dioxide approximately corresponded to those expected from respiratory calculations. It was suggested that the minimum ventilation rate associated with a carbon dioxide concentration of less than 0.4%, which could be used for any poultry, was about $1.5 \times 10^{-4} m^3/s$ per $kg^{3/4}$ live weight, though as a practical recommendation this should certainly be exceeded whenever there is the slightest risk of high ammonia levels.

An alternative method of calculation offered was $2-3 m^3/s$ per tonne of feed eaten per day.

Table 11.6 gives some maximum and minimum ventilation rates for growing turkeys. The maximum ventilation rate for the removal of metabolic heat is approximately ten times the minimum.

Physical principles of application of the requirements

It will be seen from the preceding section that practical ventilation is a matter of modulating the air change rate between the maximum and minimum requirement according to temperature. This can either be done by adjusting the fan ventilation rate in powered systems, or by adjusting the sizes of the openings in natural convection driven systems. In both types it is possible, and often desirable, that the adjustment should be automatic by means of a thermostatic sensor controlling the equipment. The physical phenomena exploited can be described, and housing conditions predicted, by simple house heat balance equations, and an example was given by Saville, Clark and Charles (1978) as follows:

$$\Delta T = H_s/(1200\,V + UA)$$

where ΔT = temperature rise inside that above outside, °C
$\quad\quad H_s$ = sensible heat output, W/bird
$\quad\quad 1200$ = volumetric heat capacity of air, J/m^3 °C
$\quad\quad\quad V$ = ventilation rate, m^3/s per bird
$\quad\quad\quad U$ = average thermal conductance of walls and roof, W/m^2 °C
$\quad\quad\quad A$ = area of walls and roof per bird, m^2 (for many building shapes this can be taken as about 1.7/stocking density in birds per m^2)

This simple equation ignores heat storage, floor heat losses, heat gain from electric lights, metabolic heat gain or evaporative heat loss from the litter, and radiative heat gain or loss through the roof, but it has nevertheless been found to give quite reliable predictions. An exception will be that it will underestimate ΔT due to solar heat gain, in the case of uninsulated turkey sheds when their roofs are exposed to intense direct sun, even in northern European latitudes (Wilson, 1985).

In order to use the equation, values for the sensible heat output of turkeys are required, and these are reviewed in *Table 11.7*. Some values for the evaporative moisture output of turkeys are given in *Table 11.8*, since these give some idea of the substantial amounts of water which must be removed by ventilation in order to prevent bad litter. *Table 11.8* also gives estimates of carbon dioxide output. Unfortunately, the production of ammonia by the litter is unpredictable, but probably depends among other things on litter moisture, temperature, the protein metabolism of the birds (i.e. more ammonia will be produced if protein is fed to excess or imbalanced, though litter capping may slow its release), and the microbial flora of the litter.

Table 11.7 Some estimates of sensible heat output of turkeys

Live weight (kg)	Temperature (°C)	Sensible heat output (W/bird)
0.11	35	0.5
0.24	32	1.4
0.42	29	2.0
0.63	27	3.7
0.96	24	5.6

The following values have been calculated at $5.8 \ W/kg^{3/4}$ body weight, i.e. based on the value for 0.96 kg birds above

2	9.8
5	19.4
10	32.6
20	54.9

Shazer, Olsen and Mather (1974)

Table 11.8 Estimated quantities of moisture evaporated by turkeys

Live weight (kg)	Water vapourized (g/day per bird at 28°C)	Carbon dioxide respired (l/day per bird)
0.052	14	4
0.23	79	23
0.45	117	34
0.91	165	48
1.4	198	57
1.8	226	65
2.3	252	72
3.2	301	87
4.5	381	110
6.8	496	143
9.1 ♂	614	176
9.1 ♀	552	159
11.3	870	250

Mitchell and Kelley (1933)

Note that the effect of this respired water on the increment of absolute humidity, mg/m^3, above that of the outside air, is given by $M = m/V$, where m is the water vapourized in g/s per bird.

Manipulation of the house heat balance equation reveals a few important general rules for house design.

(1) Increasing ventilation rate has a diminishing effect on temperature lift. Thus greatly increasing the maximum ventilation allowance has hardly any further beneficial effect on house temperature controllability in warm weather. However, at low ventilation rates, small changes in the quantity of air passing through the house have very large effects on house temperature. Therefore, in cold weather not only is the choice of minimum ventilation rate important, but also accurate and careful regulation of ventilation is important whether achieved electrically or by convection. Inlets should therefore be protected from wind interference in winter.

(2) When the economic optimum temperature is high it is essential that the insulation be of sufficient standard that U is less than about 0.5 W/m^2 °C. Such standards of insulation will also reduce solar heat gain and condensation.

   A value of U of around 0.4–0.5 W/m°C has traditionally been achieved, for example, by a composite structure of a double skinned wall or roof enclosing an air space and 80 mm of glass fibre or its equivalent in terms of thermal resistance. Wathes (1981) provided details of the physical theory of insulation and of alternative methods of achieving it. A vapour check barrier must be provided between the insulant and the moist internal air of the house, otherwise condensation within the material causes loss of insulating value and also deterioration. Wathes (1981) also provided calculations of the psychrometrics of condensation.

(3) It is easier to keep buildings warm when they are fully stocked.

Practical ventilation designs

There are numerous configurations of the inlet and outlet arrangements for both fan systems and convectional systems, and it is beyond the scope of this chapter to list them all, still less to describe them all. Design assistance can be obtained from several organizations, and from the author. However, some characteristic features deserve comment.

Fan systems

For turkeys requiring a high temperature, i.e. during brooding or when the economic optimum is high as defined above, then fully enclosed fan ventilated housing can be useful. Carpenter (1981) has classified and characterized the ventilation systems available. A useful example is the high speed jet system, for which design details have been developed in detail and are available from the author.

Natural systems

Systems depending on natural convection need openings large enough when fully open to provide sufficient air by buoyancy forces in hot windless weather. The approximate requirement for both the inlets and outlets can be estimated from Bruce (1978) at 0.3–0.5 m^2/kW of sensible heat (see *Table 11.7*).

   Despite the simplicity of convectional systems, they should be designed so that the inlets do not direct cold draughty incoming air directly onto the turkeys. Therefore inlets should be placed well above turkey height and aimed upwards in cold weather.

Monitoring

The house heat balance equation permits the calculation of the physical performance of which a given building design is capable. For any particular design and density of stocking a range of outside temperatures exists within which it should be possible to hold the desired temperature by varying the ventilation rate.

Sutcliffe, King and Charles (1985) described a monitoring scheme, based on portable computer compatible data loggers, in which the theoretically possible controllability of a building is statistically compared with its achievement.

Several years of monitoring several houses per week have shown that a house can achieve its potential, whether power ventilated or naturally ventilated, but only when wind proof, and preferably automatically controlled. The financial consequences of the errors in control can be measured by reference to the responses of the birds to temperature summarized in the review of requirements above. Improvements to buildings should be undertaken when such an analysis reveals substantial economic consequences.

Acknowledgements

The information collected at Gleadthorpe EHF was the work of many people, but in particular T. S. Bray and J. A. Binstead. The computer models of the data were by J. Gilbert. The carcass analysis was by Mrs M. Holborn. Nutritional advice and formulation was by J. R. Hopkins and statistical advice by H. H. Spechter.

References

Alburquerque, K. de, Leighton, A. T., Mason, J. P. and Potter, L. M. (1978). The effects of environmental temperature, sex and dietary energy levels on growth performance of large white turkeys. *Poultry Science*, **57**, 353–362

Anderson, D. P., Beard, C. W. and Hanson, R. P. (1964). The adverse effects of ammonia on chickens including resistance to Newcastle Disease virus. *Avian Diseases*, **8**, 369

Anderson, D. P., Solana, P., Hanson, R. P.and Cramer, C. O. (1964). Progress report on environmental studies of confinement growing of turkeys as related to respiratory disease problems. *Proceedings American Society of Agricultural Engineers*, Fort Collins. Paper No. 64-425

Benoit, J. and Ott, I. (1944). External and internal factors in sexual activity. Effect of irradiation with different wavelengths on the mechanisms of photostimulation of the hypophysis and on testicular growth in the immature duck. *Yale Journal of Biological Medicine*, **17**, 27–43

Blakely, R. M. and MacGregor, H. I. (1975). The effect of length of day and temperature on the deposition of subcutaneous fat by market turkeys. *Canadian Journal of Animal Science*, **43**, 332–336

Bray, T. S. and Binstead, J. A. (1980). Unpublished ADAS data

Bruce, J. M. (1978). Natural convection through openings and its application to cattle building ventilation. *Journal of Agricultural Engineering Research*, **23**, 151–167

Carpenter, G. A. (1981). Ventilation systems. In *Environmental Aspects of Housing for Animal Production* (Clark, J. A., ed.). London, Butterworths

Charles, D. R. and Payne, C. G. (1966). The influence of graded levels of atmospheric ammonia on chickens. 1. Effects on respiration and on the performance of broilers and replacement growing stock. *British Poultry Science*, **7**, 177–187

Charles, D. R., Scragg, R. H. and Binstead, J. A. (1981). The effects of temperature on broilers: ventilation rates for the application of temperature control. *British Poultry Science*, **22**, 493–498

Davies, C. N. (1951). Ventilation and its application to poultry housing. *World's Poultry Science Journal*, **7**, 195

Emmans, G. C. (1980). A growth model. Proceedings of conference on computers in animal production. British Society of Animal Production, Harrogate

Emmans, G. C. and Charles, D. R. (1977). Climatic environment and poultry feeding in practice. In *Nutrition and the Climatic Environment* (Haresign, W., Swan, H. and Lewis, D., eds). London, Butterworths

Foss, D. C., Carew, L. B. and Arnold, E. L. (1972). Physiological development of cockerels as influenced by selected wavelengths of environmental light. *Poultry Science,* **51**, 1922–1927

Gill, D. J. and Leighton, A. T. (1974). The effects of light environmental population density on growth performance of male turkeys. *Poultry Science,* **53**, 1927

Hellickson, M. A., Butchbaker, A. F., Witz, R. L. and Bryant, R. L. (1967). Performance of young turkeys as affected by environmental temperature. *Transactions of the American Society of Agricultural Engineers,* **10**, 793–795

Hester, P. Y., Sutton, A. L., Elkin, R. G. and Klingensmith, P. M. (1985). The effect of lighting, dietary amino acids and litter on the incidence of leg abnormalities and performance of turkey toms. *Poultry Science,* **64**, 2062–2075

Hester, P. Y., Sutton, A. L. and Elkin, A. G. (1987). Effect of light intensity, litter source, and litter management on the incidence of leg abnormalities and performance of male turkeys. *Poultry Science,* **66**, 666–675

Klingensmith, P. M., Hester, P. Y., Elkin, R. G. and Ward, C. R. (1986). Relationship of high intensity step up lighting to bone ash and growth plate closure of the tarso-metatarsus in turkeys. *British Poultry Science,* **27**, 487–492

Mitchell, H. H. and Kelley, M. A. R. (1933). Estimated data on the energy, gaseous, and water metabolism of poultry for use in planning the ventilation of poultry houses. *Journal of Agricultural Research,* **47**, 735–748

Parker, J. T., Boone, M. A. and Knechtes, J. F. (1972). The effect of ambient temperature upon body temperature, feed consumption and water consumption, using two varieties of turkeys. *Poultry Science,* **51**, 659–664

Payne, C. G. (1967). Environmental temperature and egg production. In *The Physiology of the Domestic Fowl* (Horton-Smith, C. and Amoroso, E. C., eds). Edinburgh, Oliver and Boyd

Saville, C. A., Clark, J. A. and Charles, D. R. (1978). Predicting poultry house heat balance. *World's Poultry Science Association* (UK Branch). Spring meeting

Scorgie, N. J. and Willis, G. A. (1952). In *Linton's Veterinary Hygine.* Edinburgh, Green

Shazer, J. A. de, Olson, L. L. and Mather, F. B. (1974). Heat losses of large white turkeys — 6 to 36 days of age. *Poultry Science,* **53**, 2047–2054

Siopes, T. D., Timmons, M. B., Baughman, G. R. and Parkhurst, C. R. (1983). The effect of light intensity on the growth performance of male turkeys. *Poultry Science,* **62**, 2336–2342

Siopes, T. D., Timmons, M. B., Baughman, G. R. and Parkhurst, C. R. (1984). The effects of light intensity on turkey poult performance, eye morphology and adrenal weight. *Poultry Science,* **63**, 904–909

Sutcliffe, N. A., King, A. W. M. and Charles, D. R. (1985). Monitoring poultry house environment. In *Computer Applications in Agricultural Environments.* 42nd Easter School in agricultural science (Clark, J. A., Gregson, K. and Safell, R. A., eds). University of Nottingham, Butterworths

Valentine, H. (1964). A study of the effect of different ventilation rates on the ammonia concentrations in atmosphere of broilers houses. *British Poultry Science,* **5**, 149–159

Wathes, C. M. (1981). Insulation of animal houses. In *Environmental Aspects of Housing for Animal Production* (Clark, J. A., ed.). London, Butterworths

Wilson, E. A. (1985). Solar Heat Gain. Unpublished ADAS data

Part III

Health of the turkey

Rhinotracheitis

Turkey rhinotracheitis (TRT) in Great Britain

J. C. Stuart

In late June, 1985, on the Norfolk coast facing Europe, a classic outbreak of rhinotracheitis occurred and rapidly swept through the county of Norfolk. Within 6 months the disease spread throughout the country.

East Anglia tends to be the point of entry into Great Britain of most new poultry diseases, probably because it is on one of the main bird migratory routes and has one of the highest concentrations of all species of domestic poultry in the UK.

Turkeys of any age may be affected from 1 week old to 50 weeks, when the breeders are slaughtered. It occurs on all sizes of sites, both all in — all out, one age and those with continuous multi-age production. There is usually a drop in feed consumption which is especially noticeable in the breeders. In most cases the birds remain active and interested in visitors though somewhat depressed and have an altered higher pitch voice. Respiratory symptoms vary from very mild to very severe.

There is a rapid onset of symptoms that sweep through a house within 12–24 h. Morbidity approaches 100%. However, a wire netting division will delay the spread for a few days, suggesting that spread within the house may in part be via the drinkers. Nevertheless, chlorinated water does not stop the spread, though it may result in some delay. There is also a rapid spread in a matter of a few days from house to house on a site. Occasionally an individual house will be missed. Where endemic in an area the vast majority of the flocks become affected.

The clinical syndrome varies considerably in its severity from very mild, which may be missed by an unobservant stockman, to very severe. In most uncomplicated cases, the symptoms disappear in 7–10 days but if mortality occurs they can persist much longer.

In the growing bird, the symptoms include the following.

Oedema

This is most commonly sub-mandibular but may occasionally extend over other areas of the head in a very small percentage of the birds. It is usually the first indication of the problem and may in very young birds be the only one seen.

Rhinitis

This is characterized by excess mucus in the nasal cavity that may be seen as exudate at the external nares. It rapidly becomes turbid and sticky, and, when

217

mixed with dust, forms a crust that blocks the nostrils. In some cases this exudate may be very small and only detected when the face is squeezed. The rhinitis is usually accompanied by increased snicking and head shaking. One may have to hold the bird to one's ear to hear the slight respiratory noises.

Tracheitis

The tracheal mucus is increased and becomes mucopurulent if secondary bacteria are present. It may be so severe in the very young poult, that the mucus or a plug of necrotic material completely blocks the trachea. The tracheitis is usually accompanied by coughing with moist rales and often gaping or mouth breathing. In severe cases one can hear these from outside the house.

Sinusitis

In early cases the swollen sinuses only contain air, later a clear mucus and later in some birds, white caseous material. Most sinus swellings disappear with the other symptoms. A few persist to slaughter. However, the birds do not rub their eyes or swollen sinuses over their shoulders and cause discoloration of the feathers as occurs with mycoplasmosis.

Conjunctivitis

A proportion of the flock may also show frothy conjunctivitis early in the syndrome leading to a blepharitis.

The rhinitis and tracheitis are always present in the majority of birds but other symptoms are somewhat variable in incidence.

The diseases is best diagnosed clinically. A definite diagnosis on dead birds is difficult and, of course, all birds that snick do not have rhinotracheitis.

Mortality

This is extremely variable from negligible to over 50%. On a site with many houses only a few may show an increase in mortality, occasionally all do. The eventual mortality bears no relation to the severity of the initial symptoms. The mortality tends to occur in three waves. One with the initial symptoms which may be very small, another when secondary bacteria take over, which may be very high and yet another as culls develop.

The second wave of mortality can start to occur 1–3 weeks after the initial symptoms and persists for 1–3 weeks, especially in birds of 8–11 weeks old. In these cases mortality is due mainly to secondary invaders — E. coli, Bordetella, Pasteurella-like organisms. There are typical postmortem lesions of pericarditis, perihepatitis, air sacculitis and pneumonia. In many cases the flock as a whole looks well.

A third wave develops in those houses that have shown high mortality. Frequently an increase in the number of culls develops due to leg problems — swollen hocks or adhesion between the pericardial sac and the epicardium. Mortality and culling can be very high in these cases.

Some flocks that have fully recovered also have increased condemnations in the plant especially if a high mortality occurred during the outbreak. A salpingitis is seen in some females but in general the condemnations are due to pericarditis/air sacculitis or arthritis with or without dehydration. One cannot forecast the extent of these condemnations on antemortem inspection — regardless of what some academics and red meat experts suggest under proposed changes in EEC Directive 71/118.

These condemnations can be the cause of the greatest economic loss in the whole disease outbreak.

In my experience the mortality is influenced by several factors:

(1) Age of bird: high mortality can occur in the very young during the intial stages. The excess mucus, and sometimes caseous intratracheal plugs of necrotic tissue, causes oedema of the lungs and asphyxiation. Some show an air sacculitis and pneumonia and very moist carcasses.

Mortality is invariably low in flocks older than 13 weeks when first infected.

(2) Concurrent diseases obviously influence the outcome. These include:
   (a) Haemorrhagic enteritis virus which possibly has an immunosuppressive effect. Most flocks in England convert by 8–11 weeks old — which tends to be the age of highest mortality due to secondary invaders.
   (b) *Mycoplasma gallisepticum.*
   (c) *Pasteurella multocida.*
   (d) *Moraxella.*
   (e) Coccidiosis.
   (f) Influenza A.
   (g) Debilitation from any disease.

(3) Management practices: these in my opinion have the greatest influence on mortality.
   (a) Inadequate ventilation is the most obvious. One has seen an increased severity with the onset of winter conditions when people tend to reduce ventilation rates to maintain house temperature. In general mortality is less in pole barns than in controlled environment houses.
   (b) Stocking densities, overcrowding and bad litter conditions (closely linked with ventilation); 8–12 weeks tends to be the age of greatest density on the large farms. Flocks infected at this age show the highest mortality. One rarely sees severe problems or mortality in replacement breeder flocks which are less densely stocked.
   (c) Poor hygiene.
   (d) Debeaking practices — this aggravates the problem if done at the time of the outbreak or just before.
   (e) Mixed age sites that allow continual re-exposure of susceptible stock.
   (f) Re-use of old litter for a second crop of birds due to the influence of ammonia.
   (g) Live Newcastle disease vaccination by aerosol surprisingly does not aggravate the problem to any extent.

There has been a continually changing pattern seen within some organizations. During the first wave of infection in July/August, 1985, the initial clinical symptoms were very severe but few secondary problems developed. Later more secondary problems developed, perhaps associated with winter ventilation practices. When restocking of fully depopulated sites took place with progeny from breeders that had succumbed in lay, the newly placed poults sometimes showed symptoms as early as 7–10 days of age. Later when progeny of flocks that were affected before lay, came into the programme, the initial symptoms were not seen till 3–4 weeks of age.

A few flocks have shown a second resurgence of some symptoms (coughing) and mortality, associated with a *Moraxella/Bordetella/Pasteurella*-like organism infection several weeks after the previous problems. Percarditis and air sacculitis tend to be the main lesions with some lung congestion or oedema. Many of these birds show nervous symptoms, incoordination, paralysis and die with beaks buried in the litter and legs stretched out behind them. One could almost expect this with *Pasteurella*-like organisms.

Flocks tha succumb to the initial infection near to slaughter show an increase in the number of birds that die during catching and the number of 'Dead on Arrival' at the factory. There is also an increase in the number of carcasses condemned by the Poultry Meat Inspector for extensive and acute air sacculitis.

The effect on weight gain and final weights depend upon the age of infection and severity.

So we have associated with turkey rhinotracheitis in growing birds:

(1) initial infection ± very variable symptoms in severity ± very variable mortality,
(2) 1–3 weeks later, very variable mortality, due to secondary invading organism,
(3) occasionally a resurgence of symptoms due to some of these secondary invaders,
(4) development of culls,
(5) plant condemnations.

Adult breeding flocks

These in general do not show the severe symptoms associated with rhinotracheitis in younger birds. Any present can be difficult to detect and are only seen in a few birds. Most breeders in the UK are kept in open-sided houses with more fresh air and more floor space than fatteners enjoy.

A few breeding flocks show an increased mortality, especially those of the heavier strains. Yolk peritonitis, congested lungs, air sacculitis and, very occasionally, some obscure nervous condition, the cause of which has not been found in spite of extensive investigations, have all been implicated.

The most obvious symptoms seen in infected adult flocks are a fall in feed consumption, rapidly followed by a precipitous drop in egg production. In one case this fell from 6500 eggs/day, down to 2400 within a week. Other flocks took up to 2 weeks to bottom out. All took about 3 weeks to fully regain the production which in most cases approached, and in some even exceeded, the expected point on the production curve. Affected flocks lost up to 10 eggs per bird (*Figures 12.1* and *12.2*).

Some flocks, but not all, infected as they were coming into lay were a catastrophe. They never gave any near-normal production and performed very similarly to non-vaccinated laying chickens infected with infectious bronchitis.

During the 2 weeks of recovery very large numbers of unsettable white eggs, often with very thin shells, were produced. Some of them had concretions on the shell, others were mis-shapen. These frequently amounted to 50% of the daily increase in production. Their numbers gradually decreased as production peaked again.

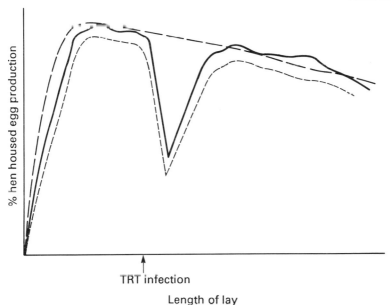

Figure 12.1 Egg production. Expected production (--), actual production (—) and hatching eggs (---)

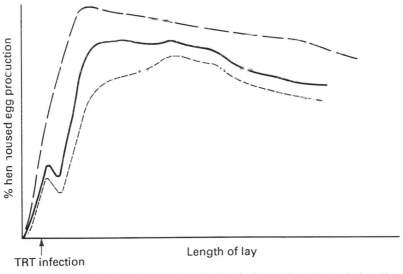

Figure 12.2 Egg production. Expected production (--), actual production (—) and hatching eggs (---)

Fertility and hatchability of settable eggs were not affected, nor was poult quality in most cases.

However, in some parts of the country where white eggs have not been a problem, poult quality has. Why?

To date no laying flock has succumbed twice and no laying flock that was infected in rearing has succumbed to the disease in lay. However, some serological investigations would suggest that the flocks will respond serologically to a second exposure.

Following the initial outbreak most breeders are naturally infected during rearing.

Transmission

Spread to other sites in most cases has been very haphazard. It does not follow any set pattern.

Feed lorries are possible culprits. Certainly circumstantial evidence would suggest that this was the case in East Anglia.

Wind-borne infection would appear to be involved in some areas. Certainly movement of infected or recovered poults has been implicated. Movement of recovered birds to another part of the country for slaughter has also been suspected of spreading the disease.

It is not until something like this happens that one discovers how much movement of stock occurs about the countryside.

Aetiology

The epidemiology of the condition certainly suggests that there has to be a virus involved and similar pneumovirus isolates have been made by several laboratories.

Bacterial complications would appear to be secondary and vary from farm to farm. *Bordetella avian* (*Alcaligens faecalis*), *Moraxella anatipestifer* Type A, various *Pasteurella*-like organisms can be found in different outbreaks during the first few days of the clinical symptoms appearing. None is common to all. They soon become swamped with *Proteus* and *E. coli*, though *Moraxella* tends to persist.

Reading the literature is confusing. It would appear that worldwide there are at least two if not three syndromes with similar clinical symptoms called turkey rhinotracheitis or turkey coryza (see *Table 12.1*).

Table 12.1

Country	First appearance	Age (weeks)	Breeders
Type I			
Canada	1960	3–7	No
USA	1960	3–7	?
Italy	1975	3–7	No
Germany	1970	3–7	No
Spain	1979	3–7	No
UK	1975	3–7	No
Type II			
Israel	1977	Any	Yes
Germany	1980	Any	Yes
Holland	1981	Any	Yes
France	1981	Any	Yes
Spain	1984	Any	Yes
UK	1985	Any	Yes
Type III			
South Africa	1976	3–7	Yes

From G. P. Wilding (personal communication)

Type I

With this type there is no rapid spread to other farms. The disease can be controlled by improved conditions and hygiene leading to eradication from the site. I propose that this should be called *turkey coryza.*

Type II

Explosive outbreaks occur with rapid spread from site to site. Improved conditions and hygiene will reduce mortality but to date cannot eradicate the disease. I propose that the description *turkey rhinotracheitis* be restricted to this clinical picture.

Type III

Very, very severe, with mortality up to 90%. Slaughtered out. Similar in many cases to Type II.

Treatment

I find it difficult to really say that any treatment is very successful. The severity of symptoms and mortality vary so much from house to house, even within a site, that the true assessment of treatments is very difficult, if not impossible. A whole battery of drugs has been tried. In general one tries to medicate against the secondary bacterial invading organisms that are associated with most of the mortality. In many cases mortality does not fall off even after medication with a drug selected on the basis of a sensitivity test. In other cases it stops long before the drug could be having any effect. We have not used Baytril (Bayer AG, FRG) as it is not licensed in the UK.

To date I do not believe that it is economically sound to treat all initial outbreaks as they occur. Some people do not agree with me. Experience shows which farms or even which houses may need treatment for the secondary bacterial infection on single age sites. On multi-age sites routine medication may be beneficial.

Prevention

I do not believe that one can keep a commercial farm, or for that matter most breeding farms, sufficiently in isolation to prevent it eventually becoming infected.

At present, improvements in all aspects of management, especially the ventilation, stocking density, litter conditions and general hygiene are the most important steps that can be taken to reduce the effect of secondary bacterial infections.

We all await the development of an effective vaccine which I believe will be a live one given to the poults during the first week of life, since maternal antibodies do not appear to protect the young bird and early infection results in fewer secondary problems. The lack of an effective laboratory challenge module does not help with the development of a vaccine.

It is now possible to detect antibodies to the TRT agent. These have been shown to be present in many broiler breeder and broiler flocks, some of which have converted at the time of an outbreak of the swollen head syndrome. The TRT agent has been isolated in France from one of these cases. However, there are many serologically positive broiler breeder flocks that have not shown any symptoms.

I am not aware of any clinical swollen head syndrome in commercial egg laying flocks though many are serologically positive. Could this virus be involved in some of the drops in egg production and poor shell quality in these flocks?

There are many serologically negative chicken flocks surrounded by infected or recovered turkey flocks.

There is also some evidence that game birds and guinea fowl can be infected with a TRT agent.

The demonstration of TRT antibodies in chickens has introduced another complication. The USA refuses to accept any chicken or turkey hatching eggs or progeny unless they come from a TRT serologically negative flock. We have no evidence of egg transmission as yet.

The isolation of the TRT agent from chickens and the export restrictions make the development of any effective vaccine even more urgent. But, will vaccination of turkeys prevent spread to chickens or has the virus already been adapted to chickens so that the chickens are now acting as a reservoir of infection to turkeys? Will we have to use the vaccine on chickens? What will then happen to the export market?

I leave you with those questions!

Laboratory investigations with turkey rhinotracheitis (TRT) virus: virus isolation, maintenance and serology

C. Baxter-Jones and R. C. Jones

Virus isolation

Primary isolation techniques

An acute and highly contagious respiratory disease affecting birds of all ages and similar to turkey rhinotracheitis (TRT), as seen in the UK from July 1985, has been present in several countries for many years (Lister and Alexander, 1986). Using conventional virus isolation methods, e.g. culture in chicken cell monolayers or embryonated chicken eggs, and despite various attempts (Heller, Weisman and Aharonovitch, 1984; Andral et al., 1985a,b) the aetiological agent was not isolated. Buys and Du Preez (1980) however, during earlier investigations of a respiratory disease of turkeys in South Africa, demonstrated the presence of a ciliostatic agent in tracheal organ culture. This agent was never fully characterized.

Organ culture has been used quite widely as a technique for propagating a range of avian viruses (see Butler, Ellaway and Hall, 1972 and Darbyshire, 1978). As a technique it is not commonly regarded as particularly sensitive for primary virus isolation. Possible exceptions are with Newcastle disease (ND) and infectious bronchitis (IB) viruses. For TRT, however, the use of tracheal organ culture greatly facilitated the primary isolation of the causative virus. The major advantage of this system over embryonated eggs or cell monolayers was the availability of a suitable marker indicating the presence of the virus, ciliostasis. The virus will grow in monolayers prepared from a range of chicken tissues but a period of adaptation is required before any cytopathic changes become evident in cell culture. Such changes do not generally become apparent during routine blind passage of respiratory tissues taken from field samples. The virus will also grow in embryonated eggs. Whereas inoculation of the ciliostatic virus into the allantoic fluid of chicken and turkey eggs did not cause any embryo abnormalities or deaths (Jones, Baxter-Jones and Wilding, 1986), a number of embryo lethal agents were isolated by Lister and Alexander (1986) from field material. These authors used the yolk sac route for attempts at virus isolation. At least one of these isolates, CVL 14/1 (Wyeth et al., 1986), after passage through turkey poults produced ciliostasis in chick tracheal organ culture.

Source of samples

Several authors have reported the isolation of pneumovirus-like agents from outbreaks of TRT in the UK (McDougall and Cook, 1986; Wilding, Baxter-Jones and Grant, 1986; Wyeth et al., 1986). The virus grows in tracheal organ cultures prepared from both turkey and chicken embryos.

In our laboratory, turkey embryo tracheal organ culture has been used for primary virus isolation. For successful isolation it is necessary to obtain samples early during the course of the disease. Once clinical respiratory signs have been present for more than a few days, the chances of isolating the virus are considerably reduced. There are no comparative published studies indicating the relative importance of different respiratory tissues for virus isolation. We have obtained good results by taking pooled material from the upper respiratory tract (usually turbinate and trachea) and homogenizing in media containing antibiotics to suppress extraneous bacterial contamination. After a low speed centrifugation, to remove cellular debris, the supernatant material can be inoculated directly into tracheal organ culture.

Virus maintenance

Tracheal organ culture

The TRT virus can be maintained in organ cultures prepared from 24-day-old turkey embryos for considerable time. Our original virus isolate, for example, BUT 1 No. 8544, was passaged 98 times in turkey tracheal rings with no apparent change in its characteristics. The virus will typically cause ciliostasis, i.e. complete cessation of ciliary movement, within 4–6 days. This may take longer in chicken rings, possibly 6 to 8 days and after a limited number of passages the ciliostasis may not be totally complete. The agent passes through membrane filters with small pore size (0.45 or 0.2 μm), albeit with a small reduction in virus titre. Organ culture fluids containing the virus do not haemagglutinate either avian or a range of mammalian erythrocytes. The virus can be neutralized by convalescent serum from affected turkey flocks; ciliostasis no longer occurs. Initially the TRT virus did not grow to very high titre in organ culture (about 10^3–10^4 median ciliostatic doses or CD_{50}/ml) although these yields have now been considerably improved.

Immunofluorescence

Indirect immunofluorescence has been used to demonstrate the virus in infected tracheal organ cultures (Baxter-Jones, Wilding and Grant, 1986) and in experimentally challenged turkeys and chickens (Jones et al., 1986, 1987). The virus shows a close association with the ciliated border of epithelial cells in the turbinates and upper trachea, although it does not persist for long periods. The tests may be performed with convalescent serum from affected birds or preferably with experimentally produced turkey or monospecific chicken sera. With high titred sera it is possible to produce a direct conjugate (fluorescein-labelled turkey anti-TRT serum). One such conjugate has recently been used to examine the respiratory and reproductive tissues of laying birds infected with TRT virus (Jones et al., in preparation).

Immunofluorescence has also been used to detect TRT virus antibodies in commercial turkey flocks (Baxter-Jones, Wilding and Grant, 1986). For this test, which will be discussed in more detail later, infected tracheal organ cultures are used. With frozen sections prepared from infected organ cultures, the best results are obtained within 2–3 days of infection. The presence of antibody in a serum sample will produce bright fluorescent staining within the ciliated epithelium of the tracheal section.

Immunofluorescence has found a variety of applications in our studies of TRT virus, i.e. detection of virus in organ culture and tissues of birds, serology, etc. Another important application of this technique was to monitor the adaptation of the virus to growth in cell culture. In the absence of a defined cytopathic effect during early passage, viral antigens could be detected in the cell monolayers.

Growth in cell culture

Very little or no cytopathic changes are observed during early passage of the TRT virus in chick embryo cell monolayers. With immunofluorescence it is possible to see evidence of virus infection. After further passage in chick embryo fibroblasts, depending slightly upon the isolate, cytopathic changes can be discerned. Syncytia, sometimes containing 20–30 nuclei, can be observed within 48–72 h and with further incubation the monolayers become more extensively damaged. After 5 or 6 days there are few cells remaining intact.

The virus will also grow in chick embryo liver cells. Using trypsin treatment, of both the virus inoculum and the maintenance medium, combined with a low speed centrifugation, it is possible to induce the virus to form syncytia within 24–48 h (R. C. Jones, unpublished information).

Once the virus was adapted to grow in fibroblast monolayers it was possible to plaque purify an isolate. The cloned virus isolate, BUT 1 No. 8544, was then transferred to a mammalian cell line (Vero) in which it also produces a characteristic syncytial cytopathic effect. Workers in France (Giraud et al., 1986a) have also used this cell line to cultivate a similar virus isolated from cases of TRT in that country. We have found the use of an immunoperoxidase staining technique particularly useful when growing the virus in Vero cells. Infected cells, which appear dark reddish-brown in colour can be readily visualized within 48 h of infecting the monolayers.

The ability to cultivate the virus in cell culture has facilitated the development of a number of serological tests, i.e. ELISA and serum neutralization. Whereas the virus titres are not significantly higher (maybe tenfold) in cells compared to tracheal organ culture it is now considerably easier to grow large quantities of the virus. Early attempts with direct or immune electron microscopy revealed only few virus particles in organ culture fluids. Large numbers of virus particles could be observed in cell culture fluids.

Serology

Development of serological tests

A number of serological tests have been developed by workers at different laboratories for detecting antibodies to TRT virus. Such methods have also been used to study the antigenic relationships of the different virus isolates.

Immunofluorescence

An indirect immunofluorescence test has been described (Baxter-Jones, Wilding and Grant, 1986). Frozen sections are cut from infected tracheal organ cultures. Serum samples can be tested at either a single (qualitative test) or a range of dilutions (quantitative test). The serum sample is layered over the section. Any virus specific antibodies present will attach to the viral antigens. The presence of antibody is revealed using a fluorescein conjugated anti-species antibody. Fluorescing cells appear bright apple green when illuminated by ultraviolet light and observed under the microscope.

ELISA

Once the virus was adapted to grow in chick embryo fibroblasts sufficient virus was obtained to produce an antigen for ELISA (Grant, Baxter-Jones and Wilding, 1987). A similar test has also been used by Wyeth et al. (1987). For this assay both virus and control (uninfected) antigens are used. For each serum sample, at a single dilution, the difference in absorbance values obtained with the two antigens is calculated. For each test the results can be standardized using a positive control serum of known titre. The results can be expressed as either optical density difference (ODD) values or after comparison with a standard curve as titre values ($\log_2$).

Workers in France (Giraud et al., 1986b) prepared an ELISA antigen from infected Vero cells. This test also utilizes a dual antigen system. More recently an isolate of the virus (Houghton strain) has been grown in tracheal organ culture and purified using an isopycnic sucrose gradient (A. P. A. Mocket, personal communication). The purified antigen is not used with a control antigen. Similar profiles were obtained when duplicate serum samples were examined using this ELISA and the one currently in use at our laboratory (Baxter-Jones et al., 1987).

Serum neutralization

Virus neutralization tests can be conducted in either organ culture or cell culture. The latter is probably most convenient. Using the constant virus (or beta method) neutralization tests have been described in chick embryo fibroblasts and liver cells (Baxter-Jones et al., in preparation) and Vero cells (Giraud et al., 1986b).

ELISA offers a number of potential advantages, particularly in terms of speed, and has been generally adopted as a routine test. The serum neutralization test may provide a useful adjunct to ELISA as a means for detecting antibody in flocks of turkeys or chickens affected by TRT virus.

Antigenic relatedness of virus isolates

Viruses isolated in the UK show a morphological similarity (Wyeth *et al.*, 1986; Baxter-Jones *et al.*, 1987). Viral particles exhibit considerable pleomorphism and spherical (*Figure 12.3*) filamentous and bizarre forms (*Figure 12.4*) can be observed in electron microscopic preparations (spherical forms 80–200 nm diameter, filamentous forms may be over 1000 nm in length). The particles are fringed with spikes (13–15 nm long). The virus has not been definitely classified, but the morphology is indicative of the family Paramyxoviridae, probably pneumovirus.

The UK isolates of the virus have been compared serologically (Baxter-Jones *et al.*, 1987). Cross neutralization tests in organ culture reveal antigenic similarity. Sera prepared against three isolates (BUT, Houghton and Weybridge) all demonstrated cross reactivity with the BUT virus isolate (BUT 1 No. 8544) as determined by ELISA, serum neutralization and immunofluorescence tests. These results indicate that the different laboratories are working with isolates of the same virus.

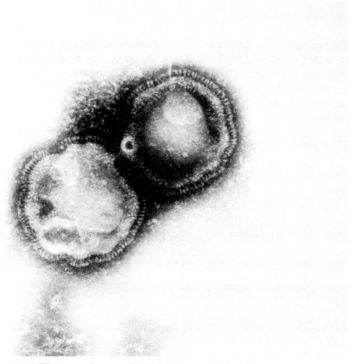

Figure 12.3 Electron micrograph of TRT virus, spherical form

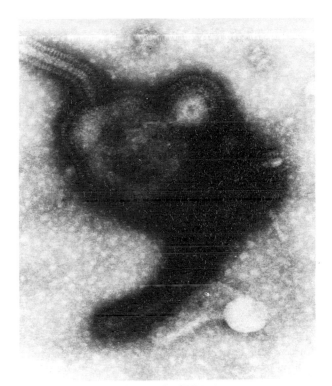

Figure 12.4 Electron micrograph of TRT virus taken from same preparation as *Figure 12.3* but showing filamentous and bizarre forms

Detection of antibody in commercial flocks

An indirect immunofluorescence test was used to detect antibodies to TRT virus in flocks of commercial turkeys in the UK affected by respiratory disease (Baxter-Jones, Wilding and Grant, 1986). Paired serum samples from five flocks were examined before and after the appearance of clinical signs of disease. Antibodies were not detected in the absence of disease. Seroconversion was demonstrated in all the flocks between 11 and 32 days after the first report of respiratory symptoms. Serum antibody titres ranged between 1:40 and 1:640 when quantitative immunofluorescence tests were performed. During a survey of commercial turkeys affected by respiratory disease in Cheshire and Buckinghamde-monstrated in sera collected from 21 flocks between 2 and 14 weeks after the appearance of clinical rhinotracheitis. All tests were performed at a single serum dilution (1 in 20) which was found sufficient to differentiate negative and positive sera. No attempt was made to titrate individual serum samples. Large numbers of infected tracheal organ culture sections are necessary to perform quantitative tests on individual sera. The use of a single serum dilution is more economic.

An ELISA has also been used to demonstrate seroconversion in flocks of turkeys affected by rhinotracheitis (Grant, Baxter-Jones and Wilding, 1987). ELISA would appear to be a sensitive and reproducible test. Antiviral antibodies can be detected in some flocks within 5 days of the appearance of clinical respiratory disease. The reproducibility of the test was assessed after repeatedly testing sera from individually identified birds. Twenty birds from each of two flocks were sampled on five occasions, before, during and after the appearance of typical rhinotracheitis symptoms. These sera were tested by ELISA on at least three separate occasions. The antibody response for each flock was similar (*Figure 12.5*). The inter-assay percentage coefficient of variation (CV) was low (M. Grant, personal communication). For individual sera CVs were below 10%, a value which is considered acceptable for serological tests.

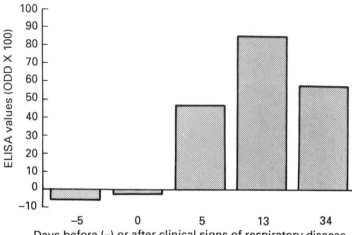

Figure 12.5 ELISA antibody response in a flock of 19-week-old commercial turkeys affected by TRT

Giraud *et al.* (1986a) used ELISA to detect antibodies to a similar virus in commercial flocks of turkeys with respiratory disease in France. ELISA has also been used to detect antibodies to TRT virus in commercial chicken flocks both in the UK and France (Wyeth *et al.*, 1987; Picault *et al.*, 1987).

A comparison was made between the ability of three serological tests (ELISA, immunofluorescence and serum neutralization) to detect antibodies to TRT virus (Baxter-Jones *et al.*, in preparation). Antibodies were detected by all tests within 5 days of the appearance of rhinotracheitis (*Table 12.2*). When data were analysed statistically the best correlations obtained were: ELISA and serum neutralization ($n = 40$, $r = 0.79$, $P < 0.001$) and immunofluorescence and serum neutralization

Table 12.2 Comparison of serological tests for TRT virus in a commercial flock of turkeys

Days before (−) or after (+) clinical signs of TRT	*Serological test*		
	Immunofluorescence[a]	*ELISA[b]*	*Serum neutralization*
−5	0[c]	−6	0
0	0	−3	0
+5	8.9	47	>10.3
+11	8.4	85	8.0
+34	5.8	58	7.3

[a] Reciprocal of mean IF or SN titres expressed as $\log_2$ values
[b] ELISA values expressed as ODD units (× 100). ELISA values less than 15 are considered negative
[c] Values represent mean titres for 20 serum samples

$(n = 40, r = 0.53, P < 0.001)$. This particular flock of birds became infected at 19 weeks of age. Antibody levels, measured by all three tests, although persistent, were generally falling by day 34 after disease signs started.

Recently a group of laying turkeys, with no previously detectable TRT antibodies, was experimentally infected with the virus inside an isolation facility (Jones *et al.*, in preparation). The sera response of five birds was monitored by ELISA and serum neutralization tests for 96 days post-infection. In contrast to the younger birds described above the antibody response measured in the mature turkeys persisted at high levels for the duration of the experiment (*Figure 12.6*). The finding of high antibody levels in sexually mature birds is consistent with field observations made during the primary wave of TRT infection in Cheshire.

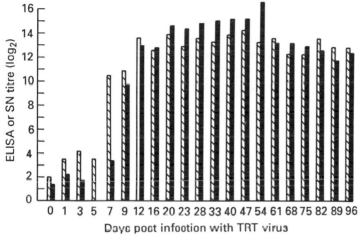

Figure 12.6 Antibody responses demonstrated by ELISA and serum neutralization in experimentally-infected laying turkeys

International survey

A respiratory disease similar to turkey rhinotracheitis has been present in several countries for many years. During the past few months we have received sera from most of these countries and tested them for antibodies to TRT virus using ELISA. Antibodies have so far been detected in samples received from France, Germany, Holland, Israel, Italy and Spain. The results of this survey will be published in more detail elsewhere.

Recently sera from turkeys and chickens experimentally infected with a ciliostatic virus isolated in South Africa (Buys and Du Preez, 1980) were tested by ELISA (virus isolate BUT 1 No. 8544). The results indicate an antigenic similarity between the virus isolates (J. Du Preez and G. P. Wilding, unpublished observations).

TRT virus in chickens

Experimental infection of chickens

Broiler and day-old SPF chickens were infected with the TRT virus (Jones *et al.*, 1987). Only mild respiratory symptoms were produced. This is perhaps not surprising since the birds were maintained within an isolation facility. The virus was re-isolated from infected birds and using immunofluorescence could be detected in the upper respiratory tract of infected SPF chicks and in sentinel birds placed in direct contact. Both infected birds and contacts were shown to possess antibodies to the TRT virus. The infection was apparently transmissible to susceptible chicks.

Examination of field sera

Antibodies to TRT virus have been detected in commercial chicken sera in the UK and France. In a study of broiler parent chickens in the UK (Wyeth et al., 1987) seroconversion to TRT virus was demonstrated in five flocks of birds after the onset of symptoms of swollen head syndrome (SHS) within the flock. No antibodies were detected before clinical signs became apparent. During a serological survey in France (Picault et al., 1987) antibodies against TRT virus were detected in SHS affected broiler and laying flocks. In our laboratory ELISA antibodies have been detected in all types of commercial chicken flocks, including commercial layers. Some of these flocks had a history of SHS or respiratory disease, others did not

Virus isolation

There have been no reports of the isolation of TRT-like viruses from chicken flocks in the UK. Recently, however, a virus similar to TRT has been isolated from broiler flocks in France (Picault et al., 1987).

Significance of virus in chickens

In summary, the TRT virus has been shown to infect chickens in isolation facilities although in absence of any secondary infection the clinical disease produced was very mild. The virus was transmitted to birds placed in direct contact. There is increasing evidence from serological studies that the virus is present in commercial chicken flocks within the UK and France. The significance of this observation is not known. Despite the recent isolation of a TRT-like virus from chickens in France more research is needed to determine the precise aetiological role of TRT virus in chickens. It is possible that there is an association between the presence of the virus in chickens and a particular disease condition, e.g. SHS. Outbreaks of respiratory disease in chickens were after all reported in the UK at about the same time that rhinotracheitis was first reported in turkeys (O'Brien, 1985; Lister and Alexander, 1986). It is equally possible, however, that the virus in chickens is not associated with any particular disease condition and maybe present also in apparently healthy flocks. Further study is required to resolve the issue.

References

Andral, B., Louzis, C., Trap, D., Newman, J. A., Bennejean, G. and Gaumont, R. (1985a). Respiratory disease (rhinotracheitis) in turkeys in Brittany, France, 1981–1982. I. Field observations and serology. Avian Diseases, 29, 35–42
Andral, B., Metz, M., Toquin, D., Lecoz, J. and Newman, J. A. (1985b). Respiratory disease (rhinotracheitis) of turkeys in Brittany, France. III. Interaction of multiple infecting agents. Avian Diseases, 29, 233–243

Baxter-Jones, C., Cook, J. K. A., Frazier, J. A., Grant, M., Jones, R. C., Mockett, A. P. A. and Wilding, G. P. (1987). Close relationship between TRT virus isolates. *Veterinary Record*, **120**, 562

Baxter-Jones, C., Wilding, G. P. and Grant, M. (1986). Immunofluorescence as a potential diagnostic method for turkey rhinotracheitis. *Veterinary Record*, **119**, 600–601

Butler, M., Ellaway, W. J. and Hall, T. (1972). Comparative studies on the infectivity of avian respiratory viruses for eggs, cell cultures and tracheal explants. *Journal of Comparative Pathology*, **82**, 327–332

Buys, S. B. and Du Preez, J. H. (1980). A preliminary report on the isolation of a virus causing sinusitis in turkeys in South Africa and attempts to attenuate the virus. *Turkeys*, **28**(3), 36 and 46

Darbyshire, J. H. (1978). Organ culture in avian virology: A review. *Avian Pathology*, **7**, 321–335

Giraud, P., Bennejean, G., Guittet, M. and Toquin, D. (1986a). Turkey rhinotracheitis in France: preliminary investigations on a ciliostatic virus. *Veterinary Record*, **119**, 606–607

Giraud, P., Bennejean, G., Guittet, M. and Toquin, D. (1986b). Turkey rhinotrachcitis (TRT) in France: isolation and characteristics of a new infectious agent. Paper presented at: Meeting of the Working Groups 7–8 (WPSA): Turkey Pathology and Waterfowl, 20–22nd August, 1986, Lyon, France

Grant, M., Baxter-Jones, C. and Wilding, G. P. (1987). An enzyme-linked immunosorbent assay for the serodiagnosis of turkey rhinotracheitis infection. *Veterinary Record*, **120**, 279–280

Heller, E. D., Weisman, Y. and Aharonovitch, A. (1984). Experimental studies on turkey coryza. *Avian Pathology*, **13**, 137–143

Jones, R. C., Baxter-Jones, C. and Wilding, G. P. (1986). Turkey rhinotracheitis. Investigations on a candidate virus. *Turkeys*, **34**(2), 23–24

Jones, R. C., Baxter-Jones, C., Wilding, G. P. and Kelly, D. F. (1986). Demonstration of a candidate virus for turkey rhinotracheitis in experimentally inoculated turkeys. *Veterinary Record*, **119**, 599–600

Jones, R. C., Baxter-Jones, C., Savage, C. E., Kelly, D. F. and Wilding, G. P. (1987). Experimental infection of chickens with a ciliostatic agent isolated from turkeys with rhinotracheitis. *Veterinary Record*, **120**, 301–302

Lister, S. A. and Alexander, D. J. (1986). Turkey rhinotracheitis: a review. *Veterinary Bulletin*, **56**, 637–663

McDougall, J. S. and Cook, J. K. A. (1986). Turkey rhinotracheitis: preliminary investigations. *Veterinary Record*, **118**, 206–207

O'Brien, J. D. P. (1985). Swollen head syndrome in broiler breeders. *Veterinary Record*, **117**, 619–620

Picault, J. P., Giraud, P., Drouin, D., Guittet, M., Bennejean, G., Lamande, J., Toquin, D. and Gueguon, C. (1987). Isolation of a TRT-like virus from chickens with swollen-head syndrome. *Veterinary Record*, **121**, 135

Wilding, G. P., Baxter-Jones, C. and Grant, M. (1986). Ciliostatic agent found in rhinotracheitis. *Veterinary Record*, **118**, 735

Wyeth, P. J., Chettle, N. J., Gough, R. E. and Collins, M. S. (1987). Antibodies to TRT in chickens with swollen head syndrome. *Veterinary Record*, **120**, 286–287

Wyeth, P. J., Gough, R. E., Chettle, N. and Eddy, R. (1986). Preliminary observations on a virus associated with rhinotracheitis. *Veterinary Record*, **119**, 139

Chapter 13

Enteric viruses of turkeys

Y. M. Saif, K. W. Theil, D. L. Reynolds and L. J. Saif

In the past decade considerable progress has been made in identifying and studying a variety of enteric viruses of turkeys. Three types of rotaviruses, as well as astroviruses, enteroviruses, parvoviruses and pseudopicorna viruses were identified. Earlier, adenoviruses, coronaviruses and reoviruses were reported.

Electron microscopy (EM) has been an important technique in facilitating this progress. Electropherotyping of genomic RNA has also been useful in identification and in studying the epizootiology of those viruses which possess double-stranded RNA (dsRNA). The use of specific-pathogen-free (SPF) turkey poults for studies on the newly identified viruses has proved valuable in determining the pathogenicity and other aspects of infection with some of these viruses. This was particularly important since natural infection is common in commercial turkeys.

Most of the newly discovered viruses were detected in poults 1–3 weeks of age and infection with some of these viruses is widespread in commercial turkey flocks. In many instances the presence of these viruses in the gastrointestinal (GI) tract of commercial poults was associated with enteric disease, but in others the correlation was not available. It was reported that more than one virus is usually detected in flocks experiencing enteric disease and that nutritional and/or environmental factors might play an important role in the pathogenesis of these viral infections. Diarrhoea is the most common clinical sign associated with enteric viral infections and malabsorption has been associated with some of these infections during the acute phase of the disease. The GI tract is usually distended with gas and its contents are watery, and the caecal contents frothy and yellowish; it seems doubtful that these changes are specific for any of these infections. Morbidity is usually high, but mortality varies depending on environmental conditions and concomitant infections.

Our knowledge of the prevalence and incidence of some of the enteric viruses has increased but the pathogenic potential of some of the viruses, or different combinations of these viruses, is not clear. Immunity apparently develops following natural infections but it is not established whether infections are eliminated or the carrier state develops. The role of passive immunity and different components of active immunity need to be characterized. The most important route of transmission is probably the oral faecal route but the possibility of egg transmission needs to be investigated. Information is lacking on the persistence of these viruses in a commercial turkey environment or on practical procedures to eliminate these viruses from that environment. Diagnostic procedures have not been developed for many of the newly discovered viruses, partially because many of them have not been adapted to replicate *in vitro*.

Considerable knowledge was gained on enteric viruses in the last decade but many questions need to be resolved and it is encouraging that several research groups around the world are involved in studies on enteric viruses of turkeys. This should lead to better understanding of the role of these viruses in enteric disease and hopefully to strategies for their control.

In this chapter, the emphasis is on the information gained on turkey enteric viruses in the last decade. Hence, the emphasis is on the newly discovered viruses. Information generated in the last decade on the earlier described viruses is also discussed.

Rotaviruses

Introduction

Rotaviruses, first established as aetiologic agents of diarrhoea in livestock in 1969 (Mebus *et al.*, 1969), are a common, widespread cause of enteric illness in the newborn of many mammalian species (Estes, Palmer and Obijeski, 1983). Moreover, they are the single most important aetiologic agent of acute gastroenteritis requiring hospitalization of infants and young children in developed countries (Kapikian *et al.*, 1980). At first, it appeared that all rotaviruses shared a common group antigen (Woode *et al.*, 1976) but later studies revealed that some rotaviruses lacked this antigen and were antigenically distinct (Bridger, 1980; Saif *et al.*, 1980; McNulty *et al.*, 1981; Chasey, Bridger and McCrae, 1986). Additional characterization of the antigenically distinct rotaviruses ultimately led to the recommendation that rotaviruses be subdivided into serogroups, with members of each serogroup sharing their own distinctive common group antigen (Pedley *et al.*, 1983). Currently, five rotavirus serogroups, designated A to E, are recognized (Pedley *et al.*, 1983; Pedley *et al.*, 1986), with the originally recognized rotaviruses belonging to serogroup A; additional serogroups likely will be identified in the future.

Avian rotaviruses were first detected by negative stain EM examination of intestinal contents of 2- to 3-week-old diarrhoeic turkey poults in the midwestern USA (Bergeland, McAdaragh and Stotz, 1977). Soon after, they were also detected by EM in intestinal contents of 2- to 5-week-old diarrhoeic turkey poults in Northern Ireland (McNulty, Allan and Stuart, 1978). Although the turkey viruses associated with these outbreaks were morphologically indistinguishable from mammalian rotaviruses, their actual antigenic relationships to other rotaviruses were not confirmed. Subsequently, some Northern Ireland turkey rotaviruses were adapted to serial propagation in cell culture and found to be antigenically related to the mammalian group A rotaviruses (McNulty *et al.*, 1979a).

More recent studies have established that turkey poults in the USA are frequently infected with rotaviruses that are antigenically distinct from the group A turkey rotaviruses (Saif, Saif and Theil, 1985; Theil, Reynolds and Saif, 1986b; Theil and Saif, 1987). Their initial description was based on a morphologic similarity to group A rotaviruses, but they failed to react with antisera to avian or mammalian group A rotaviruses. Morphologically these viruses occur as both single capsid 55 nm particles and double capsid 70 nm particles (*Figure 13.1*),

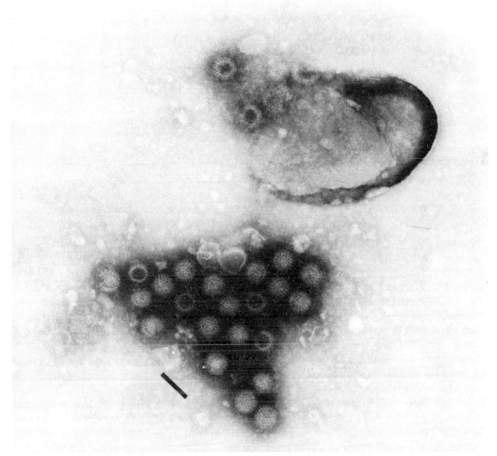

Figure 13.1 Immune electron microscopy of avian group D rotavirus showing aggregates observed after incubation of the faecal specimen with convalescent turkey anti-group D rotavirus serum. Bar = 100 nm

analogous to the situation for group A rotaviruses (Saif, Saif and Theil, 1985; Saif and Theil, 1985). These antigenically distinct rotaviruses were originally called turkey rotavirus-like viruses but comparative two-way cross immunofluorescent tests have now demonstrated that they are antigenically related to the 132 chicken rotavirus from Northern Ireland (M. S. McNulty, personal communication) which is the prototype for the group D rotaviruses (Pedley *et al.*, 1986). Although group D rotaviruses are one of the most frequently detected enteric viruses in 1- to 4-week-old diarrhoeic turkey poults, their causative role in enteric disease has not been established (Saif, Saif and Theil, 1984; Saif, Saif and Theil, 1985; Reynolds, Saif and Theil, 1987a; Reynolds, Saif and Theil, 1987b; Theil and Saif, 1987). This is mainly due to the presence of multiple enteric viruses in poults with enteritis, and to the difficulty of separating each virus type from such mixtures for pathogenicity studies (Saif, Saif and Theil, 1984; Saif, Saif and Theil, 1985; Reynolds, Saif and Theil, 1987a; Reynolds, Saif and Theil, 1987b). However, the group D chicken and turkey rotaviruses are infectious for SPF chickens and turkeys, respectively, as demonstrated by the presence of infected enterocytes or virus in specimens from experimentally exposed birds (McNulty *et al.*, 1981; Saif, Saif and Theil, 1984; Reynolds, Saif and Theil, 1987). In addition, turkeys in the USA can be infected with another antigenically distinct rotavirus that does not react with group A or group D turkey rotavirus antisera (Theil, Reynolds and Saif, 1986b). These viruses are temporarily designated as turkey atypical rotaviruses. Turkey atypical rotaviruses probably represent a third serogroup of turkey rotaviruses, but specific antiserum to these viruses must be prepared and tested against the members of each recognized rotavirus serogroup to substantiate this preliminary observation.

Classification of rotaviruses

Rotaviruses are recently characterized members of the *Reoviridae* family. Both avian and mammalian rotaviruses have been recently subdivided into at least five serogroups (A to E) based on group antigens which are common within a serogroup but distinctive outside that serogroup (Saif and Theil, 1985). In addition, distinct rotavirus electropherogroups (A to F) also have been described with characteristic genomic electropherotypes for each group, and minor genomic heterogeneity within a group (Saif and Theil, 1985). Because of the similarity in electropherotypes noted recently for isolates of serogroup B and E mammalian rotaviruses, and the finding that variation in electropherotypes does not always reflect antigenic variations (Estes, Graham and Dimitrov, 1984), the final definition of distinct rotavirus groups must rely on serological comparisons.

All rotaviruses share a common morphology. Two types of virus particle, incomplete and complete, are observed in negatively stained preparations (Estes, Palmer and Obijeski, 1983) and rotaviruses isolated from turkeys are morphologically identical to those isolated from mammalian species (McNulty *et al.*, 1979; Saif, Saif and Theil, 1985; Yason and Schat, 1985; Theil, Reynolds and Saif, 1986; Kang, Nagaraja and Newman, 1986a). Complete virus particles possess both the outer and inner capsid layers (double capsid particles) and are approximately 70 nm in diameter. Incomplete virus particles have only the inner capsid layer (single capsid layer particles) and are about 60 nm in diameter.

The group A turkey rotavirus genome comprises 11 dsRNA segments that produce a characteristic electrophoretic migration pattern (genome electropherotype) in polyacrylamide gels (Todd, McNulty and Allan, 1980; Saif, Saif and Theil, 1985; Yason and Schat, 1985). Subtle differences in the migration rates of various genome segments can be detected among the genome electropherotypes of different group A turkey rotavirus isolates (Todd, McNulty and Allan, 1980; Kang, Nagaraja and Newman, 1986b; Theil, Reynolds and Saif, 1986). Even with these minor variations, however, the group A turkey rotavirus genome electropherotypes are sufficiently distinct to permit their differentiation from the genome electropherotypes produced by mammalian group A rotavirus, group D turkey rotavirus, turkey atypical rotavirus, and reovirus (*Figure 13.2*; Saif, Saif and Theil, 1985; Theil, Reynolds and Saif, 1986a; Theil, Reynolds and Saif, 1986b; Theil and Saif, 1987).

The 11 genomic segments of mammalian rotaviruses have been classified into four size regions based on their molecular weights (Lourenco *et al.*, 1981). For avian rotaviruses genomic segments 1 to 5 are in region I; segment 6, in region II; segment 7 in region II or III; segments 8 and 9 in region III; and segments 10 and 11

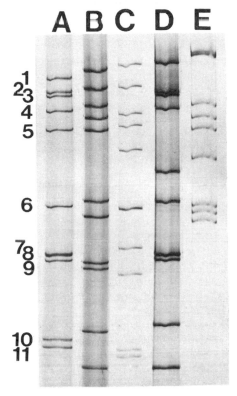

Figure 13.2 Comparison of turkey group A rotavirus, turkey group D rotavirus, turkey atypical rotavirus, and turkey reovirus genome electropherotypes in the same polyacrylamide gel slab. A mammalian group A rotavirus genome electropherotype is included for reference purposes. Numbers to the left designate segments of the turkey group A rotavirus genome. Migration is from top to bottom. Lanes: A, turkey group A rotavirus genome electropherotype; B, turkey group D rotavirus genome electropherotype; C, turkey atypical rotavirus genome electropherotype; D, bovine group A rotavirus genome electropherotype; E, turkey reovirus genome electropherotype. Segments 7 and 8 co-migrate in the turkey group A rotavirus genome electropherotype and in the bovine group A rotavirus genome electropherotype. Segments 6 and 7 of the turkey atypical rotavirus genome electropherotype co-migrate. (Adapted from Theil and Saif, 1987, with permission from the American Society for Microbiology)

in region IV. Accordingly, avian group A rotaviruses have a genomic electropherotype which can be described as a 5-1-3-2 pattern with the 7, 8, and 9 triplet being the major distinguishing characteristic. On the other hand group D rotaviruses have been described as possessing a 5-2-2-2 genome electropherotype pattern (Saif, Saif and Theil, 1985; Saif and Theil, 1985; Kang, Nagaraja and Newman, 1986a; Theil, Reynolds and Saif, 1986a; Theil, Reynolds and Saif, 1986b; Todd and McNulty, 1986) and the turkey atypical rotavirus a second distinctive 5-2-2-2 pattern characterized by a tight 6, 7 doublet (Theil, Reynolds and Saif, 1986c; Kang, Nagaraja and Newman, 1986; Todd and McNulty, 1986). Genomic heterogeneity of virus strains within electropherogroup D has been reported in turkeys (Theil, Reynolds and Saif, 1986c) and chickens (Todd and McNulty, 1986; Theil, Reynolds and Saif, 1986c).

Rotaviruses are antigenically characterized by their group, subgroup, and serotype specificities. The serotype specific antigen is located in the outer capsid layer whereas the group specific antigen is in the inner capsid layer (Bridger, 1978). Although immunofluorescent staining reactions, complement fixation tests, and immune EM (IEM) proved unequivocally that group A turkey rotaviruses share antigens with the mammalian group A rotaviruses (McNulty *et al.*, 1979a; Hoshino *et al.*, 1984; Saif, Saif and Theil, 1985; Yason and Schat, 1985; Theil, Reynolds and Saif, 1986a), the group A turkey rotavirus group antigen does differ from the mammalian group A antigen in some respects. For example, monoclonal antibodies against the mammalian group A antigen did not react with group A turkey rotaviruses (Gary, Black and Palmer, 1982; Hoshino *et al.*, 1984). Moreover, the subgroup specificity of group A turkey rotavirus Ty-1 could not be determined with monoclonal antibodies used to subgroup mammalian group A rotaviruses (Greenberg *et al.*, 1983; Hoshino *et al.*, 1984). The biological significance of this difference in the group antigen remains unclear.

At present the number of group A rotavirus serotypes infecting turkeys is uncertain. *In vivo* cross-protection studies to identify different group A turkey rotavirus serotypes have not been reported. *In vitro* neutralization tests conducted with convalescent sera derived from chicks inoculated with cell-culture-passaged group A turkey rotavirus isolates suggest that there are two serotypes in Northern Ireland (McNulty *et al.*, 1980). The recent trend, however, has been to define serotypic relationships with hyperimmune antisera prepared in guinea pigs or rabbits by intramuscular injections of semi-purified virus rather than to use convalescent sera from orally infected animals. Thus, the possible existence of two group A turkey rotavirus serotypes awaits confirmation by either *in vivo* cross-protection studies or by *in vitro* neutralization tests conducted with hyperimmune antisera. Nonetheless, reciprocal neutralization tests conducted with hyperimmune guinea pig antisera to the Northern Ireland group A turkey rotavirus Ty-1 and to selected mammalian group A rotavirus isolates have clearly established that the Ty-1 isolate is serotypically distinct from these mammalian isolates (Hoshino *et al.*, 1984).

The group D turkey rotavirus is antigenically unrelated to avian and mammalian group A rotaviruses (Saif, Saif and Theil, 1985; Saif and Theil, 1985), or to mammalian group B or C rotaviruses as determined by IEM (Saif, Saif and Theil, 1985; Saif and Theil, 1985). Turkey atypical rotaviruses were also reported to be antigenically distinct from group A and D turkey rotaviruses, but these were tested only in a one-way test with antisera to group A and D rotavirus by IEM (Theil, Reynolds and Saif, 1986b).

Epizootiology

Group A turkey rotaviruses

Group A turkey rotaviruses probably are distributed throughout the world, but the evidence to support this assumption is scant. Group A rotaviruses have been detected in young turkeys in Northern Ireland, France, and the USA (McNulty *et al.*, 1979a; Andral *et al.*, 1985; Saif, Saif and Theil, 1985; Yason and Schat, 1985). Although mammalian group A rotaviruses are ubiquitous, the prevalence of group A rotavirus in the turkey population appears to be not as great. In Northern Ireland, where turkeys are often bred and raised on the same farm, only 35% of the flocks examined by an indirect immunofluorescent staining test were seropositive for group A rotavirus antibody (McNulty et al., 1979a). However, 90% of the sera from those positive flocks were positive, suggesting that once the virus is introduced into a flock it will spread throughout it. In the USA, where turkeys are raised in large commercial flocks under intensive conditions, group A rotaviruses are frequently detected (Saif, Saif and Theil, 1985; Theil, Reynolds and Saif, 1986a; Theil, Reynolds and Saif, 1986b; Reynolds, Saif and Theil, 1987a; Theil and Saif, 1987).

Nonetheless, group A rotavirus was not isolated from turkeys reared in two small flocks at a research station in the USA (Theil and Saif, 1987) indicating that infection with this virus may not occur under some conditions.

Although natural infections with group A rotaviruses can occur in turkey poults up to 4 weeks old, many birds less than 1 week of age become infected (McNulty et al., 1979a; Theil and Saif, 1987). In fact, one study revealed that group A rotaviruses were the only rotaviruses detected in commercially-reared turkey poults less than 7 days old (Theil and Saif, 1987). The occurrence of group A rotaviral infections in 3- to 4-day-old poults raises the possibility of egg transmission, but attempts to detect virus in unhatched turkey embryos were unsuccessful (Theil and Saif, 1987). The faecal to oral route is the most probable mode of group A rotavirus transmission within a flock and experimental studies have shown that turkey poults orally inoculated with tissue-culture-passaged group A turkey rotavirus become infected with the virus (Yason and Schat, 1986b; Yason and Schat, 1987). How group A turkey rotaviruses spread from one flock to another is not known and this important question needs answering.

Little is known regarding the host range of turkey group A rotaviruses. Seven-day-old SPF leghorn chickens inoculated with cell-cultured-passaged group A turkey rotavirus TU-2 remained normal and virus could not be recovered from the intestinal contents of sacrificed birds (Yason and Schat, 1986a). However, small quantities of virus apparently were shed by some of the inoculated birds because the virus was subsequently isolated from the intestinal contents of a few non-inoculated contact control chicks. Additional studies are necessary to determine the role of other avian species in the spread of group A turkey rotaviruses.

Group D turkey rotaviruses

Both the prevalence and incidence of infection of turkey poults with group D rotaviruses have been studied. Faecal specimens from poults from different geographical locations in the USA were tested for the prevalence of group D rotaviruses by IEM and/or genome electropherotyping (Saif, Saif and Theil, 1984; Saif, Saif and Theil, 1985; Reynolds, Saif and Theil, 1987a). The same techniques were used to examine the incidence of group D rotavirus infections among turkey poults from a single operation in Ohio (Reynolds, Saif and Theil, 1987a; Theil and Saif, 1987). Few similar studies have been done in other countries with the exception of studies of group D rotaviruses in chicken flocks in the UK (McNulty et al., 1984).

At least three surveys of the prevalence of enteric viruses or dsRNA enteric viruses in turkey poults were reported (Saif, Saif and Theil, 1985; Kang, Nagaraja and Newman, 1986b; Reynolds, Saif and Theil, 1987a).

In the first study, group D rotaviruses were the most commonly detected virus in

10- to 21-day-old diarrhoeic poults, occurring in 60% of the flocks examined within five of six operations (Saif, Saif and Theil, 1984; Saif, Saif and Theil, 1985). Group D rotaviruses were detected from operations much more frequently (83% positive) than group A rotaviruses (50% positive). Group D rotaviruses were detected alone (27% of positive specimens) much less frequently than in combinations with other enteric viruses (73% of positive specimens) (Saif, Saif and Theil, 1985). The most frequently encountered combination was group D rotaviruses and astroviruses (L. J. Saif, unpublished).

In the second study, turkey flocks in Minnesota exhibiting signs of enteritis were tested for rotavirus by EM (Kang, Nagaraja and Newman, 1986). Genome electropherotyping of the faecal specimen or cell culture isolated virus was then used to confirm the electropherogroup of rotavirus present. With these techniques, 69% of the rotaviruses detected were electropherogroup A and these were the only ones which replicated in the MA104 cell cultures. About 31% of the faecal specimens contained electropherogroup D rotaviruses, and of these 73% were mixed with electropherogroup A rotaviruses. Electropherogroup D rotaviruses were most prevalent in specimens obtained in 1984 and were rarely observed in the specimens obtained in 1981 and 1983. However serology was not done to confirm the serogroups of the rotaviruses detected in the specimens examined in this study.

In the third survey, group D rotaviruses were the second most frequently detected enteric virus (after astroviruses) (Reynolds, Saif and Theil, 1987a) and were detected in about 67% of diseased flocks and 26% of normal flocks. By comparison, group A rotaviruses were detected in 22% of diseased flocks and 26% of normal flocks. Group D rotaviruses were the most prevalent enteric virus found in poults 3 to 4 weeks of age within the diseased flocks. Again the group D rotavirus–astrovirus combination was the most frequently identified virus combination among both diseased (60%) and normal (22%) flocks.

Two additional studies were conducted to determine the incidence of various enteric viral infections in turkey poults in one commercial operation in Ohio (Reynolds, Saif and Theil, 1987a; Theil and Saif, 1987). In the first study, genome electropherotyping was used to detect dsRNA enteric viruses in turkey poults from hatching to 91 days of age (Theil and Saif, 1987). In this study, 14% of specimens from turkey poults less than 29 days old were positive for electropherogroup D or A rotaviruses and these viruses were not detected in poults older than 29 days of age. Electropherogroup A rotaviruses were also confirmed as serogroup A rotaviruses using a cell culture IF test. Electropherogroup D rotaviruses were detected only in 8- to 21-day-old poults, whereas electropherogroup A rotaviruses occurred primarily in poults less than 7 days old.

This age distribution of group D and A rotaviruses was corroborated further in a second enteric virus prevalence study conducted in flocks from the same operation (Reynolds, Saif and Theil, 1987a). However, in this second study, astroviruses were detected most frequently followed by group D rotaviruses and then group A rotaviruses. The association between virus detection and diarrhoea in sampled poults was not examined in either of the two studies.

Clinical signs and pathology

Group A rotavirus

Group A rotaviruses are often detected in specimens collected from young turkey poults with enteric disturbances (McNulty et al., 1979a; Andral et al., 1985; Saif,

Saif and Theil, 1985; Kang, Nagaraja and Newman, 1986a). Clinical signs in affected poults include diarrhoea, inflammation of the vent, and vent picking. However, the precise role of group A rotavirus in the causation of these enteric illnesses of naturally-infected poults is unclear. In some instances other viruses besides the group A rotaviruses can be detected in the same flock, or even in the same poult, at the time of illness (Andral et al., 1985; Kang, Nagaraja and Newman, 1986b). Astroviruses, which can cause enteritis in young turkey poults (Reynolds and Saif, 1986), commonly infect poults in flocks concurrently with group A rotavirus (Reynolds, Saif and Theil, 1987b). Moreover, mixed infections of poults with group A and group D rotaviruses have also been detected (Theil and Saif, 1987). Furthermore, in one survey, group A rotaviruses were detected more frequently in specimens collected from normal turkey poults than in specimens collected from poults with enteric illness (Reynolds, Saif and Theil, 1987a). This latter observation suggests that the group A rotavirus requires additional factors to induce illness or that the presence of group A rotaviruses in specimens from diarrhoeic poults is coincidental.

On the other hand, there is experimental evidence that group A turkey rotavirus can induce enteric illness in turkeys.

Experimental inoculation of seronegative 7- to 42-day-old conventional turkey poults with cell-culture-passaged group A turkey rotavirus TU-2 induced moderate clinical signs consisting of watery droppings on post-inoculation days 2 to 5 (Yason and Schat, 1986b). Inoculated birds shed infective virus from 1 to 24 days post-inoculation with maximum titres detected during the manifestation of clinical signs. Concurrent with clinical signs, gross and histopathologic lesions were present within the intestinal tract. The gross lesions consisted of pallor of the intestinal tract accompanied by reduced tonicity of the jejunum and ileum, and dilated intestines filled with watery fluids containing normal solid intestinal contents. The most striking histopathological lesion was the hypercellularity of the small intestinal lamina propria due to leucocytic infiltration, but scalloping of the surface and basal vacuolation of the epithelium was also noted at the villous tips. Immunofluorescent staining revealed that the virus mainly infected the epithelium covering the villous tips throughout the small intestine, although some epithelial cells within the caecum and colon became infected after the small intestine was infected. Despite these observations, impaired intestinal absorption of D-xylose in infected poults at 2 and 4 days post-inoculation was demonstrable only if a complicated statistical analysis was used to compare the data.

In another study, essentially similar clinical signs were induced in seronegative, conventional 1-, 17-, 28-, 84-, or 112-day-old turkeys experimentally inoculated with cell-culture passaged group A turkey rotavirus TU-2 (Yason and Schat, 1987). Macroscopic and microscopic lesions developed in inoculated turkeys of each age group but were mild in birds less than 17 days of age. Lesions in older birds ranged from moderate to severe, and were most pronounced in turkeys inoculated at 84 or 112 days of age. Overall, microscopic lesions were most severe within the anterior small intestine and consisted of desquamation of enterocytes producing denuded villous tips, loss of goblet cells, fusion of villi, villous atrophy, crypt cell proliferation and crypt hypertrophy. Scanning electron microscopy of the affected regions revealed distorted villi, roughened villous surfaces, and the loss of the microvilli from the surface of the enterocytes (Yason, Summers and Schat, 1987). Taken together, these experimental results indicate that at least one group A turkey rotavirus isolate can induce diarrhoea in turkey poults.

Group D rotaviruses

The enteric disease syndrome observed in turkey poults within the first month of life has been characterized by the following clinical signs: diarrhoea, nervousness, litter eating and stunting (flock unevenness). A mortality rate of 3–15% has been observed among poults in such flocks (Saif, Saif and Theil, 1984; Saif, Saif and Theil, 1985). Group D rotaviruses have been detected frequently from diseased poults, but their common occurrence together with other enteric viruses, particularly astroviruses (Saif, Saif and Theil, 1985; Reynolds, Saif and Theil, 1987a; Reynolds, Saif and Theil, 1987b) and their detection from normal poults (Reynolds, Saif and Theil, 1987a) has made assignment of a causative role difficult.

There are no studies describing the pathogenicity of the group D rotavirus alone in turkey poults. This is due in part to the difficulty in separating this virus from other enteric viruses which are often present in faecal specimens from diarrhoeic poults. However, the pathogenicity of the group D chicken rotavirus for SPF chickens has been described (McNulty et al., 1981). The virus infected villous enterocytes inducing a mild transient diarrhoea resembling that induced by group A rotavirus.

The pathogenicity of a bacteria-free filtrate containing a mixture of group D turkey rotavirus and turkey astrovirus was tested in orally inoculated SPF turkey poults (Saif, Saif and Theil, 1984). The virus mixture induced a mild transient diarrhoea in orally inoculated 4-day-old poults, and a more profuse watery diarrhoea in poults orally inoculated at 12 or 18 days of age. Necropsied birds had frothy, gaseous intestinal contents and thin-walled intestines. Astrovirus and group D rotaviruses were detected in intestinal contents of both younger and older inoculated birds. No differences in weight were observed between inoculated and control poults and no mortality occurred. Similar findings were reported in a subsequent study when day-old poults were orally inoculated with a group D turkey rotavirus and turkey astrovirus mixture (Reynolds, Saif and Theil, 1987b). The time of the initial detection of each virus in challenged birds varied between the two studies, but this may merely reflect different doses of the component viruses present in the challenge inocula.

Diagnosis of rotaviral infections

At present, diagnosis of rotaviral infections in turkeys depends upon the demonstration of the virus, its antigens or its nucleic acids, in clinical specimens. Currently, the most useful procedures for diagnosis of turkey rotaviruses are IEM and genome electropherotyping (*Figures 13.1* and *13.2*).

The first method used to detect rotavirus in turkey specimens was the direct negative stain EM examination of faecal or intestinal contents (Bergeland, McAdaragh and Stotz, 1977). Large intestinal and caecal contents are the preferred specimen for this procedure, as the virus particles are more numerous in them than in small intestinal contents (McNulty et al., 1979b). This technique, however, does not permit the differentiation of group A and group D turkey rotaviruses and thus cannot be used as a precise diagnostic procedure. Immune electron microscopy can be used to distinguish group A turkey rotaviruses from the group D turkey rotaviruses and the turkey atypical rotaviruses (Saif, Saif and Theil, 1985; Theil, Reynolds and Saif, 1986b). Use of IEM has the advantage of greater sensitivity than genome electropherotyping (Theil, Reynolds and Saif, 1986b), the ability to determine rotavirus serogroups provided highly specific antisera are used (McNulty *et al.*, 1984; Saif, Saif and Theil, 1984; Saif, Saif and Theil, 1985; Saif and Theil, 1985) and the ability to detect other enteric viruses which may be present (Saif, Saif and Theil, 1984; Saif, Saif and Theil, 1985; Saif and Theil, 1985; Reynolds, Saif and Theil, 1987a). Because rotaviruses from each serogroup are morphologically identical, use of monospecific antisera against each virus group, prepared in SPF or gnotobiotic animals is essential for differentiating rotavirus serogroups.

The genome electropherotyping technique, which relies on the detection of viral dsRNA in specimens, is also used to detect turkey rotaviruses (Theil, Reynolds and Saif, 1986b). This technique enables one to classify rotaviruses into electropherogroups (Saif, Saif and Theil, 1984; Saif, Saif and Theil, 1985; Saif and Theil, 1985; Theil and Saif, 1987; Theil, Reynolds and Saif, 1986a; Kang, Nagaraja and Newman, 1986; Todd and McNulty, 1986). It is especially useful in detecting multiple infections with more than one rotavirus in turkey poults, characterizing the strains of rotavirus circulating within a flock at various times and identifying new rotavirus electropherogroups (Saif, Saif and Theil, 1984; Saif, Saif and Theil, 1985; Saif and Theil, 1985; Theil, Reynolds and Saif, 1986b; Kang, Nagaraja and Newman, 1986b; Todd and McNulty, 1986; Theil and Saif, 1987). However, the antigenic relationships of the various electropherogroups detected by this method still must be verified by some serologic procedure.

Group A turkey rotaviruses can also be detected by isolation in cell culture (McNulty *et al.*, 1979a; Andral *et al.*, 1985; Yason and Schat, 1985; Kang, Nagaraja and Newman, 1986b; Theil, Reynolds and Saif, 1986). One pitfall with this procedure is that group A turkey rotaviruses can be isolated in cell culture from specimens that contain predominantly the non-cultivatable group D or turkey atypical rotaviruses (K. W. Theil, unpublished data; Kang, Nagaraja and Newman, 1986b) thereby misleading the unwary.

Although there are no reports of the use of immunofluorescence for detection of group D rotavirus infections in turkeys, this method has been successfully used to detect intestinal enterocytes infected with group D rotaviruses in chickens (McNulty *et al.*, 1981). Again, such a procedure requires the use of convalescent or hyperimmune antisera, monospecific for group D rotavirus. Use of intestinal mucosal smears from infected turkeys could also serve as a source of group D rotavirus antigen for testing serum samples by indirect IF to detect group D rotavirus antibodies. Alternatively, since the group D rotavirus from chickens has been adapted to cell culture (McNulty *et al.*, 1981), cells infected with group D chicken rotaviruses might serve as the antigen source for detection of group D rotavirus antibodies in turkeys using the indirect IF test. This latter test was used to determine the prevalence of chicken group D rotavirus antibodies, which were found in 70% of the samples tested (McNulty, Allan and McFerran, 1984).

Aside from EM, genome electropherotyping, or cell culture inoculation to detect turkey group A rotaviruses, few other diagnostic methods have been tried. A coagglutination test, which relied on unfractionated rabbit hyperimmune anti-turkey group A rotavirus serum adsorbed to the surface of formalized, heat-treated *Staphylococcus aureus* (Cowan 1 strain) to detect the viral antigens, has been described (Kang, Nagaraja and Newman, 1985). Although simple to conduct, this test required that specimens be extracted with fluorocarbon and adsorbed with uncoated staphylococci to minimize non-specific reactions. Unfortunately, even then this assay's advantage of simplicity was outweighed by its unacceptably high non-specific false-positive reactions.

At present there is a real need for convenient, reliable reagents to detect and differentiate the turkey rotaviruses encountered in field specimens. Although several research laboratories have the capability of distinguishing the turkey rotaviruses, most diagnostic laboratories are apt to continue using direct EM examination of specimens or cell culture isolation for virus detection despite the limitations of these techniques. Until diagnostic reagents to detect and differentiate the group A, group D, and turkey atypical rotaviruses are widely available, our understanding of the real significance of these viruses in turkey enteritis will remain incomplete.

Prevention, control, and treatment of rotaviral infections

There are, at present, no vaccines or treatment regimens for rotaviral infections of turkeys. Methods to control this infection in young poults would include sound management practices such as regular cleaning and disinfecting of brooder houses to reduce the level of virus contamination within the poults' immediate environment. Given the rotaviruses' relative resistance to disinfectants and environmental conditions (Snodgrass and Herring, 1977; Tan and Schnagl, 1981; Moe and Shirley, 1982; Lloyd-Evans, Springthorpe and Sattar, 1986; Springthorpe et al., 1986) such practices cannot be expected to completely eliminate the virus in most cases, but they may reduce the virus dose that the poult will be exposed to early in life.

If flocks begin experiencing high mortality due to enteric disease shortly after hatch, then eventual development of vaccines for breeder hens may be needed to enhance the passive immunity transferred to poults. Further knowledge about the group D turkey rotavirus infections, and methods for their propagation in cell culture are needed before adequate control strategies can be fully developed.

Reoviruses

Introduction

Reoviruses were distinguished first as a virus group with distinct characteristics in 1959 (Sabin, 1959). Although all mammalian reoviruses shared a common group antigen, three distinct serotypes were recognized. Numerous studies promptly established that reoviruses were extraordinarily widespread in nature and that they possessed some novel characteristics including two distinct capsid shells and a segmented dsRNA genome (Stanley, 1967; Rosen, 1968; Spendlove, 1970; Joklik, 1983). Reoviruses infecting vertebrates comprise the orthoreovirus genus within the Reoviridae family (Joklik, 1983). In the decade following the establishment of the reovirus group, reoviruses infecting chickens were frequently identified or isolated (Kawamura et al., 1965; Dutta and Pomeroy, 1967; Petek et al., 1967). Soon after, turkey reoviruses were first detected during investigations of commercially-reared flocks affected with infectious enteritis, or bluecomb disease, in North America (Deshmukh et al., 1969; Fujisaki, Kawamura and Anderson, 1969; Wooley and Gratzek, 1969).

Classification of turkey reoviruses

Mammalian reovirus particles have a characteristic double-shelled capsid, 60 to 70 nm in diameter (Vasquez and Tournier, 1962; Mayor et al., 1965) and reoviruses isolated from turkeys are morphologically indistinguishable from mammalian reoviruses (McFerran, Connor and McCracken, 1976; van der Heide *et al.*, 1980; Nersessian *et al.*, 1985). Like mammalian reoviruses, turkey reoviruses possess dsRNA genomes comprising ten discrete segments that produce typical reovirus genome electropherotypes upon electrophoresis in polyacrylamide gels (*Figure 13.1*; Theil, Reynolds and Saif, 1986a; Theil and Saif, 1987). Serological studies based on *in vitro* neutralization assays indicate that there is considerable antigenic diversity among the chicken reoviruses and at least 11 serotypes have been identified (Wood *et al.*, 1980). With turkey reoviruses, however, more is known regarding their antigenic relationships to reoviruses isolated from other host species than is known about the antigenic relationships among themselves. The turkey reovirus WB-1 isolate, from Wisconsin, was found to be related to the Japanese chicken reovirus isolates by an *in vitro* neutralization assay (Fujisaki, Kawamura and Anderson, 1969). *In vitro* neutralization kinetic assays established that turkey reovirus BC-3 isolate, from Georgia, was antigenically distinct from the three mammalian reovirus serotypes but was related to the Fahey-Crawley chicken reovirus and chicken reovirus MA isolate (Munro and Woolcy, 1973). Similarly, the Northern Ireland turkey reovirus VF72-84 isolate was found to be antigenically related to the Japanese chicken reovirus Uchida isolate in a double immunodiffusion assay, but it was not neutralized by antisera to five Japanese chicken reovirus serotypes in an *in vitro* assay (McFerran, Connor and McCracken, 1976). Recent *in vitro* reciprocal cross neutralization tests revealed that three turkey reovirus isolates (NG, NC–TEV, and 82-88) were closely related but the antigenic relationships of these isolates to four chicken reovirus isolates were quite complex (Nersessian, 1987). Clearly, considerably more work is required to delineate the antigenic characteristics of turkey reoviruses.

Epizootiology and pathology of turkey reoviral infections

Reoviruses have been isolated from turkey poults with enteric diseases characterized by enteritis, diarrhoea, stunted growth, abnormal feathering, and increased early mortality, but in many instances their role in the aetiology of these illnesses remains uncertain. In Minnesota, two reoviruses were isolated in cell cultures from the caecal contents of turkeys with bluecomb, but neither isolate induced disease in orally inoculated day old poults (Deshmukh *et al.*, 1969). Moreover, poults inoculated with these isolates were not protected against a later oral challenge with an intestinal filtrate containing a non-cultivatable pathogenic virus isolate (Minnesota isolate). Subsequent EM examination of intestinal filtrates containing the pathogenic Minnesota isolate, however, disclosed that this isolate was a coronavirus, not a reovirus (Panigrahy, Naqi and Hall, 1973; Ritchie *et al.*, 1973).

Similarly, reoviruses were isolated in cell cultures from intestinal suspensions derived from turkeys with bluecomb in northern Wisconsin (Fujisaki, Kawamura and Anderson, 1969). The aetiologic role of these reoviruses in bluecomb, however, could not be convincingly established. One representative isolate, designated WB-1, was characterized and its pathogenicity for turkey poults decreased rapidly upon serial passage in cell culture. Further, young poults previously inoculated orally with cell-culture-passaged reovirus WB-1 were not clinically protected against an orally administered challenge with an intestinal contents suspension prepared from turkeys with bluecomb.

Reoviruses were also isolated from a homogenate prepared from the intestinal tracts collected from turkeys with infectious enteritis in northern Georgia (Wooley *et al.*, 1972). Two reoviruses were isolated from different regions of a sucrose density gradient after ultracentrifugation and these were designated as the BC-3 and BC-7 isolates. Both isolates were infective for cell cultures and shared the characteristics of reoviruses, but only the density gradient fractions containing the BC-3 isolate induced illness in orally inoculated day-old turkey poults. Moreover, cell-culture-passaged turkey reovirus BC-3 induced clinical signs and lesions of infectious enteritis in experimentally inoculated conventional and gnotobiotic turkey poults (Dees, Wooley and Gratzek, 1972).

Additional studies involving cross-immunofluorescent staining tests and neutralization kinetics assays established that the two isolates were antigenically identical (Gershowitz and Wooley, 1973), but the BC-3 isolate differed biologically from the BC-7 isolate as it produced alterations in the chorioallantoic membranes of inoculated chick embryos whereas the BC-7 isolate did not. Cross-neutralization tests, however, demonstrated that the reovirus BC-3 and BC-7 isolates were antigenically unrelated to the pathogenic Minnesota isolate of infectious enteritis contained in intestinal filtrates (Wooley, 1973).

On the other hand, in North Carolina a reovirus, designated as the NC-TEV isolate, was recovered in cell cultures inoculated with the intestinal tract contents of 4- to 6-week-old poults with depression, anorexia, and high mortality (Simmons *et al.*, 1972). Day-old poults orally inoculated with cell-culture passaged NC-TEV isolate became depressed and anorexic, but signs of diarrhoea and gross lesions were not detected in birds dying after infection. Although this virus was recovered from the intestinal tracts of inoculated birds, it was also isolated from many other organs indicating that it caused a systemic infection rather than just an enteric infection.

More recently another reovirus, designated as NG turkey reovirus (B. N. Nersessian, personal communication), was isolated from turkeys with infectious enteritis in northern Georgia (Goodwin *et al.*, 1984). Two-day-old turkey poults orally inoculated with cell-culture-passaged NG isolate had significantly reduced intestinal D-xylose absorption at 24 and 72 h post-inoculation but not at 120 h post-inoculation. However, compared with control birds, gastrointestinal transit time was longer in inoculated birds at 120 h post-inoculation but not at 24 and 72 h post-inoculation. Faeces passed by poults inoculated with the NG isolate were more fluid than normal. The clinical signs induced in seronegative day-old poults orally inoculated with cell-culture-passaged NG isolate were inconsistent and mild, but when present, included hyperaemic and haemorrhagic vents, increased early mortality, reduced weight gains, irregular development of the primary feathers, and distended caeca and intestines filled with watery, gaseous contents (Nersessian *et al.*, 1986). Virus spread quickly through the inoculated poults and could be recovered from many organs, including the liver, pancreas, kidney, and intestines, by 3 and 5 days post-inoculation (Nersessian *et al.*, 1985b). Reovirus could still be isolated from the intestine at 21 days post-inoculation. As with the turkey reovirus NC-TEV isolate, the NG isolate caused a systemic infection rather than an enteric infection alone.

These experimental studies have clearly documented that turkey reoviruses can be transmitted to poults by oral inoculation. Although the faecal to oral route appears to be a likely mode of transmitting the infection under natural field conditions, it is not known if other routes, i.e. the respiratory route, can be involved. Furthermore, studies have documented that reovirus could be isolated from embryos in eggs laid by broiler chickens previously inoculated subcutaneously with cell-culture-passaged chicken reovirus S1133 (van der Heide and Kalbac, 1975). The possible role of egg transmission in the spread and perpetuation of turkey reovirus infections remains unexplored at present.

While mammalian reoviruses are ubiquitous, little is known concerning the distribution of turkey reoviruses within the turkey population. Aside from the isolates in North America, turkey reoviruses have been reported only in Northern Ireland (McFerran, Connor, and McCracken, 1976) and France (Andral et al., 1985).

The natural host range of reoviruses recovered from the enteric tract of turkeys is unknown, but experimental evidence indicates that reoviruses isolated from turkeys can infect other species. For example, one turkey reovirus isolate, recovered from the livers of poults derived from a North Carolina flock affected with increased early mortality, was found to be infective for day-old chickens inoculated orally or subcutaneously (van der Heide et al., 1980). Chicks experimentally inoculated with this turkey reovirus isolate developed tenosynovitis, hepatitis, and myocarditis. More recently, four cell-culture-passaged turkey reovirus isolates, including the NG isolate, inoculated into the yolk or chorioallantoic sacs of 6-day-old embryonated hen's eggs induced high mortality (Nersessian et al., 1986). In contrast, however, day-old seronegative SPF chicks orally inoculated with cell-culture-passaged turkey reovirus NG isolate remained clinically normal although they did seroconvert, indicating a subclinical infection. Furthermore, day-old Swiss albino mice inoculated intracerebrally with some turkey reovirus isolates developed clinical signs including depression, body tremors, incoordination, lethargy, and oily coats (Nersessian et al., 1986).

The above results, combined with the close antigenic similarities of some turkey reovirus isolates to other avian reoviruses, suggest that additional studies should be conducted to determine how broad are the host ranges of other turkey reovirus isolates.

Diagnosis of turkey reovirus infections

Turkey reoviruses are most commonly detected in intestinal contents or faecal specimens by inoculation of avian primary cell cultures in which they characteristically induce syncytial cell formation (Deshmukh et al., 1969; Fujisaki, Kawamura and Anderson, 1969; Wooley and Gratzek, 1969; Simmons et al., 1972; Wooley et al., 1972; McFerran, Connor and McCracken, 1976; Nersessian et al., 1985a). However, given the turkey reovirus's ability to induce systemic infection (Simmons et al., 1972; van der Heide et al., 1980; Nersessian et al., 1986), the isolation of reovirus from turkey faeces or intestinal tracts should not automatically be construed to indicate an enteric infection, since secretions and excretions of the liver, pancreas, and kidney can also be constituents of these specimens. Attempts to isolate and serially propagate turkey reoviruses in a fetal rhesus monkey kidney (MA 104) cell line were unsuccessful (Theil, Reynolds and Saif, 1986a). Although turkey reoviruses have been detected in intestinal or faecal specimens by other assays, such as negative stain EM (Saif, Saif and Theil, 1985; Reynolds, Saif and Theil, 1987a) and the genome electropherotyping technique (Theil and Saif, 1987), cell culture isolation will probably be the most commonly used procedure and is undoubtedly the most sensitive one.

Prevention, control, and treatment of turkey reoviral infection

There are, at present, no vaccines or treatment regimens for the control of turkey reoviral infections. Common, sound management practices, such as cleaning and disinfecting the premises, should reduce the level of reovirus exposure the poults' experience early in life. The disinfectant must be selected judiciously, however, as avian reovirus is resistant to the action of many disinfectants commonly used by the poultry industry (Meulemans and Halen, 1982).

Small viruses

Introduction

Within the past decade a number of small viruses have been identified in the intestinal tracts or contents of young turkeys. Some of these viruses have been associated with enteric disease of undetermined aetiology which occurs in poults less than 4 weeks of age. Small viruses, as defined here, are those with diameters of 35 nm or less and include the astroviruses, enteroviruses, pseudopicornaviruses, and parvoviruses.

The first report of astroviruses in turkeys was made by investigators in Northern Ireland (McNulty, Curran and McFerran, 1980). Subsequently, turkey astroviruses were detected in the USA (Saif, Saif and Theil, 1985; Reynolds and Saif, 1986). Similarly, enterovirus-like viruses were identified in turkey faeces (McNulty et al., 1979a). Subsequently, others reported identifying enteroviruses from turkeys grown in the USA (Saif, Saif and Theil, 1985; Reynolds, Saif and Theil, 1987a). Small viruses resembling parvoviruses were detected in turkeys within the USA (Trampel et al., 1983). French investigators reported identifying pseudopicornaviruses in turkeys (Andral and Toquin, 1984; Andral et al., 1985).

Classifications of small viruses

Classification, and subsequent naming, of the small viruses has been done solely on the basis of particle size and morphology as determined by EM. The small viruses have been observed either by direct EM or IEM examination of faeces or intestinal contents, or by transmission EM examination of thin sections of intestinal tract.

The first report of turkey astroviruses (McNulty, Curran and McFerran, 1980) indicated the virus diameter to be between 28 nm and 31 nm, with a mean of 30.1 nm, and that about 10% of these virus particles displayed five-pointed or six-pointed star-shaped morphology. A later report (Saif, Saif and Theil, 1985) described turkey astroviruses having five-pointed star-shaped morphology. A small percentage of astroviruses which had five-pointed and six-pointed star-shaped morphology and an average diameter of 29.6 nm were reported (Reynolds and Saif, 1986).

Entero-like viruses have been described (McNulty et al., 1979a) with an average diameter of 29.8 nm and having a circular profile. Others described enteroviruses with an average diameter of 30 nm, a circular profile, and not any surface morphology (Saif, Saif and Theil, 1985). Viruses between 25 nm and 30 nm have been isolated and detected in the faeces of turkeys experiencing enteric disease and have been designated pseudopicornaviruses (Andral and Toquin, 1984).

Hexagonal virus-like particles, detected in intranuclear inclusions of absorptive epithelial intestinal cells, ranging from 15 to 20 nm, have been tentatively described as parvoviruses (Trampel et al., 1983).

Further studies are needed to classify correctly the small viruses. Currently, it is difficult to determine if many of the small viruses, reported by different investigators, are similar or different viruses.

Epizootiology

Astroviruses

The prevalence of astrovirus infection in turkey flocks from 1 to 5 weeks of age experiencing enteric disease has been reported to be high and geographically widespread across the USA (Saif, Saif and Theil, 1985; Reynolds and Saif, 1986; Reynolds, Saif and Theil, 1987a). Two separate studies concluded that astrovirus infections were the most prevalent small virus infections in poults less than 5 weeks of age with enteric disease (Saif, Saif and Theil, 1985; Reynolds, Saif and Theil, 1987a). In one study, it was reported that astrovirus infections occurred in nearly 80% of flocks with enteric disease and the astrovirus was the most prevalent virus detected (Reynolds, Saif and Theil, 1987a). Astroviruses were also detected in normal healthy flocks (Reynolds, Saif and Theil, 1987a) but far less frequently (less than 30%). Seldom were astroviruses the only virus detected in flocks experiencing enteric disease (Reynolds, Saif and Theil, 1987a). The most prevalent virus combination occurring in flocks with enteric disease was that of astrovirus and group D turkey rotavirus (Reynolds, Saif and Theil, 1987a).

Astrovirus infections often occur within the first 4 weeks of life but are rarely detected in older turkeys (Reynolds, Saif and Theil, 1987b). It has been reported that chronologically the first samples from flocks in which viruses were detected always contained astroviruses, either alone or in combination with other viruses (Reynolds, Saif and Theil, 1987b). Although astrovirus infections can occur as early as 3 days of age, it appears that they generally occur after the first week of age (Reynolds, Saif and Theil, 1987b).

It is assumed that the mode of transmission of astroviruses is a faecal-oral route, since it has been demonstrated experimentally that poults orally inoculated with astrovirus developed infection (Reynolds and Saif, 1986). However, studies addressing the transmission of astroviruses have not been reported.

Enteroviruses

The prevalence of enteroviruses is low in comparison with other viruses that infect turkeys (Saif, Saif and Theil, 1985; Reynolds, Saif and Theil, 1987a; Reynolds, Saif and Theil, 1987b). The incidence of enteroviruses appears to be sporadic. Enteroviruses (enterovirus-like viruses) have been detected in young poults from 1 to 6 weeks of age (McNulty et al., 1979a; Reynolds, Saif and Theil, 1987b). Enteroviruses have also been detected from faecal specimens obtained from adult turkeys (Reynolds, D. L., unpublished data).

Parvoviruses

To date, there has been only one report of enteropathy in turkeys incriminating parvoviruses as the aetiologic agent (Trampel et al., 1983). It was reported that all infected poults were from one geographic area within the USA (Trampel et al., 1983). The prevalence, geographic distribution, mode of transmission, and incidence of parvoviruses in turkeys are unknown.

Pseudopicornaviruses

Pseudopicornaviruses have been detected from several flocks of poults experiencing enteric disease in France (Andral and Toquin, 1984). The prevalence, incidence, mode of transmission and geographical distribution has not yet been clearly established.

Pathogenesis of small virus infections

Astroviruses

From experimental studies, it has been determined that astroviruses are capable of causing an enteric disease in turkey poults (Reynolds and Saif, 1986). When SPF turkey poults were orally inoculated with astroviruses, they gained significantly less body weight and absorbed significantly less D-xylose than uninoculated control poults (Reynolds and Saif, 1986). Astrovirus-inoculated poults had watery droppings and frothy yellow, brown droppings (Reynolds and Saif, 1986). At necropsy, characteristic pathological changes were noted including dilated caeca containing yellowish, frothy contents, gaseous fluid in the intestinal tract, and loss of tone of the intestinal tract (gut thinness) (Reynolds and Saif, 1986). It was also demonstrated that astroviruses were detected in the intestinal contents of poults prior to the onset of clinical disease and gross pathologic changes (Reynolds and Saif, 1986). This could explain why astroviruses are sometimes detected in apparently normal, healthy poults, as these poults could be in an early stage of the infection (Reynolds and Saif, 1986). In addition, it was shown that the shedding of astroviruses into the intestinal tract declines before clinical signs and pathological changes abate (Reynolds and Saif, 1986). Therefore, poults in the later stages of astrovirus disease may display clinical signs and gross pathological changes, but may not have detectable levels of astrovirus present in their intestinal tract.

   The combination of astrovirus and group D rotavirus was the most frequent combination of viruses occurring in young turkey poults (Reynolds, Saif and Theil, 1987b). SPF turkey poults experimentally inoculated with the combination of astrovirus and group D rotavirus shed astrovirus into their intestinal tract (at concentrations sufficient to be detected by IEM) prior to shedding detectable levels of group D rotavirus (Reynolds, Saif and Theil, 1987b). The clinical disease induced by this combination was much more pronounced than the disease induced by astrovirus alone (Reynolds, Saif and Theil, 1987b). Studies addressing interactions between astrovirus infections and other enteric virus infections have not been reported.

Enteroviruses

Experimental studies to establish the pathogenicity of enteroviruses have not been reported. Although enteroviruses have been detected from the faeces or intestinal contents of turkeys, they have not been incriminated as an aetiologic agent for enteric disease (McNulty *et al.,* 1979a; Saif, Saif and Theil, 1985).

Parvoviruses

Experimental studies to determine if parvoviruses are an aetiologic agent of an enteric disease have not been reported. Case history reports associating parvovirus as a cause of an enteropathy in poults have been reported (Trampel *et al*, 1983). It was reported that poults infected with parvoviruses had histories of listlessness, depression and stunting within the first 5 weeks of life (Trampel *et al.*, 1983). Histopathological examination of the intestinal tract revealed intranuclear inclusion bodies within the epithelial cells of the ileum (Trampel *et al.*, 1983). Thin sectioning and subsequent EM studies of these intranuclear bodies revealed hexagonal particles of 15 and 20 nm in diameter (Trampel *et al.*, 1983). From this observation, these particles were termed parvoviruses (Trampel *et al.*, 1983).

Pseudopicornaviruses

Pseudopicornaviruses were identified from turkey poults with respiratory and enteric disease (Andral and Toquin, 1984). SPF turkey poults experimentally inoculated with pseudopicornaviruses became infected and shed virus (Andral and Toquin, 1984). Based on serum neutralization tests, two strains of pseudopicornaviruses have been reported (Andral and Toquin, 1984).

Diagnosis of small virus infections

Astroviruses

Although astroviruses have star-shaped morphology, only a small percentage of astrovirus particles display this morphology (McNulty, Curran and McFerran, 1980). Therefore, it is quite difficult, if not impossible, to diagnose accurately astrovirus infections without the aid of IEM. A definitive determination of astroviruses can only be made by recognizing aggregates of astrovirus particles due to specific antisera employed in the IEM preparation (Saif, Saif and Theil, 1985; Reynolds and Saif, 1986). In our experience, turkey astroviruses do not display non-specific aggregation, thus one must rely on immune serum to clump the astrovirus particles.

Enteroviruses

A definitive determination of enterovirus can be made by IEM (Saif, Saif and Theil, 1985).

Parvovirus

Diagnosis of parvoviruses has been made only through the observation of small virus particles within intranuclear inclusion as described above.

Pseudopicornaviruses

Pseudopicornaviruses have been diagnosed by EM from the digestive contents of turkeys (Andral and Toquin, 1984). In addition, pseudopicornaviruses have been detected in embryonating eggs following yolk sac inoculation (Andral and Toquin, 1984).

Prevention, control, and treatment of small virus infections

To date, there are no vaccines, chemotherapeutics or other measures known to be efficacious for the control or prevention of the small viruses. Generally, good management practices emphasizing cleaning, disinfecting and litter management are recommended. However, it should be pointed out that some small viruses (astroviruses, in particular) have been troublesome even for producers with modern facilities and high management standards. Thus, contemporary management practices have not been effective in controlling some of these small virus infections (Reynolds and Saif, 1986).

Adenoviruses

Haemorrhagic enteritis virus (HEV), the causative agent of haemorrhagic enteritis (HE) of turkeys is an adenovirus. HE is one of the early recognized enteric diseases of turkey caused by a virus. The disease was first described by Pomeroy and Fesntermacher (1937). It has been reported from the major turkey producing areas of the world and almost all adult turkeys were reported to have been infected by HEV. The early work on HE has been reviewed (Domermuth and Gross, 1984).

Classifications of turkey adenoviruses

Two groups of avian adenoviruses are recognized. The chicken embryo lethal orphan virus and some isolates from turkeys are designated group I. The viruses that cause HE of turkeys, marble spleen disease of pheasants and splenomegaly of chickens are indistinguishable by agar gel diffusion tests and are designated group II and are immunologically unrelated to group I (Domermuth and Gross, 1984).

Epizootiology of HEV

Turkeys of all ages are probably susceptible to infection with HEV. In commercial flocks, the disease occurs mostly in 5- to 9-week-old birds. The faecal-oral route is probably the most common route of transmission. The HEV is relatively resistant to environmental conditions and the disease continues to reappear in consecutively raised flocks on the same premises (Domermuth and Gross, 1984).

Clinical signs and lesions of HEV

The disease is characterized by a sudden onset, depression and passage of bloody droppings, and mortality varies from 1 to 60% (Domermuth and Gross, 1984). The incubation period is approximately 1 week and the disease lasts for 1 week. Gross lesions consist of pale mucilative, congested intestines distended with bloody contents and the spleen is significantly enlarged and mottled. In addition to the intestines and spleen, microscopic lesions are detected in the pancreas, bursa of Fabricius and thymus (Fadly and Nazerian, 1982).

Pathogenesis of HEV

It was reported that an intact bursa is essential for development of disease, since chemically bursectomized turkey poults were not susceptible to the disease (Fadly and Nazerian, 1982). The viral antigen was reported in the spleen, liver, intestine, kidney and bone marrow of intraperitoneally inoculated poults (Silim and Thorsen, 1982). The virus apparently has affinity for B lymphocytes (Nazerian and Fadly,

1982). It was suggested that the virus is immunosuppressive, since it damages the bursa of Fabricius (Fadly and Nazerian, 1982) and has a predilection for B-lymphocytes. A transient suppression of lymphocyte mitogenic response was reported in turkeys infected with HEV (Nagaraja *et al.*, 1982).

Diagnosis of HEV

The acute disease can be diagnosed based on splenic and gut lesions and demonstration of development of antibodies in paired serum samples. The viral antigen can be demonstrated in spleens using an agar gel precipitation (AGP) test. The AGP can also be used to demonstrate HEV antibodies (Domermuth, Gross and DuBose, 1973). An enzyme-linked immunosorbent assay (ELISA) was also developed for detecting antibodies to HEV (Ianconescu *et al.*, 1984).

An important milestone in research on HEV occurred when the virus was propagated in cell culture (Nazerian and Fadly, 1982). Virulent and avirulent isolates of HEV were propagated in B-type lymphoblastoid cell lines of turkey origin. These cell lines were established from liver or spleen tumours of turkeys infected with Marek's disease virus (Nazerian, Elmubarak and Sharma, 1982).

Prevention and control of HEV

Birds that recover from natural HEV infection seem to be immune to reinfection (Domermuth and Gross, 1984). Passively transferred antibodies from immune hens are also effective in preventing the disease.

An avirulent strain of HEV from pheasants is being used extensively in North America to vaccinate turkeys against HE. Domermuth was instrumental in developing the procedure and demonstrating its efficacy. In that procedure, the virus is propagated in disease-free turkeys and the spleens from these turkeys are used in the drinking water to vaccinate susceptible poults (Domermuth *et al.*, 1977). The same HEV isolate of pheasant origin was adapted to propagate in cell culture and used to produce a live virus vaccine (Fadly and Nazerian, 1982). The safety and efficacy of that tissue culture vaccine was examined in laboratory and field studies (Fadly *et al.*, 1985). Currently, that vaccine is produced commercially in the USA. The use of the splenic and tissue culture vaccines is common in the USA. The rationale for the extensive use of vaccines is to induce protection from the acute disease and the possible immunosuppressive effects of the virus.

Coronaviruses

The disease caused by a coronavirus and designated, coronavirus enteritis (CE) or bluecomb, caused serious economic losses in the 1950s and 1960s in the USA and Canada. The disease was eliminated from turkey operations by depopulation and sanitation (Pomeroy, 1984). From the early 1970s until recently, diagnosis of the disease in North America was not well documented. Recent surveys of enteric viruses in the USA did not reveal the presence of coronaviruses in commercial flocks affected by enteric disease (Saif, Saif and Theil, 1985; Reynolds, Saif and Theil, 1987a). In 1988, coronaviruses were detected in flocks with mild to severe diarrhoea from Southern Quebec at a prevalence of 47.5% in 114 flocks from 42 commercial operations (Dea and Tijssen, 1988). The viruses were shown by IEM and ELISA to be antigenically similar to a Minnesota isolate of coronavirus. We detected coronaviruses in 1988 from two commercial operations in the USA (unpublished data). The viruses were detected by IEM using homologous convalescent sera. Flocks affected had severe diarrhoea and high mortality. Following recovery from the acute disease, the flocks were uneven and were significantly below expected weight at market age.

For a review of the early work in CE, the reader is referred to the article by Pomeroy (1984).

Classification of CE virus

The CE virus is a typical plemorphic, spherical coronavirus varying in size from 50 to 150 nm, with an average size of 130 nm (Panigrahy, Naqi and Hall, 1973). It is an enveloped virus manifesting large club shaped peplomers projecting from the envelope.

Epizootiology

The virus is mainly transmitted by the faecal–oral route and there is no evidence of egg transmission. It probably spreads between farms by equipment and personnel. The virus is highly contagious but relatively easily destroyed by environmental conditions and common disinfectants (Pomeroy, 1984).

Clinical signs and lesions of CE

The virus has a relatively short incubation period of 1 to 2 days. Affected birds are depressed, appear chilled and develop watery diarrhoea. Morbidity is usually 100% and high variable mortality is reported (Pomeroy, 1984). Affected birds are usually dehydrated and gut contents are watery. At the tip of the villi are large numbers of goblet cells and epithelial cells are cuboidal or squamous with loss of microvilli. The villi are shortened, and the lamina propria is denuded and infiltrated with mononuclear cells (Pomeroy, 1984; Dea and Tijssen, 1988).

Diagnosis of CE

It is difficult to diagnose CE on the basis of clinical signs and lesions. The direct IF test could be used to detect viral antigens in intestinal epithelium. The indirect IF test is used to detect antibodies in convalescing birds. An ELISA test was developed to detect viral antigens and the results were in close agreement with results of IEM (Dea and Tijssen, 1988). The virus replicates in embryonating eggs (Adams and Hofstad, 1971). More recently the virus was propagated in human rectum adenocarcinoma (HRT-18) established cell line (Dea and Tijssen, 1987).

Prevention and control of CE

Depopulation, sanitation and security are key factors in preventing and controlling the disease. It was reported that recovered birds are immune to challenge but remain carriers for life (Pomeroy, 1984).

Other viruses detected from the intestinal tract

There are few other viruses that have been isolated from the gastrointestinal tract or cloacas of turkeys. They are mentioned here to indicate their possible detection. These viruses are, paramyxoviruses 1 (Newcastle disease virus) and 3, and influenza viruses representing several haemagglutinin and neuraminidase types. These viruses were isolated from cloacal swabs in our laboratory. Certain strains of Newcastle disease virus are known to cause enteric disease, but no specific enteric disease has been attributed to the other viruses.

References

Adams, N. R. and Hofstad, M. S. (1971). Isolation of the agent of transmissible enteritis of turkeys in avian embryos. *Avian Diseases,* **15,** 426–433

Andral, B. and Toquin, D. (1984). Observations and isolation of pseudopicornaviruses from sick turkeys. *Avian Pathology,* **13,** 377–388

Andral, B., Toquin, D., L'Haridon, R., Jestin, A., Metz, M. H. and Rose, R. (1985). Les diarrhees du dindonneau: un bilan des recherches virales effectuees (rotavirus, reovirus, adenovirus, pseudopicornavirus). *Avian Pathology,* **14,** 147–162

Bergeland, M. E., McAdaragh, J. P. and Stotz, I. (1977). Rotaviral enteritis in turkey poults. In *Proceedings of the 26th Western Poultry Disease Conference,* pp. 129–130. University of California, Davis

Bridger, J. C. (1978). Location of type-specific antigens in calf rotavirus. *Journal of Clinical Microbiology,* **8,** 625–628

Bridger, J. C. (1980). Detection by electron microscopy of caliciviruses, astroviruses and rotavirus-like particles in the faeces of piglets with diarrhoea. *Veterinary Record,* **107,** 532–533

Chasey, D., Bridger, J. C. and McCrae, M. A. (1986). A new type of atypical rotavirus in pigs. *Archives of Virology,* **89,** 235–243

Dea, S. and Tijssen, P. (1987). Isolation and serial propagation of turkey enteric coronavirus in cell culture. *XXIII World Veterinary Congress Abstracts 13.7.1,* p. 324

Dea, S . and Tijssen, P. (1988). Viral agents associated with outbreaks of diarrhea in turkey flocks in Quebec. *Canadian Journal of Veterinary Research,* **52,** 53–57

Dees, T. A., Wooley, R. E. and Gratzek, J. B. (1972). Infectious enteritis of turkeys: pathogenicity of bacteria-free filtrates and a viral agent isolated from turkeys with infectious enteritis. *American Journal of Veterinary Research,* **33,** 165–170

Deshmukh, D. R., Larsen, C. T., Dutta, S. K. and Pomery, B. S. (1969). Characterization of pathogenic filtrate and viruses isolated from turkeys with bluecomb. *American Journal of Veterinary Research,* **30,** 1019–1025

Domermuth, C. H., Gross, W. B. and DuBose, R. T. (1973). Microimmunodiffusion test for hemorrhagic enteritis of turkeys. *Avian Diseases,* **17,** 439–444

Domermuth, C. H., Gross, W. B., DuBose, R. T. and Mallinson, E. T. (1975). Experimental reproduction and antibody inhibition of marble spleen disease of pheasants. *Journal of Wildlife Diseases,* **11,** 338–342

Domermuth, C. H., Gross, W. B., Douglass, C. S., DuBose, R. T., Harris, J. R. and Davis, R. B. (1977). Vaccination for hemorrhagic enteritis of turkeys. *Avian Diseases,* **21,** 557–565

Domermuth, C. H. and Gross, W. B. (1984). Hemorrhagic enteritis and related infections. In *Diseases of Poultry* (Hofstad, M. S., Barnes, H. J., Calnek, B. W., Reid, W. M. and Yoder, H. W., eds), pp. 511–516. Ames, Iowa, Iowa State University Press

Dutta, S. K. and Pomeroy, B. S. (1967). Isolation and characterization of an enterovirus from baby chicks having an enteric infection. II. Physical and chemical characteristics and ultrastructure. *Avian Diseases,* **11,** 9–15

Estes, M. K., Graham, D. Y. and Dimitrov, D. H. (1984). The molecular epidemiology of rotavirus gastroenteritis. *Progress in Medical Virology,* **29,** 1–22

Estes, M. K., Palmer, E. L. and Obijeski, J. F. (1983). Rotaviruses: a review. *Current Topics in Microbiology and Immunology*, **105**, 123–184

Fadly, A. M. and Nazerian, K. C. (1982). Evidence of bursal involvement in the pathogenesis of hemorrhagic enteritis virus of turkeys. *Avian Diseases*, **26**, 525–533

Fadly, A. M. and Nazerian, K. (1984). Efficacy and safety of cell-culture live-virus vaccine for hemorrhagic enteritis of turkeys: Laboratory studies. *Avian Diseases*, **28**, 183–196

Fadly, A. M., Nazerian, K., Nagaraja, K. and Below, G. (1985). Field vaccination against hemorrhagic enteritis of turkeys by a cell-culture live-virus vaccine. *Avian Diseases*, **29**, 768–777

Fujisaki, Y., Kawamura, H. and Anderson, D. P. (1969). Reoviruses isolated from turkeys with bluecomb. *American Journal of Veterinary Research*, **30**, 1035–1043

Gary, G. W., Black, D. R. and Palmer, E. (1982). Monoclonal IgG to the inner capsid of human rotavirus. *Archives of Virology*, **72**, 223–227

Gershowitz, A. and Wooley, R. E. (1973). Characterization of two reoviruses isolated from turkeys with infectious enteritis. *Avian Diseases*, **17**, 406–414

Goodwin, M. A., Latimer, K. S ., Nersessian, B. N. and Fletcher, O. J. (1984). Quantitation of intestinal D-xylose absorption in normal and reovirus-inoculated turkeys. *Avian Diseases*, **28**, 959–967

Goodwin, M. A., Nersessian, B. N., Brown, J. and Fletcher, O. J. (1985). Gastrointestinal transit times in normal and reovirus inoculated turkeys. *Avian Diseases*, **29**, 920–927

Greenberg, H., McAuliffe, V., Valdesuso, J., Wyatt, R. G., Flores, J., Kalica, A., Hoshino, Y. and Singh, N. (1983). Serological analysis of the subgroup protein of rotavirus, using monoclonal antibodies. *Infection and Immunity*, **39**, 91–99

Hoshino, Y., Wyatt, R. G., Greenberg, H. B., Flores, J. and Kapikian, A. Z. (1984). Serotypic similarity and diversity of rotaviruses of mammalian and avian origin as studied by plaque reduction neutralization. *Journal of Infectious Diseases*, **149**, 694–702

Ianconescu, A., Smith, E. J., Fadly, A. M. and Nazerian, K. (1984). An enzyme-linked immunosorbent assay for detection of hemorrhagic enteritis virus and associated antibodies. *Avian Diseases*, **28**, 677–692

Joklik, W. K. (1983). The members of the family reoviridae. In *The Reoviridae* (Joklik, W. K., ed.), pp. 1–7. New York, Plenum Press

Kang, S. Y., Nagaraja, K. V. and Newman, J. A. (1985). Rapid coagglutination test for detection of rotavirus in turkeys. *Avian Diseases*, **29**, 640–648

Kang, S. Y., Nagaraja, K. V. and Newman, J. A. (1986a). Primary isolation and identification of avian rotaviruses from turkeys exhibiting signs of clinical enteritis in a continuous MA 104 cell line. *Avian Diseases*, **30**, 494–499

Kang, S. Y., Nagaraja, K. V. and Newman, J. A. (1986b). Electropherotypic analysis of rotavirus isolated from turkeys. *Avian Diseases*, **30**, 797–801

Kapikian, A. Z., Wyatt, R. G., Greenberg, H. B., Kalica, A. R., Kim, H. W., Brandt, C. D., Rodriguez, W. J., Parrott, R. H. and Chanock, R. M. (1980). Approaches to immunization of infants and young children against gastroenteritis due to rotaviruses. *Reviews of Infectious Diseases*, **2**, 459–469

Kawamura, H., Shimizu, F., Maeda, M. and Tsubahara, H. (1965). Avian reovirus: Its properties and serological classification. *National Institute of Animal Health Quarterly*, **5**, 115–124

Lloyd-Evans, N., Springthorpe, V. S. and Sattar, S. A. (1986). Chemical disinfection of human rotavirus-contaminated inanimate surfaces. *Journal of Hygiene*, **97**, 163–173

Lourenco, M. H., Nicolas, J. C., Cohen, J., Scherrer, R. and Bricout, F. (1981). Study of human rotavirus genome by electrophoresis: attempt of classification among strains isolated in France. *Annals of Virology*, **132E**, 161–173

McFerran, J. B., Connor, T. J. and McCracken, R. M. (1976). Isolation of adenoviruses and reoviruses from avian species other than domestic fowl. *Avian Diseases*, **20**, 519–524

McNulty, M. S., Allan, G. M. and Stuart, J. C. (1978). Rotavirus infection in avian species. *Veterinary Record*, **103**, 319–320

McNulty, M. S., Allan, G. M. and McFerran, J. B. (1984). Prevalence of antibody to conventional and atypical rotaviruses in chickens. *Veterinary Record*, **114**, 219

McNulty, M. S., Curran, W. L. and McFerran, J. B. (1980). Detection of astrovirus in turkey feces by direct electron microscopy. *Veterinary Record*, **106**, 561

McNulty, M. S., Allan, G. M., Todd, D. and McFerran, J. B. (1979a). Isolation and cell culture propagation of rotaviruses from turkeys and chickens. *Archives of Virology*, **61**, 13–21

McNulty, M. S., Curran, W. L., Todd, D. and McFerran, J. B. (1979b). Detection of viruses in avian faeces by direct electron microscopy. *Avian Pathology*, **8**, 239–247

McNulty, M. S., Allan, G. M., Todd, D., McFerran, J. B., McKillop, E. R., Collins, D. S. and McCracken, R. M. (1980). Isolation of rotaviruses from turkeys and chickens: demonstration of distinct serotypes and RNA electropherotypes. *Avian Pathology*, **9**, 363–375

McNulty, M. S., Allan, G. M., Todd, D., McFerran, J. B. and McCracken, R. M. (1981). Isolation from chickens of a rotavirus lacking the rotavirus group antigen. *Journal of General Virology*, **55**, 405–413

McNulty, M. S., Todd, D., Allan, G. M., McFerran, J. B. and Greene, J. A. (1984). Epidemiology of rotavirus infection in broiler chickens: recognition of four serogroups. *Archives of Virology*, **81**, 113–121

Mayor, H. D., Jamison, R. M., Jordan, L. E. and Mitchell, M. V. (1965). Reoviruses II. Structure and composition of the virion. *Journal of Bacteriology*, **89**, 1548–1556

Mebus, C. A., Underdahl, N. R., Rhodes, M. B. and Twiehaus, M. J. (1969). Calf diarrhea (scours): reproduced with a virus from a field outbreak. *University of Nebraska Research Bulletin*, **223**, 1–16

Meulemans, G. and Halen, P. (1982). Efficacy of some disinfectants against infectious bursal disease virus and avian reovirus. *Veterinary Record*, **111**, 412–413

Moe, K. and Shirley, J. A. (1982). The effects of relative humidity and temperature on the survival of human rotavirus in faeces. *Archives of Virology*, **72**, 179–186

Munro, T. F. and Wooley, R. E. (1973). Neutralization kinetics study of selected reoviruses. *Infection and Immunity*, **8**, 628–630

Nagaraja, K. V., Batel, B. L., Emery, D. A., Pomeroy, B. S. and Newman, J. A. (1982). *In vitro* depression of the mitogenic response of lymphocytes from turkeys infected with hemorrhagic enteritis virus. *American Journal of Veterinary Research*, **43**, 134–136

Nazerian, K. and Fadly, A. M. (1982). Propagation of virulent and avirulent turkey hemorrhagic enteritis virus in cell culture. *Avian Diseases*, **26**, 816–827

Nazerian, K., Elmubarak, A. and Sharma, J. M. (1982). Establishment of B-lymphoblastoid cell line from Marek's disease virus induced tumors in turkeys. *International Journal of Cancer*, **29**, 63–68

Nersessian, B. N. (1987). Avian orthoreovirus: Antigenic characteristics, pathogenicity and prevention. PhD Dissertation, University of Georgia, Athens

Nersessian, B. N., Goodwin, M. A., Kleven, S. H. and Pesti, D. (1985a). Studies on orthoreoviruses isolated from young turkeys. I. Isolation and characterization. *Avian Diseases*, **29**, 755–767

Nersessian, B. N., Goodwin, M. A., Page, R. K. and Kleven, S. H. (1985b). Virus distribution in organs and serological response of poults inoculated orally. *Avian Diseases*, **29**, 963–969

Nersessian, B. N., Goodwin, M. A., Page, R. K., Kleven, S. H. and Brown, J. (1986). Studies on orthoreovirus isolated from young turkeys. III. Pathogenic effects in chicken embryos, chicks, poults, and suckling mice. *Avian Diseases*, **30**, 585–592

Panigrahy, B., Naqi, S. A. and Hall, C. F. (1973). Isolation and characterization of viruses associated with transmissible enteritis (bluecomb) of turkeys. *Avian Diseases*, **17**, 430–438

Pedley, S., Bridger, J. C., Brown, J. F. and McCrae, M. A. (1983). Molecular characterization of rotaviruses with distinct group antigens. *Journal of General Virology*, **64**, 2093–2101

Pedley, S., Bridger, J. C., Chasey, D. and McCrae, M. A. (1986). Definition of two new groups of atypical rotaviruses. *Journal of General Virology*, **67**, 131–137

Petek, M., Felluga, B., Borghi, G. and Baroni, A. (1967). The Crawley agent: An avian reovirus. *Archiv fur die Gesamte Virusforschung*, **21**, 413–424

Pomeroy, B. S. (1984). Coronaviral enteritis of turkeys (Blue comb disease). In *Diseases of Poultry*, Eighth Edition (Hofstad, M. S., Barnes, H. J., Calnek, B. W., Reid, W. M. and Yoder, H. W., eds), pp. 553–559. Ames, Iowa, Iowa State University Press

Pomeroy, B. S. and Fenstermacher, R. (1937). Hemorrhagic enteritis in turkeys. *Poultry Science*, **16**, 110–125

Reynolds, D. L. and Saif, Y. M. (1986). Astroviruses: A cause of an enteric disease in turkey poults. *Avian Diseases*, **30**, 728–735

Reynolds, D. L., Saif, Y. M. and Theil, K. W. (1987a). A survey of enteric viruses of turkey poults. *Avian Diseases*, **31**, 89–98

Reynolds, D. L., Saif, Y. M. and Theil, K. W. (1987b). Enteric viral infections of turkey poults: incidence of infection. *Avian Diseases*, **31**, 272–276

Ritchie, A. E., Deshmukh, D. R., Larsen, C. T. and Pomeroy, B. S. (1973). Electron microscopy of coronavirus-like particles characteristic of turkey bluecomb disease. *Avian Diseases*, **17**, 546–558

Rosen, L. (1968). Reoviruses. *Monographs in Virology*, **1**, 73–107

Sabin, A. B. (1959). Reoviruses. *Science*, **130**, 1387–1389

Saif, L. J. and Theil, K. W. (1985). Antigenically distinct rotaviruses of human and animal origin. In *Infectious Diarrhea in the Young* (Tzipori, S. *et al.*, eds), pp. 208–214. The Netherlands, Elsevier Science Publications

Saif, L. J., Bohl, E. H., Theil, K. W., Cross, R. F. and House, J. A. (1980). Rotavirus-like, calcivirus-like, and 23-nm virus-like particles associated with diarrhea in young pigs. *Journal of Clinical Microbiology*, **12**, 105–111

Saif, L. J., Saif, Y. M. and Theil, K. W. (1984). Detection and pathogenicity of enteric viruses recovered from diarrheic turkeys: role of a rotavirus-like agent. Proc. 17th World's Poultry Congress, Helsinki, Finland, pp. 531–541

Saif, L. J., Saif, Y. M. and Theil, K. W. (1985). Enteric viruses in diarrheic turkey poults. *Avian Diseases*, **29**, 798–811

Silim, A. and Thorsen, J. (1982). Hemorrhagic enteritis: virus distribution and sequential development of antibody in turkeys. *Avian Diseases*, **25**, 444–453

Simmons, D. G., Colwell, W. M., Muse, K. E. and Brewer, C. E. (1972). Isolation and characterization of an enteric reovirus causing high mortality in turkey poults. *Avian Diseases*, **16**, 1094–1102

Snodgrass, D. R. and Herring, J. A. (1977). The action of disinfectants on lamb rotavirus. *Veterinary Record*, **101**, 81

Spendlove, R. S. (1970). Unique reovirus characteristics. *Progress in Medical Virology*, **12**, 161–191

Springthorpe, V. S., Grenier, J. L., Lloyd-Evans, N. and Sattar, S. A. (1986). Chemical disinfection of human rotavirus: efficacy of commercially-available products in suspension tests. *Journal of Hygiene*, **97**, 139–161

Stanley, N. F. (1967). Reoviruses. *British Medical Bulletin*, **23**, 150–155

Tan, J. A. and Schnagl, R. D. (1981). Inactivation of a rotavirus by disinfectants. *Medical Journal of Australia*, **1**, 19–23

Theil, K. W. and Saif, Y. M. (1987). Age-related infections with rotavirus, rotaviruslike virus, and atypical rotavirus in turkey flocks. *Journal of Clinical Microbiology*, **25**, 333–337

Theil, K. W., Reynolds, D. L. and Saif, Y. M. (1986a). Isolation and serial propagation of turkey rotaviruses in fetal rhesus monkey kidney (MA104) cell line. *Avian Diseases*, **30**, 93–104

Theil, K. W., Reynolds, D. L. and Saif, Y. M. (1986b). Comparison of immune electron microscopy and genome electropherotyping techniques for detection of turkey rotaviruses and rotaviruslike viruses in intestinal contents. *Journal of Clinical Microbiology*, **23**, 695–699

Theil, K. W., Reynolds, D. L. and Saif, Y. M. (1986c). Genomic variation among avian rotavirus-like viruses detected by polyacrylamide gel electrophoresis. *Avian Diseases*, **30**, 829–834

Todd, D. and McNulty, M. S. (1986). Electrophoretic variation of avian rotavirus RNA in polyacrylamide gels. *Avian Pathology*, **15**, 149–159

Todd, D., McNulty, M. S. and Allan, G. M. (1980). Polyacrylamide gel electrophoresis of avian rotavirus RNA. *Archives of Virology*, **63**, 87–97

Trampel, D. W., Kinden, D. A., Solorzano, R. F. and Stogsdill, P. L. (1983). Parvovirus-like enteropathy in Missouri turkeys. *Avian Diseases*, **27**, 49–54

van der Heide, L. and Kalbac, M. (1975). Infectious tenosynovitis (viral arthritis): characterization of a Connecticut viral isolant as a reovirus and evidence of viral egg transmission by reovirus infected broiler breeders. *Avian Diseases*, **19**, 683–688

van der Heide, L., Kalbac, M., Brustolon, M. and Lawson, M. G. (1980). Pathogenicity for chickens of a reovirus isolated from turkeys. *Avian Diseases*, **24**, 989–997

Vasquez, C. and Tournier, P. (1962). The morphology of reovirus. *Virology*, **17**, 503–510

Wood, G. W., Nicholas, R. A. J., Hebert, C. N. and Thorton, D. H. (1980). Serological comparisons of avian reoviruses. *Journal of Comparative Pathology*, **90**, 29–38

Woods, G. N., Bridger, J. C., Jones, J. M., Flewett, T. H., Bridon, A. S., Davies, H. A. and White, G. B. B. (1976). Morphological and antigenic relationships between viruses (rotaviruses) from acute gastroenteritis of children, calves, piglets, mice, and foals. *Infection and Immunity*, **14**, 804–810

Wooley, R. E. (1973). Serological comparison of the Georgia and Minnesota strains of infectious enteritis in turkeys. *Avian Diseases*, **17**, 150–154

Wooley, R. E. and Gratzek, J. B. (1969). Certain characteristics of viruses isolated from turkeys with bluecomb. *American Journal of Veterinary Research*, **30**, 1027–1033

Wooley, R. E., Dees, T. A., Cromack, A. S. and Gratzek, J. B. (1972). Infectious enteritis of turkeys: Characterization of two reoviruses isolated by sucrose density gradient centrifugation from turkeys with infectious enteritis. *American Journal of Veterinary Research*, **33**, 157–164

Yason, C. V. and Schat, K. A. (1985). Isolation and characterization of avian rotaviruses. *Avian Diseases*, **29**, 499–508

Yason, C. V. and Schat, K. A. (1986a). Experimental infection of specific-pathogen-free chickens with avian rotaviruses. *Avian Diseases*, **30**, 551–556

Yason, C. V. and Schat, K. A. (1986b). Pathogenesis of rotavirus infection in turkey poults. *Avian Pathology*, **151**, 421–435

Yason, C. V. and Schat, K. A. (1987). Pathogenesis of rotavirus infection in various age groups of chickens and turkeys: clinical signs and virology. *American Journal of Veterinary Research*, **48**, 977–983

Yason, C. V., Summers, B. A. and Schat, K. A. (1987). Pathogenesis of rotavirus infection in various age groups of chickens and turkeys: Pathology. *American Journal of Veterinary Research*, **48**, 927–937

Chapter 14

The general health status of turkeys

N. E. Horrox

The general health status of turkeys is dependent on many factors that have been mentioned elsewhere in this book such as nutrition, environment, genetics and management. Also, the geographical location is important as not all diseases are truly international. There are those diseases that tend to favour certain countries or localities for a variety of reasons.

When considering the general health status of turkeys all these factors need to be taken into account as do the changes that have occurred in the methods of turkey production. Here the impact of the increase in national flock sizes over the last ten years and the even larger concurrent increase in individual flock sizes must be considered. The high concentration of turkeys in some small geographical areas also needs to be taken into account. Conversely in some countries traditional production methods including ranging of turkeys could just be starting to make a comeback. This will bring a return of some of the old diseases which the industry has now regarded for some years as a part of history.

Disease has changed in nature over the last decade or two. Originally, disease was a case of a casual agent reacting with turkeys to cause losses which were often quite dramatic. As these casual agents have been controlled, disease has become in many instances a scenario of a multitude of factors inter-reacting with the turkeys to cause losses which are far less dramatic but can, because of the size of today's flocks, be just as expensive. Also, because many factors are involved, it often depends upon which one predominates as to how the disease syndrome manifests itself. Consequently the role of the poultry veterinarian has changed somewhat from that of a diagnostician to that of the detective. This means that there is not an instant answer nor an instant cure for every disease occurrence and sometimes the farmer will have to be patient with the veterinarian as many diagnoses now take longer to arrive at than they did ten or 20 years ago.

In view of the size of many of today's flocks it is essential that the farmer has systems that enable him to detect disease at the earliest possible stage. This is so its impact can be minimized by the prompt implementation of corrective action after the poultry veterinarian has confirmed the cause of the problem. Corrective action does not automatically imply medication with antibiotics and everyone should strive to ensure that these products are only used when they are needed. Many of today's diseases can be controlled by fine tuning the management of the flock. Here feed modifications, adjustments to ventilation, changes to house temperature and initial poult quality are all important.

The maintenance of good health is dependent upon many factors and all of these must be taken into account by management. More importantly, however, consideration must be given to their interactions and interdependencies.

A lot has happened on the health front this last decade and to try and cover all of this in one chapter is a daunting task. Some diseases have been controlled and even eradicated, new treatments have been developed and, of course, new diseases and problems have arisen. The new diseases include turkey rhinotracheitis and some of the enteric viral syndromes already reviewed in this book.

In considering developments in the general health status of turkeys over the last decade each disease will be considered according to causative factors. It is obviously impossible to cover all disease so those which highlight specific concepts or principles will be considered.

Mycoplasma related diseases

Mycoplasma gallisepticum

Mycoplasmosis, due to this mycoplasma, has occurred around the world this last decade. It was once almost considered to be a disease of the past but it is making a dramatic comeback in some countries, especially in chickens. The disease has varied from a severe respiratory disease with relatively high mortality to that of an almost inapparent condition with minimal losses. Closer examination shows that productivity or fecundity is adversely affected.

A better understanding of the management of this disease by optimizing environment by factors that include temperature, ventilation and stocking rate is now appreciated. Over the last decade new antimycoplasma drugs including tiamutin, kitamycin and Baytril have become available but old favourites like tylosin and the tetracyclines have withstood the test of time and are still often used to control this disease.

Researchers around the world have consistently developed improved laboratory techniques for isolating *Mycoplasma gallisepticum*. In addition, various techniques based on fluorescent antibodies and immunofluorescent are now available for the identification of this organism. Recent work with DNA fingerprinting should allow us to know if the strain of mycoplasma that caused an outbreak is the same strain that caused other outbreaks in an area or whether it is a different one. If it is different then it should be easy to detect where else in the world that strain has caused problems. This will be an exceptionally useful management tool.

Mycoplasma meleagridis

By the early part of the 1970s all the world's primary turkey breeders had successfully cleared their stock of *M. meleagridis* by antibiotic egg injection techniques or by combining these techniques with egg dipping programmes. The benefits of this success were enjoyed throughout the industry although they have obviously been negated by the arrival of turkey rhinotracheitis in many countries. However, it would be interesting to question what the situation would be with a concurrent infection of these two agents.

With the eradication of *M. meleagridis* infection we have probably seen the eradication of the last eradicable disease from turkeys. This is because eradication is an expensive exercise and for major resources to be committed a fair degree of certainty of success needs to be guaranteed in advance. This was the case with *M.*

meleagridis and one of the factors that contributed to this was the fact that the disease was only a disease of turkeys. This meant that with good management the likelihood of reinfecting clean stock was virtually nil. This is not the case for example, with *M. gallisepticum* where clean stock can be infected from a multitude of sources, not just other turkeys.

Mycoplasma synoviae

This agent is becoming more endemic in chicken populations around the world. It is one that turkey producers have not thought too much about in recent years. It may just be ready for a comeback.

Mycoplasma iowae

In the early 1980s *M. iowae* received attention as a possible cause of depressed hatchability. This could be induced in laboratory situations but the organism dose and routes of infection involved were somewhat artificial and it would be prudent to keep an open mind as to the role this mycoplasma plays in the field.

Over the last decade the systems for isolating and identifying mycoplasmas have evolved considerably but it should always be remembered that they have been developed for the mycoplasmas we know about — could there be others that our current systems do not isolate?

Influenza

The last decade has seen a significant amount of the viral respiratory disease termed influenza. There is a reservoir of this virus in wild waterfowl populations and whenever the opportunity arises it will move into the turkey population. Also, there are many strains of this virus and there is no way of forecasting when the disease is likely to appear and which strain will be involved or what the likely losses may be.

To date, vaccination has effectively protected flocks but there is no vaccine available that will protect against all influenza strains. Vaccines tend to be specific against one or a couple of strains.

Pasteurellosis

Pasteurellosis has been reasonably widespread in the last decade but the use of effective autogenous and commercial vaccines now keeps this disease under control on most farms.

However, the picture may be very different if the disease appears as a sequel to turkey rhinotracheitis or as a component of a mixed respiratory infection.

Work in hand, especially in the USA, is likely to result in a generation of new and even better pasteurella vaccines. Even with these it will still be important to eliminate rats from the vicinity of turkeys as they invariably carry the pasteurella organism and can pass it on to the turkeys.

Respiratory staphylococcosis

Respiratory staphylococcosis is a particular problem in some areas of the USA. Workers there are using bacterial interference as a means of controlling the disease. In this technique a harmless strain of the organism is introduced to the birds and it colonizes their respiratory tracts so that there is no room for the disease-causing staphylococci when they appear at a later date. Initial results look promising and it will be interesting to see in the years ahead how effective this approach turns out to be.

Colisepticaemia

The bacterium *E. coli* is ubiquitous and whenever it comes into contact with turkeys, especially in controlled environment housing there is the potential for it to cause colisepticaemia. This disease is usually seen as a generalized infection of the bird's body with the peritoneum, liver, spleen, heart sac and lungs all being involved.

Colisepticaemia can be a disease in its own right but often it occurs as a sequel, to or in association with, another disease such as mycoplasmosis, Newcastle disease or rhinotracheitis. The severity of colisepticaemia is often greatly influenced by the environment especially the atmosphere surrounding the birds. Often the uncomplicated form of this disease can be avoided by careful management of the flock's environment.

Rickets

Rickets is a condition characterized by poor bone calcification and is typically seen at 2–4 weeks of age. Its origins lie in either a single or multiple deficiency of calcium, phosphorus and vitamin D_3. These deficiencies can be in the ration and absolute or relative in nature or they can be induced by disturbances in the physiology of the digestive tract. Such disturbances can be related to the metabolism of the liver or pancreas or to factors such as diseases that interfere with the integrity and, therefore, the absorptive efficiency of the intestinal surface.

The availability of the three key nutrients from the ration is also relevant. Therefore, many factors come into play when we consider the origin of this condition. Classic rickets is not that common but a marginal rachitic syndrome is probably more widespread than many acknowledge.

Leg conditions

Skeletal leg conditions, that is conditions affecting the leg bones of turkeys have received a lot of attention the last decade. Leg conditions, especially in teenage birds, appear to be a function of weight for age but this must be related to events in the bird's first 8 weeks of life. That is, rapid weight gain exerts pressures on the skeleton which if it is not up to its potential is likely to marginally bend or twist. Once this process has started it invariably continues until the turkey has a distorted skeletal structure accompanied by locomotory difficulties. If the skeleton is lacking in strength for example, as a consequence of an earlier rachitic episode or as a result in depression of mineral intake due to scouring it will be more prone to the pressures mentioned.

Conversely, if the pressures are excessive (as they are in a rapid spurt of growth), bone distortion is more probable. Since most growth spurts follow a period of depressed feed intake (scour or turkey rhinotracheitis) the effects are then likely to be more noticeable. However, there will be many instances when the leg bones have enough inherent strength to withstand the pressures described and then no problems ensue.

Once the original distortion to the leg bones has occurred those legs will be more likely to undergo further damage at subsequent times. Once visible leg long bone abnormalities have been detected much of the damage has been done. This condition is best managed by ensuring that the events described do not occur or if they do occur the flock should be nursed through the critical period.

Finally, unless high weights are required at an exceptionally early age, the nutrition and management in the flock's first few weeks should ensure the development of a good strong skeleton. In many instances it could well be preferable to achieve this at the expensive of weight.

Ionophorous anticoccidials

The last decade saw an increasing reliance on the ionophorous anticoccidials in modern turkey production. Monensin consolidated its position as the main ionophorous anticoccidial used for turkeys but in the second half of the period lasalocid was used quite frequently.

Eimeria species of coccidia are not the serious killer infections in turkeys that their chicken counterparts can be, but they can have a serious depressing effect on flock performance, especially if secondary entities occur.

In recent years salinomycin and narasin, two of the effective chicken ionophorous anticoccidials, have caused mortality problems when given accidentally to turkeys. Also, problems have been encountered when tiamulin, an antimycoplasma product, has been administered to turkeys receiving monensin or accidentally receiving low doses of narasin or salinomycin, as the former enhanced the toxicity of the latter. No such problems have been encountered with lasalocid.

These toxicity problems are mentioned so as to highlight one very important point that needs to be kept in mind in the future. Although the chicken and turkey are similar physiologically, they are very different animals pharmacologically. From a pharmacological viewpoint it is very dangerous to regard the turkey as an overgrown chicken.

Poor performance

In recent years work has been done to show that infectious runting and stunting syndrome of chickens also occurs in turkeys. With this observation came a trend in some of the western turkey industries that any young flock with size variation and poor feathering was deemed as having infectious stunting and runting.

However, if such flocks are examined in detail it becomes apparent that clinical signs identical to those of runting and stunting will occur if anything adversely affects nutrient uptake in the first week or so of life. Rotavirus infection will certainly cause such an effect as can nutritional imbalances. The symptoms seen at 2 weeks of age are very similar to mild rickets.

Another important lesson learnt here is that all young flocks that show uneven growth do not necessarily have infectious stunting and runting.

Mycotoxins

The possible role(s) of mycotoxins in turkey diseases are numerous but little is known about their importance. They may be very important or another ten years may show that they were one of the non-events of the 1980s.

Salmonella

Like *E. coli*, salmonella species are found widely in nature but they are not, as many think, an organism unique to poultry and poultry products. *Salmonella typhimurium* can cause serious problems in calves and many cases of human salmonella food poisoning arise from eating products such as chocolate, fish, cheese and vegetables. In the case of the latter, contamination has arisen from the spraying of crops with sewage.

Diseases caused by salmonella are rarely seen in most turkey flocks and those caused by *Salmonella pullorum*. *Salmonella gallinarum* and *Salmonella arizona* are absent from the turkey flocks in most countries.

The last decade has seen a turning point in turkey diseases. Many of the single cause entities that showed a destructive disease picture have declined and they have been replaced by multifactorial disease syndromes that show varying clinical pictures depending upon the environment in which they occur.

These require extensive and expensive research to give us a better understanding of them. To achieve this research will require adequate funding. Also, many of these syndromes do not occur overnight but their effects become slowly apparent. This creates a problem of identifying when there is a problem. The stockman can usually spot an overnight change but something that creeps in insidiously over a period of several days can be very difficult to detect by someone who is with the flock the whole time. Quite often, with these multifactorial syndromes, by the time they can be detected they can be difficult to reverse with the consequence that they leave their mark on the efficiency of that flock's performance.

Effective disease management over the next decade will require:

(1) detection of the problem as early as possible,
(2) high standards of flock management, environment control and nutrition to lessen the likelihood of the disease occurring in the first place but if it should occur these high standards should lessen its impact on the flock's performance.

Both of these factors are going to require tomorrow's stockmen to be of a high calibre and to be well versed with their subject. How this can be achieved is a problem all turkey farmers will have to tackle in the years ahead and is one which all should give attention to.

Part IV

Turkey meat science

Chapter 15

Meat yield and carcass composition in turkeys

J. D. Wood

Introduction

The aim of this chapter is to review published literature on the effects of production and processing factors on carcass yield and composition. Yield is taken to indicate the weight of eviscerated carcass in relation to live weight and the weight of parts in relation to eviscerated weight, also the weights of carcass and parts in absolute terms. Composition refers to the muscle, fat, bone and skin and the lipid, water and protein content of carcass and parts. All these characteristics are affected by production factors such as strain, sex, age and nutrition and together they determine the value of the bird to the processor and ultimately the consumer. Meat characteristics are primarily determined during growth although there is much that can be done post-slaughter to influence them.

In reviewing published data from around the world it is clear that there are no standard definitions of terms. Thus, the eviscerated carcass in some cases contains giblets and neck, the weight of the carcass may include water taken up during chilling, the weights of parts may or may not include skin, abdominal fat may include some visceral fat, parts may be separated in different ways and so on. To a large extent variation in techniques is to be expected since research may serve the interests of particular processors or follow national conventions. Even with problems of definition it is still possible to make valid generalized comparisons across experiments. However, standardized approaches such as the method of dissection developed at Spelderholt in the Netherlands and described by the World's Poultry Science Association (WPSA, 1984) which is used at the Institute of Food Research (Bristol) are particularly useful. In the future it is to be hoped that more experiments use such standard techniques so that unambiguous conclusions as to the importance of the various factors affecting carcass quality can be drawn.

Since the amount of published material in turkeys is much less than in chickens and many of the principles are similar between the two species, reference will be made to chickens where appropriate.

Importance of yield and composition in turkey marketing

In many countries during the last ten years, including the UK, there has been a marked increase in the consumption of poultry meat especially compared with that of the red meats (*Table 15.1*). The national food survey figures suggest that turkey

Table 15.1 Consumption of meats in Great Britain 1975–1984 (g/person/week)

	1975	1980	1982	1984
Beef and veal	236	230	200	178
Mutton and lamb	120	128	102	94
Pork and bacon	219	266	259	226
All poultry,	157	182	186	196
of which broiler chicken	107	121	126	129
turkey[a]	–	22	18	25

Annual Reports of the National Food Survey Committee. London, HMSO

[a] First year of records was 1978 when 15 g was recorded for turkey

constituted approximately 13% of all poultry consumed in the home in the UK in 1984 although the absolute per capita figure, 1.3 kg/annum, is lower than other estimates calculated in different ways (see Chapter 18).

Increasing popularity of poultry meat, including turkey, is due to three main factors according to surveys of consumer attitudes: low cost (value for money), a healthy and nutritious image, and availability in more interesting and convenient forms. Retail cost is dictated ultimately by the costs of production, processing and marketing and so the maximization of yield from slaughtered birds is critical in keeping costs low. The health image of poultry meat relates mainly to the perception among consumers of a low lipid and saturated fatty acid content and a belief that these should be reduced in the diet in order to cut down the risk of heart disease. It is true to some extent that replacement of white for red meat will reduce fat intake since carcasses of poultry are lower in lipid than those of the red meat species and removal of excess fat is more likely to have been done before sale. However, the point is often exaggerated. Reported values for the percentage of extractable lipid in the eviscerated carcass are not dramatically lower in chickens and turkeys than in pigs, cattle and sheep (*Table 15.2*) and there is very little difference between species in the lipid content of muscles from which subcutaneous and intermuscular fat have been removed. The data in *Table 15.2* are based on a

Table 15.2 Estimates of the carcass weight and lipid content of chickens and turkeys in comparison with red meat animals

	Chickens[a]			Turkeys[b]	
	Ref. 1	Ref. 2	Ref. 3	Ref. 1	Ref. 2
Carcass weight (kg)	1.4	1.6	1.2	9.8	10.7
Percentage lipid	20.7	15.9	17.2	17.7	11.2
	Pigs[c]	Cattle[c]	Sheep[c]		
Carcass weight (kg)	62.6	26.9	16.9		
Percentage lipid	19.4	20.2	23.5		

[a] Ref. 1 Leeson and Summers (1980a). Canadian birds aged 7 weeks
  Ref. 2 Broadbent, Wilson and Fisher (1981). UK birds aged 8 weeks
  Ref. 3 Chambers, Gavora and Fortin (1981). Canadian birds aged 7 weeks
[b] Ref. 1 Leeson and Summers (1980b). Canadian Large White strain aged 22 weeks
  Ref. 2 Bacon, Nestor and Renner (1986). US Large White strains aged 20 weeks
[c] Estimated national values for UK in 1984 (Kempster, Cook and Grantley-Smith, 1986)

similar definition of carcass weight in all the species (i.e. excluding abdominal fat and organs) and the values are averages for males and females. The data are also fairly representative of commercial production. Thus, the pig, cattle and sheep figures are average values for current British production and the chicken data are from large evaluations of commercial stock. There is apparently a wide range in percentage lipid values for turkeys, for example Hurwitz et al. (1983) reported values of 9% lipid in 19-week BUT Broad Breasted White birds.

The third factor of importance in the rising consumption of poultry meat is its availability in an ever-widening range of cut-up and further processed forms. In Britain, this applies particularly to chicken where the retail market for added-value products is now estimated to be worth £147 million, up from £25 million in 1982. However, there have also been significant changes in the turkey market and 40% of turkey is now estimated to be consumed in cut-up and further processed forms in Britain (Chapter 18), up from 10% in 1975. As with chicken, there has also been a move towards fresh rather than frozen whole carcasses and parts. However, 62% of sales in Britain are still made during the Christmas period, down from 69% in 1980.

Bearing these trends in mind, the requirements of the turkey industry in the future are likely to be for birds with the following characteristics: a heavy carcass weight without excess fat and bone — such carcasses are ideal for further processing; a high carcass and meat yield relative to live weight; and a high proportion of desirable parts, particularly breast. It is likely that 'finish' (subcutaneous fat development) will be less important as a measure of carcass quality although lipid levels within meat should not be so low as to reduce juiciness and tenderness. This review of factors affecting yield and composition will therefore concentrate on these key areas of interest.

Effects of production factors on yield and composition

The most important factors are age and weight, sex, strain, genetic selection for weight gain and nutrition.

Age and weight

Changes in yield and composition according to age and weight provide the bench marks against which the effects of other factors, for example strain and sex, can be assessed. Most studies have investigated a relatively short time period close to slaughter, for example Hartung and Froning (1968); Moran, Orr and Larmond (1970); Moran, Orr and Larmond (1971); Orr et al. (1974); Salmon, Dunkelgod and Wilson (1982b); Peng et al. (1985) and Larsen et al. (1986). The results of these investigations are in general agreement with a study conducted over a much wider age range in Large White turkeys by Leeson and Summers (1980b), some of the results of which are illustrated in Figure 15.1. Equal numbers of male and female birds were slaughtered at 2-week intervals between 2 and 24 weeks of age following rearing under commercial Canadian conditions. The important changes in yield and composition with increasing age were as follows:

(1) percentage carcass increases (not shown in Figure 15.1). Carcass weight as percentage live weight increased from 66 to 84% in males and 64 to 81% in females during the period 2–24 weeks,

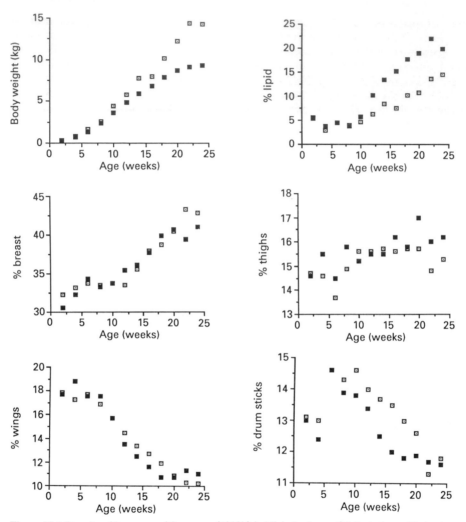

Figure 15.1 Results of Leeson and Summers (1980b) in Nicholas Large White turkeys. Birds given commercial diets *ad libitum* from birth to 24 weeks of age. Five males (□) and five females (■) analysed at 2-week intervals. Body weight obtained after 3 h (2–6 weeks) or 16 h (8–24 weeks) starvation. Lipid and parts as percentage of eviscerated carcass weight

(2) percentage breast increases,
(3) percentage thighs small increase,
(4) percentage drumsticks decrease,
(5) percentage wings marked decrease,
(6) percentage carcass lipid marked increase.

These changes are a reflection of different growth patterns within the bird and in general they are similar to changes observed in chickens (Moran, 1977; Prescott, Wathes and Kirkwood, 1985). The most important are the increase in tissues relative to viscera which cause a steady increase in carcass yield, the increase in fat stores and lipid, particularly towards the end of the finishing period and the increase in the proportion of the breast compared with other parts of the eviscerated carcass. These changes have to be balanced against one another in order to maximize carcass value whilst minimizing wasteful fat production and over-consumption of feed in relation to weight gain (feed conversion efficiency falls as fat deposition increases). However, Larsen *et al.* (1986) comment that the increase in the absolute weight and proportion of the breast seen in large modern strains in the later stages of growth, even in females, imply that these can probably be taken to older ages and heavier weights than in current US commercial practice without conferring penalties in fatness or feed efficiency.

Peng *et al.* (1985) (*see Table 15.3*) in a study conducted between 15 and 26 weeks in male turkeys, calculated 'growth coefficients' for parts and tissues of the carcass, i.e. the coefficient b in the regression of the logarithm of part weight (y) on the logarithm of carcass weight x : $\log y = \log a + b \log x$.

Table 15.3 Growth coefficients, b, in the log–log regressions of part weight, x on carcass weight, y: $\log y = \log a + b \log x$. Data from 96 male turkeys 15–26 weeks of age

	b
Wings	0.53
Shell	0.74
Drumsticks	0.81
Skin	0.83
Thighs	0.93
Breast	1.38
Fat[a]	3.06

Peng *et al.* (1985)

[a] Dissectible

The value of b describes changes in y which are independent of its size. The results confirm the conclusions reached by Leeson and Summers (1980b), i.e. low relative growth of wings and drumsticks, level growth of thighs and rapid growth of breast and dissectible fat. However, with increasing carcass weight the absolute values for b are not in agreement with those calculated by Prescott, Wathes and Kirkwood (1985) or Grey, Robinson and Jones (1982) in chickens. Work in the red meat species also shows wide variation between studies in the absolute values for growth coefficients, probably because of differences in the range of x over which measurements are made, but broad agreement as to the pattern of changes.

Moran, Orr and Larmond (1970), in the Large White turkey and Moran, Orr and Larmond (1971), in the Small White 'broiler-fryer-type' turkey, examined the changes in the meat (muscle), bone and skin content of parts as well as in the whole carcass during the later stages of growth. They concluded that changes in each part mirrored changes in the carcass as a whole. There were large differences between parts, however, which reflect their differences in value. Thus, in male Large White turkeys, the percentage of cooked meat increased between 17 and 27 weeks of age and was highest in the breast (82%) and thigh (74–80%) and lowest in the flat wing (37–46%) and lower back (42–47%). The skin content of the cooked carcass (9–11%) and parts also increased between 17 and 27 weeks due to an increase in the proportion of subcutaneous fat which is difficult to separate from skin. This changes the appearance or 'finish' of the bird which is used to assess carcass value in some commercial grading systems. In the Small White turkey similar changes occurred although at younger ages.

The problem of excessive abdominal fat deposition, which exists in the broiler chicken industry, is not so large in turkeys. Few reports quote values for abdominal fat although an exception is the study of Bacon, Nestor and Renner (1986) in a commercial US strain. In groups consisting of equal numbers of males and females, average values for the percentage of lipid in the carcass were 4.3 and 11.2% at 8 and 20 weeks respectively. Abdominal fat was zero and 1.05% of body weight at these two ages. This is a much lower figure than the 4% of body weight used by Heath, Covey and Owens (1980) to indicate an unacceptably high level of fat in broilers and is at the low end of the range 1–4% of body weight which is reported in the chicken literature (for example Chambers, Gavora and Fortin, 1981; Leenstra and Pit, 1987). There is no reason to suppose that the pattern of fat deposition is any different in turkeys than chickens so it is assumed that abdominal fat in turkeys is also a late developing depot which forms an increasing proportion of total fat as birds get heavier and fatter (Hakansson, Eriksson and Svensson, 1978a and b; Evans, 1977). As with chickens, it has been found that measures of the weight or thickness of abdominal fat in turkeys provide a useful prediction of total fat (Rose and Michie, 1983).

Subjective estimation of finish and fleshing is used in some plants (most widely in Canada) to indicate yield and meat quality. The subject has been reviewed by Moran (1977) who suggests that scoring for these characteristics provides a good prediction of composition in terms of the percentage of meat and bone. No alternative objective techniques have yet been developed. However, the relevance of finish as an indicator of eating quality is questioned by the results of Larmond and Moran (1983). Small White turkeys in finish grades A and B received the same taste panel scores for flavour, tenderness and juiciness in breast and thigh meat. Injection of coconut oil into breast meat (internal basting) improved these aspects of eating quality, although surprisingly this was most marked in the well-finished (grade A) carcasses.

Sex

Sex has marked effects on weight and composition in turkeys, more so than in most other meat species. The differences are such that males and females are used for different end-uses, i.e. males for further processing where a heavy bird with little fat is required and females for the whole bird trade in which a smaller, well-finished carcass is demanded. The changes in weight and composition with age in males and females are illustrated in *Figure 15.1*.

All studies show males to be considerably heavier than females at ages approaching the normal time of slaughter. In the study of Leeson and Summers (1980b, *Figure 15.1*) female Large White turkeys plateaued in body weight at about 10 kg and males at about 15 kg. In four strains of Small White turkeys, males were 35–37% heavier than females at 14 weeks and 47–53% heavier at 18 weeks (Orr *et al.*, 1974). There appears to be little difference between the sexes in the weight of the eviscerated carcass as a proportion of live weight (Salmon, 1979a; Hurwitz *et al.*, 1983) although some studies show a small but consistent difference in favour of males (Moran, Orr and Larmond, 1971; Leeson and Summers, 1980b).

Female carcasses contain higher concentrations of lipid, especially when taken to the same slaughter age as males (which is unlikely to be done in practice). Most studies show a gradual widening of the gap in the percentage of lipid between the sexes as age increases (*Figure 15.1*) (e.g. Hurwitz *et al.*, 1983; Bacon, Nestor and Renner, 1986) but in the study of Moran, Orr and Larmond (1970) females had consistently high values for the percentage of lipid between 14 and 24 weeks (12–13% of carcass weight) whereas males had low values up to 23 weeks (7% lipid) and much higher values at 25 and 27 weeks (17% lipid). On this evidence it was recommended that males be marketed at 23 weeks of age and females at 21 weeks. In a subsequent study with Small White turkeys, Moran, Orr and Larmond (1971) also found a large increase in the lipid content of male carcasses in the later stages of finishing, in this case at 17 weeks. They postulated that the onset of sexual maturity in males was associated with a period of rapid fat deposition. It is possible that this may have occurred later than 25 weeks of age in the Large White birds described in *Figure 15.1*.

Salmon (1979a) showed that females of a Medium White strain had higher concentrations of lipid at 18 weeks in most tissues compared with males (*Table 15.4*). However, both had a similar, low, concentration in breast meat. In a study of the lipid content of three muscles from a commercial UK broiler strain, Grey *et al.* (1983) found that the sex effect at various ages was significant only in the thigh which had the highest lipid concentration. At 364 days the values (percentage of fresh weight) were 8.7 in males and 14.3 in females. Comparable figures for breast were 1.7 and 2.2%.

Table 15.4 Weight and composition of carcass and tissues in Medium White turkeys aged 18 weeks; five birds of each sex

	Males	*Females*
Percentage of carcass weight		
Breast + back		
total	54.2	53.6
skin	6.0	7.3
meat	29.2	30.6
bone	19.1	15.7
Percentage lipid		
Breast + back meat	0.76	0.75
Thigh meat	3.52	6.42
Carcass meat	4.37	5.93
Liver	2.14	3.86
Heart	3.13	6.33

(Salmon, 1979a)

Males and females have similar proportions of parts in relation to eviscerated weight (Moran, Orr and Larmond, 1970; Salmon, 1979a; Leeson and Summers, 1980b; Perenyi, Suto and Ujvarine, 1980). Occasionally, individual studies show differences, for example the percentage of drumsticks was greater in males in the study of Leeson and Summers (1980b) and the percentage of breast was greater in males in the study of Perenyi, Suto and Ujvarine (1980) but such effects have not been found consistently. Surprisingly, there are also only minor differences in the yield of lean meat from parts and from the whole carcass despite the marked differences in lipid content (e.g. *Table 15.4*). It is clear that, apart from the skin with adhering subcutaneous fat, which is heavier in females (Salmon, 1979a), lipid is not present in larger intermuscular fat deposits in the female which would detract from saleable meat yield (Hartung and Froning, 1968).

Strain

There are many commercial strains of turkeys available to producers, as with broiler chickens, and each has advantages claimed for them. In general, it can be concluded from published reports that the important differences are in size and growth rate up to slaughter age. Yield and compositional variation mainly arise as the result of these basic differences. Thus, a small early maturing strain would be expected to have a higher carcass yield, a higher lipid concentration in the carcass, a higher proportion of breast meat, a lower proportion of wings and drumsticks and a greater degree of finish than a large strain compared at the same age (say 20 weeks) because these are all features of a more mature bird. Strain differences should only be considered remarkable when they deviate from the general rule linking yield and composition with the stage of maturity.

Moran (1977) in a review, found few differences in the yield or composition of parts between large and small turkey strains during their respective finishing periods. Orr *et al.* (1974) found a range of 1 kg (6.7–7.7 kg) in the live weight of four strains of Small White turkeys at 18 weeks of age but a range of only 1 percentage unit (33.2–34.4) in the yield of breast as a percentage of carcass weight. The meat content of cooked thigh and breast (both approximately 78%) was also similar between strains. Clayton, Nixey and Monaghan (1978) found important differences in live weight between three large UK strains between 12 and 24 weeks for males (12–18 weeks for females) but inconsistent differences in yield and composition parameters. At 24 weeks in males there was a 23% difference in live weight between the lightest (11.4 kg) and heaviest (14.3 kg) strains with the heaviest strain having 8.3% less breast meat as a proportion of carcass weight (values 42.2 and 45.7% of eviscerated weight). This finding was not repeated at 22 weeks or in females and so should be treated with caution. Small differences in yield parameters were also found by Larsen *et al.* (1986) in a comparison of females of BUT, Nicholas and Hybrid strains. The strains differed in weight gain and feed conversion efficiency up to 21 weeks but not in the yield of parts or in the meat content of breast and thighs.

Clayton, Nixey and Monaghan (1978) considered that strain differences in carcass shape (conformation) were not indicative of important differences in yield or composition. There are few definitive studies but it should be noted that in the UK it is now accepted that in pigs and cattle, breed differences in carcass conformation denote commercially important differences in meat yield at the same carcass fat content. The range of breed types available formerly was too narrow for conformation differences to be expressed and it took the introduction of 'foreign' breeds such as Pietrain pigs and Limousin cattle for these to show through. Consequently, the report of Swatland (1980) which shows large differences between two Large White turkey strains in breast yield is interesting. Males of a strain denoted N had a 6 percentage units advantage over a strain D in breast weight as a percentage of live weight (28.7 versus 22.5). This was associated with a higher ratio of breast depth to width in strain N, i.e. an improved conformation. Pectoralis muscle fibre diameter was also greater in strain N.

There is more published evidence of real strain differences in meat yield and composition in broiler chickens than in turkeys. Thus Van Middelkoop, Kuit and Zegwaard (1977) found a range of 1.65 to 2.17% abdominal fat in eight strains whose live weights ranged from 1.5 to 2.0 kg at 45 days of age. ten Have and Scheele (1981) concluded that, in general terms, strains differed more in abdominal fat than body fat. Orr, Hunt and Randall (1984) concluded that differences in yield characteristics between eight strains representing 85–90% of Canadian broilers (*Table 15.5*) were economically important. Ross birds were amongst the heaviest strains and had the highest breast and white meat yields in relation to carcass weight.

Table 15.5 Weight and carcass yield in 8 strains of Canadian broilers aged 7 weeks

	Live weight (g)	Carcass weight as percentage live weight	Percentage of carcass weight				
			Legs	Breast	White meat	Dark meat	Skin
Cobb × Cobb	1998	70.3[c]	34.0[a]	31.6[c]	21.9[a]	21.1[bc]	8.7[b]
H and N Meatnicks	1936	70.9[b]	33.8[ab]	31.8[c]	22.3[d]	21.3[b]	8.9[b]
Hubbard × Hubbard	2015	69.9[c]	33.6[b]	32.5[b]	22.6[d]	20.8[c]	9.5[a]
Peterson × Peterson	1935	71.5[a]	33.8[ab]	32.4[b]	23.1[c]	21.8[a]	8.7[b]
Peterson × Hubbard	2049	71.4[ab]	33.5[bc]	32.6[b]	23.1[c]	21.2[bc]	8.8[b]
Ross × Hubbard	2075	71.1[ab]	33.4[bc]	33.7[a]	24.5[a]	21.1[bc]	8.8[b]
Ross × Arbor Acre	2107	71.2[ab]	33.2[c]	33.9[a]	24.4[a]	21.3[b]	8.6[b]
Shaver × Shaver	2133	70.9[b]	33.4[bc]	32.6[b]	23.7[b]	21.0[bc]	8.7[b]
Ratio highest to lowest	1.07	1.02	1.02	1.07	1.12	1.05	1.10

(Orr, Hunt and Randall, 1984)

Means with different superscripts are significantly different ($P<0.05$)

Genetic selection for weight gain

In turkeys, as in chickens, there has been an impressive trend towards increased weight gains and higher body weights at marketing during the last 10 years or so (Fisher, 1984) and much of this is due to genetic selection for growth rate itself which has a 'moderately high' heritability of 0.3–0.5 (McCarthy and Siegel, 1983). It has been widely speculated that in chickens this has resulted directly in increased fat deposition particularly in the abdomen. Evidence for the view was presented by Chambers, Gavora and Fortin (1981) who compared two modern commercial Canadian strains with an unselected strain representative of commercial birds in 1958. The modern strains weighed about 1700 g at 47 days of age and contained 17.7 and 14.3% lipid in the carcass. The unselected strain weighed 717 g and contained 11.3% lipid; whereas a strain selected from this base population for high 63-day weight weighed 1088 g and contained 14.6% lipid.

Griffin, Butterwith and Goddard (1987) compared male broiler chickens with layer-strain chickens. At 10 weeks of age the broilers contained 60 g of abdominal fat, 1.5% of body weight and the layers contained 5 g, 0.5% of body weight. Part of the 'metabolic' reason for this fast growth and associated over-fatness in meat strains could be an altered hypothalamic control of appetite, resulting in overeating as suggested by McCarthy and S iegel (1983). Evidence that highly selected strains eat so as to almost reach their physical capacity for food was presented by Nir *et al.* (1978).

Despite the evidence supporting the view that selection for rapid growth necessarily increases fat deposition, it has not always been found. In *Table 15.6*, the results of five experiments involving *ad libitum* feeding of male birds of different selection lines are presented. The values for weight and lipid are not directly comparable between experiments because of different procedures. In three cases, birds selected for rapid growth were both heavier and fatter than those selected for slow growth or unselected controls. In the other two cases, selected birds were heavier but had the same composition.

Table 15.6 Body weight and fatness in male broilers from strains selected for high and low growth rate

| | Ref. 1 | | Ref. 2 | | Ref. 3 | | Ref. 4 | | Ref. 5 | |
	H	L	H	L	H	L	H	L	H	L
Final body weight (g)	672	345	1363	571	1624	525	1565	1254	1088	717
Body lipid (%)	6.9	4.8	12.8	13.0	10.9	7.6	9.6	9.8	14.6	11.3
Abdominal fat (%)	–	–	4.4	4.2	1.4	0.6	–	–	1.4	1.2

1 Proudman, Mellen and Anderson (1970). White Plymouth Rocks aged 44 days. Selected for high or low 56-day weight for 15 generations
2 Burgener, Cherry and Siegel (1981). White Plymouth Rocks aged 63 days. Selected for high or low 56-day weight for seven generations
3 Cherry *et al.* (1987). White Plymouth Rocks aged 61 days. Selected for high or low 56-day weight for 23 generations. Same base material as in Ref. 2
4 Pym and Solvyns (1979). Synthetic line aged 63 days. Selected for 5–9 week gain or unselected control line
5 Chambers, Gavora and Fortin (1981). Meat-strain chickens aged 47 days. Selected for high 63-day weight or unselected control line

Pym and Solvyns (1979) found that selection based on feed conversion efficiency was as effective in reducing the percentage of carcass fat as selection for food consumption alone was in increasing it. More recently, Leenstra and Pit (1987) have confirmed this. Only selection directly against abdominal fat was more effective in reducing its contribution to live weight (*Table 15.7*) and this approach carried a penalty in weight gain. Selection for weight gain alone produced the heaviest and fattest birds.

If metabolic differences between strains caused there to be different levels of fat at the same stage of maturity, such differences would also exist at full maturity. Few

Table 15.7 Live weight, fatness and feed conversion ratio in males of four broiler selection lines after four generations

Line[a]	Live weight at 42 days	Abdominal fat (% live weight)	Body fat (% whole bird)	Feed conversion ratio (21–42 days)
AF	1887	1.04	9.3	2.04
FC	1967	1.47	10.3	1.95
GR	2113	2.25	13.9	2.24
GL	2193	2.28	12.9	2.21

(Leenstra and Pit, 1987)

[a] Lines selected from same base population for: ratio AF, abdominal fat (sib selection); FC, Feed conversion; GR, body weight on restricted feeding (70% *ad libitum*); GL, body weight on *ad libitum* feeding

comparisons have been made in mature birds although Chambers, Gavora and Fortin (1981) (*Table 15.6*), found that abdominal fat content in 68-week-old hens was actually lower in the strain selected for high 63-day weight than in the unselected control line. Oritsegbubemi (1987), whose data are discussed by Emmans (1988) in this volume, also considered that chemical composition was essentially similar between seven turkey selection lines at maturity. There was a range in body lipid of 15.7–20.6%, the differences between lines being non-significant.

Although it has not been widely suggested that excessive fatness in the carcass or abdomen is a problem in rapidly-growing turkeys, Nestor (1982) and Bacon, Nestor and Renner (1986) have shown that selection based on 16-week body weight increases fat deposition. Results in *Table 15.8* show that males and females of a strain F selected for 14 generations on the basis of 16-week body weight had more abdominal fat than a random-bred control line (RBC). Subsequent work (Bacon, Nestor and Renner, 1986) showed that after 17 generations the selected birds also had higher concentrations of carcass lipid (8.0 versus 6.0% at 14 weeks in combined groups of males and females). The values for lipid and abdominal fat are low compared with those for chickens (*Tables 15.6* and *15.7*) but the results serve to indicate that the same principles apply. Perhaps selection for feed conversion efficiency should be instituted in turkeys to preserve their advantage over chickens in lipid content.

Table 15.8 Weight and abdominal fat in turkeys selected for 16-week body weight for 14 generations – 102–105 birds in each group

		Live weight (20 weeks, kg)	Abdominal fat (percentage of live weight)
Random-bred	Males	9.9	0.28
Control line	Females	6.7	0.78
Selection line	Males	12.5	0.49
	Females	8.9	1.33

(Nestor, 1982)

To examine the long-term effects of selection on the yield of carcass and carcass parts, Prescott, Wathes and Kirkwood (1985) compared results in a modern UK commercial broiler strain with those in the published literature since 1946. They concluded that whereas growth rate had been dramatically improved by selection during that time, there was little evidence of changes in the allometric relationships between carcass weight and live weight or breast muscle weight and live weight. All the data could be plotted in a straight line with little variation after logarithmic transformation.

Nutrition

Turkeys, like chickens, but unlike the red meat species, are usually fed *ad libitum* and so the nutritional variables of interest are the concentrations of nutrients in the diet with the aim of maximizing growth rate and feed conversion efficiency from birth to slaughter. Less attention has been paid to nutritional effects on yield and composition *per se* although in general the most rapid and efficient growth is achieved when fat forms a low proportion of the weight gained and meat yield is consequently high (because of the high energy cost of depositing fat).

Growth rate and feed conversion efficiency are affected most importantly by protein and energy concentration in the diet and the ratio between these. There appears to be broad agreement in the literature that protein concentration in the prestarter period should be around 28–30% of high quality protein and this should be stepped down gradually to around 16–17% in the finishing period (Potter, Shelton and McCarthy, 1981; Summers *et al.*, 1985; Larsen *et al.*, 1986; Hester *et al.*, 1986). In US and Canadian reports, energy concentration is typically 12–12.5 MJ ME/kg in the prestarter period increasing to about 14 MJ ME/kg at finishing. This increase in energy density is the result of substituting maize for soyabean meal as the concentration of protein is reduced. In UK diets with lower maize and higher barley and wheat inclusions, energy levels are lower on average and do not increase during growth (Rose and Michie, 1987). There seems little point in consciously raising the ratio of energy to protein at the time when fat deposition is becoming more significant.

A recent British compilation of data on nutrient requirements recommends 30% crude protein (1.95% lysine), 12.25 MJ ME/kg in the prestarter period and 17.5% crude protein (0.85% lysine), 12.50 MJ ME/kg in the finishing period with six feeding periods in all (Portsmouth and Marangos, 1986). A recent Canadian report also suggests that energy concentration can be reduced below 13–14 MJ ME/kg on average whilst still obtaining high growth rate and meat yield. However, at 11–12 MJ ME/kg, feed efficiency was reduced as birds compensated by consuming more feed (Summers *et al.*, 1985).

Table 15.9 Effects of protein regime on growth and composition of male Large White turkeys

Protein regime[a]	Live weight at 20 weeks (kg)	Feed:gain 0–20 weeks	Percentage of live weight		Fat (percentage deboned carcass)[b]
			Abdominal fat	Meat yield	
1 (20–8)	5.50[1]	3.47[1]	0.69[3]	42.3[1]	6.2
2 (24–12)	11.44[2]	2.73[2]	1.66[1]	48.3[2]	11.0
3 (28–16)	13.42[3]	2.52[2]	0.98[2,3]	51.8[3]	10.4
4 (32–20)	13.39[3]	2.55[2]	1.32[1,2]	51.8[3]	11.2

(Summers *et al.*, 1985)

[a] Figures in brackets are percentage crude protein in first and last (prestarter and finisher) periods
Energy concentration and protein to energy ratio in the 5 periods for the optimal regime (No. 3) were 12.6, 12.7, 12.9, 13.2 and 13.4 MJ ME/kg and 22.2, 19.7, 17.0, 14.4 and 11.9 g CP/MJ ME
[b] Calculated from other results

Means with different superscripts are significantly different ($P<0.05$)

The results in *Table 15.9* are from the study of Summers *et al.* (1985) in which Large White turkeys were given four diffferent 'protein regimes' between birth and 20 weeks. The regimes differed in protein concentration, differentials between them being retained over five periods, each of which lasted 4 weeks, during which overall concentrations were gradually reduced. ME concentrations were the same for each protein regime in each period, increasing from 12.6 to 13.4 MJ ME/kg from the prestarter to the finisher periods (i.e. standard Canadian practice).

Regime 3 (28 16) won the bout in terms of weight gain, food efficiency, abdominal fat content and meat yield. The leanest carcasses were obtained on the lowest protein regime (20–8) although this was associated with subnormal growth. There was no benefit in this study in moving to the highest protein concentrations although strains with higher potential rates of body protein deposition might benefit from such regimes.

Salmon, Dunkelgod and Wilson (1982a) questioned the necessity of so many dietary changes during growth. In a comparison of different protein concentrations they found that growth and feed conversion efficiency were as high with two as with eight changes so long as protein concentration was high, i.e. 29–30% during 0–12 weeks and 22–24% during 12–24 weeks for males. Clearly protein was provided in excess towards the end of each period. The number of dietary changes (two, four or eight) had little effect on meat yield or the proportions of skin, bone or fat although both high protein regimes produced the highest meat yields and lowest proportions of bone and skin. Salmon, Dunkelgod and Wilson (1982b) made the important observation that the effect of protein concentration on meat content was particularly marked in the high-value breast which is perhaps not surprising in view of its potential for high relative growth during the finishing period (Table 15.3). Other workers have observed this positive effect of high protein levels on breast yield (Nixey, personal communication).

Salmon (1974), on the basis of his own data and published reports, considered that variation in the ratio of protein to energy concentrations was less critical in its effects on fat deposition in turkeys than in chickens. In his own study, different concentrations of dietary fat (2.9, 6.0 and 14.5% of diet) were given during the period 0–24 weeks. The diets also differed in protein to energy ratio. Growth rate was higher in birds given the high fat diets as was the lipid content of thigh meat and breast meat. In breast meat the average values between 4 and 24 weeks for the lipid content of dry matter were 1.7, 2.6 and 3.5% for the diets with 2.9, 6.0 and 14.5% fat respectively. The proportion of grade A finish carcasses was 84% for the low fat and 98% for the high fat diets. The effects of protein to energy ratio were less marked than this although the range in the ratio was smaller than in other studies (for example, Summers et al., 1985, Table 15.9).

Effects of pre-slaughter and processing factors

Moran (1977) reviewed the effects of holding, dressing, evisceration and chilling on broilers and turkeys of different sizes. He concluded that holding for a 10–12 h period before slaughter produced a 3–6% weight loss in small turkeys and a 2–8% weight loss in large turkeys, the lower figure representing the value at slaughter age and the higher some 8–12 weeks previously. Moran (1977) concluded that if losses greater than these, which represent the disappearance of gut contents, are to be avoided, birds should be processed within 12 to 16 h of food and water withdrawal.

Salmon (1979b) investigated the effects in Small White turkeys of a 12- or 24-h holding period with and without both food and water. The results (Table 15.10) showed that eviscerated carcass weight was lower at 24 h than at 12 h and was lower if both food and water were withheld. He concluded that holding should be limited to 12 h and birds should have access to water. The extra weight lost, presumably by dehydration, was not recovered on chilling since the weight gain in that process was the same for all treatments.

Table 15.10 Effects of food and water deprivation on carcass yield in Small White turkeys. Six birds per treatment held in battery pens at 27°C

Treatment		Carcass weight (percentage of live weight)
Fed and watered		75.1
Food deprived	12 h	74.8
	24 h	73.2
Food + water deprived	12 h	72.9
	24 h	72.0

(Salmon, 1979b)

Veerkamp (1986) showed that loss of tissue weight was increased if birds were tightly packed in crates during the holding periods and suggested that this was due to a high temperature and relative humidity. Previously, Chen *et al.* (1983) showed that holding loss increased in broilers from 1.6% of prehold weight after 8 h at 10°C to 8.3% after 16 h at 32°C. Jensen (1981) has shown that transport time has an effect on reducing carcass weight greater than that due simply to time without feed.

The changes in weight from a posthold condition to an oven ready carcass or to a stage when cutting up commences depend greatly on processing procedures. Moran (1977) found that under Canadian conditions, dressing loss (blood and feathers) was about 8% in large and 9% in small turkey strains and decreased as age increased. Evisceration loss was about 14% in large and 16% in small strains and these losses similarly declined as age increased during the finishing period. For these reasons, carcass weight as a proportion of liveweight increases as birds get older and heavier.

Salmon (1980) in female Large White turkeys, examined the effects of various changes in processing procedures, for example plucking, evisceration and chilling. Small but commercially significant effects were observed, for example dry plucking reduced chilled carcass yield.

Finally, it is obvious that different procedures during the preparation of processed products will have a large effect on the final retail yield of cuts, in many cases overwhelming the effects of the factors discussed in this review. Nakai and Chen (1986) for example, found that the weight of fried broiler breasts varied between 61 and 85% of raw weight depending on the coating used during preparation for frying.

Concluding remarks

It is clear that meat yield and carcass composition in turkeys are affected by many factors in production and processing. In the future, in order for turkey to continue to compete successfully with other meats, more attention will need to be paid to combining all the factors in optimal and economic ways.

As the demand for turkey as a source of lean meat for use in added-value products increases, there is likely to be a trend towards higher slaughter weights.

This emphasizes the need for improved genetic strains which grow rapidly and efficiently to heavy weights.

It is necessary to continually reassess the optimum slaughter weights for new strains. If they are slaughtered when immature, carcass yield and percentage breast will be low. The concentration of lipid may be so low as to reduce eating satisfaction, particularly in the breast. On the other hand, slaughtering birds when too mature reduces feed efficiency and may increase the concentration of lipid to undesirable levels. It should be emphasized that an important reason for the current popularity of turkey is a perceived low fat content compared with other meats.

The current evidence suggests that turkey strains selected for increased growth rate to an early age reach correspondingly heavier mature weights and are similar in body composition to other strains when compared at the same stage of maturity. In other words there is no strong evidence that selection increases body fatness for 'metabolic' reasons as it appears to have done in some broiler chicken strains. Nevertheless, continuous monitoring should be done to check on this point. If fatness does increase, alternative selection strategies will have to be devised, on the experience with chickens.

Despite the importance of variation in yield and composition to profitability in the processing industry, the practical difficulties of obtaining and recording data in plants have militated against any developments in the objective measurement of these characteristics. There are therefore few schemes which base producer payments on carcass quality (this applies to broiler chickens as well as turkeys). Development of cheap and accurate techniques for assessing weight, meat and fat content and some aspects of meat quality would greatly assist in matching future production to changing consumer requirements.

References

Bacon, W. L., Nestor, K. E. and Renner, P. A. (1986). The influence of genetic increases in body weight and shank width on the abdominal fat pad and carcass composition of turkeys. *Poultry Science*, **65**, 391–397

Broadbent, L. A., Wilson, B. J. and Fisher, C. (1981). The composition of the broiler chicken at 56 days of age: output, components and chemical composition. *British Poultry Science*, **22**, 385–390

Burgener, J. A., Cherry, J. A. and Siegel, P. B. (1981). The association between sartorial fat and fat deposition in meat-type chickens. *Poultry Science*, **60**, 54–62

Chambers, J. R., Gavora, J. S. and Fortin, A. (1981). Genetic changes in meat-type chickens in the last twenty years. *Canadian Journal of Animal Science*, **61**, 555–563

Chen, T. C., Schultz, C. D., Reece, F. N., Lott, B. D. and McNaughton, J. L. (1983). The effect of extended holding time, temperature and dietary energy on yields of broilers. *Poultry Science*, **62**, 1566–1577

Cherry, J. A., Nir, I., Jones, D. E. Dunnington, E. A., Nitsan, Z. and Siegel, P. B. (1987). Growth-associated traits in parental and F_1 populations of chickens under different feeding programs 1. *Ad libitum* feeding. *Poultry Science*, **66**, 1–9

Clayton, G. A., Nixey, C. and Monaghan, G. (1978). Meat yield in turkeys. *British Poultry Science*, **19**, 755–763

Emmans, G. C. (1988). The growth of turkeys. In *Proceedings 21st Poultry Science Symposium. Recent Advances in Turkey Science*, edited by C. Nixey and T. C. Grey. London, Butterworths

Evans, A. J. (1977). The growth of fat. In *Growth and Poultry Meat Production* (Boorman, K. N. and Wilson, B. J., eds), pp. 29–64. Edinburgh, British Poultry Science Ltd

Fisher, C. (1984). Fat deposition in broilers. In *Fats in Animal Nutrition* (Wiseman, J., ed.), pp. 437–470. London, Butterworths

Grey, T. C., Robinson, D. and Jones, J. M. (1982). Effect of age and sex on the eviscerated yield, muscle and edible offal of a commercial broiler strain. *British Poultry Science*, **23**, 289–298

Grey, T. C., Robinson, D., Jones, J. M., Stock, S. W. and Thomas, N. L. (1983). Effect of age and sex on the composition of muscle and skin from a commercial broiler strain. *British Poultry Science*, **24**, 219–231

Griffin, H. D., Butterwith, S. C. and Goddard, C. (1987). Contribution of lipoprotein lipase to differences in fatness between broiler and layer-strain chickens. *British Poultry Science*, **28**, 197–206

Hakansson, J., Eriksson, S. and Svensson, S. A. (1978a). *The Influence of Feed Energy Level on Feed Consumption, Growth and Development of Different Organs of Chicks. Report No.57*. Swedish University of Agricultural Science, Department of Animal Husbandry

Hakansson, J., Eriksson, S. and Svensson, S. A. (1978b). *The Influence of Feed Energy Level on Chemical Composition of Tissues and on the Energy and Protein Utilisation by Broiler Chicks. Report No.59*. Swedish University of Agricultural Science, Department of Animal Husbandry

Hartung, T. E. and Froning, G. W. (1968). Variation of physical components of turkey carcasses as influenced by sex, age and strain. *Poultry Science*, **47**, 1348–1355

Heath, J. L., Covey, R. C. and Owens, S. L. (1980). Abdominal leaf fat separation as a result of evisceration of broiler carcasses. *Poultry Science*, **59**, 2456–2461

Hester, P. Y., Peng, I. C., Adams, R. L., Furumoto, E. J., Larsen, J. E., Klingensmith, P. M., Pike, O. A. and Stadelman, W. J. (1986). Comparison of two lighting regimens and drinker cleaning programmes on the performance and incidence of leg abnormalities in turkey males. *British Poultry Science*, **27**, 63–73

Hurwitz, S., Frisch, Y., Bar, A., Eisner, U., Bengal, I. and Pines, M. (1983). The amino acid requirements of growing turkeys. 1. Model construction and parameter estimation. *Poultry Science*, **62**, 2208–2217

Jensen, O. (1981). Influence of transport-time on yield of broilers. In *Quality of Poultry Meat* (Mulder, R. W. A. W., Scheele, C. W. and Veerkamp, C. H., eds), pp. 38–43. Spelderholt Institute for Poultry Research, The Netherlands

Kempster, A. J., Cook, G. L. and Grantley-Smith, M. (1986). National estimates of the body composition of British cattle, sheep and pigs with special reference to trends in fatness. A review. *Meat Science*, **17**, 107–138

Larmond, E. and Moran, E. T. (1983). Effect of finish grade and internal basting of the breast with oil on sensory evaluation of small white toms. *Poultry Science*, **62**, 1110–1112

Larsen, J. E., Adams, R. L., Peng, I. C. and Stadelman, W. J. (1986). Growth, feed conversions and yields of turkey parts of three strains of hen turkeys as influenced by age. *Poultry Science*, **65**, 2076–2081

Leenstra, F. R. and Pit, R. (1987). Fat deposition in a broiler strain. 2. Comparisons among lines selected for less abdominal fat, lower feed conversion ratio, and higher body weight after restricted and *ad libitum* feeding. *Poultry Science*, **66**, 193–202

Leeson, S. and Summers, J. D. (1980a). Production and carcass characteristics of the broiler chicken. *Poultry Science*, **59**, 786–798

Leeson, S. and Summers, J. D. (1980b). Production and carcass characteristics of the Large White turkey. *Poultry Science*, **59**, 1237–1245

McCarthy, J. C. and Siegel, P. B. (1983). A review of genetical and physiological effects of selection in meat-type poultry. *Animal Breeding Abstracts*, **51**, 87–94

Moran, E. T. (1977). Growth and meat yield in poultry. In *Growth and Poultry Meat Production* (Boorman, K. N. and Wilson, B. J., eds), pp. 145–173. Edinburgh, British Poultry Science

Moran, E. T., Orr, H. L. and Larmond, E. (1970). Production efficiency, grades and yields with the Large White turkey as related to sex and age. *Poultry Science*, **49**, 475–493

Moran, E. T., Orr, H. L. and Larmond, E. (1971). Sex and age related production efficiency, grades and yields with the Small White broiler-fryer type turkey. *Poultry Science*, **50**, 411–425

Nakai, Y. and Chen, T. C. (1986). Effects of coating preparation methods on yields and compositions of deep-fat fried chicken parts. *Poultry Science*, **65**, 307–313

Nestor, K. E. (1982). The influence of genetic increases in body weight on the abdominal fat pad of turkeys. *Poultry Science*, **61**, 2301–2304

Nir, I., Nitsan, Z., Dror, Y. and Shapira, N. (1978). Influence of overfeeding on growth, obesity and intestinal tract in young chicks of light and heavy breeds. *British Journal of Nutrition*, **39**, 27–35

Oritsegbubemi, A. A. (1987). The relationship between mature body size and body composition of different turkey strains. MSc thesis, University of Glasgow, UK

Orr, H. L., Gillis, W. A., Usborne, W. R. and Stevens, R. W. C. (1974). Influence of strain and age on the grade and yield of component parts of turkey broilers. *Poultry Science*, **53**, 1382–1386

Orr, H. L., Hunt, E. C. and Randall, C. J. (1984). Yield of carcass, parts, meat, skin and bone of eight strains of broilers. *Poultry Science*, **63**, 2197–2200

Peng, I. C., Adams, R. L., Furumoto, E. J., Hester, P. Y., Larsen, J. E., Pike, O. A. and Stadelman, W. J. (1985). Allometric growth patterns and meat yields of carcass parts of turkey toms as influenced by lighting programs and age. *Poultry Science*, **64**, 871–876

Perenyi, M., Suto, Z. and Ujvarine, J. (1980). Changes in the proportion of the carcass parts of male and female heavy type turkeys between 4 and 20 weeks of age. In *Proceedings 6th European Poultry Conference*, pp. 514–519. World's Poultry Science Association

Portsmouth, J. and Marangos, A. (1986). Rations to meet all requirements. *Poultry World*, December, 9–11

Potter, L. M., Shelton, J. R. and McCarthy, J. P. (1981). Lysine and protein requirements of growing turkeys. *Poultry Science*, **60**, 2678–2686

Prescott, N. J., Wathes, C. M. and Kirkwood, J. K. (1985). Growth, food intake and development in broiler cockerels raised to maturity. *Animal Production*, **41**, 239–245

Proudman, J. A., Mellen, W. J. and Anderson, D. L. (1970). Utilization of feed in fast and slow-growing lines of chickens. *Poultry Science*, **49**, 961–972

Pym, R. A. E. and Solvyns, A. J. (1979). Selection for food conversion in broilers: body composition of birds selected for increased body-weight gain, food consumption and food conversion ratio. *British Poultry Science*, **20**, 87–97

Rose, S. P. and Michie, W. (1983). Estimation of abdominal fat in laying hens, turkeys and broilers using calipers. *Journal of Agricultural Science, Cambridge*, **101**, 345–350

Rose, S. P. and Michie, W. (1987). Environmental temperature and dietary protein concentrations for growing turkeys. *British Poultry Science*, **28**, 213–218

Salmon, R. E. (1974). Effect of dietary fat concentration and energy to protein ratio on the performance, yield of carcass components and composition of skin and meat of turkeys as related to age. *British Poultry Science*, **15**, 543–560

Salmon, R. E. (1979a). Slaughter losses and carcass composition of the Medium White Turkey. *British Poultry Science*, **20**, 297–302

Salmon, R. E. (1979b). Effect of food and water deprivation on live-weight shrinkage, eviscerated carcass yield and water absorption during chilling of turkey carcasses. *British Poultry Science*, **20**, 303–306

Salmon, R. E. (1980). Effects of method of processing and chilling of turkey carcasses on processing losses, water absorption and yields. *British Poultry Science*, **21**, 253–256

Salmon, R. E., Dunkelgod, K. E. and Wilson, B. J. (1982a).Influence of dietary protein concentration and frequency of diet changes on rate of growth efficiency of food utilization and carcass quality of Large White turkeys. *British Poultry Science*, **23**, 501–517

Salmon, R. E., Dunkelgod, K. E. and Wilson, B. J. (1982b). Nutrition, age and strain effects on carcass quality and meat yield of Large White turkeys. *British Poultry Science*, **23**, 519–526

Summers, J. D., Leeson, S., Bedford, M. and Spratt, D. (1985). Influence of dietary protein and energy on performance and carcass composition of heavy turkeys. *Poultry Science*, **64**, 1921–1933

Swatland, H. J. (1980). A histological basis for differences in breast meat yield between two strains of white turkeys. *Journal of Agricultural Science, Cambridge*, **94**, 383–388

ten Have, H. G. M. and Scheele, C. W. (1981). A comparison of the effects of different nutritional factors on the carcass composition of three broiler strains at two ages. In *Quality of Poultry Meat* (Mulder, R. W. A. W., Scheele, C. W. and Veerkamp, C. H., eds), pp. 386–396. Spelderholt Institute for Poultry Research, The Netherlands van Middelkoop, J. H., Kuit, A. R. and Zegwaard, A. (1977). Genetic factors in broiler fat deposition. In *Growth and Poultry Meat Production* (Boorman, K. N. and Wilson, B. J., eds), pp. 131–143. Edinburgh, British Poultry Science Ltd

Veerkamp, C. H. (1986). Fasting and yield of broilers. *Poultry Science,* **65**, 1299–1304

WPSA (1984). Method of dissection of broiler carcasses and description of parts. WPSA European Federation. Working Group V. Editor: Professor J. Fris Jensen, Roligheddsvej 25, 1958 Frederiksberg C, Denmark

Chapter 16

Turkey meat texture

T. C. Grey

Introduction

Most consumer complaints about turkey meat have been concerned with meat texture and over the years considerable effort has been expended in elucidating the causes of variability in the texture of turkey meat. Much of the research was concentrated over a period of 20 years up to the mid 1970s. Our knowledge of the factors influencing turkey meat texture has increased since then, but the inherent problems are still present and considerable research effort is still required to guarantee the production of a product acceptable to the consumer. Unfortunately, the momentum of research effort has diminished over recent years, although the reasons for this reduction are not clear.

In this review on turkey meat texture, it is therefore proposed to highlight earlier findings in the field and to update more recent research on mainly whole bird production.

Effects of breed, sex, age, conformation and diet

Breed, sex, age, etc. are included under one heading because there is new evidence to show that there is possibly an interaction between some of these factors which, when taken in isolation, would result in duplicated discussion.

As shown in *Table 16.1*, Marsden *et al.* (1952) found considerable variation in breast muscle texture in four turkey strains. Uneviscerated Broad Breasted Bronze, Beltsville Small White, Standard-bred Bronze and White Holland were aged in air at 1–2°C for periods between 1 and 15 days. Of these four strains, Beltsville Small White received the highest taste panel rating. The important finding from this work was that even after an excessive ageing period, tough birds were still obtained and leg muscles were more tender and less variable than breast. Marsden *et al.* (1957) suggested that juicier breast muscle tended to be more tender and that plump turkeys cooked under similar conditions to those turkeys with smaller breast muscles were less tender. In this study no consistent effect of diet on texture, was found, irrespective of whether the diets were predominantly cereal, edible oil-meal or linseed oil-meal.

Carlson *et al.* (1962) reached a similar conclusion using birds fed diets containing combinations of corn, grain, oats and fat, and found no measurable effects of diet, strain or sex in their studies. Harkin, Kitzmiller and Gilpin (1958) had also

Table 16.1 Tenderness of breast and leg of roasted turkeys of different varieties, as described by five judges (12 males and 12 females of each variety)

Variety	Sex	Tenderness of breast, percent of 60 samples described as					Tenderness of leg, percent of 60 samples described as		
		Very tender	Tender	Moderately tender	Tough	Very tough	Very tender	Tender	Moderately tender
Beltsville Small White	Male	20	42	33	5	–	37	55	8
	Female	40	35	22	3	–	60	40	–
Broad Breasted Bronze	Male	23	59	10	8	–	25	72	3
	Female	25	47	23	5	–	37	60	3
Standard bred Bronze	Male	12	25	48	15	–	23	72	5
	Female	16	47	22	15	–	35	60	5
White Holland	Male	27	31	22	18	2	32	60	8
	Female	20	27	17	31	5	25	70	5

Courtesy of Marsden *et al.* (1962)

previously found no dietary effects on texture after comparing diets containing animal or vegetable protein supplemented with vitamins A and D and lard. The effects of high and low energy levels on meat texture (Goertz *et al.,* 1955) were also not significant with Broad Breasted Bronze turkeys, however, a slight preference for birds grown on the high density diet was obtained. Goertz *et al.* (1961) using male and female Beltsville White turkeys could find no significant effect on texture as a result of feeding different combinations of cereal grains. Goodwin (1966) using an Allo-Kramer shear press evaluated six strains of male and female Broad Breasted Bronze turkeys aged 26 weeks and found that females were more tender than males.

Although only three birds of each sex and strain were studied, the data obtained indicated that a taste panel would have difficulty in differentiating the meat texture between the sexes. No textural difference was found between breast and thigh muscle. Stadelman, Mostert and Harrington (1966) compared two sexes and five strains at 12, 18 and 24 weeks of age after postmortem ageing in ice-slush for varying periods up to 24 h. No significant differences in shear force values were found between strains or sexes, although the period of ageing had a significant effect. A reduced resistance to shear occurred with increasing age and thigh meat was tougher than breast. Larmond, Petrasovits and Moran (1971) found that at the onset of sexual maturity, 22 weeks for males and 17 weeks for females, the toughness of breast muscle suddenly increased whether evaluated by an experienced taste panel or the Warner-Bratzler shearing device.

Ngoka *et al.* (1982) found no difference in breast muscle texture between the sexes of 16- and 20-week-old birds. However, 16-week turkeys were significantly tougher than the 20-week birds.

Seemann and Bohn (1983) compared both sexes of five strains of turkey, i.e. BUT 5, BIG 5, BUT 8, BUT 6 and Nicholas. The females were killed at 72 and 101 days and males at 139 and 160 days. *M. pectoralis profundus* (minor muscle) and *m. biceps femoris* (leg muscle) were removed and grilled to an internal temperature of 70°C.

Statistically significant differences in shear values were found between strains and ages in the minor and leg muscles of females and between strain only in the males as shown in *Tables 16.2* and *16.3*. It was not possible to compare the sexes because of the age effect nor was it feasible to compare the texture of the leg muscle

Table 16.2 Means of shear values (kg) of *m. pectoralis profundus* and *m. biceps femoris* from female turkey

	M. pectoralis profundus		*M. biceps femoris*
	Parallel sample	*Vertical sample*	
Strain 1	1.87[b]	1.08	2.44[a,b]
2	2.04[b]	1.25	2.73[a]
3	2.02[b]	1.08	2.49[a,b]
4	2.20[a,b]	1.27	2.29[b]
5	2.41[a]	1.25	2.72[a]
Age (days)			
72	2.02[b]	1.22	2.63[a]
101	2.19[a]	1.16	2.44[b]

After Seemann and Bohn (1983)

[a,b] Values not having the same superscripts within each column are significantly different at the 5% level

Table 16.3 Means of shear values (kg) of *m. pectoralis profundus* and *m. biceps femoris* from male turkey

	M. pectoralis profundus		M. biceps femoris
	Parallel sample	Vertical sample	
Strain 1	1.79[a]	1.35[a, b]	3.20[a]
2	1.86[a]	1.54[a]	3.06[a, b]
3	1.55[b]	1.28[b]	2.91[a, b]
4	1.61[b]	0.97[c]	2.58[b]
5	1.58[b]	1.17[b]	2.99[a, b]
Age (days)			
139	1.64	1.30	2.91
160	1.72	1.23	2.98

After Seemann and Bohn (1983)

[a,b,c] Values not having the same superscripts within each column are significantly different at the 5% level

with that of the minor muscle because of the difference in sample size used for the Warner Bratzler shear press. Grey *et al.* (1986) found a significant diet versus strain interaction in one experiment and generally found that a high energy, low protein diet resulted in more tender breast muscle (*Tables 16.4* and *16.5*). Taste panel evaluation demonstrated considerable variability within a treatment and evidence was obtained, which indicated that this variability was related to muscle structure. Seemann *et al.* (1986) found that tough samples were found to have more giant cells, fibre defects and larger cell size.

Summary

There is conflicting evidence as to whether particular strains of turkey produce meat which significantly differs in texture. The variability in texture within a treatment is indisputable. However this variability associated with samples of insufficient size may have resulted in research workers finding no significant effects. Both age and weight factors influence texture. Younger turkeys have a much wider range of texture values and some are extremely tough.

This contrasts with the heavier birds which tend to be more tender and have less variable texture. There is also some evidence to indicate that strains respond differently to diets with differing energy/protein contents, particularly those strains which are currently in commercial production. There are considerable problems associated with comparison of the sexes, not least of these are the age/weight effect and composition.

Effects of stress, catching, transport, transfer and killing

With regard to stress and its effect on meat texture, the question is: how do we measure stress and can it be related to the postmortem quality of the carcass? Freeman (1984) and Freeman *et al.* (1984) have examined the effects of transportation as a stressor and obtained evidence of increased adrenal cortical activity and marked hyperlipacidaemia which was a glucagon mediated response.

Table 16.4 Taste panel scores for texture of turkey breasts

Diet	Mean	panel	scores
	Strain A	Strain B	Strain C
1	4.11[a]	4.22[a]	3.28[b]
2	2.99[a]	3.80[a]	3.82[c]
x =	3.55	4.01	3.55

Courtesy of Grey *et al.* (1986)

Diet 1. Low energy UK-type ration containing wheat and barley
Diet 2. Commercial diet containing 200 g/kg protein
Both diets fed from week 16 to killing.

[a] $n = 10$
[b] $n - 11$
[c] $n = 9$

Table 16.5 Taste panel scores for texture and juiciness, male turkeys fed different diets

		Experiment 2[a]		Experiment 3[b]		
		Strain C	Strain D	Strain C	Strain D	Strain E
Texture						
Diet 1	Mean	3.89	3.75	3.85	4.29	3.96
	Range	2.1–5.9	2.2–4.6	2.9–5.2	2.9–6.4	3.1–5.6
Diet 3	Mean	3.47	3.47	3.77	3.65	3.91
	Range	2.4–5.8	2.0–5.8	2.1–6.1	2.5–6.5	2.3–5.6
Juiciness						
Diet 1	Mean	4.93	4.59	4.55	4.52	4.86
	Range	3.6–6.0	3.4–5.6	3.6–6.0	3.6–5.2	3.6–5.8
Diet 3	Mean	4.75	4.75	4.99	4.88	5.20
	Range	3.6–5.6	3.5–6.2	3.8–5.8	3.9–6.0	3.7–6.4

Courtesy of Grey *et al.* (1986)

$n = 10$ treatment

[a] Birds 16 weeks of age held chilled until sampled
[b] Birds 20 weeks of age frozen until sampled

Taste panel scores   1 = Extremely tender   8 = Extremely tough
                     1 = Extremely juicy   8 = Extremely dry

Diet 1. Low energy UK-type ration containing wheat and barley
Diet 3. High energy American-type ration containing maize up to 800 g/kg

Birds prior to transportation are always deprived of food for a minimum of 6 h and this depletes liver glycogen to negligible levels, at least in broilers (P. D. Warriss, personal communication). As far as can be ascertained, none of these physiological changes have been directly related to muscle texture. However, studies have been made of the effects of struggle on the subsequent rates of glycolysis and muscle texture, and these will be discussed in the biochemistry section below. van Hoof (1979) studied the influence of the antemortem and perimortem factors on the biochemical and physical characteristics of turkey muscle.

Turkeys slaughtered on the farm without transportation were significantly tougher than those transported before three other treatments involving electrical stunning and varied delay before manual or mechanical slaughter. Because of practical difficulties in this study, manually farm slaughtered birds were not plucked and were cooled at ambient temperature for 3 h before being placed in a chill-room at +2°C. These birds may have undergone accelerated glycolysis through being held longer at high temperatures, resulting in heat shortening and hence toughening, whereas industrially processed birds were more tender due to the effectiveness of the stunning procedure.

Ma and Addis (1973) also studied the effects of struggle using male turkeys aged 5 months which, in this study, were bled but not plucked or eviscerated and stored at +2°C. They found that struggling decreased the time course of rigor and that some unrestrained birds had completed glycolysis (pH 5.5) within 5 min post mortem. Breast muscles removed after 24 h ageing and cooked to an internal temperature of 80°C showed no significant difference in shear value between treatments. Birds processed similarly but electrically stunned before exsanguination again showed no significant textural differences. As with Van Hoof's study, the greatest variation in texture was found in the muscle from birds which had struggled. Ma and Addis (1973) commented on the difficulty in eliminating struggle completely and that emotional stress as well as heat stress may also be contributory factors.

Although not discussed by the authors, 6-month-old male turkeys were considerably more tender than 3-month-old birds used in this study. Froning, Babji and Mather (1978) with 6-month-old turkeys, examined the effects of preslaughter temperature, stress, struggle and anaesthetization, on breast muscles cooked to 82°C. Allo-Kramer shear press values were significantly higher in heat stressed and free struggle birds when compared with anaesthetized and cold-stressed birds after normal processing and overnight ageing in ice-slush. Goodwin, Mickelberry and Stadelman (1961) studied different methods of human slaughter in 20-week-old male and female Broad Breasted Bronze turkeys. They compared oral administration of nembutal, debraining, electric knife, carbon dioxide immobilization, reserpine tranquillization and a control group of no special antemortem treatment. All were killed by severing the carotid arteries and jugular vein and birds were aged for 4 and 24 h.

Method of humane slaughter had no significant effect on shear values of breast muscles; however, all the humane treatments resulted in an increase in shear value of the high muscles. Tenderness improved with increase in ageing time. Babji, Froning and Ngoka (1982) also examined the effects of preslaughter environmental temperature. Holding birds at 38°C for 4 h prior to slaughter resulted in significantly increased breast muscle shear values when compared with cold-stressed (4.4°C) birds, suggesting that a cool preslaughter environment produces meat with better quality characteristics. Ngoka et al. (1982) found that anaesthetization prior to slaughter produced more tender breast meat when compared with a non-anaesthetized free struggle control group. They also found that excitation prior to anaesthetization also resulted in significantly more tender meat. No differences in texture were found between the sexes and 16-week-old turkeys were tougher than 20-week birds. All the birds in this study were aged in ice-slush overnight and frozen. These results are in agreement with Landes, Dawson and Price (1971) who found that even after ageing in ice-slush for 72 h, the mean shear value for ten breast muscles from anaesthetized turkeys was half the value obtained for ten control birds.

Summary

Of the factors which have been shown to influence meat texture, struggle, preslaughter heat stress and possibly the cooling rate would all seem to be implicated and to increase toughness to a significant extent. Electrical stunning if carried out correctly may reduce the adverse effects of struggle, although emotional stress and the bird's reaction to stress may also result in variation in the rate of *postmortem* glycolysis and the ultimate texture of the muscle.

Scalding and plucking

No recent studies have been carried out on the effects of scalding and plucking on the texture of turkeys. Most of the work was completed between the late 1940s and the early 1960s and researchers have not felt the need to re-examine the conclusions reached in these earlier studies. Initially, efficiency of feather removal and carcass finish were evaluated (Pool *et al.*, 1954) and subsequently carcass quality after up to 12 months' frozen storage (Klose and Pool, 1954). The effects of temperature and duration of scalding on the tenderness of broilers were also studied by Shannon, Marion and Stadelman (1957). Klose *et al.* (1959) summarized their earlier findings on texture; increased scalding time and temperature had significant although small toughening effects on breast meat texture even after ageing up to 70 h.

Table 16.6 Toughening effect of machine picking versus hand picking for turkey fryers[a]

Picking procedure	Shear force of pectoralis super.		Fraction with shear force $\leqslant 20\,lb$
	Average of 12 fried halves (lb)	Range (lb)	
Hand	23	16–50+[c]	9/12
machine[b]	44	16–50+[d]	2/12
	Average of 16 fried halves[f]		
Hand	12	8–16	16/16
machine[b]	38	29–50+[e]	0/16
	Average of 12 roasted halves[g]		
Hand	11	7–18	12/12
machine[b]	22	9–34	6/12

Courtesy of Klose *et al.* (1959)

[a] Six to eight Beltsville White 14–15-week old hen turkeys per group scalded at 138–139°F for about 45 s; after picking and warm evisceration, chilled for 24 h (7 h in ice-slush and 17 h in drained ice); frozen and either fried or roasted from the frozen state
[b] Commercial line of double drum pickers, consisting of 8 ft rougher, 8 ft reverse picker and 3 ft neck finisher all acting on birds suspended by feet; and a 3 ft hock picker, 8 ft finisher and 7 ft washer all acting on birds suspended by neck
[c] One of 12 shear values in excess of 50 lb, and averaged in as 50 lb
[d] Nine of 12 shear values in excess of 50 lb, and averaged in as 50 lb
[e] Two of 16 shear values in excess of 50 lb, and averaged in as 50 lb
[f] Least significant difference (1%) = 4
[g] Least significant difference (1%) = 7

Mechanical plucking resulted in a considerable increase in breast muscle toughness when compared with hand plucking (*Table 16.6*). The effect of the number of pluckers used was cumulative and the differences in texture were not resolved after ageing for up to 24 h. As can be seen in *Table 16.6* a considerable range of shear values was obtained both within and between treatments. Wise and Stadelman (1959) using 16-week-old Leghorn pullets clarified the situation by keeping plucking conditions constant and varying the time and temperature of scald. These authors found that variations due to temperature, time and depth of muscle layer were all highly significant. The outer 0–2 mm layer was most affected by treatments, being the toughest while the innermost layer was the most tender. Wise and Stadelman (1961) then repeated this work with turkeys using thicker slices of breast and again found that the outer layer (0–6 mm) toughened faster at temperatures above 50°C than the rest of the breast when the scald time was kept constant at 12 min.

They concluded that the toughening effect of excessive scalding was a direct function of the tissue temperature during the early postmortem period and that the presence of skin or a lower environmental temperature during this critical postmortem period decreased the scald effect. It should be noted that the scald times used by Wise and Stadelman (1961) were excessive and in a later study (Stadelman, Mostert and Harrington, 1966) when turkeys aged between 12 and 24 weeks were scalded at 60°C for 45 s, no variation in texture with depth of muscle was found. Goodwin (1966) using 26-week-old males and females scalded at 60°C, only observed a significant sex effect on the texture of breast muscle, although the outer 0–3 mm layer was marginally tougher. No differences were found between the six strains studied and males were tougher than females.

Summary

There is unequivocal evidence that mechanical plucking and an extended period of scalding above 50°C result in an increase in toughness of the breast muscle. The effects of both treatments seem to be additive and this is reflected in the increased shear values found in the outer 6 mm of the breast muscle. There is a likelihood that the increase in toughness may be due to heat shortening since it is reduced by the presence of skin and the effects of cooling in the immediate environment.

Chilling, ageing and chill storage

The problem of bird to bird variability in breast meat texture has been mentioned earlier and Klose *et al.* (1959) encountered the same problem in studies on turkey processing. Ageing of turkeys in ice-slush resulted in a rapid but very variable reduction in toughness during the first 4 h, tenderization continued up to 12 h post mortem, however, very little change occurred beyond 12 h. Deep fat frying of turkey halves resulted in tougher meat, the authors commenting that deep fat frying from the frozen state required about one-fifth of the time to cook when compared with roasted whole birds. It may be that the disruption of muscles attached to bone during the halving of the birds rather than the method of cooking resulted in increased toughness during cooking from the frozen state. Holding turkeys in a thawed state (1–2°C) after frozen storage had a similar tenderizing effect to an equal period of chilling before freezing. Dodge and Stadelman (1959) compared 14-week-old chickens and turkeys after ageing in air at 3.9°C for 2, 5 and 8 h. Significant differences in the shear values were found and the authors concluded that these were due to the variation in the time sequence of rigor between the two groups of birds.

In a later study, Dodge and Stadelman (1960) could find no effect of the rate of cooling, in either water or air at 1–2°C, on meat texture. Air-chilled carcasses took 250 min and water chilled 152 min to reach 4.4°C and all were aged for periods up to 16 h. A significant improvement in texture with ageing time was found, however, in one treatment: holding birds at 24°C prior to slush-ice chill resulted in less tender breast meat even after 10 h ageing. Although the authors attributed this to dehydration, it may have resulted from heat shortening rather than dehydration. Klose et al. (1961) confirmed that the rate of cooling does not have any effect on tenderness. This study suggested that longer ageing periods than used in conventional chilling were not necessary for turkeys over 9.0 kg eviscerated weight.

Goodwin, Mickelberry and Stadelman (1962a) examined rate of cooling using agitation and tumbling during chilling which resulted in an increase in the time taken to develop optimum tenderness. After ageing for 32 h significant differences in texture were found. In this study the turkeys weighed between 2.5–3.5 kg and it should be noted that the outside layer (0–3 mm) was significantly tougher at all stages of chilling and that the breast muscle was more tender than the thigh. Commercial processing procedures were studied by Marion and Goodman (1967) using turkeys ranging in eviscerated weight from 3.2 to 10.0 kg. Normal two-stage chilling of 1 h duration was compared with birds additionally aged in ice-slush for 3 and 23 h. Whole birds were cooked and the texture of breast and thigh measured using the Lee-Kramer shear press. Significant treatment effects were found with 15-week-old turkeys weighing approximately 3.3 kg and clearly indicated the necessity for a longer ageing period to tenderize the muscle before freezing.

Scholtyssek and Klose (1967) also highlighted the problem of variability associated with the measurement of texture in various weights and ages of turkey, aged for different periods in ice-slush as shown in *Figure 16.1*. The variability in mean texture values of the birds far outweighed the variability between strips of muscle or shear values and the authors stressed the need to use a large enough sample in order to obtain meaningful results. Brodine and Carlin (1968) repeated the chilling regime used by Marion and Goodman (1967) this time with 18- and 24-week-old male turkeys and compared taste panel tenderness scores with Lee-Kramer shear press data. Both methods of evaluation of texture were comparable and produced no significant effects of chill period, method of thawing and cooking rate. The authors commented that after commercial processing, which included 1 h spin-chill, turkeys were adequately aged before freezing. Three cooling procedures were studied by Welbourn et al. (1971).

(1) 16°C for 3 h,
(2) 16°C for 45 min, 8°C for 45 min and 0°C for 90 min,
(3) 0°C for 3 h.

No significant effects on shear value, modulus of elasticity, modulus of toughness and maximum stress were found in cooked muscles although there were some differences in raw muscle. Wiskus, Addis and Ma (1973) studied the postmortem changes in dark turkey muscle. They initially compared m. biceps femoris with m. peroneus longus. Shear values were considerably higher for m. biceps femoris and considerable variation was found in the time for rigor completion in both muscles.

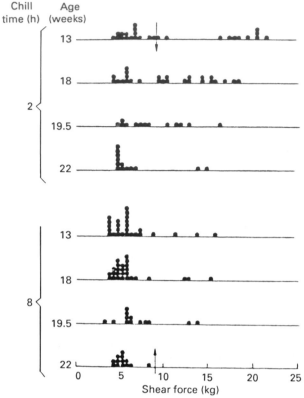

Figure 16.1 Distribution of shear values on the basis of individual birds. The arrows designate the shear value above which consumer-type panels object to toughness (courtesy of Scholtyssek and Klose, 1967)

With commercially processed turkey the *m. biceps femoris* from birds frozen without chilling and in rigor, was significantly tougher than pre-rigor muscle given the same treatment. The reverse was found with the *m. gastrocnemius* which was tougher in the pre-rigor state even after chilling for 3 h at 2°C before freezing. A high standard deviation was found in the *M. gastrocnemius* shear values clearly indicating considerable variation in the rates of glycolysis particularly after only 3 h chill.

Hegarty and Allen (1976) demonstrated the toughening effect of muscle removal immediately post mortem. It took 3 and 7 days of ageing for turkey breast and leg respectively before the muscles had reached similar shear values to controls dissected post rigor. No difference was found between unaged and aged muscles (7 days at 2°C) which were dissected after rigor completion. Chilling or freeze thawing of breast muscle dissected pre-rigor or in rigor similarly resulted in no increase of shear values. A very important observation by these authors was related to the *m. semitendinosus* which was found to have significantly higher shear values when allowed to enter rigor after pre-rigor dissection, when compared with the contralateral muscles allowed to enter rigor in a stretched, undissected position (*Table 16.7*).

Table 16.7 Effect of postmortem muscle length and subsequent ageing on the shear force of turkey semitendinosus muscle

	Shear force (kg)		
	Unaged (n = 11)	Aged (n^a = 7)	Significance due to ageing
Stretched[b]	3.87 ± 0.31	2.67 ± 0.13	P<0.001
Dissected	5.46 ± 0.36	3.02 ± 0.16	P<0.001
Significance due to dissection	P<0.001	NS	

Courtesy of Hegarty and Allen (1976)

[a] Samples were aged for 7 days at 2°C
[b] Stretched maximally until rigor completion or dissected post mortem

Electrical stimulation and chilling

A considerable amount of research on electrical stimulation has been carried out on red meat and has recently been reviewed by Chrystall and Devine (1986). Unfortunately, there have been few detailed studies on poultry meat. Jensen, Jul and Zinck (1979) examined the effects on broilers using equipment which was capable of applying a variable pulse rate (1.25–50 pulses/s) at any voltage up to 800 V. Stimulation was applied for 1 min after bleeding (3 min *post mortem*) and also after scalding and plucking (6 min *post mortem*). Their overall conclusions were that electrical stimulation although lowering the pH did not have any clear effect on texture and there was no trend in the results.

Dransfield *et al.* (1984) and Lockyer and Dransfield (1986) have reported studies carried out in commercial processing plants on turkeys and broilers. A Medal Junior low voltage electrical stimulation unit set to apply unidirectional pulses of 5 ms duration at 14.3 pulses/s for 30 s duration was used. Comparison was made between air and immersion-chilled turkeys. The shear value data indicated that immersion-chilled turkeys were marginally tougher than air-chilled. Electrical stimulation very slightly reduced the toughness in immersion-chilled turkey but increased the variability in air-chilled turkey. However, no significant differences were obtained between the shear values of electrically stimulated turkeys chilled by either method. It should be noted that small turkey hens, 3.5 kg live weight were used in this study. The broiler study utilized air-chilled broilers which were frozen either immediately after chilling or after overnight ageing. Ageing tenderized non-stimulated birds and had no effect on electrically stimulated birds which were tougher than unstimulated birds. It appears that any benefit to be obtained from electrical stimulation will depend on an interaction between several factors such as degree of struggle, stunning and plucking in the commercial situation.

Chill storage

The effects of chill storage of uneviscerated turkeys (Traditional Farm Fresh) on flavour and texture have recently been studied (Griffiths *et al.*, 1984; Grey and Mead, 1985; Grey *et al.*, 1986). These investigations have shown that uneviscerated hand-plucked turkeys can be stored for extended periods at chill temperatures without any adverse effect on texture and that cooling in an air flow at ambient temperature for a few hours before chilling in air, did not result in an increase in toughness.

Summary

It has been clearly demonstrated that the period of ageing at chill temperatures is important in allowing for the tenderization of turkey particularly with very young birds. What seems to be debatable is the effect of rate of cooling. There is evidence which suggests that fast cooling leads to tougher meat however some studies have found no effect. The actual removal of the muscles from the bird immediately *post mortem* has a considerable toughening effect and a prolonged period of ageing, up to 7 days, is required to reduce this effect.

In conclusion therefore, any interruption of muscle connections immediately post mortem, or during rigor must result in the toughening of the meat. There is also good evidence to suggest that the variability in texture is possibly related to the variation in the time post mortem of the onset of rigor in various carcass muscles. What is difficult to prove *in situ* is the temperature at which the onset of rigor has occurred. The outer 6 mm of breast muscle, for example, has been shown to be tougher than the inner part. Whether this is due to the differential in temperature during the early stages of chilling or the previous treatments of scalding and plucking is not known. To counter this, it has been shown that holding machine plucked turkeys at 24°C before chilling resulted in tougher meat, yet with hand plucked Traditional Farm Fresh turkey, slow cooling did not result in tough meat.

Freezing, frozen storage and comparison with fresh birds

Most of the earlier studies on the freezing of turkey were on conditions necessary to obtain a visually acceptable product (Klose and Pool, 1956; Lentz and van den Berg, 1957; van den Berg and Lentz, 1958) and also on the use of a two stage freezing procedure (Farrell and Robinson, 1969). Marion and Stadelman (1958) examined four freezing methods involving liquid immersion freezing, combined immersion, plate freezing and a commercial air circulation freezer found no significant effect on the texture of the breast muscle after ageing in ice-slush for 24 h.

Goodwin, Mickelberry and Stadelman (1962) studied the effect of cooking before freezing on turkey halves from birds aged in ice-slush for 72 h. Cooking before freezing when compared with cooking after freezing resulted in significantly higher shear values, thigh muscles were more affected than breast. Barrie, Goertz and Fry (1964) compared the acceptability of blast-frozen and liquid immersion frozen male and female turkeys and concluded that there was no significant difference in flavour, juiciness and tenderness scores between the two methods of freezing. Shrimpton (1965) commented that when toughness occurs unexpectedly, neither freezing nor any other single stage during processing is solely responsible and that the problem may be associated with the birds themselves.

Klose *et al.* (1959) demonstrated that frozen storage at −18°C for up to 9 months had no tenderizing effect although holding at −3°C for 1 to 2 weeks produced appreciable tenderization. Behnke and Fennema (1973) repeated some of the latter work. Ageing whole Leghorn hens for periods up to 2.5 h at −3°C without conventional chilling, resulted in tenderness equivalent to that obtained with a conventional chilling period and freezing. All the birds aged at −3°C were wrapped and frozen pre-rigor after commercial processing. Seemann *et al.* (1986) tried to repeat the tenderizing effect of storage at −3°C with 13 week BUT Big 6 turkeys. Storage times of 0, 4 and 24 h at −3°C in air, were evaluated; no improvement in texture was obtained as a result of the treatments.

Ristic (1980) studied the effects of frozen storage time and temperature on turkey quality, although tenderness was evaluated no actual data were given. The author, however, recommended that at −10 and −20°C satisfactory quality can still be obtained after 9 and 21 months storage respectively. In an earlier study Ristic (1977) found no effect on tenderness after 24 months' storage of turkey at −20°C. Grey *et al.* (1982), using broilers, found that air-chilled frozen broilers slightly increased in toughness after 6 months' storage at −12°C or 9 months at −20°C. Cunningham (1975) has reviewed the acceptability and use of frozen poultry.

Comparison of fresh with frozen 16-week-old turkeys was made by Hoke, McGeary and Lakshmanan (1968). Birds were stored frozen for 5 or 10 months, thawed and cooked from the same starting temperature (9°C). *M. pectoralis major* shear values were marginally higher after 5 months' storage when compared with fresh or 10 months' frozen stored birds. In contrast, thigh muscles increased in tenderness during frozen storage. Baker and Darfler (1981) compared fresh with frozen broilers, turkeys and ducks. All the birds were halved and opposite halves used for fresh and frozen samples. No significant differences in texture between fresh and frozen birds were found after modified triangle taste-panel tests and shear value measurements. The authors commented that of those judges who distinguished between fresh and frozen meat, a greater percentage preferred the fresh samples.

Summary

The studies on the freezing of turkey have demonstrated that minimal changes in quality occur after freezing and frozen storage for up to 24 months at −20°C. With respect to texture, it would seem that there may be a likelihood of a small increase in toughness of breast muscle after 5 months' storage which was reduced after 10 months. Comparison of fresh versus frozen storage is difficult to assess particularly after a period of frozen storage. Nevertheless, there would seem to be no detectable difference between the texture of fresh and frozen turkeys, stored for up to 30 days. The continuation of the ageing process during the thawing of frozen turkey has been shown to tenderize the meat, although holding at −3°C for short periods does not seem to appreciably tenderize birds which have been properly aged.

Cooking procedures

Goertz, Hooper and Harrison (1960) compared fresh with frozen turkey hens thawed at ambient temperature for 18 h and roasted at 163°C to final temperatures of 90 and 95°C in breast and thigh respectively. Cooking times were significantly longer for fresh frozen birds roasted to 95°C in the thigh (33 min/kg) than for fresh unfrozen birds cooked to 90°C in the breast (30 min/kg). Tenderness scores were not significantly different between cooking treatments or fresh and unfrozen birds. Cooking breast up or breast down had no significant effect on any of the palatibility scores. Goertz and Watson (1964) also found no difference in palatibility and doneness between right and left sides of turkey and suggested that a final internal temperature of 95°C in the thigh was preferable, since breast at 85°C and thigh at 90°C were considered underdone. Holmes (1986) also found no difference between right and left side of turkey breast muscle.

Ultimate temperature was also studied by Goodwin *et al.* (1962) who found no significant difference in shear values for light and dark meat after cooking to 77, 82, 88 and 94°C ultimate temperatures in aluminium foil. Two oven temperatures were used, 121 and 149°C and the variation in heating rate did not significantly affect shear values. Smith and Cunningham (1971) studied three cooking methods for breaded breast fillets and found that microwave cooking resulted in a juicier, more tender meat with less cooking loss when compared with deep fat and pan-fried fillets.

Deethardt *et al.* (1971) compared open-pan cooking with foil wrapped half turkey at two oven temperatures, 163 and 233°C. At 163°C oven temperature, foil wrapped halves took twice as long as open-pan cooked halves to cook to 85°C in the thigh. Cooking losses were found to be significantly higher in fresh turkey cooked by the open-pan method at 163°C, although these birds were considered juicier by the taste panel. Tenderness differences were not significant between the two cooking methods.

Mostert, Harrington and Stadelman (1966) cooked turkey halves after ageing whole birds in ice-slush for variable periods up to 24 h and freezing. After cooking from the frozen state at 190°C oven temperature to internal temperatures of 88 and 90°C in breast and thigh respectively, slush-ice chilled birds were found to require less cooking time than controls frozen after evisceration. As the age of the bird increased, the time to cook decreased, 12-week-old birds required 118 min/kg and 24-week birds 65 min/kg. Masaquel and Travnicek (1968) compared braising (moist heat) and roasting of turkey dark meat quarters from the frozen state in a preheated oven at 163°C to a final cooked temperature of 85°C. Shear values were lower for roasted leg muscles and the *m. biceps femoris* was found to be more tender than the *m. quadriceps femoris*. Travnicek and Hooper (1968) found no difference in texture between braised and roasted breast muscles cooked to an internal temperature of 80°C.

Johnson and Bowers (1974) compared freshly cooked and reheated excised turkey breast muscle which was injected with either water or phosphate solution. No indication was given as to when the muscles were excised after death and this may account for the negative result with respect to texture, since Grey, Robinson and Jones (1978) obtained a significant decrease in toughness of broilers after polyphosphate injection into the breast of birds which were subsequently roasted whole. Berry *et al.* (1980) studied cooking times and yields with roasted turkeys thawed to an initial starting temperature of 5°C. Cooking was started in a cold oven set to a uniform temperature of 163°C and cooking was continued until the thigh temperature reached 82°C. Cooking times are shown in *Table 16.8* for each of four weight ranges and are longer than those given by Goertz, Hooper and Harrison (1960). Cornforth *et al.* (1982) evaluated six different methods of cooking whole birds from the frozen-state until the lowest of four thermocouple readings was 71.1°C. Roasting in a foil tent at an oven temperature of 93.3°C produced the most tender breast meat when assessed by taste-panel and shear value. However, cooking times were excessive, 253 min/kg at an oven temperature of 93.3°C compared with 86 min/kg at 163°C in foil tents.

Table 16.8 Cooking time[a] for turkeys as influenced by size, stuffed or not stuffed (min/kg)

Size (kg)	3.6–5.4	5.5–7.3	7.4–9.1	9.2–10.9
Not stuffed	52.7	49.3	42.2	42.2
Stuffed	60.6	57.1	48.9	42.7

After Berry *et al.* (1980)

[a] Cooked in oven at 163°C, started from room temperature to end-point temperature at 82°C in deep thigh

More recently Martinez, Maurer and Arrington (1984) noted considerable differences in cooking rates of turkey with initial temperatures varying between −2.2 and +2.8°C and highlighted the importance of standardizing the initial temperature of the bird in the determination of cooking times. They also commented that the temperature in the thigh after cooking was always 5–8°C higher than the breast and that if the recommended practice of ultimate temperature measurement in the thigh of 82–85°C was followed then the breast temperature would only be 77–79°C which in the author's view may result in undercooking. Ehrcke *et al.* (1985) compared eight cooking treatments after thawing to 6°C and concluded that panel ratings for acceptability were significantly higher after cooking in a convection oven at 135°C, when compared with a conventional oven at 190°C. An end point temperature of 79°C in the breast was used in all treatments and only with the conventional oven did the thigh meat appear to be insufficiently cooked.

Summary

Measurements of texture usually require the product to be cooked. Although cooking rate does not seem to have too much influence on texture, the ultimate temperature needs to be standardized. All the evidence relating to yield, degree of cooking and acceptability of whole turkey would indicate a minimum deep breast muscle temperature of 85°C should be obtained preferably using an oven temperature of 163°C. Further research is required to elucidate the differences that may be found with halves, quarters or portions compared with whole birds since the cutting or trimming of muscle leads to an increase in toughness after cooking. The effects of wrapping in aluminium foil do not seem to be consistent, particularly with regard to yield and juiciness. In the UK, commercial processors always recommend to consumers that the turkey should be thoroughly thawed usually at refrigerator temperature. Cooking instructions are usually given for a specific oven temperature and the cooking time according to a weight range. Presumably the data given has been based on a particular initial starting temperature.

Biochemical changes and texture

Glycolysis

De Fremery (1963, 1966) reviewed the earlier studies on biochemical properties and texture carried out at the Western Regional Laboratory, USA. His general conclusions were that acceleration of postmortem glycolysis increased toughness in aged meat and that elimination of, or reduced, *postmortem* glycolysis did not result in an increase in toughness although it resulted in the rapid disappearance of adenosine triphosphate (ATP) and consequent rapid onset of rigor. Most of the published work had been carried out on muscle excised immediately after death.

Dodge and Stadelman (1960) demonstrated a positive relationship between pH at the end of the ageing period and texture ($r = 0.71$). An initial mean pH of 6.40 had declined to 5.89 after 12 h in ice-slush and shear values from 27.3 kg/g to 7.8 kg/g. A similar pattern was found with air-chilled turkey. Ma, Addis and Allen (1971) found that out of 20 turkey hens, eight took on average 221 min, eight took 93 min and four took 37 min to the completion of rigor and that sarcomere length began to increase in length after 1 h post mortem in the fast rigor group, 2 h in the intermediate group and 6 h in the slow rigor birds. They then compared two groups, (a) struggled, and (b) restrained and found that the struggled group had a decreased time course of rigor (mean value 93 min) compared with the restrained group (250 min). No stunning, scalding, plucking or evisceration were carried out in this study. The authors commented that there was a possibility that some commercially processed birds which have a slow time course of rigor may be frozen too soon resulting in less tender meat.

Ma and Addis (1973) found that lactate, pH and ATP were significantly different between struggled and restrained groups of turkey during the first 3 h post mortem. Sarcomere length was significantly shorter in the restrained group during the first 2 h post mortem. Vanderstoep and Richards (1974) studied the biochemical changes in excised muscle from turkeys aged 15 and 25 weeks. Muscles were removed after bleeding, placed in ice and sampled at intervals up to 180 min. Considerable variation in ATP, lactate content and pH were found at the postmortem times sampled and the authors concluded that there were two groups of turkey; i.e. fast and slow glycolysing. Their conclusion was based on the rate of ATP disappearance measured at 0 and 60 min and expressed as a proportion of the initial value.

van Hoof (1979) also found considerable variation in ATP content as antemortem and perimortem conditions changed and stipulated that elimination of struggle by electrical stunning delayed the breakdown of ATP. Ngoka et al. (1982) found no significant difference in pH and glycogen content between excited and non-excited turkeys prior to killing after anaesthetization. However, excitation resulted in meat with a higher water holding capacity and reduced shear values. Muscles from birds which were allowed to struggle freely and given no anaesthesia had a significantly lower initial pH, lower water holding capacity, increased shear value and the muscles were darker and redder. Babji, Froning and Ngoka (1982) found that pre-slaughter heat stress (4 h at 38°C) resulted in significantly lower ultimate pH and water holding capacity and higher shear values. Heat stress also affected the breast muscle colour which was significantly lighter, having lower aL and higher L tristimulus values than control or cold stressed turkey and the authors concluded that a cool pre-slaughter environment resulted in meat of better quality.

pH_{20} and texture

The relationship between the pH measured at about 15–20 min post mortem and the subsequent quality of the meat has been used in the red meat industry for many years. It has more recently been applied to broilers (Kijowski and Niewiarowicz, 1978; Seemann, 1985) and turkeys (Dransfield et al., 1984) and both turkeys and broilers (Lockyer and Dransfield, 1986). From the evidence presented in these studies it is debatable as to whether a PSE type or DFD type of meat is produced in poultry muscle. There is no doubt that fast, normal and slow rates of glycolysis are found which can result in heat shortening if the glycolytic rate is fast and the carcass is not cooled sufficiently or a type of cold shortening if the rate is slow. Both may lead to meat which is tougher and which cannot always be resolved by prolonged ageing. The presence of a small proportion of these tougher muscles in studies of commercial processing and in laboratory investigations can lead to erroneous conclusions because of (a) the high variance and (b) the possibility that an unequal distribution of these birds has been obtained. For example, when Lockyer (personal communication) compared texture and pH at 20 min post mortem in turkey using individual bird data a non-linear relationship was obtained. However

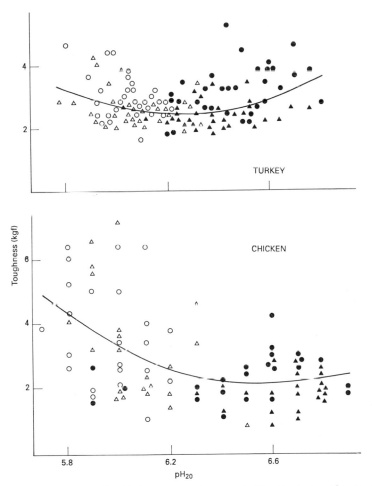

Figure 16.2 The relationship between toughness and pH_{20}. For turkey: ● = immersion chilling; ▲ = air-chilled and for chicken: ● = un-aged; ▲ = aged overnight. Closed symbols represent non-ES carcasses and open symbols represent ES carcasses. All toughness values are corrected for ageing effects and the fitted curves are the common curves calculated from the parallel curve analyses using the equation: toughness = $a - b(pH_{20}) + c(pH_{20})^2$ (courtesy of Lockyer and Dransfield, 1986)

the data fitted a quadratic function (Ross, 1975). The results of these studies with and without electrical stimulation for broilers and turkeys are shown in *Figure 16.2*.

Muscle shortening and temperature

Since Locker and Hagyard (1963) first described cold shortening in freshly excised beef muscles, considerable research has been carried out on this subject. With respect to poultry, de Fremery (1963) in his review, reported the effects of holding excised cockerel muscles at various temperatures. The rate of ATP disappearance and relative toughness were plotted against postmortem temperature. Both curves followed the same general course and were minimal between 10 and 20°C. Smith, Judge and Stadelman (1969) measured the actual shortening of excised broiler, hen and turkey muscles at various temperatures. Excision of the muscles resulted in an initial contraction of 10–12% and after incubation, shortening was virtually complete after 3 and 5 h in broiler and turkey respectively. Shortening of Leghorn hen muscles at 0°C increased from 14.8% at 30 min to 20.7% at 3 h whereas over the same period no shortening occurred at 16°C.

Turkey muscles stored under similar conditions for 5 h shortened by 19.9% at 0°C compared with 13.7% at 16°C. It should be noted that all measurements were made with respect to intact length. A more sensitive method of measuring the tendency to contract was reported by Jungk and Marion (1970) using an isometer (Jungk *et al.*, 1967). This instrument measures postmortem tension load at constant length thus simulating conditions that may exist on the carcass. A total of 121 muscle strips from 30 turkeys, incubated at various temperatures from 2 to 37°C, were evaluated. No linear relationship between temperature and the time to maximum tension was found. However, when shortening experiments without tension were carried out at temperatures between 4 and 35°C and measurements made after excision of the muscles a significant linear relationship ($P<0.01$) was found between extent of shortening and temperature. The authors concluded that there was no evidence for cold shortening in turkey muscle when attached to the carcass.

Wood and Richards (1974) using broiler breast muscle found that the tension which developed in 3 min at 2°C had disappeared within 15 min. When strips of muscle were incubated at 2°C then brought to 23°C considerable tension was developed as a result of the continuation of the normal time course of rigor. The authors suggested that 'cold shock' released calcium ions, the sarcoplasmic reticulum then removed the calcium ions and since ATP was still present the muscle returned to its original tension.

Welbourn, Harrington and Stadelman (1968) had previously found that chilling turkeys for 3 h at 0°C resulted in a significant increase in thigh muscle shear values and that chilling resulted in a progressive shortening of sarcomere length in breast and thigh with decreasing temperature. However, no significant correlations between shear values and sarcomere length were obtained. Lee and Rickensrud (1978) found minimum shortening with broiler muscle strips excised pre-rigor, after incubation at temperatures between 4 and 10°C. A small cold shortening effect was demonstrated at 0°C and was greater in the thigh than in the breast muscle. The percentage shortening increased as the temperature was increased from 10 to 43°C, particularly in the thigh (*Figure 16.3*). The conclusions from this study, strongly indicated that high post-mortem muscle temperature (>20°C) induced much more

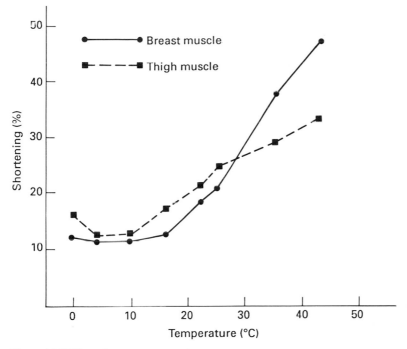

Figure 16.3 Effect of temperature on the extent of shortening in chicken muscles excised pre-rigor (courtesy of Lee and Rickansrud, 1978)

severe shortening and that reduction in body temperature to below 20°C was required as early as possible after death to prevent heat shortening.

Jeacocke (1984) has recently shed some light on the cause of the variability in the time to onset of rigor in red meat. Using membrane-free single muscle fibres he found that there was considerable variation in the delay to onset of rigor suggesting that individual muscle fibres within a whole muscle enter rigor at different times. If, however, the single fibres are allowed to go into rigor by metabolic depletion then the onset of rigor mortis is much more rapid than in the whole muscle. A small bundle of fibres is intermediate in rate of onset between that for a single fibre and whole muscle. Since individual fibres vary in glycogen content, the rapid onset of rigor in some of them may reflect the rapid decline of intracellular ATP. With turkey and broiler muscle there is of course an additional factor, that of temperature during commercial processing, where heat is applied during scalding and subsequently heat is removed during chilling. When temperatures are monitored it is usually in the deep breast; however there is always a temperature gradient between the deep muscle and the muscle immediately under the skin. The extent of shortening of muscle will therefore depend not only on the levels of available metabolites but on its thickness, location within birds and whether it is a 'white' or 'red' muscle since the latter have been shown to be more susceptible to cold shortening (Offer, 1984).

Muscle structure has not been discussed here because of space limitations but there are indications that the variability in muscle bundle size (Grey et al., 1986; Seemann et al., 1986) found within birds of the same strain may be another genetically linked factor which can influence the ultimate texture of the meat.

Overall conclusions

At attempt has been made to summarize the important conclusions reached in each of the sections. However, of the many factors which influence turkey texture, some may or may not be additive and some may be more important than others. Future research should therefore be directed towards the resolution of the importance of the separate effects and the standardization of methods of evaluation. In addition, the influence of breeding on muscle structure, the response of the bird to stress and the consequent effects of these factors on muscle texture should receive more attention. Present commercial production of turkeys produces a small proportion of birds which are regarded as tough even after overnight ageing. This situation will continue unless the various factors which produce the variability in muscle texture can be controlled.

References

Babji, A. S., Froning, G. W. and Ngoka, D. A. (1982). The effect of preslaughter environmental temperature in the presence of electrolyte treatment on turkey meat quality. *Poultry Science,* **61,** 2385–2389

Baker, R. C. and Darfler, J. M. (1981). A comparison of fresh and frozen poultry. *Journal of American Dietetic Association,* **78,** 348–351

Barrie, P. J., Goertz, G. E. and Fry, J. L. (1964). Acceptability of blast-frozen and liquid-frozen turkey hens and toms. *Food Technology, Champaign,* **18,** 163–165

Berry, J. G., Stadelman, W. J., Pratt, D. E. and Sweat, V. E. (1980). Estimating cooking times and meat yields from roasted turkeys. *Journal of Food Science,* **45,** 629–631

Behnke, J. R. and Fennema, O. (1973). Quality changes in prerigor poultry at −3°C. *Journal of Food Science,* **38,** 275–278

Brodine, M. V. and Carlin, A. F. (1968). Chilling and thawing methods and their effect on quality of cooked whole turkeys. *Food Technology, Champaign,* **22,** 607–610

Carlson, C. W., Adams, A. W., Wilcox, R. A., Gastler, G. F. and Burrill, L. M. (1962). Dietary energy, sex, strain, and storage as influencing composition and/or palatibility of Broad Breasted Bronze turkeys. *Poultry Science,* **41,** 150–160

Chrystal, B. B. and Devine, C. E. (1986). Electrical stimulation: its early development in New Zealand. In *Advances in Meat Research, Vol. 1* (Pearson, A. M. and Dutson, T. R., eds), pp. 73–119. Westport, AVI Publishing Company

Cornforth, D. P., Brennand, C. P., Brown, R. J. and Godfrey, D. (1982). Evaluation of various methods for roasting frozen turkeys. *Journal of Food Science,* **47,** 1108–1112

Cunningham, F. E. (1975). Acceptability and use of frozen poultry — a review. *World's Poultry Science Journal,* **31,** 136–148

De Fremery, D. (1963). Relation between biochemical properties and tenderness of poultry. In *Proceedings of Meat Tenderness Symposium,* pp. 99–120. New Jersey, Campbell Soup Company

De Fremery, D. (1966). Some aspects of postmortem changes in poultry muscle. In *The Physiology and Biochemistry of Muscle as a Food* (Briskey, E. J., Cassens, R. G. and Trautman, J. C., eds), pp. 205–212. University of Wisconsin Press, Madison, Wisconsin

Deethardt, D., Burrill, L. M., Schneider, K. and Carlson, C. W. (1971). Foil-covered versus open-pan procedures for roasting turkey. *Journal of Food Science,* **36,** 624–625

Dodge, J. W. and Stadelman, W. J. (1959). Post mortem aging of poultry meat and its effects on the tenderness of the breast muscles. *Food Technology, Champaign,* **13,** 81–84

Dodge, J. W. and Stadelman, W. J. (1960). Relationships between pH, tenderness, and moisture levels during early post-mortem aging of turkey meat. *Food Technology, Champaign,* **14,** 43–46

Dransfield, E., Down, N. F., Taylor, A. A. and Lockyer, D. K. (1984). Influence of electrical stimulation and slow chilling on the texture of turkey breast muscle. In *Proceedings of the 30th European meeting of Meat Research Workers, Bristol,* pp. 180–181

Enreke, L. A., Rasdall, J. U., Gibbs, S. U. and Haydon, F. C. (1985). Comparison of eight cooking treatments for energy utilization, product yields, and quality of roasted turkey. *Poultry Science,* **64,** 1881–1886

Farrell, A. J. and Robinson, J. E. (1969). Time:temperature profile during turkey freezing. In *Proceedings of the 1st International Congress of Food Science and Technology, Vol. 1 Chemical and Physical Aspects of Food* (Leitch, J. M., ed.), pp. 667–678. New York, Gordon and Breach

Freeman, B. M. (1984). Transportation of poultry. *World's Poultry Science Journal,* **40**(1), 19–30

Freeman, B. M., Kettlewell, P. J., Manning, A. C. C. and Berry, P. S. (1984). Stress of transportation for broilers. *Veterinary Record,* **114,** 286–287

Froning, G. W., Babji, A. S. and Mather, F. B. (1978). The effect of preslaughter temperature, stress, struggle and anesthetization on colour and textural characteristics of turkey muscle. *Poultry Science,* **57,** 630–633

Goertz, E. G., Vail, G. E., Harrison, D. L. and Sanford, P. E. (1955). Organoleptic and histological characteristics of fresh and frozen stored turkey fed high-density and low-density rations. *Poultry Science,* **36,** 640–648

Goertz, G. E., Hooper, A. S. and Harrison, D. L. (1960). Comparison of rate of cooking and doneness of fresh unfrozen and frozen, defrosted turkey hens. *Food Technology, Champaign,* **14**(9), 458–462

Goertz, G. E. and Watson, M. A. (1964). Palatability and doneness of right and left sides of turkeys roasted to selected end point temperatures. *Poultry Science,* **43,** 812–817

Goertz, G. E., Weathers, B., Harrison, D. L. and Sanford, P. E. (1961). Tenderness scores and Warner-Bratzler shear values for broilers and white turkeys fed different cereal grains. *Poultry Science,* **40,** 488–493

Goodwin, T. L., Mickelberry, W. C. and Stadelman, W. J. (1961). The influence of humane slaughter on the tenderness of turkey meat. *Poultry Science,* **40,** 921–924

Goodwin, T. L., Mickelberry, W. C. and Stadelman, W. J. (1962). The effect of freezing, method of cooking, and storage time on the tenderness of pre-cooked and raw turkey meat. *Poultry Science,* **41,** 1268–1271

Goodwin, T. L., Mickelberry, W. C. and Stadelman, W. J. (1962a). Methods of aging and muscle flexing and their effects upon the tenderness of turkey meat. *Poultry Science,* **41,** 193–198

Goodwin, T. L., Bramblett, V. D., Vail, G. E. and Stadelman, W. J. (1962). Effects of end-point temperature and cooking rate on turkey meat tenderness. *Food Technology, Champaign,* **16,** 101–102

Goodwin, T. L. (1966). The influence of strain on the tenderness of twenty-six-week-old turkeys. *Poultry Science,* **45,** 594–596

Grey, T. C., Robinson, D. and Jones, J. M. (1978). The effects on broiler chicken of polyphosphate injection during commercial processing. *Journal of Food Technology,* **13,** 529–540

Grey, T. C., Griffiths, N. M., Jones, J. M. and Robinson, D. (1982). The effect of chilling procedures and storage temperatures on the quality of chicken carcasses. *Lebensmittel-Wissenschaft und Technologie,* **15,** 362–365

Grey, T. C. and Mead, G. C. (1985). Quality characteristics of traditional turkeys. *Turkeys,* **33,** 13

Grey, T. C., Griffiths, N. M., Jones, J. M. and Robinson, D. (1986). A study of some factors influencing the tenderness of turkey breast meat. *Lebensmittel-Wissenschaft und Technologie,* **19,** 412–414

Grey, T. C., Mead, G. C., Griffiths, N. M. and Jones, J. M. (1986). Effects of evisceration and storage temperature on changes in meat quality of traditional farm-fresh turkeys. *British Poultry Science,* **27,** 463–470

Griffiths, N. M., Mead, G. C., Jones, J. M. and Grey, T. C. (1984). Effects of storage on meat quality in uneviscerated turkeys held at 4°C. *British Poultry Science,* **25,** 259–266

Harkin, A. M., Kitzmiller, C. and Gilpin, G. L. (1958) Quality of the cooked meat of turkeys fed animal or vegetable protein diets with vitamin and fat supplements. *Poultry Science,* **37,** 1328–1339

Hegarty, P. V. J. and Allen, C. E. (1976). Comparison of different postmortem temperatures and dissection procedures on shear values of unaged and aged avian and ovine muscles. *Journal of Food Science,* **41,** 237–240

Hoke, I. M., McGeary, B. K. and Lakshmanan, F. (1968). Muscle protein composition and eating quality of fresh and frozen turkeys. *Journal of Food Science,* **33,** 566–571

Holmes, Z. A. (1986). Comparison of meat quality between the right and left roasted turkey halves. *Poultry Science,* **65,** 497–500.

Jeacocke, R. E. (1984). The control of post-mortem metabolism and the onset of rigor mortis. *Recent Advances in the Chemistry of Meat, (Bristol, 1983)* (Bailey, A. J., ed.), pp. 23–27. The Royal Society of Chemistry, London

Jenson, J. H., Jul, M. and Zinck, O. (1979). Electrical stimulation of chickens. In *Proceedings of the Fifth International Congress of Food Science and Technology, Kyoto, Japan* (Chiba, H., Fujimaki, M., Iwai, K., Mitsuda, H. and Morita, Y., eds), p. 124. Tokio, Kodansha, Elsevier, Amsterdam

Johnson, P. G. and Bowers, J. A. (1974). Freshly cooked and reheated turkey breast muscle. *Poultry Science*, **53**, 343–348

Jungk, R. A., Snyder, H. E., Goll, D. E. and McConnell, K. G. (1967). Isometric tension changes and shortening in muscle strips during post mortem aging. *Journal of Food Science*, **32**, 158–161

Jungk, R. A. and Marion, W. W. (1970). Post-mortem isometric tension changes and shortening in turkey muscle strips held at various temperatures. *Journal of Food Science*, **35**, 143–145

Kijowski, J. and Niewiarowicz, A. (1978). Effect of initial pH in broiler breast muscles on gel forming capacity of meat proteins, and on rheological characteristics of frankfurter-type sausage. *Journal of Food Technology*, **13**, 461–468

Klose, A. A., Campbell, A. A., Hanson, H. L. and Lineweaver, H. (1961). Effect of duration and type of chilling and thawing on tenderness of frozen turkeys. *Poultry Science*, **40**, 683–688

Klose, A. A. and Pool, M. F. (1954). Effect of scalding temperature on quality of stored frozen turkeys. *Poultry Science*, **33**, 280–289

Klose, A. A. and Pool, M. F. (1956). Effect of freezing conditions on appearance of frozen turkeys. *Food Technology, Champaign*, **10**, 34–38

Klose, A. A., Pool, M. F., Wiele, M. B., Hanson, H. L. and Lineweaver, H. (1959). Poultry tenderness 1. Influence of processing on tenderness of turkeys. *Food Technology, Champaign*, **13**, 20–24

Landes, D. R., Dawson, L. E. and Price, J. F. (1971). Protein extractability of turkey breast muscle exhibiting different rates of post-mortem glycolysis. *Journal of Food Science*, **36**, 122–124

Larmond, E., Petrasovits, A. and Moran, E. T. (1971). Eating quality of Large White turkeys as influenced by age and sex. *Canadian Institute of Food Technology Journal*, **4**, 75–79

Lee, Y. B. and Rickansrud, D. A. (1978). Effect of temperature on shortening in chicken muscle. *Journal of Food Science*, **43**, 1613–1615

Lentz, C. P. and van den Berg, L. (1957). Liquid immersion freezing of poultry. *Food Technology, Champaign*, **11**, 247–250

Locker, R. H. and Hagyard, C. J. (1963). A cold shortening effect in beef muscles. *Journal of the Science of Food and Agriculture*, **14**, 787–793

Lockyer, D. K. and Dransfield, E. (1986). Poultry texture: effects of electrical stimulation, chilling, maturation and further ageing. In *Proceedings of the Meat Chilling Symposium (Bristol, 1986)*, pp. 53–57. International Institute of Refrigeration (in press)

Ma, R. T. and Addis, P. B. (1973). The association of struggle during exsanguination to glycolysis, protein solubility and shear in turkey pectoralis muscle. *Journal of Food Science*, **38**, 995–997

Ma, R. T., Addis, P. B. and Allen, E. (1971). Response to electrical stimulation and post-mortem changes in turkey pectoralis major muscle. *Journal of Food Science*, **36**, 125–129

Marion, W. W. and Goodman, H. M. (1967). Influence of continuous chilling on tenderness of turkey. *Food Technology, Champaign*, **21**, 307–309

Marion, W. W. and Stadelman, W. J. (1958). Effect of various freezing methods on quality of poultry meat. *Food Technology, Champaign*, **12**, 367–369

Marsden, S. J., Alexander, L. M., Schopmeyer, G. E. and Lamb, J. C. (1952). Variety as a factor in fleshing, fatness and edible quality of turkeys. *Poultry Science*, **31**, 433–443

Marsden, S. J., Alexander, L. M., Lamb, J. C. and Linton, G. S. (1957). Relationships among diet composition, fleshing, fatness and edible quality of female roasting turkeys. *Poultry Science*, **36**, 646–657

Martinez, J. B., Maurer, A. J. and Arrington, L. C. (1984). Heating curves during roasting of turkeys. *Poultry Science*, **63**, 260–264

Masaquel, C. and Travnicek, D. M. (1968). Effect of cooking methods on palatability, hypoxanthine and uric acid content of dark turkey meat. *Poultry Science*, **47**, 1284–1289

Mostert, G. C., Harrington, R. B. and Stadelman, W. J. (1966). The effect of aging time, sex, strain and age on cooking of turkey meat. *Poultry Science*, **45**, 359–362

Ngoka, D. A., Froning, G. W., Lowry, S. R. and Babji, A. S. (1982). Effects of sex, age, preslaughter factors, and holding conditions on the quality characteristics and chemical composition of turkey breast muscles. *Poultry Science*, **61**, 1996–2003

Offer, G. (1984). Progress in the biochemistry, physiology and structure of meat. In *Proceedings of the 30th European Meeting of Meat Research Workers, Bristol*, pp. 87–94

Pool, M. F., Mecchi, E. P., Lineweaver, H. and Klose, A. A. (1954). The effect of scalding temperature on the processing and initial appearance of turkeys. *Poultry Science*, **33**, 274–279

Ristic, M. (1977). Effect of storage time and temperature on the quality of poultry meat. *Kalte*, **30**, 464, 469–472, 474

Ristic, M. (1980). Dependence of meat quality on storage temperature and storage time of turkeys. *Fleischwirtschaft*, **60**, 1894–1895

Ross, G. J. S. (1975). Simple non-linear modelling for the general user. In *Proceedings of the 40th Session International Statistics Institute, Warsaw, Poland*, **2**, 585–593

Scholtyssek, S. and Klose, A. A. (1967). Sources of variability in turkey tenderness. *Poultry Science*, **46**, 936–938

Seemann, G. and Bohn, M. (1983). Age and strain influences on meat quality of male and female turkeys. In *Proceedings of the 6th European Symposium on Quality of Poultry Meat*, pp. 78–86. Ploufragan France

Seemann, G. (1985). Changing of the pH value and other meat parameters after slaughtering. In *Proceedings of the 7th European Symposium on Quality of Poultry Meat*, pp. 128–136. Vejle, Denmark

Seemann, G., Jones, J. M., Griffiths, N. M. and Grey, T. C. (1986). The influence of storage time and temperature on turkey breast meat quality. *Archiv für Geflügelkunde*, **50**, 149–153

Shannon, W. G., Marion, W. W. and Stadelman, W. J. (1957). Effect of temperature and time of scalding on the tenderness of breast meat of chicken. *Food Technology, Champaign*, **11**, 284–286

Shrimpton, D. H. (1965). The influence of freezing on the quality of poultry meat. In *Proceedings of the International Institute of Refrigeration Commission*, **4**, pp. 237–242. Karlsruhe

Smith, M. C., Judge, M. D. and Stadelman, W. J. (1969). A 'cold shortening' effect in avian muscle. *Journal of Food Science*, **34**, 42–46

Smith, M. L. and Cunningham, F. E. (1971). Preparing and cooking turkey breast fillets. *Poultry Science*, **50**, 1434–1437

Stadelman, W. J., Mostert, G. C. and Harrington, R. B. (1966). Effect of ageing time, sex, strain and age on resistance to shear of turkey meat. *Food Technology, Champaign*, **20**, 960–964

Travnicek, D. and Hooper, A. S. (1968). Effect of cooking method on the quality of turkey breast meat cooked from the frozen state. *Poultry Science*, **47**, 1281–1283

van den Berg, L. and Lentz, C. P. (1958). Factors affecting freezing rate and appearance of eviscerated poultry frozen in air. *Food Technology, Champaign*, **12**, 183–185

van Hoof, J. (1979). Influence of ante- and peri-mortem factors on biochemical and physical characteristics of turkey breast muscle. *Veterinary Quarterly*, **1**, 29–36

Vanderstoep, J. and Richards, J. F. (1974). Post-mortem glycolytic and physical changes in turkey breast muscle. *Canadian Institute of Food Science and Technology Journal*, **7**, 120–124

Welbourn, J. L., Harrington, R. B. and Stadelman, W. J. (1968). Relationships among shear values, sarcomere lengths and cooling procedures in turkeys. *Journal of Food Science*, **33**, 450–452

Welbourn, J. L., Harrington, R. B., Haugh, C. G., Aberle, E. D. and Stadelman, W. J. (1971). Effects of cooling procedures on shear values, instron measurements, protein solubility and pH of turkey. *Poultry Science*, **50**, 1870–1875

Wise, R. G. and Stadelman, W. J. (1959). Tenderness at various muscle depths associated with poultry processing techniques. *Food Technology, Champaign*, **13**, 689–691

Wise, R. G. and Stadelman, W. J. (1961). Tenderness of poultry meat 2. Effect of scalding procedures. *Poultry Science*, **40**, 1731–1736

Wiskus, K. J., Addis, P. B. and Ma, R. T. (1973). Post-mortem changes in dark turkey muscle. *Journal of Food Science*, **38**, 313–315

Wood, D. F. and Richards, J. F. (1974). Cold shortening in chicken broiler pectoralis major. *Journal of Food Science*, **39**, 530–531

Chapter 17

Flavour and taint in turkey meat

J. M. Jones

Introduction

Flavour, consisting of several factors such as odour and taste, is one of the major criteria of the eating quality of turkey meat. Since flavour is developed during the cooking process, it is usually evaluated on the cooked meat using subjective methods, namely sensory or consumer panels. While there is a continuing interest in relating panel results with the many chemical components of poultry meat flavour, currently there does not appear to be an acceptable and accurate alternative to the human assessor as a means of evaluating turkey meat flavour. A number of authors have stressed the importance of using the most appropriate sensory method to assess the flavour of poultry meat (Land and Hobson-Frohock, 1977; Froning *et al.*, 1978; Tellefson *et al.*, 1982).

Both subjective and objective techniques are commonly used to assess the rancidity of meat. A feature of rancidity development is an increase in the concentration of carbonyl compounds present in the meat, and this fact has been employed in the most widely used objective method, i.e. the estimation of malonaldehyde using thiobarbituric acid (TBA).

Many stages and processes are involved in the production of turkey meat, and the purpose of this chapter is to discuss how these various factors may influence the turkey meat flavour and how quality problems might arise.

Relationship between sensory and objective methods of assessing flavour deterioration

The objective assessment of meat 'off-flavour' is frequently given in terms of TBA numbers, or values (mg malonaldehyde/kg meat): a TBA value of about 1 is commonly taken as the point where oxidative rancidity may be detected by the human subject. However, experience with poultry meat has shown that there is not always a significant relationship between the subjective and objective methods. For instance, while Jacobson and Koehler (1970) reported a high negative correlation ($r = 0.77$) between the flavour and TBA number of roasted and cubed turkey meat held for 1 days at 1°C, this was not the case with chilled turkey meat loaves, where sensory ratings showed a 'slight' to 'moderate' rancidity after 3 days, although TBA values were very high (Younathan, Marjan and Arshad, 1980). Similarly, no significant correlations between TBA numbers and taste panel responses for precooked frozen meat were found by Webb, Marion and Hayse (1972a) who suggested that insufficient training of their sensory panel may have been a factor responsible for the lack of correlation. Further complicating factors are that whereas panellists may detect rancidity only in one area or at the edge of the meat sample (Cash and Carlin, 1968), TBA values might be measured on samples from other sites in the tissue, while in some instances TBA numbers may actually decline during chilled or frozen storage, but over the same period panellists might detect increased rancidity in the meat (Cash and Carlin, 1968; Igbinedion et al., 1981).

Effect of bird strain, sex and age on meat flavour

There is little evidence that the 'finish' (degree of fattening) of the carcass influences the flavour of turkey meat (Larmond and Moran, 1983), although MacNeil and Dimick (1970) had earlier implied that the flavour of turkeys yielding large quantities of skin might differ from that of thin-skinned birds. A number of studies have suggested that thigh meat has a greater flavour intensity than breast meat (Brodine and Carlin, 1968; Moran et al., 1984). On the other hand, the sensory panel used by Jacobson and Kohler (1970) gave higher flavour scores to breast meat.

No consistent effects of strain or sex on meat flavour were noted by Carlson et al. (1962) in their study of three strains of Broad Breasted Bronze turkey. Similarly, Moran et al. (1984) found that there was no difference in the flavour of meats from 20-week-old large males of the Nicholas and BUT strains.

Brodine and Carlin (1968) concluded that the meats of 18- and 24-week-old turkey males were similar in flavour. The fact that there was no difference in the flavour of meats from 14-week-old male and female turkeys (Larmond, Salmon and Klein, 1983) was perhaps not surprising in the light of the earlier work of Larmond, Petrasovits and Moran (1971), who found no difference between the flavour of breast meat from Large White turkey males slaughtered at intervals between 17 and 27 weeks of age and that of hens of the same strain killed between 14 and 24 weeks of age. However, with both sexes, sensory panel ratings for flavour increased during the first 4 weeks of the experiment, but declined in the age periods immediately preceding the onset of sexual maturity (22 weeks for males, 19 weeks for hens), and improved thereafter, leading the authors to suggest that changes in hormonal secretions might directly influence turkey meat palatability.

Effect of diet on meat quality

Influence of ingredients on flavour

The effect on turkey meat flavour of feeding various diets has been extensively investigated over several decades. In an early investigation using female birds aged between 26 and 34 weeks, Marsden et al. (1957), found that the type of cereal used in the growing diet had little effect on the flavour, but that in the case of thigh meat at least, cereal-fed birds were rated more highly than those fed growers diets high in edible oil or linseed meal. Breast meat flavour was largely unaffected by the composition of the growers diet.

No consistent effects on flavour were noted by Carlson *et al.* (1962) who used diets of differing energy levels. However, the meat of males fed corn was consistently preferred over that from male birds raised on oats, oats plus fat or corn and fat diets, whereas hens fed oats were preferred in one experiment and corn-fed in another. More recently, Moran *et al.* (1984) found no difference in the flavour intensities of meat from turkeys fed a high energy diet containing corn, soyabean meal and fat, and those fed on a lower energy diet formulated with wheat, barley and fishmeal. The inclusion of triticale in diets fed to male breeder turkeys from 28 to 45 weeks of age did not influence meat flavour (Savage *et al.*, 1987).

There has been interest in finding alternatives to cereals as feed ingredients, largely on a cost basis. In addition to assessing the effect of such alternatives on aspects of bird performance such as growth rate, there is a need to ascertain their effect, if any, on meat quality.

Moran, Larmond and Somers (1973) fed several forms of whole soyabeans to male turkeys from 8 to 23 weeks of age and compared the sensory properties of the meat with that from birds fed control diets containing added soyabean oil or animal tallow. The experienced taste panel found flavour differences to be more associated with the source of dietary fat rather than with the state in which the soyabeans were fed to the birds. The flavour of turkeys receiving soyabean oil was significantly better than those fed tallow. The inclusion of up to 500 g/kg yellow peas in a corn–soyabean meal diet, or the addition of corn oil or lysine to such a basal diet, did not significantly influence the flavour of cooked turkey meat (Carlson *et al.*, 1969; Savage *et al.*, 1986).

Larmond, Salmon and Klein (1983) found no effects on meat flavour when turkeys were fed varying amounts of canola (rapeseed) meal, although there was a slight incidence of off-flavour at 73 g meal/kg diet compared with control or diets containing higher levels of canola. The authors, however, concluded that feeding canola was unlikely to cause taint in turkey meat.

The effect on flavour of diets containing animal or vegetable protein and supplemented with vitamins and fats, was investigated by Harkin *et al.* (1958) who showed that the flavour of thigh meat from turkeys fed a vegetable protein diet containing vitamin A plus 80 g/kg lard had higher flavour scores than any other diet examined. No significant differences were noted in the case of breast meat.

The inclusion of live yeast culture as a growth factor in a corn–soyabean meal diet fed for 20 weeks to turkey males had no effect on the flavour of cooked breast or thigh meat (Savage, Nakaue and Holmes, 1985).

Taints

While there is little evidence that dietary constituents markedly affect the flavour of poultry meat, it has been known for some 50 years that the presence of fish oil or meal in the bird's diet can impart an off-flavour or taint to turkey meat.

Crawford *et al.* (1975) showed that there was no significant difference in the 'fishy' flavour of thigh meat from birds fed diets containing 10 or 20 g/kg tuna oil, but that the breast meat from turkeys on the diet containing the higher level of tuna oil had a significantly greater 'fishy' flavour. The 'fishy flavour' scores with tuna oil were significantly different from those obtained when the diet contained 40 g/kg beef fat. Chemical analysis showed the presence in tuna oil of high levels of ω-3 fatty acids, i.e. those fatty acids with a double bond at the third carbon from the methyl end of the carbon chain. These were C20:5ω3, C22:5ω3 and C22:6ω3. Since such acids were virtually absent from beef fat, Crawford and Kretsch (1976) concluded that their oxidation was the factor responsible for the 'fishy' flavour of meat.

Recent evidence suggests that 'fishy' flavour may still be a problem to the modern turkey processor: Moran *et al.* (1984) concluded that the 'off-flavour' detected in the thigh meat of a number of 20-week-old male turkeys was probably a consequence of the birds having been maintained on diets containing varying levels of fish meal.

Improvement of meat stability

Turkey meat is generally considered to be oxidatively less stable when compared with chicken meat. This difference between species may in part be due to the greater concentration of phospholipids in turkey meat (Allen and Foegeding, 1981), since it is the levels of these lipids which decrease as oxidative changes occur during storage. In general, these changes are greater in thigh than in breast meat (Sklan, Tenne and Budowski, 1983; Whang and Peng, 1987). However, it is well established that the underlying reason for the poorer stability of turkey meat is the birds' poor efficiency in depositing tocopherol (vitamin E) in their fat and muscle (Mecchi *et al.*, 1956). Sklan, Bartov and Hurwitz (1982) concluded that the lower tocopherol levels found in turkey tissues were explained in part by the greater production and excretion of tocopheryl glucuronides — major catabolic products of tocopherol metabolism — being some two to nine times higher in the turkey than in the chicken.

In the light of the above, it is not too surprising to find that attempts have been made to improve meat stability by the administration of vitamin E to live turkeys and to establish the best means of presenting the compound to the birds. Webb, Marion and Hayse (1972b) concluded that injection of tocopherol weekly for 12 or 16 weeks prior to slaughter was more effective in reducing TBA numbers than was oral application. On the other hand, investigations by Uebersax, Dawson and Uebersax (1978a) led the authors to conclude that dietary supplementation with vitamin E was more effective in retarding rancidity development than was the bi-weekly injection of tocopherol.

The level of tocopherol in the bird's tissues is significantly affected by the concentration of the compound in its diet (Marusich *et al.*, 1975; Sheldon, 1984). The latter study showed that thigh muscle may contain up to six times more tocopherol than breast or skin and fat, presumably because of the better vascularity of the turkey leg.

Diets supplemented with vitamin E at levels up to 400 IU/kg feed and administered to turkeys for 1–4 weeks prior to slaughter were found to delay the onset of rancidity in breast meat (Marusich *et al.*, 1975). TBA analysis suggested that 200 IU vitamin E/kg feed given for 4 weeks, or 400 IU/kg feed for 3 weeks had optimal effects. More recently, Rethwill *et al.* (1981), using leg meat, found that whereas the low levels of vitamin E (10 IU/kg) which may be commonly added to turkey rations, gave a low level of protection from oxidation when administered over the entire 14-week growing period, supplementation at 300 IU/kg feed significantly improved the shelf-life (as judged by TBA values) of turkey carcasses refrigerated at 3°C for 3 weeks. This was particularly the case with birds whose dietary source of added fat was of animal origin.

Sheldon (1984) raised female turkeys on standard starter and grower rations for 16 weeks before splitting the batch into four groups which were then fed diets containing different levels of tocopherol. In the case of Diet A, 1.63 IU tocopheryl acetate/kg were fed for weeks 16–18, B; 1.63 IU for weeks 16 and 17, followed by 275 IU at week 18; C, 55 IU for weeks 16–18, and D, 275 IU for weeks 16–18. Following slaughter at 19 weeks, each carcass was deboned and the breast, thigh meat, and the skin and subcutaneous fat covering them were ground together. TBA analysis was carried out shortly after processing, and again after refrigerated or frozen storage in air or nitrogen. All levels of tocopherol supplementation (Diets B to D) were effective in reducing TBA values, although a level of 275 IU tocopheryl acetate/kg feed administered for 1 or 3 weeks prior to slaughter was most effective. Overall, packaging in nitrogen had no statistically significant effect on TBA numbers when compared to air, although lower numbers for control samples in nitrogen led the author to conclude that nitrogen-packaging of meat containing normal levels of tocopherol might help reduce oxidation during storage.

Effect of processing

There is little evidence that the primary processing of turkey carcasses influences the flavour of the resulting meat. A possible point where changes might be expected is at the 'tanking' stage, when carcasses are held for a number of hours in ice or ice/water, hence providing conditions where chemical compounds may be leached from the tissues. However, the flavour of meat of male turkeys was not significantly affected by immersion of carcasses in slush ice for up to 23 h (Brodine and Carlin, 1968).

In a number of countries, 'self-basting' turkeys are produced by injecting the eviscerated carcasses with various solutions, usually oil-based. Cornforth et al. (1982) using turkeys basted with solutions of unspecified composition, found that both broth- and oil-basted breast meats were preferred over the meat from unbasted controls with the broth-basted carcasses receiving a significantly higher rather than the others. Similarly, the use of coconut oil as the internal basting medium for the breast improved meat quality (Larmond and Moran, 1983). On the other hand, thigh meat did not benefit from basting.

Regulatory authorities in some countries allow the use of certain enzymes as tenderizers of poultry meat, and on examining the effect of papain injection on the sensory properties of turkey breast meat Chambers and Bowers (1981) found off-flavour to intensify as the enzyme concentration was increased from 1 to 2 mg/kg. However, incorporation of the papain in a flavour marinade prior to injection may overcome the problem of off-flavour (Cunningham and Tiede, 1981).

Of the numerous products formulated from turkey, rolls may be prepared from white or dark meat blended with salt and other ingredients. A series of investigations into the effects of meat type and ingredients on the flavour of rolls showed that light meat received higher scores than dark meat, while the addition of 4.5 g/kg phosphate, and the inclusion of 20 to 30 g/kg of soya protein isolate in the product formulation improved its flavour (Kardouche and Stadelman, 1978; Kardouche, Pratt and Stadelman, 1978). Further work confirmed that the flavour of turkey breast meat rolls was improved by the incorporation of sodium chloride and various phosphates into the product and revealed that there was no significant difference due to the type of phosphate used (Froning and Sackett, 1985).

Effect of storage on meat flavour

Whole carcasses

As with most turkey products, eviscerated carcasses may be held in the chilled ('fresh') or frozen states. There is little to suggest that the flavour of chilled carcasses is enhanced during the normal shelf-life period. As regards frozen turkeys, Hoke, McGeary and Lakshmann (1968) found that the flavour score of thigh meat of carcasses held for 5 months at −20°C was greater than those of fresh turkeys. However, there was evidence of flavour deterioration between 5 and 10 months of storage.

While much of the poultry currently produced is in the form of oven-ready, i.e. eviscerated carcasses, in some countries such as the UK, there is a sizeable market, notably at Christmas, in turkey carcasses which have been stored uneviscerated under dry, cool conditions. Consequently, there have been a number of recent studies into how the flavour of meat from such carcasses is influenced by the storage conditions.

Griffiths *et al.* (1984), using a 5-point scale to rate the size of the flavour difference between a test sample and the control, found that the flavour scores of cooked breast meat from turkeys held uneviscerated for 8 days at 4°C overlapped those of day 1, although there was a significant overall difference between the two periods of storage. The perceptual difference found by a trained taste panel between a control and samples from carcasses stored for 8 days was very slight however, and being less than one scale unit, probably would not have been perceived by the average consumer. Results are shown diagrammatically in *Figure 17.1*, where it is seen that a clear flavour difference was evident at 16 days of storage, with meat flavours being described as 'strong', 'livery' and 'gamey'. At 24

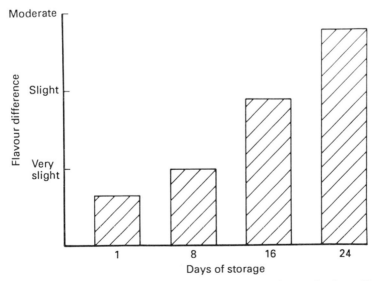

Figure 17.1 Effect of hanging at 4°C on the flavour of uneviscerated turkeys. The flavour differences are between a control and the test sample and were on a scale where 0 = no difference, 1 = very slight, 2 = slight, 3 = moderate and 4 = large. (Reproduced by courtesy of Forbes Publications Ltd)

days of storage the flavours were more intense, leading the authors to conclude that flavour acceptance was a matter of the panellists' personal preferences.

A later study (Grey *et al.*, 1986) showed that while there were no flavour differences between turkeys held at 4°C for 1 day and those stored for 10 days, subsequent evisceration and storage at −2°C for a further 20 days resulted in a significantly stronger flavour. In contrast, there was no flavour difference when uneviscerated carcasses were held under the same conditions.

Portions in modified atmospheres

A major growth area in turkey meat production is in the development of products which are marketed in the chilled state. However, these generally have a relatively short shelf-life due to the proliferation of spoilage bacteria on the meat. While spoilage of poultry may be considerably delayed by holding the meat at temperatures below 0°C (Barnes *et al.*, 1978), there is also commercial interest in the use of various packaging techniques to extend shelf-life. However, there is relatively little published experimental information on the effects of such techniques on the flavour of turkey products.

Jones *et al.* (1982) studied the effect of packaging method on the flavour of turkey meat held at 1°C. In the case of skinless breast fillets (*m. supracoracoideus*) packaged in oxygen-permeable material, there was little difference between initial samples and those stored for 10 days, but by day 14 all samples were considered to be 'gamey' or 'livery'. Breast fillets held in vacuum packs showed no clear differences up to 14 days of storage, but thereafter up to 25 days, variable flavour changes were detected, with some samples showing no difference from the initial samples, while others held under the same conditions were 'slightly' to 'moderately' different. At day 32, all samples were 'stronger', 'stale' or 'gamey'. It was found that flavour changes could be detected well before the appearance of 'off'-odours, indicating that such odour assessment was not necessarily a suitable criterion for judging the shelf-life of poultry products.

Table 17.1 Effect of gaseous environment on the flavour of turkey breast meat

Type of pack	Day 8[a]	Day 18
20 % carbon dioxide	Sweet Metallic Stale Less flavour	Bland Bitter Strong Sulphur
20% carbon dioxide + 20% oxygen	Stale, fishy Strong, fishy	Fishy Bitter Burnt Sour
20% carbon dioxide + 10% oxygen	Fruity Gamey Bitter	Sour Burnt Rancid

Data of Mead *et al.* (1983). (Courtesy of Forster-Verlag AG)

[a] Days of storage at 1°C

Drumsticks held with skin intact in oxygen-permeable packs had more flavour after 10 days than controls, and at 14 days, were 'gamey', 'sweet' or 'gutty'. As with breast meat held under the same conditions, vacuum-packed drumsticks showed a wide variation between samples up to 16 days of storage, although the reasons for the sample variation were not established. At 18 days the acceptable storage time had been exceeded.

Further studies with breast fillets (Mead *et al.*, 1983) confirmed that few flavour changes occurred during 21 days of storage in the case of vacuum packs or in packs containing differing levels of carbon dioxide in nitrogen. However, if oxygen was added to the carbon dioxide/nitrogen mixture in an attempt to improve meat colour, strong, and generally unpleasant, flavours were detected after as little as 4 days of storage at 1°C. The rate of development of unpleasant flavours in the cooked meat appeared to be related to the level of oxygen in the packs. Examples of flavour descriptions applied by the sensory panel to fillets held under varying storage conditions are given in *Table 17.1*. Interestingly, the 4-day period when flavour changes were first noted by Mead *et al.* (1983) falls within the shelf-life period normally allowed by commercial processors who hold turkey portions in packs containing mixtures of nitrogen, oxygen and carbon dioxide.

Irradiation

Although the irradiation of poultry carcasses to prolong shelf-life is permitted in a number of countries and the process is known to cause odour and flavour changes in the irradiated product, there appears to be little published information relating to turkey meat.

Cured products

Cured turkey products are also available on the market and there have been a number of studies designed to evaluate the effects of curing mixture ingredients, such as salt, nitrite, ascorbate, erythorbate and spices, on product flavour. Although the presence or absence of erythorbate did not significantly affect the flavour scores of turkey hams (Hasiak *et al.*, 1984), the presence of 550 mg/kg of erythorbate significantly increased the cured flavour and overall acceptability scores of frankfurters (Wesley, Marion and Sebranek, 1982). In both cases there was evidence that erythorbate acted as an anti-oxidant in that the TBA values of the products in which it was incorporated were reduced.

It is well known that nitrite can react with amines to form nitrosamines, some of which have been implicated as causes of cancer in experimental animals. Thus there has been public concern about the presence of nitrosamines in cured meat, although according to Hotchkiss and Cassens (1987), these compounds are not routinely found other than in fried bacon. Nonetheless, there have been a number of recent studies on the possible effects of reducing nitrite levels in the curing mixture on the overall quality of cured turkey products.

The flavour of smoked turkey drumsticks was unaffected by the presence or absence of added nitrite in the curing brine (Olson *et al.*, 1979). Later, Sheldon, Ball and Kimsey (1982), used an untrained taste panel to study the effects of various curing procedures and nitrite levels on the organoleptic quality of smoked turkey breast meat. The panel found no effect of curing method, and while the panel scores for the cured meat flavour of turkeys cured with reduced nitrite levels were numerically higher, indicating an improved flavour, they were not statistically significantly different.

Similarly, the hedonic (preference) scores for the flavour of turkey hams containing levels of nitrite ranging between 0 and 156 mg/kg were not significantly different when assessed over an 11-week storage period, although the most undesirable flavour scores were found in samples containing no nitrite (Hasiak *et al.*, 1984). In contrast, Wesley, Marion and Sebranek (1982) concluded that a nitrite level between 50 and 100 mg/kg was required for full flavour development in turkey frankfurters, but that no further flavour enhancement occurred on the addition of higher levels of nitrite.

Sales, Bowers and Kropf (1980) on testing turkey frankfurters stored for up to 4 weeks, observed that while consumers preferred frankfurters cured with nitrite to those without nitrite, the flavour of the frankfurters containing no added nitrite did not differ significantly from those containing nitrite. In the same study, a trained taste panel found the flavour of nitrite-containing products to be significantly different, and that cured meat flavour increased with increasing nitrite concentration, while rancid flavour decreased under the same conditions. Turkey breast emulsions (sausages) prepared with (a) sodium chloride, (b) nitrite, (c) ascorbate, (d) b + c, or (e) none of these additives, were stored in the raw or cooked state for 5 weeks at −18°C prior to being assessed for meaty and stale aromas (Tellefson *et al.*, 1982). When raw emulsion was heated after storage, those samples containing no additives, or with both ascorbate and nitrite present, had more meaty aroma than those containing only one of the ingredients. Emulsions containing nitrite plus ascorbate had less stale aroma than other treatments. A greater stale aroma was noted when sodium chloride was present in the product, suggesting that salt was exerting a pro-oxidant effect, although estimation of the TBA value indicated that this was not the case. On the other hand, this study confirmed earlier work from the same laboratory (Tellefson and Bowers, 1981) that both nitrite and high levels of ascorbate acted as anti-oxidants in turkey meat products.

The replacement of nitrite with sorbate, another inhibitor of *C. botulinum*, was said to lead to adverse flavour changes in turkey frankfurters (Bauermann, 1979).

Flaked turkey thigh meat was used by Graham and Marriot (1986) as the principal raw ingredient in the manufacture of smoked, restructured products, either being used alone or in combination with 100 g/kg dry-cured ham or fresh pork. Sensory evaluation of the cooked products showed that flavour desirability did not differ between the various products, either when freshly prepared, or after holding for 84 days at −23.3°C. While none of the meats changed in flavour desirability between 21 and 84 days of frozen storage, the product containing only turkey as the meat ingredient, and which had been stored for 21 days, was considered to be less desirable than the corresponding product containing fresh pork. The panel's view was supported by the fact that the sample containing only turkey meat had a higher TBA value.

It seems likely that the differing results obtained by various research groups may reflect the variation in the type of cured product under investigation. However, the preponderance of evidence reviewed suggests that providing good manufacturing practice is observed, cured turkey products of acceptable colour, flavour and microbiological quality could be achieved using sodium nitrite at levels between 50 and 100 mg/kg.

Rancidity of mechanically recovered meat

Mechanically recovered meat (MRM) is the material removed from turkey necks or from the skeleton ('frame', 'rack') after the bulk of the meat has been removed from the carcass, and is widely used in chopped emulsion products. Mechanical deboning may be achieved either by forcing the meat off the bones by the application of high pressure, or by using an auger to force the carcass parts against screens through which the meat passes (Jones, 1986).

In addition to the heat generated in the product, the physical processes involved in the preparation of MRM result in considerable cell damage and introduce air, haem pigments and varying levels of fat into the purée-like material (Froning, 1981). Therefore, it is not too surprising to find that poultry MRM may only be held for 5–6 days at 3 or 4°C before the detection of rancidity, due largely to autoxidation of poly-unsaturated fatty acids located in the phospholipid fraction. In turkey MRM, 62–64% of the fatty acids in this fraction are unsaturated, with oleic, linoleic and arachidonic acids predominating (Dawson and Gartner, 1983). These latter compounds decrease in concentration during turkey meat storage (Salih *et al.*, 1986; Whang and Peng, 1987). Uebersax, Dawson and Uebersax (1978) investigated the storage stability of turkey MRM cooled with carbon dioxide prior to being held in air-filled or vacuum packs. While there was no significant difference due to packaging, the carbon dioxide-cooled meat exhibited higher TBA values than controls. Generally, MRM exposed to air or mixed under a stream of carbon dioxide, had higher TBA values than unmixed controls or meat mixed under nitrogen (Uebersax, Dawson and Uebersax, 1978b). Vacuum packaging resulted in lower TBA numbers than did packaging in air. Although treatment with carbon dioxide may have caused an increase in the TBA values of the MRM, the fact that the initial pH value of the carbon dioxide-treated meat (pH 5.76) was much lower than that of the control (pH 6.14) suggested that such treatment may be useful in maintaining the microbiological quality of MRM. Blending poultry MRM in nitrogen containing various levels of carbon monoxide has also been shown to improve its storage stability, although in the case of chicken meat at least, the product becomes redder following treatment with the monoxide (McNeill, Kakuda and Findlay, 1987).

While the subsequent onset of rancidity in poultry MRM held at refrigeration temperatures may be delayed by the inclusion of tocopherol in the diets of the birds (Webb, Marion and Hayse, 1972a; Hayse, Marion and Paulson, 1974; Uebersax, Dawson and Uebersax, 1978a), more commonly, anti-oxidants are introduced into products containing MRM. Such anti-oxidants include synthetic compounds such as butylated hydroxyanisole (BHA), butylated hydroxytoluene (BHT), citric acid and polyphosphates, as well as naturally occurring materials such as rosemary extracts or egg fractions.

Barbut, Josephson and Maurer (1985) investigated the effect of added rosemary oleoresin (20 mg/kg) on the refrigerated shelf-life of turkey breakfast sausages prepared with three parts hand-deboned meat and one part MRM. In the presence of the oleoresin, TBA values of the sausages remained fairly constant over a 15-day storage period and were substantially lower than those of sausages which did not contain an anti-oxidant. Assessment by a sensory panel showed that the degree of oxidative rancidity increased with storage time in the case of raw sausages with no additives, and also that after 10 days of storage such sausages were significantly different from those containing spices alone or in combination with anti-oxidant.

However, the spice containing samples could not be differentiated on the basis of oxidative rancidity, due to the masking effect of the spice mix. Similarly, the panel could not distinguish any difference in the off-flavour intensity of fried sausage containing spice and those that also contained rosemary oleoresin, although gas chromatography had shown the former to contain higher concentrations of oxidatively-derived carbonyl compounds.

The level of rosemary derivative added to the product formulation may have an important bearing on the resulting flavour, since MacNeil, Dimick and Mast (1973) found that although rosemary spice extract improved the flavour of simulated turkey MRM when present at a level of 10 mg/kg, with 50 mg/kg added extract the flavour was less acceptable than that of untreated control MRM.

According to Lu and Baker (1986), addition of egg yolk at levels of 10, 20 and 30 g/kg, or phosvitin (625 mg/kg) to the product significantly decreased the TBA values of both cooked and uncooked patties derived from neck MRM, but did not enhance the oxidative stability of patties prepared from turkey drumstick MRM. However, egg white, particularly the conalbumin fraction, may be an effective anti-oxidant when added to turkey thigh meat (Froning, Ragan and Niemann, 1986).

Some evidence suggests that turkey MRM may also undergo adverse quality changes due to oxidation when stored in the frozen state. Froning et al. (1971) found the incorporation of 150 g/kg turkey MRM which had been stored at −24°C for 90 days, into beef frankfurters, reduced the flavour of the resulting product. In a later study, Johnson, Cunningham and Bowers (1974) stored MRM derived from whole eviscerated carcasses at temperatures between −13 and −32°C for up to 14 weeks prior to cooking and assessment by a sensory panel. Flavour scores were constant, and in the range of 'slightly to moderately desirable' during the first 10 weeks of storage, but deteriorated thereafter. There was no significant effect of storage temperature on flavour. On the other hand, TBA values increased with both temperature and time, the increase being accelerated after 6 weeks of storage. Uebersax, Dawson and Uebersax (1978) reported no significant increases in the TBA values of MRM held over a 3-month period at −18°C, although here the initial TBA values were rather high (3.10, compared with the values of less than 2.0 observed by Johnson, Cunningham and Bowers, 1974).

Subjective and objective measurements on summer sausages containing 500 g/kg turkey MRM which had been maintained at −25°C prior to use revealed that there was a slight decline in product quality with meat held frozen for 6 months. However, the sensory panel did not report adversely on flavour (Dhillon and Maurer, 1975). The results of this study suggested that fermented products such as summer sausages may behave differently from cooked turkey products.

'Warmed-over flavour'

Some precooked and refrigerated poultry products may become unacceptable to the consumer because of adverse flavour changes which occur on subsequent re-heating of the foods. The resulting off-flavour is often described as 'warmed-over flavour' (WOF) and seems to particularly affect turkey meat. In their comprehensive review of the occurrence of WOF in meats and fish Pearson, Love and Shorland (1977), reported that WOF could also be encountered in refrigerated raw ground meat. According to Addis (1986), WOF is now a more significant problem than is lipid autoxidation.

Sensory analysis of roasted and cubed turkey meat showed that while the flavour was unimpaired by storage for 4 days at $-20°C$, at $4°C$ there was a marked deterioration in flavour during storage, especially in the case of leg meat where panel ratings fell from 7.0, on a scale with 10 representing the best turkey flavour, before storage to 3.6 after 4 days (Jacobson and Koehler, 1970). There was a concomitant increase in the TBA numbers of both breast and leg meat, particularly in the case of the latter. Since the panellists accepted leg meat with higher TBA values than breast meat, the authors concluded that the rich, meaty flavour of dark meat masked or supplemented the initial development of oxidative flavour changes.

The experienced sensory panel used by Cipra and Bowers (1970) rated the flavour of freshly braised turkey breast meat superior to that of braised meat reheated after 24 h at $6°C$. Rancid and stale flavours in the reheated meat were related positively to the intensities of sulphur, ammonia, bitter and acidic flavour and aroma components. Storage and reheating had no significant effect on the TBA value of the meat. It was suggested that changes in both lipid oxidation and ninhydrin-positive compounds were involved in adverse flavour changes. In contrast to the foregoing, Cremer (1986) reported that the flavour intensity of cooked turkey rolls increased slightly after 24 h refrigerated storage, and that reheating to $66°C$ did not result in the production of 'off-flavour'.

Wilson, Pearson and Shorland (1976) assayed breast and leg meat for total lipids and phospholipids, as well as measuring the TBA values of the raw meat, of meat immediately after cooking to $70°C$, and of cooked meat held refrigerated for 48 h. From these studies the authors concluded that since WOF became more serious as the proportion of phospholipids to total lipids in the meat increased, the phospholipids apparently played a major role in causing the quality defect in cooked meat.

Ruenger, Reineccius and Thompson (1978) roasted half turkeys to an internal temperature of $82°C$; some of these samples were stored for 48 h at $4°C$ prior to reheating. On using triangle tests to compare fresh with reheated meat, the authors found that their sensory panel could distinguish between the two, and that they had equal success in selecting WOF in breast and leg meat. This latter result did not support the hypothesis of Wilson, Pearson and Shorland (1976) that red meat would be more susceptible to WOF than white meat. In the same study by Ruenger, Reineccius and Thompson (1978), volatile constituents of the raw and cooked meats were assayed by gas chromatography, and the results submitted to computer analysis. Such analysis showed one peak (heptaldehyde) to be different in white meat, but this plus two others (one being identified as n-nona-3,6-dienal) to be different in dark meat. The concentrations of all three components increased in the reheated samples, indicating that WOF was due to the formation of additional volatile compounds rather than to a reduction in the components of 'fresh turkey' flavour. Both heptaldehyde and the dienal were believed to be products of lipid oxidation, their presence providing further evidence for WOF resulting from such oxidation. Thirty volatile compounds were identified as potential products of fatty acid oxidation by Sheldon and Wu (1986) in their study of WOF in cooked turkey breast meat rolls which showed that there was a correlation between flavour deterioration and increasing TBA numbers. Further work revealed that five volatiles, pentane, pentanal, hexanal, 2-heptanone and 2-hexenal, were correlated with oxidative deterioration (Wu and Sheldon, 1986).

Einerson and Reineccius (1977) compared the flavour and TBA values of ground turkey breast meat precooked to 82°C, refrigerated and then reheated, with those of canned and retorted meat similarly refrigerated and reheated. While the sensory panel found no significant difference between the degree of WOF of 'fresh' and retorted meats, there were significant differences between these and 'warmed-over' meats. The TBA values showed a similar pattern (*Table 17.2*). It was shown that the anti-oxidant substance responsible for the inhibition of WOF in retorted turkey meat was water soluble, of low molecular weight, and probably resulted from 'browning' interactions which occurred in the meat during retorting (Einerson and Reineccius, 1977, 1978).

Table 17.2 Organoleptic and chemical evaluation of fresh, warmed-over and retorted turkey

	Treatment		
	Fresh	Warmed-over	Retorted
Mean flavour score[a]	0.84	3.63	1.00
Mean TBA value[b]	0.518	0.689	0.500

From Einerson and Reineccius (1977) (courtesy of Food and Nutrition Press Inc.)

[a] Scale from 0–5, with 0 representing no 'warmed-over flavour' (WOF) and 5 representing very strong WOF
[b] TBA value in absorbance

Roasted meat obtained from birds treated with tocopherol was stored at −25°C for 4 months prior to reheating and examination by sensory evaluation and TBA analysis (Webb, Marion and Hayse, 1972a). Significant differences in off-flavour were found due to muscle type and tocopherol treatment. In both sexes breast meat had lower off-flavour than thigh meat. *Table 17.3* shows that overall, meat from males injected with 10 IU of tocopherol had the lowest off-flavour scores, while in the female group, birds injected with 100 IU vitamin E had the least amount of off-flavour. In some cases the sensory panellists preferred turkey meat which was partially rancid because it had more flavour than fresh turkey. Subsequent TBA analysis of leg meat from male turkeys fed varying levels of vitamin E (Rethwill *et al*, 1981), provided further evidence that the inclusion of tocopherol in the diet gave some protection against the subsequent development of WOF.

Table 17.3 Effect of tocopherol administration on flavour and off-flavour of turkey meat

	Sex	Vitamin E treatment				
		Control	Oral		Injected	
			10 IU	100 IU	10 IU	100 IU
Flavour	F	4.79[a]	5.01[a,b]	5.50[c]	5.16[b,c]	5.21[b,c]
	M	4.90[a]	4.89[a]	4.90[a]	5.22[a]	4.88[a]
Off-flavour	F	2.89[a]	2.66[a,b]	2.13[a,b]	2.41[b,c]	2.04[c]
	M	2.26[a]	2.06[a]	2.11[a]	1.67[b]	2.26[a]

Reprinted from *Journal of Food Science* (1972), **37**, 853–856. Copyright of The Institute of Food Technologists

[a,b,c] Values not followed by a common letter are different at the $P = 0.01$ level of significance

Flavour and off-flavour evaluated on an ascending scale of 1 to 8

Effect of cooking method on flavour

The development of institutional food-services, together with a need to conserve energy, has stimulated renewed interest in the methods of cooking poultry products and in the determination of the optimal temperatures to be used for cooking. In particular, the increasing popularity of microwave ovens for cooking, or for reheating convenience foods, has led to a number of investigations into the possible effects of such a cooking method on the sensory qualities of turkey meat.

Turkey carcasses oven-roasted at 93.3°C had higher flavour scores than birds roasted at higher temperature, or cooked in a microwave oven (Cornforth et al., 1982). Although all samples were cooked to a nominal internal temperature of 71.1°C, the carcasses roasted at 176.6 or 204.4°C had a final temperature of 76.7°C and had lower flavour scores. On the other hand, the study of Hoke, McGeary and Lakshmann (1968) had shown that the flavour of turkey meat intensified as the end-point temperature rose from 74 to 85°C. This latter view tended to be supported by Cremer (1986), who after examining the white meat component of rolls prepared from mixed breast and leg meats, concluded that flavour was not fully developed in rolls cooked to an end-point temperature of 77°C. Flavour intensity increased significantly when slices of the cooked rolls were held at 66°C for a further 60 min. This latter study also showed that rolls cooked to an internal temperature of 77°C using an oven temperature of 135°C had a more intense flavour than was the case when the oven temperature was 105°C.

Evaluation of the flavour and aroma of precooked frozen turkey meat following reheating in microwave or conventional gas ovens (Cipra and Bowers, 1971) showed that 'meaty-brothy' flavour and aroma were more intense in the meat reheated by microwaves. The intensities were greater in dark than in light meat: indeed, light meat reheated in a microwave oven tended to have a bland flavour.

In contrast to the above, roast turkey flavour was higher and off-flavour lower, when breast meat was cooked in a rotary hearth oven than when a microwave appliance was used (Chambers and Bowers, 1981). Similarly, the flavour of drumstick meat roasted in an electric oven was rated more highly than that of meat cooked in a microwave oven (Cunningham and Tiede, 1981).

Further evidence that microwave cooking resulted in lower flavour scores for breast meat than did conventional roasting methods was produced by Ehrcke et al. (1985) in their study of eight cooking treatments. Panel scores were significantly higher for turkeys cooked in a convection oven at 135°C than in a conventional oven at 190°C, microwave apparatus at various power settings, or a microwave-convection oven. Those panellists owning microwave ovens tended to give a lower turkey flavour rating than those who did not own such equipment.

Chambers and Bowers (1981) suggested that the slower heating that occurred in a conventional oven may have allowed for the development of 'roasted flavour' more readily than did the faster microwave cooking process.

Conclusions

There is little evidence to suggest that the flavour of turkey meat is affected markedly by the characteristics of the bird, by its diet, or by the various stages employed in the commercial processing of the carcass. The flavour of the eviscerated carcass can be enhanced by the injection of suitable solutions, and that of the formulated product can be influenced by the ingredients added during manufacture. Currently, such treatments will generally be the only available means of enhancing turkey meat flavour, although holding the carcass for some days prior to evisceration will intensify the flavour of the resulting cooked meat.

Studies indicate that flavour acceptability depends on the personal preferences of the taster.

The high susceptibility of turkey meat, especially in the ground form to lipid oxidation, may present problems to the food manufacturer developing new products. There is a need to develop a reliable objective means of determining rancidity in poultry meat.

References

Addis, P. B. (1986). Poultry muscle as food. In *Muscle as Food* (Bechtel, P. J., ed.), pp. 371–404. London, Academic Press

Allen, C. E. and Foegeding, E. A. (1981). Some lipid characteristics and interactions in muscle foods — a review. *Food Technology*, **35**(5), 253–257

Barbut, S., Josephson, D. B. and Maurer, A. J. (1985). Antioxidant properties of rosemary oleoresin in turkey sausage. *Journal of Food Science*, **50**, 1356–1359 and 1363

Barnes, E. M., Impey, C. S., Geeson, J. D. and Buhagiar, R. W. M. (1978). The effect of storage temperature on the shelf-life of eviscerated air-chilled turkeys. *British Poultry Science*, **19**, 77–84

Bauermann, J. F. (1979). Processing of poultry products with and without sodium nitrite. *Food Technology*, **33**(7), 42–43

Brodine, M. V. and Carlin, A. F. (1968). Chilling and thawing methods and their effects on quality of cooked whole turkeys. *Food Technology*, **22**, 607–610

Carlson, C. W., Adams, A. W., Wilcox, R. A., Gastler, G. F. and Burrill, L. M. (1962). Dietary energy, sex, strain and storage as influencing composition and/or palatability of Broad Breasted Bronze turkeys. *Poultry Science*, **41**, 150–160

Carlson, C. W., Guenther, E., Schneider, K. C., Guild, L. P., Deethardt, D. and Greichus, Y. A. (1969). Effects of corn oil and lysine on growth, fatty acid composition and palatability of Large Broad White turkeys. *Poultry Science*, **48**, 1027–1033

Cash, D. B. and Carlin, A. F. (1968). Quality of frozen boneless turkey roasts precooked to different internal temperatures. *Food Technology*, **22**, 1477–1480

Chambers, E. IV and Bowers, J. A. (1981). Sensory characteristics of papain injected turkey cooked conventionally or by microwaves. *Journal of Food Science*, **46**, 1627–1628

Cipra, J. S. and Bowers, J. A. (1970). Precooked turkey. Flavor and certain chemical changes caused by refrigeration and reheating. *Food Technology*, **24**, 921–923

Cipra, J. S. and Bowers, J. A. (1971). Flavor of microwave- and conventionally-reheated turkey. *Poultry Science*, **50**, 703–706

Cornforth, D. P., Brennand, C. P., Brown, R. J. and Godfrey, D. (1982). Evaluation of various methods for roasting frozen turkeys. *Journal of Food Science*, **47**, 1108–1112

Crawford, L. and Kretsch, M. J. (1976). GC-MS identification of the volatile compounds extracted from roasted turkeys fed a basal diet supplemented with tuna oil: some comments on fishy flavor. *Journal of Food Science*, **41**, 1470–1478

Crawford, L., Kretsch, M. J., Peterson, D. W. and Lilyblade, A. L. (1975). The remedial and preventative effect of dietary α-tocopherol on the development of fishy flavor in turkey meat. *Journal of Food Science*, **40**, 751–755

Cremer, M. L. (1986). Sensory quality of turkey rolls roasted and held in an institutional convection oven with and without chilled storage. *Journal of Food Science*, **51**, 868–872

Cunningham, F. E. and Tiede, L. M. (1981). Properties of selected poultry products treated with a tenderizing marinade. *Poultry Science*, **60**, 2475–2479

Dawson, L. E. and Gartner, R. (1963). Lipid oxidation in mechanically deboned poultry. *Food Technology*, **37**(7), 112–116

Dhillon, A. S. and Maurer, A. J. (1975). Quality measurements of chicken and turkey summer sausages. *Poultry Science*, **54**, 1263–1271

Ehrcke, L. A., Rasdall, J. O., Gibbs, S. O. and Haydon, F. C. (1985). Comparison of eight cooking treatments for energy utilization, product yields and quality of roasted turkey. *Poultry Science*, **64**, 1881–1886

Einerson, M. A. and Reineccius, G. A. (1977). Inhibition of warmed-over flavor in retorted turkey by antioxidants formed during processing. *Journal of Food Processing and Preservation*, **1**, 279–291

Einerson, M. A. and Reineccius, G. A. (1978). Characterization of antioxidants responsible for inhibition of warmed-over flavor in retorted turkey. *Journal of Food Processing and Preservation*, **2**, 1–7

Froning, G. W. (1981). Mechanical deboning of poultry and fish. In *Advances in Food Research* (Chichester, C. O., Mrak, E. M. and Stewart, G. F., eds), Vol. 27, pp. 109–147. London, Academic Press

Froning, G. W. and Sackett, B. (1985). Effect of salt and phosphates during tumbling of turkey breast muscle on meat characteristics. *Poultry Science*, **64**, 1328–1333

Froning, G. W., Ragan, L. F. and Niemann, L. (1986). Conalbumin as an antioxidant in turkey meat. *Poultry Science*, **65** (Suppl. 1), 45

Froning, G. W., Arnold, R. G., Mandigo, R. W., Neth, C. E. and Hartung, T. E. (1971). Quality and storage stability of frankfurters containing 15% mechanically deboned turkey meat. *Journal of Food Science*, **36**, 974–978

Froning, G. W., Maurer, A. J., Hale, K. K. and Carlin, A. F. (1978). Sensory properties of poultry meat. *North Central Regional Research Report No. 254*. Lincoln, University of Nebraska

Graham, P. P. and Marriot, N. G. (1986). Value enhancement of turkey dark meat through restructuring techniques. *Poultry Science*, **65**, 2056–2064

Grey, T. C., Mead, G. C., Griffiths, N. M. and Jones, J. M. (1986). Effects of evisceration and storage temperature on changes in meat quality of traditional farm-fresh turkeys. *British Poultry Science*, **27**, 463–470

Griffiths, N. M., Mead, G. C., Jones, J. M. and Grey, T. C. (1984). Effects of storage on meat quality in uneviscerated turkeys held at 4°C. *British Poultry Science*, **25**, 259–266

Harkin, A. M., Kitzmiller, C., Gilpin, G. L. and Marsden, S. J. (1958). Quality of the cooked meat of turkeys fed animal or vegetable protein diets with vitamin and fat supplements. *Poultry Science*, **37**, 1328–1339

Hasiak, R. J., Chaves, J., Sebranek, J. and Kraft, A. A. (1984). Effect of sodium nitrite and sodium erythorbate on the chemical, sensory and microbiological properties of water-added turkey ham. *Poultry Science*, **63**, 1364–1371

Hayse, P. L., Marion, W. W. and Paulson, R. J. (1974). The effectiveness of tocopherol in controlling oxidative rancidity in turkey. *Poultry Science*, **53**, 1934

Hoke, I. M., McGeary, B. K. and Lakshmann, F. (1968). Muscle protein composition and eating quality of fresh and frozen turkeys. *Journal of Food Science*, **33**, 566–571

Hotchkiss, J. H. and Cassens, R. G. (1987). Nitrate, nitrite and nitroso compounds in foods. *Food Technology*, **41**(4), 127–134 and 136

Igbinedion, J. E., Orr, H. L., Johnston, R. A. and Gray, J. I. (1981). The influence of packaging in flexible films and light on the shelf-life of fresh chicken broiler carcasses. *Poultry Science*, **60**, 950–955

Jacobson, M. and Koehler, H. H. (1970). Development of rancidity during short-term storage of cooked poultry meat. *Journal of Agricultural and Food Chemistry*, **18**, 1069–1072

Johnson, P. G., Cunningham, F. E. and Bowers, J. A. (1974). Quality of mechanically deboned turkey meat. Effect of storage time and temperature. *Poultry Science*, **53**, 732–736

Jones, J. M. (1986). Review: application of science and technology to poultry meat processing. *Journal of Food Technology*, **21**, 663–681

Jones, J. M., Mead, G. C., Griffiths, N. M. and Adams, B. W. (1982). Influence of packaging on microbiological, chemical and sensory changes in chill-stored turkey portions. *British Poultry Science*, **23**, 25–40

Kardouche, M. B. and Stadelman, W. J. (1978). Effect of rigor state, phosphate addition and aging on quality of turkey rolls. *Poultry Science*, **57**, 425–432

Kardouche, M. D., Pratt, D. E. and Stadelman, W. J. (1978). Effect of soy protein isolate on turkey rolls made from pre- and post-rigor muscle. *Journal of Food Science*, **43**, 882–884

Land, D. G. and Hobson-Frohock, A. (1977). Flavour, taint and texture in poultry meat. In *Growth and Poultry Meat Production* (Boorman, K. N. and Wilson, B. J., eds), pp. 301–334. Edinburgh, British Poultry Science Limited

Larmond, E. and Moran, E. T., Jr (1983). Effect of finish grade and internal basting of the breast with oil on sensory evaluation of Small White toms. *Poultry Science*, **62**, 110–112

Larmond, E., Petrasovits, A. and Moran, E. T., Jr (1971). Eating quality of Large White turkeys as influenced by age and sex. *Canadian Institute of Food Technology Journal*, **4**, 75–79

Larmond, E., Salmon, R. E. and Klein, K. K. (1983). Effect of canola meal on the sensory quality of turkey meat. *Poultry Science*, **62**, 397–400

Lu, C.-L. and Baker, R. C. (1986). Effects of egg yolk and phosvitin on extending the oxidative stability of patties made from mechanically deboned turkey meat. *Poultry Science*, **65** (Suppl. 1), 83

MacNeil, J. H. and Dimick, P. S. (1970). Poultry product quality. 1. Compositional changes during cooking of turkey roasts. *Journal of Food Science*, **35**, 184–186

MacNeil, J. H., Dimick, P. S. and Mast, M. G. (1973). Use of chemical compounds and a spice extract in quality maintenance of deboned poultry meat. *Journal of Food Science*, **38**, 1080–1081

Marsden, S. J., Alexander, L. M., Lamb, J. C. and Linton, G. S. (1957). Relationships among diet composition, fleshing, fatness and edible quality of female roasting turkeys. Part 2. Fish products in starters; cereal grains and oilcake meals in growers. *Poultry Science*, **36**, 646–657

Marusich, W. L., Ritter, E. de, Ogrinz, E. F., Keating, J., Mitrovic, M. and Bunnell, R. H. (1975). Effect of supplemental vitamin E in control of rancidity in poultry meat. *Poultry Science*, **54**, 831–844

McNeill, J., Kakuda, Y. and Findlay, C. (1987). Effect of modified atmosphere blending on the oxidative stability and color of frozen mechanically separated poultry meat. *Journal of Food Science*, **52**, 568–570, 583

Mead, G. C., Griffiths, N. M., Jones, J. M., Grey, T. C. and Adams, B. W. (1983). Effect of gas-packaging on the keeping quality of turkey breast fillets stored at 1°C. *Lebensmittel-Wissenschaft und — Technologie*, **16**, 142–146

Mecchi, E. P., Pool, M. F., Behman, G. A., Hamachi, M. and Klose, A. A. (1956). The role of tocopherol content in the comparative stability of chicken and turkey fat. *Poultry Science*, **35**, 1238–1246

Moran, E. T., Jr, Larmond, E. and Somers, J. (1973). Full-fat soybeans for growing and finishing Large White turkeys. II. Effect on tissue fatty acids and organoleptic evaluation. *Poultry Science*, **52**, 1942–1948

Moran, E. T., Jr, Poste, L. M., Ferket, P. R. and Agar, V. (1984). Response of large tom turkeys differing in growth characteristics to divergent feeding systems: performance, carcass quality, and sensory evaluation. *Poultry Science*, **63**, 1778–1792

Olson, V. M., King, N. A., Langbehn, J. A. and Stadelman, W. J. (1979). Acceptability of smoked turkey drumsticks with and without nitrite addition. *Poultry Science*, **58**, 587–590

Pearson, A. M., Love, J. D. and Shorland, F. B. (1977). 'Warmed-over' flavour in meat, poultry and fish. In *Advances in Food Research* (Chichester, C. O., Mrak, E. M. and Stewart, G. F., eds), Vol. 23, pp. 1–74. London, Academic Press

Rethwill, C. E., Bruin, T. K., Waibel, P. E. and Addis, P. B. (1981). Influence of dietary fat source and vitamin E on market stability of turkeys. *Poultry Science*, **60**, 2466–2474

Ruenger, E. L., Reineccius, G. A. and Thompson, D. R. (1978). Flavor components related to the warmed-over flavor of turkey. *Journal of Food Science*, **43**, 1198–1200

Sales, C. A., Bowers, J. A. and Kropf, D. (1980). Consumer acceptability of turkey frankfurters with 0, 40 and 100 ppm nitrite. *Journal of Food Science*, **45**, 1060–1061

Salih, A. M., Price, J. F., Smith, D. M. and Dawson, L. E. (1986). Effect of salt and metal ions on lipid oxidation in turkey breast. *Poultry Science*, **65** (Suppl. 1), 117

Savage, T. F., Nakaue, H. S. and Holmes, Z. A. (1985). Effects of feeding a live yeast culture on market turkey performance and cooked meat characteristics. *Nutrition Reports International*, **31**, 695–703

Savage, T. F., Nakaue, H. S., Holmes, Z. A. and Taylor, T. M. (1986). Feeding value of yellow peas (*Pisum sativum L* Variety Miranda) in market turkeys and sensory evaluation of carcasses. *Poultry Science*, **65**, 1383–1390

Savage, T. F., Holmes, Z. A., Nilipour, A. H. and Nakaue, H. S. (1987). Evaluation of cooked breast meat from male breeder turkeys fed diets containing varying amounts of triticale, variety Flora. *Poultry Science,* **66**, 450–452

Sheldon, B. W. (1984). Effect of dietary tocopherol on the oxidative stability of turkey meat. *Poultry Science,* **63**, 673–681

Sheldon, B. W. and Wu, T. (1986). Flavor components and factors associated with the development of off-flavor in cooked turkey rolls. *Poultry Science,* **65** (Suppl. 1), 125

Sheldon, B. W., Ball, H. R. and Kimsey, H. R., Jr (1982). A comparison of curing practices and sodium nitrite levels on the chemical and sensory properties of smoked turkey. *Poultry Science,* **61**, 710–715

Sklan, D., Bartov, I. and Hurwitz, S. (1982). Tocopherol absorption and metabolism in the chick and turkey. *Journal of Nutrition,* **112**, 1394–1400

Sklan, D., Tenne, Z. and Budowski, P. (1983). Simultaneous lipolytic and oxidative changes in turkey meat stored at different temperatures. *Journal of the Science of Food and Agriculture,* **34**, 93–99

Tellefson, C. S. and Bowers, J. A. (1981). Effects of ascorbate and nitrite concentration in turkey frankfurter-type products. *Poultry Science,* **60**, 579–583

Tellefson, C. S., Bowers, J. A., Marshall, C. and Dayton, A. D. (1982). Aroma, color, and lipid oxidation of turkey muscle emulsions. *Journal of Food Science,* **47**, 393–396

Uebersax, K. L., Dawson, L. E. and Uebersax, M. A. (1978). Storage stability (TBA) and color of MDCM and MDTM processed with CO_2 cooling. *Poultry Science,* **57**, 670–675

Uebersax, M. A., Dawson, L. E. and Uebersax, K. L. (1978a). Storage stability (TBA) of meat obtained from turkeys receiving tocopherol supplementation. *Poultry Science,* **57**, 937–946

Uebersax, M. A., Dawson, L. E. and Uebersax, K. L. (1978b). Evaluation of various mixing stresses on storage stability (TBA) and color of mechanically deboned turkey meat. *Poultry Science,* **57**, 924–929

Webb, R. W., Marion, W. W. and Hayse, P. L. (1972a). Effect of tocopherol supplementation on the quality of precooked and mechanically deboned turkey meat. *Journal of Food Science,* **37**, 853–856

Webb, R. W., Marion, W. W. and Hayse, P. L. (1972b). Tocopherol supplementation and lipid stability in the turkey. *Ibid,* **37**, 496

Wesley, R. L., Marion, W. W. and Sebranek, J. G. (1982). Effect of sodium nitrite concentration, sodium erythorbate and storage time on the quality of franks manufactured from mechanically deboned turkey. *Journal of Food Science,* **47**, 1626–1630, 1653

Whang, K. and Peng, I. C. (1987). Lipid oxidation in ground turkey skin and muscle during storage. *Poultry Science,* **66**, 458–466

Wilson, B. R., Pearson, A. M. and Shorland, F. B. (1976). Effect of total lipids and phospholipids on warmed over flavor in red and white muscle from several species as measured by thiobarbituric acid analysis. *Journal of Agricultural and Food Chemistry,* **24**, 7–11

Wu, T. and Sheldon, B. W. (1986). Influence of phospholipids on the development of oxidative off flavors in cooked turkey rolls. *Poultry Science,* **65** (Suppl. 1), 147

Younathan, M. T., Marjan, Z. M. and Arshad, F. B. (1980). Oxidative rancidity in stored ground turkey and beef. *Journal of Food Science,* **45**, 274–275, 278

Chapter 18

Further processing of turkey meat

R. I. Richardson

Introduction

The term further processing encompasses such processes as deboning, size reduction, tumbling, massaging, reforming or emulsifying. Other processes such as breading, battering, cooking or freezing may also take place. Whole carcasses which are basted, marinaded or smoked could also be referred to as further processed. It leads to a better utilization of carcass meats, can upgrade off-cuts or poorer cuts, offer portion control, convenience, variety and relatively consistent product quality.

Turkey meat is physiologically younger than most processing red meats and has a more rapid rate of glycolysis and postmortem tenderization. It also has less fat and collagen. Deboning can begin earlier and processing treatments are gentler and of shorter duration. Turkey meat is now used for making many traditional products previously made from red meats as well as many recently developed turkey products.

The types of products now available are increasing, ranging from cut-up portions to reformed roasts, rolls, escalopes, grillsteaks, burgers, turkey hams, sausages, frankfurters, salamis, bolognas, etc. More recently ready-prepared meals have utilized an increasing amount of turkey meat (Anon, 1987a).

This review will deal with the growth in the further processed turkey market, the functional properties of turkey meat relevant to product manufacture, current and potentially new methods of processing, advances in packaging, breadings, coatings, shelf-life studies and the production and utilization of mechanically deboned turkey meat (MDTM). As this is a very large topic, only summaries and highlights of recent studies are presented.

Production statistics

World turkey meat production has continued to increase over the last few years with the USA still producing half the total world production. The expansion of the turkey industry in a number of countries has progressed at variable rates. Production and consumption data for the EEC, USA and Israel are shown in *Table 18.1*. It is noticeable that countries with high consumption have a large proportion of cut-up or further processed production. In Italy for instance, turkey meat has always been sold as cut-up in direct competition to veal and pork and only latterly

Table 18.1 World turkey production and consumption

| | Production (10³ tonnes) | | Consumption (kg/head) | Percentage cut-up or further processed |
	1975	1986	1986	1986
Belgium/Luxembourg	6.8	4.4	1.5	31
Denmark	1.7	4.0	0.4	3
Eire	ND	16.0	4.4	ND
France	93.0	289.0	4.5	87
Greece	ND	3.0	0.3	ND
Italy	ND	234.0	4.1	95
Netherlands	14.6	22.0	1.3	10
UK	85.0	155.6	3.0	55
West Germany	17.0	73.0	1.9	73
Portugal	19.0	20.0	2.0	ND
Spain	ND	19.0	0.4	ND
Israel	ND	43.0	9.5	95
USA	981.8	1790.0	6.1	76

Data from USDA (1987) and Anon (1987b). ND, no data available

Table 18.2 Turkey market for the UK (10⁶ birds)

	1976	1980	1981	1982	1983	1984	1985	1986
Whole birds:								
Retail	15.5	15.9	17.2	14.9	16.8	17.8	16.0	16.3
Catering	1.0	1.0	1.0	1.0	1.0	1.2	1.5	2.0
Total	16.5	16.9	18.2	15.9	17.8	19.0	17.5	18.3
Further processing and cut-up	0.9	5.5	6.0	7.0	8.0	8.5	9.0	10.0
Total birds	17.4	22.4	24.9	22.9	25.8	27.5	26.5	28.3
Further processing and cut-up as percentage of total	5.2	24.6	24.8	30.6	31.0	30.9	34.0	35.3

Data supplied by British Turkey Federation and revised from 1982 to Audits of Great Britain data

has a small proportion (6%) been further processed. In the USA, in 1975, 29% was further processed, in 1985, 46%. The growth of the turkey industry in the USA is shown in *Figure 18.1*. In the UK whole bird consumption is still seasonable, with more than 60% being sold in the Christmas and New Year periods. *Table 18.2* shows how, in the UK, total bird production has increased, mainly due to an increase in the numbers cut-up and further processed.

Functional properties of turkey meat

Functional properties of muscle constituents in comminuted meat products have been reviewed by Acton, Ziegler and Burge (1983) and by Bøgh-Sørensen at a recent poultry meat quality symposium (Bøgh-Sørensen, 1985). The main functional properties relevant to the further processing of meat are conferred by the gelation of meat proteins and are fat, water and meat particle binding (Kinsella, 1982). Only a brief summary and recent findings will be included here.

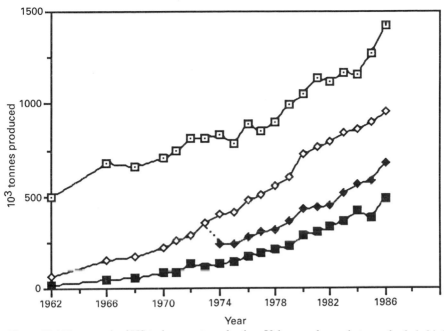

Figure 18.1 The growth of US turkey meat production. Values are for ready-to-cook whole birds (⊡), further processed whole birds and deboned meat (◇), further processed deboned meat (◆) and cut-up portions (■)

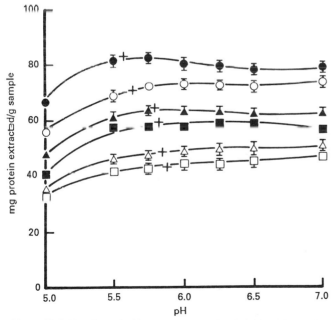

Figure 18.2 The effect of pH upon protein extractability of turkey breast (●–●, ○–○), thigh (▲–▲, △–△) and drumstick (■–■, □–□) meat. Open symbols are in the presence of 0.5 M sodium chloride, and closed symbols in the presence of 1.0 M sodium chloride. + values at unadjusted pH. Values are the means of samples from five turkeys. Standard errors are represented by vertical bars

Protein extractability

Turkey breast meat has a higher protein content than leg meats and more of it is extractable by salt solutions (McCready and Cunningham, 1971; Prusa and Bowers, 1984). Richardson and Jones (1987) have shown that, in a highly comminuted system with solution to meat ratio of 20:1, protein extraction increases with both pH (*Figure 18.2*) and salt concentration (*Figure 18.3*), the main effect of pH was in the range pH 5.00–5.75. In a study of turkeys aged from 10 to 22 weeks, protein extractability was more dependent upon the ultimate pH of the meat than upon the age of the turkeys (Richardson, in preparation). Taste preference dictates that salt concentrations used in product manufacture are lower than those which will give optimum protein extraction. However, in the initial mixing of salt and meat the concentration of salt at meat surfaces will be higher than at equilibrium in the final product.

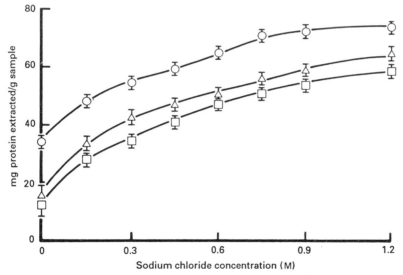

Figure 18.3 The effect of sodium chloride concentration upon protein extractability of turkey breast (O–O), thigh (△–△) and drumstick (□–□) meat at unadjusted pH. Values are the means of samples from five turkeys. Standard errors are represented by vertical bars

Extractability is greater with smaller meat particles (Acton, 1972a). In a patent for making a reformed poultry meat product a temperature of −2 to −1°C was recommended for optimum protein extraction (Hansen, Schwall and Colburn, 1966). Salt and polyphosphates significantly increase protein extraction during the tumbling of turkey breast meat and help to improve bind (Froning and Sackett, 1985). Polyphosphates normally act through their effect on pH and ionic strength (Trout and Schmidt, 1986). They may also have a role in removing sarcoplasmic proteins which have been precipitated onto the myofibrillar proteins in those muscles with rapid rates of postmortem glycolysis, such as PSE (pale, soft, exudative) pork, and thus make them more available for extraction (Lewis, Groves and Holgate, 1986). This study also showed that polyphosphates have a reduced effect in meats with a pH above 5.9. Some poultry breast meat is in the pH range

5.8–6.0 with leg meats often having a pH above this, whether this has an effect on the role of polyphosphates in poultry meat requires further study.

Protein gelation

Protein gels upon heating at which time fat, water and meat particle binding takes place. Montejano, Hamann and Lanier (1984) have compared gel development in surimi, pork, beef and turkey pastes in a model system. Gelation was monitored as temperature increased at 0.5°C/min in a thermal scanning rigidity monitor. Final rigidity of turkey gels was twice that of beef and pork and about the same as surimi. Results also suggested that turkey gels had a near perfect elastic character. The greater strength of the turkey gels may indicate a higher protein functionality when compared with beef or pork. Electron microscopy showed that the turkey gels had a higher proportion of strands and interconnections than the pork or beef gels.

Water holding

Water holding in meat has been reviewed by Hamm (1975). Salt and polyphosphates improve the cook yield of products by reducing cooking losses (Froning and Sackett, 1985). In a recent study Richardson and Jones (1987) have shown how water uptake and retention by finely comminuted turkey meat is affected by the pH, concentration of salt, the type of meat and by cooking. These results are shown in *Figures 18.4* and *18.5*. At higher salt concentrations raw breast

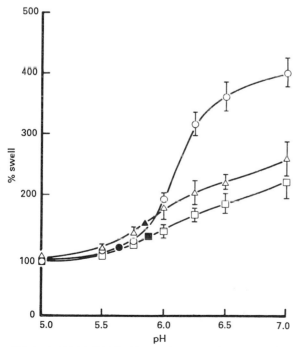

Figure 18.4 The effect of pH upon the percentage swell of turkey breast (○–○), thigh (△–△) and drumstick (□–□) meat in the presence of 0.5 M sodium chloride. Closed symbols are values measured at unadjusted pH. Values are the means for samples from five turkeys. Standard errors are represented by vertical bars

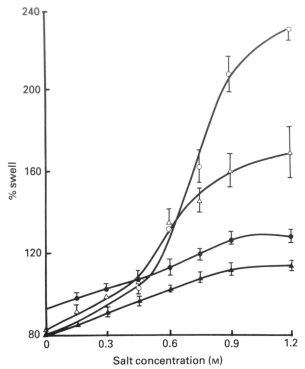

Figure 18.5 The effect of salt concentrations upon percentage swell of turkey breast (○–○, ●–●) and thigh (△–△, ▲–▲) meats adjusted to pH 6.0. Open symbols are for raw meat (water binding potential), closed symbols for cooked meat (water holding capacity). Values are the means for samples from five turkeys. Standard errors are represented by vertical bars (courtesy of Richardson and Jones, 1987)

meat retained more salt solution than leg meat, especially at higher pH. Upon heating, breast meat retained more salt solution than leg meat at all salt concentrations.

Emulsification capacity

Measurements of emulsification capacity (EC) have been used in conjunction with measurements of salt extractable protein and the total protein content of meat to produce bind constants which can be used in emulsion product least-cost formulations (Acton, 1979). Although these are empirical they seem to be of practical use. The EC values derived by Hudspeth and May (1967, 1969) for various meat types from different poultry species are often quoted. However, these authors found a higher EC for leg meat than breast meat despite the former having a lower protein extractability. EC is reduced with increasing protein concentration in model systems (Saffle, 1968).

More recent functionality tests such as surface hydrophobicity, protein solubility or sulphydryl content may be more precise tests for emulsion systems (Li-Chan, Nakai and Wood, 1984, 1985). In a recent study Brock and Enser (1987) have shown that the proteins added as part of the fat for emulsion products must also be taken into account.

Methods used for product manufacture

Technologies used for product manufacture range from reforming of large or whole muscle chunks through size reduction, such as mincing for burgers or flaking for grillsteaks, to emulsion technologies used to make traditional European-type sausages or frankfurters.

Many early poultry products were based upon traditional European sausage technology. Minced meat was mixed with cures, stuffed into casings and cooked. These products bore little resemblance to roasted whole meat. Large deboned red and white turkey meat pieces in natural proportions were also assembled in casings but upon cooking and slicing they fell apart. Many early patents claimed the use of mechanical action and/or the addition of salts, or the inclusion of salted emulsions of skin and meat trim, as means of effectively binding muscle pieces in reformed products causing them to resemble whole muscle in appearance and texture (Torr, 1965; Aref and Tape, 1966; Hansen Schwall and Colburn, 1966; Schlamb, 1970).

It is now well documented that salt and mechanical action are necessary to extract protein from meat pieces which, upon heating, will bind the pieces together in poultry (Schnell, Vadera and Baker, 1970; Acton, 1972b) and pork or beef (Theno, Siegel and Schmidt, 1976, 1977; Siegel et al., 1978). Turkey breast meat muscles can be tumbled or massaged whole in brine and stuffed into casings or moulds. Some size reduction or the addition of a matrix of smaller particles may be employed to fill spaces in the product. Fat, which is non-wettable, or collagen sheaths may interfere with bind. Thigh meat is composed of a number of smaller muscles each with its own collagenous sheath however blade tenderization can be employed to slit this sheath and improve bind (McGowan, 1970). Other turkey meats such as drum or outer-wing sections are less easy to debone as whole pieces. Mincing them would destroy fibre structure whilst still leaving collagen intact. Flaking is a more recent technique for particle size reduction which also cuts collagen. The correct flaking temperature must be chosen (bringing a frozen block of meat up to a higher subzero temperature suitable for machine slicing, dicing or flaking is known as tempering), too low a temperature and the meat shatters into smaller particles, too high and meat comes out in strands like mince (Koberna, 1986; Jolley et al., 1986). Discrete flakes of meat of various sizes can be obtained by using different flaking head sizes. A combination of flake sizes can be used, larger flakes add to the texture whilst smaller flakes are used as a bind matrix. The technique is used in the UK for several products including the growing grillsteak market. Grillsteaks have eating qualities closer to that of whole meats than minced products such as burgers.

Finely comminuted skin or trim is often added to the above product types to improve juiciness and eating quality.

Emulsion technology is used for producing continental-type sausages and frankfurters from finely comminuted meat which may be trim but more particularly mechanically deboned turkey meat (MDTM) (see below).

New developments in meat binding

To date reformed meat products have been formed by extracting meat proteins, using mechanical action in the presence of salts, which bind meat pieces together upon cooking. They must therefore be sold either pre-cooked or frozen in a natural or synthetic casing. Some products are now sold fresh, e.g. burgers or escalopes, where the breading or other coating helps to hold the product together and in addition flash-frying results in some surface setting of the meat pieces.

Meat proteins produce a better bind than other non-meat additives (Siegel, Church and Schmidt, 1979). Milk proteins, already used as additives, enhance colour, flavour and juiciness. Recently, a new milk protein has been introduced which is composed of a mixture of casein and whey proteins (Anon, 1986). An emulsion of the derivative recommended for poultry products (TMP 1350) with skin, fat and trimmings when added to whole muscle pieces is claimed to produce a good cooked bind in the absence of salt and also to lighten the colour of products made from finely comminuted dark thigh meat.

High-temperature short-time (HTST) extrusion cooking may be one way to reform mechanically deboned poultry meat (MDTM) for use in other products. HTST cooking of mechanically deboned chicken meat (MDCM) has so far failed to produce bind without the use of other additives such as wheat flour or pregelatinized corn starch (Megard, Kitabatake and Cheftel, 1985).

Two recent developments have introduced the concept of using chemically, rather than thermally, induced gels for developing bind in raw fresh products without salt or polyphosphates. The Netherlands Centre for Meat Technology, TNO-CIVO Institutes, has patented a method for binding pieces of meat with a gel containing fibrinogen, thrombin and a transglutaminase enzyme as essential components (Paardekooper and Wijngaards, 1987). After these components have been mixed with the meat pieces they are put in a mould and allowed to stand overnight at chill temperature by which time a sliceable coherent mass is obtained (Paardekooper, 1987).

Another patented process, from Colorado State University, uses the seaweed polysaccharide sodium alginate as binder (Schmidt and Means, 1986). Trimmed meat is reduced in size and placed in a mixer, alginate is added followed by a calcium source, such as calcium carbonate, and an acidulant such as lactic acid. The whole mass is placed in a mould or stuffed into a casing and allowed to set. Initial reports on the system suggest good raw bind development, good but variable cooked bind, good storage stability but reduced palatability scores when compared with a salt/polyphosphate system (Means and Schmidt, 1986; Means *et al.*, 1987). The system is being developed in the USA and also in the UK at IFR-Bristol where improvements in cooked bind and palatability have already been made.

Hot-deboning and electrical stimulation

Turkey rolls made from hot-deboned meat were tougher than conventional rolls (Nixon and Miller, 1967). The use of salt and polyphosphates, adequate tumbling and a 3-day ageing period of the prepared rolls, did however produce a product assessed by a trained panel as being indistinguishable from conventionally prepared rolls (Kardouche and Stadelman, 1978). Salting and mixing alone were not adequate to tenderize hot-deboned turkey meat (Furumoto and Stadelman, 1980).

Electrical stimulation of poultry meat has been mentioned in the previous chapter. It is used in the red meat industry to allow hot stripping of carcasses, earlier processing and to reduce energy costs for cooling (Cuthbertson, 1980). In our own studies (Richardson, Taylor and Buxton, in preparation), hot-deboned turkey breast or thigh meat tumbled in salt and polyphosphates and made into rolls which were subsequently not aged, were significantly tougher than rolls made from cold-deboned meat. Thigh rolls also had higher cooking losses and shrink. Low voltage electrical stimulation failed to significantly improve rolls made from stimulated, hot-deboned breast or thigh meat. Hot-deboning also produced less tender breast minor muscle fillets whether or not the carcass had been electrically stimulated.

Improving turkey meat acceptability

Consumer demand appears to be for white turkey meat products, but a manufacturer must balance his production to use all edible parts of the carcass. Cook out and eating quality of dark meats can be improved by restructuring techniques such as flaking (Graham and Marriott, 1986) and by correct blends of salt and polyphosphates or other additives such as egg white (King, Patel and Earl, 1986). Because of its higher myoglobin content turkey dark meat has been used very successfully in cured products such as turkey ham (Baker and Darfler, 1981). Attempts have also been made to develop washing procedures to reduce the colour of dark meats either from MDTM (Hernandez, Baker and Hotchkiss, 1986) or strips of chicken thigh meat (Ball and Montejano, 1984; Acton, Bowie and Dick, 1985). The use of calcium caseinate instead of sodium caseinate has been shown to lighten the colour of chicken nuggets (Hendrickx, 1987).

In the past a number of colour problems have occurred with turkey breast meat. A pink coloration after cooking, that gives the impression of under-cooking, is sometimes found in whole turkey breasts or breast rolls. Nitrite from curing procedures in other areas of the plant or in the water supply have sometimes been implicated. Other causes have been leakage of refrigerant gases (Everson, 1984), inhalation of gases during transportation (Froning, 1983), gases from cooking ovens (Poole, 1956), spray dried albumin as an additive (Froning, Hargus and Hartung, 1968), different concentrations of muscle myoglobin (Froning, Daddario and Hartung, 1968), and pre-slaughter stress leading to higher levels of cytochromes in muscle (Ngoka and Froning, 1982; Babji, Froning and Ngoka, 1982). Cornforth et al. (1986) have shown that pinkness may also be caused by reduced, denatured haemochromes. This reduction is probably caused by nicotinamide already present in the meat. Production of pinkness will then depend upon the redox potential of the meat. Factors governing variability in redox potential are still to be determined.

Product shelf-life and presentation

The cutting, deboning, handling, mixing and packaging of turkey meat increases the likelihood of microbial contamination or proliferation. Studies of poultry plants have shown that bacterial numbers increase during further processing (Brant and Guion, 1972; Denton and Gardner, 1981).

Mechanical deboning of carcass residues leads to increased bacterial numbers but no more so than in minced meat (Maxcy, Froning and Hartung, 1973) since both cause cellular disruption and provide an ideal medium for bacterial growth. For precooked products there is a conflict between cooking temperatures being high enough to kill vegetative pathogenic bacteria, yet not too high as to cause unnecessarily high cooking losses. If 80–85°C is attained all vegetative pathogens are destroyed. At lower temperatures there is an increased chance of bacterial survival but cook losses are reduced. If final cook temperatures are less than 70°C then cook time to kill is very long. This problem with respect to salmonella is considered by Simonsen et al. (1987) and Roberts and Gibson (1988). Many further processed products have the advantage that they can be cooked from frozen thus minimizing the possibility of bacterial proliferation during and after thawing.

Salting and curing

Salting, curing and smoking are traditional methods for preserving meat products but are now mainly used to give diversification in product appearance and flavour. Reduced levels of cure and smoking are now used to allow the milder poultry flavours to come through and to meet consumer desire for reduced levels of salt and nitrite. Acceptable colour and flavour of smoked turkeys can be produced with only 25% of the USDA permitted maximum of nitrite (156 ppm), provided good cure distribution is obtained by the use of multi-needle injection (Sheldon, Ball and Kimsey, 1982). Present cure levels are inadequate to allow unrefrigerated storage (Mast, 1978; Wisniewski and Maurer, 1979) or extended refrigerated storage (Oblinger *et al.*, 1978). Thigh meats need higher levels of nitrite than breast to prevent microbial proliferation due to the higher iron content (Bushway, Ficker and Jen, 1982).

There have been several studies aimed at reducing the levels of salts and nitrite in products, particularly frankfurters, whilst retaining microbiological stability. Sorbic acid has been suggested as a partial replacement for salt and/or nitrite. Its use has been reviewed by Sofos (1981). One problem associated with the use of sorbic acid is that it lightens the colour of products (Larsen, McNeil and Mast, 1986). Cooking during the processing of these products will destroy bacteria, as outlined above, but does not destroy spores of such pathogens as *Clostridium botulinum*. Spores will not grow below 10°C. Nitrites are traditionally used in cured products to prevent spore growth and thus allow the storage of such products above 10°C. Whilst the effect of reducing the levels of individual components of a cure mix on spore development is readily assessed, the interactions between the components are more complex and merit further study before reduced levels of cure are used in new poultry products (Roberts and Gibson, 1986, 1987).

Irradiation

Irradiation is another method used to reduce bacterial levels and thus extend shelf life. It is not a new technique and has already been accepted in some 28 countries. Recent reviews on the irradiation of poultry meat include Mead and Roberts (1986) and Faw and Chang-Mei (1987).

Irradiation with doses of 250–500 krad (2.5–5.0 kGy) are designed to reduce the levels of viable non-sporing pathogens to undetectable levels, this dose could be increased to 750 krad for frozen poultry. Irradiation uses doses up to 250 krad and is designed to reduce the numbers of organisms responsible for spoilage of chill-stored product and will also reduce the numbers of salmonella.

The development of radiolytic products or the loss of vitamins such as thiamine at these low doses is no greater than found after other processing methods. However, some colour and odour changes occur.

Irradiation of turkey fillets at 250 krad under chill conditions produced a pinker meat with a distinct odour. These effects were minimized after cooking (Mead and Roberts, 1986). The choice of packaging material was also important, vacuum packs of oxygen-impermeable material produced fillets of a more intense red colour and a more obvious radiation odour when first opened compared with fillets in oxygen-permeable polyethylene packs.

Packaging

Packaging has become increasingly important in recent years and has improved the presentation of foods, particularly fresh meat. It adds to customer appeal and the use of new packaging materials and printing techniques allows good product presentation, visibility and added information. Red meat packaging has been reviewed by Taylor (1985), similar principles have been applied to poultry meat (Dawson, 1987).

One of the greatest innovations in the red meat industry in the last 20 years has been the introduction of vacuum packaging for the transport of large primal joints from slaughterer to processor. Vacuum packaging in a gas impermeable covering reduces evaporative losses, prevents further microbial contamination and reduces proliferation of microbes already present due to the natural production of carbon dioxide as a result of tissue respiration. Because of vertical integration in the turkey industry there has not as yet been the same demand for this process although it is used in Europe for the distribution of portions to stores and butchers.

Packaging for retail display

Overwrapping is carried out on rigid or expanded plastic trays with a clear film of material which has a high oxygen and a low water vapour permeability. It is still the most popular method and relies upon good refrigeration, efficient distribution chains and quick turnover.

Vacuum packing can also be used for fresh retail display but the pressure exerted during vacuum packing can mis-shape large raw meat portions and squeeze out meat juices. It is used for pre-cooked, pre-sliced products.

In controlled (CAP) or modified (MAP) atmosphere packs the gaseous atmosphere in the pack is controlled by the packer, but the atmosphere will also change due to meat respiration. Much higher levels of carbon dioxide are achieved than in vacuum packs. MAP is becoming more popular for cut-up, diced or minced meat.

Jones et al. (1982) compared the storage of turkey breast fillets or drumsticks in either oxygen-impermeable vacuum packs or oxygen-permeable polyethylene overwrap at 1°C. In oxygen-permeable overwrap packs 'off' odours were detected after 14 days for drumsticks and 16 days for breast fillets, the spoilage flora being predominantly pseudomonads. In vacuum packs 'off' odour development was delayed a further 6 days for drumsticks and 9 days for breast fillets. The 'off' odours were commonly described as sour rather than putrid and spoilage organisms were predominantly atypical lactobacilli. In a further experiment (Mead et al., 1983), vacuum packed breast fillets were compared with modified atmosphere packed breast fillets. Various combinations of carbon dioxide with or without oxygen were made to volume with nitrogen. The appearance and keeping quality of the fillets were similar in the vacuum packs and the MAP containing carbon dioxide/nitrogen mixtures, although the ultimate 'off' odours were different. The spoilage microflora were atypical lactobacilli. The presence of oxygen in the packs resulted in 'off' odours by 15 days compared with 18 days for the other packs, this odour was described as being cheesy rather than sour. However, the fillets in these packs had developed marked flavour changes as early as 4 days, this was put down to the development of rancidity. The inclusion of oxygen also caused colour changes. An initially acceptable bloom was noted on these fillets which was often pink but very variable between samples. However, pinkness remained in some of the samples after cooking giving them a raw appearance.

Breadings, batters and coatings

Breadings and batters have been reviewed by Cunningham and Suderman (1981), and breadings and coatings were the topic of a recent symposium held in the UK (Anon, 1987c). Coatings enhance product appearance (Zwiercon, 1974; Elston, 1975) and add to the pleasure of eating (Vickers and Bourne, 1976). Flavourings in a coating or a glaze serve to extend the product range, whilst breadings act as a moisture barrier, improve yield and reduce unit costs. The Japanese crumb was developed because of a desire by the poultry industry to differentiate its products from those of the fish industry. It has a crisper, lighter bite and will allow longer cooking times but finish with a lighter colour than traditional fish breadings. Wholemeal crumbs and potato based crumbs have followed and the incorporation of gums, modified starches and other additives help to stabilize batters, alter crumb texture and reduce frying oil uptake.

Mechanically recovered meat

Production and properties

Mechanical deboning of poultry has been reviewed by Froning (1981). With the increase in the number of turkeys being cut-up and used in further processed products, a large number of carcass shells and bones with meat still adhering are produced. Early deboning machines scraped ground bones over the surface of a perforated drum. In a second type, pressure from an auger screw forces meat from the inside to the outside of a perforated drum. The third type of deboner works as a batch operation. Pressure from a ram forces meat to flow from the bones through a sieve screen, the bone cake is then ejected and a new batch introduced. This latter type of machine uses whole bones and has more variable settings. Machines are also available specifically for recovering meat from necks.

Table 18.3 shows the variability in chemical composition of mechanically recovered turkey meat (MDTM) from different sources. The composition is affected by the type of machine used and its settings, the type of bones used, the amount of meat left on the bones and the amount of skin (for references see *Table 18.3*). Skin does not contribute to an increased collagen content as it tends to stay with the bones, but will add considerably to the fat content (Satterlee, Froning and Janky, 1971). The protein recovered is of similar amino acid composition to hand deboned meat (Essary and Ritchie, 1968) and is of good nutritional quality (Hsu *et al.*, 1978; Babji, Froning and Satterlee, 1980). Any bone particles found are smaller in size than in hand deboned meat (Froning, 1979) but the overall calcium content is higher. It has been suggested that this may be beneficial in the diet of many individuals (Froning, 1981).

MDTM differs from hand deboned meat in the extent to which the myofibrillar structure has been destroyed. Screen size will determine residual structure (Schnell *et al.*, 1974) and protein functional properties may also be reduced if operating temperatures are too high. If long bones are deboned then some bone marrow will be present and colour will be darker due to the presence of more haemoglobin (Froning and Johnson, 1973). The high levels of fat, increased haem content, the

Table 18.3 Chemical composition of mechanically deboned turkey meat

Source	Percentage protein (P)	Percentage fat (F)	Percentage moisture (M)	M/P	F/P	Reference
Frame, no skin	16.3	15.8	65.9	4.04	0.97	1
Racks	14.5	14.7	63.7	4.39	1.01	2
US turkey plant						
Number 1	16.0	12.0	70.8	4.43	0.75	3
2	14.8	15.2	69.5	4.70	1.03	3
3	16.2	15.6	67.5	4.17	0.96	3
4	17.4	10.0	72.5	4.17	0.57	3
Frame	15.5	13.5	70.6	4.55	0.87	4
Frame	12.8	14.4	70.7	5.52	1.13	5
Frame, machine A	11.8	18.4	68.8	5.83	1.56	6
Frame, machine B	13.5	11.5	73.3	5.43	0.85	6
Frame	12.8	12.7	73.7	5.76	0.99	7
Racks	13.5	16.0	68.9	5.10	1.19	8
Backs and necks	16.2	15.6	67.8	4.17	0.96	9
Breast cage	15.4	10.2	71.3	4.63	0.66	10
Rack some skin	13.4	17.0	67.9	5.07	1.27	10
Back some skin	13.0	21.7	65.9	5.07	1.67	10
Necks	12.4	4.5	81.7	6.59	0.36	11
Necks	15.7	5.2	79.0	5.07	0.33	11
Frames	13.9	13.1	79.0	5.06	0.94	11
Range of ten samples of frames in Protecon						
Highest	15.7	8.4	79.3			11
Lowest	12.7	4.1	72.6			11
Typical hand-deboned meat						
Breast	23.6	1.2	74.2	3.14	0.05	12
Thigh	19.6	8.6	70.8	3.61	0.44	12
Drum	20.5	6.8	71.9	3.51	0.33	12

M/P Moisture to protein ratio
F/P Fat to protein ratio

References: 1 Babji, Froning and Satterlee (1980); 2 Barbut, Arrington and Maurer (1984); 3 Dawson (1975); 4 Essary (1979); 5 Froning et al. (1971); 6 Froning and Janky (1971); 7 Grunden, MacNeil and Dimick (1972); 8 Hamm and Young (1983); 9 McMahon and Dawson (1976), 10 MacNeil, Mast and Leach (1979), 11 Mecch and Kirk (1986), 12 Grey et al. (1983)

presence of metal ions, an increase in temperature during deboning, the mixing in of oxygen and the highly comminuted nature of MDTM all contribute to a susceptibility to microbial spoilage and oxidative rancidity. Turkey meat is more prone to oxidative rancidity than broiler meat due to its higher phospholipid content and lower natural tocopherol content (Moerck and Ball, 1974; Dawson and Gartner, 1983). Turkeys require much higher levels of vitamin E in their diet than broilers to improve natural meat stability (Marusich et al., 1975). It has been suggested that MDTM should not be stored for more than 6 days at 3–4°C (Dimick, MacNeil and Grunden, 1972; Moerck and Ball, 1974) or 10 weeks in frozen storage (Johnson, Cunningham and Bowers, 1974). Smith (1987) has shown that TBA values of frozen MDTM increased rapidly in the first 7 weeks of storage, but this was prevented by the inclusion of an anti-oxidant mixture. This mixture was not able to prevent the loss of protein functionality. After 26 weeks frozen storage gels made from isolated myofibrils were less able to retain water and the gel microstructure had changed from a continuous filamentous to a globular matrix.

Froning and Johnson (1973) have advocated centrifugation of the MDTM to reduce the fat and haem content but this has also been reported to confer no advantage (Dhillon and Maurer, 1975).

Cooling MDTM by the application of carbon dioxide snow would appear to be acceptable but its use for freezing is not recommended as it can lead to increased rancidity as measured by TBA and peroxide values (Uebersax, Dawson and Uebersax, 1977, 1978; Mast, Jurdi and MacNeil, 1979). Liquid nitrogen tunnels, plate or blast freezers give rapid rates of freezing without this problem. MDTM used in comminuted products can be tempered, reduced in size by flaking and added to the mixer in the frozen state. This would reduce oxidation and microbial proliferation during thawing and preclude the need to add ice during mixing. In the USA, MDTM is often dispatched preblended with the correct level of salt and half the desired nitrite level.

Use of MDTM

MDTM is used in the manufacture of soups, meat balls or patties but because of its highly comminuted nature it is best suited to emulsion type products such as bolognas, salamis, frankfurters and other sausages. Poultry MDM can be incorporated into sausages of other meat types up to a level of 15% but by far the greatest usage in the USA is in 100% poultry frankfurters. By 1980 poultry frankfurters had captured market shares of 15–25% in some areas (Marsden, 1982). Froning (1981) has reviewed the functional characteristics of mechanically deboned poultry meat for use in frankfurter production. The major differences between the preparation of poultry frankfurters and red meat frankfurters are that poultry frankfurters need less added water due to the high moisture content of MDTM (see Table 18.3), end-point chopping temperatures are lower at around 12°C because of the lower melting point of poultry fat (Froning, 1970) and cooking at a higher humidity helps to avoid a tough external skin caused by the higher protein content (Marsden, 1982). Smoke houses can also be dispensed with if liquid smoke is added during formulation (Schneck, 1982).

The use of MDTM in other products is limited by its lack of texture. Acton (1973), texturized MDM by cooking 4 mm diameter strands at 100°C. Lampilla, Froning and Acton (1985) used such strands, cut into chunks, to add texture to roasts made with MDTM or hand-deboned turkey meat (HDTM). Roasts with up to 50% texturized MDTM did not show an increase in product shear values but visually had higher fibre levels. Similarly, texturized MDTM was used in the production of summer sausages (a fermented and smoked sausage product). Formulations using one-third HDTM, one-third MDTM and one-third turkey heart meat, or substituting texturized MDTM for HDTM resulted in very acceptable products. These were further improved by darkening the product colour by the addition of beetroot juice extract (Barbut, Arrington and Maurer, 1984). Morphology and texture were rated good with this formulation and were as acceptable as traditional sausages made with beef but at half the cost (Barbut, Cassens and Maurer, 1985). MDTM has also been used successfully in sloppy toms (a meat in gravy sandwich filling) again at half the price of the traditional beef product (Laughren and Maurer, 1985).

Conclusions

The market for turkey meat continues to grow, aided by the expansion in further processed products. With consumer preferences changing towards fresh, reduced additive products, research is required into new methods of making reformed products without the use of salt and polyphosphates whilst retaining cook yields and eating quality. New packaging methods must be defined for these and other fresh products. A clearer definition of how rearing and processing conditions affects the functional properties of turkey meat and whether any such variability has an effect on product quality is also required.

References

Acton, J. C. (1972a). The effect of meat particle size on extractable protein, cooking loss and binding strength in chicken loaves. *Journal of Food Science*, **37**, 240–243

Acton, J. C. (1972b). Effect of heat processing on extractability of salt-soluble protein, tissue binding strength and cooking loss in poultry meat loaves. *Journal of Food Science*, **37**, 244–246

Acton, J. C. (1973). Composition and properties of extruded, texturized poultry meat. *Journal of Food Science*, **38**, 571–574

Acton, J. C. (1979). Functional properties of sausage raw materials related to comminuted product systems. In *Proceedings of the 21st Annual Meat Science Institute* (Carpenter, J. A., ed.), pp. 14–18. University of Georgia

Acton, J. C., Bowie, B. M. and Dick, R. L. (1985). Alteration of meat color. In *Proceedings of the 27th Meat Science Institute* (Carpenter, J. A., ed.), pp. 48–58. University of Georgia

Acton, J. C., Ziegler, G. R. and Burge, D. L. (1983). Functionality of muscle constituents in the processing of comminuted meat products. *CRC Critical Reviews in Food Science and Nutrition*, **18**, 99–121

Anon. (1986). New binder for restructured meat products. *National Provisioner*, November 8th issue, 17

Anon. (1987a). *The Further Processed Poultry Report*. London, Iain Smyth Associates for Sun Valley Poultry

Anon. (1987b). EEC facts and forecasts 1987. *Poultry World*, September issue, 11–22

Anon. (1987c). In *Savoury Coatings*, (Parry, R. and Fuller, D. B., eds) (Manchester Polytechnic, 1986) London, Elsevier

Aref, M. and Tape, N. W. (1966). Method for producing a composite body of poultry meat. *Canadian Patent*, 864,447

Babji, A. S., Froning, G. W. and Ngoka, D. A. (1982). The effect of preslaughter environmental temperature in the presence of electrolyte treatment on turkey meat quality. *Poultry Science*, **61**, 2385–2389

Babji, A. S., Froning, G. W. and Satterlee, L. D. (1980). The protein nutritional quality of mechanically deboned poultry meat as described by C-PER assay. *Journal of Food Science*, **45**, 441–443

Baker, R. C. and Darfler, J. M. (1981). The development of a poultry ham product. *Poultry Science*, **60**, 1429–1435

Ball, H. R. and Montejano, J. G. (1984). Composition of washed broiler thigh meat. *Poultry Science*, **63**(1), 60–61

Barbut, S., Arrington, C. C. and Maurer, A. J. (1984). Optimum utilization of turkey in summer sausages. *Poultry Science*, **63**, 1160–1169

Barbut, S., Cassens, R. G. and Maurer, A. J. (1985). Morphology and texture of turkey summer sausages. *Poultry Science*, **64**, 932–936

Brant, A. W. and Guion, C. W. (1972). Microbiology of commercial turkey deboning. *Poultry Science*, **51**, 423–427

Bøgh-Sørensen, L. (1985). Objective methods for measuring functional properties of poultry meat. In *Proceedings of the 7th European meeting on Poultry Meat Quality* (Vejle 1985) (Ambrosen, T., ed.), pp. 111–125

Brock, C. J. and Enser, M. B. (1987). Identification of the interfacial proteins in meat emulsions. In *Proceedings of the 33rd International Congress of Meat Science and Technology* (Helsinki 1987) (Pelaja, E., ed.), pp. 258–260

Bushway, A. A., Ficker, N. and Jen, C. W. (1982). Effect of nitrite and sorbate on total number of aerobic microorganisms in chicken white and dark meat patties. *Journal of Food Science, 47*, 858–860, 863

Cornforth, D. P., Vahabzade, F., Carpenter, C. E. and Bartholomew, D. T. (1986). Role of reduced hemochromes in pink color defect of cooked turkey rolls. *Journal of Food Science, 51*, 1132–1135

Cunningham, F. E. and Suderman, D. R. (1981). Use of batters and breadings on food products — a review. In *Proceedings of the 5th European Symposium on Poultry Meat Quality* (Wageningen 1981) (Mulder, R. W. A. W., Scheele, C. W. and Veerkamp, C. H., eds), pp. 314–343. Wageningen, Pudoc

Cuthbertson, A. (1980). Hot processing of meat: A review of the rationale and economic implications. In *Developments in Meat Science*, Vol. 1 (Lawrie, R., ed.), pp. 61–88. London, Applied Science Publications

Dawson, L. E. (1975). Utilization of mechanically deboned meat from turkeys. In *Proceedings of the 2nd International Symposium on Poultry Meat Quality* (Erdtsieck, B., ed.), pp. 53(1)–53(8). Wageningen, Pudoc

Dawson, L. E. (1987). Packaging of processed poultry. In *The Microbiology of Poultry Meat Products* (Cunningham, F. E. and Cox, N. A., eds), pp. 223–233. Orlando, Academic Press

Dawson, L. E. and Gartner, R. (1983). Lipid oxidation in mechanically deboned poultry. *Food Technology, 7*, 112–116

Denton, J. H. and Gardner, F. A. (1981). Effect of further processing systems on selected microbial attributes of turkey meat products. *Journal of Food Science, 47*, 214–217

Dhillon, A. S. and Maurer, A. J. (1975). Stability study of comminuted poultry meats in frozen storage. *Poultry Science, 54*, 1407–1414

Dimick, P. S., MacNeil, J. H. and Grunden, L. P. (1972). Poultry product quality. Carbonyl composition and organoleptic evaluation of mechanically deboned poultry meat. *Journal of Food Science, 37*, 544–546

Elston, E. (1975). Why fish fingers top the market. *Fishing News International, 14*, 30–34

Essary, E. O. (1979). Moisture, fat and mineral content of mechanically deboned poultry meat. *Journal of Food Science, 44*, 1070–1073

Essary, E. O. and Ritchie, S. J. (1968). Amino acid composition of meat removed from boned turkey carcasses by use of commercial boning machine. *Poultry Science, 47*, 1953–1955

Everson, C. (1984). Inside stuff. *Meat Industry (USA), 30*, 2

Faw, E. R. and Chang-Mei, T. (1987). Radiation preservation of poultry meat. In *The Microbiology of Poultry Meat Products* (Cunningham, F. E. and Cox, N. A., eds), pp. 235–273. Orlando, Academic Press

Froning, G. W. (1970). Poultry meat sources and their emulsifying characteristics as related to processing variables. *Poultry Science, 49*, 1625–1631

Froning, G. W. (1979). Characteristics of bone particles from various poultry meat products. *Poultry Science, 58*, 1001–1003

Froning, G. W. (1981). Mechanical deboning of poultry and fish. *Advances in Food Research, 27*, 109–147

Froning, G. W. (1983). Color of processed turkey. *IFT Muscle Foods Division Newsletter, 9*, 2–4

Froning, G. W. and Janky, D. (1971). Effect of pH and salt preblending on emulsifying characteristics of mechanically deboned turkey frame meat. *Poultry Science, 50*, 1206–1209

Froning, G. W. and Johnson, F. (1973). Improving the quality of mechanically deboned fowl meat by centrifugation. *Journal of Food Science, 38*, 279–281

Froning, G. W. and Sackett, B. (1985). Effect of salt and polyphosphates during tumbling of turkey breast muscle on meat characteristics. *Poultry Science, 64*, 1328–1333

Froning, G. W., Daddario, J. and Hartung, T. E. (1968). Color and myoglobin concentration in turkey meat as affected by age, sex and strain. *Poultry Science, 47*, 1827–1835

Froning, G. W., Hargus, G. and Hartung, T. E. (1968). Color and texture of ground turkey meat products as affected by dried egg white products. *Poultry Science, 47*, 1187–1191

Froning, G. W., Arnold, R. G., Mandigo, R. W., Neth, O. D. and Hartung, T. E. (1971). Quality and storage stability of frankfurters containing 15% mechanically deboned turkey meat. *Journal of Food Technology*, **36**, 974–978

Furumoto, E. J. and Stadelman, W. J. (1980). Influence of salt addition on tenderness of hot boned pork, chicken, turkey, and beef rolls. *Journal of Food Science*, **45**, 1062–1063

Graham, P. P. and Marriott, N. G. (1986). Value enhancement of turkey dark meat through restructuring. *Poultry Science*, **65**, 2056–2064

Grey, T. C., Robinson, D., Jones, J. M. and Pritchard, R. (1983). Observations on the composition and nitrogen factors of poultry meat. *Journal of the Association of Public Analysts*, **21**, 1–5

Grunden, L. P., MacNeil, J. H. and Dimick, P. S. (1972). Poultry product quality: Chemical and physical characteristics of mechanically deboned poultry meat. *Journal of Food Science*, **37**, 247–249

Hamm, R. (1975). Water holding capacity of meat. In *Meat* (Cole, D. J. A. and Lawrie, R. A., eds), pp. 321–328. London, Butterworths

Hamm, D. and Young, L. L. (1983). Further studies of commercially prepared mechanically deboned poultry meat. *Poultry Science*, **62**, 1810–1815

Hansen, L. J., Schwall, D. V. and Colburn, J. T. (1966). Method of preparing a poultry product. *US patent*, 3,285,752

Hendrickx, A. C. M. (1987). Valorization of fatty ingredients for poultry in processed poultry products. In *Proceedings of the 8th European Symposium on Poultry Meat Quality*, pp. 149–154. Budapest

Hernandez, A., Baker, R. C. and Hotchkiss, J. (1986). Extraction of pigments from mechanically deboned turkey meat. *Journal of Food Science*, **51**, 865–867

Hsu, H. W., Sutton, N. E., Banjo, M. O., Satterlee, L. D. and Kendrick, J. G. (1978). The C-PER and T-PER assays for protein quality. *Food Technology*, **32**, 69–73

Hudspeth, J. P. and May, K. N. (1967). A study of emulsifying capacity of salt soluble proteins of poultry meat. 1. Light and dark meat tissues of turkeys, hens and broilers and dark meat tissues of ducks. *Food Technology*, **21**, 1141–1142

Hudspeth, J. P. and May, K. N. (1969). Emulsifying capacity of salt soluble proteins of poultry meat. 2. Heart, gizzard and skin from broilers, turkeys, hens and ducks. *Food Technology*, **23**, 373–374

Johnson, P. G., Cunningham, F. E. and Bowers, J. A. (1974). Quality of mechanically deboned turkey meat: Effect of storage time and temperature. *Poultry Science*, **53**, 732–736

Jolley, P. D., Ellery, A., Hall, L. and Sheard, P. (1986). Keeping your temper: Why it is important for the manufacturer. In *Proceedings of a Subject Day, 'Meat thawing/tempering and product quality'*, Institute of Food Research, Bristol

Jones, J. M., Mead, G. C., Griffiths, N. M. and Adams, B. W. (1982). Influence of packaging on microbiological, chemical and sensory changes in chill-stored turkey portions. *Poultry Science*, **23**, 25–40

Kardouche, M. B. and Stadelman, W. J. (1978). Effect of rigor state, phosphate addition and aging on quality of turkey rolls. *Poultry Science*, **57**, 425–432

King, A. J., Patel, S. B. and Earl, L. A. (1986). Effect of water, egg white, sodium chloride, and polyphosphate on several quality attributes of unfrozen and frozen, cooked, dark, turkey muscle. *Poultry Science*, **65**, 1103–1111

Kinsella, J. E. (1982). Protein structure and functional properties: emulsification and flavor binding effects. In *Food Protein Deterioration, Mechanisms and Functionality*, ACS Symposium series 206 (Cherry, J. P., ed.), pp. 301–326. Washington DC, American Chemical Society

Koberna, F. (1986). Tempering temperature requirements for cutting and processing equipment. In *Proceedings of a Subject Day, 'Meat thawing/tempering and product quality'*. Bristol, Institute of Food Research

Lampilla, L. E., Froning, G. W. and Acton, J. C. (1985). Restructured turkey products from texturized mechanically-deboned turkey. *Poultry Science*, **64**, 653–659

Larsen, J. E., MacNeil, J. H. and Mast, M. G. (1986). Sensory and quality characteristics of poultry frankfurters containing nitrite or sorbate. *Poultry Science*, **65**, 1542–1546

Laughren, C. M. and Maurer, A. J. (1985). Sloppy toms made from mechanically deboned turkey meat. *Poultry Science*, **64**, 1907–1913

Lewis, D. F., Groves, K. H. M. and Holgate, H. H. (1986). Action of polyphosphates in meat products. *Food Microstructure*, **5**, 53–62

Li-Chan, E., Nakai, S. and Wood, D. F. (1984). Hydrophobicity and solubility of meat proteins and their relationship to emulsifying properties. *Journal of Food Science,* **49**, 345–350

Li-Chan, E., Nakai, S. and Wood, D. F. (1985). Relationship between functional (fat binding and emulsifying) and physicochemical properties of muscle proteins. Effects of heating, freezing, pH and species. *Journal of Food Science,* **50**, 1034–1040

MacNeil, J. H., Mast, M. G. and Leach, R. M. (1979). Protein efficiency ratio and amounts of selected nutrients in mechanically deboned turkey meat. *Journal of Food Science,* **44**, 1291–1293, 1298

Marsden, J. L. (1982). Technological developments in the manufacture of poultry frankfurters. In *Proceedings of the Reciprocal Meat Conference (1981),* **34**, 126–134

Marusich, W. L., De Ritter, E., Ogrinz, E. F., Keating, J., Mitrovic, M. and Bunnel, R. H. (1975). Effect of supplemental vitamin E in control of rancidity in poultry meat. *Poultry Science,* **54**, 831–844

Mast, M. G. (1978). Curing and smoking poultry products. *Worlds Poultry Science Journal,* **34**, 107–111

Mast, M. G., Jurdi, D. and MacNeil, J. H. (1979). Effects of CO_2-snow on the quality and acceptance of mechanically deboned poultry meat. *Journal of Food Science,* **44**, 346–349, 354

Maxcy, R. B., Froning, G. W. and Hartung, T. E. (1973). Microbial quality of ground turkey meat. *Poultry Science,* **52**, 486–491

McCready, S. T. and Cunningham, F. E. (1971). Salt-soluble proteins of poultry meat 1. Compositional and emulsifying capacity. *Poultry Science,* **50**, 243–248

McGowan, R. G. (1970). Method of preparing a poultry product. *US patent,* 3,503,755

McMahon, E. F. and Dawson, L. E. (1976). Effects of salts and phosphates on some functional characteristics of hand and mechanically deboned turkey meat. *Poultry Science,* **55**, 573–578

Mead, G. C. and Roberts, T. A. (1986). Irradiation of poultry meat. *Turkeys,* **34**, 27–29

Mead, G. C., Griffiths, N. M., Jones, J. M., Grey, T. C. and Adams, B. W. (1983). Effect of gas-packaging on the keeping quality of turkey breast fillets stored at 1°C. *Lebensmittel-Wissenschaft und Technologie,* **16**, 142–146

Means, W. J. and Schmidt, G. R. (1986). Algin/calcium as a raw and cooked binder in structured beef steaks. *Journal of Food Science,* **51**, 60–65

Means, W. J., Clarke, A. D., Sofos, J. N. and Schmidt, G. R. (1987). Binding, sensory and storage properties of Algin/Calcium structured beef steaks. *Journal of Food Science,* **52**, 252–256, 262

Meech, M. V. and Kirk, R. S. (1986). Chemical characteristics of mechanically recovered meat. *Journal of the Association of Public Analysts,* **24**, 13–26

Megard, D., Kitabatake, N. and Cheftel, J. C. (1985). Continuous restructuring of mechanically deboned chicken meat by HTST extrusion-cooking. *Journal of Food Science,* **50**, 1364–1369

Moerk, K. E. and Ball, H. R. (1974). Lipid autoxidation in mechanically deboned chicken meat. *Journal of Food Science,* **39**, 876–879

Montejano, J. G., Hamann, D. D. and Lanier, T. C. (1984). Thermally induced gelation of selected comminuted muscle systems — rheological changes during processing, final strengths and microstructure. *Journal of Food Science,* **49**, 1496–1505

Nixon, D. M. and Miller, B. F. (1967). Evaluation of turkey boning techniques. *Poultry Science,* **46**, 1088–1093

Ngoka, D. A. and Froning, G. W. (1982). Effect of free struggle and preslaughter excitement on color of turkey breast muscles. *Poultry Science,* **61**, 2291–2293

Oblinger, J. L., Koo, L. C., Koburger, J. A. and Janky, D. M. (1978). Changes in the microbial flora of smoked chicken during storage. *Poultry Science,* **57**, 123–126

Paardekooper, E. J. C. (1987). Recent advances in fresh meat technology. In *Proceedings of the 33rd International Congress of Meat Science and Technology* (Helsinki 1987) (Petaja, E., ed.), pp. 170–174

Paardekooper, E. J. C. and Winjngaards, G. (1987). Composite meat product and method for the manufacture thereof. *European patent application Nr,* 32,766

Poole, M. F. (1956). Why does some turkey turn pink? *Turkey World,* **Jan**, 68

Prusa, K. J. and Bowers, J. A. (1984). Protein extraction from frozen, thawed turkey muscle with sodium nitrite, sodium chloride, and selected sodium phosphate salts. *Journal of Food Science,* **49**, 709–713, 720

Richardson, R. I. and Jones, J. M. (1987). The effects of salt concentration and pH upon water-binding, water-holding and protein extractability of turkey meat. *International Journal of Food Science and Technology,* **22**, 683–692

Roberts, T. A. and Gibson, A. M. (1986). Chemical methods for controlling *Clostridium botulinum* in processed meats. *Food Technology*, **40**, 163–176

Roberts, T. A. and Gibson, A. M. (1988). Some aspects of the role of food preservatives and the microbiological consequences of their omission. *Turkeys*, **32**, 29–32

Saffle, R. L. (1968). Meat emulsions. *Advances in Food Research*, **16**, 105–160

Satterlee, L. D., Froning, G. W. and Janky, D. M. (1971). Influence of skin content on the composition of mechanically deboned poultry meat. *Journal of Food Science*, **36**, 979–981

Schlamb, K. F. (1970). Methods of binding large pieces of poultry. *US Patent*, 3,499,767

Schmidt, G. R. and Means, W. J. (1986). Process for preparing algin/calcium gel structured meat products. *US Patent*, 4,603,054

Schneck, J. C. (1982). Liquid smoke application to cured meat. In *Proceedings of the Reciprocal Meat Conference* (1981), **34**, 101–103

Schnell, P. G., Vadera, D. V. and Baker, R. C. (1970). Mechanism of binding chunks of meat. Effect of physical and chemical treatments. *Canadian Institute of Food Science and Technology Journal*, **3**, 44–48

Schnell, P. G., Vadehra, D. V., Hood, L. R. and Baker, R. C. (1974). Ultra-structure of mechanically deboned poultry meat. *Poultry Science*, **53**, 416–419

Sheldon, B. W., Ball, H. R. and Kimsey, H. R. (1982). A comparison of curing practices and sodium nitrite levels on the chemical and sensory properties of smoked turkey. *Poultry Science*, **61**, 710–715

Siegel, D. G., Church, K. E. and Schmidt, G. R. (1979). Gel structure of nonmeat proteins as related to their ability to bind meat pieces. *Journal of Food Science*, **44**, 1276–1279, 1284

Siegel, D. G., Teno, D. M., Schmidt, G. R. and Norton, H. W. (1978). Meat massaging: The effects of salt, phosphate and massaging on cooking loss, binding strength and exudate composition in sectioned and formed ham. *Journal of Food Science*, **43**, 331–333

Simonsen, B., Bryan, F. L., Christian, J. H. B., Roberts, T. A., Tompkin, R. B. and Silliker, J. H. (1987). Preservation and control of food-borne salmonellosis through application of Hazard Analysis Critical Control Point (HACCP). *International Journal of Food Microbiology*, **4**, 227–247

Smith, D. M. (1987). Functional and biochemical changes in deboned turkey due to frozen storage and lipid oxidation. *Journal of Food Science*, **52**, 22–27

Sofos, J. N. (1981). Nitrite, sorbate and pH interaction in cured meat products. In *Proceedings of the Reciprocal Meat Conference*, **34**, 104–120

Taylor, A. A. (1985). Packaging fresh meat. In *Developments in Meat Science*, Vol. 3 (Lawrie, R., ed.), pp. 89–114. London, Elsevier Applied Science Publications

Theno, D. M., Siegel, D. G. and Schmidt, G. R. (1976). Microstructure of sectioned and formed ham. *Journal of Animal Science*, **42**, 1347 (abstract)

Theno, D. M., Siegel, D. G. and Schmidt, G. R. (1977). Meat massaging techniques. In *Proceedings of the Meat Industry Research Conference*, pp. 53–57. Chicago, American Meat Science Association and American Meat Institute Foundation

Torr, D. (1965). Method of preparing an edible meat product. *US Patent*, 3,173,795

Trout, G. R. and Schmidt, G. R. (1986). Effect of phosphates on the functional properties of restructured beef rolls: The role of pH, ionic strength, and phosphate type. *Journal of Food Science*, **51**, 1416–1423

Uebersax, K. L., Dawson, L. E. and Uebersax, M. A. (1977). Influence of 'CO_2-snow' chilling on TBA values in mechanically deboned chicken meat. *Poultry Science*, **56**, 707–709

Uebersax, K. L., Dawson, L. E. and Uebersax, M. A. (1978). Storage stability (TBA) and color of MDCM and MDTM processed with CO_2 cooling. *Poultry Science*, **57**, 670–675

USDA (1987). *Poultry and egg statistics, 1960–1986*. USDA/ERS.

Vickers, Z. and Bourne, M. C. (1976). Crispness in foods — a review. *Journal of Food Science*, **41**, 1153–1157

Wisniewski, G. D. and Maurer, A. J. (1979). A comparison of five cure procedures for smoked turkey. *Journal of Food Science*, **44**, 130–133

Zwicroth, G. A. (1974). Case of the weeping pies (and others). *Food Engineering*, **46**, 79, 81

Chapter 19

The place of the turkey in the animal industry of the future

T. R. Morris

The title of this chapter presupposes that there will be an animal industry in the future. Whether this is a safe assumption, or a controversial one, must depend upon the time scale which we wish to consider. Few of us would have any confidence in predicting what humans will be eating a thousand years from now and many of us may feel doubtful about predicting the course of events over the next century.

My own assumption is that there will, one day, be an end to the raising of animals for slaughter and consumption. I do not suppose that this will come about because everyone is persuaded that eating a vegetarian diet is a healthier way of life or that, in the first instance, people will agree that eating animals is wrong (except in the case of horses, dogs, pigs or guinea pigs in particular societies). It seems to me more likely that, in the fullness of time, food technologists will develop a range of products which consumers come to regard as cheap and perfectly satisfactory alternatives to real meat (and, probably, real eggs and real milk). I envisage the decline of the meat market resulting from quite straightforward economic competition from alternative foods derived from field crops or obtained by microbial synthesis or by tissue culture from inorganic starting materials using factory processes. Once we reach a stage where the majority in our society are eating non-animal products most or all of the time (because they are cheaper), there will soon be a majority view that it is morally wrong to raise animals for slaughter just to satisfy those who (like me) want to go on eating roast beef and stuffed turkey. These stages are clearly discernible in the fur trade and, though selling a real mink coat is not yet a crime, it may become so in some countries in the not too distant future.

However, I regard the decline and eventual disappearance of the animal industry as a distant prospect and a slow process. For the next 20 years or so I assume that meat-eating will be common in many societies around the world and that, in most of those, *per capita* consumption of meat will expand as the standard of living rises. The increase in poultry meat consumption, in particular, is likely to continue and the prospect for those working in the turkey industry today I regard as particularly rosy.

There is a strong contrast between the outlook for the turkey industry and that for most other agricultural commodities. We know that there are declining markets for milk and eggs in most developed countries. The *per capita* consumption of beef has fallen in the UK and elsewhere and there seem to be no technical developments in prospect which will dramatically reduce the cost of producing beef. The

351

production of lamb in Europe happens to be highly profitable at the present time, but this is entirely due to price support from EEC taxes and presumably cannot last very long.

Pork, chicken and turkey are the three meats which have not 'enjoyed' price support and all three have become cheaper, relative to beef and lamb, and have increased their share of the market correspondingly. Annual rates of genetic improvement in the efficiency of turning animal feed into edible meat (a calculation which includes reproductive efficiency as well as growth rate and carcass composition) are still largely determined by selection intensity which depends on reproductive rate. Here, chickens and turkeys will continue to have an advantage compared with pigs and so the gap in price between pig and poultry meat is likely to widen.

Nevertheless, pig meat represents serious competition for the poultry industry and the pig industry should be watched carefully by those planning to invest more in turkeys. Some argue that the leanness of poultry meat is an added factor in its favour but others are busy expanding turkey sales by putting a knob of butter or lard on top of a turkey steak while others are arguing that pigs are now too lean for some of the market outlets. Fatness and leanness are not clear-cut issues.

What is clear is that when a poultry carcass is cut up and sold in pieces, the yield of saleable meat is higher and the costs of obtaining 1 kg of meat are lower from large carcasses. For further processing, the large turkey will always be a better starting point than a chicken and this is why there is great potential for expansion in turkey meat consumption.

In proportional terms, turkey meat consumption has been expanding faster than any other livestock commodity in the USA and in many European countries in the past ten years. In Europe and the USA, turkey now accounts for about 5% of the meat eaten and it does not seem outrageous to suggest that the turkey industry's share of the meat market might be expanded to 25% of the total over the next 20 years. This would represent a fivefold expansion of turkey production in the countries where turkey meat is already a familiar product. In addition to this there is potential for expanding sales of breeding stock and technology in those Muslim countries of the world which produce (or can afford to buy) grain for livestock feeding and where there is no competition from pig meat.

With such a glorious prospect of expansion ahead, what can stop the turkey industry (or slow it down)? One factor is probably over-concentration. It is distressing to hear (Chapter 1) of a processing plant now being built in the USA to handle 20 million turkeys a year. Production units to feed this plant would need to be within easy transport distance of the factory, which would make it impossible to prevent diseases spreading from one site to another. Added to this are the problems of keeping a market supplied when such a large plant has a serious breakdown. There are economies of scale up to a point, but surely two plants each with capacity of 10 million turkeys a year would not cost more to build than one of 20 million? The benefits of dispersion are difficult to quantify, but they are real enough and should be weighed against the small (though easily calculated) savings in capital and operating costs associated with concentration of a livestock industry in one area.

The main aim of this book is to review technical progress and to consider future technical developments and the remainder of this chapter will be devoted to considering whether and how science may be able to help the turkey industry grow.

Buss (Chapter 2) has related how bigger turkeys have been bred simply by picking out the heaviest individuals at a fixed age and Owatland (Chapter 9) has pointed out that selection for a dimple-breasted bird has limited keel size and thereby the potential for further increasing the proportion of breast meat on a turkey carcass. Increasing weight at a given age is relatively easy and, in the large populations maintained by international poultry breeding companies, there is no sign that rate of improvement in this trait is slowing down. But it is time to recognize that selection for useful skeletal characteristics may be just as profitable as increasing mature body weight. A longer keel, relative to other skeletal dimensions, could carry more breast meat for further processing and it might be helpful to the big males in walking and in mating. The chunky, broad-breasted turkey looks very nice when dressed and entered in a carcass competition but may not be the most sensible shape to select in sire lines which are to be used to breed turkeys for further processing.

The possibility of going back to natural mating is an intriguing one. Many in the turkey industry argue that artificial insemination is now a well-understood art, giving entirely satisfactory fertility at reasonable cost; but it cannot be cheaper than natural mating if only natural mating would give the same fertility. It has been suggested that present-day strains of meat turkeys are simply too big to mate satisfactorily, but the ostrich is bigger and broiler males mated to dwarf females have a wider male:female body weight ratio. What would be the result of restricting feed supply to turkey males to make them smaller and perhaps fitter? Perhaps they would then achieve satisfactory natural mating and so do away with the need for artificial insemination? It does seem that some exploratory trial in this area would be worthwhile, particularly if this were combined with a selection programme designed to improve the skeletal conformation of the large turkey.

The hatchability of turkeys is not nearly as good as that of hens. Christensen and Bagley (Chapter 5) have quoted an overall figure of 73% hatch of all eggs set for a typical hatchery. Improving this figure probably requires attention to incubator design and operation rather than more research. The non-genetic causes of poor hatchability are well understood and operational research within a large hatchery will usually result in marked improvements. Genetic improvement of fertility and hatchability is more difficult, but progress can be made by applying consistent selection pressure and, no doubt, this is being done within lines today.

Conventional genetic selection has become unfashionable as a topic for research in this age of molecular biology, but is still the fastest way of achieving defined targets in poultry breeding. It is very unlikely that techniques based on molecular biology will replace quantitative genetics in turkey breeding in the next ten years. Buss (Chapter 2) commented that, so far, only one turkey gene has been fully sequenced, but the problem is not in sequencing a gene but in thinking of one which is worth pursuing. There seem to be no useful single genes in the turkey which we would want to manipulate, though there may be genes elsewhere which it would be interesting to transfer to the turkey genome. The sex-linked dwarf gene from chickens would be one example and the gene(s) for lysine synthesis taken from a bacterium might be another.

It seems more likely that the early examples of the application of molecular biology to turkey production will come through immunology rather than gene insertion. For example, immunization of female breeding turkeys against endogenous prolactin production may be a potent way of eliminating broodiness.

The turkey industry should be aware that the promised revolution in biotechnology may pose a threat as well as a promise. In the longer run it may be possible to produce turkey breast muscle in unlimited quantities by tissue culture techniques at a price which undercuts the old-fashioned process of feeding turkeys and watching them grow.

This brings me to the question of feed resources and nutrition. There does not seem much likelihood that maize and wheat and soyabean meal will be displaced as the principal feedstuffs for turkeys in the next 20 years. Abundant supplies are likely to be available on the world market and there are powerful economic and political reasons why those developing countries which have rapidly expanding populations will not buy up, or be given, grains on a scale which will leave the livestock industries in temperate countries short of feedstuffs. Some expansion of rapeseed and other high-protein crops may occur in Europe and more fish may be taken from the oceans, but it is unlikely that either of these trends will markedly reduce the use of soyabeans as the major source of protein for poultry feeding. There will probably be some increase in the use of synthetic amino acids to achieve a desirable amino acid profile at lower protein concentrations and Nixey (Chapter 10) has suggested that we should pay more attention to threonine in particular.

It does seem that nutritional knowledge has now reached a stage where we can predict with sufficient accuracy the nutrient requirements of an animal once its performance characteristics (including voluntary food intake and carcass composition) have been specified. The phrase 'sufficient accuracy' is chosen advisedly. We probably do not know the vitamin A requirement of a particular strain of turkeys at all accurately and we certainly do not have good information about the effect of environmental circumstances on the bird's response to vitamins. But so long as feed manufacturer's incorporate wide safety margins in vitamin provision, there is nothing to be gained by measuring requirements more precisely under carefully controlled experimental conditions. If we are to improve our knowledge about cost-effective safety margins, intended to allow for the requirements of flocks kept under less-than-perfect conditions, we shall need large scale trials conducted under a wide range of industrial conditions and these trials can only be worth doing for the vitamins which are costly to supply.

In defining optimal levels of amino acids for turkey diets, one of the problems is that the optimum changes rather quickly as the bird grows and its rate of protein accretion changes relative to its energy needs for maintenance and for fattening. It has been pointed out by Rose and Michie (1982) and others that allowing the growing turkey to balance its own diet is a neat and efficient solution to this problem. Why the industry has not developed effective systems for choice feeding turkeys is something of a mystery. It is not unusual to have two chain feeders in large turkey houses and the opportunity to develop choice feeding with no extra investment is there waiting to be grabbed.

Charles (Chapter 11) and Noll (Chapter 7) have shown that the environmental responses of birds, including turkeys, are well understood and can be modelled in a way that will lead to optimal economic solutions to problems of building design and operation. There is perhaps not enough good information about the responses of breeding flocks to patterns of daylength change, but it is unlikely that much improvement in fertility or production of hatching eggs would result from further trials in this area and so the expected benefit:cost ratio is not very encouraging.

Emmans (Chapter 8) has made the interesting calculation that fast-growing male turkeys in the 8–16 week stage are usually too hot (even in a British winter) to eat the amount of food needed to reach their full growth potential. This has led him to speculate that the turkey industry might move to Iceland, but experience in the

USA has been that California and the Carolinas have enjoyed a greater expansion of turkey meat production than Wisconsin and Minnesota. This serves to remind us that a turkey business has to optimize its whole operating system and not simply go all out for maximum growth rate. Higher environmental temperatures do limit growth but they also lead to lower feed conversion ratios and this is one of the main reasons why the North American poultry meat industry has moved towards the southern states. British turkey production is more likely to move to Spain than to Iceland.

Speculating about technical developments is interesting, but the expansion of turkey meat production depends upon the food technologists and the marketing men, not upon marginal improvements in productive efficiency which may result from research into genetics, nutrition or the environment. The question is whether the turkey industry can keep on inventing new turkey-based products which the supermarkets can handle and the housewife will buy.

I believe that the industry will continue to develop its product range, no doubt with help from the food technologist but probably without much need for food science research.

Does this mean that research relating to turkeys should stop? Certainly not! Agricultural science research is a proper intellectual pursuit and every bit as respectable as archaeology or astronomy. Some of it will turn out to be useful, though which bits (and when) it is very hard to predict. When workers in the 1930s first collected chicken semen and showed that artificial insemination was feasible they had no vision that the turkey industry would come to depend on it. Of course, those of us engaged in research for a living must persuade both government and industry that future success in a competitive world depends upon maintaining investment in scientific research. But those working in the business know that, even with our present level of technical knowledge, the turkey industry has a glorious future before it.

Reference

Rose, S. P. and Michie, W. (1982). The food intakes and growth of choice-fed turkeys offered balancer mixtures of different compositions. *British Poultry Science*, **23**, 547–554

Chapter 20

Poster papers

Effect of Baytril^R (Bay Vp 2674) on young turkeys affected with respiratory infections

W. W. Braunius
Regional Animal Health Service, PO Box 10, 6880 BD Velp, The Netherlands

In July 1986, an increased mortality was observed on a turkey farm when rearing flocks of birds of various ages. During the first 2 weeks of life the main symptom was a white diarrhoea followed by respiratory problems such as sneezing, mucoid nasal excretion and the development of 'swollen heads' in the third and fourth week. The most common findings after the necropsy of some birds was an inflammation of the airsacks, sometimes associated with an extensive pericarditis and perihepatitis. In some cases pneumonia was found.

A bacteriological examination of the material showed in most cases an *E. coli* infection, insensitive against chloramphenicol, tetracycline, ampicillin and trimethoprim. Serological tests on *Mycoplasma gallisepticum* and *Mycoplasma synoviae* were always negative, as well as agglutination against influenza. The titres against Newcastle disease were always 4.0. Because of the high mortality rate, the relative insensitivity of the isolated *E. coli* strains and because of the risk of a *Mycoplasma* infection it was decided to start an initial treatment with tylosin.

Because of the poor results with this treatment it was decided to continue with colistin. In the beginning, this treatment produced a decrease in mortality and stopped the white diarrhoea. But immediately after the completion of the colistin treatment, mortality as well as symptoms increased again. Therefore, one pen was treated for about 4 weeks. Because leg problems became apparent, the colistin treatment was stopped and a supply of vitamins via drinking water was initiated. The mortality increased again.

The second postmortem examination was carried out 2 months later. Again the diagnosis was the 'swollen head' symptom and an inflammation of airsacks and lungs. A strain of *Pseudomonas aeruginosa*, resistant against chloramphenicol, tetracycline, ampicillin, furazolidon, flumequine and trimethoprim could be isolated. A sensitivity against neomycin and colistin still existed.

So far virus isolation had not been successful. The serological test against *Mycoplasma* revealed a positive result for *Mycoplasma meleagridis*.

Considering the positive results and good efficacy of the quinolone carboxylic acid derivate enrofloxacin (Baytril) against *E. coli*, mycoplasmoses and others under experimental conditions (described by Scheer, 1986), it was decided to test this new synthetic chemotherapeutic agent on the affected animals of the different flocks.

For 5 days the animals received 50 ml of a 10% oral formulation per 100 litres drinking water which is equivalent to 50 ppm per day. Mortality decreased rapidly and the symptom of white diarrhoea could no longer be observed. A flock of poults was treated, beginning with the fifth day of life, for 5 days with the recommended dosage of 50 ppm. This flock did not show the 'usual' mortality rate of 10% in the first 2 weeks.

Discussion

Increasing problems are to be expected especially on farms with flocks of birds of different ages. This was also the case on the farm studied: in spring results were good, but later in the year problems increased. In summer 1986, the mortality rates increased so much that even rhinotracheitis had been considered to be present, but no specific tracheal abnormalities were to be seen. *Mycoplasma meleagridis* could have played a role; this organism can cause air sacculitis and osteodystrophy in turkeys. Secondary *E. coli* infections can aggravate the problems. However, *Mycoplasma meleagridis* agglutination tests are known to be unreliable sometimes, especially in young birds (Gordan and Jordan, 1982).

Considering the poor effect of tylosin and the high resistance of the *E. coli* isolates, there was little choice of antibiotic therapy. The owner's use of colistin is understandable because he considered the gut condition to be primary. However, colistin is not resorbed and is therefore certainly not indicated for respiratory infections. Until now, Baytril has not been used in turkeys, but was found to be well tolerated by these birds and reduced mortality rates very well.

References

Gordan, R. F. and Jordan, F. T. W. (1982). *Poultry Diseases,* 2nd Edition. London, Bailliere Tindall
Scheer, M. (1986). Bay Vp 2674 — ein neues Chemotherapeutikum, **20**, 591–593

Effect of dietary protein, energy and supplemental fat on reproductive performance of turkey breeder hens

S. Touchburn, P. De Henau and W. Chan
Department of Animal Science and McGill Nutrition and Food Science Centre, Macdonald College of McGill University, 21,111 Lakeshore Road, Ste Anne de Bellevue, Quebec, Canada H9X 1CO

Three experiments with broiler breeder turkey hens in cages tested dietary crude protein levels of 11–15%, metabolizable energy (ME) levels of 11.3–13.0 MJ/kg (2700–3100 kcal/kg) and supplemental animal fat blend levels of 0–7%. Overall, the best reproductive performance was obtained with a diet containing 14% crude protein, 12.1 MJ/kg (2900 kcal/kg) and a calorie:protein ratio of 864 (kJ) 207 (kcal). These are similar to the values recommended in *Nutrient Requirements of Poultry* (NRC, 1984). Supplemental fat, assigned an ME value of 37.7 MJ/kg (9000 kcal/kg) and added isocalorically to the diet consistently improved reproductive performance. This effect was apparent when intake of protein and energy were not affected and thus appears to be a truly physiological phenomenon. None of the dietary manipulations prevented the decline in feed consumption and body weight at onset of lay. Plasma triglyceride levels preceded and tended to parallel the egg production curve.

Changes in egg composition and eggshell characteristics during the first laying cycle of turkey hens

N. A. French and D. J. Shaw
British United Turkeys Ltd, Hockenhull Hall, Tarvin, Chester CH3 8LE, UK

The fresh egg weight, wet and dry yolk weight, wet and dry albumen weight, shell weight, shell thickness and water vapour conductance were measured on eggs from a Large White turkey flock at 2-weekly intervals over a 20-week laying cycle.

All the measured traits showed significant changes over the laying cycle. Total egg weight showed a curvilinear increase throughout lay. Wet and dry yolk weight and water vapour conductance likewise increased through lay and also increased as a proportion of the total egg weight. Wet and dry albumen weight showed a slight increase up to 16 weeks in lay and then decreased. As a proportion of total egg weight, both wet and dry albumen content decreased through lay. There was also a corresponding decrease in the percentage total water content of the egg. Over the first few weeks in lay, shell weight and shell thickness increased, but thereafter decreased.

Total egg weight is highly correlated with wet albumen weight within groups of eggs collected at one period in the laying cycle. The correlation between total egg weight and wet yolk weight was weaker, although still significant. However, the increase in the average total egg weight during the laying cycle would appear to be primarily caused by the increase in wet yolk weight.

Processing full-fat canola (low glucosinolate, low erucic acid rapeseed) as a high energy feedstuff for turkeys

R. E. Salmon and V. I. Stevens and B. D. Ladbrooke
Research Branch, Agriculture Canada, Box 1030, Swift Current, Saskatchewan, S9H 3X2
POS Pilot Plant Corporation, Saskatoon, Saskatchewan, S7N 2R4, Canada

Full-fat canola seed, containing 400 g/kg of oil, is a potential high energy feedstuff but must be processed to render its nutrients available to the bird. To determine the level of processing required, canola seed either whole or flaked in a roller mill, either raw or cooked, or extruded, was compared with fully extracted canola meal plus oil at up to 200 g/kg canola meal equivalent (on oil-adjusted basis) in mash or steam pelleted diets for turkeys to 6 weeks of age.

Cooking was ineffective but both flaking and extrusion improved live weights and feed efficiency. Steam pelleting was even more effective and resulted in similar food efficiencies with whole and processed seed. Slightly reduced live weights with whole or flaked seed, even when pelleted, were not improved by increased total protein or supplementary amino acids and do not appear to be due to reduced availability of protein.

Neither lysine nor arginine affected performance with control, canola meal or full-fat seed diets. Response to methionine was much less with canola than with soyabean meal control diet.

Whole canola seed at 165 g/kg in pelleted turkey broiler diets supported growth of Medium White turkeys equal to that of control or canola meal diets, but 330 g/kg reduced live weights at 12 weeks. Levels of 165 and 330 g/kg of full-fat canola are equivalent, on an oil-adjusted basis, to 100 and 200 g/kg of canola meal.

Choosing an optimal hatcher temperature for turkey eggs

A. Ar and M. Meir
Tel Aviv University
and A. Nir
Ministry of Agriculture, Tel Aviv, Israel

To establish hatchability parameters in hatchers, one must eliminate from analyses incubator factors that influence hatchability. Effects of five temperatures (T) ranging between 36.5°C (97.7°F) and 38.5°C (101.3°F) were tested in hatchers (ventilated at 0.3 l/(min egg); kept at egg–air humidity difference of 17 Torr) on hatchability (HA), late mortality (LM), class A hatchlings (CA), fresh hatchling weight (HW), timing and synchronization, of 4800 eggs (Big 6 BUT; 88 g ± 6 SD) incubated at 37.5°C (99.5°F); 55%RH (84.9°F WB) conditions. Mean shell conductance was 22.2 mgH$_2$O/(100 g day Torr) ± 4.5 SD. Eggs lost 11.6% ± 2.3 SD of their initial weight (W) on day 25. Best HA and lowest LM (90.2 and 7.3% respectively) occurred at 37.0°C (98.6°F). Highest CA proportion (67.8% from hatched; rigid inspection) was at 38.0°C (100.4°F). Highest CA/fertile (60.9%) was at 37.5°C (99.5°F). HW decreased with increasing water loss (WL) and T from 72.4% of W and 9.3% WL at 36.5°C to 67.6% W and 13.9% WL at 38.5°C. HW of 70.5% W was associated with best CA proportion. Pipping on day 26 (34.4%) and hatching on day 27 (23.9%) increased to 83.2% and 64.3% with T from 36.5°C to 38.5°C. Late (day 29) hatches were minimal (3.1% and 4.0%) at 37.0°C and 37.5°C, respectively. We thus recommend a hatching temperature of 37.5°C (99.5°F) for turkey eggs with 12% WL on day of transfer.

Self-selection of protein and energy by turkey breeder hens

D. E. Emmerson, D. M. Denbow and R. M. Hulet
Department of Poultry Science, Virginia Polytechnic Institute and State University, Blacksburg, Virginia, USA

Forty-eight Large White turkey hens were individually caged and provided 14 h light per day for a 23-week production cycle. Half of the birds were provided with a split-diet in which they had a choice between a high protein (34.8% protein, 1854 kcal ME/kg) and a high energy (8.1% protein, 3219 kcal ME/kg) feed source. The two feed sources were balanced for all other nutrients. The control birds were fed a diet prepared by blending the high protein and high energy diets to produce a feed intermediate in protein and energy (18.5% protein, 2707 kcal ME/kg). Feed consumption, egg production, egg weights, body weight and the incidence of broodiness were measured throughout the period.

Birds fed the split-diets produced an equal number of eggs as control birds but consumed approximately 10% less feed. While energy intake was equal for the two groups, protein consumption was lower for birds on the split-diet treatment. Therefore, birds on the split-diet treatment selected a diet with a higher energy/protein ratio. While 25% of the control birds experienced broodiness, only 10% of the choice-fed birds became broody. There were no significant differences in the egg weights or body weights of the two treatment groups. These data suggest that diets with a higher energy/protein ratio might be more appropriate for the feeding of turkey breeder hens.

Effects of limiting the photoperiod and of restricting the body weight of Large White turkey males on the efficiency of semen production

P. M. Hocking
AFRC Institute for Grassland and Animal Production, Poultry Department, Roslin, Midlothian, EH25 9PS, Scotland, UK

Three groups of Large White turkey males were reared in floor pens. Two groups of 18 males were fed *ad libitum* throughout and given a photoperiod of 14L:10D (AL14) or 7L:17D (AL7) from 10 to 18 weeks of age. The body weights of a third group of 20 males given the 7L:17D photoperiod were limited to about 0.5 of *ad libitum* males by restricting food allocation from 6 to 18 weeks (R7). Daily food intake was increased to 480 g per bird at 25 weeks and resulted in average body weights of 0.65 and 0.78 of *ad libitum* males at 30 and 54 weeks respectively. All birds were given 14L.10D from 18 weeks and semen collection started at 20 weeks. Sexual maturity occurred earliest in AL14 but the averages of AL14 and AL7 were similar and earlier than R7 (23 vs 27 weeks, $P<0.001$). The development of normal semen production was more rapid in AL7 than in AL14 males. Individual semen yields were lower ($P<0.001$) in R7 than in AL7 and AL14 and semen quality was similar (proportion of sperm). Mortality to 54 weeks in the *ad libitum* groups was high (0.5 versus 0.1, $P<0.01$) and resulted in lower total semen yields compared with restricted males. Semen (spermatozoa) production from 32–54 weeks was 46.3(12.5), 43.4(12.5) and 60.1(15.3) mg/male housed at 6 weeks for AL14, AL7 and R7 males respectively. Corresponding production efficiencies (out/input) were 315(85), 347(80) and 452(115) mg/kg food.

Effect of insemination frequency and number of spermatozoa inseminated on reproductive results obtained with turkey semen, stored for different times

G. Huyghebaert and F. Van Wambeke
Rijksstation voor Kleinveeteelt Burg, Van Gansberghelaan 92, 9220 Merelbeke

Semen from a heavy turkey strain was used to study the effect of different storage times (0, 6, 24 and 48 h at 6°C and with intermittent agitation: 10 min/h at 200 rpm), frequency of insemination and number of spermatozoa inseminated (7 days, 140×10^6, 14 days, 140×10^6, 14 days, 280×10^6, respectively) on fertility, embryonic mortality (EM: 0–7 days; 7–24 days; 24–28 days) and hatchability during a 14-week breeding period. Each treatment consisted of four replications of seven medium-weight caged hens each.

All main treatment effects were significant ($P<0.05$) for fertility, early EM and hatchability. There was also a significant ($P<0.05$) interaction, 'storage time' × 'AI-dose/frequency of insemination', for fertility and hatchability. This significant interaction revealed that the reproductive performances decreased after (1) longer storage times (age related decline in sperm viability), and (2) insemination of lower numbers of spermatozoa.

Insemination of fresh semen resulted in high fertility (>97%) and hatchability (>86%) results, which were not affected by age, AI dose or frequency. After short-term storage (6 h) the weekly performances were comparable with those obtained with fresh semen, but during the second half of the experimental period higher AI doses were necessary at fortnightly intervals of insemination. However, after longer storage periods (24–48 h) higher numbers of spermatozoa had to be used to obtain optimal reproductive performances during the whole experimental period: at fortnightly intervals after 24 h of storage and at both AI intervals after 48 h of storage.

Safety of lasalocid for turkeys and its compatibility with tiamulin

Nigel Lodge
Roche Products Ltd, Broadwater Road, Welwyn Garden City, Hertfordshire, UK

This poster presentation refers to an independent trial carried out by Huntingdon Research Centre on 640 male and female turkeys between July and November 1985.

Eight hundred SVII turkeys were allocated to 40 pens. After 14 days, birds in each pen were reduced from 20 to 16 in number. Birds were individually wing-tagged and reared according to standard practice.

Males and females were allocated to each of the following dietary levels of lasalocid continuously from day old to 16 weeks of age: 0 ppm, 125 ppm, 187.5 ppm, 250 ppm, 375 ppm (equivalent to 0, 1, 1.5, 2 and 3 times maximum recommended level).

In addition, further pens of birds receiving dietary 125 ppm lasalocid were medicated with tiamulin (250 ppm via drinking water) for a 5-day period at ages 4, 8, 12 and 16 weeks respectively. Extra pens on dietary 125 ppm lasalocid acted as controls.

Results at 16 weeks showed a dose-related improvement in body weight in birds given lasalocid, up to and including the 375 ppm dose groups. No adverse treatment-related effects were observed compared to control (unmedicated) birds on parameters including FCR, haematology, biochemistry, organ weights and general postmortem examination.

In addition administration of tiamulin produced no adverse effects at any of the four treatment ages in terms of body weight, food consumption, water intake and postmortem findings.

The response of growing turkeys to lysine

T. S. Bray

ADAS, 66 Ty Glas Road, Llanishen, Cardiff CF4 5ZB, Wales, UK

In two contiguous experiments at Gleadthorpe Experimental Husbandry Farm (MAFF), the responses to amino acids of two large body sized strains of turkeys were examined (BUT Big 6 Stags and BUT T6 Stags and Hens).

Lysine was used as the 'marker' amino acid with others being at a constant ratio to it. Dietary treatments were based on the calculated lysine requirements (g/day) at 12°C, using the formula $20 \Delta W + 0.12 W^{0.75}$, where ΔW = liveweight gain (kg/day) and W = live weight (kg).

The responses in performance are presented for two differing experimental designs.

The first experiment in a converted cattle shed containing 12 pens, used nine diets/period, with lysine being 0.8–1.6 times the calculated level and with no replication of six of these diets. This proved to be a satisfactory experimental design for computing the responses in liveweight gain. Two examples are presented, namely:

(a) for the first period (age: 8–12 weeks)
$$y = 6.9328 + 54.697x - 6.0201x^2$$
(b) for the response to dietary regime (age: DO–24 weeks)
$$y = -30.471 + 77.295x - 11.665x^2$$

where both lysine intake (x) and liveweight gain (y) are in g/bird.

In the second experiment, the effects of a factorial design comprising four environmental temperatures and four dietary lysine levels were examined, in eight climate rooms. Temperature treatments were 11, 15, 19 and 23°C and the lysine levels were pitched at 0.9, 1.1, 1.3 and 1.5 times the calculated level. For both stags and hens at each temperature, the computed response to lysine confirmed that no interactions occurred between temperature and lysine intake. There was a trend however for the response to be less at the coolest temperature. Equations for the response to lysine at each temperature are presented.

In both experiments, increasing the amino acid intake:

(1) increased the live weight, feed consumption and improved the feed conversion of stags,
(2) increased the quantity and percentage of white meat and therefore the total meat and meat:bone ratio of stags. The protein content of the white meat tended to be increased also,
(3) improved the 'finish' of stags.

Index

Acrosome reaction, 61
Actin, *see* Muscle growth
Added-value products, *see* Further processing
Adenoviruses
    classification of, 254
    clinical signs and lesions of HEV, 254
    diagnosis of HEV, 255
    epizootiology of HEV, 254
    pathogenesis of HEV, 254–255
    prevention and control of HEV, 255
Adrenal function, embryonic, 84
Age
    flavour and, 314
    of hen
        at first egg, 18–19, 20
        embryonic mortality, 70
        incubation egg weight loss, 74
    meat texture and, 296–300
Agriocharis ocellata, 11
Air sacculitis, 220
Alacaligens faecalis, 222
Albumen phenotypes, 15
Alginate, polysaccharide sodium, 338
Amino acids
    arginine, 194–195
    balance, 192–194
        antagonisms, 194
        imbalances, 194
        toxicities, 194
    in breeding hens, 102–104
    calculated response
        bodyweight gain, 188
        Edinburgh model, 187–190
        growth rate, 187
        Israeli model, 187, 188
        maintenance, 187–188
        predicted requirements, 190
        profiles, 188–189
        Reading model analysis, 190–192
    commercial diets, 194–195
    empirical experimentation
        interpretation method, 185–187
        plateau or upper limits, 185
        previous plane of nutrition, 185

Amino acids (*cont.*)
    leucine, isoleucine and valine interrelationship, 195
    lysine, 184, 186, 190, 191, 194–195
    lysine–arginine antagonism, 194–195
    metabolizable energy, 185, 189–190
    methionine, 186, 189
    requirement expression, 184–185
    sequences, 15
    sulphur amino acids (TSAA), 186, 187, 189, 190, 191, 192
    synthetic, 354
Anti-prolactin serum, broodiness and, 48
Aortic rupture, 15
Ar, A., 360
Arginine, 194–195
Artificial incubation
    altitude and, 76
    humidity, 73–74
    temperature and, 71–73
    turning of eggs, 74–75
    ventilation, 75–76
Artificial insemination, 20, 353
    historical development, 4
    see also Natural mating
Astroviruses
    diagnosis, 253
    epizootiology, 251
    pathogenesis, 252
Atresia
    differential, 32
    of yellow-yolky follicles, 33
Autosomes, 15

Bagley, LG, 69–90
Batters, 342
Baxter-Jones, C, 224–232
Baytril, 357–358
Binding, 337–338
    chemical induced gels, 338
Biotin transfer mechanism, 108–109
Blepharitis, 218
Blood pressure, 15

Bluecomb, *see* Coronaviruses
Body characteristics, 17–18, 21
    repeatability of measurement, 18
Body conformation, 16–17
Body weight, 16, 18, 21
    breeding hens and feed intake, 96–98
    lighting and, 124
    selection for, 279–281, 352–353
Boning
    hot, 338–339
    see also Further processing; Mechanically
        recovered turkey meat
Bordetella avian, 218, 220, 222
Braunius, W.W., 357–358
Bray, T.S., 363
Breadings, 342
Breast muscle, *see* Muscle growth
Breast width, 16–17
Breeding
    primary, 6
    programmes, 23–24
Breeding stock
    rhinotracheitis in, 220–224
    see also Lighting; Nutrition
Broodiness, 19, 21, 42–49
    early detection, 127
    elimination by immunization, 353
    endocrine interactions, 43–46
        neuroendocrine control mechanisms, 46–47
    environmental effects, 128
    flock control, 128
    high ambient temperature and, 46
    identification, 126
    lighting effects, 126–128
        bright lights, 127
        continuous lights, 127
        treatment length, 127
    pharmaceutical treatment, 47–49, 127–128
Buss, E.G., 11–30

Calcium, 60, 61
    for breeding hens, 105–106
Calcium caseinate, 339
Canola seed, 359–360
Catching, meat texture and, 293–294
CE, *see* Coronaviruses
Chan, W., 358–359
Chapman–Enskog relation, 80–81
Charles, D.R., 201–214
Chemical composition, of mature turkey, 136–138
Chilling
    ageing and meat texture, 296–300
    chill storage, 299   300
Chloride
    for breeding hens, 106
    see also Salt
Choice feeding, 160–161, 354, 360–361
Christensen, V.L., 69–90
Clomiphene citrate, broodiness and, 47–48
Coatings, 342

Coccidiosis, 267
Colisepticaemia, 266
Colour problems in processing, 339, 341–342
Commercial diets, 194–195
Conjunctivitis, 218
Cooking procedures
    flavour and, 326
    high temperature short-time extrusion *see*
        HTST
    texture and, 301–303
Coronaviruses, 255–56
    classification, 256
    clinical signs and lesions, 256
    diagnosis, 256
    epizootiology, 256
    prevention and control, 256
Coryza, 222, 223
Cryopreservation, 59–60, 300–301
Cured products
    flavour and taint in, 320–321
    nitrites, 320–321
    smoked, 320–321
    sorbate, 321
Curing, 340
Cytogenetics, 14–15
    2N chromosome number, 14–15
    idiogram, 15
Cytoskeleton, 179–181

Daylength, *see* Photoperiodic responses
De Henau, P., 358–359
Deboning, mechanical, *see* Mechanically
        recovered turkey meat
Desmin, 180
Dienal, 324
Diet, *see* Nutrition
Diffusion, *see* Embryology, respiration
Dopamine, broodiness and, 47, 49
Dressing losses, 284

E.coli, 218, 222, 357
Economic traits, 16–25
    body characteristics, 17–18, 21
    body conformation, 16–17
    body weight, 16, 18, 21
    broodiness, *see* Broodiness
    edible meat yield, 22–23
    egg numbers, 19–20, 21
    egg weight, 22
    feed efficiency, 22
    fertility, 20–21
    hatchability, *see* Hatchability
    livability, 22
    phenotype deformation, 23
    sexual maturity, 18–19
Economies of scale, 352

Edinburgh model, 187–190
Egg lines, *see* Egg production
Egg production
  age at first egg, 18–19, 20
  broodiness, *see* Broodiness
  numbers, 19–20, 21
  ovarian function, *see* Ovarian function
  persistency, 20
  physiology of, 31–54
  selection for increased, 33
  see also Artificial incubation; Embryology;
      Photoperiodic responses
Egg weight, 22
  humidity and, 73–74
Eggshell
  characteristics during first laying cycle, 359
  environmental interaction with, 81
  gas tension across, 80
  hard-shelled, 35
  permeability, 78–79
  surface area, 79–80
Eimeria species, 267
ELISA, 227, 228, 229, 230, 231
Embryology, 69–90
  egg composition during first laying cycle, 359
  embryonic lethals, 16
  environment and eggshell interaction, 81
  mortality
    domestication and, 71
    genetic selection for reduced, 70
    hen age and, 70
    lay time of day, 71
    malpositions, 70
    multiple clutches and, 71
    peaks, 69–70
    pre-incubation storage and, 70–71
  physiology
    adrenal and thyroid function, 84
    haematology, 82–83
    heart, 81–82
    intestinal digestive function, 84
    liver, 83–84
    lung, 83
  respiration, 77–81
    Chapman–Enskog relation, 80–81
    diffusion, 78
    eggshell permeability, 78–79
    eggshell surface area, 79–80
    gas tension across shell, 80
  see also Artificial incubation; Hatchability
Emmans, G.C., 135–166
Emulsification capacity, 336
Endocrine control
  broodiness, 43–46
  ovarian function, 31–35
Enteric viruses, 235–261
  enteroviruses
    diagnosis, 253
    epizootiology, 251
    pathogenesis, 252
  see also individual viruses e.g. Adenoviruses

Environmental requirements, 201–214, 354–355
  automatic adjustment and thermostatic sensors,
      210
  broodiness, 128
  evaporative moisture output, 210, 211
  for growth, 161–162
  heat output, 210, 211
  house heat balance equations, 210, 211–212
  light, *see* Lighting
  monitoring, 212–213
  spermatozoa and, 57–58
  temperature, 201–207
    feed balance, 163
    limits, 354–355
  ventilation, *see* Ventilation
Evisceration loss, 284
Exercise, spermatozoa output and, 58

Fats
  deposition, 272–273, 276, 277, 280, 281
  dietary fat, 101–102
  essential fatty acids, 100–101
Feathers
  growth, 152–154
  pigmentation, 12, 14
Feeding, *see* Nutrition
Females, *see* Age, of hen; Nutrition, breeding
      hens; Reproduction, females
Fertility, 20, 21
Fibrinogen, 338
Fick's Law, 78, 79, 81
Flaking, 337, 339
Flavour and taint, 313–330
  cooking method and, 326
  cured products, 320–321
  processing effects, 317
  rancidity of MRM, 322–323
  sensory and objective testing, 313–314
  sex and age of turkey and, 314
  storage
    irradiation, 320
    in modified atmospheres, 319–320
    whole carcasses, 318–319
  turkey diet and
    fish taints, 315–316
    ingredients, 314–315
    meat stability, 316–317
  'warmed over flavour', 323–325
Fleshing, degree of, 17
Flight, energy and muscle fatigue, 171
Follicle stimulating hormone, *see* FSH
Foot pad lesions, 23
Fowl pest, *see* Newcastle disease
Fowl pox vaccinations, 16
Freezing and frozen storage, 59–60, 300–301
  turkey quality, 300–301
  turkey semen, 59–60
French, N.A., 359
Fructose, glucose conversion to, 59
FSH (follicle stimulating hormone), 34

Further processing, 331–349
  binding, 337–338
  breading, batters and coatings, 342
  colour problems, 339, 341–342
  emulsification capacity, 336
  flaking, 337, 339
  functional properties of turkey meat, 332–336
  grill steaks, 337
  hot-boning and electrical stimulation, 338–339
  HTST (high temperature short-time extension),
    338
  improving acceptability, 339
  MRM, see Mechanically recovered meat
  need for larger turkeys, 352–353
  packaging, 341
    for retail display, 341–342
  production statistics, 331–332
  protein extractability, 333, 334–335
  protein gelation, 335
  shelf-life, 339–341
    bacterial numbers, 339
    irradiation, 340
    salting and curing, 340
  water holding, 335–336
  see also Meat; Processing effects
Future developments, 351–355

Gascoyne, J., 3–9
General health, 263–268
  poor performance, 267–268
  see also individual aspects and diseases e.g.
    Nutrition and Reoviruses
Genetics, 11–30
  body weight selection, 352–353
  breeding programmes, 23–24
  cytogenetics, 14–15
  economic traits, see Economic traits
  feed conversion efficiency selection, 280
  gene mutations, 12–14
  history of wild turkey, 11
  parthenogenesis, 15–16
  physiological assessments, 15
  reduced embryonic mortality selection, 70
  skeletal characteristics selection, 353
  weight gain selection, 279–281
Gleadthorpe Experimental Husbandry Farm, 202,
  363
Glucose, to fructose conversion, 59
Glycogen, 176
  cardiac, 82
  flight energy and, 171
  in liver, 84, 293
Glycolysis, texture and, 303–304
GnRH (gonadotrophin releasing hormone), 34,
  37, 40
  broodiness and, 47
Gompertz functions, 143, 144, 152
Gonadal steroids, broodiness and, 47

Gonadotrophin, 34
  broodiness and, 47
  photoinduced release, 36–38
Grey, T.C., 289–311
Grill steaks, 337
Growth, 135–166
  environmental requirements, 161–162
    negative aspects, 162–164
  feather-free chemical body, 145–147
  feather growth, 152–154
  Gompertz functions, 143, 144, 152
  mature state, 135–141
    body protein and carcass bone weights, 138,
      140, 141
    chemical composition, 136–138
    non-carcass components, 140
    physical composition, 138, 139, 140
  nutritional requirements, 154–161
    amino acid, 155, 157
    choice feeding, 160–161
    effective energy, 155
    metabolizable energy, 154–155
    negative aspects, 162–164
    variation in, 158–160
  physical body growth, 149–150, 151
    carcass bone and body protein relationship,
      150, 152
  potential growth curve, 141–144
  rate, genetic selection for, 33, 279–281
  temperature and feed balance, 163
  testing and parameter estimation, 148–149
  see also Environmental requirements; Muscle
    growth; Nutrition

Haematology, embryonic, 82–83
Haemorrhagic enteritis virus, see Adenoviruses
Hatchability, 7, 21, 353
  optimal hatcher temperature, 360
  see also Artificial incubation; Embryology,
    mortality
Hatcheries, 6–7.
Health, see General health and individual viruses
Heart, embryonic, 81–82
Hens, see Age of hen; Nutrition, breeding hens;
  Reproduction, females
Heptaldehyde, 324
HEV, see Adenoviruses
High-temperature short-time extrusion cooking
  (HTST), 338
Hocking, P.M., 361
Holding, 283–284
  texture and, 294
    chilling and, 296–300
Horrox, N.E., 263–268
HTST (high temperature short-time extrusion),
  338
Humane killing, 294
Humidity, artificial incubation and, 73–74
Huyghebaert, G., 361–362
Hybrids, 14

Idiogram, 15
Immunofluorescence, 226, 227, 245
Immunology, 353
Incubation
    behaviour, see Broodiness
    historical development of incubators, 3, 4
    see also Artificial incubation
Influenza, 265
Intestinal digestive function, embryonic, 84
Ionophorous anticoccidials, 267
Irradiation
    product shelf-life and, 340
    storage flavour and taint, 320
Israeli model, 187, 188

Jones, J.M., 313-330

Killing, see Slaughter methods

Lactobacilli, 341
Ladbrooke, B.D., 359-360
Lake, P.E., 55-61
Lasalocid, 362
Leg conditions, 266-267
Leucine, isoleucine and valine interrelationship,
    195
LH (luteinizing hormone), 34, 63
    atmospheric negative ion and, 57
    photoinduced release, 37
    pre-ovulatory release, 35
Lighting, 200
    breeder hens
        light intensity and source, 122-123
        photoperiod, 121-122
    broodiness and, see Broodiness
    males
        age at lighting, 123-124
        optimum body weights, 124
        photostimulation, 124-125
        semen production and, 58, 59, 63-64, 125-126,
            361
    prebreeder hens, 119-121
        light intensity, 120
        light sources, 120-121
        photoperiod, 119-120
    see also Photoperiodic responses
Lipoproteins, very low density, 32, 33
Livability, 22
Liver, embryonic, 83-84
Liveweight gains, 168, 169, 188
Lodge, Nigel, 362
Lung, embryonic, 83
Luteinizing hormone, see LH
Lysine, 184, 186, 190, 191, 194-195, 207, 363

M.biceps femoris, 297-298, 302
M.gastrocnemius, 298

M.pectoralis major, 301
M.peroneus longus, 297
M.quadriceps femoris, 302
Magnesium, for breeding hens, 107
Males, see Lighting; Reproduction, males; Semen
Malpositions, 70
    turning eggs and, 75
Management practices
    rhinotracheitis mortality and, 219-220
    see also Lighting; Ventilation
Marketing
    added-value products, 273
    competition from pig meat, 352
    healthy image, 9, 272-273
    low cost, 272
    whole birds, 8
    yield and carcass composition, 271-273
Mating
    artificial insemination, see Artificial
        insemination
    natural, 353
Maturity, see Growth
MDTM, see Mechanically recovered turkey meat
Meat, 8-9
    ability to be flavoured, 8
    functional properties of, see Further processing
    lower fat, 9, 272-273
    quality versus quantity, 175-176
    texture, see Texture
    yield, see Yield and carcass composition,
        271-288
    see also Mechanically recovered meat
Mechanically recovered turkey meat
    chemical composition, 342, 343
    deboning, 342
    oxidative rancidity, 343
    production and properties, 342-344
    rancidity of, 322-323
    temperature effects, 343, 344
    uses of, 344
Meir, M., 360
Meleagris gallopavo, 11
    races of, 11
Metabolizable energy, 154-155, 189-190, 207
    breeding hens, 98-100
    rearing diets, 94-95
Methionine, 186, 189, 207
Microwave cooking, 326
Microwave radiation, spermatozoa and, 57
Minerals
    for breeding hens, 105-107
        trace elements, 107-108
    for growing turkeys, 184
Monensin, 267
Moraxella, 220
Moraxella anatipestifer Type A, 222
Morris, T.R., 351-355
Mortality
    embryonic or post-hatching, 14
    rhinotracheitis, 218-220
        concurrent diseases, 219

MRM, *see* Mechanically recovered meat
Multipliers, 6–7
Muscle growth
  actin, 168
  aerobic features, 171–172
    fast-contracting, 173
    slow-contracting, 173, 178
  anaerobic, fast-contracting, 173, 178
  appearance of muscularity, 169, 170
  breast muscles, 168, 169
  cytoskeleton, 179–181
  fatigue and, 171
  filaments, 168
  formation of muscle fibres, 178–181
  gross anatomy, 168–170
  histology of skeletal muscle, 179
  intrafascicularly terminating, 177–178
  length of breast, 170
  liveweight gains, 168, 169
  longitudinal, 176–177
  M.pectoralis, 171
  M.supra coracoideus, 170, 177
  mitochondria, 175
  mitosis, 178
  muscle fibre, 168
  myoblast, 178, 180
  myofibrils, 168, 171, 174–5, 177, 178
  myosin, 168, 171
  myotubes, 178
  numbers of fibres, 177–178
  oxygen movement, 175
  physiology of, 167–182
  premyoblasts, 179
  radial growth of muscle fibres, 173–176
  red and white muscle fibres, 170–173
    histological features, 172–173
  sarcomere, 168, 177, 304
  sarcoplasmic reticulum, 168, 174, 306
  transverse tubular system, 168
  width of breast, 170
Muscles, 17
  dark, post mortem changes in, 297–298
  see also Meat; Muscle growth; Texture
Mycoplasma gallisepticum, 6, 264, 357
Mycoplasma iowae, 265
Mycoplasma meleagridis, 6, 264–265, 357, 358
Mycoplasma synoviae, 6, 265, 357
Mycoplasmosis, 264
Mycotoxins, 268
Myofibrils, *see* Muscle growth
Myosin, *see* Muscle growth

Narasin, 267
Natural mating, 353
Nesting behaviour, *see* Broodiness
Neuroendocrine control
  of broodiness, 46–47
  of photorefractoriness, 40–42
Neuropeptide, 34
Newcastle disease, 209, 219

Nir, A., 360
Nitrites in cured products, 320–321
Nixey, C., 183–199
Nutrition, 91–117
  amino acids, 102–104, 155, 157, 354
  breeding hens
    amino acids, 102–104
    body weight and feed intake, 96–98
    dietary fat, 101–102
    dietary protein, energy and supplemental fat
      and, 358–359
    effect of dietary protein, energy and
      supplemental fat, 358–359
    essential fatty acids, 100–101
    metabolizable energy, 98–100
    minerals, 105–108
    protein, 104–105
    self-selection of protein and energy, 360–361
    vitamins, 108–113
  choice feeding, 160–161, 354, 360–361
  diet and flavour and taint, 314–317
  diet and meat texture, 292
  during rearing, 91–95
    females, 91–94
    metabolizable energy, 94–95
    protein, 95
  effective energy, 155
  feed efficiency, 22
  full-fat canola, 359–360
  future prospects for, 354
  growing turkeys, 183–199
    amino acids, *see* Amino acids
    commercial diets, 194–195
    food intake, 195–197
    lysine, 207, 363
    methionine, 186, 189, 207
    minerals, 184
    recommended nutrient ratios, 197
    types of response, 183
    vitamins, 183–184
  metabolizable energy, 94–95, 154–155,
    189–190, 207
  potential growth and, 154–161
  restricted feeding and semen production, 62–63
  temperature, 203–207
  variation in requirements, 158–160, 283, 354
  yield and carcass composition and, 281–283

Oedema, 217
Off-flavour, *see* Flavour and taint
Origin, 11–12
Ovarian function
  differential atresia, 32
  endocrine control of, 31–35
  follicular growth, 32–34
  ovulatory cycle, 34–35
  see also Photoperiodic responses
Ovarian weight, 15
Oxidation, *see* Stabilization

Packaging, 341
    for retail display, 341–342
    vacuum, 341
Parthenogenesis, 15–16
Parvoviruses
    diagnosis, 253
    epizootiology, 251
    pathogenesis, 252–253
Pasteurella-like organisms, 218, 220, 222
Pasteurellosis, 265
Pause days, 34, 35
Pericarditis, 220
Permeability, eggshell, 78–79
pH, and texture, 304–306
Phenotype deformation, 23
Phosphate injections, 302, 317, 334, 335
Phosphorus, for breeding hens, 106
Photoperiodic responses, female, 34, 35–42
    extraretinal photoreceptors, 38
    gonadotrophin release, 36–38
    light wavelength, 38
    photorefractoriness
        adult, 39–42
        juvenile, 38–39
        neuroendocrine control, 40–42
        progressive development, 40, 42
Photoperiodic responses, males, 58, 59, 63–64,
    361
Physical composition, 138, 139, 140
Physiological assessments, 15
Physiology, of muscle growth, *see* Muscle growth
Plucking, 284
    meat texture and, 296
Polyembryony, 16
Poor performance, 267–268
Potassium, for breeding hens, 107
Pre-slaughter effects, 283–284
    meat texture and, 294
    texture, 304
Prebreeder hens, lighting, *see* Lighting
Primary breeding, 6
Processing effects
    dressing losses, 284
    evisceration loss, 284
    flavour and taint, 317
    plucking, 284
    see also Further processing; Meat
Processors, 7–9
Proctodael gland, 56
Product manufacture, *see* Further processing;
        Processing effects
Production statistics, 331–332
Progesterone
    broodiness and, 44
    pre-ovulatory release, 35
Protein
    breeding hens, 104–105
    extractability, 333, 334–335
    gelation, 335
    rearing diets, 94–95
Proteus, 222

Pseudomonas aeruginosa, 357
Pseudopicornaviruses
    diagnosis, 253
    epizootiology, 252
    pathogenesis, 253

Rapeseed, 359–360
Reading model analysis, 190–192
Reoviruses
    classification, 246–247
    diagnosis, 249
    epizootiology and pathology, 247–249
    host ranges, 249
    prevention, control and treatment, 249–250
    transmission, 248–249
Reproduction, females
    dietary protein, energy and supplemental fat
        and, 358–359
    nutrition and performance, 91–94
    sexual maturity, 18–19
Reproduction, males, 55–61
    anatomical features, 55–57
    sexual maturity, 19
    see also Semen
Respiration, embryonic, *see* Embryology
Respiratory infections, use of Baytril, 357–358
Respiratory staphylococcosis, 266
Reynolds, D.L., 235–261
Rhinitis, 217, 218
Rhinotracheitis, 217–233
    adult breeding flocks, 220–224
        aetiology, 222–223
        prevention, 223–224
        transmission, 222
        treatment, 223
    antibody detection, 223–224
        in commercial flocks, 229–231
    bacterial complications, 222
    in chickens
        experimental infections, 231–232
        field sera examination, 232
        virus isolation, 232
    international survey, 231
    mortality, 218–220
        concurrent diseases, 219
        management practices, 219–220
    serology
        ELISA, 227, 228, 229, 230, 231
        immunofluorescence, 227
        serum neutralization, 227–228
        test development, 227
    symptoms, 217–218
    virus isolation, 224–225
        antigenic relatedness of, 228
    virus maintenance
        growth on cell culture, 226–227
        immunofluorescence, 226
        tracheal organ culture, 224
Richardson, R.I., 331–349
Rickets, 266

Rigor onset, 307
Rosemary oleoresin, 322–323
Rotaviruses, 236–250
    ages distribution, 241–242
    clinical signs and pathology, 242–243
    diagnosis, 243–246
        cell culture innoculation, 245, 246
        EM examination, 244–245, 246
        genome electropherotyping technique, 245
        immunofluorescence, 245
    epizootiology, 240
    group A, 236–237, 238–240, 240–241
    group D, 237–238, 240, 241–242, 244
    prevention, control and treatment, 246
    transmission, 240–242
Runting, 267–268

Saif, L.J., 235–261
Saif, Y.M., 235–261
Salinomycin, 267
Salmon, R.E., 359–360
Salmonella, 268, 339
Salpingitis, 218–219
Salt, 334, 335–336
    see also Chloride
Salting, 340
Sarcomere, see Muscle growth
Sarcoplasmic reticulum, see Muscle growth
Scalding, 295
Selection, see Breeding programmes; Genetics
Self-basting, 317
Semen
    ageing of male and, 61
    collection by massage, 56, 57, 60, 61–62
    extraction limits, 61–62
    light intensity effects, 125–126
    onset of production, 19
    photoperiodic responses, 58, 59, 63–64, 361
    restricted feeding and production of, 62–63, 361
    spermatozoa
        acrosome reaction, 61
        body reserves of, 61–62
        concentration, 19
        density, 55
        environmental factors and, 57–58
        maturation, 56
        oviductal survival, 60
        physiological and biochemical factors, 65–66
        plasma membrane of, 59–60
    storage
        cryopreservation, 59–60
        glucose to fructose conversion, 59
        lighting and, 59
        oxygenation during, 59
        times and, 361–362
    volume of, 19
    yellow, 59
Serotonin
    broodiness and, 47, 49
    spermatozoa and, 57

Sex chomosomes, 15
Sex differences
    effect on texture, 291
    flavour and, 314
Sexual maturity, see Reproduction, females;
        Reproduction, males
Shanks, 17–18
Sharp, P.J., 31–54
Shaw, D.J., 359
Shelf-life, see Further processing, shelf-life
Short-day treatment, 38–39
Shortening of muscles, temperature and,
        306–307
Sinusitis, symptom of rhinotracheitis, 218
Skeletal characteristics selection, 353
Skeletal deformation, 23
Slaughter methods
    humane killing, 294
    morality of, 351
    texture and, 294
Small viruses
    classification, 250–251
    diagnosis, 253
    epizootiology, 251–252
    pathogenesis, 252–253
    prevention, control and treatment, 253–254
Smoked turkey, see Cured products
Sodium, for breeding hens, 106–107
Sodium caseinate, 339
Sodium chloride, 334–336
    see also Salt
Sorbate, 321
Spermatozoa, see Semen
Stabilization
    fatty acid oxidation, 324
    flavour and, 316–317
    oxidative rancidity in MRM, 343
    tocopherol treatment, 325
    vitamin E and, 316, 343
Staphylococcosis, respiratory, 266
Stefan's Law, 81
Stevens, V.I., 359–360
Stocking densities, 219
Storage
    chill, 299–300
    flavour and taint
        irradiation, 320
        portions in modified atmospheres,
            319–320
        whole carcasses, 318–319
    frozen, 300–301
    pre-incubation, and mortality, 70–71
    of semen, see Semen, storage
    see also Further processing, shelf-life
Stress
    meat texture and, 292–295
    pre-slaughter heat stress, 304
Stuart, J.C., 217–224
Stunting, 267–268
Swatland, H.J., 167–182
Swollen head, 357

Taint, see Flavour and taint
Temperature
    artificial incubation and, 71–73
    broodiness and, 46
    changing genetic material and, 207
    environmental limits, 354–355
    for growing turkeys, 201–207
    in MRM, 343, 344
    muscle shortening and, 306–307
    nutrients and, 203–207
    optimal hatcher temperature, 360
Texture, 289–311
    breed, sex, age, conformation and diet effects,
        289–292
    chilling
        ageing, 296–300
        chill storage, 299–300
        electrical stimulation and, 299
    cooking procedures, 301–303
    freezing and frozen storage, 300–301
    glycolysis, 303–304
    muscle shortening and temperature, 306–307
    pH and, 304–306
    pre-slaughter effects, 304
    rigor onset, 307
    scalding and plucking and, 295–296
    stress, catching, transport, transfer and killing
        effects, 292–295
Theil, K.W., 235–261
Thighs, 17–18
Thiobarbituric acid (TBA), 313
Thrombin, 338
Thyroid function, embryonic, 84
Tiamulin, 267, 362
Tocopherol treatment, 325
Touchburn, S., 358–359
Trace elements, for breeding hens, 107–108
Tracheal organ culture, 224
Tracheitis, 218
Transglutaminase enzyme, 338
Transport and transfer, meat texture and,
        293–294
TRH, 47
TRT, see Rhinotracheitis
Turkey coryza, 222, 223
Turkey industry
    geographical concentration, 4–5
    historical development, 3
    see also individual aspects e.g. Further
        processing
Turkey meat, see Meat

Vacuum packaging, 341
Van Wambeke, F., 361–362
Ventilation, 208–210, 219
    artificial incubation, 75–76
    excess ammonia, 209
    fan systems, 212

Ventilation (cont.)
    minimum air requirement, 209
    natural systems, 212
Vimentin, 180
Virus isolation, rhinotracheitis, 224–225, 228, 232
Vitamins
    breeding hens, 108–113
        allowances, 111–113
        biotin transfer, 108–109
        chlorine, 111
        folic acid, 111
        nicotinic acid, 110, 111
        pantothenic acid, 110, 111
        pyridoxine, 110, 111
        riboflavin, 110, 111
        thiamin, 110, 111
        vitamin A, 109–110, 111
        vitamin D, 110, 111
        vitamin E, 110, 111
        vitamin K, 110, 111
    growing turkeys, 183–184
    incorporation into eggs
        age effects, 109
        biotin transfer mechanism, 108–109
VLDL, see Lipoproteins, very low density

'Warmed over flavour', 323–325
    and heptaldehyde and dienal, 324
Water holding, 335–336
Weight gain, genetic selection for, 279–281
Whitehead, C.C., 91–117
Wild turkeys
    energy and flight, 171
    origins, 11–12
Wood, J.D., 271–288

Yield and carcass composition, 271–288
    edible meat yield, 22–23
    fat deposition, 272–273, 276, 277, 280, 281
    finishing and fleshing estimates, 276
    importance in marketing, 271–273
    low fat image, 272–273
    nutrition and, 281–283
        dietary changes during growth, 158–160, 283,
            354
    pre-slaughter effects, 283–284, 294
    processing factors, 284
    production effects
        age and weight, 273–276
        feed conversion efficiency, 280
        genetic selection for weight gain, 279–281
        sex differences, 276–278
        strains of turkeys, 278–279
    skin content, 275

Zinc, 60, 107